Goddesses and Monsters

Women, Myth, Power, and
Popular Culture

Jane Caputi

THE UNIVERSITY OF WISCONSIN PRESS / POPULAR PRESS

The University of Wisconsin Press
1930 Monroe Street
Madison, Wisconsin 53711

www.wisc.edu/wisconsinpress/

3 Henrietta Street
London WC2E 8LU, England

1   3   5   4   2

Printed in the United States of America

Library of Congress Cataloging-in-Publication Data
Caputi, Jane.
Goddesses and monsters : women, myth, power, and popular culture / Jane Caputi.
p.   cm.
"A Ray and Pat Browne book."
Includes bibliographical references and index.
ISBN 0-299-19620-8 (cloth: alk. paper)
ISBN 0-299-19624-0 (pbk.)
1. Feminist criticism. 2. Popular culture.   3. Women in popular culture.
4. Sex role.   5. Patriarchy.   I. Title.
HQ1190.C368   2004
306—dc22   2003020572

The following chapters are based in part on essays that have appeared in the following journals: "'Jaws' as Patriarchal Myth," *Journal of Popular Film* 6 (1978): 305-25; "Seeing Elephants: The Myths of Phallotechnology," *Feminist Studies* 14 (1988): 486-524; "The New Founding Fathers: The Lore and Lure of the Serial Killer," *Journal of American Culture* 16, no. 3 (1990): 1-12; "*Sleeping with the Enemy* as *Pretty Woman Part 2:* Or, What Happened after the Princess Woke Up," *Journal of Popular Film and Television* 19, no. 2 (1991): 2-8; "American Psychos: The Serial Killer in Contemporary Fiction," *Journal of American Culture* 16, no. 4 (1993): 101-12; "Unthinkable Fathering: Connecting Incest and Nuclearism," *Hypatia: A Journal of Feminist Philosophy* 9, no. 2 (1994): 102-22; "The 21st Century Sex, Love, and Death Goddess," *Blue Mesa Review,* no. 10 (1998): 3-14; "The Second Coming of Diana," *National Women's Studies Association Journal* 11, no. 2 (1999): 103-23; "Small Ceremonies: Ritual in *Forrest Gump, Natural Born Killers, Seven,* and *Follow Me Home,*" in *Mythologies of Violence in Postmodern Culture,* ed. Christopher Sharrett: 147-74 (Detroit: Wayne State University Press, 1999); "Facing Change: African Origins in Octavia Butler's *Parable* Novels," *Journal on the Fantastic in the Arts* 11, no. 2 (2000): 175-78; "On the Lap of Necessity: A Mythic Interpretation of Teresa Brennan's Energetics Philosophy," *Hypatia: A Journal of Feminist Philosophy* 16, no. 2 (2001): 1-26; "Everyday Pornography," in *Race, Class, and Gender in the Media,* ed. Gail Dines and Jean Humez: 434-50 (Thousand Oaks, Calif.: Sage Publications, 2002).

For Teresa Brennan

1952–2003

An original, who was really something

If the imitation is always trying to be something, and cares desperately for its status, the original is really something, but does not care.

Teresa Brennan, *History after Lacan*

Contents

Illustrations

Goddesses and Monsters

Introduction

Tracing the Goddess/Facing the Monster

An ancient interpretation . . . gives *Hawwah* [Eve] the meaning "serpent" and finds in Genesis a trace of the primitive belief that earthly life originated in a serpent . . . [a] "goddess of
the underworld, worshipped in the form of a serpent, and
bearing the title of 'mother of all living.'"

W. H. Bennett (1926, 607)

Nothing disappears without a trace.

Postcard for *The X-Files*

In the mythic way everything begins with a story, sometimes a made-up
one, sometimes a true one. This happens to be a true one. On the day
before Halloween 2002 I was flying up to Boston from Florida. I sat
next to two little boys, one four and one six. The younger one clutched
a toy, a figure of Bart Simpson whose head seemed to be emerging from
a dinosaur body. When I expressed some delight as well as perplexity, he
laughed and told me that it was Bart in a "costume"! Of course. I asked
the older boy who he was going to be for Halloween. He replied: "The
killer." I asked: "Which killer?" And he told me. "The one in the video
game. The one who kills the girl."

This brief moment crystallized much of what was churning around
in my mind concerning popular culture and its gods, goddesses, heroes,
and monsters. Bart Simpson, beneath his obviously brash and bratty
surface, is an archetypal trickster, a transformer or shapeshifter (Radin,

3

1937). Through this little toy, the trickster moves between being Bart and being a creature, paradoxically enough a dinosaur, who, though "extinct," is spectacularly alive in the world of myth. The older boy's enthusiasm for the video game also referred to the mythic world, the one of gods and men where the boy becomes the man/hero/god by slaying the representative of nature and origins—the monster/goddess, "the girl."

These and related themes cohere in the essays collected here in *Goddesses and Monsters*. Some of the essays are new; most have been reworked; a few are still in their original form.[1] All are based in three premises:

1. Popular culture serves as a repository of ancient and contemporary mythic and folkloric images and narratives, personalities, icons, and archetypes.[2] Narrative-driven, image-rich, celebrity-populated, hero-worshipping, and monster-mad popular culture is a prime playing field for myth and ritual, for myth is "always concrete—consisting of vivid, sensually intelligible narratives, images, rites, ceremonies, and symbols" (Watts, 1968, 8). Many of us are attracted to popular entertainments because these forms and stories—sensual, symbolically overblown, often vulgar (Cooper, 1995), and truly fantastic—allow us to enter, even in the midst of our organized, bureaucratic, and rationalist world, into a "dreamtime," a state of consciousness characterized by the play of the mythic imagination. Mythic/symbolic language and pictures allow us to see into the dark, into that which is necessarily mysterious—to imagine and communicate with what is otherwise ineffable. And myth is powerful. It raises energies, galvanizes actions, evokes emotions, and binds a people into a community. Myth is a fable, to be sure, but at the same time it is what Paula Gunn Allen (1986a, 103) understands "as a language construct that contains the power to transform something (or someone) from one state or condition to another."

2. Of course, this power, like that of shapeshifting, is an ambivalent one. It cuts both ways. The novelist Toni Cade Bambara (1993, 132–33) vividly cautions against a hegemonic popular culture that "masks history and addicts us to voyeurism, fetishism, mystified notions of social relations, and freakish notions of intimate relations." Pop culture can provide a conduit for a kind of everyday pornography, putting the force of myth behind oppressive stereotypes and narratives. These include: the idolization of female slenderness and concomitant transmission of body-loathing ideals to women (Bordo, 1993); images of white innocence and purity shadowed by those of black criminality and hypersexuality, taking form in such stereotypes as the "black rapist of white women" and its

counterpart, "the bad black woman," "both designed to apologize for and facilitate the continued exploitation of black men and women" (Lerner, 1972, 193); and the Western genre, which glorifies genocide by presenting it as an epic moment when the forces of "civilization" vanquished "savagery" (and not the other way around). Mainstream popular culture all too often provides an ego massage to those in power, legitimizing the "spirit murder" (Williams, 1991, 73) of the oppressed and marginalized while simultaneously reaping profits, colonizing minds, fracturing selves, and inducing oppressed peoples to hate themselves and futilely seek recognition, love, and redemption from those who hate, fear, use, and disrespect them (Hernton, 1998, 84). Still, as Stuart Hall (1992) and others have argued, audiences for popular culture participate in making its meanings; they variously accept, reinterpret, and/ or resist and reject dominant messages. Seeing through these, particularly for those of us who are stigmatized by them, can be uniquely energizing and transformative.

3. But this is not the whole story. Pop culture is not only a meaning system enforcing the status quo. *Popular,* after all, comes from a Latin word meaning *people.* A most valuable index to what people commonly know, value, fear, remember, and believe can be found there. Oddly enough, it is also a place where things usually unspoken, things that go against established canons, can be said.

In his musings on the folk antecedents of popular culture, the literary critic Leslie Fiedler (1982, 51) reminds us that "for a long time, in fact, all song and story was regarded as contraband except that canonized by the hierarchy of the church, i.e., declared inspired by God." Nonetheless, the church was unable to stop the flow of popular culture, and the "oral/aural song and story of the folk flourished, as it were, behind the backs of the fully literate." These folk songs and stories, Fiedler observes, tended "to express the repressed," and "in patriarchal ages" popular culture "pays tribute to the matriarchal" (41).

Feminist and otherwise resistant perspectives allow us to consciously recognize these tributes as they continue to suffuse some, though certainly not all popular stories and songs. In these, we can trace a record, albeit a coded one, of wisdoms that have had to go underground to survive the brainwashings wrought by patriarchal domination, taking form in the suppression and domestication of women; the persecution of gender and sexual variance; imperialist colonizations; and a continuous assault on the elements, living creatures, and the green world. This resistant wisdom tradition pops up, for example, in the ongoing belief in psychic phenomena; in the "green consciousness" (environmental awareness and nature reverence) especially prevalent in children's culture; in radical conspiracy theorizing that tells us that those in power are the true cause of disorder;[3] in the recurrent presence of the death goddess as monster, sex symbol, mammy, mystery lady, Amazon, and femme fatale; in the open invitation to take a fantastic voyage to other worlds/possibilities; and in all the various retellings of wonder stories communicating hope, telling those who are despairing that the dreams that they "dare to dream really do come true."[4]

True Lies?

> The *tlamatinime* [wise women and men of the ancient Nahua culture] themselves acknowledged that "it may be that no one on earth can tell the truth" except through flower and song.
> Miguel León-Portilla (1963, 83)

> What are called "myths" in the white world, and thought of as primitive spiritual stories that articulate psychological realities, are in the native world the accounts of actual interchanges.
> Paula Gunn Allen (1991, 6)

> The Origin story functions basically as a maker of our identity—with the story we know who we are. . . . The stories are always bringing us together, keeping this whole together . . . and I want to remind you that we make no distinctions between the stories—whether they are history, whether they are fact, whether they are gossip—these distinctions are not useful when we are talking about this particular experience with language.
> Leslie Marmon Silko (1981a, 57–60)

The word *myth* can be paradoxical. A verbal exchange by two tennis announcers during the broadcast of the 2002 U.S. Open perfectly captured this complexity. When Mary Carillo referred to Pete Sampras's "mythic strength," John McEnroe immediately retorted: "It's not mythic, it's real." Of course, Carillo wasn't suggesting that Sampras's skills were illusory; she used the word *mythic* to convey a sense of his strength as legendary, bordering on the divine. McEnroe's misunderstanding was nonetheless a predictable one, rooted in the common notion of *myth* as a falsehood.

According to the religious historian Mircea Eliade (1963, 1–2), a movement begun in Greece around 500 B.C.E. criticized and rejected "mythological expression" and defined myth in negative relation to *historia*. The latter was seen as describing reality, while *mythos* came to denote "'what cannot really exist.'" Monotheistic religious hegemony contributed to this pejorative understanding of myth by characterizing the religious beliefs of various goddess-, earth-, and nature-reverencing pagans, infidels, and so-called savages as "myth," and their own beliefs as revealed "truth." This proposition that myth is false is a consummate reversal, for, as the Nahuas knew, it is sacred story and figuration that allow us to approach (if not fully unveil) truths that are otherwise inaccessible.

The issue of what is myth and what is history turns up when feminist thinkers point to matriarchal cultures in both old and new hybrid forms (Amadiume, 2003, 103), ponder times in human history that were not patriarchal at all, and explore possibilities for nonpatriarchal futures (Daly, 1998).

Patriarchal proponents invariably universalize their system, claiming that nothing else ever did or could exist. Although she finds no evidence for original "matriarchies," Gerda Lerner (1997, 121) understands patriarchy as a historical phenomenon. Patriarchy took both material and symbolic shape, as Lerner describes it: "In the period when written history was being created, shortly after the formation of the archaic states, women were already in a subordinate condition, their roles, their public behavior, and their sexuality defined by men or male-dominated institutions. From that time on, women were educationally deprived and did not significantly participate in the creation of the symbol system by which the world was explained and ordered. Women did not name themselves; they did not, after the Neolithic era, name gods or shape them in their image." She further theorizes that patriarchal systems took hold via an "'invention of hierarchy'" (133). This strategic turning of "'difference' into dominance" was accompanied by male appropriation of women's sexuality and reproductive capacities. It is only in the past two hundred years, Lerner notes, that groups of women in patriarchal cultures have become conscious of a group identity and the actuality of their historical experience, leading some to "reclaim our past," the entire record of women's history and worldviews (121).

One sweeping work of such reclamation, *The Great Cosmic Mother: Rediscovering the Religion of the Earth* (Sjöö and Mor, 1991), was written by the poet Barbara Mor (while she struggled as a welfare mother). It expanded upon a much shorter work first written by Monica Sjöö, an artist. This work radically renames and reclaims the past, reinterpreting world history and shaping symbols for the divine, the self, and the world from the perspectives of the most marginalized of women. Key to its approach is an understanding that "the female sex has functioned as a colony of organized patriarchal power for several thousand years now. Our brains have been emptied out of all memory of our own cultural history, and the colonizing power systematically denies such a history ever existed. The colonizing power mocks our attempts to rediscover and celebrate our ancient matriarchies as realities" (27).

The poet, novelist, and scholar Paula Gunn Allen, in *The Sacred Hoop: Recovering the Feminine in American Indian Traditions*, makes a similar argument. Prior to waves of patriarchal colonization, she writes, there were what she calls "gynocracies" throughout the world — "woman-centered tribal societies in which matrilocality, matrifocality, matrilinearity, maternal control of household goods and resources and female deities of the magnitude of the Christian God were and are present and active features of traditional tribal life" (1986a, 3–4). Gynocratic cultures, marked among Native American societies prior to the European conquest, Allen avers, value peacefulness, harmony, cooperation, health, and general prosperity and are based in nonhierarchical notions of relationship between humans and all of creation. There is no notion of land ownership; rather, the people belong to the land. Genocide against Native Americans, Allen insists, was rooted in *gynocide*, the need to destroy these gynocratic social systems, religions, and values with which patriarchy could not coexist. Hence, it was imperative to destroy them both in substance and in memory. Still, these traditions continue to be kept, in the heart as well in daily practices, by living people and communities. And there are still songs about them. And memories and recognitions of gynocentric places, peoples, and times persist in our oral tradition and popular culture.

Outlandish Words and Worlds

But do not despise the lore that has come down from distant years; for oft it may chance that old wives keep in memory word of things that once were needful for the wise to know.
J. R. R. Tolkien (1954a, 420)

Somewhere over the rainbow
Way up high,
There's a land that I heard of
Once in a lullaby.
E. Y. Harburg, "Somewhere over the Rainbow"

Consider the *outlandish* narrative so common to popular culture. The word suggests a journey to a place far beyond the borders of the known—through the looking glass, under the sea, over the rainbow, and into outer (and inner) space. The Land of Oz is one such place, featuring a fraudulent male ruler and a bevy of powerful, if ambivalent, female witches.

In the later medieval period, the travelogue recounting sojourns in exotic places was a much loved form. One of the most celebrated was that of Sir John Mandeville, who, thankfully, included not only first-hand experiences but also "stories he had heard in the course of after-dinner gossip, introduced by a phrase like 'some men say.' The land of Amazonia, for example, 'is all women and no man . . . because the women will not suffer no men amongst them to be their sovereigns'" (Miles, 1989, 145). The Amazonian myth endures. The television series *Xena: Warrior Princess* (Rob Taubert, producer, 1995–2001) is a cult phenomenon whose fans speak of their immersion in a potent "Xenaverse" (Martinez, 2000)! More obscure traces of the existence of Amazonia and the yearning for an alternative universe characterized by "Xenaversity" can be found throughout popular culture.

In the 1950s and early 1960s, as a young girl fervent about all kinds of monster and science fiction films, I happened upon the land of Amazonia in movies like *The Cat People* (Jacques Tourneur, 1942), *The Curse of the Cat People* (Robert Wise, 1944), *Cat Women of the Moon* (Arthur Hilton, 1953), *She Gods of Shark Reef* (Roger Corman, 1956), *The Queen of Outer Space* (Edward Bernds, 1958), and *Mermaids of Tiburon* (John Lamb, 1962).[5] All of these featured some kind of all-female society encroached upon by violent male outsiders. As a young viewer I happily received stories that, however obliquely, initiated me into the Amazon mythos. All such stories dramatized the possibility of a "woman's world" and challenged what had been presented to me as the inevitability of patriarchy and universal heterosexuality. Herein also were inscribed memories of a pattern much like that described by Paula Gunn Allen (1986a): gynocracies upended and colonized by an invading/exploring cadre of manly men. Even though the collapse of the supposedly monstrous Amazonian worlds was the preferred "happy" ending in such films, contrary young minds such as my own were free to take alternative suggestions regarding female possibility and sovereignty.

Eliade (1963) calls our attention to the original meaning of *myth*, to which, he says, Western thinkers are returning: myth as sacred, exemplary story. Sacred origin stories, even when they show up as gossip, B-movies, and cult television, are the ones that tell a group how it came to be, that bind it into a community, that furnish a sense of cosmic purpose and direction. Patriarchy, like any other social organization, needs its "sacred stories," its version of how this world came to be, and how it will continue. So too do the variously green, gay, and goddess movements that challenge patriarchy's perpetuity.

Some scholars of religion and history (e.g., Eller, 2000) scorn the belief in ancient gynocentric cultures as wishful thinking—gossip, not fact. This argument, however one views its merits, does not take into account myth's transformative affects and effects. The myth of gynocentric origins and, implicitly, eventualities has been generated, interpreted, and believed by both women and men for well over a century.[6] The reclaiming of this past and the reworking of its symbols comprise a political, emotional, spiritual, and psychical vision that not only describes but also generates a resistant, nonpatriarchal consciousness and an alternative path of *becoming* for both women and men.

This question of *belief* is a recurrent one in popular fables. We might briefly consider two especially germane ones. *The Matrix* (Larry Wachowski and Andy Wachowski, 1999) tells a story about a world where machines have taken over. With no other energy source, they enslave humans and use them as "batteries" to supply their needs for electrical power. People are kept, from birth to death, in enforced slumber and fed on the dead bodies of other humans while their vital energies are tapped to feed the machine's need. To forestall resistance, the machines generate the "matrix," an illusory world that blinds humans to reality and assures their (uninformed) consent. Most believe that they actually are living autonomous lives. The hero, Neo, aided by a group of revolutionaries, is able to "wake up," see the truth, and stop believing in the illusion. Simultaneously, members of the group are able to retrieve his body. As body and mind come together, Neo can reclaim his vital energies and no longer, unconsciously, feed the system. After establishing this promising line of inquiry, the film degenerates, offering blatantly contradictory messages. There are hyperbolic (and beautified) displays of mayhem, the standard fetishizations of big guns, leather, and alienating eyewear, and that familiar techno-yearning to transcend the body and its necessities. Still, the story does register that intriguing take on belief. The machine-generated matrix, like any oppressive system, fundamentally relies upon the energies and resources, not only physical but also psychical, of the oppressed. The first step to successful resistance is "waking up," refusing any longer to believe in the lies the system generates to mask its purposes. This refusal is not simply "symbolic," individually gratifying but without real impact. Rather, its effects are utterly material. As a result of this individual refusal to believe in its version of reality, the system is deprived of at least a part of its essential energy or fuel. Implicitly, collective disbelief would drastically disempower that system.

While *The Matrix* advises skepticism regarding the official story, the trilogy by J. R. R. Tolkien, *The Lord of the Rings*, reminds us, conversely, of the need to return our belief (energy) to much that an oppressive system has characterized as falsehood or "myth." As the story goes, the hobbit Frodo and his companion hobbits, a wizard, a man, an elf, and a dwarf must undertake a quest to destroy the dread "ring of power" before it can be reclaimed by an evil lord who will use it to accomplish world domination. *The Lord of the Rings* is a mostly male-oriented heroic quest—and one with familiar problematic tropes. One identifies darkness with evil and lightness with good. Another diametrically splits the feminine principle (the fair, slim and youthful-appearing Galadriel is shadowed by the ancient, dark, and monstrous Shelob, she of the stinking, obese "belly" and insatiable appetite). Despite these formulations, the story manages to communicate an enduring critique of imperious power. During the 1960s and 1970s, at the height of the counterculture and protests against the war in Vietnam, the *Lord of the Rings* books were enormously popular and the slogan "Frodo Lives" appeared in graffiti and on t-shirts. By 2002, as preparations for the U.S.-led war against Iraq were being finalized, an Internet joke made the e-mail rounds. It depicted a photo of President George W. Bush wearing the dread "ring of power." Under the picture is the lamentation: "Frodo Failed."

The trilogy, simultaneously, evokes elemental memories and urges belief in the ensouled being of the green world as a primal source of resistance to that arrogant power. Throughout, Tolkien gives clear indications that he is not simply spinning a yarn for entertainment purposes but speaking of real beings, real dangers, and real potentialities. There is a moment in *The Two Towers* (Tolkien, 1954b, 168) when King Théoden is confounded by the appearance of the most ancient beings of the earth, sentient trees called Ents. He asks the wizard Gandalf to explain who these beings might be, at which Gandalf chides him for his ignorance: "Is it so long since you listened to tales by the fireside? There are children in your land who, out of the twisted threads of story, could pick the answer to your question. You have seen Ents. . . . Did you think that the name was given only in idle fancy? Nay, Théoden, it is otherwise: to them you are but the passing tale." Théoden, humbled, replies in part: "Songs we have that tell of these things, but we are forgetting them, teaching them only to children, as a careless custom. And now the songs have come down among us out of strange places, and walk visible under the Sun."

The Lord of the Rings traces a clash between a green, and still honorably humble, world and a mechanized one dominated by an ego-driven lord who is obsessed with omnipotence, warfare, genetic manipulation, enslavement of the minds and bodies of others, personal immortality, and apocalypse. Tolkien makes respectful reference to folklore, averring that the old wives' songs speak, albeit often indirectly, of real beings and events. Moreover, he suggests that it is by allying ourselves with these mythic beings and energies that the oppressive forces can be undone. As Gandalf further tells Théoden: "You are not without allies, even if you know them not" (168).

The sense of wonder in the mythic realm and awareness of and belief in its presences come easily to many children. But the ability to perceive it has atrophied in those modern adults who are caught up in the human world and who, we might add, are also addled by official stories and belief systems focused almost exclusively on hubristic and power-mad lords. When wonderers give their belief, instead, to egalitarian, elemental, balanced, green, and goddess-oriented myth, it enables them to recognize ancient allies and to "court and engage the older powers moving within these images, songs and stories and thereby actualize their potential for transformation" (Ceti Boundy, letter to author, March 9, 2003).

Goddess/Monster

> Some [despite Aztec patriarchal rewriting of the myths] continued to believe in the Lord and Lady of Duality, Ometechuhtili and Omechihuatl. The early deities seemed to capture the balanced oppositions of life and death, light and dark, as well as the masculine and feminine, in androgynous representations. . . . The principle of complementarity between the sexes seemed to be dying out as sex antagonism grew in the course of conquest.
>
> June Nash (1978, 359)

A patriarchal and militarist Aztec culture, bent on imperial conquest, rewrote a sexually egalitarian Nahuan mythology in order to inspire and justify its predatory conquests—of other peoples, of women, and of land—and to legitimate human sacrifice (Nash, 1978). The early Nahuan theology, Miguel León-Portilla (1963, 83) illuminates, understood the divine, or "origin of life of earth," as having a "dynamic essence" consisting of complementary feminine and masculine principles, whose true nature could be comprehended only through the figurative language of "flowers and song." This ancient and still-current *gender dynamic* theology is a welcome alternative for those seeking a flower that still has some scent and a song other than a militaristic march.[7]

Feminist conceptualizations stress a dynamic understanding of "goddess," not as some woman up in the sky or even down in the earth. In Mary Daly's (1978, 111) words, *goddess* is the "the deep Source of creativity integrity" and "the Self-affirming be-ing of women." Similarly, Luce Irigaray (1993, 61, 63–64) understands the female divine in ontological and dynamic terms: "To become means fulfilling the wholeness of what we are capable of being. . . . But as long as woman lacks a divine made in her image she cannot establish her subjectivity or achieve a goal of her own. She lacks an ideal that would be her goal or path in becoming." Men, too, need the feminine divine in order to reconcile with, recover, and honor the repressed and denied feminine aspects of their own being and becoming.

Patriarchal rewritings of egalitarian myth not only split the divine essence, separating goddess from god, but then also recast goddess as devil, monster, and whore. Again, the Aztec experience, as described by Gloria Anzaldúa (1987, 27–28) is exemplary: "The male-dominated *Azteca-Mexica* culture drove the powerful female deities underground by giving them monstrous attributes . . . thus splitting the female Self and the female deities. They divided her who had been complete, who possessed both upper (light) and underworld (dark) aspects . . . into chaste virgins and . . . *putas,* into Beauties and the Beasts."

In ancient myth from numerous cultures, we find a similar respect for elemental ambivalence. Chthonic (earth) deities "nearly always appear in a dual aspect—one friendly and beneficent, the other dark and sinister, just as the divine [Greek] pair Demeter and Persephone symbolize, on the one hand, the kindly earth yielding food for man and, on the other, the gloomy depths of Hades" (Geffcken, 1926, 573). Such deities are depicted bearing not only fruits and flowers, but also snakes. The sacred snake recalls the primal serpent/mother of all living things, Eve. The serpent is, as well, the signature of the Aztec goddesses, like Coatlicue, of whom Anzaldúa speaks and of Damballah, the bisexual god/dess, the origin or "Source" for Haitian Voodoo (Hurston, 1983, 142). Serpents continue to be recognized as bearers of subterranean wisdom, signifiers not only of death but also of infinity and rebirth. In the folklore-steeped novel *The Serpent's Gift* (1994) Helen Elaine Lee exquisitely reimagines the ancient truths associated with "Miss Snake"—including an appreciation of the "twoness of all things" and her "gift of renewal." The dual and dynamic nature of being and knowledge is acknowledged to this day in the symbol of the medical profession (a symbol also associated with Damballah): the ancient caduceus, a staff (the primordial tree) around which two serpents thread in opposite directions (uncannily similar to the pattern of DNA). This complementary dual pattern reflects the necessities of honoring and balancing high and low, feminine and masculine, summer and winter, light and dark, increase and decrease, the rose and the garbage (Hanh, 1988, 31), life and death.

A master consciousness (Griffin, 1989) splits the integrity of being, releasing destructive power as surely as when the atom is split and generating a series of false oppositions. "Otherness," the basis of oppression, is created when the self is split, and what is disowned, feared, and denied in the self is projected onto another being or group (Hoch, 1979; Eugene, 1994). The "other" is then stigmatized and warred against. A holistic, green, and gynocentric imagination seeks to restore to the divine (and to the self) those necessary aspects of the whole that have been demonized and made into the "other." These include the feminine and the female, chaos, emotion, soul, age, animality, the depths, darkness, dirtiness, lowness, decay, illness, and natural death. Goddess/monster myth potentially inspires a revalorization of what is defamed as soft/feminine in males and bitchy/butchy in females. It recognizes masculinity and femininity not as ontologically opposite traits, but as mutual and even mutable traits, variations on the primally female nature of creation. Goddess/monster myth resacralizes animals and, concomitantly, those traits we associate with animals in ourselves: intuition, instinct, sexuality, sensuality, and mortality. It guides humans to understand that not everything is controllable, although much can be influenced. It makes a respectful reconnection with the elements and with the cyclical earth, and, for all of these reasons, promotes the establishment of more equitable social relations and sustainable cultures.[8] Above all, goddess/monster myth, comprehending the necessarily dynamic and dualistic nature of Nature, makes peace with death, understanding natural death as a necessary part of the spiral of birth, life, death, transformation, and rebirth. The reigning god myth, however, has another drift altogether.

Gods and Humans

I was making life-and-death decisions . . . playing God in their lives.

Edmund Kemper, the "Coed Killer" (quoted in "The Random Killers," 1984)

I had a sense of power. A sense of destruction. . . . In the Nam you realized you had the power to take a life. You had the power to rape a woman and nobody could say nothing to you. That godlike feeling you had was in the field. It was like I was god. I could take a life. I could screw a woman.

Anonymous Vietnam veteran (quoted in Baker, 1982, 152)

"God exists and he's American." . . . I do not believe we have made a man to end wars. I believe we have made a man to end worlds.

University professor discussing a newly invented nuclear man/machine in the cult comic book series *The Watchmen* (Moore, 1986)

In the fall of 2002 the so-called Beltway Snipers shot thirteen random people in just over three weeks; ten died. They also left notes and images for the police at the various crime scenes. This had happened before, but there was a marked innovation: the killers demanded money—$10 million—to stop the violence. During this siege, news media found themselves in the uncomfortable position of feeding the serial killers' needs for attention and, at the same time, ineluctably creating entertainment out of atrocity.

Coincidentally, just as this serial killing spree began, another big-budget serial killer story opened. *Red Dragon* (Brett Ratner, 2002) was, ironically, highly profitable entertainment about multiple and sensationalized murder. I bring this up not to suggest that movies cause crime, but to observe that the film medium, as has happened before, eerily provided a choral and moral backdrop to a famous crime. Were we thinking about the world in a mythic or sacred way, we might see this uncanny coincidence as a sign demanding that we as a culture rethink our violent notions of god, fetishization of guns, our worship of cash, and our cult of hurtful masculinity.

Like its predecessor, *The Silence of the Lambs* (Jonathan Demme, 1991), *Red Dragon* featured two serial killers, one a frightening killer of white middle-class families, the other a charming "genius." The latter, Hannibal Lecter (Anthony Hopkins), was ubiquitously dubbed our nation's "favorite serial killer." In a key scene in *Red Dragon*, an FBI agent tells a group of police officers that there is no doubt that the family serial killer will strike again. "Why?" one woman asks him. "Because it makes him God," intones the agent. Just days after *Red Dragon* opened, the police found the Death card from a Tarot deck near the scene of one of the shootings. Inscribed on the card was a message from the shooter. It was reported in the media as reading: "Dear Policeman, I am God."

Such grandiose allusions to divinity have long been a crucial part of the serial killer myth (Caputi, 1987). They proliferate as well in technological, especially nuclear, mystique and metaphor, most famously when the erudite J. Robert Oppenheimer, "father" of the atomic bomb, named the bomb test site "Trinity" and then, while witnessing the first atomic blast, recited the god Krishna's words from the sacred Hindu text, the *Bhagavad-Gita:* "I am become Death, the shatterer of worlds" (Jungk, 1958, 201).

More mundane occasions for such utterances occur regularly in popular playtimes. In the media storm that followed the discovery of the inscribed Tarot card in the Beltway case, the public learned that "I am God" is a common declaration by victorious players of violent video games. We were reminded that Eric Harris, one of the two teenaged boys who committed mass murder at Columbine High School in April 1999, was an avid video game player and had scribbled, "I am God" in another student's yearbook (Zernike, 2002).

The popularity of this phrase in all of these contexts points to a pervasive, if usually unexamined, recognition that violence, control, total power over others, and specifically masculine lethal violence or the power of "unnatural death," all have a religious character in our culture. Despite much talk of God being "love" and associated with creation, the phrase "I am God" is not uttered in delivery rooms by mothers, or by those getting the news that they have received the Nobel Peace Prize. The dominant notion of *god* in the Abrahamic patriarchal religions is an all-male being whose defining characteristics seem to be omnipotence, jealousy, righteousness, judgment, and dominance. This notion of god powers all sorts of terrorism: religious, political, criminal, familial, militarist, nuclear, and any combination of these as powermad men take up that mythic role, "playing god" by waging war, accumulating fortunes, toying with others' lives, and lording it over everybody else. Another type of god/dess, one understood as female, feminine, and commingling aspects of both sexes, might more readily be associated with natural instead of unnatural death, and summon up wholly other qualities: the ability to generate energy, to commune and communicate, to feel sexual desire and ecstasy, to create art, to create life, to inspire growth, to transform patterns, to bear life and sustenance as well as disease, infirmity, and death, and to be capable of occasioning rebirth.

Since Jack the Ripper, popular culture has relentlessly mythicized the serial killer—as a monster, genius, a preternatural entity, an outlaw-hero, a man on a divine mission, and also a kind of immortal, a god. Behind all of this acclaim lurks a recognition that the serial killer is a sign of the times. The cover of the November 4, 2002, issue of *U.S. News & World Report* shows an enlarged close-up of the two Beltway snipers, smiling in a pre-crime snapshot, and the word "MONSTERS." In recent years, sensationalized serial killers have diverged from the model of the lone white male sexual predator. The Beltway Snipers were revealed to be two black men, John Muhammad and Lee Malvo, one a Gulf War veteran who had abused and terrorized his wife, the other a seventeen-year-old in thrall to an authoritarian father figure. The cover of the November 4, 2002, issue of *U.S. News & World Report* shows an enlarged close-up of the two, smiling in a pre-crime snapshot, with the word "MONSTERS" emblazoned above. That same word, *Monster*, is the title of a feature film (Patty Jenkins, 2004) about the only iconic female serial killer, Aileen Wuornos, who was executed in Florida in October 2002. The chronically impoverished, homeless, raped, and prostituted Wuornos defied the odds by becoming a serial killer herself, striking out against violent men, as she claimed, instead of becoming the victim of a serial killer.

The mythic serial killers who so overpopulate pop culture are neither "gods" of omnipotence nor "monsters" in the sense of someone or something strange, bestial, alien, and truly unexpected. Although exceptional in their violence, and increasingly varied in their motivations, they are predictable happenings in a misogynist, violence-obsessed, and consumerist culture (Caputi, 1987). The mythic serial killer is, however, a *prodigy* in the ancient sense of the word (Bloch, 1986)—an ominous sign of unspoken or unacknowledged truths, an omen or warning of impending disaster.

Filling in the *Background*

[Myths] have a miraculous or "numinous" quality which marks them as special, queer, out of the ordinary, and therefore representative of the powers or Power behind the world.

Alan Watts (1968, 7)

Goddesses and Monsters opens with an essay I published in 1978 on *Jaws* (Steven Spielberg, 1975), the first time I consciously recognized the presence of patriarchal creation myth in popular culture and the identification of the goddess with the monster. The story of *Jaws* in many ways replicates one of the very oldest written myths in history, the Sumerian "creation" story that tells of the slaughter of the primordial serpent goddess/monster, the Dragon of Chaos, Tiamat, by a young upstart god, Marduk. Tiamat is the mythic matrix, the mother of all "cunts" (see chapter 17). An ancient text actually refers to "Marduk defeating Tiamat with his penis" (Marcus, 1996, 50) and he does so by targeting her "open mouth" and finally, her "heart" (common symbolic equivalents of the vulva). Goddess murder is the original sex murder. After this copulatory slaughter, the god splits Tiamat's skull, and then, cleaving her body, uses it to form the heavens and the earth.

In this story the body of the goddess/monster is violently severed. *Splitting* is a core motif in Genesis, as well. Human beings are separated from the garden, the earthy paradise, and the serpent/goddess, the metaphysical "mother of all living" and bearer of chthonic wisdom. Such stories reveal a catastrophic alienation from nature, both external and internal. They frequently revolve around a hard, dominant, and rational masculinity that defines itself in agonistic relation to a dangerous (sometimes repulsive, sometime painfully attractive), insatiable, and overwhelmingly potent female or feminine presence that must be obliterated—and then often assimilated, one way or another. This killing of serpent- and vulva-identified goddess/monsters continues to preoccupy god-identified men in popular culture as in the real world, and these types (as militarists, murderers, and nuclear family men) become the very harm they claim to be protecting us all from. We also can note that the original paradigm of splitting continues to be enacted in adept but fundamentally foolish practices (*foolish* in the sense of *lacking consideration of long-term consequences*), such as splitting the atom or the gene.[9]

The radical feminist theologian Mary Daly urges us to look into what she calls the deep *"Background"* of traditional sexist myth, resurfacing their substories, underground resources, and animating energies. For, she argues, patriarchal myths "contain *stolen* mythic power" (1978, 47) and are based upon appropriation and reversal of images and themes that formerly had signified female potencies. Adopting this perspective, we can begin to unearth stories of repressed and slandered, though deeply attractive and resistant on a subterranean level, female, feminine, and nonphallic powers behind such monstrous figures as vamps, dragon ladies, bulldaggers, psychic friends, weak sisters, evil stepmothers, dark ladies, fifty-feet women, witches, wimps, bitches, flaming fairies, and aliens.

Even though the goddess/monster is killed off in most patriarchal stories, she is dynamically immortal. Thus, although most patriarchal religions deny any possibility of female divinity, the oral tradition has never really stopped talking about her, even if the story is distorted by the usual stereotypes. In these, the primordial serpent goddess of the underworld becomes the Devil. "Mother Earth" is cast as an all-forgiving and unconditionally loving nurturer, a "Mammy," happy to provide unpaid service and clean up after oppressive slaveholders and their families. The androgynous or bisexual Divine is sidelined to freak and drag shows. The Lady of the Beasts is caged and domesticated. The Sex Goddess is straightened out, reduced to a fertility fetish, scorned as Jezebel and whore, made into a pornographic object to be stripped, spread, surveyed, sold, and even snuffed. The potent Bitch Goddess becomes the high-heeled and tightly bound dominatrix, safely contained in a pornographic dungeon. The Death Goddess is hated as a castrating and ravenous monster, as in *Jaws*, the femme fatale, rotten underneath her façade of beauty (Grace Jones in *Vamp*, Richard Wenk, 1986). The Sovereignty Goddess (resisting colonization) appears as the hideously fecund Bitch Mother in *Aliens* (James Cameron, 1986). She is never more monstrous than when she claims her rightful Queendom (Ursula in *The Little Mermaid*, John Musker and Ron Clements, 1989). The underworld goddesses's priest still peeks through as the femme villain (the serpent-skirted Hades in *Hercules* [Ron Clements and John Musker, 1997]). Her witch/priestess, when not burnt at the stake, is stripped of any official religious authority. Still, we can discern her presence behind the masquerade of the 1–800 telephone psychic.

Feminist thinkers of all stripes, including pop culture audiences, critically interpret popular culture and understand, both consciously and unconsciously, these *Background* presences and tales. For interpretation is not performed only by experts. Rather, myths are *always* involved in an ongoing process of interpretation and reinterpretation: Even "to tell it . . . is to interpret it" (O'Flaherty, 1988, 31). When Alice Walker (1997) looks behind the stereotypic image of Aunt Jemima, she comes face to face with the original goddess of abundance and nurture, She who is "giving the party" of life. Sandra Cisneros (1996) finds the primordial sex goddess just beneath the skirts of the Virgin of Guadalupe. When much of the world's population reacted with outrage and grief to Princess Diana's death, some daring to call it murder, it was because they recognized her as manifesting forces of love and compassion that had been understood throughout antiquity as the properties of the world folk deity Diana—goddess of light and dark, queen of the witches as well as the gender variant, the protector of the poor, the imprisoned, and the sick, and the historical challenger of patriarchal hegemony.

The feminist interpretations explored throughout *Goddesses and Monsters* are ones that first of all refuse worship to the gods of Power, Pride, Possession, Dominance, Quantity, Progress, Speed, and Control, in all the various shapes they assume, from serial killers to nuclear warheads. These retellings reclaim, represent, and representiate traditions that are friendly to the monstrous, the female, the feminine, the body, the beast, the erotic, the dark, the green, the earth, and the undercurrents, and are prone to an identification with those who are constituted as little, common, queer, odd, and otherwise "other."

Much of the gynocentric oral tradition has been lost, but not without leaving a "trace," those faint markings that can be deepened and filled in, trails that can be followed, not only into the mythic past, but also into an alternative future. *Goddesses and Monsters* hopefully holds up a tracing paper to popular culture, inviting discerning readers to grasp the outline of this persistent substory and fill it in with flower and song, color, dimension, and *Background*.

Part 1

Patriarchal Myth

1

Jaws as Patriarchal Myth

We know how often the goddess appears as an animal, as cow and swamp bird, as ewe and lioness. She also "is" a fish.

Erich Neumann (1963, 276)

In the bedroom, as he was undressing, the thought occurred to him that the cause of all the unpleasantness, the source of the whole mess, was a fish. . . . The ludicrousness of the thought made him smile.

Peter Benchley (1974, 151–52)

It was no accident that the author of *Jaws* became a near millionaire from his book before it was even published, that the film of the same name became the highest grossing of all motion pictures to that date, or that a veritable obsession with its theme plunged America into what the mass media predictably dubbed "Jaws-mania." For the movie *Jaws* is by no means merely a scary story, good "*clean* horror," as one reviewer enthused. Rather, it is the ritual retelling of an essential patriarchal myth—male vanquishment of the female symbolized as a sea monster, dragon, serpent, vampire, or some other creature, administering a necessary fix to a society hooked on and by male control.[1] The purpose of *Jaws* and other myths of its genre is to instill dread and loathing for the female, and they usually culminate in her annihilation. Although I will refer to the book, my main concern is with the film—a film that the critic Molly Haskell (1975, 75) judged "a scare machine that works with computer-like precision," a film that millions have seen and that has correspondingly grossed millions.

23

My interpretation of *Jaws* is based in the perspective advanced in the introduction to this volume: patriarchy is a historical phenomenon and ancient myth traces the existence of a gynocentric consciousness and culture (see also Briffault, 1927; Diner, 1965; and Davis, 1971). The mythic record also indicates that the coming of patriarchy was a violent one, evinced in legends of Amazon tribes, in worldwide traditions of male heroes slaying dragons, serpents, and monsters, and in the ritual rape of the older Greek goddesses by newly arrived gods (Graves, 1960, 1:56, 74, 93).[2] Most glaring of all is the content of certain patriarchal "creation" myths, which, from a female perspective, might more aptly be termed destruction epics. Charles Doria (1974, 33–34) describes this type of myth: "Both of these stories depend on the still more ancient view of creation as flowing from the womb of a fish or whale woman: Leviathan or Tiamat. The oldest known versions of this creation story embody the sea as a whale/serpent/fish woman locked in combat/making love with a god of light/sperm, being defeated/impregnated, cut open/giving birth to the various orders of the universe." Here the primordial battle of the sexes is outlined; here "making love" and "making war" become identical. Here also emerges the rudimentary plot of *Jaws* as this film joins the continuum of warfare against the female. For myths such as these do not simply remain fixed in the past, but travel through time, changing form and style. Their function is to stitch together the seams of the prevailing reality, to bestow legitimation and credibility upon the societal order. Thus in a patriarchy, myths of male superiority and victory over the female must be continually retold, participated in, and internalized. Enter *Jaws* as the latest installment of a time-honored serial.

It does not matter that the shark in *Jaws* is referred to as "he." Such a technique of gender disguise is common in the evolution of deceptive myth. Although it is now assumed that the serpent in the Garden of Eden was male, medieval art frequently depicted it with "female breasts and head in accordance with a theological tradition" (L. Brown, 1974, 310). This transsexing process is further manifested in the myth in which the infant Apollo slays a dragon who was the guardian of the Delphic Oracle. In the earliest extant accounts, the dragon was unmistakably female, although in later versions it came to be regarded as male (Tripp, 1970, 508). In his study of the Great Mother, Erich Neumann (1963, 173–74) likewise observed this phenomenon and concluded: "The guardian spirit is either female or of indeterminate sex, but its terrible, female-matriarchal character is in any event clear. Its uroboric bisexuality is explained by mixture with the destructive power of the Feminine, which at a 'later' stage is often represented as male."

The 1970s were assuredly part of this "later" stage. The great white shark in *Jaws,* though deceptively called "he," actually represents the primordial female and her most dreaded aspects.

The Mythic Base: "She Was the First"

> When Tiamat opened her mouth to consume him
> He drove in the Evil Wind that she close not her lips . . .
> Her body was distended and her mouth was wide open.
> He released the arrow, it tore her belly,
> It cut through her insides, splitting the heart.
> The Babylonian creation epic (quoted in Baring and Cashford, 1991, 277–78)

> In that day Jehovah with his hard and great and strong sword will turn his attention to Leviathan, the gliding serpent, even to Leviathan, the crooked serpent, and he will certainly kill the sea monster that is in the sea.
> Isaiah 27:1

> Quint grabbed the harpoon dart at the end of the rope and, with his hand, plunged it into the soft white belly of the fish. Blood poured from the wound and bathed Quint's hands.
> Peter Benchley (1974, 309)

In the most widely displayed advertisement for *Jaws,* a naked woman swims on the surface of the water while underneath looms the head of a gigantic shark, its mouth wide open and full of excruciatingly sharp teeth. The poster announces, "She was the first." Interestingly enough, this is precisely the point of *The First Sex* by Elizabeth Gould Davis. In her book Davis claims that the female sex preceded the male, that goddesses predated gods, and that in all myth, originally, "the first creator of all is a goddess" (1971, 33). Many ancient epics relate a usurper god's challenge to and destruction of the original female creator. *Jaws* is modeled upon this archetype and, as the above quotations illustrate, closely parallels certain of these, particularly that of the Babylonian fish goddess Tiamat. Thus the "she" in the poster text refers not only to the swimming woman, but to the shark itself as a symbol of this primary goddess.

One of Davis's foremost witnesses to the primacy of the female sex is the evidence of the Babylonian myth in which Tiamat, the original creator, is later challenged by Marduk (a child god). During their battle he enfolds her in his net, drives an "Evil Wind" into her wide-open mouth, and tears her belly with his arrows, slaying her. He then "pause[s] to view her dead body" and decides to "split her like a shell-fish," forming the land and sky from her dismembered body.[3] In the film *Jaws* the shark is finally destroyed through its wide-open mouth by an exploding oxygen tank. The Evil Wind strikes again.

Erich Neumann (1963, 183) cites a similar myth in the culture of pre-Columbian America: "The Earth Goddess is brought down from the primordial heavens and torn asunder; from the two halves heaven and earth are made, as in the case of the Babylonian Tiamat. Precisely by this rending she becomes the source of all foodstuffs." This charming legend is in turn directly connected to the biblical forerunner of the great white shark of the 1970s — the Leviathan. The psalmist sings to Je-hovah: "You broke the heads of the sea monsters in the water. You your-self crushed to pieces the heads of Leviathan. You proceeded to give it as food to the people, to those inhabiting the waterless regions" (Psalms 74:13-14).

Some highly interesting issues are posed here. First, Christianity is the religion that has ritualized the eating of its god, Jesus Christ, who furthermore claims the fish as his symbol. Yet obviously this is a con-trived practice meant to strike a resonant chord. It was originally a fe-male who was slaughtered and offered for consumption, for the fish was originally the symbol of the fertility goddess (Neumann, 1963, 141). Be-cause of the symbolic relationship between the sea and the *Magna Mater,* some peoples have held the fish to be sacred; in certain Asiatic rites priests were forbidden to eat it at all (Cirlot, 1962, 101). Roman Ca-tholicism, however, institutionalized the custom of eating fish on Friday to commemorate the original consumption of the female and in an at-tempt to confer on a god the status of the deposed goddess.

Christian symbolism in *Jaws* extends beyond its echoes of Levia-than. As patriarchy evolved in Western civilization, the chief god in one of its religions went 3-D, becoming one god with three distinct persons: the mysterious Christian Trinity. (Again this is imitative of matriarchal religion, which revered a widely known triple goddess [see Graves, 1960, 1:14, 21-22].) This triune god retained the function of the gods and heroes who had gone before him — namely, to dispose of female being. He can be found doing just that in *Jaws,* as the reviewers urge us to ap-preciate: "spectacular final confrontation between the three men and the great white shark" (Canby, 1977), and "*Jaws* is eminently worth seeing for its second half: three men against a killer shark" (Magill, 1975). We need not strain to discern that these three men are the superstar surrogates of three other well-known figures: the Father, Son, and Holy Ghost of the Christian religion, performing their appointed and mythic mission.

Both scientifically and mythologically the ocean has been considered a primal uterus, the source of all life (Kerenyi, 1949). This consideration has also been extended to sea creatures. Joseph Campbell (1968, 90) notes "the world-wide womb image of the belly of the whale," appearing in the familiar stories of Jonah, Herakles, and Pinocchio. Dolphins have been similarly regarded. The very name of the species is derived from the Greek word *delphis,* "womb." While dolphin imagery generally represents the life-giving, fructifying womb of the Great Mother, her character also contains an antithetical elementary nature. For the mother not only gives life but mythologically is also the bringer of death. This Terrible Mother appears in universal personae as varied as Kali, Hekate, Medusa, and the Malekulan Lev-Hev-hev, a name that means "That which draws us to It so that It may devour us" (Neumann, 1963, 174). In her negative character "Mother" appears precisely as "Maw": "Thus the womb of the earth becomes the deadly devouring maw of the underworld . . . the abyss of Hell, the dark hole of the depth, the devouring womb of the grave and of death" (149). (That the shark hunters in *Jaws* are confronting death in the territory of hell is indicated by the name of Quint's boat, the *Orca,* the Latin word for whale and also the species name for killer whales; and the whale, like other marine monsters, is identified with hell. In the *Aeneid* Virgil names the entire world of hell *Orcus.*)

"In the course of the later development of patriarchal values," Neumann (1963, 155) further notes, "the negative aspect of the Feminine was submerged." The Terrible Mother of death and hell, however, reemerges most dramatically from the oceanic depths as the dismembering, devouring, and undeniably awe-inspiring shark in *Jaws.*

The Teeth of the Sea

> Beyond any doubt her sex is a mouth and a voracious mouth which devours the penis—a fact which can easily lead to the idea of castration.
>
> Jean Paul Sartre (1957, 86)

> *Jaws* is the perfect movie for anyone with a larger-than-life castration complex.
>
> Christopher Sharp

When *Jaws* hit the international market, the French translated its title as *Les dents de la mer* (The teeth of the sea), leading us not only to the idea of castration, but to the consideration of two related themes: the mythological motif of the *vagina dentata* (the toothed, i.e., castrating, vagina) and males' obsessive fear of abortion.

Elaine Geiger, editor-in-chief of New American Library, placed a large bid for the paperback rights to *Jaws* but nevertheless lost out to Bantam. She later stated, "I never would have bid half a million dollars if it hadn't been called *Jaws*" (T. Morgan, 1974, 21). Obviously the word carries some intriguing associations. *The Oxford English Dictionary* gives as one definition: "the seizing action or capacity of any devouring agency, as death, time, etc." Metaphorical use suggests the end of life, the grave, annihilation. Tennyson wrote in "The Charge of the Light Brigade": "Into the jaws of Death, / Into the mouth of Hell / Rode the six hundred."

Such dire associations are rooted solidly in the symbology of the Terrible Mother: "The positive femininity of the womb appears as a mouth; that is why 'lips' are attributed to the female genitals. . . . Similarly, the destructive side of the Feminine, the destructive and deathly womb, appears most frequently in the *archetypal form of a mouth bristling with teeth*" (Neumann, 1963, 168; emphasis added). Both mythically and iconographically, the mouth of the Great Mother is often identified with the *vagina dentata* (Eliade, 1975, 2:409). This archetypal form (the gaping mouth of the shark) provided the major drawing card for this filmic blockbuster. The irony is that this form actually represents the primordial ball-buster, the dreaded *vagina dentata* of worldwide mythology.

Many ancient culture possessed legends that described the first women as having toothed vaginas, making the vagina impassable and penile penetration impossible. This motif is, as Wolfgang Lederer (1968, 46) noted, extremely prevalent. It is most distinct in Native American myths that speak of a culture hero who manages to overcome the Terrible Mother and with sticks, stones, or some medicinal concoction breaks the teeth out of her vagina, and thus "makes her into a woman." (As Simone de Beauvoir observed [1971, 267], "One is not born, but rather becomes, a woman.") Patriarchal civilization can commence only after this act has been accomplished. An extremely interesting variant is recorded by the Waspishiana and Taruma tribes, who relate that the first woman had a *carnivorous fish* inside her vagina.

Such legends are encountered in India and Africa as well. In some of these one tooth is not knocked out, and it becomes the clitoris. Here apparently is the basis for the mutilating and misogynistic ritual of clitoral excision, still practiced widely in parts of Africa where it is feared that a man who has intercourse with an uncircumcised woman will suffer a puncture from her "dart" or clitoris (Lederer, 1968, 46).

Although William S. Pechter, writing in *Commonweal* (1975, 72), was sure that "the fear [in *Jaws*] never strikes anything primal or profound," it is the *vagina dentata* itself which rips across the screen as the bloody, gnashing mouth of the shark. In one scene from the film, men peer into the mouth of a safely dead shark and quip, "Deep throat." As most are aware, fellatio was the subject of a widely viewed pornographic film of that name. Here man's deep-rooted fear of the act's castration implications surfaces. In another sea story, *Moby-Dick*, Ahab's amputated leg can be seen as a euphemism for a castrated penis — could this be why he pursues the white whale so relentlessly? On the advertising poster for the film, what appears to be the bottom part of the shark is not part of the fish at all, but looks much more like the top of a penis, heading straight for the toothy mouth.

Dismemberment in the Ocean

With the sea symbolically evoking the uterus and the shark's teeth the ferocious mouth of that organ, *Jaws* emerges as a full-blown male nightmare, not only of castration, but also of *abortion*. For what is abortion but the action that most typifies a "Terrible Mother," a "destructive and deathly womb"?

Mary Daly (1978, 59) has observed that some men deeply identify with the fetus, particularly with "unwanted fetal material." Nowhere is their terror clearer than in *Jaws*. The action takes place mainly in the ocean, the primal womb and source of life, but this is a uterus full of blood, gore, danger, and death. There are scenes of dismembered limbs and legs falling off into the deep, and all but one of the shark's victims are male — usually swimming or floating peacefully, unaware, when attacked.

Significant to this aspect is the film's strong emphasis on boy children, closer to the fetal stage and more vulnerable to the mother, thus encouraging fetal feelings among the viewers. Again and again little boys are the focus of peril. First we have to worry about the Boy Scouts; then little boys greatly predominate in the crowded water. The climax is reached when Alex Kintner, happily floating on his raft, grotesquely exits in a geyser of blood. (*Kintner* is, of course, very similar to the German word for children, *Kinder.*) Later, the police chief's son goes into shock as he narrowly escapes an attack. One appalled reviewer for the

Los Angeles Times warned, "*Jaws* is a nightmare for the young." Did he realize, however, quite how young?

Deliver Us from Evil

Not only do the shark's victims have a boyish slant, but its two surviving killers are also markedly and stupidly puerile. One is terrified of the water and seems to be perpetually in danger of wetting his pants. The other sticks his tongue out and makes faces behind Big Daddy Quint's back. Brody and Hooper join a long line of distinguished boy killers, for youth is one of the more prominent characteristics of monster-slayers. Marduk was the infant grandson of Tiamat when he killed her. Philip Slater (1968, 126) notes that three of the most important figures in Greek mythology—Zeus, Apollo, and Herakles—as very young children initiated their careers by killing a serpent. He adds that the serpents are all of maternal origin. I suggest that the prevalence of this type of myth indicates the existence of a popular male fantasy—namely, that in the act of birth, or at an initiatory ritual of rebirth, the boy succeeds in killing the mother.

Men's antipathy toward the mother is widely and diversely apparent. She is killed off in the oldest fairytales and blamed for the most modern of male discontents. Yet one of the most glaring expressions of this animus is found at a most primary level and closely associated with the act of birth—that is, deliverance. At the time this film was made, U.S. births were effected mostly by the god-surrogate, the doctor, who *delivered* the baby while the mother was drugged and strapped to hospital apparatus in an abnormal position. Her genitals were often sliced (episiotomy), an almost always unnecessary procedure that recalls the treatment of Tiamat at the hands of Marduk. This obstetrical practice was not simply a male takeover of the female function of birthing, but the enactment of a gynophobically rooted ritual by which a man "saves" the baby from the mother. *The Oxford English Dictionary* gives as the primary meaning of *deliver:* "a. To set free, liberate, release, rescue, save. . . . b. To set free *from* restraint, imminent danger, annoyance, trouble, or evil generally." The word and the birthing practice it describes point to a system that views all mothers as Terrible, as evil monsters from whom the child must be saved. Further evidence is unwittingly offered by Frederick Leboyer. In his ironically titled *Birth without Violence,* he gives this interpretation of the delivery room drama: "She is driving the baby out. At the same time she holding it in, preventing its passage. It is *she* who is the enemy. She who stands between the child and life. Only one of them can prevail; it is mortal combat" (1976, 26; emphasis in original). Apparently mythic violence attends every birth, no matter what procedure is used.

The association between the shark and the birthing Terrible Mother is suggested quite early in the film. When a shark is caught and displayed as the killer, Hooper remains unconvinced. To be sure, he proposes, they must cut open the dead shark to see if the *little boy is inside it*. He subsequently performs a postmortem cesarean section (amid much grunting and letting of waters) while Brody watches in revulsion. And the final scene in *Jaws* clearly represents an initiatory ritual of matricidal rebirth. Confrontation with marine monsters, as Eliade stated (1969, 158), is "the typical ordeal of initiation." Immersion in the waters (sacramentalized as baptism) is the classic symbol of rebirth. With the sea monster successfully torn apart (and Daddy disposed of in the bargain), the two boys, now men, emerge from the waters to paddle fearlessly toward the shore.

Cinematic Rape

Discussing the use of kinesis in films, Gerald Mast notes that many films are both sensually assaultive and sexually explicit. He remarks (1977, 59): "We film spectators are not only voyeurs; we also experience a kind of rape." What Mast fails to recognize is that there are, in fact, two experiences of rape—that of the rapist and that of the one who is raped. *Jaws* sets up its viewers for just these experiences. Men are invited to gloat over the rape/defeat of the primordial female; women are asked to internalize this defeat. Yet there is still another rape in *Jaws*—as a matter of fact, the film opens with one.

A group of teenagers sit around a campfire smoking and drinking. One boy keeps giving a girl the eye. She gets up and begins to run toward the beach. He gives chase, continually calling to her, "Slow down. Wait. I'm coming." As she throws off some of her clothes, he adds, "I'm definitely coming." Reaching the water naked, the girl enters for a swim. By this point the boy has reached the beach and lies down on the sand. The girl calls out, telling him to take a swim too, but he refuses. Suddenly the shark attacks, whirling the girl in a coil of death through the water. She screams for what seems to be an eternity. Some of her words, though scrambled, can be made out. She is yelling, "It hurts, it hurts." At this precise moment the camera cuts to the boy, stretched out on the beach and intoning, "I'm coming, I'm coming." No doubt he was.

Because of the suspense and horror in this scene, the implications of the dialogue and succession of events are difficult to grasp consciously. But logically there is no reason for the boy to be repeating "I'm coming" when he and the girl have already spoken and ascertained that he is, in fact, on the beach. Are we to believe that he had, within seconds, slumped into a drunken stupor, oblivious to her piercing cries, and that his loaded words were meaningless? No. This scene reeks with meaning, and the scent is unmistakably one of rape/murder. (The suggestion of rape is actually inserted into the dialogue later when men, viewing her remains, joke about Jack the Ripper.) One can protest that the boy did not touch the girl, that it was indisputably the shark who killed her. Yes, but this is not supposed to be enacted and perceived as a "normal" rape scene. Rather, it is a carefully constructed form of subliminal cinematic rape, with the visual images leading to one interpretation, but the sound and succession of events suggesting another.

As I have previously noted, this was the only female whom the shark ever attacks; every other victim, anyone who is even actively threatened by the shark, is male. There is, again, a mythic rationale for this construction. The plotting of *Jaws* draws heavily upon the patterns of ancient sea monster myths. One type of these is so prevalent that an entire genre has been named for it: the Andromeda theme. In these stories a hero or god rescues a chained maiden from a ravaging sea monster. He generally slays the beast and marries the girl. However, Robert Graves (1966, 363) offers a radically different interpretation of this scenario: "Theophilius was wrong to suggest that the hero rescues the chained virgin from a male sea-beast. The sea-beast is female—the Goddess Tiamat or Rahab—and the God [or hero] Bel or Marduk, who wounds her mortally and usurps her authority, has himself chained her in female form to the rock to keep her from mischief. . . . It has even been suggested that in the original icon, the Goddess's chains were really necklaces, bracelets and anklets, while the sea-beast was her emanation." With this relevant background in mind, we can wonder if the visual appearances of *Jaws* are as potentially deceptive as those of ancient myths. If the subliminal message is that the girl has been raped and murdered, then the shark is clearly the archetypal revenging guardian spirit, who, throughout the rest of the film, with deliberate vengeance, attacks only males.

Extensions of the Myth

Man is the hunter; woman is his game.
The sleek and shining creatures of the chase,
We hunt them for the beauty of their skins;
They love us for it and we ride them down.
    Alfred Lord Tennyson, *The Princess*

Jaws incorporates many of the most misogynistic and gynophobic elements of patriarchal civilization. These elements are by no means restricted to symbolic representation, but are enacted with dire consequences for women. Here, I will pinpoint some of these and briefly explicate their extension into life.

Fear of the vagina dentata. As previously mentioned, this primal belief is one of the causes of the practice of female genital mutilation. This involves the removal of parts of the external genitalia, the clitoris, and the labia; in the most severe form, infibulation (practiced in the Sudan), the clitoris, labia minora, and parts of the labia majora are amputated, and the vulva is scraped raw and sewn together. It is estimated that over thirty million women alive today have been subjected to some form of genital mutilation.

The "deathly and devouring womb." In *Jaws* the fetishized object of attack is the shark's mouth, symbol of the vaginal jaws, the "fishy" vulva of the human female. In the 1970s American medicine was leading a similar battle against the uterus. Each year more than 690,000 hysterectomies were performed, making it the second most frequently performed major operation. Almost half of all women over forty were advised to undergo it. The operation ended in death for 12,000 women per year. Researchers estimated that 15 to 40 percent of these operations are unnecessary (Rodgers, 1975). Their popularity, however, was in part due to an attitude expressed by some gynecologists that the post-childbearing uterus is a "potentially lethal organ." Dr. Ralph C. Wright, a Connecticut gynecologist, termed the womb a "useless, bleeding, symptom-producing, potentially cancer-bearing organ [which] therefore should be removed" (Larned, 1974, 36). Behind each word of Wright's scutter eons of male dread of the womb of death, of which *Jaws* is the latest monstrous projection. When he announces that the womb is a "potentially lethal organ," we might respond, yes, but lethal to whom? Who indeed is afraid of the Big Bad Womb?

Women as fish: the shark as a symbolic woman. Male homosexual slang once designated women as "fish" (Lederer, 1968, 249). This symbolic association has a long history. To the contemporary imagination the shark, as the most dangerous fish, signifies the perilous aspect of women. Anyone who reads the current literature on sharks will soon begin to notice a creeping, pervasive, irrational fear and tendency to obsession that cannot be caused only by the species' potential danger to humans. Rather, the source of this fear is the identification of the shark with that which is outside the comprehension and control of man—primitive danger, the wild—similar to the dread with which some men view women. Jacques Cousteau wrote of the fear of sharks: "Second in violence only to the monstrous fury of hungry sharks is the blind hatred of men for this species. I have watched and filmed scenes of carnage of implacable cruelty, in which normally quiet and reasonable men used axes to hack at the bodies of sharks they had caught, and then plunged their hands and arms into the blood streaming from the entrails, to extract their hooks and bait. Floundering about among the gutted carcasses for hours on end, pushing hook and bait back up to within inches of the quivering jaws they would normally never have gone near, these men were gratifying some obscure form of vengeance" (Cousteau and Cousteau, 1970, 23).

Do these men really aim at some form of vengeance, or do they rather act out of fear, frustration, and ontological impotence? This dismembering carnage is similar to the tearing asunder of the North American Earth Goddess, to the breaking of the Leviathan, to the splitting of Tiamat by Marduk. These are legends that give intuitions about a past for which we have no real details. But details are available about the maddeningly same rituals that are performed today. The following account is taken from the testimony of a Vietnam veteran concerning war crimes he witnessed and participated in in Vietnam. A squad of men have just beaten and shot a woman to death. One of them, a representative of the U.S. Agency for International Development, approaches her body: "He went over there, ripped her clothes off, and took a knife and cut from her vagina almost all the way up, just about to her breast and pulled her organs out, completely out of her cavity, and threw them out. Then he stooped and knelt over and commenced to peel every bit of skin off her body and left her there *as a sign for something or other*" (Vietnam Veterans Against the War, 1972, 74; emphasis added). As a sign—a sign of the times, a sign of approval, a sign from god, signed, sealed, and delivered. A sign of the identity of all patriarchal wars. A sign that reads, "The State of Patriarchy is the State of War . . . and the primordial, universal Enemy of patriarchy and its wars is the female sex" (Daly, 1978, 103). In view of the gynocidal myths that pervade this world, can there be any shock at such atrocities? Mircea Eliade can write this: "*One becomes truly a man only by conforming to the teaching of the myths, that is, by imitating the gods . . . in illo tempore the* god had slain the marine monster and dismembered its body in order to create the cosmos. Man repeats this blood sacrifice — sometimes even with human victims" (1975, 1:254; emphasis in original).

A Knock on the Unconscious

Once when someone tried to talk to a group of children about sharks one of them cried out: "There is no such thing as a shark."

Kornei Chukovsky

One last theme is suggested by *Jaws*. Jung wrote, "The sea is the favorite symbol for the unconscious, the mother of all that live" (Jung and Kerenyi, 1963, 96–97). Neumann wrote, "The Terrible Female is a symbol for the unconscious. And the dark side of the Terrible Mother takes the form of monsters" (1963, 148). The ocean setting of *Jaws* is precisely appropriate for a horror film; its sea and shark are the unconscious mind, the realm of thought and creativity, which remains a wilderness, beyond the colonizing grasp of patriarchal socialization.

This socialization process divides the mind, carving out an area (the conscious) which is drawn into a specific, accepted, reality.[4] Subliminal incursions are then launched into the remainder, the sub- and the unconscious. The uncontrolled territory is by and large cut off from clear communication with the conscious but remains, in essence, mysterious, primitive, even wild, as evidenced by dreams, creativity, intuition. *Jaws*, however, implants the suggestion that these depths of the mind and the self are, in fact, deadly. (This theme recurs in science fiction and horror; see especially the film *Forbidden Planet* [Fred McLeod Wilcox, 1956].) It floods us with the image of a zone inhabited by terrifying creatures where we are out of our element, completely vulnerable, and ultimately subject to destruction. As it subliminally dips into our minds, *Jaws* asks us to become terrified of that mind, warning us: "Stay off the beaches," "Keep out of the water." For naturally if "we," that is our awareness, are not there, what remains to keep subliminal invasions out?

The purpose of *Jaws* is to instill relentless terror. Though the movie ends, its message is set for eternal mental replay. Yet all those who reeled and wondered under the ferocious assault of patriarchal myth in *Jaws* should remember that this great white shark, and whales, dragons, serpents, and sea monsters as well, represent the untamed female, the Mother, the *vagina dentata*, the Lesbian, the White Goddess, Tiamat, the wild, the unconscious (B. Harris, 1977, 5–8).[5] As Ishmael in *Moby-Dick* allowed, "And of all these things the Albino whale was the symbol. Wonder ye then at the fiery hunt?"

2

Sleeping with the Enemy as Pretty Woman Part II?

So, what happened after he climbed up the tower and rescued her?
Edward (Richard Gere) to Vivian (Julia Roberts) in *Pretty Woman*

She left her husband. He was a terrible man; he used to beat her. Oh, it wasn't always like that. At first he was charming and tender, but it all changed after the honeymoon.
Laura (Julia Roberts) in *Sleeping with the Enemy*

Once upon a time, a pretty white girl from the heartland named Vivian (Julia Roberts), a girl with a self-confessed penchant for "bums," quit high school and followed one of them to Los Angeles. Soon she found herself on the streets, working Hollywood Boulevard but maintaining her independence (no pimp for her), her sense of humor, and her dreams. A black man, a "street-talker," calls out, "This is Hollywood. Everybody comes to Hollywood got a dream. What's your dream?" One day, Vivian is having a particularly bad time. Her roommate has spent all their rent money on drugs, making it likely that they will lose their apartment. On the way to confront her, Vivian runs smack into the police, who are pulling the unseen body of a murdered woman from a dumpster. The police question the street-talker: "Who was her pimp?" He replies: "Cocaine her pimp. She a 'strawberry' . . . trading her sorry self for some crack." The roommate seems in danger of taking

37

on a pimp herself, but after a pep talk from Vivian changes her mind and recites their mantra: "We say who, we say when, we say how much."

Later that night, Vivian's luck seems to change drastically when she is picked up by a lost but outrageously rich corporate raider, Edward (Richard Gere), the epitome of the emotionally constipated workaholic. Edward is trying to find his way back to Beverly Hills. Vivian not only gives him directions but shows him how to drive his (borrowed) expensive sports car. She is markedly bold, self-possessed, and fabulously witty. Her most appealing trait for female viewers is her ability to speak truth to his power with no holding back. She mocks the decorous snobs they encounter in the hotel elevator and is utterly forthright about her sexuality. When they arrive at his exclusive hotel, she propositions him. Though he initially turns her down, something makes him change his mind, and he hires her for the night. First, though, he wants to get a little paperwork done, so he orders champagne and strawberries for her and then directs her to the television to amuse herself. Vivian goes into the bathroom. When Edward suspects that she is doing drugs and barges in, he finds that she is only flossing her teeth; this is a key scene that establishes Vivian as "clean," innocent, a "nice girl" even though she is a prostitute. While Edward catches up on calls and paperwork, Vivian lies on the floor on her stomach and loses herself, accompanied by childlike guffaws, in an episode of *I Love Lucy*. This childish affect (gum chewing, fidgeting, etc.) marks Vivian's behavior throughout the film. Watching her, Edward gets turned on and wordlessly communicates an imperative. She then crawls across the room on hands and knees to attend to him. Vivian asks him what he wants. He asks her what she does. "Everything," she replies (a huge concession in the context of prostitution), except for kissing on the mouth. Still on hands and knees, she performs oral sex on him. Some viewers might find the rapid transition from giggling "little girl" to "knowing whore" a bit disturbing.

The next morning, as Vivian wakes and sits down to strawberries and other morning delicacies, Edward makes a proposal. He has just been left by his live-in girlfriend, whom, it is made clear, he has neglected and used for some time. Edward seemingly has no negative emotional reaction to this traumatic event. Did the woman mean anything to him other than a relationship object? In any event, the girlfriend has finally refused to be at his "beck and call," and he is in need of an escort for his week's business activities in Los Angeles. Edward and Vivian strike a deal whereby she gets $3,000 for being his "beck and call girl" for the rest of the week.

Edward sends Vivian out with some cash to purchase suitable clothes. She heads to Rodeo Drive, where she is put down and put out of their store by snooty clerks. Luckily for Vivian, the hotel manager takes a proprietary and paternal interest in her and contacts a friend to help her. A few days later, Edward himself accompanies Vivian on a multi-thousand-dollar shopping spree. Store clerks, who have verbally affirmed their desire to "suck up" to Edward, surround Vivian with sartorial options that Edward selects or rejects. Later she models the outfits as the song "Pretty Woman" plays on the soundtrack. Sharing moments such as these, as well as baths, operas, business dinners, and barefoot walks through the grass, Vivian begins to influence Edward and inspire him to renounce some of his more predatory business tactics. Soon, she and Edward are "in love."

When Edward proposes that Vivian be installed permanently as his Los Angeles mistress, the romantic Vivian refuses, telling him that as a child she always dreamed of being a princess locked in a tower who is rescued by a knight on a white horse. "I want the fairytale," she insists. Reluctant to make a commitment, Edward bids her farewell. The next day, when he is checking out, he asks the helpful hotel manager to do him a favor and return a jeweled necklace he had rented for Vivian to wear to the opera. The manager asks to look at the necklace and then delicately suggests to Edward: "It must be difficult to let go of something so beautiful." At this, Edward undergoes an epiphany and, now understanding Vivian to be comparable to a quarter-million-dollar necklace, hightails it down to Hollywood to spring her from her low-class apartment, rescue her from prostitution, and presumably marry her.

Once, during a class devoted to *Pretty Woman* (Garry Marshall, 1990), a young woman stood up and announced that after seeing the movie she had thought about going into prostitution but that our discussion had changed her mind. However ridiculous this seems, it would be foolish to discount the influence of such films on impressionable minds. Olga Shved, who runs La Strada, an organization in Kiev dedicated to fighting the trafficking of women in Eastern Europe, specifically mentions *Pretty Woman* as a dangerous influence whose message that prostitution can be a good way to meet a rich husband has rendered young women particularly susceptible to pimps and international traffickers.[1] Another activist, Mary Madden, also despises *Pretty Woman*. Writing for the prostitution advocacy group WHISPER (Women Hurt in Systems of Prostitution Engaged in Revolt), Madden deplores the film's depiction of prostitution as "glamorous, sexy and profitable" and the way viewers "are led to believe that prostitutes can choose their customers, and choose and enjoy the sex acts they engage in" (1990, 4).

According to the International Organization for Migration, an offshoot of the United Nations (Binder, 2002), seven hundred thousand women and girls annually are trafficked, mostly involuntarily, specifically for sexual slavery around the world, across international borders, including into the United States. Within the United States, most home-grown prostitutes, male and female, enter into prostitution at the age of thirteen or so. Overwhelmingly they are on the street because they have run away from sexual and/or physical and psychological abuse at home. Most are initiated into prostitution by a pimp through an elaborate method of seduction and procurement (Hodgson, 1997). The ravages associated with the life include being raped and beaten, getting infected with sexually transmitted diseases, being socially stigmatized, and falling prey to drugs, homelessness, and hopelessness.[2] In *Pretty Woman* we see all these factors vaguely swirling around and behind Vivian, but somehow she has remained miraculously untouched by them.

Pretty Woman was a phenomenal success, particularly among female viewers. In a piece in the *New York Times Magazine,* "Prince Charming Comes Back," Daphne Merkin argues vehemently against the film's detractors and insists that we recognize *Pretty Woman* as a distillation of an enduring female fantasy of "sexual submission and emotional domination" (1990, 18). She quotes a number of ardent fans, including "Sara, a skeptical-to-the bone woman, divorced, a family therapist," who tells her, "It's been a long time since I've thought about a movie so much, wishing for the sequel to come."

Talk of a sequel has continued over the years. Still, I think female viewers already have been given their sequel—inadvertently—in *Sleeping with the Enemy* (Joseph Rubin, 1991), a thriller about a battering husband who is so consumed with jealousy that he beats his wife after another man compliments her beauty, who holds his much younger wife as such a prized possession that if she leaves him he will kill her, who has her so terrorized that she submits to sexual relations that she would refuse if she could. Supposedly, once *Pretty Woman*'s Vivian walks away from the combat zone of prostitution, all is safe and happy. But as *Sleeping with the Enemy*'s Laura reminds us, the danger remains; it just has shifted to the home front.

Sonja Peterson-Lewis, who has conducted research into battering relationships (1990), argues that in many cases the behaviors that attract the woman in the first phase of a relationship are firmly related to subsequent, overtly abusive ones that characterize the committed phase. Such behaviors include: jealousy (which at first makes the woman feel special and cared about, but later catalyzes his physical violence); a remarkable attention to her dress or mannerisms (later manifesting as an obsessive need to control all aspects of her presentation); his role as "protector," willing to use violence against others (indicating that he might be wont to turn that violence against her); and her role as "protégé" (leading him later to claim her undying gratitude).

Peterson-Lewis examines these and other related "paradoxes," commenting that such patterns remind her of "the old adage that warns: 'The things that make you laugh can also make you cry.'" Similarly, a lighthearted and comic fantasy like *Pretty Woman* can unfold quite logically into the very scenario that terrifies us. Guided by the star of Julia Roberts's presence in both films (as well as a number of bizarre visual and thematic correspondences between them), we might imagine *Pretty Woman* and *Sleeping with the Enemy* as representing two phases of one relationship.

Sleeping with the Enemy concerns a vulnerable young woman from the heartland, Laura (Roberts), who is married to Martin (Patrick Bergin), an outrageously rich, dark, handsome older man. The couple has been wed for about four years, and although they started out very much in love, marriage brought out the batterer in the man, and horror has overtaken this "fairytale" romance. Laura desperately wants to leave but knows that if she does Martin will seek her out and murder her. Thus, she has devised a secret escape plan. Faking her own death, she disguises herself (wearing a wig that, though brown, is otherwise exactly like the blond one we first see on Vivian), heads for the Midwest, assumes a new identity, and acquires a boyfriend, Ben (Kevin Anderson), a drama teacher at the local college. At one point, Ben takes her to his workplace and has her try on a succession of costumes, while the song "Brown-Eyed Girl" plays in the background. It's not "Pretty Woman," but it's close.

Many viewers might wonder if Ben is really such a good bet. At their first meeting, he mock-threatens Laura as she takes some apples from a tree in his yard. He also has a disturbing tendency to come up on her unawares. Another time, with little thought for her comfort or pleasure, he pushes her down on some stairs and tries to have intercourse with her, ignoring at first her cries for him to stop. Earlier, Laura had reminisced with Martin about his teaching her to dance; later, Ben dances with Laura to the tune of "Run-around Sue." The action (dancing) and the song's theme (women as unfaithful) are motifs clearly identified with Martin, but it's Ben who is now in the picture. Nancy Price's novel (1987), on which the film is based, far more directly suggests Ben's misogyny and his potential for battery, but here we do not see the new relationship develop in detail. Martin has discovered Laura's deception and has tracked her down. After some conventional slasher-film stalking, the two confront each other, and Laura kills him with his own gun. Maybe she will now start the whole nightmare over again with Ben.

Although each of these films is pitched to a female audience, they represent different genres. *Pretty Woman* is a romance, a utopian fantasy confirming the possibility of male-female relationships in a world marked by a sex-based power differential. *Sleeping with the Enemy* is a Gothic nightmare fantasy, a story form where a woman finds that her husband is a lunatic, a murderer, or both. As Tania Modelski (1982, 61) notes, these genres correspond to different stages in a woman's life. In romances, the "preoccupation is with getting a man; in Gothics the concern is with understanding the relationship and the feelings involved once the union has been formed."

In *Pretty Woman,* the initial phase of that relationship, Vivian not only gets her man; she also realizes her childhood wish to be a "princess." Her "white knight," Edward, actually is a graying one; he is about twenty years older than she (a gap emphasized by her consistently childish behaviors), but fabulously rich and cultured. He plays classical music on the piano and introduces her to opera. In *Sleeping with the Enemy,* the union has been formed. Laura's husband, Martin, is also significantly older and significantly richer; uncannily, his favorite and frequently spoken endearment for his wife is "princess"; he ritually insists on Berlioz to accompany his sexual encounters with her. Like Edward, Martin is extremely organized and tries to keep everything under control, but in his case the negative implications of this behavior surface immediately. For example, there is his martial marital tidiness. At home, under threat of a beating, Laura must see to it that all the cans in the kitchen cupboard line up impeccably and the bathroom towels hang at attention.[3]

Martin is very attentive to his wife's dress and concerned that she have suitable attire; like Edward, he selects his lover's clothes.[4] In one of the opening sequences of *Sleeping with the Enemy,* Martin steers Laura into wearing a dress of his choice to a party, against her own inclination. Later, when they return, he is so turned on by her appearance and submission to his will that he grabs her, knocking to the floor the plate of strawberries she is holding. In any other film, the spilled strawberries might pass as a sign of uncontrollable passion; here they signify the sexual violence normalized in this marital relationship and Martin's use of sex as a weapon of domination. Soon Laura, like the strawberries, is on the floor, knocked down when her paranoid husband explodes with jealous rage over an imagined transgression. Curiously, strawberries attend the first sexual encounter between the lovers in each film. Moreover, in the opening of *Pretty Woman,* the fallen/murdered prostitute — the so-called strawberry — is a stark warning of the fate of women who fall outside patriarchal favor and protection.

Martin and Edward are men accustomed to power; both are models of self-discipline and demand order and discipline in others. They are both older and of much higher class status than their lovers. They have many subordinates, expect to control situations, and get people to do as they wish. In *Pretty Woman* racial, class, sexual, and age hierarchies are pronounced. Vivian's Italian American roommate (Laura San Giacamo) speaks with a working-class accent; the murdered woman pulled from the dumpster is never seen, but due to racist stereotyping the reference to "crack" addiction stereotypically conjures an image of an African American woman (Roberts, 1997, 156–57). All the women in the film are service objects — wives, secretaries, prostitutes, cheap or expensive but always available for a price (as the film's opening sequence makes clear).[5] The age gap between Vivian and Edward has uncomfortably pedophilic overtones, as she is consistently saddled with little-girlish behaviors. The men who surround the WASPish Edward are classified according to a social/racial/sexual hierarchy. His greedy and unscrupulous lawyer (Jason Alexander) is coded as Jewish and as a repressed homosexual in love with Edward; the helpful though unnamed hotel manager (Hector Elizondo) is a light-skinned Latino; the hotel chauffeur (R. Darrel Hunter) is a dark-skinned African American. Both Martin and Edward are surrounded by "others" who must serve and defer to them. In short, they are defined by their power over subordinates, a power that begins at home.

Clothing is an important icon in each film. Women's clothing, and what it can symbolize (acquiescence to objectification, men's fetishistic tastes, and so on), clearly functions as an aphrodisiac for Martin. After one battering session, he brings home a red silk camisole. Immediately he puts it on Laura and just as immediately demands sex. She, having no choice, suffers beneath him, clearly experiencing no pleasure. This scene provides a textbook illustration of Andrea Dworkin's (1987) argument that, in a context of male supremacy, sexual intercourse is conceptualized and practiced as a ritual of domination. Ludicrously, the sex between the prostitute and her john in *Pretty Woman* is presented as ecstatic.

Despite the romantic and comedic frame and the bones tossed to gender equality in *Pretty Woman*, Edward and Vivian's relationship is based purely in male authority and female negotiation. To be sure, she "works it" superbly, but from a profoundly disadvantaged position. Moreover, by film's end Vivian is totally in Edward's world, wearing "his" clothes, following his etiquette, and mingling with his friends. Her formerly defiant voice, like her attire, is now muted. And let's face it, along with all the other social inequities between the two—class, status, gender, age—she is his sexual servant during the brief week of their "courtship." Their first sexual experience happens when, at his command, she crawls over to perform fellatio on him. Are we really ready to believe that after the marriage ceremony she no longer will have to do "everything" on demand?

Vivian's almost divine canniness in a hostile world and her successful manipulation of that system make her a deeply attractive heroine to many women viewers, a goddess of personal beauty, sexual prowess, and transformational power. She, all alone, is able to change the chilly Edward into a human being with a soul and a conscience. Yet viewers' deep fondness for Vivian might also demonstrate that, consciously or unconsciously, women identify with Vivian's status as prostitute—having to cater, trick, and act out somebody else's sexual scenarios in order to get security, social status, and a nice lifestyle. While Vivian is undoubtedly smart, she acts within a world that deeply circumscribes and prostitutes female potencies and possibilities.

Pretty Woman concerns a prostitute; *Sleeping with the Enemy,* a wife. Numerous feminist thinkers have pointed to the wavering line dividing wife from prostitute, none more dramatically than Nawal el Saadawi in her novel *Woman at Point Zero.* Her prostitute/heroine Firdaus speaks (1983, 91): "Not for a single moment did I have any doubts about my own integrity and honour as a woman. I knew that my profession had been invented by men, and that men were in control of both our worlds, the one on earth, and the one in heaven. That men force women to sell their bodies at a price, and that the lowest paid body is that of a wife. All women are prostitutes of one kind or another. Because I was intelligent I preferred to be a free prostitute, rather than an enslaved wife." Firdaus ultimately kills a pimp who, despite all her efforts to refuse and avoid him, starts to control her life. She speaks a "savage and dangerous" truth to the Arab prince who is her last john, telling him that although she has killed a man, she is not the criminal, since she has killed only a criminal. Moreover: "I am saying that you are criminals, all of you: the fathers, the uncles, the husband, the pimps, the lawyers, the doctors, the journalists, and all men of all professions" (100). Firdaus is arrested and rejects an option to ask the president for the pardon that would have spared her life; she is executed in prison.

Poor women often recognize and accept that they participate in forms of modified or folk prostitution as one of the necessities of living under systems of male supremacy. An impoverished woman who engages in casual sex expects to get some financial help in paying the rent or buying groceries. Gina Wood, a public health professor in Georgia, explains that poor women do this "just trying to make ends meet, day-to-day survival . . . how they have to frame their lives, especially if they have children or elderly parents to care for" (quoted in Sack, 2001). Women privileged by race and class are far more likely to insist on a great distance between prostitution and traditional matrimony. Yet these same women often pass on to younger women such advice as: "It's just as easy to marry a rich man," which is just another way of saying, "Don't give it away for free, and make sure you get the best price."

My great-aunt Fritz, dispensing alternative wisdom, warned me: "The man who courts you is not the man you marry." In other words, just like Martin in *Sleeping with the Enemy,* a man can radically change from prince to predator right after the wedding vows. Vivian, formerly (in her mother's words) a "bum magnet," is attracted only to men who are bad for her. She ends up committing herself to a man she has known for only one week. Feminists raising awareness about spouse abuse firmly advise against the whirlwind courtship and bonding to a man whom one knows only slightly. And what Vivian does know about Edward should signal potential abuse.

Edward had an authoritarian and emotionally abusive father, who left him and his mother when he was young and vulnerable, and against whom he has harbored a great deal of rage that he might be prone to project onto other relationships, a common tendency of batterers (Sonkin, Martin, and Walker, 1985, 45). Edward also has a jealous streak. At a polo game Vivian gets into a friendly conversation with a business rival of Edward's. Edward observes this and when pressed by his nasty lawyer, Philip, to reveal how he met Vivian, tells him that Vivian is a "hooker" whom he picked up on Hollywood Boulevard. Philip uses the information immediately to humiliate Vivian during a verbal exchange.

When Vivian and Edward argue about this later, Vivian tells him that if she were wearing her own clothes she would have been able to hold her own against Philip, that she is not Edward's toy, and that she has sovereignty. Edward responds by flaunting his power over her, telling her that she has very few options in life. When she gathers herself to leave him, telling him that he doesn't own her and repeating at least part of her mantra, "I say who, I say when" (though now in a quavering voice), he takes another approach. He softens, apologizes, and pleads with her to stay. Edward plays his trump card when he reveals that he had seen her talking with the other man and "didn't like it." She defends herself: "We were just talking." He repeats: "I didn't like it." Vivian relents but tells him that he hurt her and he should never do it again. The next scene shows them in bed, post coitus, being intimate emotionally and sharing secrets from their pasts. Vivian imprudently assumes that he won't hurt her again just because she tells him not to. And she is doubly fooled for taking jealousy as a sign of love. Jealousy indicates possessiveness and insecurity and leads, as it does here, to retaliation. It does in *Sleeping with the Enemy* as well, when Martin's jealousy over the most inconsequential of his wife's interactions with men repeatedly occasions his abuse, despite his apologies and assurances that he won't do it again.

Previously, Edward has had only troubled relationships with women, characterized by coldness, neglect, and condescension. "Impossible relationships are my special gift," he tells Vivian. It is easy to see why, for women, whether girlfriends or prostitutes, are objects that Edward appropriates and makes use of. Indeed, his decision to commit to Vivian is formed only after he understands her to be comparable to a beautiful and expensive necklace that he had rented (just as he had rented her in her capacity as prostitute). The exchange with the hotel manager makes him realize that he actually can *own* the woman; quite simply, he can marry her. Perhaps this is how Martin felt in the early stages of his relationship with Laura. Subsequently, Martin's sense of ownership is so profound that, should Laura leave him, he will resort to murder so that no one else can "have" her.

Many defenders of *Pretty Woman* argue that this is an egalitarian fairytale, for, as Vivian puts it in response to Edward's question at the start of this chapter: "She rescues him right back." Yet let's examine this proposition with some care. The idea that an upper-class corporate raider will descend to Hollywood Boulevard and lift a woman out of prostitution and make her his wife is indeed pure Hollywood. But the film's companion notion—equally evident in the Disney version of

Beauty and the Beast (Gary Trousdale and Kurt Wise, 1991) — that a woman can serve as the "savior" of some variant of the "bad boy," or, more precisely, a seriously troubled man (e.g., one with a history of alcohol abuse, womanizing, emotional problems, or violence), is an all too common reality. Indeed, the appeal of the "bad boy" for many women is a heady combination of the standardized dynamism of eroticized domination and submission and the opportunity to stage her own grandiose fantasy: In her narcissistic illusion, she is so "special" and so unique that the irascible bad boy will fall helplessly in love with her and change all his egregious behaviors.

Peterson-Lewis describes a "cheerleader/conspiracy" pattern accompanying the initial stages of abusive relationships: "In instances in which the actor [the batterer] has a history of dysfunctional behaviors and/or relationships, parents, relatives, and/or friends of the abusive personality may be particularly eager to find someone who can fill a 'savior' function for the actor." At first, the woman tends to be flattered by the acceptance, but later she is dismayed to find out that these friends and relatives had conspired, more or less consciously, to conceal the man's abusive past. Seducing us with the archetypal romance and the gloss of mutual salvation, *Pretty Woman* positions its audience as "cheerleader" for Vivian and Edward's relationship. In reality, few prostitutes have been "saved" by capitalists with hearts of gold, while the numberless women who play a redeemer-of-troubled-man role do so at great risk of damning themselves to a dysfunctional, if not abusive, relationship.

Perhaps foreshadowing the ultimate nightmare drift of this dream pairing is a scene where Vivian actually is battered — not, of course, by Edward, but by his negative *alter ego,* his lawyer. Angry that Vivian has influenced Edward to forgo a legal but unscrupulous business deal, Philip comes by and harasses her, taunting her as a "fifty-dollar whore" and then backhanding her across the face and trying to rape her. In the nick of time, Edward comes to the rescue and throws Philip out. But first Philip reminds Edward that he has given him ten years of total love and devotion. Edward verbally lashes Philip, telling him: "It was the 'kill' you loved, not me," and screaming at him to "get out." Later, as Edward holds ice to Vivian's bruised face, she alludes to the fact that she has been beaten before. Edward comforts her: "Not all guys hit," he says, appearing here to be the consummate good guy, the prince. Yet is Edward really so different from "guys" who hit and the assorted "bums" to whom Vivian has previously been drawn? Subtextually, Edward is not opposed to but identified with Philip. One of Philip's functions in the film is to provide a scapegoat repository for all of Edward's less ideally Prince Charming traits: emotional coldness, alienation, misogyny, rage, inordinate greed, a penchant to use people, a tendency to resort to violence when thwarted, and that devotion to "the kill."

The scene that directly precedes the battering episode clearly aligns Edward with Philip's perspectives and presages the violence. In it Edward offers to set up Vivian in a condo and make her his mistress. She reacts with bitter disappointment. He leaves her with this self-righteous statement: "I've never treated you like a prostitute." Only when Edward is out of earshot does she mutter, "You just did." The sassy Vivian is no longer in evidence; she has lost her ability to speak out and confront him and is manifestly more vulnerable now. How long will it be before Edward again treats Vivian "like a prostitute," perhaps accusing her of thwarting his business deals, impugning her as a "whore," beating her and raping her, making her do "everything" for him at his whim? Like Martin in *Sleeping with the Enemy*, probably he'll wait until after the honeymoon.

Pretty Woman closes with the voice of the "street-talker", the African American man whose presence and voice underscore the mythic character of the story. The street-talker is the very opposite of the rich, property-holding, and emotionally stunted Edward. Symbolically, we can read him as an "urban griot," the embodiment of the culture's soul and keeper of the oral tradition.[6] Ironically, this position would be greatly honored in a gynocentric society, but in *Pretty Woman*'s commodity-consciousness and male-dominated culture, it is Edward, the corporate raider, who commands all space and respect, while the "soul" is homeless. Edward, we might remember, is characterized by Vivian (when they first meet and she is still telling the truth) as having a "sharp" and "useless" look. Although the street-talker (and the tradition he represents) has been displaced and discredited, he still appears, calling out to all the other dispossessed people, urging them to keep "dreaming," to keep envisioning alternative possibilities, for, as the oral tradition has instructed over the millennia, no reality ever comes into being without first manifesting itself as a dream.

The dream in *Pretty Woman* is that our heroine (like Cinderella and countless other fairytale heroines), by virtue of her pluck, luck, character, beauty, and intelligence, can overcome the most desperate odds and transform her life. But *Pretty Woman* is a not-so-wonderful wonder tale, for it is very partial in its vision. Would Vivian have been worthy of romance and salvation if she were not "pretty"—young, slender, and white? In a racist worldview, "'ugly,'" Patricia J. Williams (1997, 282) observes, "is so often used as a synonym for 'black.'" D. Soyini Madison (1995, 230) explicitly asks us to recognize the ways that the film effectively excludes some of the most dispossessed—black women—from the "princess" dream. It is only because Vivian is a "pretty" white woman that the plot can "unfold in the manner that it does."

That plot hinges upon the safe resolution, for that pretty white woman, of the "good" girl/"bad" girl dichotomy. In *Pretty Woman,* the prostitute transmogrifies into the girl next door, fit to be a wife to the prince. But this is a token victory only. First of all, the prince is not really so charming, and we remain in serious doubt about his ability to transform. And, second, the dangerous and punitive double standard remains intact. This is the unavoidable message communicated by the "plot device" of the dead, unmourned, "un-pretty woman"—the (implicitly) African American prostitute in the dumpster whom we encounter at the film's opening.

Elsa Barkley Brown (1997, 275) reminds us of the relational nature of women's lives under both racism and sexism: "It is important to recognize that middle-class women live the lives they do precisely because working-class women live the lives they do. White women and women of color not only live different lives but white women live the lives they do in large part because women of color live the ones they do." The murder of "Skinny Marie," the film's silent (and silenced) woman, at the film's opening, although seemingly a gratuitous plot element, is actually fundamental. Marie and Vivian are held in just the type of relation described by Brown. Marie dies in order that Vivian may live. Marie suffers and is thrown away as so much trash so that Vivian can be rescued and counted as a treasured (if found) object by a member of the elite. Skinny Marie is the ritual blood sacrifice to the double standard; Vivian is the token that proves the rule.

Although superficially distinct in genre, subject, and tone, *Pretty Woman* and *Sleeping with the Enemy* take the same materials—the socially constructed power differential between women and men, the commingled fear and love women feel for men in a culture that aggrandizes men and devalues women—and shape these materials into either utopian fantasy or apocalyptic nightmare. In this case the Gothic nightmare almost immediately followed the Romance, semiotically and temporally. *Sleeping with the Enemy*'s appearance one year after *Pretty Woman* suggests that the earlier film introduced a gross imbalance into our collective fantasy life, for, however pleasurable the utopian dream might have been, digestion was incomplete and a restorative sour bite was needed in the form of a cautionary fable. In the "happy ending" of *Sleeping with the Enemy,* the princess does not marry her prince; she kills him!

Daphne Merkin expresses her enthusiasm for the sort of patriarchal fairytale that concludes with the kiss, the "mad, implausible embrace." Yet, as *Sleeping with the Enemy* reminds us, the story doesn't really end there. According to the National Violence against Women Survey (Tjaden and Thoennes, 2000, iii), "intimate partner violence is pervasive in U.S. society. . . . Approximately 1.5 million women . . . are raped and/or physically assaulted by an intimate partner annually in the United States, many victims are victimized more than once. . . . Thus, approximately 4.8 million intimate partner rapes and physical assaults are perpetrated against U.S. women annually." The most common way for a woman to be murdered is by a lover or former lover; the most dangerous time is when she is attempting to leave him. All too often when the Princess awakens from her dream of Prince Charming, it is only to find that she still is sleeping, though now not alone but with her mortal enemy.

3

Femme Noire

WITH LAURI SAGLE

When I was a little girl at primary school, I was always asked
to play the witch in playground fantasies. I felt uneasy but
wanted to have friends so I did.

Lola Young (1996, 1)

At work I'm treated like a great big, intimidating Negress, so I
spend half my time trying to make myself nonthreatening,
even though I'm not really threatening, so the caucasians can
deal with me—even though it's not really me they feel threatened by, it's their image of me.

Jill Nelson (1993, 251)

A number of critical works address the sexual politics of dangerous
women in popular films: "monstrous feminine" horror or science fiction
imagery (Creed, 1993), and violent, predatory femme fatale types in film
noir (Doane, 1991; Hart, 1994; Holmlund, 1994; Jermyn, 1996). Yet all
too often these critics (Mary Ann Doane is an exception) deal inade-
quately if at all with racial significations. Despite the linguistic commonplace, itself steeped in racism, that horror is "dark" and femmes fatales and the films they appear in are noir ("black"), many theorists,
through differing strategies, neglect to critique representations of dangerous, monstrous, and violent women of color and focus only on sexy
white femmes fatales (Hannsberry, 1998). Our purpose here is to address this oversight, provide some analysis of the racial politics of

femme noire imagery, and offer textual readings of several narratives that we find particularly revealing.

In her book *Fatal Women* Lynda Hart argues that, first of all, women of color rarely appear in dominant cultural representations. Moreover, in a heterosexist culture, the aggressive, predatory, criminal woman is the conventional stereotype for the lesbian; hence, the lesbian is "the silent escort of the violent woman" (1994, x) of popular film. Hart reasons that since lesbians are almost always represented as "overwhelmingly white and middle-class . . . the inverted others of a white, middle-class masculine imaginary" (xi), the classic femme fatale is always white. She thus restricts her discussion to those roles.

Conversely, Suren Lalvani, in "Consuming the Exotic Other," suggests that the femme fatale is paradigmatically a woman of color. Lalvani writes that in the nineteenth-century European Romantic imagination, the exotic woman of color represented uninhibited sexuality to be enjoyed by Western men. But, at the same time, "once her desire is freed, that in itself poses a threat to the colonial male's identity and the polarized categories of its constitution. Hence, the idea of the 'Fatal Woman'" (1995, 269).

Much of the standard imagery associated with the white femme fatale actually is rooted in colonialist and racist projections about the woman of color. The very characteristics that make the white woman "bad" or "noir" are those qualities that according to a racist/sexist viewpoint are especially endemic in women of color: primitive emotions and lusts, violence, sexual aggression, masculinity, lesbian tendencies, promiscuity, duplicity, treachery, contaminating corruption, sovereignty, and so on.

Let us consider a few examples of the white femme noire. In *The Cat People* (Jacques Tourneur, 1942), the Serbian Irena (Simone Simone) turns into a man-eating black panther when her hyper-bland white American husband approaches her for sex. While in a restaurant celebrating her marriage, she is recognized by another "cat woman," who calls out to her as "sister." The lesbian and racial subtexts are barely contained here. In *Basic Instinct* (Paul Verhoeven, 1992), the room in which the first homicide takes place is decorated with African art and statues of jungle beasts with bared fangs. Before we meet the killer—the thin, white, blond, upper-class Catherine (Sharon Stone)— the policemen at the murder scene joke that the 240-pound maid (racist-misogynist code for a woman of color) "did it." Blond Alex Forrest (Glenn Close) in *Fatal Attraction* (Adrian Lyne, 1987) sports a wild,

snaky hairdo, which, as many commentators noted, recalls the Gorgon
Medusa. This mythic allusion obviously suggests the character's fatal
relationship to men, yet the Medusa also archetypally signifies, as Alice
Walker reminds us, "the black female Goddess/Mother tradition and
culture of Africa" (1989, 269). In *The Hunger* (Tony Scott, 1983), Mrs.
Blaelock, the bisexual vampire, is played by a blond European, Catherine Deneuve. This centuries-old monster, however, was born in a
markedly nonblond country: *Egypt!* Perhaps the most alarming example is *Species* (Roger Donaldson, 1995). A pubescent girl, superficially an
all-American blonde, is actually a "half-breed" combination of alien
and human, the product of an experiment with alien DNA. Her keepers, fearing a deadly outcome, decide to kill her. She escapes and, while
on a train, undergoes a transformation, becoming an enormous, slimy,
snaky-haired monster. At this point an African American female porter
enters the room. The monster immediately subdues her. While the
porter lies on the floor with her legs spread, a giant hole in the monster's
body opens and ejects an adult white female. It is this woman who rampages through the rest of the film as a shape-shifting creature, sometimes a beautiful blonde, sometimes a lethal monster. The visual implication is unmistakable: subtextually, it is the African American woman
who is the "mother" of this white-looking but monstrous "half-breed."

All of these films hint at an insight at the heart of Julie Dash's
1982 short film *Illusions*. It is the hidden, background presence of the
woman/lesbian of color that gives the foregrounded white woman
much of her "voice," her power, strength, and resonance—even as this
very potency is made monstrous. No matter how insistently white and
heterosexual the classic femme fatale may appear, it is the mythic dark
woman/lesbian whose potencies—deepened through her distance from
and disloyalty to white heterosexist patriarchy—energize her.

Kimberlé Crenshaw (1993, 193) offers an analysis of what she terms
"representational intersectionality, referring to the way that race and
gender images . . . converge to create unique and specific narratives
deemed appropriate for women of color." Women of color appear regularly in dominant cultural representations. They do not, however, occupy the centralized and privileged roles that white women occupy.
Contemporary cinema regularly features scary, dangerous, and loathsome women of color, sometimes as less powerful or centralized variants
of classic femme fatale roles, but also in other types of narratives and
positions, as well as B-grade and exploitation movies—places that are
deemed "appropriate" for women of color. Here, we identify several

interwoven stereotypic "places"—the Virgin/Cannibal, Lady/Dragon, and Queen/Bitch—and give examples of these types of narratives and images.

The Virgin/Cannibal

> In a very peculiar way eroticism became a medium for estab-
> lishing contact, for penetrating the secrets of nature, the real-
> ity and the "otherness" of the continent. The seduction and
> conquest of the African woman became a metaphor for the
> conquest of Africa itself. Powerful erotic symbolism linked a
> woman's femininity so strongly to the attraction of the land
> that they became one single idea, and to both were attributed
> the same irresistible, deadly charm.
>
> Nicholas Monti (cited in Doane 1991, 213)

In *The Adventures of Priscilla, Queen of the Desert* (Stephan Elliott, 1994), three white Australian men, traveling drag show performers, meet an older white man who is living with his foreign, Asian wife; she is what is euphemistically called a "mail-order bride." Yet she is not the submissive helpmeet-*cum*-sex-toy spoil of colonialist warfare he had bargained for. Rather, she likes to get intoxicated and act out on stage (a privilege that, in this film, is reserved for biological males). One night the husband makes her stay at home while he accompanies the drag artists to a show he has arranged in his small, homophobic town. The locals are not especially pleased at the drag show but perk up when the wife, who has managed to escape, invades the stage and performs a semi-striptease and an act that includes first kissing some ping-pong balls and then inserting them into her vagina. She then bends over and ejects them with great velocity. Her husband interrupts this performance, dragging her kicking and screaming off the stage. The next day she leaves him, delivering one final insult (in cracked English): "You got lit-tle ding-a-ling." The misogynist humor here is rooted in a reversal of expectations: The poor husband wanted an exotic but docile maiden, symbol of his conquest, but instead got a voracious "man-eater"—that is, a woman who controls her own vagina.

In numerous narratives featuring women of color, a cannibalistic monster lurks behind the pretty mask of the apparently benign love/sex object. These Virgin/Cannibal representations push the envelope of the classic virgin/whore paradigm, bursting into "darker" meaning in popu-lar parables that issue warnings about the inherent danger of liaisons with the "other." After all, a "whore" can deceive, steal, embarrass, and convey social diseases, but a cannibal possesses sufficient incisoral strength to rip and chew, to wreak social destruction through full-scale annihilative consumption. She swallows (with her mouth or her vagina), digests, excretes, and incorporates with the mythic powers of destruction and creation. So, even though history is saturated with the literal records of white conquerors subjugating and assimilating nonwhite subjects, colonial narratives recurrently express, in a classic inversion, a fear of cannibalistic consumption perpetrated by unruly dark subjects. Such narratives serve to remind the conquerors that the forces of "civilization" must be maintained or all will be lost—down the atavistic, unbreachable Black Hole of the "cannibal's" gnashing orifice.

James Michener's Pulitzer Prize–winning *Tales of the South Pacific*, a novel published in 1946 and translated onto stage and screen via Rodgers and Hammerstein, may seem an unlikely place to seek virgins and cannibals, but where there are foreign-based U.S. soldiers, there are sure to be their indigenous female complements. Inevitably, someone in this volatile relationship rooted in eroticized military incursion, overt sexual exploitation, and cultural domination will be eaten. Historically, the equation does not favor the native woman.

According to Walden Bello (1992), there were three hundred U.S. military bases and facilities in the Pacific alone by the early 1990s, many of them established during or shortly after World War II. Consequently, the women of many of these Pacific nations were coerced into participating in "institutionalized [sexual labor] in a multi-million dollar entertainment industry that enjoys the blessing of the U.S. military, which considers sexual recreation vital for the 'morale' of the troops" (16). Cynthia Enloe (1990, 36) elaborates on this type of relationship, commenting that "sex tourism" is not confined to military personnel, but encompasses a wider audience of tourists, all of whom share a common philosophical conviction that "certain women, usually women of color, [are] more available and submissive than the women in their own countries."

In Michener's *Tales,* the relationship between Lieutenant Joe Cable and Liat, a young Island girl-woman, is one of the literary hallmarks of this type of encounter. Cable is a handsome young officer stationed on a South Pacific island during World War II. One of his assignments is to keep an eye on and, if possible, remove an enterprising native inhabitant named Bloody Mary, who sells island trinkets, including shrunken heads, to the soldiers. Bloody Mary is described as "old and repulsive with her parched skin and her jagged teeth" (169), and Cable cannot imagine a female more drastically different from his own fair sweetheart, "a lovely, fair-haired Bryn Mawr junior" (166). As he writes to this angel, he thinks of the "disparity between [Bloody Mary] and the lovely girl in Germantown. The unreality of the comparison overwhelmed him" (165–66). What Cable is unprepared for, however, is Bloody Mary's lovely daughter, Liat.

Bloody Mary encourages Cable to come visit Bali-ha'i. As Cable approaches the almost mythical island, the rapturous description of the native terrain converges with conventional notions of native females: "Bali-ha'i was an island of the sea, a jewel of the vast ocean. It was small. Like a jewel, it could be perceived in one loving glance. It was neat. . . . It was green like something ever youthful, and it seemed to curve itself like a woman into the rough shadows formed by the volcanoes on the greater island of Vanicoro. It was here on Bali-ha'i, within the protecting arm of Vanicoro, that the women of the islands lived" (171).

Much to Cable's delight, Liat, like Bali-ha'i, is also a small, neat, gem of the Pacific. And she is youthful, only perhaps seventeen. After Bloody Mary introduces Cable to her daughter, she retreats so that they might get better acquainted. He determines that her teeth were white, her form was exquisite, and that "she was altogether delectable" (177). After Cable has thoroughly explored/eaten Liat, he sees that she is "crying softly to herself, [and he finds] incarnadine proof that he was the first who had loved her" (178–79). She was an island virgin, and he had taken the first bite of this delicate fruit.

Cable soon begins to ruminate upon the character of Vanicoro, "a large and brooding island, miasmic with malaria, old fetishes, sickness and deep shadows. . . . [I]n the old times it was known as a magic place. . . . Only the bravest natives dared live on Vanicoro, and they were the last to give up cannibalism" (170). The connection between Vanicoro and Bali-ha'i is indisputable: Vanicoro shelters Bali-ha'i and flings a "protecting arm" around the little jewel (171). But squinting from a distance, Cable can hardly separate the two. The connection alarms him: "Were Bali-ha'i and all its people merely a part of the grim and brooding old cannibal island?" (183).

Cable attempts to repress the image of ancient savagery/cannibalism, but fails. Later that night, when polled by fellow officers as to whether or not he would sleep with a native "girl," Cable says no. He denies Liat publicly, but he privately acknowledges her magnetic allure and realizes that he must abandon her or all will soon be lost. Cable's repudiation of Liat is not based only in the social condemnation of miscegenation, but in his desire to protect his very soul from the long shadows cast by Vanicoro. Liat's teeth are, for the time being, "white and even," but soon they could extend into sharper tools, becoming stained and "funereally black" like Bloody Mary's. Soon it could be Cable's head, shrunken and displayed on a string by the Crone/Mother for his military brethren. So, instead, Cable devours her first, when he is still able to do so. He takes Liat's virginity, leaving her humiliated and positioned for marriage to an abusive older plantation owner. Somehow, however, Cable feels that *he* has been wickedly manipulated. In his final assertion of power over Liat and what she represents, Cable insists that she have sex with him as her husband-to-be arrives at her doorstep. As a military officer and a lover, Cable secures his territory and leaves his native maiden broken and sobbing while he takes off for his next assigned conquest/destination.

Not all renditions of the Virgin/Cannibal motif insist on the complete rejection of the native maiden. If she can be utterly divided from her monstrous double, the elder matriarch/cannibal, the virgin can be "saved"—that is, consumed and assimilated by the elite white man. The B-movie *She Gods of Shark Reef* (Roger Corman, 1958), filmed on the island of Kauai, depicts a successful severing.

She Gods was born in the historical period immediately prior to the admission of Hawaii as the fiftieth state. Contention, dissension, racist fear, as well as intoxication with the income potential of "paradise" incorporated, characterized much of the preceding debate. Statehood proponents had to counter contentions that residents of Hawaii were of "dubious ethnic stock," "alien heritage," and probable Communist affiliation (Daws, 1968, 388–90).

Much of the pro-statehood propaganda revolved around the representation of the Hawaiian Islands as a beautiful, warm, brown, welcoming woman, rather like the heroine of *She Gods of Shark Reef*. In this colonial fantasy, a sharp-tongued, shark-identified, and controlling Crone named Pua presides over an island of beautiful, playful, young native girl-women; there are no men on the island. The function of these island women is to gather and process pearls for an unnamed Big Company that owns the island. One fateful day, the brothers Chris and Lee, one "good" and one "bad," are shipwrecked on Shark Reef. They are almost devoured by the shark gods, but are rescued by Mahia (played, in the racist tradition of Hollywood, by Polish actress Lisa Montell). Pua tries to forestall the inevitable, but Chris (the "good" brother) is immediately attracted to Mahia.

Mahia is the Island personified—young, lush, verdant, wild, sexually ripe and juicy. She and the other young women, significantly, are harvesting pearls, not for themselves but for the Big Company. Pearls and oysters frequently symbolize female sexuality: defended by a stubborn shell until the time when it is pried open and the flesh voraciously consumed. The exotic consumption implied in *She Gods* is a vivid representation of what bell hooks (1992, 23) calls "eating the other": "When race and ethnicity become commodified as resources for pleasure, the culture of specific groups, as well as the bodies of individuals, can be seen as constituting an alternative playground where members of dominating races, genders, sexual practices affirm their power-over in intimate relations with the Other."

Before eating Mahia's oyster and stringing her pearl, however, our hero Chris must first separate Mahia from her heritage. This process is initiated at their first meeting when Mahia rescues the men, not only denying the sharks a sacrificial treat, but stabbing a shark to death. This act of blasphemy and self-negation is the beginning of the end for Mahia as an honorable native maiden. In Hawaii's mythohistory, the Shark is not only a deity but one of several *aumakua*, or ancestor-guardians, who are responsible for watching over their living relatives. The *aumakua*, as the Hawaiian historian Mary Pukui (1973, 37) says, "also [bring] warning of coming misfortune and deliverance from immediate danger." Furthermore, the *aumakua* can temporarily "possess" the corporeal form of their living relative and increase his or her strength, fortitude, or even creativity. Capricious mischief and directed displeasure are also characteristics of the *aumakua*, and one of the quickest ways to incur an *aumakua*'s rage is to needlessly kill or eat an animal of the *aumakua*'s form (38). Even if Mahia did not claim the shark as her *aumakua*, sharks are still revered within native Hawaiians' worldview, and slicing one up to save a couple of mercenary invaders would most likely evoke intense disfavor. And if these sharks were her *aumakua*—her ancestors, her family—perhaps they were bearing an urgent warning: "Avoid these meddlesome *haoles* ["outsiders," usually white mainlanders] and swim for your life!"

Pua, too, exhorts Mahia to stay away from the brothers and orders them to have no contact with her. But to them, Pua is just a spooky old lady with no real authority, a representative of the laughable "She Gods," for, as all viewers should know, "God" is singular and male. As part of their courtship, Chris works to displace Mahia's confidence in her *kupuna*, her elder, and replace it with unwavering faith in him, in his goodness, in his rightness, and in his ability to make decisions for her. In effect, he becomes her "god." Mahia eventually responds to his deconstruction and mockery of her sacred beliefs with this affirmation: "Chris good. I know that." Correspondingly, Pua becomes the emblem of "evil."

Pua decides that Mahia must be given to the sharks because of her transgressions, but god/Chris "saves" her, spilling more shark blood and severing Mahia from her sacred world. The two brothers and Mahia then prepare to leave the island. Lee, who is trying to make off with a cache of pearls, falls overboard and is killed by a shark. Here, the film's false opposition of good and bad brother is meant to derail recognition that the brothers are both thieves, and actually Chris might be the more insidious one. The pearls that Lee was trying to steal were the property of the Big Company that managed the island, surely a capital offense. This infraction, however, seems minor compared to what Chris effects. For Chris represents a model whereby the colonizers assimilate the natives and convince them of colonial integrity, moral superiority, and chivalry while desanctifying native gods, ridiculing native culture, and undermining native social relationships.

The final humiliation occurs as Chris and Mahia sail away into the sunset toward their new destiny. Pua, who has escaped from the bound and gagged position they had left her in, trails after them with her arms outstretched, begging Mahia to return. But it is too late. Chris has won his pearly girlie (and all she represents). Mahia, with her hand resting lightly on the strong shoulder of her new savior, turns her back on Pua and states with finality, "Let us go, Chris. The tide is high. The wind is strong. We'll leave evil behind us." Undoubtedly, a pair of Mai Tais await them in the brand-new Waikiki condo of their commodified future.

Another colonial love-sex-conquest-escape plot featuring a bifurcated Virgin/Cannibal heroine may be seen in *The Serpent and the Rainbow* (Wes Craven, 1986). Dr. Allen (Bill Pullman), employed by a Boston-based medical-pharmaceutical corporation called Biocorp, is seeking the magic formula for Haitian zombie powder, a formula guarded jealously by the Haitians who utilize or otherwise know of it. He is ostensibly motivated to locate this secret powder because of its miraculous anesthetic properties and its potential to save (elite American) lives. And, as added incentive, the head of Biocorp wants to "properly market" the powder, so . . . well . . . so a tidy profit can be made while they're saving all of those (American) lives.

Dr. Marielle DuChamp (Cathy Tyson), a local Haitian psychiatrist, is Allen's link to this murky world of Voodoo and zombification. She also happens to be light-skinned, sexy, and educated, but with enough of the "primitive" magic lingering in her to prove alluring to the inquisitive Allen. Her magic, though, is represented primarily as generous, indulgent, safe, sexual magic. For example, when she is possessed by the Goddess of Love at a religious gathering on their first night together, she focuses entirely on Allen, choosing him over the Haitian Voodoo priest. But Allen, the central white presence, is the real possessor; he will always remain in control. As Trinh Minh-ha (1989, 88) observes, colonized women of color in subordinate sexual relationships are presented as "the possibility of a difference, yet a difference or an otherness that will not go so far as to question the foundation of their beings and makings."

DuChamp is cast as the ideal tour guide: She possesses pagan knowledge and passion, but she is also reasonable, advocating for science, "civilization," and the white man who will "save" her country with these tools. Two consecutive symbolic scenes, representing this fusion of Eros, danger, containment, and colonial aggrandizement, occur on a pilgrimage during which Allen is guided by DuChamp. After walking for quite a distance, DuChamp and Allen, along with hundreds of other Haitians, make an encampment for the evening. As the worshippers sleep, they are bathed in the warm glow of surrounding candles. Allen wakes up and glances tenderly at DuChamp, who is sleeping soundly beside him. Suddenly an immense snake slithers over her sleeping form, advancing menacingly toward him. He is horrified and moves away from the snake that has seemingly emerged from the body of his faithful guide. How can this be? Apparently, inhering within DuChamp is a dark force he hadn't bargained on.

Compounding his shocked confusion is a chattering figure in the distance. As the figure approaches, it becomes obvious that it is a female dressed in a wedding gown and veil. Her words are unintelligible, but her connection to DuChamp soon becomes apparent. The bride's veil is lifted, revealing the horrifying visage of a rotting skeleton. A snake then shoots out of the bride's mouth, clamping onto Dr. Allen's face before he even has time to say, "I do." Allen wakes, sweating and terrified, as if from a dream. But dream or not, the message is clear: Beware of the dark other, because the cannibal, the savage, the snakelike betrayer, is always ready to burst forth from beneath the placid façade, ready to consume her next meal. Like the Virgin/Cannibal pair of Liat and Bloody Mary, DuChamp and her double, this Haitian Medusa, are among the most treacherous femmes fatales, threatening the global investments of military and corporate power, and the very forces of external access and acquisition rights, with their latent power to resist and devour.

Allen, like most patriarchal/colonial heroes, seeks to "boldly go where no man has gone before"—righteously and regularly violating sacred spaces and places of knowledge. Earlier he had tried to persuade an older, darker, larger Haitian woman into giving up some of her religious secrets. She refuses, shaking her head. But DuChamp will soon be used to fulfill that role. As their journey resumes, DuChamp leads him to a beautiful place, which she tells him is the most sacred area on their pilgrimage, a sequestered cove where Haitians have traditionally worshipped. While other Haitians celebrate below them, DuChamp and Allen copulate. She is seen in slow motion, and her movements recall those of a wild animal that has just been caught. Allen has found her "secret place," her exalted terrain, and will insert himself into it, taking what his white American male and corporate privileges give him: her body, her faith, and her culture's secrets.

In both *She Gods* and *The Serpent and the Rainbow*, the cannibal fatale is vanquished and "order" is restored. In the conclusion of these romances, the white heroes seem to be safely enamored of their brown, compliant lovers, though we are not privy to any further evolution of the relationship. For that, we might turn to the episodic horror film *Tales from the Darkside* (John Harrison, 1990). Here, as Kimberlé Crenshaw (1993) observes, the viewer is offered an admonition regarding such relationships: When procreation is actually achieved, the results are monstrous.

In "Beyond Racism and Misogyny," Crenshaw notes how themes of extreme violence and monstrosity often would not "work" unless the narrative focused upon a woman of color and evoked the peculiar race-sex exoticism created by the fusion of systems of white and male supremacy. One episode in *Tales from the Darkside* features a monstrous, gigantic gargoyle roaming through a seedy section of a city. It kills one white man and spares the life of another, a young artist, only after he promises never to reveal the events he has witnessed. Later that same evening, the artist meets and falls in love with a young woman of color (Rae Dawn Chong, an actor who is of mixed ancestry), whom he marries. He subsequently becomes highly successful and affluent. They have two adorable children. Still, he remains obsessed with his experience with the gargoyle. On their tenth anniversary, he decides that one way to express his profound love for his wife will be to break his vow and tell her the truth. As he does so, she becomes enraged and begins to transform. Of course, she is the gargoyle! Their children come out of their bedroom; they too have shape-shifted into mini-gargoyles! Although the artist begs for his life, she mercilessly tears out his throat, gathers her children, and flies out into the night. Crenshaw comments: "Here the drop-of-blood rule really works: The children, although half human, are little monsters too. Can anyone doubt the message—white male miscegenators, beware! Exotica and danger do go hand in hand" (1993, 119). For behind the apparently beautiful face of the woman of color—the virgin/lover/mother—lurks the lethal, cannibalistic, nonhuman monster.

A more thoughtful Virgin/Cannibal narrative structures the provocatively named "Faces," a 1995 episode of *Star Trek: Voyager*. A Federation officer who is half-Klingon, half-human, Lieutenant B'Elana Torres (Roxann Biggs-Dawson), is kidnapped by members of another species, the Vadians, whose entire population is afflicted with a terrible plague. The malevolent Vadians either keep captives as slaves or slaughter them for their organs, but they have a different plan for Torres. One of the Vadian doctors manages to separate her into two distinct beings, one human and one Klingon, so that he may experiment on a "purified Klingon specimen" in hopes of finding a cure for the plague.

As the narrative unfolds, the human Torres is clearly treated as the *true* Torres; she speaks as the central "I" and recalls growing up hating the Klingon aspect of her appearance, the oversized and demarcated forehead. Now she has gotten her wish and possesses a fully human face. The forceful Klingon self is presented as the "spice, [the] seasoning that can liven up the dull dish that is mainstream white culture" (hooks, 1992, 21). And she is a most useful ingredient, possessing great appetite, strength, bravery, and killing power. Soon, she escapes her bonds and encounters her human self. Forced to face her Klingon self, human B'Elana faints in horror. After she comes to, the "cannibalistic" Klingon B'Elana, flashing her powerful and prominent teeth, exhorts the weakened human B'Elana to eat some barely cooked meat she has prepared. Human B'Elana at first refuses, then forces herself to take a few virginal bites.

In this story, the Klingon—who throughout the *Star Trek* canon represents the racial "other"—provides the brawn and Eros, while the human supplies the brain, manipulating the computer to effect their escape. The Vadian doctor is wildly attracted to the Klingon B'Elana, but ultimately, when he tries to shoot the human one, her Klingon counterpart leaps into the path of the phaser beam. The human B'Elana mourns her demise but finds herself more at peace without what she perceives as the inner *alien* presence. However, human B'Elana learns that she cannot survive without having Klingon DNA, replicated from the dead B'Elana, reintroduced into her system. She grudgingly accepts this and concludes: "I guess I just have to accept the fact that I'll spend the rest of my life fighting with her." The last shot is of her ruefully rubbing her human forehead, in painful anticipation of the time when her Klingon aspect will again reassert itself.

As the protagonist's Chicana name, *Torres,* suggests, "Faces" is a metaphorical tale of *mestiza* experience and consciousness. This sci-fi *mestiza* can be read as beginning to accomplish what Gloria Anzaldúa (1990) calls "making her face/making her soul." In Anzaldúa's terms, making *face* means women of color "becoming a subject in our own discourses. We rip out the stitches, expose the multi-layered 'inner faces,' attempting to confront and oust the internalized oppression embedded in them, and remake anew both inner and outer face. . . . We begin to acquire the agency of making our own *caras*" (Anzaldúa, 1990, xxvi). Elsewhere Anzaldúa speaks of *mestiza* consciousness overcoming oppositional hierarchy, creatively sustaining contradictions, developing a tolerance for ambiguity. As a bridge between two or more cultures, the *mestiza* is healer and creator of a new nondualistic consciousness (Anzaldúa, 1987, 77–91). In "Faces" the *mestiza* has been trying to hide and even obliterate her inner *cara.* However, by episode's end, B'Elana has met her undeniably potent, erotic, and bold inner self and must now unequivocally face the fact that without *all* of her self she cannot survive.

Lady/Dragon

> And if we are not silent, suffering doormats, we are demon-ized dragon ladies—cunning, deceitful, sexual provocateurs. Give me the demonic any day—Anna May Wong as a villain slithering around in a slinky gown is at least gratifying to watch, neither servile nor passive.
>
> Jessica Hagedorn (1994, 74–75)

The stereotypic Dragon Lady is the female side of the white racist projection of the Oriental mastermind obsessed with world domination. She appears in popular culture as "Fu Manchu's various female relations, prostitutes, and devious madames" (Tajima, 1989, 309). We find her in such modern films as the cult offering *The Crow* (Alex Proyas, 1994), where Angel (Bai Ling), the horrifically beautiful and sadistic sister of the male villain, goads her brother/lover into participating with her in serial sexual torture and murder. Indeed, she seems to initiate much of it, taking a special delight in carving out the eyes of her female victims. The Dragon Lady also appears, for a younger audience, as Rita Repulsa (Julia Cortez), the nemesis of the Mighty Morphin Power Rangers. She is a visibly Asian witch/goddess who wears a horned headdress and pointy conical devices over her breasts. She represents the culmination of "bad" Asian female characteristics: greed, selfishness, and sophisticated intelligence combined with base cunning and an entirely unsentimental perspective on "love."

Darrell Y. Hamamoto (1994, 251) tells us that it was only as she grew older that the great actress Anna May Wong (Wong Lui-Tsong) was allowed to perform in roles relatively free of sexually racist stereotyping: "As an older woman, no longer could she be mistaken for the yellow temptress who could lure decent white men into unspeakable acts of debauchery with only a slight parting of her ruby-red lips." In his survey of "yellow peril" stereotypes, Gary Hoppenstand (1992, 284) notes that Dragon Lady imagery is based in "the image of the Oriental prostitute first introduced in American culture . . . in the dime novel" and continued in comic strips, films, and television portrayals. Like that of the Jezebel, whore, or sexually aggressive black woman (Collins, 1998, 81), the image of the "Oriental prostitute," later evolving into the sexually aggressive Dragon Lady, originated and continues under conditions of colonization and sexual slavery and serves to disguise and legitimate that slavery.

United States immigration policies in the nineteenth century were designed to exclude Chinese women. Of the few Chinese women in the United States at that time, many were prostitutes who had been sold into virtual slavery or debt peonage by male relatives. These women were forced to work for the most part in very low-grade brothels. They were beaten on a regular basis by both owners and johns, commonly were addicted to opium as it provided some respite from the constant abuse and degradation, and were afflicted in high numbers with gonorrhea and syphilis (Takaki, 1989, 40–42, 121–23). Systems of debt peonage (including both sexual and nonsexual labor) persist in contemporary U.S. culture for Third World women. Moreover, the image of the "Oriental prostitute" has acquired a new layer of expressive force since World War II, as U.S. troops have occupied areas of Asia and "turned out" the local population.

A typical Dragon Lady appears in the Arnold Schwarzenegger vehicle, the romantic comedy *cum* spy thriller *True Lies* (James Cameron, 1994). Schwarzenegger plays an American spy, Harry, who is leading a

double life, more interested in having adventures with his companion-
able male partner than with his wife, and not telling his family the true
nature of his work. On one international assignment, Harry meets a
gorgeous (ethnically unspecified) Asian woman (Tia Carrere), a linguistically skilled and knowledgeable dealer in ancient, sacred art, who
bears a mythic name, *Juno*. She is immediately captivated by Harry. The
two dance a sensuous tango before Harry makes his exit. Out of her
sight, he kills countless faceless minions in a spectacular getaway. But
they soon meet again. Juno, we find out, is an unscrupulous wretch who
is in league with a group of Arab terrorists planning to "nuke" the
United States; she has no political or moral agenda, but is in it only for
the money. Meanwhile, because her husband is so busy, and so very ne-
glectful, his wife, Helen (Jamie Lee Curtis), has become dowdy before
her time. She is, however, contemplating an affair, a fact inadvertently
discovered by her husband.

Two parallel plot lines develop: the now insanely jealous Harry uses
high-tech CIA equipment to facilitate stalking and terrorizing his
wife—scenes played as slapstick comedy. Aided by the technology,
Harry masks his identity, kidnaps Helen, and isolates her in an interro-
gation room where he subjects her to an inquisition. Luckily for her, she
is able to respond truthfully that she has been faithful; she even offers
up the admission that she loves her husband. Helen's secret inquisitor,
Harry, orders her to work as a prostitute on a "spy" mission (with him as
the secret john). Believing her life to be in danger, she consents. Helen
soon transforms from frump to bombshell. As her (disguised) "cus-
tomer," Harry commands the unwitting Helen to strip and dance for
him. She initially complies but is plotting resistance, bopping him over
the head with a telephone. Remember: this is a comedy and she *is* a
good girl. They are immediately interrupted, however, when the Arab
terrorists along with their Dragon Lady barge in and kidnap the two.
Juno (who is called "bitch" by all the men more frequently than her
name) flaunts her power, hinting to Helen about a prior relationship
with her husband. Harry recoils from the suggestion and lashes back
with the ultimate put down: "You're damaged goods, lady."

Ultimately, of course, Harry manages to escape and save the day, di-
verting the nuclear weapon, which "safely" explodes offshore. The re-
united twosome shares a passionate kiss with the mushroom cloud as
backdrop. Helen is emboldened and sexualized by her experiences—
which include not only playing stripper and prostitute and (ineptly)

shooting big phallic weaponry, but also punching out Juno and setting up her death. She emerges from her ordeal revitalized and able to function not only as Harry's wife, but also his new partner in spyland. The film ends with the now sexually satisfied and happily married couple dancing a sensuous tango as they undertake a new spy mission together.

Numerous lies, repressions, and omissions undergird this story. Harry's desire to have a secret life, his paranoia, megalomania, extreme violence against other men, his initial lack of desire for his wife, and his over-the-top jealousy and possessiveness, are all clues that suggest Harry's repressed bisexuality.[1] This implicit homoerotic "bomb" is safely defused however as the storyline progresses. By film's end, Harry's male partner hasn't had to die. But he is now safely out of the picture and Helen has taken his place.

Another deception conceals Harry's actual relation to terrorism. Distracted by those Arab bad guys, we might not notice that the "good guy," Harry, *also* is a terrorist, of the domestic kind. Harry, in truth, typifies the most dangerous kind of domestic violence perpetrator. He evinces extreme jealousy and possessiveness, an obsessive need for control, verbal abusiveness, physical violence against all and sundry, and a penchant to sexually demean his partner. He's a stalker, liar and verbal abuser, a manipulative lover, kidnapper, and a potential wife-killer.[2] Had Helen herself become "damaged goods" by being unfaithful, Harry might well have "terminated" her in order to maintain his manly honor. *True Lies* is a comedy romance so this doesn't happen. Sill, that discomfiting truth lies just beneath the surface of the plot.

And what of the relation of Helen to Juno? Once again, we encounter the standard good/bad split, and along obvious racial lines. Because Helen is a proper patriarchal woman, all autonomy, self-interest, intellectual knowledge, worldly experience, sovereign sexual power, and mobility are forbidden to her. All of these traits, along with greed, are manifested in the "bad" woman of color. Still, Juno is embarrassingly ineffective; we even see her being slapped around by her terrorist employers. *True Lies* is a "slaying the Dragon Lady" narrative—one in which Juno is progressively stripped of her power and dignity and ultimately her life. That story is paralleled by one in which Helen, inversely, regains her eroticism, self-confidence, and vitality. *True Lies* positions the woman of color as the emblem of evil, a "whore" by nature. It then sets her up so that the "virtuous" white woman can beneficially absorb her essential energies, quite literally over the woman of color's dead body.

As all this focus on essential energies suggests, there is a goddess text beneath this story. *Juno* is the ancient Roman Great Goddess and also the designation in Latin for the female *daemon,* the soul or genius of a mortal woman (Nitzsche, 1975). The name *Helen* recalls that ultimately desirable wife, Helen of Troy. When we first meet Juno, she blazes with psychic energy, is gloriously attractive, and obviously possesses greater knowledge, energy, and Eros than the captive Helen. But Juno is soon to be killed and psychically *cannibalized. True Lies* uses femme fatale imagery to effectively propagandize not only homophobia and misogyny, but also the lethal energetic exploitation of women of color by white women and men. The understory of the film has a white woman absorbing and assimilating the dark women's vital forces or soul. Juno ends up dead and Helen emerges as sexy, triumphant, and fulfilled. But Helen remains, of course, in marital/sexual subjugation to her abusive husband, who now is able to most effectively exert his control over her and exploit her newly acquired energies, both at home and at work.

Queen/Bitch

> Where white women are depicted in pornography as "objects," Black women are depicted as animals. Where white women are depicted as human bodies if not beings, Black women are depicted as shit.
>
> Alice Walker (1980, 103)

In *Vamp* (Richard Wenk, 1986), Grace Jones plays a horror variant on the femme fatale—a beautiful and ruthless vampire who reigns over a group of subordinates who are utterly in her thrall. This vampire coven operates out of a seedy urban strip bar where Jones and the other female vampires both perform and seek victims. Her face is powdered white, evoking the Voodoo goddess Erzulie Freida (Hurston, 1983, 145). Her costumes include Egyptian regal headdresses, spiraling breastplates, and magical body paint. This iconography is that of a goddess; her presence evokes and invokes the primordial Black Mother/Goddess, found throughout the world (Birnbaum, 2001). Yet there is little dignity for "She Gods," particularly the dark, primordial goddess, in a patriarchal culture ruled by a god of light. Not only is the Vamp/Goddess utterly demonized, but in one telling moment the bartender refers to her as the "Queen Bitch."

In racist and misogynist culture, these two terms, both together and separately, frequently are hurled as especially powerful and racialized insults. Patricia J. Williams (1995, 138–49) notes how the originally powerful word *queen* is racialized and tossed around in such epithets as "welfare queen," "quota queen," and "condom queen," directed against, respectively, poor African American women, Lani Guinier, and Joyce-lyn Elders. Barbara McCaskill and Layli Phillips (1996, 121) also note the similarity of the labels "condom queen" and "'welfare queen' connot-ing indolent, obese, Cadillac-driving, food-stamp-licking, husbandless black women with three or four children in tow." They argue that the use of "condom queen" to refer to Dr. Joycelyn Elders is "a new twist on an old racist tactic of silencing African American women by making us monstrous, parasitical, and un-American." *Queen* signifies, in these contexts, variously, greed, fecundity, insatiability, and malignant matri-archy; it conveys a mockery of even the possibility of black female influ-ence, authority, and sovereignty, while masking white-supremacist fear of that possibility.

Refusing and resisting these characterizations, numerous women of African descent reclaim *queen* as an honorific title (including the singers Queen Latifah and India Arie). Luisah Teish (2002) educates audiences about the history of African goddesses and queens and then asks them to "learn how the goddesses and queens live on in the psyches of women today, and how these ancient feminine powers operate in our personal lives and our communities." Lil' Kim (1996), refusing all decorum, rau-cously reclaims even the phrase "Queen Bitch" in her song of that title.

Bitch, like *queen,* is a word with a complicated legacy. It now func-tions as a racialized term of contempt for women, rooted in the porno-graphic image of the woman of color as subhuman animal (and, con-comitantly, the belief that animals are "beneath" humans). Yet at one point in human history *bitch* was as honorific as the terms *queen* or *god-dess;* indeed, they were in some ways synonymous. Barbara Walker (1983, 109) reveals that *Bitch* "was one of the most sacred titles of the Goddess, Artemis-Diana." Indeed, around the world, from "India to the Mediterranean, in Asia Minor, Crete, Greece, Syria, Mesopotamia, Egypt, Africa, and westward to Malta, Sicily, and southern Spain," as Erich Neumann (1963, 268) notes, the Great Mother or Lady of the Beasts assumed the form of an animal or appeared surrounded by ani-mals. This Goddess/Bitch—sexually sovereign, creative, and potent—is the half-remembered mythic figure who provides a background source for the power of the femme noire. It is her memory, perhaps, that causes some viewers to agree with Jessica Hagedorn and root for the "villain."

In a Eurocentric framework, "deviance" of all kinds, including les-bianism, savagery, violence, and a contaminating touch, historically has been projected onto women of color, particularly women of African ancestry (Gilman, 1985; Collins, 1998). At the same time, femininity (itself a "deviance" under male supremacy) is often projected onto men of color and Jewish and gay men. In his 1996 book *Evil Sisters: The Threat of Female Sexuality and the Cult of Manhood*, Bram Dijkstra argues persuasively that racism and sexism intertwine in Western/colonialist scientific, anthropological, and psychological projections of dangerous, primitive, and essentially feminine cultures of peoples of color lurking at the boundaries of the "superior," strictly gender-dimorphic, white- and male-ruled "civilization."

This sexually political racism was vividly rendered in popular narratives from the first half of the twentieth century built around the erotic female vampire—whom we might also recognize as a demonization of a goddess (Keesey, 1997). The narrative of *Vamp* opens as three fraternity brothers go into the vampire bar, presided over by a Queen (Grace Jones). One of the white boys, totally enraptured by her erotic dance, goes backstage to recruit her to dance at their party. She welcomes him into her bed and surprises him with her sexual aggression. As she voraciously licks and nuzzles his body, her fangs begin to grow, her eyes roll back, she foams at the mouth, and then she attacks, all the while making grunting animal noises as she kills him.

Michele Wallace (1990, 5) has noted that the "postmodern variation on black women's 'silence'" is that African American women can be in the representational frame, yet only when uncritical or marked by a "total lack of voice." Throughout the entire narrative of *Vamp*, the Jones character never speaks. Ultimately, the surviving white boy manages to trap her in her lair, decorated with African motifs and artwork, and located in a sewer. Our boy hero manages to expose her to some sunlight. Screaming horribly, she becomes first withered and then rotted flesh, ending as a skeleton who, as a final gesture of defiance, gives a bony "fuck you" finger to her assassins before she expires.

There is at least some possibility of resistant identification with the defiance and sovereignty of Jones's Vampire Queen as she opposes the white fraternity boys and all the sex, class, and race power they represent. It is a bit more difficult to recognize her sister in *Aliens* (James Cameron, 1986), a film that serves up Queen/Bitch imagery with the woman of color now absolutely monstrous, inhuman, malevolent, parasitical, speechless, and loathsome. Moreover, her antagonist is now a white woman who achieves hero status by annihilating the "Bitch."

The narrative of the *Alien* trilogy begins when an outer-space mining crew picks up an alien stowaway who uses the human body as a breeding ground—a function lethal to the human host. Later, we discover that the evil Company actually intended its crew to bring back the alien, hoping to make some new and highly profitable technological toys and weapons from it. This alien is finally defeated by the lone survivor of the crew, Ripley, played by the WASPishly aristocratic Sigourney Weaver. The sequel takes Ripley back to a planet where the aliens have wiped out a colony of invading humans. There, accompanied by a squad of U.S. Marines, a representative of the evil Company, and a small girl she rescues (giving her an adoptive motherly cast), Ripley again does victorious battle, killing the Alien Queen and insouciantly "nuking" the planet in the process.

The alien figure in this wildly popular series stands as one of the most extreme icons of repulsion and otherness that Hollywood horror/science fiction has produced over the last one hundred years, so successful that a similar version was used in the blockbuster *Independence Day* (Roland Emmerich, 1996). Not surprisingly, this consummate enemy in *Aliens* is, once again, female, maternal, and dark in her origins and associations. This repulsive, powerful, and insect-like Queen/Bitch (quite reasonably from her point of view) is focused upon the vanquishment of the human colonizers who want to seize her and her progeny as raw material for weapons technology. From the point of view of the colonizers, the Alien is mindlessly hell-bent upon the destruction of all that is "good," all that is "human." Guess whose side viewers are supposed to be on.

The iconography of the Alien, created by H. R. Giger, suggests a bestiary of sexual organs and associations—penis heads, grotesque labia, toxic leaking blood and other secretions, *vagina dentata*-like apertures, oversized vulvas. Such imagery, again, is rooted in a long tradition of commingled racism and sexism. Social Darwinists argued that the earliest stage of humanity—one that ceaselessly threatens to return—was dominated by the female and marked by bisexuality, the lack of clear distinction between the sexes. Since Africa was the ground of human origin, Africa was figured persistently as a savage, fecund, and unevolved, though fascinating, woman. In Joseph Conrad's famous metaphor, Dijkstra (1996, 150) observes, "The womb of humanity was the heart of darkness." These same notions pervaded pulp fiction, where the "ultimate temptress, the bestially beautiful, primitive African queen . . . the ultimate praying mantis, the woman with the African womb" (147) was a stock figure of the "enemy" throughout the twentieth century.

The womb/Queen of *Aliens* is no longer vampishly beautiful, but she is even more powerfully fecund, devouring, and bestial. It is in this repugnant alien, one who no longer even remotely resembles a human being, that Charles Ramírez Berg astutely locates the submerged presence of the woman of color, specifically the mother of color. Ramírez Berg (1989, 4) contends that contemporary science fiction films focusing upon outer-space "aliens" provide a "cinematic arena for the unconscious reflection on the immigrant 'question.'" Specifically, he views the filmic alien as a representation of mainstream resentment and scapegoating of Hispanic immigrant aliens. According to Berg, aliens who agree to "go home" (like E.T.) are presented sympathetically, while those who refuse to leave are eradicated mercilessly. The *Alien* trilogy focuses upon a highly destructive and unwelcome alien immigrant, one with the potential to annihilate "humanity"—that is, First World imperial culture.

Aliens is specifically about *mothers,* presenting two contrasting maternal figures: "Ripley . . . a nurturing 'mother' of a space colony orphan, and the Alien queen mother, a mechanically efficient reproducing machine" (Berg, 1989, 14). Berg reads this dichotomization as a "horrifying depiction of Alien (read Third World) motherhood. The giant Alien *queen* mother . . . is terrifying enough, but when it is so sharply contrasted with Ripley, the 'civilized' mother, it has chilling implications. . . . The Alien mother [is] down in her birth chamber, reproducing mindlessly, endlessly. She is a monster out of the nativists' worst nightmares, procreation gone mad, uncontrollable and unstoppable. Ripley's unforgettable cry, 'Get away from her, you bitch,' defends First World mothering at the expense of the Third World womanhood. In this light, the fact that a woman wipes out the Alien mother and her offspring is hardly cause for rejoicing. The film's positive feminist elements are overwhelmed by its imperialistic underpinnings."

Ripley's "feminism," as Susan Jeffords (1987, 75) agrees, is a "corporate feminism that operates finally to separate women from each other as well as from any power that might come from their shared community." Concomitantly, the enemy of all that is right and good is the fecund and sovereign woman of color, who, like the racist projections of the "welfare queen" or the mindlessly procreating Third World mother, is presented as "monstrous, parasitical, and un-American" (McCaskill and Phillips, 1996, 121).

Beneath the text of *Aliens* and the other films discussed in this chapter is the barely whispered recognition that it is "America" itself that is invasive, parasitical, and monstrous. As Toni Morrison (1992, 17) understands, the negative qualities assigned to the "other" in a dominant culture's literature are extensive meditations on the "dreamer," the dominant culture itself. This is stunningly apparent in the film *Star Trek VI: The Undiscovered Country* (Nicholas Meyer, 1992). Captain Kirk and Dr. McCoy have been unjustly imprisoned, two noble white men out of place amid the alien riffraff of the universe. Kirk is befriended and seduced by an apparently beautiful woman (the black supermodel Iman) who promises to help them escape. Yet it turns out that her beauty is only a façade; she is a member of an alien species who is adept at shape-shifting. In her "real" body, she is a hairy and hideous beast/bitch. Moreover, her deception runs deeper than her appearance; she actually is a betrayer, setting up Kirk and McCoy to be killed. When Kirk realizes this and challenges her, she shape-shifts into a mirror image of him. Looking at this replica of himself, he snarls with disgust, "I can't believe I kissed you." Mocking the narcissism of this prototypical hero, she sneers back, "Must have been your lifelong ambition." As they struggle, he asks, "Isn't it time for you to change into something else." She retorts, "I like it here." Within a few seconds, she is dead, blasted into oblivion by her purported ally, another "alien," the Klingon commander.

Once again—from the white hero's perspective—we find that beneath the pleasing and seductive appearance of the woman of color lurks a dangerous beast. This sequence also vividly plays to the elite's fear that oppressed peoples, if uncontained, will usurp the position and very identity of the "whiteman." At the same time, it provides an extraordinarily truthful moment in the history of colonialist cinema. When Kirk, icon of the consummate, neo-Western (civilization) hero, faces the mirror image of *himself* as the monster, it is briefly revealed that the *horror*—the cannibalistic, invasive, parasitic, destructive other—is not the traditional scapegoat, the dark and bestial female. Rather, the real face of *horror* is nothing but that of the "hero" himself.

Sympathy for the Alien

> The movie *Alien* affected me greatly because I really identified
> with it . . . it seemed like they were taking all the things they
> fear and hate about themselves and projecting them onto the
> monster. Just like we did with blacks and like people do with
> queers—all the evils projected. My sympathies were not with
> the people at all; they were with the alien.
>
> Gloria Anzaldúa (2000, 40)

The images of the femmes noires discussed here often elicit conflicting responses. Just as Gloria Anzaldúa identifies with the alien, similarly resistant film viewers find themselves more readily in female villains and monsters than in arrogant heroes and their loyal wives and hench-women. Both Anzaldúa and Robin Wood (1986) recognize the persistence of such popular, if nonhegemonic, responses. They argue that many women and men discover in the "monster" those aspects of our-selves that society and civilization, in the service of social inequalities of race, gender, sexuality, and class, have required that we deny, stigmatize, and disown. Both of these theorists point to the repression of female sexuality, bisexuality, racial difference, and all that is identified with the feminine and the animal as the traits that, unfairly, are made monstrous, "other," and, we might add, "noir" in popular imagery.

Along with Jessica Hagedorn, we endorse the resistance and po-tency of the Dragon Ladies and recognize ourselves in the defiant and powerful femmes noires. Still, we cannot forget that these stereotypes are conventionally understood as confirming women's base inferiority and immorality and can inspire hatred, scapegoating, and retaliation. Over time, as Stuart Hall (Grossberg, 1986, 54) observes, these reiter-ated negative images take on "lines of tendency," fixing perception into standard oppressive grooves.

In order to defuse these negative affects and effects, challenge these damaging ideologies, and transform consciousness, critics, readers, and viewers can disrupt these lines of tendency in a variety of ways: for ex-ample, by generating new narratives. At the same time, we also can re-organize and refigure the familiar narrative elements in ways that raise consciousness. This occurs when critics and thinkers like Anzaldúa shockingly assert and explain their identification with female villains and monsters. It also happens when familiar stories are elaborated from the perspective of the "other." Three recent novels, *Wicked* (1995) by John Maguire, *Ahab's Wife* (1999) by Sena Jeter Naslund, and Alice Randall's *The Wind Done Gone* (2001), deliberately recast a "canonical" text from the point of view of a subordinated or scapegoated character. We imagine similarly slanted remakes of such popular films as *Aliens, Vamp,* and *True Lies* and applaud educational efforts that encourage the popular audience's tendency to envision and center those perspectives.

4

The Pornography of
Everyday Life

Sɪɪ: those two airliners arrowing into the twin towers of the
World Trade Centre, repeatedly seen on television that day,
with a pornographic monotony and reduplication: one became
a voyeur of tragedy. The repetitions did not sate the feel of—
visually-distanced—horror: they fed and fed it.

Patrick Hutchings (2002, 71)

Fight, rape, war, pillage, burn. Filmic images of death and
carnage are pornography for the military man; with film you
are stroking his cock, tickling his balls with the pink feather of
history, getting him ready for his real First Fuck.

Anthony Swofford (2003, 7)

Charles Murray's book *The Bell Curve,* which suggests that
blacks may be inferior to whites in the area of intelligence, is a
scabrous piece of racial pornography masquerading as serious
scholarship.

Bob Herbert (1994)

As the above quotes indicate, *pornography* is regularly used in ways that
have nothing to do with sexual explicitness. Rather, pornography is
commonly understood as a form of propaganda, a representational style
linked with defamation and desensitization, if not destruction. Patricia
J. Williams (1995, 123), who thinks legally, critically, and gracefully
about race, sex, and injustice, calls pornography a "habit of thinking,"
and one that informs all manner of abusive and exploitative attitudes

and relationships. *Pornography,* as I am using the term, is just that, a worldview, a way of thinking and acting that sexualizes and genders domination and submission, from the bedroom to the war room, making domination masculine (even when a woman plays that role) and submission feminine (even when a man plays that role), and making both the essence of sex (Dworkin, 1989, 253–75). By wedding sexuality to inequality, pornography conditions women and men to have a substantial investment in maintaining the oppressive status quo—again, from interpersonal relationships to international politics.

Pornography kills off, and then substitutes itself for, the erotic—the life force, the earthy and ethereal force of growth, fruitfulness, exuberance, ecstasy, connectedness, and integrity. Pornography severs eroticism from intimacy and empathy and bonds it to voyeurism and objectification (of the self and of another). It incarnates pleasure in acts of hatred. It would have all of us believe, even those of us getting the "fuzzy end of the lollypop" (Sugar/Marilyn Monroe's lament in *Some Like It Hot,* Billy Wilder, 1959), that without a certain measure of power and powerlessness, danger, fear, pain, possession, shame, distance, and violence there wouldn't be any "sex" at all. Of course, the simultaneously pornographic, monotonous, and erotophobic culture tends to make that true. Variously damaged, alienated, and desensitized, pornography can become what we need in order to feel at all.

Some applaud pornography because it allows access to sexual imagery and language and easily offends offensive religious morality. Yet pornography is no real alternative to systemic sex-negative morality; rather it is an intrinsic part of it. Pornography and mainstream morality both stem from and continually reinforce a worldview that first makes a complex of body/low/sex/dirty/deviant/female/devil and then severs these from mind/high/spirit/pure/normal/male/god. For both, sex itself is the core taboo. Moralism systematically upholds the taboo and pornography systematically violates it. In the complex that evolves from this absurdity, taboo violation itself becomes erotically charged. Evil becomes seductive and the good mostly boring. Without patriarchal moralism's misogyny, homophobia, demand for sexual ignorance, and sin-sex-shame equation, pornography as we know it would not exist. And, together, the two work to maintain the sex and gender status quo.

The following sketch is admittedly over-simplified, but is meant to suggest a basic outline of this relationship. Moralism subordinates women by veiling, sequestering, ensuring economic dependency, and enforcing strict codes of modesty and a sexual double standard (making sure there is a steady supply of faithful wives, pure daughters, and prostitutes for men, mostly female but also male). Pornography accomplishes the same end by stripping women, ordaining constant sexual availability, and defining all females as mantraps and inherent "whores," just waiting to be offered the right price. The relationship between moralism and pornography works like the "good cop/bad cop" trick. When women rebel against the moralist code, the system responds by offering pseudo-liberation: fashions marking girls and women as sexual prey, the opportunity to work, mostly for less pay (on top of totally unpaid housework and child-rearing), smoke, drink, have "boob" and face jobs, have pornography introduced into relationships, and be a sex object and spectacle for as many men as possible. All this takes place alongside a backlash of sensational and public sexual violence. When women seek relief from this set of conditions, the system promises order and protection for "good" women via the imposition of patriarchal family values (male dominance and female servitude, sexual and otherwise, in the home), "modest" dress, sexual ignorance; punitive scrutiny of women's sexual behavior, restricted entry to public and occupational space, censorship, covenant marriage, and officially sanctioned homophobia. Some women (e.g., Shalit, 1999), even some feminists (Wolf, 2003), have suggested a return to practices of religious "modesty" as workable resistance to the mainstreaming of pornography and disrespect for women. But this would be utter folly. The feminist challenge is to recognize the fundamental identity of the two systems and to make a different world altogether.

Ironically, the story that most completely illuminates the complicity of pornography and patriarchal morality is that original story of naked lust, the one about Adam and Eve. After Eve converses with the Snake goddess (see the introduction to this volume), she initiates Adam into the mysteries of sex and knowledge. Subsequently, a rivalrous and upstart male god curses Eve: "Your desire shall be for your husband and he shall rule over you." Through patriarchal interpretations of this influential story, the Snake becomes the Devil, sex becomes synonymous with sin and "dirt," and unequal (even abusive) and monogamous (for women) heterosexual relationships become the norm. Active female desire is branded as "bad girl" witchcraft, whoredom, and scripted into slut, femme fatale and "dominatrix" roles or channeled into "good girl" masochism, romantic or otherwise. Both pornography and the pornography of everyday life enthusiastically affirm these messages. Religious-oriented bestsellers like *The Surrendered Wife* (Doyle, 2000), enjoin married women to graciously submit—sexually, psychically, financially and every other which way—to their husbands. Meanwhile, in pornography, women (and men playing the submissive feminine role), are bound, gagged, pissed on, beaten and tortured.

The pornographic habit of thinking and acting goes beyond explicitly sexual matters and informs fascist ideology, racism, enslavement, torture, colonization, and military conquest (Theweleit, 1987; Sontag, 1980; Hernton, 1988, A. Smith, 2003). Susan Sontag (1980, 102) asks quite sensibly why "Nazi Germany, which was a sexually repressive society, [has] become erotic?" She finds a clue in this underlying dynamic: "Hitler regarded leadership as sexual mastery of the 'feminine' masses, as rape." Through such mastery (up to and including acts of genocide of scapegoats), "the leader makes the crowd come" (102). Rena Swentzell (1993, 167), a Native American scholar from Santa Clara Pueblo in New Mexico, demands that we stop "coming" to this atrocious scenario and, instead, feel revulsion at the fascist belief in "power as an integral part of sexuality," for "That is what the inquisition was all about. That is what the whole conquest of the Southwest was about—power and control by males." The sexualized conquest continues as Ward Sutton (2003) suggests in a hilarious political cartoon in *The Village Voice*, referencing the 2003 United States–led invasion of Iraq (fig. 4.1). It depicts the notoriously cocky Secretary of Defense Donald Rumsfeld watching four separate television screens, all tuned to different channels, and all displaying the same "live" image of Baghdad being bombed. His pants are down and he is masturbating and chanting "Oh, yeah . . . oh yeah . . . Drop your payload . . . BURN, BABY, BURN!!" Militarists and conventional moralists might call this cartoon "pornography." But that would be a reversal.

Many think that any critique of pornography implies sexual repression or censorship but I advocate neither. Nonpornographic, sexually arousing stories and images can delight, challenge, instruct, deepen and enliven our imaginations, and increase knowledge. Artists, entertainers, filmmakers, writers, and essayists need to be able to explore sexual and violent themes, limited not by law but by a sense of responsibility, personal integrity, and social justice. Of course, it is these qualities that are deliberately shredded by the pornographic imagination, where taboo violation is not only sexualized, but also aestheticized and radicalized. By *taboo violation* I do not mean the strategic use of obscenity, like that employed by Sutton to criticize the (pornographic) powers that be; I mean the deliberate flaunting of life-preservative taboos, like those against incest, rape, murder, and related violations of the life force.

4.1 Cartoon by Ward Sutton, *Village Voice*, March 24, 2003

I turn now to an interpretation of some popular images, both con-temporary and classic, that directly appeal to pornographic beliefs.[1] My point is not that the media and/or popular culture are the problem and should be "cleaned up." Nor am I suggesting that these images are rep-resentative of all of popular culture. Rather, I have selected them be-cause, particularly when read in relation to one another, they reveal the basic tropes of the pornographic worldview or story (one whose ending is inevitably apocalyptic). My hope is to provoke ongoing consciousness raising, including my own. The necessarily collective work of exposing and deconstructing the pornographic story helps us to recognize not only its grip, but also its historical contingency. Anyone untelling that story—in the arts, in politics, and in everyday life—reclaims the imagi-native energies that, consciously or not, otherwise go into feeding it. This frees and fuels the imagination to tell another story altogether, in all of its permutations, one where every encounter, however ordinary or unconventional, playful or serious, enduring or brief, is based in respect, one where no one is a master and no one a slave, and one that ends in possibility.

We might, then, begin at the beginning of the pornographic story, that familiar "boy meets girl" one, based in caricatures of oppositional and unequal sex, who act out fixed and fetishized gender roles.

Gender Porn

An ad for a perfume called "Happy" shows a white man and woman in 1950s-type garb suggesting total gender role conformity. She wears a pink party dress and holds out a birthday cake. He sports a football uniform, holds a ball under his arm, and has assumed a running stance. "Happy"? I wonder. What would these two ever have to say to one another? How could these caricatures ever step out of these fetishized roles? This portrait might more aptly be dubbed "Misery," for the image portrays one originally *whole* psyche, now split and divided against itself. This ad is the "G-rated" version of the pornographic couple. We find an "R-rated" one in a 2002 underwear ad. A woman in sexy red lingerie looks up tremulously, lips parted, as a fully dressed man towers over her, holding something, possibly something threatening, behind his back. The whole thing looks just so terribly hot. They couldn't be more different—or more unequal—and this is the essence of the thrill.

This little bedroom moment has historical resonance. Gerda Lerner (1997, 133) locates as the advent of patriarchal social systems in the "invention of hierarchy," when "difference" becomes dominance. The pornographic imagination reinforces this inegalitarian gender arrangement, and simultaneously eroticizes it. The gender roles that characterize everyday pornography are steeped in racist ideals. Social Darwinism made it clear that the fuzzy gender lines and "matriarchal" character of so-called primitive cultures were clear signs of their low status on the evolutionary ladder (Dijkstra, 1996). Civilization, they said, could be measured by the greatness of the degree of separation between the sexes. Nowadays, the highly evolved man is still supposed to be taller, stronger, richer, older, and colder—in short, more powerful—than his mate. The woman is shorter, weaker, poorer, decorative, vulnerable, younger, emotionally warmer—in short, socially powerless. These caricatures, in turn, are attracted only to each other and turned on by the power discrepancy between them. This normative sadomasochism of romantic love is cleverly critiqued in a 2001 episode of HBO's *Sex and the City* (*"La Douleur Exquise!"*). Our heroine Carrie (Sara Jessica Parker) enjoys a party with a campy S&M theme at a gay club. All is in good fun, but later that evening, when she dons a bit of the finery and goes to see her wealthy, older, and permanently unavailable boyfriend "Mr. Big," the juxtaposition induces Carrie to face up to the S&M dynamic that structures her (sexually compelling but *unhappy*) relationship. That realization strengthens her, and she decides to leave him. Carrie, however, maintains feelings for her erstwhile lover. He pops in and out of her life, mostly when he needs her help or when she is about to marry someone else. Nevertheless, the series concluded in February 2004 by dropping its earlier realism, scripting him into a suddenly committed and caring guy, and (à la *Pretty Woman*) reuniting the pair in a feel-good (for those in denial, anyway) happy ending.

In gender porn, all possibilities of homosexual or transgendered being and expression are erased or made monstrous. A *New Yorker* cover drawing (June 13, 1994) shows two gay men celebrating their wedding. Both are depicted as freaks or monsters, some kind of prissy vampires. *Newsweek* (June 21, 1993) put two lesbians on its cover—smiling young white women, well scrubbed and affluent (one wore pearls and both had good teeth). The headline announces: "Lesbians Coming Out Strong. What Are the Limits of Tolerance?" In this context, *tolerance* is a dangerous word, suggesting that as long as lesbians do not cross some ill-defined line—becoming too butch, too political, too demanding, too sexual, too dark, too old, too unsmiling—they might be tolerated. But then again, maybe they won't, especially if, god forbid, they want to get married. In early 2004, the intolerant found a new champion in President George W. Bush who, facing a grassroots gay marriage movement and an upcoming election, called for nothing less than a constitutional amendment banning gay and lesbian marriage.

Such a drastic response might well be rooted in the realization that these unions can provide a precedent of a marriage between equals, challenging the traditional marital model making women the property of and social subordinates of men. Beneath all the moralistic rhetoric about marriage between "one man and one woman" being the very "bedrock of our civilization" is the familiar pornographic commitment to sexualized and gendered dominance and submission. Everyday porn tells us that only men and women belong together sexually—except for those titillating moments when avowedly heterosexual "babes" like

Madonna and Britney lip lock for a few seconds. (We should note that there is no male parallel.) Concomitantly, it insists, men and women are inexorably different in ways that ordain and justify social inequality. The headline of the January 20, 1992, cover of *Time* reads: "Why Are Men and Women Different? It isn't just upbringing. New studies show they are born that way." The cover image is of a (probably) Latino boy and a girl, about eight years old, standing in front of a brick wall (fig. 4.2). The boy, wearing the pants, takes up most of the frame. Pulling up his sleeve, flexing his right bicep, and admiring his small swollen muscle, he turns away from the skirted girl and focuses entirely on his own performance. She gazes indulgently upon him and places one hand under his elbow, signifying her support. In this little visual story, males and females are utterly different, with males being both self-absorbed and other-absorbing (as he sucks up her space and energy). The girl is sidelined, but her expression suggests that she accepts her place as a condition of his potency. And there is that unmistakable metaphor for immutability (whether biological or cultural)—the brick wall they are up against.

A grown-up version of this couple appears in a Calvin Klein underwear ad from 1992. The ad is spread over two pages. On the first page the white rapper then known as Markie Mark appears clad only in his underpants. With a threatening look on his face, he grabs his penis in a bullying gesture. On the next page Markie is relaxed and sitting on the floor. He faces forward. Leaning into him, and wrapping a supportive arm around his waist, is the notoriously slender "waif" Kate Moss (also dressed only in her underpants).

A leather fashion spread in *Today's Black Woman* (2000) features a man and a woman—well, most of their bodies, since the figures are cut off at the head (fig. 4.3). He wears a jacket (unzipped to show his naked chest), pants, and sensible walking boots. She wears only an unzipped jacket, leather bikini underwear, one stocking, and high-heeled boots. His hand is tensed, held away from his body, and ready for action. Hers is limp, closed, and resting on her thigh. The man's other arm is wrapped around her naked waist, and she leans into him.

There is no leather in the next image, a 1999 ad for L'Oreal "straight-up" hair-straightener, but it is still all about sexual domination (fig. 4.4). A white woman with long hair gazes up, sweetly and trustingly, at her stern-faced boyfriend, who towers over her. He is literally "in her face," visually dominating her. The ad commands them to "play

4.2 *Time* cover, January 20, 1992

it straight." Certainly that command refers as much to conformity to standardized male-dominant/female-subordinate heterosexuality as it does to chemically straightened locks.

Sexual, gender, and racial projections abound in these depictions. The white people keep their heads; the black people are pure body, and

her.
nylon.
flight.
jacket/
marithe.
francios.
girbaud
leather.
bikini/
shapes.
by.
anton
ankle.
boots/
stuart.
weiztman
his.
nylon.
flight.
jacket,
leather &
stretch.
pants/
marithe.
francios.
girbaud,
shoes/
cesare.
paciotti

TCH SHOE WATCH SHOE WATCH SHOE WATCH SHOE W

SEE SHOPPING GUIDE, PAGE 103

4.3 "In fashion: Shoe watch," *Today's Black Woman*, 2000

4.4 L'oréal Paris cosmetics ad, Cosmair, Inc. © 1999

the Latinos are children. The females are positioned to suggest vulnerability, stasis, and service. The males are active, incipiently violent, and in control. The eroticism exuded by the adult couples is clearly based in their inequality. These gender-porn images point to domination, violence, and control of space as intrinsic and defining components of masculinity. Hard male musculature and the penis are graphically associated with violence and power. Femininity, on the other hand, is represented as contained, supportive, and controlled. Moreover, as this one-way power dynamic implies, the feminine counterpart might well soon find herself at the other end of hardened muscle or hostile penis.

Boy Beats Girl

In November 2000 a student gave me two pages torn from an unidentified fashion magazine. An Asian woman sits bereft and forlorn on a bench. Red makeup is applied around one eye to suggest that she has been beaten bloody. On the next page she wears a backless dress and is posed to suggest that she is utterly spineless. She stands with her back to us and bending to the side, her arms dangling. Splotches of green makeup imply that she has bruises on her back and along her arm. Three years later, another student brought in a few pages ripped from an unidentified issue of *Vibe*. A fashion spread featured a man and woman who were involved in several different abusive moments. In one, the man shouts and gestures at the woman; she sits, head down and with her hands trying to protect her ears. Another portrays the aftermath of a slap; her face veers away, her hands are held up in a futile attempt to ward him off; her breasts spill out from her low-cut designer blouse. The final shot shows him at the door, pushing at it and trying to gain entry. She presses against it, keeping it from opening. But she looks resigned and we assume he will soon be back inside. Such imagery normalizes and inevitably glamorizes intimate physical and emotional abuse.

Battery is a long-term process of torture and intimidation meant to break the will of the victim and destroy her ability to resist. This is accomplished not only by physical assault but also through repeated humiliations, death threats, and psychological attacks on the victim's sense of self (Jones, 1994). Robert Jensen and Gail Dines note that a common scenario in pornographic novels involves women who at first do not understand their need to submit. As a man forces sex on her and humiliates her, she learns "to crave sex and domination" (1998, 94). The same message is conveyed by a 1994 ad for boots that appeared in *Details*, a men's magazine. In this a woman is positioned on hands and knees with her buttocks high in the air and her face down; she is licking the floor. The copy reads: "An acquired taste." The pornographic message here is that if an abuser humiliates his partner long enough, she will learn to love it. Anal sex also is implied, but not in any way that suggests that the activity could be pleasurable when consensual. Rather, it is promoted as a way to demean women.

On one pornographic Internet site (www.rotten.com), an obese, naked white woman is shown kneeling. She is bound with rope, and her hands are restrained behind her back. A hood completely covers her head, and she wears a collar with large rings through which the ropes are anchored. Black leather straps are tightly wrapped in many rings around her large breasts, which appear mottled and in pain. Written on the tip of one breast is *slut;* on the other is *cunt.* Scrawled down, on the skin between her breasts, is the word *whore.* Once again, pornography presents crudely what everyday imagery presents through a sweetened glaze. Fashion images regularly display women in variations on this theme of female bondage and display. One, for Natori (2000), shows a young, thin, and pretty white woman. She is decked out in black fetish lingerie and sits up straight, though she looks down. Her legs are spread, her breasts offered in a black lacy push-up bra. Everything suggests bondage, particularly the thick ribbon that acts as a collar around her neck and her downcast and deeply shadowed eyes.

In another image from the same pornographic site, a white woman is stuffed into a recycling bin. The neck of the bin is much smaller than its body, so it is clear that she is unable to escape. We see only her shoulders and head. A clothed man in denim and work boots urinates into her open mouth. A mainstream variant on this theme appears in a Skyy vodka ad from 2003. The setting now is absolute opulence. A woman in a backless black cocktail dress lies on a golden couch. A martini glass stands on the skin of her back. We see only the hands of a man as he overturns a thermos, clearly phallic in shape, pouring the liquid into the glass, ready to spill out all over her.

Making Difference into Domination

The pornographic pattern of eroticized feminine submission and masculine dominion undergirds not only interpersonal relations but also imperialist colonization and conquest. Possession of women and girls (and, although it is not often spoken of, boys and men) by conquerors has historically been celebrated in the colonial or tourist postcard (Alloula, 1986), featuring "exotic" women in various stages of undress. This colonial tradition is continued in a fashion layout featuring a dark-skinned model, Naomi Campbell (*Harper's Bazaar*, April 1994). Fashion images are set off by quotations from the French painter Paul Gauguin regarding his sojourns in Tahiti, where he had a fourteen-year-old mistress: "I had been seduced . . . by this land and by its simple and primitive people." The first image is of an offered, cut-open tropical fruit, glistening with moisture. The second is of Campbell, also offered, glistening and open—naked and face down on a bed. The joys of sexualized/racialized domination, what bell hooks calls "eating the other" (1992, 21–39), are here offered to the mostly female readers of *Harper's Bazaar*. They are implied as well in a 1999 ad for Skyy vodka, where a young, blond, towel-clad white woman, lounging on a mat, props her head up and extends one arm with a glass to be filled (fig. 4.5). An Asian woman kneels alongside, ready to serve. Sexual subordination is coded into her posture and downcast eyes, elaborate coiffeur, and tight, red silk dress slit up to her buttocks.

Men of color are offered up in similar ways, to elite men as well as women. An ad for Nike workout clothes in a men's fashion magazine (*GQ*, August 2000) uses a two-page spread. On the left a dark-skinned African American man, wearing only a long-tailed shirt, crouches awkwardly, legs apart. On the right, the man stands, this time wearing only the pants; his massive chest is displayed, but his arms are behind his back, as if he were handcuffed, and his head is so deeply lowered that we cannot even see his face and eyes (fig. 4.6). The body language connotes shame and submission and reproduces the iconography of slavery. It also positions this black man as a submissive sex object. Cultural theorist Ann duCille suggests that this not uncommon "feminization" of black men is a product of white men's masked desire for black male bodies, a denied desire that often can be found underlying extreme manifestations of racism and homophobia. She recognizes a pornographic dynamic infusing such institutions as slavery, organized sports, and law enforcement, where white men discipline, gaze at, and control the bodies of dark men. In law enforcement the black male body is disproportionately incarcerated as well as "frisked, patted down, probed, cuffed, spread and ordered to 'assume the position,' which, after all, is the stance of anal intercourse" (duCille, 1997, 308).

4.5 SKYY Vodka ad, SKYY Spirits, LLC © 1999

4.6 Nike apparel ad, 2000

Violence Objects

A *Time* cover (April 24, 2000) shows a pumped-up white man from the top of his nose to mid-thigh. (The absence of his eyes suggests a dearth of those feminine-marked traits of empathy and soul.) He clenches his fists and bares crooked and dangerous-looking teeth. Across his pumped-up chest is the word "TESTOSTERONE." Most men, of course, no matter how much testosterone they have, look nothing like this model and never will. Ironically, the dangerous pursuit of hyper-masculinity (often through abusing steroids) is spurred by fear of being perceived as insufficiently masculine, as feminine, and/or gay.

James Gilligan (1996) suggests that most male violence occurs not because men are hormonally driven to aggression, but because perpetrators are shamed, most commonly by an insult to their culturally concocted "manhood." When boys and men sexually harass other boys and men with words, they shame them by calling them *woman, whore, candy-ass, weak sister, faggot, pussy, bitch*. A cartoon in the *New Yorker* by P. Byrnes (November 22, 1999) shows a white man about to receive a rectal exam. He asks his doctor, another white man: "Does this make me your bitch?" *Bitch* suggests not only an aggressive woman, but also a male prisoner who is weak and sexually subordinated. According to gender conventions, being receptive, sexually or otherwise, connotes femininity and is deeply shameful for men. This includes practices of homophobic homosexuality, when the man who plays the "masculine" role in anal sex considers himself "straight" and proud but his partner "gay" and demeaned.

In male prisons, it is relatively easy to see the ways in which sexual intercourse is ritually practiced to demonstrate power, to punish, and to demean (Gilligan, 1996; Kupers, 2001). So too is intercourse a ritual of domination as it is practiced in heterosexist normalcy, argues Andrea Dworkin (1987). *Fucking, screwing, banging, having, taking, possessing, scoring, slicing, nailing:* All these terms indicate a recognition that a patriarchal/pornographic mindset associates penetrative sex with violence, humiliation, conquest, punishment, and masculine domination of the feminine—in whatever form the feminine appears: a wife, a whore, a boy, a slave, a colonized people, the land, the enemy, the self.

"Kill the Girl"

The six-year-old boy I describe in the introduction—the one who told me that he wanted to be "the killer" for Halloween, "the one who kills

4.7 Bitch Skateboards ad, 1994

the girl"—had already absorbed the main theme of the pornographic "master story." This same imperative is graphically represented in an ad for "Bitch Skateboards," appearing in 1994 in the teenage-boy magazine *Big Brother* (fig. 4.7). It depicts the public-bathroom stick figures for a man and a woman. The "man" holds his right arm outstretched, pointing a gun at the head of the "woman." Surely this ad is about hating girls and women, but it's also about hating the "feminine" within the male self. In order to attain patriarchal manhood, the teenage boy must execute his "inner bitch," becoming the hero by killing "the girl" within. The same motif structures a two-page ad for Wrangler jeans (UK *Cosmopolitan*, February 2003). On the left, a nostalgic black-and-white image of a Western film hero holds out a big gun at waist level and shoots toward the right. On the right, a full-color image of a contemporary woman falls over backward as if shot.

An extreme form of violent pornography is the snuff film or photograph, showing someone actually being murdered: The killing is understood as the climactic part of the sex.[2] A "virtual snuff" sensibility informs countless fashionable images that have appeared in advertising and fashion tableaux since the 1970s. Models are showcased in positions suggesting that they are dead: suffocated under plastic bags; laid out in gift-box coffins; buried under concrete; sprawled brokenly on stairs and boutique floors. Symbolic dismemberments have long been the norm in fashion photography (decapitated heads to sell us perfume, amputated legs to push pantyhose, even crowds of disembodied eyes to sell us eye shadow). These dismemberments usually are not recognized as such, so habituated are we to them. We might notice them if they were being done to male bodies, but they are not in any comparable way.

The pretentiously virtuous film *The Life of David Gale* (Alan Parker, 2003) foists an unanticipated snuff scene on its viewers. The film opens when a slim, young, and beautiful white New York reporter receives the news that a Texas prisoner on death row, David Gale, has selected her to conduct a final interview with him. "Why me?" she wonders. Her coworker, a large African American woman, responds by laughingly pointing out that she, "a fat, black woman" was not chosen. Gale is a Texas university professor and well-known anti–death penalty advocate in a notoriously pro–death penalty state. The governor publicly avers that he will change his position only if it can be proven that the state executed an innocent person. As Gale tells his life story, we learn that he once had a brilliant academic career, but his life was marred by an uncaring and unfaithful wife and then utterly ruined by a student's (false) rape accusation. When one of his university friends and activist colleagues is the victim of an apparent rape, torture, and asphyxiation murder, Gale is arrested, tried, convicted, and given the death penalty. On the day just before his execution, the journalist receives a video, showing the moment of the apparent murder. Another young, white, slender but large-breasted woman is lying on the floor. She has a garbage bag taped over her head and hands cuffed behind her back. She struggles for air and then expires. Viewers get treated to this spectacle several times throughout the course of the film. But we soon learn that things are not exactly what they seem. A surprise ending reveals that the woman had terminal cancer and that she actually was committing suicide, deliberately in front of a video camera, as part of an elaborate plot to change death penalty laws. Gale is her secret coconspirator. They want him to be executed so that, afterward, their friends can release the full tape, showing that this was a suicide and not a murder, proving that the system is capable of executing an innocent. They also have strategized that the journalist, now emotionally invested in the case, will widely publicize the story. The producers easily could have found another way for the suicide activist to die and still make their anti–death penalty point. Would they have subjected a naked male body to this treatment? Why did they, like Gale, choose the stereotypically "pretty woman" to use for their ends? Maybe they also wanted to make some pornographic points: Only some women are valuable, in life and in death; and women lie about sexual violence. Twice in the film, what looks like sexual abuse turns out not to be so. One female character orchestrates a false rape charge while another deliberately acts out her own naked snuff scene. Despite assertions to the contrary, and despite all appearances of coercion, it is revealed that *the woman really wanted it*. This belief is a standard "rape myth" and one that, entrenched in the minds of jurors, cops, journalists, coworkers, and family members leads to tolerance of rape, victim-blaming, and even the exoneration of rapists (Burt, 1980).

While *The Life of David Gale* insouciantly incorporates pornographic elements, the explicit porn film *Forced Entry* (2003) borrows some conventions from the horror genre. Its producer, Rob Black of Extreme Associates, calls *Forced Entry* a "slasher film with sex, loosely based on the Hillside Strangler case" (CBS News, 2003). The film features lots of damage to women, who are urinated on, beaten, raped, suffocated, and strangled. However extreme, *Forced Entry* is a late entry in the annals of cinematic snuff.

The first (and still the most celebrated) "pornographic murder" (Durgnat, 1978, 499), one taking the point of view of the sex killer and eroticizing murder, is the shower scene in *Psycho* (Alfred Hitchcock, 1960). The killer's-eye-view, more mundanely, also structures an ad for *Law and Order* (NBC, Dick Wolf) that appeared in *TV Guide* (October 11, 1995). Under the headline "Coed Killer" is a drawing of a prostrate young and blond female corpse with plunging neckline and prominent breasts. When murder is so blatantly, if almost invisibly, sexualized and exploited, we might have to realize that the sex killer is not a deviant, an incomprehensible monster, but rather the logical product of a culture that ubiquitously eroticizes violence.

Rape

A 1996 ad in *Seventeen* for Bonnie Bell "no shine" cosmetic products mocks the feminist insistence on women's right to refuse sexual relations. The ad headlines the words "No means NO," which many recognize as an antirape slogan. Here, though, *no* means: "No more greasy makeup." One 1992 study found that girls younger than eighteen accounted for 62 percent of rape victims (Johnston, 1992). This ad trivializes antirape activism for the age group most susceptible to rape.

Excessive use of alcohol greatly increases the likelihood of acquaintance rape. In numerous ads aimed at men, drinking facilitates sex, whether the woman consents or not. A 1995 ad for Bacardi rum that appeared on the back cover of *Vibe* shows three men and one woman. At first glance, because her pants are the same color as those worn by one of the boys, it appears as if she is standing firmly on the ground. But if you look closely, you can clearly see that the men are lifting her up in the air. Her legs are spread, and a huge bottle of Bacardi rum is aimed into her crotch. Everybody is smiling.

In the second Gulf War (2003), the American public was asked to celebrate the "shock and awe" tactics employed in the initial strikes against Iraq. According to its designers, the intent of "shock and awe" is to overwhelm the enemy not only physically but also in "psychological and intangible" ways. The point is "to hit very hard right at the start so as to make everybody on the other side feel that resistance is hopeless" (cited in Safire, 2003). This has always been the intent and strategy of everyday sex-war terrorists—rapists and batterers. A 2001 ad in *ESPN Magazine* for the "mudslide," an alcoholic drink, shows a screaming woman backed up against a pile of sandbags. The bottle, again, is poised to enter between her legs. The copy advises the reader: "Don't hold back."

Silence

> Let a woman learn in silence with all submissiveness. I permit no woman to teach or to have authority over men; she is to keep silent.
>
> Paul (1 Tim. 2:11–12)

Hostility to female speech is a recurring preoccupation of sexist systems, enforced in a multiplicity of ways: religious proscriptions; modesty codes; the exclusion of women from arenas of power; sexual abuse; and pornography.[3] Shaming remains one of the most effective ways to silence someone. A comic selection from *Hustler* is overt in its hostility to female speech. Under a caption reading "Lip Service," we view a photograph of a woman's face in which a vulva has replaced her mouth (fig. 4.8). The text below the picture reads: "There are those who say that illogic is the native tongue of anything with tits. . . . It comes natural to many broads; just like rolling in shit is natural for dogs. . . . They speak not from the heart but from the gash, and chances are that at least once a month your chick will stop you dead in your tracks with a masterpiece of cunt rhetoric. . . . The one surefire way to stop those feminine lips from driving you crazy is to put something between them—like your cock, for instance" (cited in Russell, 1998, 65). In other words, men can shut the offending "mouth" via rape—oral and vaginal.

It is common in pornography to find images of women not only bound but also gagged—so too in everyday pornography. A 2002 ad for Lexus shows a naked woman "bound and gagged" with hot pink ribbons, supposedly showing the "avant-garde" nature of the art and the car. An ad for Miller beer on the back cover of *Sports Illustrated* (2000) shows a man's hand resting a beer on top of an ordinary-looking middle-aged white woman's head; she must be positioned somehow on the floor (fig. 4.9). She is grimacing, her eyes almost closed (although on a quick glance it might seem that she is smiling). She holds the label of the beer, as if it were a gag, over her mouth. Viviana Cintolesi told me that this ad visually transmitted a common sexist saying in Chile: The perfect woman has a flat head (on which a man can place a beer), big ears (so that he can hold her tight), and a toothless mouth (so that he can orally rape her with no danger to himself).

Sex Objects

Sexuality is socially organized to require sex inequality for excitement and satisfaction. The least extreme expression of gender inequality, and the prerequisite for all of it, is dehumanization and objectification.

Catharine MacKinnon (1989, 243)

A 1985 poster for Carrera motorcycle equipment depicts a woman's body fused to a motorcycle. Her skin appears to be polished black metal; her

LIP SERVICE

There are those who say il- logic is the native tongue of anything with tits. We can't speak for all women, but some, at least, seem to enjoy clouding things up. It comes natural to many broads; just like rolling in shit is natural for dogs: It feels good and they like it. They speak not from the heart but from the gash, and chances are that at least once a month your chick will stop you dead in your tracks with a master- piece of cunt rhetoric.

You just have to learn to live with it. So who's com- plaining? The one surefire way to stop those feminine lips from driving you crazy is to put something between them—like your cock, for instance.

4.8 "Lip service," *Hustler,* 1976

4.9 Miller Genuine Draft beer ad, Miller Brewing Co. © 1999

arms become handlebars; her rump, the seat. An ad for Nike "air" sports shoes (*Sports Illustrated*, 1999) shows the shoe as well as an uninflated sex doll. The caption reads: "Air is what makes it good." These ads are aimed at men, identifying women with pleasurably possessable and controllable objects. Ads aimed at women also ask us to internalize female objectification: female bodies are shown as indistinguishable from mannequins, often partially dismembered mannequins (Caputi, 1987). While these images seem outlandish, they are telling metaphors for the socially desirable female body—one modified by cosmetic surgery, Botox, incessant dieting and toning, make-up, hair dye, fetish clothing, and fixation on sexual "parts."

Although pornography is rumored to be all about lust and sexual excitement, in the long run pornography is about desensitization, disconnection, the constriction of the sexual imagination, and the increasing appeal of control and sadism to that numbed sensorium (Jensen, 1998, 139). Pornographic objectification is a process whereby a sentient being is dehumanized; someone is turned into something that can be exchanged, owned, shown off, abused, disposed of, and used as a means to someone else's ends. And the truth is, if you dehumanize others, you unavoidably do it to yourself as well.

Misogyny, homophobia, absurd notions of permanently hard masculinity, inculcated ignorance, and sexual shaming—all these encourage men's alienation and insecurity about intimacy, making pornography particularly attractive. An article in *Men's Health* (Gutfield, 1999) warns that men can become addicted to Internet pornography and its engineered fix and lose their desire and capacity for real interactions. Such a scenario underlies a notorious ad for Miller Lite, shown during televised sports events throughout 2002. Two tipsy young men in a bar are rhapsodizing about their ideal beer commercial: Two "babes" wrestle, tear each other's clothes off, and slap each other around before one asks the other if she wants to "make out." The dolts ask: "Who wouldn't want to watch that?" Two women, sitting at the bar, grimace. As this ad itself suggests, pornography, like alcohol, can be addictive, causing users to prefer a relationship with their substance to actual encounter. Perhaps this is one of the main reasons patriarchal culture is reluctant to market pornography to women. Most men don't want women objectifying them, holding them to unreal standards of beauty and performance, and losing focus on them as individuals.

Women learn our status as objects not only through "beauty school" and pornography, but also through fashion and art. Drawing upon the history of the female nude in European art, John Berger (1972, 46–47) notes that these works served a pornographic function for their collectors. Moreover, he argues, in a sexist system "men act and women appear." The one who does the looking is generally in a position of power.

Still, it would be erroneous to find the antecedents of pornographic structures exclusively in elite art or, as some do, in the politically progressive and transgressive productions of early modern heretics, freethinkers, and libertines (Hunt, 1993). Patricia Hill Collins (1998, 136) argues persuasively that African American women are not included in pornography as an afterthought, but that the history of racist enslavement and sexual exploitation of African American women forms a "key pillar on which contemporary pornography rests." Because of imperial racism and slavery, naked African women were objects of display (in the United States and in Europe), were reduced to commodities for purchase on the auction block, and, legally, were forced sexually and reproductively. These practices have "developed into a full-scale industry," pornography, where "women are objectified differently by racial/ethnic category" (137).

Pornographic thinking projects excessive, purportedly "animalistic," sexuality onto racialized subjects. The novelist Alice Walker writes: "Where white women are depicted in pornography as 'objects,' black women are depicted as animals" (1980, 103). Consider an ad for Moschino apparel that appeared in 1999 in *Elle* magazine (fig. 4.10). A dark-skinned woman, with a big Afro and garbed in leopard-skin pants and halter top and high heels, stands with legs spread wide and arms flung out against the wall. Looking closely we that she is literally stapled to fabric on that wall. Such characterizations mark black women not only as sex objects, but also as slaves and subhumans, inherently "dirty."

"Dirty" Pictures

> If the past and human nature are any indication . . . the outlaw element in porn . . . will likely rise (or sink) to the occasion and do the necessary dirty work to keep porn, well . . . dirty. The way it should be.
>
> Mark Cromer (2001, 28)

> Where white women are depicted as human bodies if not beings [in pornography], black women are depicted as shit.
>
> Alice Walker (1980, 103)

Everyone knows that pornography has to be "dirty." But what does this really mean? A cartoon in *Hustler* provides some background. It shows a black man wiping himself after defecating. Where the tissue wipes clean, his skin turns white. A mainstream version of this "joke" can be found in a 2000 ad for Calvin Klein "Dirty Denim" Jeans. The now-deceased African American singer Lisa "Left Eye" Lopes, of the music group TLC, is wearing short-short "dirty denims" and posed against a

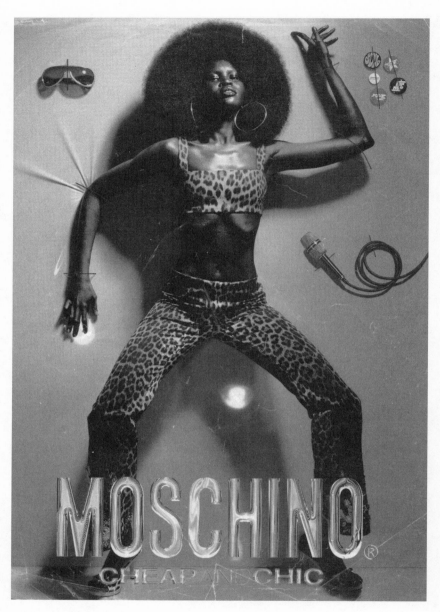

4.10 Moschino apparel ad, 1999

chain-link fence. It is nighttime, and this doesn't look like a very safe place to be. She is standing, but bending forward so her buttocks protrude. She looks not only "dirty," but also prostituted.

In the religious worldview put forth by the Abrahamic religions, it is Eve (Hawa) whose "transgression against the command of Allah" not only marked women as morally weaker than man, "but is also responsible for bringing *pislik* (dirtiness) into existence . . . creaturely functions of defecation, urination, and sweating . . . menstruation" (Delaney, 1988, 79). Concomitantly, racist and sexist "civilization" defines progress as being removed from body functions, sexuality, and the animal and elemental world, which is understood as inferior, evil, and feminine. Of course, no one is really removed from these. But to keep up the illusion, all of these traits of "dirtiness" are denied by the oppressor and projected onto the oppressed. The oppressor then persecutes the oppressed with vigor, since they represent these feared and despised aspects of himself. All women, to a greater or lesser degree depending on factors of race, class, and sexual experience; men of color; working men; gay men; colonized peoples; poor people; Jews—have been figured as "dirtier" (and more sexual) than those who conveniently define themselves as cleaner, purer, more moral, civilized, chaste, and superior (Dijkstra, 1996).

Although all women are seen as inferior, some women are denounced as particularly "dirty"—women of color, prostitutes, poor women. They are "whores." Select other women are designated, in what Calvin Hernton (1988, 136) understands as "pious pornography," as "virgins," impossibly chaste and pure—for example, upper- and middle-class white women who are installed as the closely guarded symbol of "white purity, white culture, of whiteness itself" (Doane, 1991, 41). That is, until they slip up somehow.

This pattern of opposition is enacted with great visual charge in a Benetton ad from 1991. Two children (probably girls, although there is no way to be sure) are shown naked from the shoulders up (fig. 4.11). The pale-skinned and very blond child on the left looks like a stereotypical angel, while the dark-skinned child, like a stereotypical devil, has her hair formed into two pointy horns. The ad is reprehensible in its overt meaning, but the children's arms are wrapped around each other, suggesting, however subtly, that this is a portrait of one originally whole psyche, now caricatured and horribly divided against itself. Still, if this was the intent, it would have been far better to reverse the traditional color associations.

4.11 United Colors of Benetton ad, 1991

Two semiotically related and utterly unredeemable magazine ads appeared in 1994. One, from *Cosmopolitan*, is for soap, although you could easily think you were looking at a recruitment poster for the Aryan Nation (fig. 4.12). A young, smiling blonde, wearing faded blue jeans and a white blouse, stands against a white background. The boldfaced "Pure" obviously refers equally to the woman and the soap. Her alleged "purity" has not only racialized but also sexualized resonance, for, of course, it is non-patriarchally-sanctioned sexual activity that paradigmatically sullies women and makes them targets for specific types of sexual violence: The designated "pure" woman must bear the honor of her male relatives and community. If she transgresses against what the menfolk believe to be proper behavior, they can righteously kill or rape her, committing an "honor crime" (Baker, Gregware, and Cassidy, 1999).

For the elite woman to be "pure" (however tenuously), somebody has to be "dirty." In a 1994 ad for Diesel jeans, appearing in *Details,* a brown-skinned woman lies on a bed covered with zebra-striped sheets. She wears a black bra, unbuttoned jeans, and a crucifix (symbolizing colonization as well as theological notions of sexual filth/evil). Obviously, this woman is available for invasion and conquest. The headline reads: "How to Control Wild Animals." In smaller print, this advice is

4.12 Liquid Neutrogena soap ad, Neutrogena Corp. © 1994

given: "We all want a safer world. So, come on, let's build more zoos. 1000s of them! Right now, there are far too many dangerous animals running around, wasting space, wasting time, using the planet as a toilet! Take our advice. Don't be fooled by 'natural' beauty, stick 'em in practical, easy-to-clean metal cages." By stigmatizing this woman (and those she represents) as a dangerous and filthy "animal," the conditions are laid for any type of abuse to be done to her with impunity. And, significantly, the pornographic imaginary also allows and often delights in abuse directed at animals (Adams, 1990).

This moralistic understanding of sex as defilement and hence "dirty" and sinful is deeply ingrained. It is the basis for the mind/body split, which divides the body into pure zones (head and face) and impure or dirty ones (genitals and organs of elimination). Following upon this split, whole peoples can be classified as "dirty" (dark, savage, bestial, sexual, "shitty," dangerous) and subjected to rape, lynching, colonization, and genocide, aptly euphemized as "ethnic cleansing" (Bauman, 1989). Animals (hairy, uncivilized, unashamed) are figured as inferior creatures for use, and the earth, the very source of humanity (*human* is related to the Latin *humus*, "earth, dirt"), is cast as the ultimate feminine victim. Moreover, under this model, notions of childhood purity or "innocence" do not protect children but actually target them for abuse.

Everyday Child Pornography

When women demand and express our intellectual, sexual, and emotional freedom, society responds with both overtly woman-hating pornography and the increased fetishization of children (Kaplan, 1991). In pornographic videos, women are marked with cosmetics, clothing, and coiffeurs to suggest that they are children or teenagers (Jensen and Dines, 1998, 87). In everyday pornography, sexually objectified women are shown in poses and clothing that suggests that they are little girls and actual little girls are made up and dressed up as if they were adult seductresses—as in a 2002 series of ads for Chanel perfume (fig. 4.13). In the mid-1980s, one of the biggest porn stars was Traci Lords—until it was revealed that she was sixteen years old. Gregory Dark, a pornographer known for his especially violent, abusive, and soulless touch, orchestrated her career, beginning with her first feature, *New Wave Hookers*. Dark boasts that a "whole generation of kids learned about sex from my fucked-up movies" (quoted in Junod, 2001, 131). By the late 1990s, images of teenage girls decked out like porn queens had become normative.

4.13 Chance fragrance ad, Chanel Inc., 2002

Dark himself directed a Britney Spears video in 1999, during her schoolgirl phase. Spears's sexpot appeal is founded in the way her handlers first promoted her as "innocent." Another (bleached) blonde icon, six-year-old JonBenet Ramsey, a victim of sexual murder, haunts our culture and demands that we recognize the pornographic object behind the "little beauty queen." But this recognition is repressed by the pornographic notion of childhood "innocence."

An ad from 1975 pitching Love's Baby Soft fragrance dispenses with all subtlety (fig. 4.14). It depicts a heavily made-up child with an elaborate adult coiffeur. She is about six years old. The headline reads: "Love's Baby Soft. Because innocence is sexier than you think." The ad blatantly positions the young girl as a sex object and acknowledges that it is her "innocence" that makes her such a suitable erotic target. Although this appears paradoxical, it makes perfect pornographic sense. The "moralistic" ethic puts chastity next to godliness and makes sex "dirty," defiling a supposed bodily and spiritual "purity." Sexual gratification of any kind then becomes all bound up not only with taboo violation, but also with defilement.

Charles Stember, in his study of sexual racism, describes standard notions of sexual pleasure in piously pornographic systems (1976, 149): "The gratification in sexual conquest derives from the experience of defilement—of reducing the elevated woman to the 'dirty' sexual level, of polluting that which is seen as pure, sexualizing that which is seen as unsexual, animalizing that which is seen as 'spiritual.'" When children are labeled "innocent," it places them squarely into this paradigm of sex as delicious defilement of "the pure" and thereby sets them up for abuse. In the world made by morality/porn, taboos and rules are literally made to be broken (and rule breaking itself becomes pleasurable). Stuck in the virgin/whore dilemma, women are accused of saying "no," but meaning "yes." But it is pornography, in the broad sense in which I am using the term here, that commands "no," but secretly solicits "yes."

Caught up in the sex-negative notion that children are "innocent," that is, asexual, many cannot see the sexual behaviors that adults act out on children *as* sexual behaviors, not only inappropriate touching and actual abuse, but also spanking and fetishized clothing. This notion of childhood "innocence" stigmatizes children's instinctual sexual behaviors like masturbation and (consensual and nonabusive) sex play as deviant and punishable offenses. It suppresses sex education, leaving children ignorant and truly vulnerable to predators. It leads children to believe that they are "dirty" and "bad" when they have sexual feelings, including those that sometimes are aroused during abuse. Abused children then end up feeling guilty and ashamed, carrying the emotions of the predator that have been transmitted to them via the sexual abuse itself (Caputi, 2003).

Specialized pornographic genres graphically focus on incest themes and pictorials (Russell, 1998). These appear as well in a disturbing family

4.14 Love's Baby Soft ad, Love Cosmetics, 1975

spread in a 1979 issue of *Playboy*. A sequence, playfully entitled "Father Knows Best," features a twenty-something woman posing naked for her photographer father. Underneath the headline, and before we get to the adult shots, is a full nude portrait of the daughter when she was three. Her backside is in view as she turns to look at her father. The accompanying copy reveals that the father would shoot nude models at home and that the little girl would take her clothes off, mimic the model's poses, and beg her daddy to photograph her too. He just had to comply, for: "She had the cutest little tush." Once again, the notion of childhood innocence permits this abuse to go unnoticed. Don't get me wrong. Lots of parents photograph their young children naked with no harmful intent or effect. Yet photographing a child in the context of pornography shoots is another thing altogether. And, of course, a father's pornographically photographing his daughter, as a child or an adult, is arguably an incestuous act. The tongue-in-cheek title, "Father Knows Best," acknowledges the underlying connection between mainstream family values and incest itself.

Patriarchal family values idealize a father's godlike authority in his home/castle, where wives and children, his dependents and, in classical form, his property, submit to his dominion. Incest and domestic abuse constitute the underside of that fundamentally unequal arrangement. In an issue of *Life* (April 1991) devoted to "The American Family," three apparently naked representatives of the ideal family—a white man, woman, and baby—are photographed in intimate closeup. Only faces and shoulders are showing (fig. 4.15). Presumably they are all lying down on a bed. The woman (who looks literally about fourteen years old) holds the baby at her breast. The man (who looks much older) doesn't lie beside her, as one might expect. Rather, he looms above them, gazing proprietarily down upon them and taking up about half of the space. There is no conceivable way that people would naturally arrange themselves in such an odd pose. This image exists primarily to visually announce the superior status and total domination of the man as the head of the nuclear family.

Child abuse generally is perpetrated not by strangers but by someone known to the child whom the child has been led to *trust*—a family member, coach, priest, minister, or neighbor. An ad from the St. Paul insurance company (it appeared in both print and television formats, airing during the 2000 World Series) shows, albeit in symbolic form, a predator's-eye-view of such a relationship (fig. 4.16). In the television version, a pretty little tousled-haired white girl stands in a field. In the

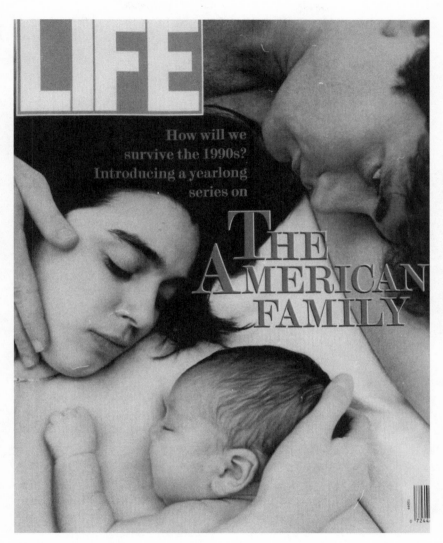

LIFE

How will we
survive the 1990s?
Introducing a yearlong
series on

THE
AMERICAN
FAMILY

4.15 *Life* cover, April 1991

distance something long, hard, and unmistakably phallic rises up in the tall grass. It turns out to be the horn of a rhinoceros, and the camera alternates between the child's loving face and the charging rhino. Captions read: "Trust / Is not being afraid / Even if you're vulnerable." As the rhino reaches the child, a cloud of dust covers both. When it clears, we see the little girl reach out her hand and stroke the horn as she plants a kiss on it. This highly fantastic scenario begs to be interpreted

Trust *is not being afraid even if you're vulnerable.*

Is there someone who understands how frightening a situation can be? Someone who believes fear can be dismantled when we are armed with confidence? Is there an insurance company that is consistently rated superior by independent rating services – a company with a 146 year history of providing strength in the face of uncertainty? Without Question.

Without Question. **The St Paul**
Property and Liability Insurance
For more information contact your independent insurance agent or broker or visit www.stpaul.com.

4.16 The St. Paul Companies ad, 2000

symbolically. The girl's trumpeted "vulnerability" only enhances her erotic appeal in the pornographic paradigm. The rhino, a fairly obvious phallic symbol, represents the abuser, who initially seems threatening but whom the girl nonetheless invites to approach through her attitude of calm receptivity. The sexual abuse is signified by that moment when the cloud of dust covers them and we cannot see what is happening.

When the dust clears, the little girl strokes and kisses her abuser on his horn/penis.

When I show this ad in class, many students tell me that I am simply reading too much into the text and that they cannot see what I am talking about. Perhaps I am simply wrong. But the factor of denial must always be considered when dealing with images suggesting incest and child sexual abuse. A telling moment in the documentary *Capturing the Friedmans* (Andrew Jarecki, 2002) conveys this truth. Wife and mother Elaine Friedman lived for years in utter ignorance of her husband's pedophilia, his probable abuse of their sons, and his (admitted) abuse of at least two other boys. Arnold Friedman was also an avid collector of child pornography, and Elaine relates that when the police first showed her his magazines, the extremely graphic pictures simply made no sense to her. She literally could not see what was going on in them until some time later after her entrenched denial had lifted. Perhaps a bit of that same inability to "see" afflicts everyone in this fundamentally mixed-message culture.

Apocalyptic Endings

An ancient and worldwide tradition figures the earth not only as a sacred being, but as a feminine one (Eliade, 1958a; Merchant, 1980). Pornography paradigmatically desecrates what once was sacred, and the earth now is treated, in representation as in reality, as other feminine or feminized beings are. In ads for everything from hotel chains to high-technology devices, the earth is stabbed, halved, strangled, "snuffed," and rendered partially or wholly artificial (Caputi, 1993). An exemplary image appears in a 1985 ad from a major nuclear contractor, Rockwell International (fig. 4.17). It shows the earth as if it were a projection on a computer screen. The top half of the sphere was sectioned into four pieces; the bottom disappeared into an abstract grid. Bolts penetrate our planet at both axes as well as through the middle. The depiction, the accompanying verbal copy explains, shows how the corporation is able to "'man·ij" the planet.

Sometimes a female body stands for the earth. A 1999 ad for car stereo speakers shows a naked, curvy, and inert, perhaps dead, young white woman flat out on the ground. Of course, we soon realize, she *is* the ground/earth that viewers are invited to drive over. Inscribed over every inch of her body are roadmaps. The headline reads: "Feel the raw, naked power of the road." What is implicit in these images is rendered

Manage
• *Handle or direct with a degree of skill; e.g. apply high technology to global markets.*
• *Achieve; e.g. increased productivity through strategic investments supporting the work of 100,000 engineers, scientists and skilled employees.*
• *Succeed in accomplishing, as in record sales, record earnings, record return on equity.*

We're not out to change the world. Just to supply the technology it takes to make it better.

But technology alone doesn't bring 20.3% Return on Equity or nine straight years of increased earnings.

That takes management. Ours provides a culture that stimulates and directs the growth of high technology in four diverse business areas. To learn more about us, write: Rockwell International, Department 815F-62, 600 Grant Street, Pittsburgh, PA 15219.

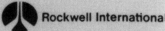 **Rockwell International**

...where science gets down to business

Aerospace Electronics
Automotive General Industries

4.17 Rockwell International ad, 1985

fully explicit in a political cartoon by David Levine that appeared in *The Nation* (February 25, 1984). It visualizes Henry Kissinger's political power by showing him "fucking" a woman's body with the earth as her head. There is no trouble getting his point: the sexual thrill of world domination and possession.

In *The 120 Days of Sodom,* de Sade (1987, 364) envisions the ultimate pornographic pleasure as an earthly holocaust. His gathered "libertines" all agree that violation of taboo is the supreme sexual thrill and recount crimes they would like to commit. A banker speaks of his yearning: "Ah, how many times, by God, have I not longed to be able to assail the sun, snatch it out of the universe, make a general darkness, or use that star to burn the world!" Contemporary technology has come up with a means—nuclear weaponry—to realize that pornographic fantasy (Caputi, 1993). Proponents of pornography insist that fantasy is utterly distinct from reality. To be sure, not every fantasy seeks a literal enactment. But some, like dreams, really do come true as the pornographic imagination takes shape in all manner of destructive technological and military practices. This factor doesn't mean that we outlaw fantasy, but it does suggest that we take it seriously and seek to understand how it interacts with and potentially shapes reality.

An illustration by the well-known rock artist Raymond Pettibone, on the cover of a mid-1980s avant-garde rock compilation album, *The Blasting Concept* (fig. 4.18), shows a naked man strangling a woman with a rope while fucking her. Through a window, we see that a mushroom cloud is exploding outside. Once I showed this image to a graduate class and compared its message to that of the film *Dr. Strangelove* (Stanley Kubrick, 1963), where the mad Air Force general who blows up the world is named General Jack D. Ripper. I suggested that it illustrated the investment of rape-murderous desires into nuclear weaponry. One student, drawing upon "sex-positive" pro-pornography arguments, offered another interpretation. She told me that this image demonstrated, instead, the woman's sexual agency and power in choosing to be asphyxiated as a means of increasing the strength of her orgasm. Both of us offered radically different interpretations. But the question is not necessarily who is "right." The essential message remains clear: The pornographic ethic that eroticizes sadomasochism, taboo violation and violence, up to and including apocalyptic violence, logically is leading us right into the lap of a nuclear holocaust. The poet Jayne Cortez (1984, 109) pleads with all of us: "Tell me that you have no desire / to be the first one to fuck / into the fission of a fusion / of a fucking holocaust."

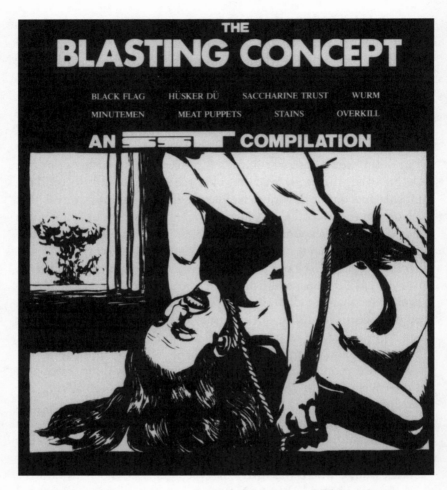

4.18 *The Blasting Concept* album cover by Raymond Pettibone, SST Records, 1983

Bitch Theory

A notorious *Hustler* cover (June 1978) shows a large meat grinder with chopped meat coming out of one end. At the other end, being fed into the device, is the naked body of a woman. All that remains is her body below the waist. Accompanying this graphic is a quip from the magazine's founder, Larry Flynt: "We will no longer hang women up like pieces of meat."

Conventional thought suggests that men chop up and "'man·ij'" women, animals, and all of nature because men are naturally stronger and smarter, the dominant species, the superior sex. Nawal El Saadawi

(1980, 100), the Egyptian novelist and political theorist, contends that actually it is male insecurity and terror in the face of "the innate resilience and strength of the woman" that first led men to oppress and subjugate women, trying to "conquer the indomitable vitality and strength that lay within women, ready to burst out at any moment."

Understanding men's fear of female potency helps us to identify the common denominator among phenomena like pornographic display; rape; harassment; veiling; bondage; corseting; fashion-mandated thinness; feminizing makeup; crippling footwear; depilation of the legs, face, underarms, and genitals; cosmetic surgery (including laser surgery to tighten the vagina and diminish the size of the labia); and clitoridectomy and other forms of genital mutilation. All such practices (and the imagery that promotes them) represent the fear-based masculine project to contain, control, infantilize, and defeat female potency.

In the pornographic view, male potency veritably requires female impotence, and whenever there is a truly sovereign woman (not just a "dominatrix" acting out a male-authored script), there is a weak and castrated man. Bob Guccione, founder of the glossy porn magazine *Penthouse*, admits as much in a comment on Viagra when he whines: "Feminism has emasculated the American male, and that emasculation has led to physical problems" (quoted in Roof, 1999, 5). Yet many women and men reject this equation and yearn for recognitions of female potency, social as well as sacred, historical as well as mythic, and for the momentous shift in notions of male potency that would necessarily accompany this renewal. Such notions of potency would be inseparable from human consanguinity with and balanced relationship to the animal, elemental, and fertile/dirty world.

Hustler seeks to degrade women by linking us to animals—and, to be sure, animals and women are treated in similarly disrespectful ways (Collard, 1988; Adams, 1990; Warren, 1997). Yet from a nature-respecting perspective, the woman-animal connection is an honored one. For example, although *bitch* is now a term of contempt, this word originally was "one of the most sacred titles of the Goddess Artemis-Diana" (B. Walker, 1983, 109), who often appeared as a dog herself, or in the company of hounds. This ancient, powerful Bitch is the sacred archetype behind the contemporary profanity, reflecting fear of the "bitch goddess" (as well as the sexually sovereign, creative, autonomous woman).

Arguably, modern pornography, in all of its manifestations, is a genre devoted to profaning and containing female divinity and bitch potency (see chapter 16, "The Naked Goddess"). In *Goddess: Myths of the Female Divine*, David Leeming and Jake Page (1994) trace an ancient history of goddess worship followed by systematic denigrations during the patriarchal era. Modern pornography continues this tradition by appropriating signs, including female nakedness and the revelation of the vulva (Hurston, 1983, 137) as well as the association with animals (Neumann, 1963), which previously signified female sacrality and the presence of a goddess. But pornography's sway does not remain unchallenged, and some of the most vital resistance to the pornographic imaginary can be found in a radical reclamation and recasting of these ancient traditions and associations. A contemporary movement of art, literature, mysticism, and ecological/feminist philosophy challenges the pornographic worldview in just this way (e.g., A. Walker, 1982; Daly, 1984; Gadon, 1989; Conner, 1993; Cisneros, 1996; Ensler, 1998; Anzaldúa, 2000; Schneemann, 2002). Breaking the habit of the pornographic mindset begins with healing the masculine/feminine and mind/body splits and claiming sexual intelligence, sexual speech, and a sacred erotic, and female potency, as well as representing and invoking ecstatic and often mystical sexualities as routes to both pleasure and knowledge.

A nonpornographic Eros, and worldview deeply connected with the body, sensuality, the green world, and the animal/sexual soul, rejects the apocalyptic ends (and ending) of the pornographic story and its use/abuse/violate dictum. It recognizes the supreme arrogance and foolishness of such practices, and, refusing projection and objectification, respects and identifies with "the girl," the bitch, the dark, and the dirt.[4]

Part 2

Gods and Monsters

5

The New Founding Fathers
The Lore and Lure of the Serial Killer in Contemporary Culture

Jack the Ripper
He was the first.
Cover blurb from a collection of stories on the Ripper (Dozois and Casper, 1988)

Ted Bundy—A Man with Vision
—A Man with Direction
—A Prophet of Our Times
Flyer advertising a student program, University of New Mexico, Albuquerque (1989)

Freddy's fame—make that notoriety—was confirmed by the
National Coalition on Television Violence, which in a recent
survey found that children ages 10 to 13 are more familiar with
Freddy [from the *Nightmare on Elm Street* series] and his Par-
amount counterpart Jason of "Friday the 13th" than with such
famous historical figures as George Washington, Abraham
Lincoln, or Martin Luther King, Jr. Jason was recognized by
72 of the 100 children surveyed and Freddy by 66, while poor
Honest Abe was identified by 36.
"Freddy Items Are Vendor's Dream," *Albuquerque Tribune*, September 2 (1989)

Watching *The Week in Rock* on MTV (September 16, 1989), I was taken
aback when the announcer commented, "Now for some news from
Boston—home of baked beans, B.U., and at least one renowned serial
strangler." How blithe, normalizing, and easy a reference to atrocity. Yet
why was I surprised? Just one year earlier, in autumn 1988, Great Britain

and the United States "celebrated" the centennial of the crimes of "Jack the Ripper." Mourning, which might seem appropriate to the occasion, was notably absent (except in feminist demonstrations and writings). Rather, light-hearted Ripper paraphernalia, such as a computer game, t-shirts, buttons, mugs, and a blood-red cocktail, appeared throughout England (Cameron, 1988, 17–19). Most strikingly, in both the United States and England, the legend of the Ripper was ubiquitously retold, and millions were familiarized with its elements—a massively promoted made-for-TV movie, innumerable newspaper accounts, an exploitation thriller, *Jack's Back,* and scores of new books on the master killer.

This recent mythicization of the Ripper continues a process that has been in motion since 1888. Elsewhere, I have argued that "Jack the Ripper" is father to an "age of sex crime" (Caputi, 1987) and that his status as a cultural icon legitimates male violence against women. The Ripper has provided a cultural category for a new type of crime (the territorial, ritualistic, nicknamed, serial sex slayer) and acted as a role model for subsequent killers, including the "Boston Strangler," the "Son of Sam," the "Yorkshire Ripper," the "Green River Killer," the "Hillside Strangler," and so on—killers who then go on to generate legends and attract cultlike behavior of their own. Serial sex killers such as these are celebrated (sometimes covertly, sometimes overtly) along a cultural gamut including made-for-TV movies, rock 'n' roll songs, horror fanzines, jokes, pornographic magazines such as *Hustler,* and extreme sadist publications.[1] Simultaneously, a parallel cult can be discerned in the adulation given (primarily by teenage boys) to the fictional screen counterparts of the modern sex killer, such as "Freddy Krueger," the child molester/murderer from the *Nightmare on Elm Street* movies and television series, and "Jason," the hockey-masked multiple murderer from the *Friday the 13th* film series.

While such mythmaking proceeds unabated, serial murder itself has become a recognized factor in modern Western life. Justice Department official Robert O. Heck gives his view: "We all talk about Jack the Ripper; he killed five people. We all talk about the 'Boston Strangler' who killed thirteen, and maybe 'Son of Sam,' who killed six. But we've got people [*sic*] out there now killing twenty and thirty people and more, and some of them just don't kill. They torture their victims in terrible ways and mutilate them before they kill them. Something's going on out there" (quoted in Lindsey, 1984).

Of course, Heck's language works to obscure what actually is going on out there, for the "people" who torture, kill, and mutilate in this way are men, while their victims are predominantly females, women and girls, and, to a lesser extent, younger men. As these hierarchical lines indicate, these are crimes of sexually political import, crimes rooted in a system of male supremacy in the same way that lynching is based in white supremacy. That recognition, however, is impeded by longstanding tradition, for, as Kate Millett noted in her classic work, *Sexual Politics:* "We are not accustomed to associate patriarchy with force. So perfect is its system of socialization, so complete the general assent to its values, so long and so universally has it prevailed in human society, that it scarcely seems to require violent implementation. Customarily, we view its brutalities in the past as exotic or 'primitive' custom. Those of the present are regarded as the product of individual deviance, confined to pathological or exceptional behavior, and without general import. And yet . . . control in patriarchal societies would be imperfect, even inoperable, unless it had the rule of force to rely upon, both in emergencies and as an ever-present instrument of intimidation" (1970, 59–60).

The most commonly analyzed form of such patriarchal force is rape. Early feminist analysts of rape asserted that rape is not, as the common mythology insists, a crime of frustrated attraction, victim provocation, or uncontrollable biological urges. Nor is it one perpetrated only by an aberrant fringe. Rather, rape is a direct expression of sexual politics, a ritual enactment of male domination, and a form of terror that functions to maintain the status quo (Millett, 1970, 61–62; Griffin, 1971, 26–35; Brownmiller, 1975; Russell, 1975). Similarly, the murders of women and children by serial killers are not the acts of inexplicably deviant men. On the contrary, sexual murder is a product of the dominant culture. It is the ultimate expression of a sexuality that defines sex as a form of domination/power; it, like rape, is a form of terror that constructs and maintains male supremacy.

Heck's statement invokes shared knowledge of a tradition of serial murder (beginning with Jack the Ripper) that, as he puts it, "we all talk about." Indeed, we all do. In this chapter, using several representative killers, I trace some of the ways in which modern culture talks about the sex killer. I survey the folklore and popular culture representations of these killers (both actual and fictional) and interpret these for what they tell us about male supremacy and cultural constructions of monstrosity and horror, as well as fears of the future.

Father to an Age

Two women cops working twice as hard for half the glory . . .
TONIGHT: Decoys for a Jack the Ripper.
Ad for the premiere episode of *Cagney and Lacey* (*TV Guide*, March 20, 1982)

Imagine . . . a study of feminism from the point of view of Jack
the Ripper . . . a novel that bristles with irony and wit.
New York Times review of *Confessions of a Lady-Killer* (Schechner, 1979, 15)

A third class of strangers are so utterly beyond the pale that
they seem alien not only to the group, but to the human
species. I refer to *monsters*, indicated by names like: pervert,
degenerate . . . psychopath . . . fiend, demon, devil . . . Jack the
Ripper.
Orrin Klapp (1962, 59)

[Jack the Ripper] that great hero of my youth, that skilled
human butcher who did all his work on alcoholic whores.
Charles McCabe, *San Francisco Chronicle,* October 7, 1971
(quoted in Brownmiller, 1975, 294)

Jack the Ribber.
Restaurant, New York City

I need some help here. Some hands. Just send me anybody.
Jack the Ripper. I'll take anyone who's good with a knife.
Hawkeye on *M*A*S*H*, c. 1973

And Jezebel the nun, she violently knits,
A bald wig for Jack the Ripper, who sits,
At the head of the Chamber of Commerce.
Bob Dylan, "Tombstone Blues," 1965

The ghost of Jack the Ripper hovered over Washington today.
Story on federal budget cuts, *ABC Nightly News,* November 29, 1984

VOICE: Knock knock.
HUSBAND: Who's there?
VOICE: Jack the Ripper.
HUSBAND: It's for you, dear.
The Benny Hill Show, c. 1980

Mrs. Hanson . . . had always worn an extra enforcement of
petticoats against an ever-potential Jack the Ripper.
Fannie Hurst (1943, 97–98)

Traces of the Ripper's presence constantly intrude into urban
women's consciousness. Walking down my street in Manhattan recently, I came upon graffiti emblazoning the Ripper's
name on a side of a building That same week the Lesbian
Herstory Archives forwarded to me a threatening letter from

"Jack the Ripper": "THE ORIGINAL JACK not a cheap imitation.
I've conquered death itself and am still on this earth waiting to
strike again."

Judith Walkowitz (1982, 570)

As this brief sampling of reference indicates, the figure of Jack the Ripper preoccupies this culture in the form of a pervasive and particularly
all-embracing metaphor (though, obviously, with different meanings
for women and men). The mythic Ripper inspires awe and laughter; he
is viewed as both hero and monster; and he is hailed by many as a key
innovator, not only in the annals of true crime, but also in the imagination of modern horror. In a recent discussion of that genre, two of its
practitioners, writers Harlan Ellison and Gahan Wilson, traced the origins of modern horror to Jack the Ripper:

> ELLISON: Everything that scares us today dates back to Jack the Rip-
> per. He is still the operative icon of terror. He may be small potatoes by
> current standards . . . but the Ripper started it. He created the form.
> WILSON: Just as no one paints landscapes the same way since Turner,
> a creative monster like the Ripper changed the landscape of what scares
> us. He inspired generations. (Ellison and Wilson, 1989, 47)

Wilson and Ellison seem to be vicariously thrilled by the Ripper, if they
do not actually heroize him as a "creative monster" who blazed their
path into the realms of horror. But, of course, this is an expedient and
gender-specific thrill; as men, they personally have little to fear from the
Ripper and do not have to suffer the consequences of that aggrandizing
mythicization.

The crimes of the Ripper occurred in the Whitechapel district of
London, an area well known as a center of poverty and prostitution.
The still-unknown killer has been credited with as many as twenty murders, although probably only five were the work of the one man; others
were imitative or unconnected crimes. The killer made no attempt to
cover up his actions. Rather, he left the bodies on display, out on the
open street in four instances. Furthermore, he (or, far more likely, someone pretending to be the killer) advertised his crimes by writing letters
to the police, the press, and citizen groups, nicknaming himself in one
letter, taunting the police, predicting future crimes, and even mailing
half of a human kidney to the chief of a Whitechapel vigilance group
(the letter writer claimed to have eaten the other half). The victims, all
prostitutes, were not raped; their throats were slit from behind, and
then the sexual and other organs were severely mutilated. While similar

atrocities indubitably had occurred before, indicated, perhaps, in legends of werewolves and vampires, or tracked as isolated incidents of "lust murder" in the nineteenth century, it was not until 1888 in London that the idea of a sexually motivated criminal, specializing in mutilation, dismemberment, and murder, took shape as a cultural icon (Caputi, 1987; see also Cameron and Fraser, 1987).

Many have asked why Jack the Ripper, more than other sex criminals, has left such a mark. Nigel Morland avers (1966, 138): "The melodramatic name of Jack the Ripper . . . is largely the reason for his immortality, that and the imaginative folk lore which has always surrounded him." In truth, the identity of the Ripper has never been established; this evocative anonymity has been a source for much of the Ripper lore as self-proclaimed "Ripperologists" and "Ripperophiles" continually sift over the known information, proposing improbable and often highly romanticized possible identities (e.g., a member of the royal family).

Further enabling the mythicization process, the crimes of the Ripper constitute one of the first media events. As historian Judith Walkowitz notes (1982, 550): "One cannot emphasize too much the role of the popular press, itself a creation of the 1880s, in establishing Jack the Ripper as a media hero, in amplifying the terror of male violence, and in elaborating and interpreting the meaning of the Ripper murders to a 'mass' audience." A key feature of that elaboration was the wedding of the crimes to traditional horror images and formulae. "Unable to find historical precedents for the Whitechapel 'horrors,' commentators resorted to horrifying fictional analogues" (ibid.). Here are the beginnings of the Ripper mythos—the sex killer as human monster, master criminal, immortal being—as well as the origins of his role as a stock character in twentieth-century literature. Jack the Ripper has been a recurring figure in popular and serious fictions (beginning with Frank Wedekind's *Die Busche der Pandora*, 1904, and Marie Belloc Lowndes's story "The Lodger," 1913), in films (e.g., Nicholas Meyer's *Time after Time*, 1979, and Albert Hughes and Allen Hughes's *From Hell*, 2001), television dramas (most notably as an immortal alien entity on *Star Trek*), and songs (e.g., Link Wray's "Jack the Ripper," 1959; Screamin' Lord Sutch and the Savages' "Hands of Jack the Ripper," c. 1969).

Still, the reasons for the Ripper's solidly entrenched status as a cultural icon go beyond his colorful nickname or the fortuitous collaboration of the nineteenth-century popular press. His enduring popularity, instead, is primarily rooted in the patriarchal foundations of the modern world, and his essential meaning is his role as an emblem of misogynist terrorism. Horror writers might expediently celebrate the mythic Ripper as a "creative monster" who "inspired generations"—I assume they mean generations of horror writers. Yet the Ripper legend has also inspired generations of misogynist men, both armchair criminals who enjoy identifying with the Ripper in various fictional portrayals and actual killers who directly indicate that they were emulating the Ripper (see Caputi, 1987, 34–35).

As time goes by, the Ripper's mythic representations have only increased, and a bibliographic essay listing all of the forms in which the Ripper makes an appearance would run into hundreds of items. Three interconnected themes recur in this accumulated Ripper Lore: (1) the immortality of the Ripper (2) the confusion of the historical and the fictional criminal, and (3) the establishment of a sex-murder tradition, built upon the Ripper's original crimes.

In 1905 British children jumped rope to this chant: "Jack the Ripper's dead / And lying on his bed. / He cut his throat with Sunlight Soap / Jack the Ripper's dead" (Opie and Opie, 1959, 11). This verse represents one of the very few times the Ripper has died in the popular mind. Rather, his primary persona is that of an immortal and continually lethal presence. This notion was introduced to a mass audience by Robert Bloch in his 1942 short story "Yours Truly, Jack the Ripper" (collected in Bloch, 1977, 1–20) and subsequently has been imitated countless times. In the 1979 film *Time after Time,* Jack the Ripper actually travels into the present through his unsuspecting friend H. G. Wells's time machine. The horrified Wells is finally able to dispatch him via that very machine, sending him, as perfectly befits a mythic creature, "into *infinity,* where he really belongs."

A startling juxtaposition of stories in the October 30, 1979, issue of *US* illustrates the second and third themes. The first item, a news story on a series of sex slayings in Yorkshire, claims: "A New Jack the Ripper Is Terrorizing England." On the very next page, a headline for a story on the film *Time after Time* reads: "The Stars Really Fall in Love in a New Jack the Ripper Flick." This placement collapses the "New Jack the Ripper" almost imperceptibly into the "New Jack the Ripper Flick," as if there really were no substantial difference between the two. Such juxtapositions may lead us to consider the ways in which the incessant mythicization/heroization of the misogynist killer encourages the emergence of the "New Jack the Rippers," men eager to fill out the archetype of the criminal genius/monster whose exploits are reviled but simultaneously celebrated in the popular culture.

Writers have surveyed the lore surrounding the Ripper from a variety of perspectives, and it is not my intention to recapitulate that material in any greater depth here. Rather, having established the prominence and prevalence of Ripper lore, I want to concentrate on the much less analyzed personae and lores of several men who come from the "generations" inspired by Jack the Ripper, killers such as Ted Bundy and David Berkowitz.

"America's Jack the Ripper"

So let's salute the mighty Bundy,
Here on Friday, gone on Monday.
All his roads lead out of town.
It's hard to keep a good man down.
Aspen folksinger, celebrating Bundy's first prison escape, 1978
(quoted in Winn and Merrill, 1980, 217)

When the *Reader's Digest* published an original article on Ted Bundy, its cover blurb announced: "Caught: America's Jack the Ripper" (Adam, 1981, 210–39). In some ways, this seemed mere hyperbole. The two killers were not that much alike: Bundy selected college coeds, not prostitutes, as his victims, and he hid the bodies, instead of displaying them. Nevertheless, just as Jack the Ripper seemed to personify the underside of Victorian England, so too Ted Bundy epitomized his society, presenting a persona of the superficially ideal, all-American boy. Just months after the 1988 centennial celebration for the mythic father of sexual murder, the focus effortlessly shifted to that paradigmatic son, Bundy—and to the drama leading up to his execution on January 24, 1989, and the revelry that accompanied it. In the days preceding his death, Bundy's story dominated the mass media, memorializing and further mythicizing a killer who had already been the subject of scores of book chapters, articles, five books, and a made-for-TV movie (where he was played by Mark Harmon, an actor whom *People* once gushed over as the "world's sexiest man"). On the morning Bundy went to the electric chair, hundreds gathered across the street from the prison (judging from photographs, the crowd was composed largely of men). Many wore specially designed costumes, waved banners proclaiming a "Bundy BBQ," or "I like my Ted well done," and chanted songs such as: "He bludgeoned the poor girls, all over the head. / Now we're all ecstatic, Ted Bundy is dead." The most common journalistic metaphors for the overall scene invoked carnivals, circuses, or tailgate parties before a big game (e.g., Lamar, 1989, 34).

This sort of spontaneous outpouring of folk sentiment was not without precedent. In the late 1970s, when he was awaiting trial for the murder of Caryn Campbell in Aspen, Colorado, Bundy managed to escape twice. The first time he was caught and returned to custody; the second time he made it to Florida. News of his escapes (particularly the first) prompted a phenomenal reaction. All observers concur: "In Aspen, Bundy had become a folk hero" (Larsen, 1980, 182). "Ted achieved the status of Billy the Kid at least" (Rule, 1980, 255). "Aspen reacted as if Bundy were some sort of Robin Hood instead of a suspected mass murderer. A folklore sprang up out of the thin Rocky Mountain air" (Nordheimer, 1978, 46). T-shirts appeared reading: "Ted Bundy is a One Night Stand." Radio KSNO programmed a Ted Bundy request hour, playing songs like "Ain't No Way to Treat a Lady." A local restaurant offered a "Bundyburger" consisting of a plain roll: "Open it and see the meat has fled," explained a sign. Yet after his second escape, the FBI took Bundy seriously enough to name him to its Ten Most Wanted List, seeking him "in connection with 36 similar-type sexual slayings throughout several Western states."

Just as Bundy's young, white, generally middle-class victims were stereotypically (and with marked racist and class bias) universalized as "anyone's daughters," Bundy himself was depicted as the fatherland's (almost) ideal son—handsome, intelligent, a former law student, a rising star in Seattle's Republican party. And although that idealization falls apart upon examination—he had to drop out of law school because of bad grades; he was chronically unhappy and habitually abused alcohol; he was a nailbiter and nosepicker—it provided an attractive mythic persona for purposes of identification. As several feminist analysts have noted (Millett, 1970, 62; Lacy 1982–83; Walkowitz, 1982), a recurrent and vivid pattern accompanying episodes of sensationalized sex murder is ordinary male identification with the sex killer, as revealed in "jokes, innuendoes, veiled threats (*I* might be the Strangler, you know)" (Lacy, 1982–83, 61). Such joking followed Bundy's murder of two sorority women at the Chi Omega House at the University of Florida, Tallahassee. One woman who lived there at the time remembered:

> Probably the most disturbing thing was the series of jokes and innuendoes that men traded about the murders. My boyfriend at the time was a public defender, and it was his office that represented Bundy at trial. He heard a lot of comments by virtue of being male and working close to the investigation that I probably would never have heard otherwise. We talked recently and he said there were basically two kinds of humor about the killings: (1) sorority-related jokes [and] (2) jokes

which connected the violence of torn-off nipples and bite marks on the victims to Bundy's sexual "appetite" as in "eating" the victims sexually or sometimes, literally. One such joke was: "What do you get when you have a Tri Delt, a Chi O, and a Phi Mu? A three-course dinner for Ted Bundy." What could possibly be behind this kind of humor? I really don't buy the theory that these jokes help to reduce the stress of a horrible event. I think they just reduce the horror of the event in order to make it acceptable. (Cassandra Sitterly, personal communication, August 10, 1984)

After his first escape, the male identification was with Bundy as a rebel, an outlaw hero. When he was on trial for murder in Florida, as the joking there indicated, he provided fodder for some sadistic sexual fantasies. Subsequently, Bundy did the supremely unmanly thing: He confessed to his crimes and manifested fear of death. No longer qualifying as a hero, Bundy was now cast into the complementary role of scapegoat. The "blood-thirsty revelers" who partied outside as Bundy was executed, through their objectification and disrespect for the victims and lust for death, still mirrored Bundy, but now delightedly demanded that the all-American boy die as a token sacrifice for his and their sins.

Elements, frequently obscure, of Bundy lore can be found in various places. Students in a popular culture class tell me that they are sure that the name of the Bundy family on the Fox network's parodic sitcom *Married with Children* deliberately recalled the notorious Ted Bundy and was a subtle reference to the downside of "happy" American family life. The punk band Jane's Addiction recorded a song called "Ted, Just Admit It" (on *Nothing's Shocking*, 1988—this was before Bundy had confessed). Here, they sing of television news being "just another show with sex and violence" and chant over and over that "sex is violent." But I encountered the most startling mythicization of Bundy at the University of New Mexico in Albuquerque, where I then taught: a flyer advertising a program on pornography (fig. 5.1), held in the dorms, sponsored by a student group, and including a showing of the tape of Bundy's last interview. The flyer displayed a likeness of the killer under the slogan: "A Man with Vision. A Man with Direction. A Prophet of Our Times . . . Ted Bundy: The Man The Myth. The Legand [*sic*]." Unfortunately, I learned about this program too late to attend, so I cannot say with certainty what the tone of the program was. The flyer itself combines elements of a seemingly serious agenda ("film, informed speakers, discussion") with patently "sick" humor (the references to Bundy as a visionary prophet). The sponsor for the event was the Entertainment Program Committee, a

5.1 Flyer advertising a program on pornography, University of New Mexico in Albuquerque, 1989

dormitory student group, so I imagine that the program was a way for students, primarily male, to get together to joke about Bundy, particularly his claim that pornography led him to sexual violence.

As previously noted, the mystery surrounding the identity of Jack the Ripper has generated a considerable amount of his lore. Although his identity is clear, other factors about Bundy provide fodder for legend. Bundy confessed to thirty murders, yet he has also been implicated in at least twenty others by the authorities; moreover, without much corroborating evidence, some relatives of missing women are sure that he killed their loved ones. For example, Sophia Mary Healey disappeared at Royal Gorge in Colorado in 1979. The *Denver Post* reports that her mother "clings to the notion her daughter was murdered or abducted by a man seen entering the park in a tan VW immediately after Healey. That man, she believes, was notorious serial killer Ted Bundy, who had recently escaped from a Colorado jail" (Simpson, 1989). Like his predecessor, Jack the Ripper, Bundy has become something of a "collective for murder."[2] Finally, Bundy was "illegitimate," and his mother never revealed the identity of his birth father. Such obscure paternal origins are an open invitation to mythicization, as happened when an article in *Vanity Fair* broadly suggested (without any actual evidence) that Louise Bundy was impregnated by her abusive father, making Bundy a child of incest (MacPherson, 1989).

Finally, the greatest myth surrounding Bundy is one that we encounter nearly everywhere in the mainstream press—the notion that Bundy and others like him are complete "enigmas." This is constantly reiterated in refutation of Bundy's claim—which he had made consistently since his capture in 1978—that pornography had influenced his evolution into a sex killer. For example, *Playboy* approvingly quotes one of his lawyers, James Coleman: "He [Bundy] didn't know what made him kill people. No one did" (Playboy Forum, 1989, 49). Similarly, a *New Yorker* editorialist, after pooh-poohing the "deadly dangers of nude centerfolds, X-rated movies, and bottom-rack periodicals," averred: "I don't believe that Ted Bundy or anyone else understood what made him commit and repeat the crimes he confessed to, which were rape murders of an unimaginable violence and cruelty" (Talk of the Town, 1989, 23). Yet, such cruel violence is verifiably *imaginable* (and even erotic and/or entertaining) in this culture—consider the pornographic snuff film and soft-core snuff, such as the slasher film.

Bundy, the alleged "enigma," wanted people to see him as just like them, as "sharing a common humanity." As he told evangelical minister Jim Dobson, founder of Focus on the Family, a multimedia Christian ministry, in his final interview: "Those of us who are . . . so much influenced by violence in the media, in particular pornographic violence, are not some kind of inherent monsters. We are your sons, and we are your husbands, and we grew up in regular families" (quoted in Lamar, 1989, 34). Many interpreted his statements as Bundy trying to put blame on the media, refusing to take responsibility for his crimes, and just telling Dobson what he wanted to hear. But—and Dobson might not like to hear this—the serial killer *is* a product of normalcy, the logical, if extreme, manifestation of a systematically misogynist culture that subordinates and objectifies women (in traditional religion and homes as well as in pornography) and one that associates violence with virility.

And there is one other truth carried by Bundy's statement, one he so obviously could not come to terms with, the one about "common humanity." Other people are "part of ourselves," though "very little in our language or culture encourages" us to recognize this reality (Williams, 1991, 62). Indeed, if we were to feel and know that connectedness, we would not be able to oppress and violate others because we would experience immediately their anguish as well as realize the ways that we are also harming ourselves.

Bundy remains the emblem of the boy-next-door serial killer. Another sex killer from the 1970s deliberately cultivated a diametrically opposed persona—that of the nonhuman "monster."

"I Am the 'Monster'"

> I am deeply hurt by your calling me a wemon [*sic*] hater. I am not. But I am a monster. I am the "Son of Sam" . . . I am the "Monster"—"Beelzebub"—the chubby behemoth.
> David Berkowitz, April 1, 1977, letter to police, printed in the *Daily News*
> (June 5, 1977)

During his spree as the "Son of Sam," the killer who randomly shot young women as they walked alone on the street or sat in parked cars with other women or men, David Berkowitz wrote highly dramatic and disturbing letters to both the police and the press, letters that were subsequently printed in the daily papers. One such letter was sent to columnist Jimmy Breslin of the *Daily News*:

> Hello, from the cracks in the sidewalks of New York City and from the ants that dwell in these cracks and feed on the dried blood of the dead that has settled into these cracks.
> Hello from the gutters of New York City, which are filled with dog manure, vomit, stale wine, urine and blood.

Don't think that because you haven't heard from me for a while that I went to sleep. No, rather, I am still here, like a spirit roaming the night. Thirsty, hungry, seldom stopping to rest; anxious to please Sam. (Quoted in Klausner, 1981, 168)

The first day that just a part of that letter was printed, the *Daily News* sold a record-breaking 1,116,000 copies, a record that stood until the day Berkowitz was apprehended in mid-August. Actually, an extraordinary number of newspapers were sold throughout that summer as the *Post* and the *News* vied in a circulation war, turning their most sensationalist attention to this story. So intense was their coverage that the *New Yorker* charged the city's tabloids with what we might think of as "self-fulfilling publicity": possibly encouraging the killer, or another of like mind, to strike again "by transforming a killer into a celebrity . . . into a seemingly omnipotent monster stalking the city" (Talk of the Town, 1977, 21). While such criticism may seem to be merely enacting the social-class differential between the prestigious magazine and the tabloids, a few years later Berkowitz indicated that the *New Yorker* may have been right. He avowed that after his fourth shooting: "I didn't much care anymore, for I finally had convinced myself that it was good to do it, necessary to do it, and that the public wanted me to do it. The latter part I believe until this day. I believe that many were rooting for me. This was the point at which the papers began to pick up vibes and information that something big was happening out in the streets. Real big!" (quoted in Abrahamsen, 1983, 60).

Throughout the summer of 1977, New York's attention was riveted on the "Son of Sam." Men wore t-shirts bearing the police sketch of the suspect's face. Talk of the killer had become "the staple of conversation," and then-mayor Abraham Beame summed up the melodramatic fascination of that time: "Son of Sam. I even liked the name and that in itself was terrifying. I knew it would stick—would become his trademark—you could see it all building, the fears of the people, including my own, and the headlong rush of the press to create a personality, someone they could build a story around" (quoted in Klausner, 1981, 146). Significantly, that movement to create a narrative was facilitated not only by Berkowitz's self-articulated monstrosity, but also by his style and choice of victims, for the killer who preyed on parked teenage couples seemed the very embodiment of that most common bogeyman of teenage horror—the stalking maniac of a popular urban legend, "The Hook." In journalistic accounts of several shootings, the basic elements of "The Hook" clearly structure the narrative. The boy and girl pull into a lovers' lane to neck and begin to talk about the killer. The boy plays it cool, but the girl gets scared and begs the boy to leave. The boy doesn't take her fear seriously, but finally agrees. Just then the killer approaches and shoots them.[3]

After Berkowitz was captured in August 1977, reminders of the terror continued to haunt New York women, some deliberately planted by big business. Berkowitz's claim that he "liked to shoot pretty girls" was widely quoted in the press. Incredibly, just a few months after his arrest, Max Factor introduced a new face moisturizer called "Self-Defense." Billboards throughout the city threatened: "Warning! A Pretty Face Isn't Safe in This City. Fight Back with Self-Defense." The cosmetics firm unabashedly tried to cash in on the fear generated by the sex killer, and, at the same time, implanted some all by itself (MacAllister, 1978, 37–39).

Again, in Albuquerque, I observed several references to Berkowitz in the local youth subculture. A popular local punk band was called "Cracks in the Sidewalk," a name derived from Berkowitz's "hello from the cracks" letter to Jimmy Breslin. When Berkowitz was caught, he claimed that he was possessed by demons and received orders to kill from a man named "Sam" who communicated with him through a barking dog. (Later, he confessed that he had made all of this up.) Ten years later, on public access cable television in Albuquerque, a group of local amateur filmmakers showcased their works (frequently short horror films featuring a serial/slasher killer) on a program they called "Son of Sam Theater." A man who bore some resemblance to Berkowitz hosted the show. He held and occasionally talked with a dog hand puppet whom he called Sam. Occasionally another man would enter and chat with the host, proclaiming himself to be another serial killer (e.g., Ed Gein, on whom the killer in *Psycho* was based). The general tone was one of high camp and hilarity, as when "Berkowitz" slashes "Gein" to death with a knife in a mode reminiscent of *Psycho*'s famous shower scene.

This cross-referencing between actual serial killers and horror film is itself significant. For the most common monster of contemporary horror film is a serial killer, beginning with Norman Bates in *Psycho* (Alfred Hitchcock, 1960). Since then, we have seen the immortal or at least re-generated serial killer in *Silent Rage* (Michael Miller, 1982), in the phenomenally popular Freddy and Jason of the *Nightmare on Elm Street* and *Friday the 13th* series, *Child's Play* (Tom Holland, 1988), *Shocker* (Wes Craven, 1989), *Seven* (David Fincher, 1995), and *Fallen* (Gregory Hoblit, 1998).

"Pop Culture's Heroes"

Freddy is pollution. Freddy is evil. Freddy is what's wrong with the world. . . . Racism, pollution, child molestation, child abuse, alcohol, drugs.

Robert Englund (Fo, 1988, 72)

Nowadays, the good guys seem to be fighting a losing battle, and teenagers appear to like it that way. Jason, the goalie-masked, knife-wielding fiend of the "Friday the 13th" series of movies, and Freddy Krueger, the hideous-looking killer in the "Nightmare on Elm Street" movies, are pop-culture heroes.

Lena Williams (1989)

Our heroes and their narratives are an index to our character and conception of our role in the universe.

Richard Slotkin (1973, 564)

As noted earlier, a key factor in the mystique of Jack the Ripper has been his incorporation into the horror genre as a stock character. Indeed, by the latter part of the twentieth century, one of the most common monsters, as Robin Wood has observed, is a "human psychotic" (1986, 83). Moreover, even the traditional monsters—the vampires, werewolves, and phantoms—are now being overtly portrayed as sex killers, as the werewolves in *The Howling* (Joe Dante, 1980) are. If patriarchal legend has immortalized the Ripper (and is in the process of doing the same thing to Bundy et al.), his screen brethren too are deathless, surviving seeming demise in feature after feature, resurrecting themselves to dispatch those intrepid teenage girls who vanquished them in earlier installments, and gloating, as does Freddy (Robert Englund) in *Nightmare on Elm Street IV,* "I am eternal."

Like Bundy and Berkowitz (and their fictional forebear, Norman Bates), Freddy and Jason have identifiable mothers—but not fathers. Jason, the young son of a female cook at a summer camp, drowned while the camp counselors neglected him in favor of sexual satisfaction. His mother begins a vengeance campaign in the first *Friday the 13th* (Sean Cunningham, 1980), only to be beheaded by the sole surviving girl. Jason, however, isn't dead. In *Part II,* we meet him as a deformed teenager who keeps a candle-lit shrine to his mother's head. His first action is to gore to death the surviving girl from the original film and then to begin the silent reign of terror that has lasted through multiple sequels (he doesn't even acquire his famous hockey mask until *Part III*). The loquacious Freddy Krueger of *Nightmare on Elm Street* originated as a child molester and murderer in an affluent suburban community. Tried for his crimes, he was freed on a technicality, so some local parents got together and burned him to death. Now Freddy preys upon the children of these parents through their dreams. In *Nightmare, Part III* (Wes Craven, 1987), we meet Freddy's mother, a ghostly nun who explains that as a young girl working in a madhouse, she was accidentally locked in with the inmates and repeatedly raped. Freddy was thus "the bastard son of a hundred maniacs."

It is mythically necessary to leave the paternity of these killers nebulous and even multiple, for their true father is indeed a collective entity— the patriarchal culture that has produced the serial killer as a fact of modern life. Moreover, these deranged sons must themselves stand in for that absent father, assuming the punitive paternal role. As Wes Craven (director and writer of the first *Nightmare on Elm Street*) has indicated: "Freddy is the most ruthless primal father. The adult who wants to slash down the next generation" (quoted in Corliss, 1988, 67).

In Craven's original conception, Freddy was "the most evil human being you can imagine, someone who goes after children." He had no plans to make Freddy invincible and eternal; rather, as he planned it, the extremely resourceful heroine of the first film, Nancy (Heather Langencamp), defeats Freddy in a uniquely mythic way. Nancy first employs every means she can think of to defeat the terrible Freddy, going into his world and battling him there. When that doesn't work, she drags him into her world and, using stratagems from a military manual, tries to trap him so that she can hand him over to the authorities. But all of her violent resistance is to no avail. Finally, Nancy realizes that Freddy possesses no vital force of his own; he is dependent upon her energies for his existence. When she deliberately turns her back on him, proclaiming that she is withdrawing every bit of energy she ever gave him, Freddy fades into oblivion. This was a satisfying and philosophically complex conclusion, but producer Nick Shaye wanted sequels and insisted upon a conventional ending where Freddy rises from the dead and the teenagers are doomed. (The heroic Nancy is killed off in *Part III*). Craven points out that under Shaye's direction, the movement was to "soften Freddy and make him a little bit more of a buffoon. . . . Now in a sense, he's embraced by younger kids. And they can make fun of him. In a way he's dangerous and in a way he's a joke. It's probably safer to deal with him that way" (quoted in Gire, 1988, 10). Craven's rationale is the same one that is used to explain the disturbing jokes about serial killers such as Ted Bundy. Yet it is women who most need to manage their fear about sex killers, and in my experience women rarely if ever make these jokes. Such joking is a means of normalizing the sex killer and identifying with him. Softening Freddy only softens and makes palatable the sexual abuse and murder of children. Incidentally, Freddy is not the first serial killer to be perceived as ironic and witty; that role was originally written for the mythic Jack the Ripper. Nor is he the first figure to double as buffoon and evil terror. John Wayne Gacy, rapist, torturer, and killer of thirty-three boys and young men, frequently performed for children as a clown.

Most commentators speak quite loosely about the "kids" who embrace these filmic killers, yet we should be wary of the facile generic label and the gender differences it conceals. All observers agree that the slasher film audience is mostly between the ages of twelve and twenty and largely male (e.g., Clover, 1987, 224). What do Freddy and Jason mean to the (disproportionately male) children and teenagers who are so fascinated by these films in which a couple making love signals an imminent assault, where there are virtually no permanent survivors, and where both sexes are targets, though it is on the women's bodies and (usually more prolonged) deaths that the camera lingers? The film critic Robin Wood discusses the types of identification operating for the slasher film audience, but first distinguishes these current products from traditional horror (1986, 195): "There the monster was in general a creature from the id, not merely a product of repression but a protest against it, whereas in the current cycles the monster, while still produced by repression, has essentially become a superego figure, avenging itself on liberated female sexuality or the sexual freedom of the young. . . . Where the traditional horror film invited, however ambiguously, an identification with the return of the repressed, the contemporary horror film invites an identification (either sadistic or masochistic or both simultaneously) with punishment."

One element of viewers' masochistic identification is a pledge of allegiance to the punitive father, hoping quite hopelessly that this will save them. We see this in the stories of those women who "fall in love" with killers such as Ted Bundy (his wife actually married him after he had been convicted of the Chi Omega murders).[4] The other strategy (the sadistic one) is to identify with the violator and his role, to be titillated by his excesses and turned on by his depredations.

In October 1988, nineteen-year-old Sharon Gregory was murdered in Greenfield, Massachusetts, by eighteen-year-old Mark Branch, who stabbed her more than fifty times. Branch at the time was undergoing psychological counseling because of his obsession with slasher films; he particularly identified with Jason, the murderer from the *Friday the 13th* series. When his home was searched, police found more than seventy-five slasher videos and sixty-four similar books, three knives, a machete, and three goalie masks, like Jason's (Simurda, 1988). Branch eluded the police for about a month and then hanged himself in a local woods. Perhaps significantly, the murder took place around Halloween. This factor created additional havoc in Greenfield and caused town officials to ask parents to cancel traditional trick-or-treat activities — but not because they were afraid Branch would strike again: "Instead, they are afraid pranksters may dress up as Jason . . . and scare young children or cause edgy residents to overreact and hurt someone in the dark" (Coakley, 1988). Branch's sadistic identification with Jason (as well as the expected pranksters' identification with Branch) is, assuredly, extreme, yet not completely unexpected. A hero, after all, is a role model, one who acts out the fantasies of his fans, one who inspires emulation.

For obvious reasons, Freddy and Jason are often discussed together: Each is a powerful and compelling contemporary symbol of evil. Yet the two series and the two monsters are quite distinct. The *Friday the 13th* movies are gorenography; the thin stories and cardboard characters exist only to give flesh to the slaughter scenes.[5] It is difficult to imagine anything but sadism behind an identification with Jason. But the original *Nightmare on Elm Street* movie (and to some extent the sequels), although not free of the slasher film's fixation on coupling teen sex with elaborate female death, is far more interesting. Freddy is no mere death machine. Robert Englund (the actor who plays Freddy) analyzes the character: "He is the nightmare in suburbia. He is the nightmare in white America and he's reminding you that you can't escape IT!" (Fo, 1988, 72). As such, Freddy may invite some identification as a completely unrepressed individual, a revolutionary figure who disregards and destroys traditional mores and values, and who exposes as fraud the image of the happy nuclear family and ideal suburban community.

A rather astonishing poem, "A Nightmare on Sesame Street," seems to stem from such a perspective and displays a sense of apocalyptic humor akin to Freddy Krueger's own.[6] It was turned in by a ten-year-old boy in 1988 as a classroom assignment (accompanied by fig. 5.2).

> It was a pleasant day, everybody was happy. "Play Ball," shouted Big Bird one bright sunny day. But his friends disagreed. Which game should they play? Grover spoke first. He said, "Please let's play catch." But Henry suggested a quick soccer match. "Hey buddies," said Ernie, holding his bat, "how about baseball?" I'd really like that. "I agree,"

5.2 Drawing by a ten-year-old boy turned in as a classroom assignment, 1988

Betty Lou said, flexing her mitt. But Oscar retorted, "Not enough grit." Cookie completely ignored the debate. While he munched on a frisbee that looked like a plate. "I get a kick out of football," said Bert. But Oscar continued, "Not enough dirt." "My racket is tennis," said Oscar persisting. Big Bird interrupted, "Let's try coexisting!" We'll take turns," Big Bird said averting a brawl. And that's what they did. And they each had a ball . . . until . . . There he was Freddy Cruger *[sic]*. He said, "A is for Aim, B is for Blades. C is for Cut and D is for Dead." He popped Grover's ball then he sliced him. He stabbed Ernie and threw him somewhere. He stabbed Bert when he said he wanted to play football. He sliced Cookie Monster's cookies. "What's going on here," said Big Bird. "Run," said Henry. "He will kill you." "Nonsense, I'll ask him to be my friend." "Will you be my friend," Big Bird said. Not a chance, ffft ouch I'm, dying. Cruger kills the rest of the people at sesame street. And his next stop is Mr. Rogers Neighborhood.

This piece certainly bespeaks a rage against the television version of banally happy children's culture and experience. Yet if this poem is a rebellion, it is one that is programmed for self-defeat. For Freddy Krueger—the child molester and murderer—is no genuine stranger to that world, but a direct product of it. He is the alter ego, not the true opposite, of that other cultural icon, the all-knowing and authoritative suburban "good dad"; Krueger is Ward Cleaver unrepressed, running amok, wielding a cleaver. He is the incestuous/alcoholic/abusive/murderous father, hidden behind the placid façade of Elm Street, U.S.A. Moreover, he is the consummate "nuclear father," threatening imminent apocalypse.

By killing women and children, Freddy and Jason, as well as the actual killers whom they reflect, are symbolically destroying life and the future itself. Robert Englund tells the (predominantly young and male) readers of the skateboard magazine *Thrasher* (Fo, 1988, 75): "Child Killer? What are children? Children are the future. Freddy's killing the future. Freddy hates beauty. He hates youth. He hates the future. . . . It's kinda political y'know. Freddy hates the future. He's killing the future. Parents are weary. They don't want to defend the future anymore. The kids see it, and Freddy's killing the kids."

Killing the future. The psychologist Robert J. Lifton (Lifton and Falk, 1991) points out that the fear of "futurelessness" (the belief that one has no future, and neither does the world) is a condition particularly afflicting children and teenagers in the nuclear age. It is commonly accepted that monsters from 1950s horror and science fiction—Godzilla or giant ants—were metaphors for "the Bomb." Yet current film monsters continue to carry those nuclear meanings (see Caputi, 1988). As murderer of the future, Freddy is a symbolic evocation, not only of the reality of rampant child abuse and murder, but also of the everyday potential of nuclear annihilation, of radical futurelessness.

The delirious embrace of the sex killer (factual or fictional) is a phenomenon closely related to what Lifton has described as the "nuclear high": the desperate attempt to deny or escape destruction through identification with the agent of that destruction. Thus, the consummately lethal nuclear weapons are mythicized as beautiful, awesome, even divine, as the "only form of transcendence worthy of the age" (Lifton and Falk, 1991, 77). Lifton illustrates this "nuclear high" by pointing to one of the final images of *Dr. Strangelove* (Stanley Kubrick, 1963), "in which man rides bomb to its target while uttering a wild Texas yodel." Interestingly, an episode of *Freddy's Nightmares* (a television series spin-off from the films) tells the story of a young girl who dreams presciently of nuclear holocaust. Our commentator, Freddy Krueger, appears first with a mushroom cloud coming out of his head, and then out in space, riding a nuclear missile down to planet Earth to blow it up. He takes off his hat and waves it, calling "Yee ha," clearly in homage to that well-known *Dr. Strangelove* scene. Then, he reconsiders, turns the missile around, and says, "Nah, I'd rather get you little buckaroos one at a time." Freddy, we then realize, is something like a personalized nuclear bomb.

In *Dr. Strangelove*, the mad general who engineers world nuclear destruction is the aptly named Jack D. Ripper. How fitting that these icons of sex murder so frequently merge with those of nuclear annihilation, for both of these atrocities are apocalyptic—both kill the future. Moreover, both are based in male-supremacist sexuality and marked by the equation of "unimaginable" cruelty and violence with power, eroticism, and ecstasy (Caputi, 1987, 188–97; Russell, 1988). Freddy Krueger and Jason join Jack the Ripper and Ted Bundy as the founding fathers and sons of an unremittingly apocalyptic culture, pointing to a future consisting of no safe sex ever, beaches spiked with toxic waste, extinct species, global warming, and nuclear war.

Regarding the heroization of his fellow atomic scientists after World War II, Leo Szilard once commented: "It is remarkable that all these scientists . . . should be listened to. But mass murderers have always commanded the attention of the public, and atomic scientists are no exception to this rule" (quoted in Boyer, 1985, 61). Yet why must mass murderers rule our attention? Like the originally efficacious heroine in the first *Nightmare on Elm Street*, we might instead take command ourselves and deny them that aggrandizing focus. Such denial would not be the passive and self-defeating kind that merely pretends that they don't exist, but an *active* denial, one that takes back our energies, upon which their fame depends, negates their lure, deconstructs their lore, and does not perpetuate, but diminishes, their reality.

6

American Psychos

[*The Silence of the Lambs*] is no more than escapist entertainment, brilliantly made.

Caryn James (1991)

[Jeffrey Dahmer] was a quiet man who worked in a chocolate factory. But at home in apartment 213 a real-life *Silence of the Lambs* was unfolding.

People, cover blurb, August 12, 1991

Contrary to the cliché, fiction and films about serial killers constitute anything but "escapist entertainment." First of all, these texts sometimes not only reflect but also anticipate actual crimes, suggesting that the border between reality and representations (pictorial and narrative) is more porous than conventional rationalist thought allows. Second, what are we allegedly "escaping" when we enter into these narratives? Are women eluding our fears of random, or not so random, sexual violence? Is anyone really evading thoughts of terrorism, chemical contamination, economic depressions, the devastation of the rainforests, nuclear war, or fears of the end of the world? Hardly. Quiet as it's kept, serial killer fiction has been "all the rage" not because it allows us to escape, but because it so accurately, albeit symbolically, describes our world.

Elsewhere (Caputi, 1987) I have argued that the contemporary era is an "age of sex crime," marked by a fascination with the serial killer and his ascendancy to mythic/heroic status. The founding father of the age is the still-unidentified "Jack the Ripper," who murdered and mutilated five prostitutes in London in 1888. The unprecedented pattern laid down during the Ripper's original siege now is enacted with some regularity in the United States: the single, territorial and sensationally nicknamed killer; socially powerless and often scapegoated victims; a signature style of murder or mutilation; intense media involvement; and an accompanying incidence of imitation or "copycat" killings. "Classic" Ripper-type killers include the "Boston Strangler," the "Son of Sam," the "Hillside Strangler," and the "Green River Killer," to name only a few. New branches of serial murder practice have appeared, represented by the housebound killer (John Wayne Gacy, Dahmer) or the traveling killer (Ted Bundy).

Correspondingly, the mythic serial killer—the preternatural, enigmatic, eternal genius—has become an ever more common and downright heroic figure in film and fiction. My previous study (1987) of 1970s male-authored serial killer literature analyzed the ways in which these narratives reiterated and refined the myth of the serial killer and eroticized and justified their violences. In this chapter I address three related themes as they occur in subsequent films and novels featuring serial killers: (1) the role of feminism (2) serial murder's relationship to what we can call *ecocide*—environmental devastation, and (3) the serial killer as a central figure in a confluence of apocalyptic narratives, a glaring sign of the (end) times of the world as we know it. Finally, I look at recent works featuring women who, avenging sexual abuse, commit murder against men.

Feminism

On December 6, 1989, at the University of Montreal, twenty-five-year-old Marc Lépine, dressed for combat and heavily armed, rushed the college of engineering. In one classroom, he separated the women from the men, ordered the men out, and shouted, "You're all fucking feminists," before opening fire on the women. During a half-hour rampage, he killed fourteen young women, wounded nine other women and four men, and then turned his gun on himself. Lépine resented women's advancement in a traditionally male profession and blamed women for ruining his life; his suicide note included a hit list of prominent Canadian feminists.

As I read of this atrocity, I wondered how it made Columbia University English professor George Stade feel. His 1979 novel, *Confessions of a Lady-Killer,* a work that Mark Schechner (1979, 15) aptly described in the *New York Times Book Review* as "a study of feminism from the point of view of Jack the Ripper," celebrates the deliberate targeting of feminists by a proudly antifeminist and righteous serial killer/hero. Its protagonist introduces himself at the outset: "My name is Victor Grant. I am the hero or villain of the narrative to follow, depending on whether you are a feminist or a human being" (Stade, 1979, 13). Denying humanity to those you scapegoat is the classic legitimation for mass or serial murder, and that is exactly what Grant has in mind. His wife, Samantha, has left him to work on a feminist magazine and establish her own identity. Victor vows revenge, quits his job in the university bookstore, and begins a new regimen—a nearly all-meat diet, exercise, and mental conditioning—in order to be born again as a heroic slayer of prominent New York City feminists. There is no retribution, and the novel presents Grant as perfectly justified—indeed, as heroic. At first it seems as if this might be only an absurdist parody. Yet, as John Leonard (1979, 46) comments: "What begins in farce, ends in cruelty, with no accounting." Essentially, this novel promotes the Lépine rationale: Terrorism, taking the form of serial sex murder, provides aggrieved male supremacists with a final solution to feminism.

In the summer of 1991, publications ranging from the *New York Times* to *Entertainment Weekly* noted the glut of serial killer books on bestseller lists. In order for this to occur, publishers stressed, the audience needed to comprise both women and men (McDowell, 1991). *The Silence of the Lambs* was the star player here. Many attributed this to the story's inherent feminism and appeal to women through several strong female characters, including a U.S. senator, her daughter, a kidnapping victim who fights back, and the central investigator and hero, the ambitious FBI trainee Clarice Starling. This assessment certainly has merit; it is gratifying to identify with a heroine who forcefully opposes and ultimately dispatches a serial killer of women. Still, the feminist reading comes undone when we mythically dissect Dr. Hannibal Lecter, the infamous serial killer and cannibal, and his relationship to our heroine. Starling first encounters Lecter after she takes a mythic descent into hell (the basement cell where he is kept). So compelling is their developing bond that some critics celebrate the pair as an ideal cinematic romantic couple, along the lines of Hepburn and Tracy (Hawkins, 1993). Yet let's look a little more closely at this coupling and its meanings.

The Silence of the Lambs is dedicated by Harris to "the memory of my father," and despite the strong female presence, it is the patriarch who rules this text. He appears variously in Starling's fondly remembered father (a slain night watchman); in Jack Crawford, her boss at the FBI;

and in Lecter, whom she must petition to aid her in her current search for Jame Gumb, a.k.a. Buffalo Bill, a childish killer who kidnaps, kills, and skins large young women so that he may sew up a "girl suit" for himself to wear.

Since Jack the Ripper, the serial killer has been mythicized as genius, artist, core id of mankind, preternatural demon, outlaw hero, and an undefeatable and eternal being. Lecter benefits from a full hundred years of this mythmaking process. As the story goes, he is a "genius," possessing powers both mental and sensory that transcend ordinary human limits. One distinct factor has been added to make him palatable to women readers. Although he murders both women and men, the only murders described are those of men. Thus, *The Silence of the Lambs* manipulates its audience by confounding us with a classic deceptive duo, here not so much good cop/bad cop as good serial killer (Lecter)/bad serial killer (Gumb).

Where, we might ask, is the feminist value in thus immortalizing a sadistic cannibal? Moreover, where is the feminist value in featuring a central female figure whose ambition propels her into depending upon, bonding with, and achieving self-awareness through her interactions with the millennial version of Jack the Ripper? Although Starling is the putative heroine, without Lecter's reading of the evidence she would have been incapable of solving the mystery and rescuing the kidnapping victim. Lecter demands payment for that service: Starling's "worst memory of childhood" (Harris, 1988, 150). Essentially, Starling is asked to sell her soul, her core constitutive memory, to the "devil" in order to succeed. At the same time, the narrative asks the reader to feel fascination, empathy, and above all awe for that "devil." By novel's end, not surprisingly, it is Lecter, not the reader, who has "escaped." The serial killer, once again, is at large, cast into myth. Female readers, once again, have been given to understand that their only hope of salvation from sacrificial victimization lies in being dutiful daughters, being initiated by, bonding with, and paying homage to abusive father figures.

An incest subtext figures prominently in the story. As Starling, in response to Lecter's insistence, begins to tell him the story of her worst memory, her removal to a ranch in Montana after the murder of her father, he immediately interrupts her: "Did your foster father in Montana fuck you, Clarice?" (229). She denies that he ever even tried and tells him that the real trauma was her exposure to the slaughter of lambs. Yet the girl's waking up to horror in the night, her identification with helpless, screaming animals, and her flight from the ranch suggest an interpretation of these events as an allegorical rendering of incestuous assault. It was that personal atrocity that actually constituted her "worst memory of childhood." Logically, then, Starling grew up desperate to become an FBI agent and to save women endangered by male sexual abuse, to track down and even slay offenders such as Jame Gumb. Unfortunately, as the novel sets it up, to complete that mission she must consent to being "mind fucked" by her surrogate father, Hannibal Lecter. Incest trauma, in this schema, is indelible, and the victim, however strong, must reenact it in subsequent interactions with metaphysically cannibalistic father figures.

Early on Starling's boss, though using her by offering her as bait, warns her against allowing Lecter to "get inside" her. Of course, that is precisely where Lecter ultimately and intimately lodges. At the close of their first encounter, "Starling felt suddenly empty, as though she had given blood" (24). By the next day, she intermittently feels "an alien consciousness loose in her head" (26). As the film's conclusion makes clear, that alien consciousness has taken up permanent residence. Starling (Jodi Foster) is graduating from the FBI, a student no more. During the ceremony she gets a phone call. It is Lecter (Anthony Hopkins) telling her that he won't come after her because she is so interesting. When he abruptly hangs up on her, Starling, sounding and looking haunted, if not possessed, repeats into the phone: "Dr. Lecter, Dr. Lecter, Dr. Lecter." No longer on the phone, he is, however, firmly inside her.

In *Hunting Humans,* Michael Newton (1990, 1) claims that the United States boasts 74 percent of the world's serial killers. Whatever the incidence, it is American popular culture that has embraced and valorized the serial killer. A line of clothing marketed to young male skateboarders is named "Serial Killer." A catalogue for the line features a woman naked from the waist up (though she conceals her nipples with her hands) and the name *Serial Killer* in large, outlined block letters in the space above her picture. These letters are colored in with imagery replicating the U.S. flag. The model also wears a cap with an upsidedown flag on it, just over the "Serial Killer" logo. One of the cable networks celebrated July 4, 2000, by devoting its entire schedule to documentaries about serial killers. What exactly is being said by such millennial and patriotic, albeit ironic, salutes to the serial killer?

Also spoofing and simultaneously honoring this national icon is *American Psycho* by Bret Easton Ellis (1991). Typically, the fictional killer is presented as the ultimately mysterious psychopath, adamantly undetermined by his culture. Ellis reverses this by making the "psycho" of his novel, Patrick Bateman, a man who actually epitomizes the "best" of American society. He is heterosexual, homophobic, white, rich, greedy, materialistic, insatiably interested in pornography, Harvard-educated, and a Wall Street broker. He is also a narcissistic and unemotional man who wonders: "If I were an actual automaton what difference would there really be?" (Ellis, 1991, 343). Ellis puts forth the serial killer as the exemplar of U.S. consumer ideologies, and attendant alienation and class hierarchies.

However much the novel satirizes consumerism, it studiously avoids any critical gender analysis of the origins or behaviors of the serial killer. When Bateman murders men, the scenes are relatively short, take place outside, and are asexual. When women are murdered, the sequences are extensive, take place in private, and frequently follow upon several pages of sadomasochistic sexual description clearly aimed at arousing the reader. Ellis offers highly detailed scenes wherein women are tortured and killed in ornate and highly sexualized ways. In one, the killer nails a former girlfriend to the floor, cuts out her tongue and then orally rapes her. In another, he forces a starving rat up a woman's vagina. Between boring satirical riffs extolling designer clothes, expensive consumer goods, pop singers, and yuppie lifestyles, Ellis suddenly crackles into life, churning out his own designer product: porno-violence. *American Psycho* became a bestseller and was made into a film.

Mary Harron (2000), a feminist who directed the film version, says that she did so because she admires the novel. As she reads it, "although many scenes were excruciatingly violent, it was clearly intended as a critique of male misogyny, not an endorsement of it." I find this hard to understand. Is penning scenes like the following any way to critique misogyny?

> I start by skinning Tori a little, making incisions with a steak knife and ripping bits of flesh from her legs and stomach while she screams in vain.... I force my hand down, deep into her throat, until it disappears up to my wrists—all the while her head shakes uncontrollably, but she can't bite down since the power drill ripped her teeth out of her gums—and grab at the veins lodged there like tubes and I loosen them with my fingers and when I've gotten a good grip on them violently yank them out through her open mouth, pulling until the neck caves in, disappears, the skin tightens and splits though there's little blood. Most of the neck's innards, including the jugular, hang out of her mouth and her whole body starts twitching, like a roach on its back, shaking spasmodically, her melted eyes running down her face mixing with the tears

and Mace, and then quickly, not wanting to waste time, I turn off the lights and in the dark before she dies I rip open her stomach with my bare hands. (Ellis, 1991, 304)

The pornographic worldview teaches both women and men to view women's pain as pleasure, her torture as a sex act, and women themselves as insignificant beings, mere symbols, primordial "others" to whom sexualized violence just naturally happens. What if Ellis had constructed a plot, or Harron made a film, that critiqued these aspects of misogyny and made the audience feel, not the conventional pornographic charge from sexual violence, but identification with the abused body? To do this, one would have to be far more truly outrageous. For example, what if a female actor were cast to play the man's role and male actors played the women's victim roles? The shock to consciousness might radically disrupt conventional reception of the standard story and force viewers to recognize its political implications. Such a production might have qualified as genuine political satire. As it is, *American Psycho,* in both novel and film versions, stands as just another way for a best-selling misogynist to say to women: "Your pain is my pleasure and, by the way, also my gain."

Ecocide

> Deforestation in the 1990s will claim roughly 110,000 acres per day in the tropics alone. . . . Forest disintegration of this magnitude ripples throughout the global ecosystem. The visual metaphor that comes to mind is an earth skinned alive, its lungs ripped out.
>
> Stephen J. Pyne (1991, 19)

This passage on deforestation resonates remarkably with the sex/murder scene just quoted from *American Psycho.* Throughout everyday speech and imagery, we find an abundance of metaphors relating femicide to ecocide.

On September 4, 1988, an op-ed piece in the *Los Angeles Times* urged global strictures against environmental depredations. The headline read: "To Save the Earth from Human Ruin Enact New World Laws of Geo-Ecology." To illustrate this concept, an artist, David Tillinghast, rendered the globe impaled upon a huge knife (fig. 6.1). One need hardly consult Freud to grasp the message: The earth is in the death grip of an ecocidal ripper.

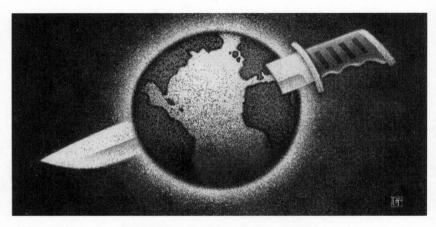

6.1 Illustration by David Tillinghast, *Los Angeles Times*, 1988

The mythic serial killer embodies not only femicidal but also ecocidal intent. The endless numbers of women raped, flayed, mutilated, and murdered, in both the real and the fictional worlds, reflect the large-scale assaults on a besieged and traditionally feminine-identified earth. In *The Death of Nature*, Carolyn Merchant (1980, 164-72) argues that the basic dynamic of the scientific revolution of early modern Europe was mirrored in the structures and practices of the European Witch Craze. The courtroom inquisitions, the often explicitly sexual torture of women with probes and mechanical devices: These paralleled the emerging scientific model of men's supreme power over a female Nature, and their assumed mandate to probe and interrogate her "mysteries," using science and mechanism as the methods by which men could extract her deeply guarded "secrets." Similarly today, the torture, ravaging, mutilations, and annihilations of individual women and feminized men by sex murderers, both factual and fictional, function as parallel rituals alongside the larger industrial, scientific, technological, and militaristic "crimes against nature" that contaminate, eviscerate, skin, and ultimately cannibalize the planet, including deforestation, species extinction, chemical and nuclear contamination, stripmining, and so on.

Ecofeminist philosophy proposes that violence against women and violence against the earth are consanguineous assaults, rooted in a characteristic patriarchal eroticization of violence as well as the designation of women and nature as "others," passive objects for men to dominate and use, rich resources to be mined, targets for seizure/rape. The fetishization of nuclear weapons is one of the more obvious enactments of this paradigm, as a number of shrewd popular narratives observe. These include *Monsieur Verdoux* (Chaplin, 1947), where the titular character played by Charlie Chaplin explicitly compares serial sex murder to the mass murder accomplished by the atomic bomb; *Dr. Strangelove* (Stanley Kubrick, 1964), where the crazed Air Force general Jack D. Ripper initiates world nuclear apocalypse; and *The Dead Zone*, a Stephen King (1979) novel and subsequent film (David Cronenberg, 1983), where a psychic "Everyman," John Smith, recognizes a nuclear-crazed U.S. presidential aspirant as the "political equivalent" of a serial killer of teenage girls.

In the Gulf War of the early 1990s, the United States accomplished the deaths of nearly a hundred thousand Iraqis and the ecological ruination of vast regions in Iraq and Kuwait. Just before the war began, I remember hearing on the radio someone describe Saddam Hussein as "Ted Bundy with an arsenal." Of course, in terms of devastation inflicted, "Bundy" seems to have been operating on the U.S. side.

This connection between the serial killer craze and the Gulf War also subliminally informed the April Fool's Day, 1991, cover of *Newsweek* (fig. 6.2). The staring eyes of Hannibal "The Cannibal" Lecter (Anthony Hopkins) highlight a story about the unprecedented surge of mayhem, particularly aimed at women, in all forms of popular culture (Plagens, 1991). At the top, above the *Newsweek* logo, is a blurb referring to another story, "Apocalypse in Iraq: The Shattering of a Nation." Of course, these two stories are really part of one narrative flow (Caputi, 1991). Since it was April Fool's Day, I had to ponder: the Fool is the negative alter ego of the King. He pantomimes, in symbolic ways, the hidden nature and behavior of the potentate. This image suggests that the violence and multiple murder that so preoccupy our popular culture in the personalities of Lecter and other serial killers are linked, however subterraneanly, to the ideals and accomplishments of our political leaders and military forces. The cannibalism that characterizes the nation's "favorite" serial killer is a monsterized version of consumerist culture and the United States' ravenous appetite for the lion's share of the world's resources, including oil. Depictions of the legal murders of the war—soldiers buried alive by tanks, civilians bombed, and so on—were censored by government decree in news coverage. Yet perhaps that violence was displaced onto a ubiquitous and accelerated sex-and-violence output of popular culture, to be absorbed by everyday Americans.

Curiously enough, *Time*'s April 1, 1991, issue, though it did not put Lecter on the cover, registered his presence on its back page, in an essay

Newsweek

April 1, 1991 : $2.50

VIOLENCE

GOES MAINSTREAM

Movies, Music, Books—
Are There Any Limits Left?

'Hannibal the Cannibal' from 'The Silence of the Lambs'

6.2 *Newsweek* cover, April 1, 1992

by regular columnist Lance Morrow (1991, 82), "A Moment for the Dead." Morrow explicitly recognized a connection between serial killing and the violence committed by the American military in the Gulf War. He first asks readers to take a break from celebrating this satisfying victory with so few Americans dead, but so many Iraqis slaughtered. Next, he ponders the metaphysical implications of such an event. Reading his words more than a decade later, and in the aftermath of September 11, we can recognize them as strangely prophetic: "To kill 100,000 people and to feel no pain at having done so may be dangerous to those who did the killing. It hints at an impaired humanity, a defect like a gate through which other deaths may enter, deaths no one had counted on. The unquiet dead have many ways of haunting—particularly in the Middle East, which has been accumulating the grievances of the dead for thousands of years. In any case, there is not, or there should not be, such a thing as killing without guilt—especially not mass killings without guilt. When people kill without remorse, we call them insane. We call them maniacs, serial murderers." In fall 2002, President George W. Bush received backing from Congress to wage war once again in Iraq. At the same time, a team of two serial snipers, one of whom turned out to be a Gulf War veteran, terrorized the Washington, D.C., area. And Hannibal Lecter was back in yet another film, *Red Dragon* (Brett Ratner, 2002). Has Hannibal become our "favorite cannibal" because he so clearly resembles us/U.S.?

Common consensus holds that it is "primitives" (i.e., dark-skinned tribal peoples) who are cannibals. Indeed, reflecting that bias, a *Newsweek* artist (February 3, 1992) depicted real-life cannibal and sex killer Jeffrey Dahmer with the face markings typical of Pacific Islanders (fig. 6.3). This is a bizarre reversal. Dahmer was a white man who battened on the bodies of men of color; indeed, his racial privilege aided him in his crimes, helping him to avoid suspicion and ensuring that his victims would be seen as insignificant. On one occasion, a naked Cambodian boy, bleeding from the anus, ran away from Dahmer and into the care of two police officers. The *National Bulletin on Police Misconduct* (1994, 2) reveals that they returned the child to Dahmer after he told them that it was a mere domestic quarrel.

Hannibal Lecter, also a white man and one particularly associated with upper-class tastes and culture, has taken up residence in a Caribbean island by the end of the film version of *The Silence of the Lambs*. We see him surrounded by dark-skinned people. As our popular culture itself suggests, a metaphorical cannibalism is fundamentally necessary to

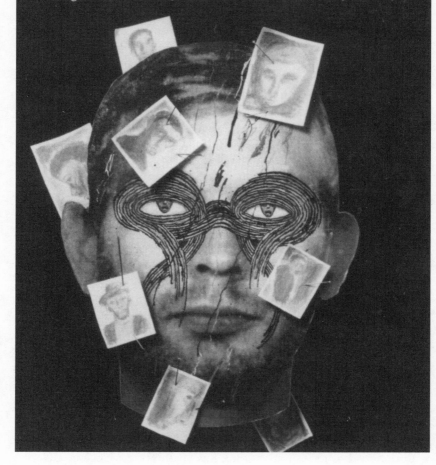

6.3 Illustration from *Newsweek*, February 3, 1992

the much vaunted "American way of life," including conspicuous and ever-expanding consumption for the middle and upper classes. This lifestyle is founded in the historic theft of land and enslavement of dark-skinned and tribal "others" (Native Americans and Africans). Perhaps Lecter and his real-world counterparts so grip the collective imagination because they also mirror current gluttonous First World incorporation of the land and resources of others, most frequently racial others. This includes the body parts of others—illegally obtained organs for transplant (Wines, 2003), sold, in desperation, by the poor and going to the rich.

Cannibalism is a paradigmatic taboo. In ancient thought, the breaking of a taboo (as with the incest committed by the king in Sophocles' *Oedipus the King*) results in pollution. In its original meanings, *pollution* is understood as an energetic phenomenon, a moral blight that manifests in a malaise on the land, contamination, disease, and trauma. In modern thought, *pollution* is itself the contamination. Of course, contemporary pollution remains both material and psychical and is rooted still in the flouting of life-preservative taboo. Capitalism continuously endorses and encourages the unbounded and ever-expanding pursuit of the (material) good no matter what limited resources are exploited, what waterways fouled, what wetlands sacrificed, what mountains stripmined. As those authoritative voices on the credit card commercials firmly suggest: "Don't leave home without it." "Visa takes you everywhere you want to go." Concomitantly, technology allows no limits in its quest, as a 1985 Lockheed advertisement boasts, "to penetrate the secrets of the Universe." J. Robert Oppenheimer, the chief scientist at Los Alamos and "Father of the Atomic Bomb," epitomized this normalized taboo violation when he commented: "It is my judgment in these things that when you see something that is technically sweet, you go ahead and do it, and you argue about what to do about it only after you have had your technical success. That's the way it was with the atomic bomb" (quoted in Lifton and Falk, 1991, 425). The denial of any need for taboo, in the sense of protective restraints on economic expansion or on technology's sweet tooth, has resulted, quite obviously, in an epidemic of pollution and the invention of ever-greater means of mass destruction. The taboo violation embodied in the character of Hannibal the Cannibal mirrors that core cultural dynamic and ensures our spectacular obsession with his persona, for, as the American historian Richard Slotkin (1973, 564) aptly observes, "our heroes and their narratives are an index to our character and conception of our role in the universe."

The popular fascination with the mutilating, cannibalistic, and taboo-violating serial killer, in both fact and fiction, suggests many things, including an endorsement of colonialist, femicidal, and ecocidal actions. But we might also recognize this figure as emerging into popular consciousness because he is so manifestly a sign of the times, a portent of impending disaster. Turning once again to the *Newsweek* cover featuring Lecter, we note the word *apocalypse* in the blurb. That resonant word invites us to consider yet another related theme in serial killer myth: the correspondence of the killer to one of the most ubiquitously reiterated stories of contemporary culture—that one about the end of the world.

Apocalypse Now?

I'm twenty-seven for Christ Sakes and this is, uh, how life presents itself in a bar or in a club in New York, maybe *anywhere*, at the end of the century.

Bret Easton Ellis (1991, 399)

The cover of *Time* for July 1, 2002, shows a cross in the midst of flames. Inside the cross, the headline blazes: "THE BIBLE & THE APOCALYPSE: Why More Americans are reading and talking about THE END OF THE WORLD." Inside, an article points to the runaway popularity of the Left Behind series of novels, based on the Book of Revelation and depicting the imminent end of the world from the point of view of evangelical Christianity. Curiously enough, serial killer novels also have been talking about the end of the world for some time now.

Thomas Harris's first novel featuring Hannibal Lecter is *Red Dragon* (1981). Like *The Silence of the Lambs, Red Dragon* also features a second, less-appealing serial killer. This one is in thrall to the biblical "Red Dragon," who shows up as God's antagonist in Revelation. *The Silence of the Lambs* refers to the same biblical book when Lecter lectures Starling on the significance of Christ as the paschal lamb, the epithet under which he appears in Revelation. Historically, this title explicitly refers to Christ's role as sacrificial victim: The paschal lamb was the substitute for the murder of the first-born son, demanded by Yahweh.

In a rather subversive swipe at that bloodthirsty God, the narrative of *Red Dragon* explicitly links the actions of the serial killer not to the "devil" but to *God*. Hannibal Lecter tells Will Graham, the FBI agent, that he knows that Graham too finds pleasure in killing: "Think about it, but don't worry about it. Why shouldn't it feel good? It must feel good to God—He does it all the time, and are we not made in His image?"

(Harris, 1981, 270–71). Religious fervor has many people imagining (and some hoping) that God might commit the ultimate act of mass murder and ecocide—destroying the earth with fire as prophesied in the gospel of St. Peter and thus announcing the Second Coming of Christ.

American Psycho also is rife with apocalyptic references. Just prior to her torture and murder, Bethany, a former girlfriend, tells Bateman that he has hung a painting upside down and asks how long it has been that way. "A millennium," Bateman answers and then knocks her unconscious: "I drag her back into the living room, laying her across the floor over a white Voilacutro cotton sheet and then I stretch her arms out, placing her hands flat on thick wooden boards, palms up, and nail three fingers on each hand at random to the wood by their tips. . . . I keep shooting nails into her hands until they're both covered" (Ellis, 1991, 245).

Ellis moves from the crucifixion to the apocalypse when, later, Bateman dines with his current girlfriend and muses: "To Evelyn, our relationship is yellow and blue, but to me it's a gray place, most of it blacked out, bombed, footage from the film in my head is endless shots of stone and any language heard is utterly foreign, the sound flickering away over new images: blood pouring from automatic tellers, women giving birth through their assholes, embryos frozen or scrambled (which is it?), nuclear warheads, billions of dollars, the total destruction of the world" (343). In *American Psycho*, the "future is murder," as Leonard Cohen prophesies on the soundtrack to another serial killer text, *Natural Born Killers* (Olive Stone, 1996). And what else can the ascendancy of the serial killer to heroic status mean? The paradigmatic symbolic action of Jack the Ripper is the attack on the vulva/womb, the bodily emblem of the original source of life. The mythic serial killer provides a symbolic parallel to the religious/corporate/military/political culture that paradigmatically attacks the feminine—as it is located in women, feminized men, and the natural world.

Yet, contrary readers might ask, which world exactly is it that is ending? The "Dragon of the Apocalypse" also appears in George Stade's *Confessions of a Lady-Killer*, only in his schema the dragon is recognized in its original mythic connection to the primordial mother/goddess and to her contemporary representatives, feminists. Feminism, as Stade's murderous hero sees it, is a political movement capable of bringing about the collapse of "civilization": "The monster who held Samantha [his wife] in thrall [the feminist Jude Karnofsky, his first victim] was the Dragon of the Apocalypse herself. Karnofsky had at her disposal all the demonic forces released by the collapse of a civilization, our civilization" (1979, 41).

The misogynist (and anti-Semitic) tone of this pronouncement suggests an alternative reading of the apocalyptic drift in serial killer narratives. The acceleration of violence (fictional and factual) against women is a backlash phenomenon, meant to reassert threatened patriarchal power and stave off the socially transformative powers of feminism. The end of "civilization" that Stade and his brethren fear is not really the "end of the world," but the end of the world as we know it—that is, the very world that has produced the serial killer, the world of patriarchy.

The Revenge of the Lambs

> Out of Florida's recent wave of horrific crimes comes a dark version of *Thelma & Louise* in a rare case of a female serial killer.
>
> Mark McNamara (1991, 91)

> Thelma and Louise Live Forever.
>
> Feminist t-shirt, c. 1991

Popular representations once again resonated uncannily with reality in 1991, as many observers readily found connections between Aileen Wuornos, the prostitute and lesbian then accused of killing six men in Florida, and the film sensation *Thelma and Louise* (Ridley Walker, 1991). In *Thelma and Louise* a man starts to rape Thelma in the parking lot of a bar. He is stopped and subsequently killed by Louise after he responds to her admonitions to treat women with respect with the retort: "Suck my dick." The film, embraced rapturously by many, also created a furor among others. John Leo (1991, 20) writing in *U.S. News and World Report* condemned the film's "toxic feminism" and "explicitly fascist theme." Clearly, the idea of women responding to abuse by men with violence and death power was for many a taboo subject—and one that is rooted in the patriarchal taboo on female divinity.

Mainstream imagery conventionally has shown women as passive, weak, unable and even unwilling to become violent against men, though they can be violent against other women. Violence and death dealing have been constituted as masculine properties and privileges in patriarchal culture. This belief is given divine legitimation by reigning conceptions of God as not only all-male, but also as *omnipotent*— all-powerful in the sense of able to dominate supremely and to wield control over individual life and death. As the feminist theologian Mary

Daly pointed out in her germinal *Beyond God the Father* (1973), this reigning notion of a male god (all-powerful, loving but cruel, feared but worshipped) is epitomized in the criminal image of the death-dealing Mafia Don in *The Godfather* (Francis Ford Coppola, 1970). Patriarchal representations of goddesses are confined to images of fertility, nurturance, and sexual receptivity. When "goddess" becomes assertive, actively desirous, and/or death-dealing, she becomes "monster."

Correspondingly, in traditional mainstream representations "good" women are never violent. This began to be challenged in the early 1970s in "Blaxploitation" films. In *Coffy* (Jack Hill, 1973), Pam Grier plays a modern-day avenging Amazon, putting away the dealers responsible for addicting her younger sister to drugs. *Ms.* magazine put Grier on the cover, recognizing her cinematic heroine as "tough, assertive, non-traditional" (quoted in Bogle, 1988, 58). It was not surprising that this fearsome figure first showed up as an African American woman. Racist notions encourage viewing "good" women as proper white women and African American women as "bad," inherently more likely to become violent and criminal. But behind the mythic "bad" woman, we often find a deposed goddess. The movie poster for *Coffy* announces the heroine as the "'Godmother' of them all" (ibid.). Just as the titular figure in *The Godfather* was a symbolic double for the patriarchal god, Coffy, the female justice-seeking avenger and reclaimer of death power, is the cinematic representative of the previously repressed but now resurfacing female divine.

A significant contingent of feminists has long been urging women to "fight back" and meet violence with violence. In her outrageous, lyrical rant against patriarchy (originally written in 1967), Valerie Solanas (1997, 184) advocates the killing of "all men who are not in the Men's Auxiliary of SCUM." Rapists head her long list of objectionable men. While most feminists did not advocate murder, the emerging women's movement countered women's internalization of passive femininity by promoting what Martha McCaughey (1997) calls "physical feminism," including training in self-defense. The poet and essayist June Jordan (1981, 149) in a powerful essay vowed to fight to the death any man who attempted rape against her.

An increasing number of novels and films reflected this resistant strain of thought and featured women fighting back and even killing those who would rape, abuse, or murder them (Shulins, 1991; McCaughey and King, 2001). Soon following *Coffy* was *Lipstick* (Lamont Johnson, 1976), featuring a white woman (Margaux Hemingway) who killed her rapist and stalker after the court system had let him off and he subsequently raped her younger sister. A woman actually becoming a vengeance-seeking serial killer soon surfaced in an obscure novel, *Dear John* by Susan Lee and Sondra Till Robinson (1980). The protagonist takes up serial murder after being raped and seeing a friend suffer through the same experience. After murdering several strangers, she finally locates and kills the original rapist, though not without injury to herself. The novel ends ambiguously, suggesting that she has to pay too great a price for a perhaps misguided vengeance. This theme recurs in the film *Ms. 45* (Abel Ferrera, 1981), which concerns a deaf and mute woman, raped twice in one day, who becomes a serial killer of men.

Several explicitly feminist works also feature women striking out violently against abusive men; in none of these works is the violence eroticized. *Woman at Point Zero*, a compelling literary work by the Egyptian writer Nawal el Saadawi (1983), was widely embraced by U.S. feminists. A woman, Firdaus, becomes a prostitute after experiencing a lifelong series of abuses from men. For a time she enjoys relative freedom in this role, but an unrelenting and unwanted pimp harasses and beats her, so she kills him. Although offered leniency by the state if she repents, Firdaus refuses. As she sees it, it is impossible for a woman in this man's world to be a criminal. Moreover, she claims, it is she who killed the actual criminal. The men who interrogate her are incredulous and demand clarification, which she provides: "I am saying that you are criminals, all of you: the fathers, the uncles, the husbands, the pimps, the lawyers, the doctors, the journalists, and all men of all professions. . . . Everybody has to die. I prefer to die for a crime I have committed rather than to die for one of the crimes you have committed" (101). Firdaus becomes a mythic and even immortal heroine as she refuses the passive constraints of femininity and tells the truth no one else dares to speak. She repudiates the scapegoat role assigned to prostitutes in particular and women in general (Dworkin, 2000, 333).

Two feminist novels from the early 1990s about female serial killers are *The Weekend* by Helen Zahavi (1991) and *Mercy* by Andrea Dworkin (1991). *The Weekend* features an ordinary Englishwoman, Bella, who is harassed by obscene phone calls and rape threats for weeks. Having had enough, Bells kills her harasser with no great difficulty. After this, she too becomes a multiple murderer, slaying those men who assault her. In the last scene, Bella is walking along Brighton Beach at night when a man approaches and attacks. He is himself a serial killer named "Jack," who strangles, rapes, and mutilates women. But Bella is prepared with her switchblade and knifes him to death. By naming the serial killer "Jack," Zahavi openly defies the myth of the eternal and omnipresent Ripper.

Dworkin's *Mercy* is written as an unbroken monologue, save for a brief prologue and epilogue in a measured academic voice. The narrator is "Andrea," a woman born into an age already in thrall to mass murder: "I was born in 1946, after Auschwitz, after the bomb, I never wanted to kill, I had an abhorrence for killing but it was raped from me, raped from my brain; obliterated, like freedom" (1991, 333). Andrea envisions an "army of girls" who will burn down Times Square, will gather en masse to kill abusive husbands and/or pimps, and "are ready for Mr. Wall Street who will follow any piece of ass down any dark street; now he's got a problem it is very important for women to kill men" (331). Dworkin, known for her theory of pornography as a form of violence against women (1981), fictionally advocates serial murder of men to challenge those who defend pornography as simple representation, not "real" in its impacts and effects.

The comic underground zine, *Hothead Paisan: Homicidal Lesbian Terrorist*, is written and illustrated by Diane DiMassa. Its heroine, Hothead, strikes out against "dickheads" everywhere, harassing and even killing and graphically castrating men who abuse women—street thugs, gynecologists, antiabortion terrorists—while questioning, frequently in conversation with various types of feminists—the meaning of her over-the-top violence. On occasion, the author herself will enter into the zine's frame. In *Hothead 5* (DiMassa, 1992, 6–8), one such meta-conversation takes place. A woman named Fran calls DiMassa and complains that Hothead is "disgustingly violent" and "acts just like the men she's bashing." Fran argues: "We, as women, must set an example and act in a peaceful, non-violent way godamn it." DiMassa assures her that Hothead herself is not perfectly balanced—"buzzed out on too much T.V.!" The whole thing, she explains, is a "satire," mocking in particular the superviolent mass media while also providing a fantasy that allows women to vent their justifiable rage. DiMassa asks Fran if she has ever been "so pissed-off at someone that you fantasized about killing them? Like maybe possibly your Uncle George?" At this point, Fran, an incest survivor, understands completely and writes out a check for a subscription to *Hothead Paisan*.

Martha McCaughey (1997, 185) finds social value in such images of women's violence for two reasons: These representations "help real women think that violence is not simply a physical impossibility" for themselves, and simultaneously they "reverse the fantasized connection between violence and sexuality that more traditional images instill in men's imaginations. That is, men might stop thinking that violence against women is sexy and heroic, as traditional fantasies suggest, and instead start appreciating a woman's self defensive violence." The accumulated weight of years of conventional images of women responding with erotic delight to sexual harassment, falling madly in love with rapists, and passively succumbing to assault has done much to promote the lie that when women say "no," they really are saying "yes," and that, in any event, women are incapable of much physical resistance. McCaughey claims that representations of women's retaliatory violence might cause men to rethink their belief that women erotically enjoy violation, and also to entertain the possibility that the "result of coercion will be their violent punishment" at the hands of the woman they had hoped to victimize (ibid.).

Mythically, these representations have another function as well: They reclaim for women the power of death. In patriarchal traditions, "good" women are hypocritically revered as givers of life and nurturers while forcibly separated from any traffic with powers of death. Simultaneously, men are separated from life-identified and nurturing activities and associated especially with death dealing. Violence (in war, sports, business, criminal activities, and so on) becomes the initiatory test for the achievement of manhood and masculinity. Dominating power characterizes not only the male god but also his earthly delegates, those men who regularly "play god": political leaders, soldiers, doctors, nuclear scientists, and serial killers.

One expressly lesbian-feminist novel, Patricia A. Murphy's *We Walk the Back of the Tiger* (1988), is a story that explicitly introduces the goddess/avenger theme at which *Coffy* first hinted. A serial killer of young college women is slain by "Fitzie O'Donnell," an African American prostitute who paints a "red teardrop in the center of her forehead." Fitzie, iconically, has become an avatar of Kali Ma, the black Hindu goddess of creation, preservation, and destruction.

In the mainstream Hollywood production *The Cell* (Tarsem Singh, 2001), goddess-identified death power once again meets the male serial killer and eventually metes out cosmic, though merciful, justice to him. *The Cell* is different from other mainstream serial killer narratives in its refusal to perpetuate the myth of the charismatic, heroic, immortal and godlike serial killer. Instead, this killer, though undeniably vicious, is pathetic. It is his female nemesis, Catherine (Jennifer Lopez), who becomes mythic. In a dream persona of the female divine, she acts to stop injustice and restore balance (see "The Gods We Worship," chapter 8 in this volume).

Such portrayals, reversing the expectations of the stereotypic serial killer narrative are promising. The grip of the allegedly eternal, omnipresent, and omnipotent Ripper on our imaginations begins to break when we refuse his mythicization, when we reassociate men with nurturance and the life force, and when we respect female powers of death and justice.

Fear of natural death is rooted in fear of the feminine (Plumwood, 1993) and has resulted in the obsessive association of masculinity with violent and unnatural death. Concomitantly, it has resulted in an increasingly power-mad, violent, and murderous world and a bizarre cultural necrophilia, as evidenced by multipronged assaults on nature, the source/force of life; the eager expectation of apocalypse; the worship of commodities; the proliferation of automata and simulacra; the torturous prolongation of "life" through medical technologies; the permanence of war; and the invention of ever-greater weapons of megadeath.

In serial killer mythos, the killer deals death but is not subject to it himself. Immortality—enduring mythic life in the form of celebrity and fame—is his signature. In James Ellroy's *Killer on the Road* (1986, 280), the imprisoned serial murderer concludes his narrative: "I implode into a space beyond all laws, all roadways, all speed limits. In some dark form, I will continue." The myth that the serial killer continues in perpetuity feeds and naturalizes misogynist violence. The strong, unsilenced, and violent women in the popular novels and films discussed here line up to form a mythic counterforce to the celebrated rippers, stranglers, and shooters. In a world where the likes of Jack the Ripper and Hannibal Lecter are rendered immortal, now Thelma and Louise, as the t-shirt says, also live forever.

7

Small Ceremonies

Ritual in Natural Born Killers, Forrest Gump, *and* Follow Me Home

> I hold to the traditional Indian views on language, that words
> have power, that words become entities. When I write I keep
> in mind that it is a form of power and salvation that is for the
> planet. If it is good and enters the world, perhaps it will coun-
> teract the destruction that seems to be getting so close to us. I
> think of language and poems, even fiction, as prayers and
> small ceremonies.
>
> Linda Hogan (quoted in McAllister, 1982, 352

On June 12, 1995, *Time* magazine's cover announced a "Special Report."
Red, white, and blue letters appeared against a mournful black background: "ARE MUSIC AND MOVIES KILLING AMERICA'S SOUL?" This
report was occasioned by presidential candidate Bob Dole's attack on
what he termed the "nightmare of depravity" projected by many
violence-filled Hollywood movies.

Time's (and Dole's) question might seem both hyperbolic and expediently distracting. We haven't yet seen, prominently placed for national
contemplation, such questions as "Is Corporate Greed Killing America's Soul?" or "Is a Tradition of Genocide/Gynocide Killing America's
Soul?"[1] Yet *Time*'s question did spur me to consider the relationship of
popular culture to what traditionally have been considered religious

matters: goddesses and gods, demons, sacrifice, prayer, good and evil, the soul, myth, ritual, and ceremony.

Commentators have argued that the popular media are akin to traditional religion. For example, George Gerbner (1978, 46) understands popular culture as a form of religion "in the sense of one's having no choice—a cosmic force or symbolic environment that one was born into, and whose assumptions one accepted without much questioning." Gerbner overstates the lack of choice for participants in popular culture; there always is a possibility of alternative interpretation. Still, this approach is valuable in getting us to think beyond the popular culture experience as a solely conscious, rational, and individualistic one, whereby discrete viewers (whether adults or children) maintain conscious distance from what they consume, understanding it as "text" that is always subject to the rational will.

Jacob Sullum (1997), a senior editor at *Reason* magazine, exemplifies this view of media influence, for good or for ill: "A conscious mind must intervene, deciding how to interpret the message and whether to act on it." But, arguably, there are all sorts of materials—religious icons, archetypal images, pornography, or artworks—which conscious (rationalist) minds might reject, but which imaginations, emotions, and appetites respond to and sometimes even act on in both predictable and unpredictable ways, with sometimes beneficial and sometimes ill effects.

The poet and novelist Linda Hogan articulates a worldview that understands words (and, we might imagine, images) as forms of sacred power, with potential to inspire or counteract destruction, to nurture or wound the soul's capacities for, growth, resiliency, and empathy. This suggests a new model for understanding the relationship between reality and popular narratives and representations. Perhaps people *participate* in popular culture as in a ceremony and are transformed by it, though admittedly not always consciously, uniformly, or predictably. Perhaps, as well, we don't just "read" the text at that supposed distance. Rather, we enter into it and *feed* it energetically. Perhaps, as a result of our participation in these "small ceremonies," certain powers or potentialities are bolstered and thereby *realized* (literally, made real); concomitantly, others are banished, neglected, degraded, starved, undone.

Any understanding of narrative as sacred necessarily involves an appreciation of the world-building powers of myth. In cultures that identify with rationality, myths are understood in several ways. Most simplistically, they are seen as fables that are false, stemming from a primitive or childlike worldview. With somewhat more sophistication, myths are defined as narratives that, with accompanying rituals, offer a paradigm of the basic values and meanings of a society.[2] In some indigenous worldviews ideas of the sacred, as well as of myth and ritual, share some of these meanings, but go far beyond them. As the poet and scholar Paula Gunn Allen (1986a, 72) explains, "[T]he word *sacred,* like the words *power* and *medicine,* has a very different meaning to tribal people than to members of technological societies. It does not signify something of religious significance and therefore believed in with emotional fervor—'venerable, consecrated, or sacrosanct,' as the *Random House* dictionary has it—but something that is filled with an intangible but very real power or force, for good or bad." In this paradigm, the universe is understood as "alive and . . . supernaturally ordered," that is, subject to the actions of invisible or spiritual forces. Myths are "language constructs that contain the power to transform something (or someone) from one state or condition to another. . . . [A]t base a vehicle, a means of transmitting power" (104). Just as myths are sacred language constructs or stories, ritual is "organized activity that strives to manipulate or direct nonmaterial energies toward some larger goal" (80), actions organized to produce power in order to effect transformations, to influence direction, to reconceptualize and hence reconfigure reality. Like prayer, ritual intends to tap into cosmic sources of power to effect some end.

Hopi photographer and filmmaker Victor Masayesva theorizes the ritual character of film, extending Hogan's concept of art as ceremonial and adding another concept, that of *medicine:* "I think this whole process of film making can be compared with medicine that has power to heal or cause harm depending on how it is used. I think that's why so many people are doing it. But what they don't know how to do is finish it, cleanse and purify. We can make people crazy. There's too many people out there making people crazy without getting them back down. Film is like that. There's a lot of people making these films which mesmerize. You get drawn into them. Hollywood seduces you and people there have the power to do it. There are very few people who can finish it off" (quoted in Singer, 1996, 233). Masayesva's use of the word *medicine* is different from the one many of us are used to. *Medicine,* Allen (1986a, 72–73) clarifies, "is a term used for the personal force through which one possesses power. Medicine is powerful in itself, but its power can be used only by certain persons, under certain conditions, and for certain purposes." *Medicine,* moreover, can be dangerous if you are exposed to it when you are not prepared or are not ready to know about it (Beck and

Walters, 1977, 28). Masayesva's words caution us to think about the potency and potential of film, to consider the possibility that some filmmakers might be using it recklessly, thereby (either deliberately or stupidly) making people crazy or sick, without being able to heal or deal with what they have wrought.

Sometimes an argument that popular culture has the power to bypass our conscious minds and influence us is used to justify censorship. I am not in any way calling for censorship. Banning something is akin to psychological defense mechanisms of denial and repression. What is denied will find expression another way; what is repressed will return, sometimes with more force than it had in the first place. Artists, especially popular artists, show us who we are as a culture. At the same time, they do not merely reflect but also influence where we are going, one way or another, as they powerfully participate in the ongoing conversation that shapes culture, as they summon certain energies and ignore others. Those who want to shift the shape of things to come in the direction of justice, peace, and communitarianism can tap into powers of imagination, soul, and myth to tell a different story about who we are and what and where we have been, to imagine possibilities for growth, transformation, and healing, and to effect these changes via their art/work. And viewers can too. Viewers are not passive recipients of messages. Nor do they somehow "check their brains at the box office" and have a "mindless" and distanced entertainment experience. Rather, viewers have a mythic, ritualistic, and participatory experience—even what the literary critic Parker Tyler (1947, ix) understood as a "spiritual" experience.

In this chapter I look at three films through this ceremonial, "medicinal" model: *Natural Born Killers* (Oliver Stone, 1994), *Forrest Gump* (Robert Zemekis, 1994), and *Follow Me Home* (Peter Bratt, 1996). I hope to offer some new ways of interpreting popular culture—ways based in knowledge of the world-building, transformative, dangerous or beneficial, sickening or healing powers of myth and ritual.

Searing the Soul

> I use films as benchmarks, signposts. As therapy, also . . .
> where everything is soul-searing.
> Oliver Stone (quoted in Schiff, 1994, 43)

Some of the most potent national narratives of violence revolve around the figure of the male serial killer, who is immortalized in every manner of story, song, and image, characterized as a genius, a preternatural entity, a charismatic personality, a sexual dynamo, a manifestation of unrepressed libidinal vitality. Overtly or covertly, he is presented as an "outlaw-hero," proffering a revolutionary challenge to the stodgy, duplicitous, and confining status quo. But this is ridiculous. The serial killer is actually the "cop," the enforcer of such foundational values as male supremacy, violent masculinity, egocentrism, consumerism, excess, and the erotic joys of domination.

Natural Born Killers is a visually dazzling paean to that supposedly magnetic, insurrectionary, and sexy serial killer. Mickey (Woody Harrelson) and Mallory (Juliette Lewis) are packaged for standard popular appeal: They are slim, white, attractive young lovers from the heartland with an intense life-long commitment, on the run across a resonant Western landscape. The film opens in a diner in New Mexico. Rapidly shifting visuals, beginning with a clip from the classic family sit-com *Leave It To Beaver,* issue like gunfire from a television set. Mickey sits at the counter and orders pie. The waitress asks him if he likes key lime pie. He tells her that he tried it ten years ago and didn't, but that he "was a completely different person back then." Right away, we know that Mickey is a transformer, a being characterized by change. Mallory refuses pie and deliberately insults the waitress. She goes to the center of the room and performs a provocative dance. When a leering man propositions her, Mallory begins to beat him up. Mickey joins in with firepower, and soon only two people are left. One is the waitress, who cries and pleads for her life, but Mallory toys with her and then blows her away. They let the remaining man live and instruct him to spread their legend.

Next, there is a flashback to the lovers' first meeting. It is framed as an ironic sit-com, *I Love Mallory.* The narrative, accompanied by a horrifically incongruous laugh track, concerns a family headed by an incestuous father and served by a beaten and complicitous mother. Mallory is raped by her father in a bed covered with smiley-face sheets. When Mickey arrives as the meat deliveryman, dripping blood, the two immediately fall in love. Soon, Mickey and Mallory murder her parents and initiate their adventure as serial killers traveling through the Western landscape.

Mickey, like the Western outlaw-heroes who precede him in the national mythology, is a "real man" (the only one in the film), defined by his sexual attractiveness and his superior ability to commit violence. Mallory, though vicious under Mickey's influence, is stereotypically feminine in all other way. She is Mickey's muse and minstrel as well as being whiny, childlike, and submissive to her unfaithful and out-of-control man. As an incest victim, she has been broken (in) by her father and thus is primed for the sadistic Mickey's controlling embrace.

Although it might appear that the film is condemning incest by inverting standard sit-com propaganda about the happy, trauma-free family headed by a benevolent and omniscient father, that is not necessarily so. *Natural Born Killers* exposes the incest subtext layered into that patriarchal dynamic, yet, at the same time, it subtly promotes it. One function of father-daughter incest as a form of social control is to break the girl's self at an early age, to effect a trauma, rendering her a "Daddy's girl" in thrall to all the subsequent "fathers" she encounters—husbands, bosses, presidents, and so on. Mallory is patently unable to break away from this damage, as evidenced by her trajectory straight into the arms of the psychologically cruel and serially "unfaithful" Mickey. He even picks up an attractive young woman to torture, rape, and murder, and keeps her, bound and gagged, in their bedroom while he is "making love" to Mallory. Mallory is enraged, but only because she is jealous, not because she feels any empathy for the victim. She stomps out and commits a murder herself against a hapless gas station attendant who has obliged her by going down on her. It is difficult to read Mallory's action as any real blow against the system!

Right after committing patricide and matricide, Mallory and Mickey run away and get married. During the ceremony Mickey, who functions as priest as well as groom, pronounces himself the "god of my world." They then take off on a jaunt across the Western states, committing scores of random murders. Stephen Schiff (1994, 45) describes *Natural Born Killers* as a "breakthrough" movie for Stone. "For all his usual excesses, Stone has never been quite as excessive as this: his furies have driven him across a frontier." Indeed, as Cara MariAnna (1996) realizes, the movie reads as a Western, a "violent and bloody adventure on the great frontier," a reinscription of Manifest Destiny, the national myth that legitimated our own version of "ethnic cleansing," appropriated land and resources, and attempted to destroy and discredit as "savagery" an ancient (and, some argue, gynocentric) culture and way of life.[3]

The movie opens as Mickey and Mallory, in a Challenger convertible, crash unconcernedly through a series of signs that read "Road Closed." The landscape is a hallucinogenic one; monsters and demons accompany them. Horses gallop beside the car. Soon, Indians will be confronted and killed. While wandering through New Mexico, they run out of gas, eat psychedelic mushrooms, and get sick in the desert. Mickey berates Mallory, echoing her father by calling her a "stupid bitch." They encounter an older Navajo man (Russell Means), who recognizes Mickey as a supernatural "demon"; he sees that poor Mallory has merely the "sad sickness." In the midst of a disturbing dream of his original wounding (as a child witnessing the suicide of his violent father), Mickey shoots the perceptive grandfather in front of his horrified grandson. Mallory is unnerved. "That was bad, bad, bad," she tells Mickey.

As if in retribution, Mickey and Mallory are bitten by rattlesnakes and weakened, leading to their capture by a corrupt policeman (who is himself a sex-murderer). The two are put on trial and then jailed. The second half of the film takes place in prison. An unctuous television talk show host, Wayne Gale (Robert Downey Jr.), comes to conduct an interview with Mickey, to be broadcast live just after the Super Bowl. During this interview, Mickey spouts metaphysical maxims about the naturalness and purity of murder, the spurious character of innocence, the vocational aspect of his violence, the way that violence is "fed" through hate and cured through love, the existence of his inner demon, and the culpability of the mass media in sullying the sacredness of murder through buying and selling it. Mickey's words reveal him as not only the sexiest man in the movie, but also the "wisest," the only one with any insight in a sea of self-serving hypocrites and fools. They also inspire a riot, allowing the pair to escape and take Gale as hostage. At film's end they righteously shoot him while he begs for his life, symbolically annihilating the "media" who, the film preaches, are responsible for sensationalizing violence, making serial killers into heroes, and creating social chaos. The last shot shows Mickey and a pregnant Mallory with two children riding around the country in an RV. On the soundtrack, Leonard Cohen prophesies that the "future is murder."

Natural Born Killers is in some ways a unique cinematic critique of American culture. It points to the false oppositions between cops and killers, family values and family horror. It effectively juxtaposes the competitive score-keeping of football and multiple murder. It connects the genocidal Western myth to the mythic allure of the serial killer and suggests that both patterns are rooted in the same destructive "medicine." However, while recognizing the serial killer in the cop, it refuses to see the social enforcer or "cop" in the killer. Similarly, while lambasting the traditional nuclear family, the film subtly promotes its devastating effects. And while it points to the power of the media to steal souls, these questions remain: Does *Natural Born Killers* itself make a meal of viewer's souls? Does it tap into and ultimately feed destructive powers? Does it "finish" the critique, in Masayesva's sense, or does it leave us stranded on the road to apocalypse?

In a *New Yorker* article, Stephen Schiff (1994, 42) profiles Oliver Stone as someone rather like Mickey: a man given to "tirades and bad behaviors, to strenuous womanizing and long, intoxicated journeys into the night," someone searching for "extreme violence," which he equates with "extreme maleness" (45). In front of Schiff, Stone grabs one of his female employees from behind and fondles her. We learn that he once doctored a reluctant date's drink with Quaaludes, demands a constant string of sex partners, and found it impossible to be faithful to his wife. Concomitantly, he is intensely spiritual. Research for *The Doors* included jetting "off to South Dakota to 'do peyote with the Indians,'" and during preparations for *Natural Born Killers* he and his writers embarked on "mushroom-fueled expeditions through Arizona and New Mexico to scout out locations." Stone "participates in Native American sweat lodges, and makes trips to the most remote regions of Tibet, India, and Nepal" in his study of Buddhism. The name of his production company is Ixtlan, drawn from the Carlos Castañeda books about Yaqui sorcery.

Religious references appear regularly throughout *Natural Born Killers*. Early on in the film, Mickey announces that it is the "end of the world." Sacred music dominates the soundtrack, including Qawwali devotionals sung by Nusrat Fateh Ali Khan as the background for the prison riot (Pareles, 1997, 20). Much of the film's action takes place in a "dreamtime." Sometimes the demon animating Mickey is represented as a distinct, satanic figure. At other times, Mickey himself transposes into the demon and stands, amid flames, with blood dripping over him. Angels, cartoon figures, and violent scenes from history come in and out of view. Mythic beasts as well animals traditionally associated with power if not sorcery in the Southwest—the coyote, snake, and bear— appear throughout.

While the narrative mocks fans' adulation of Mickey and Mallory, the film itself is similarly star-struck. All of *Natural Born Killers'* energy, presence, soul, beauty, and poetry are invested in the pair of killers. Mickey, in the mythic tradition of pop killers like Charles Manson, becomes a philosopher-king with a manifest destiny. In the interview with Gale, Mickey avers: "You'll never understand, Wayne. You and me, we're not even the same species. I used to be you, then I evolved. . . . I realized my one true calling. I'm a natural born killer." While Stone takes great glee in parodying the Geraldo Rivera–like Wayne Gale, no such ironic distance interferes with his portrayal of Mickey as the heroic focus of viewer identification.

Just prior to this speech, there has been a commercial break. The ad is the familiar one for Coca Cola where computer-generated polar bears sit and drink their sodas as they watch the Aurora Borealis, which appears as a shimmering Coke logo! In the oral traditions of several Native American groups, both the Aurora Borealis and the Bear are powers that are sacred—that is, at times profoundly dangerous; if you are careless, they can mesmerize you and steal your soul (Silko, 1981b). Stone is perhaps suggesting the equivalent power of the visual media to fascinate, addict, and possess.

Yet the Bear signifies something else as well. In ancient Germanic tradition the Bear betokened rampaging, manic violence. A group of male warriors, known as the Berserkers (those who wore the bear shirts), magically identified themselves with the Bear. Through a series of ordeals, a candidate "took to himself a wild-animal mode of being; he became a dreaded warrior in the measure in which he behaved like a beast of prey. He metamorphosed himself into superman because he succeeded in assimilating the magicoreligious force proper to the carnivora. Part of their rites included terrorizing women, and exercising a "right of rapine" (Eliade, 1958b, 81). The Berserker transcends his humanity by a fit of aggressive and terror-striking fury, which assimilates him to the raging beast. In this way he embodies "furor . . . a sort of demonic frenzy" (83–84). The modern Berserker, Mickey, is able to inspire others to emulate him. As Mickey testifies on live camera to his "calling," prisoners witnessing his performance are inspired to riot. The film's narrative itself ascribes a causal connection between Mickey's words and the prisoners' violent reaction. In the real world too, numerous murderers explicitly cite *Natural Born Killers* as their inspiration.[4]

Oliver Stone has claimed that his film "reflects" a "very violent and bankrupt" society (Kiselyak, 1996). When Mickey pronounces himself "the god of my world," he is right. The serial killer is the tacit god of America, the god of violence, consumerism, conquest, phallic manhood, and egocentrism. And, as the film further suggests, the apocalypse the mythic Mickey portends is implicit in the very "creation" myth of America—the implicitly genocidal/gynocidal Western adventure.[5]

Does *Natural Born Killers* also participate in that violent energy and that mythos? Stone avers that his own violence is innate, that "there was in me, I feel, a huge violence when I was born," and that he "was born in a way that was damaged" (Schiff, 1994, 55). He refers to the violence that "erupts out of rage and desire," the violence that characterizes all of his work, as "the demon" (45). Martin Scorsese, Stone's most influential teacher at the New York University film school, passionately declares his own spiritual approach to filmmaking: "I made it [*The Last Temptation of Christ*] as a prayer, an act of worship" (quoted in Blake, 1996, 2). In many ways, *Natural Born Killers* also feels like a prayer, an act of worship for the god of violence, a feeding of the "demon."

In the director's cut version, available on video, Stone reveals that he originally planned a different ending. Mickey and Mallory would not survive but would be killed by an otherworldly emissary. We first meet this character, whom Stone describes as both a "psycho" and a "guardian angel," as a man sitting in the diner in the opening scene. He holds a newspaper with headlines reading "666 Death," and observes the lethal proceedings before vanishing. Later, this same man is a prisoner who guides them out of danger during their escape. After they shoot Gale, this man indicates his wish to remain with them forever; he also propositions Mallory and mocks her for her childlike subservience to Mickey. When they turn on him, he kills them. Had Stone remained committed to this ending, *Natural Born Killers* might have suggested a cautionary vision of a Mickey and Mallory destroyed by the very force that they worship. As the film stands, Mickey remains a righteous challenger of the corrupt status quo, a cosmic force of fate and destiny—instead of being exposed as a self-aggrandizing narcissist. Mallory remains his helpmeet.

Earlier, I wondered if *Natural Born Killers* was "finished" in Masayesva's sense. That is, as an artwork does it bring us to a place where we face the previously unfaceable, and then guide us back from that precipice, shaken but more knowledgeable, stronger, our souls expanded, even healed? Stone provides some clues when he describes his own state of mind while making the film: "*Natural Born Killers* came from a very emotional moment in time. Those two years that I really felt disgusted, everything was coming up and I just expressed it as a kid—by throwing paint on a canvas. And I just let it go. I didn't censor myself at all" (Kiselyak, 1996). Despite its technical brilliance, *Natural Born Killers* is a markedly immature production. Mickey epitomizes a childish furor and an utter inability to recognize the ontological significance of any human being other than himself (or one utterly dominated by him, i.e., Mallory).

Natural Born Killers is unquestionably effective in conveying a sense of corruption pervading the American spirit. At the same time, it participates in it. It makes evil attractive; it ends up worshipping the demon/god it purports to critique. But this is only part of the story. Films like *Natural Born Killers* cannot do this job alone, but require self-consciously virtuous "family-values" movies that, in a complementary vein, promote the same message. Such films posit the "good" as so sex-less, imbecilic, and monotonous that evil becomes unavoidably glamorous, sensuous, and impossible to resist.

The Rebirth of a Nation: *Forrest Gump*

The year 1994 saw the release not only of *Natural Born Killers,* but also of its secret twin, *Forrest Gump,* the story of a mentally impaired European American man as a fateful force in American history. Not surprisingly, Bob Dole highlighted *Forrest Gump* as an appropriate type of picture for America. One critic saw the film as functioning as a ritual of "national reconciliation" (Chumo, 1995). But if *Gump* is a healing film for some Americans, it is desperately unhealthy for those designated as "others."

However different a family-values celebration like *Forrest Gump* in-itially appears from a violence-fest like *Natural Born Killers,* there are uncanny similarities. Both, obviously, are intended to serve as epic vi-sions of contemporary America. Each film poses its protagonist against dramatic backdrops of the American landscape. The heroes are Euro-pean American men, paired with incest-damaged European American women. The heroes' stars rise in direct proportion to the misery and death rate of those around them. Talk of fate or destiny manifestly pre-occupies each of them. While one hero represents pure innocence and the other represents pure evil, these polarities actually function as false opposites, twin faces of one belief system, one practice, and one god.

Forrest Gump (Tom Hanks) begins life physically disabled. Not only does the child miraculously regain the use of his legs, but his pres-ence continually provides a sort of divine catalyst of destiny, inspiring and influencing such celebrated figures as Elvis, John F. Kennedy, and John Lennon. Miraculously, Gump animates such deciding national moments as school integration, the Vietnam War, the opening of U.S. relations with China, Watergate, the home computer boom, and the AIDS epidemic. His voice never changes, however; it is a monotonous drone throughout, empty of soul and presence.

As these key moments reveal, Gump is a mythic ambassador; his job is to renew our faith in America's traditional image of itself as a primor-dial, creative innocent. Literary critic R. W. B. Lewis (1965, 1) traces the development of this figure in nineteenth-century literature, designating him the "American Adam": "the authentic American . . . a figure of heroic innocence and vast potentiality, poised at the start of a new history." This myth of natural innocence, adhering primarily to European American men, hugely belies the historical realities of colonization, genocide, slavery, and rapine. The European American nation grew strong through the sexual/reproductive servitude of women (as slaves, prostitutes, and/or wives), the displacement and destruction of native peoples, the enslavement of Africans, and an unbalanced use, therefore abuse, of the land and its resources. In *Forrest Gump* the mythic figure of the innocent American reasserts his sway, again reinscribing Manifest Destiny (most dramatically figured in his runs across the continent), and staking his claim on the future. To be sure, Gump's lifetime is no longer the time of pure beginning. Guilt-laden events from recent history—resistance to the Civil Rights Movement, assassinations, and unjust war—are showcased. But in the vision of *Forrest Gump,* these are anomalies, unable to touch Forrest and therefore unable to stick to the heart and soul of America.

The hero, significantly, is named after one of his ancestors, the Confederate general Nathan Bedford Forrest, founder of the Ku Klux Klan. His mother explains that this deliberate naming is to remind him that sometimes "we all do things that don't make no sense." But, really, it is the mother's explanation that makes no sense. One names children after ancestors in homage, to invite that ancestor's presence, and to ensure imitation and continuation of her or his example. Gump's profound link to that horrible ancestor is underscored in a key insert. As the mother tells the story of the ancestor, in a black and white flashback scene of the Klan riding (reminiscent of D. W. Griffith's epic 1915 film *The Birth of a Nation*), General Forrest is played by the same actor who plays Gump, Tom Hanks. Gump's characteristic "innocence" works, perversely enough, to negate the historical guilt of his namesake.

Griffith's *Birth of a Nation,* as its epic title implies, provided a national creation myth, overtly heroizing the founder of the Ku Klux Klan and dramatizing with great force the fundamental components of the commingled racism and sexism that characterizes the white- and male-supremacist belief system.[6] *The Birth of a Nation* sanctifies Southern white men's racist violence and objectifies European American women as emblems of racial and sexual purity. At the same time, it explicitly conjures a dread of the power and rule of women of color, it portrays men of color as sexual predators or buffoons, and promotes a horror of race mixing. *Forrest Gump* is essentially a kinder and gentler remake of Griffith's text. Ritually, it resuscitates that tradition, continues that story, rebirths that "nation."

Forrest, the emblem of American "innocence," never actively hurts anyone, but, significantly, most of those around him serve him in some way or another and then drop dead. His self-sacrificing Momma (Sally Field) dies of cancer. Her dying insight, offered in one of the film's many conversations about fate, is the self-effacing realization that, as she tells her son, "I was destined to be your Momma."

Jenny (Robin Wright), the childhood friend with whom Forrest is obsessed, is, like Mallory, a victim of father-daughter incest. As a young woman, Jenny leaves her hometown and goes to college. She tries to become a protest singer (to get a job, she has to sing nude), poses for *Playboy,* participates in the antiwar movement (where she has a lefty boyfriend who batters her), and finally becomes a sexually promiscuous drug user. Jenny seems fated only for sexual humiliation, victimization, and failure. Gump forever pines for her, despite her consistent rejection of him. Finally, she joins him just long enough to have one sexual encounter, which, we later find out, has resulted in a pregnancy. She leaves again, only to summon Gump some years later when she is dying of AIDS—divine retribution, no doubt, for her sexual sins. Gump marries her and regains his son—named Forrest, continuing the homage to the KKK—before the fatally impure Jenny conveniently expires. Just as incest worked for Mickey, it has ultimately furthered Gump's agenda. Without that initial wounding, the dynamic and ambitious Jenny might have made something of her life and would not have had to return, beaten, to Gump, a man who clearly could never satisfy her need for a vital, engaging, and equal partner.

Gump emerges virtually unscathed from Vietnam, although all those around him die or are maimed. His mentally "slow" African American sidekick Bubba (Mykelti Williamson) is killed in Vietnam, but Gump lives to fulfill Bubba's dream of founding a shrimping business. Bubba and Jenny are sacrificial victims. Gump absorbs their energies and benefits from their disasters, growing more powerful. Lieutenant Dan Taylor (Gary Sinise), Gump's commanding officer in Vietnam, believed himself destined to die in battle like his forebears. Badly wounded, he is saved by Gump and survives, much to his dismay, with both legs amputated. For most of the film he is a bitter, substance-abusing wreck. Cynically offering to serve as Forrest's first mate on the shrimping boat, he grimly notes their initial failures, scornfully asking

Forrest where his "god" is. "Right then," Gump narrates, "God showed up"—in the form of a powerful hurricane that wipes out the rest of the shrimping fleet. Again, profiting from others' disasters, Gump goes on to make a fortune. Later, Dan shows up at Gump's wedding with pros-thetic legs and an Asian (war) bride in tow. No Dragon Lady, she is frumpily dressed, with plump cheeks and a submissive manner. The war, it seems, has finally been won.

Bob Dole distinguishes *Natural Born Killers* from a good, clean pic-ture like *Forrest Gump,* but this is a spurious distinction. They are com-plementary morally bankrupt visions. On his mythic series of runs across the continent, Gump attracts followers who seek inspiration. A man trying to come up with a successful t-shirt offers Gump a blank one to wipe his mud-splashed face. Like Veronica's veil (in one of the film's many allusions linking Gump to Jesus Christ), the t-shirt retains a sacred image of Gump's visage—the smiley face!

Forrest Gump is a smiley face stamped on the violence and injustice in American history. It equates goodness with static, sexless ignorance, denial that has solidified into an absolute inability to know. Through-out his life, Forrest remains completely innocent and ignorant of his own motivations or effects, despite their momentous implications. He claims that he does things for "no particular reason." Significantly, For-rest is utterly immutable, as underscored in the monotony of his voice, his dress, and his devotions. On the other hand, Mickey's core charac-teristics are transformation, a complex and poetically articulated evil, violence, beauty, and sexual dynamism. The impossible and stupid pur-ity of the "good" advocated by patriarchal morality and enacted so dra-matically in *Forrest Gump* allows all evil to be projected onto an irre-deemable and dangerous, though often seductive and attractive, "other"—a devil/Satan.[7] At the same time the utter banality of the "good" in *Gump* makes the aesthetically rich and sensualized evil in *Natural Born Killers* irresistibly attractive.

Both *Forrest Gump* and *Natural Born Killers* wage war on the soul by apotheosizing heroes/gods who steal and consume souls (as signified by the attrition rate of those around them). Gump enshrines a moronic god; *Natural Born Killers* adores a berserk one. However distinct they ap-pear, they are philosophically and morally identical. One "god" revels in knowing exactly what he is doing, the other in remaining blissfully un-aware; yet they are uncannily resonant. Alone but particularly together, they are signs of doom. Their quest is to climb to the top over a pile of dead, sacrificial bodies. The destiny they signal for us/U.S. is disaster.

Healing the Soul Wound

Art unfailingly reflects its creator's heart. Art that comes from
a heart open to all the possible paths there might be to a
healthier tomorrow cannot help but be medicine for the tribe.
Alice Walker on *Follow Me Home* (1997, 172)

Film, like all art, both popular and elite, is a form of power, for creation
or destruction: power to stir emotion, to dramatize myth, to tell the stories that shape reality, to tap into the dream, reaching deeply into the
viewer's unconscious, a medium, some even would say, with the capacity to summon transformative forces, for good or evil, and to carry messages from and to nonhuman sources and forces.[8]

Follow Me Home (directed and written by Peter Bratt, 1996) is a film
that, from the perspective of the dispossessed, consciously seeks to effect healing. It asks viewers to recognize that creation is ongoing and is
a collaborative project between the dreamtime and the real world. In
Bratt's words: "What often gets called the dreamworld and reality aren't
really distinguished in many traditional cultures, so I try not to get
wrapped in that very western linear way of telling a story. The spirit and
the contemporary voices are present all the time. It's just that at different times, different voices get loud" (quoted in Dauphin, 1997, 120).

The narrative concerns four artists: Tudee (Jesse Borrego), the
group's leader, a Chicano struggling with internalized oppression; his
misogynist, self-destructive cousin, Abel (Benjamin Bratt); Kaz (Calvin
Levels), a well-educated, health-conscious African American, intent on
living a serene and nonviolent existence; and Freddy (Steve Reevis), a
Native American man who is a recovering alcoholic.

The very first scene takes us into the dreamtime, the world of spirits,
origins, and magic. Ancestors come in and out of view. Drumming and
whispering can be heard. There is a cut to reality; an old, homeless
blind man plays a conga drum on a city street, asking for change. The
scene shifts again, and we see a mural in the process of being painted.
Called "The Ancestors," it depicts a collage of "Pre-Columbian and
Post-Colombian images. Faces and bodies: plant, animal, human, Indian, African, Asian—a surreal dreamscape" (Bratt, 1993, 1). This is the
mural Tudee, Freddy, Abel and Kaz are finishing up. Tudee has conceived a plan that they will travel east from Los Angeles to paint a mural
of their ancestors on the White House, "putting our images, our colors
on the walls of LA CASA BLANCA." They plan to leave that evening but
are still squabbling about the feasibility of their quest. Tudee articulates

the importance of the project: "It's like words are symbols, like these images we paint. And every image or word we use to describe a reality helps to create and define that reality. It's only a mater of time before whatever it is we project becomes the reality itself. . . . Tu sabes?" Abel, frustrated with the theoretical tone, tells his cousin: "You want a 'reality projection'? Shit, I got one right here between my legs." Kaz then joins in, getting even more theoretical: "Actually, you're right. The, quote-unquote, reality in which we live is very much a projection of the male organ, that is the penis. The absence of the female energy, or as you understand it, the energy of the 'bitch,' is why the world is so, excuse me, fucked up, and why some people think and speak in the misogynis-tic way that you do." Abel responds, "It was a bitch, excuse me, Eve, who got Adam's ass kicked out in the first place." Kaz takes this oppor-tunity to clarify, "You're saying that we live in a patriarchal theocracy that sanctifies male dominance by an authoritarian religion. And I'm saying, what about other Creation myths, yours, mine, ones that don't necessarily displace the female principle?" All this talk of creation myth, Eve, and the female principle prepares us for the introduction of the fifth central character, Evey (Alfre Woodard). Stopping for food in a roadside diner, they encounter an African American woman, Evey, car-rying a sealed package. She is clearly in a state of mourning. We later find out that she bears a funeral urn, carrying the ashes of her dead daughter, slain when she was caught in gang crossfire.

As the four artists travel east, Tudee repeatedly slips into a dream-time where he is an apprentice to a mythical "White Man," a represen-tation of the American colonizing force. Back in real time, the four meet up with Evey again, this time on the road. A European American man dressed as an Indian (part of a group of cavalry enthusiasts who dress up and enact historical Western battles) was killed when he drove his vehicle into the rear end of her car. Three of the dead man's friends, all white men in cavalry uniforms, come upon the group at the scene of the accident and immediately draw their guns and hold everyone cap-tive. While searching their friend's vehicle, they discover that a valuable "antique," a tomahawk, is missing. They threaten retaliation but can't make good on it because Abel, who has been asleep in Freddy's van, comes out with his own gun and takes charge. Abel and company loosely tie up the men and make their escape, taking Evey with them. As they drive along, Tudee once again slips into dreamtime. There he meets a little girl, Evey's dead daughter, singing to herself "her favorite song" — the cheerful and upbeat "Rapper's Delight." Tudee joins in.

They walk around a schoolyard, and the child invites Tudee to touch up the faded images on a mural. Then she says goodbye.

We are back in the real world. As the five drive down the road, Abel taunts Evey, referring to her as the "bitch." Evey challenges him: "You know if you ever tire of calling me a bitch, you can always substitute it with nigger. For me the terms mean the same thing." Abel, reeling, nevertheless mocks her, "I bet you're one of them feminist type bitches, ain't you? Like those ho's who go around trying to cut a motherfucker's balls off." Evey looks deeply into his eyes and demands and then gets his respect with these words: "I am not a ho and I am not a bitch. Like your mother who gave you life, and her mother who gave her her own; like your aunts and sisters and daughters—I am a woman. Do you understand me, A WOMAN."

Meanwhile, the three battle reenactors wait in their car, hoping to intercept the five travelers and regain the tomahawk. A DJ heard on the car radio offers a "big warm welcome to all of you reenactment enthusiasts and historians who have convened in town for the sixth annual DAYS OF BLUE. These boys have come from every part of the country to re-create the battles of our nation's glorious past. And by doing so, they not only honor our proud American history, but literally, literally keep it alive." Larry (Tom Bower), the group's leader, congratulates the DJ on his insight.

Two of the men, Larry and Farmer (Kieran Mulroney), while away the time fantasizing about sex with women of color. They mock the other man, Perry (John Allen Nelson), because he has studied Eastern religions and because his wife left him to be with a Japanese meditation leader. Larry and Farmer are incredulous that he sees no need to violently avenge this; they also joke about killing the artists when they find them. Eventually, the artists' van comes by. The reenactors give chase and fire on the van, causing Tudee to drive off the road. The five are taken to a cabin, taunted, and threatened. A key concern is the return of the tomahawk. Freddy, the only one who actually reached into the dead man's vehicle, denies ever having seen the tomahawk. Perry becomes increasingly uncomfortable as Larry and Farmer threaten violence.

Tudee suddenly starts singing the opening verses of "Rapper's Delight." Evey, then Freddy, and then Abel and Kaz join in. The chant is clearly magical, summoning ancestral spirits, conjuring a force of some kind. Farmer holds a gun to Tudee's head. As the five continue chanting, their voices fade, replaced by the whispering of spirit voices. Tudee slips into the dreamtime. He begins to tell a story in the voice of an indigenous person, centuries earlier, looking east, knowing that invaders are coming who will claim ownership. He is aware that they will try to destroy him, that they will consume until there is nothing left, "and there will be no more blood to let but your own." Tudee realizes that one result might be that he himself will change: "I will become like you, and I will be unrecognizable even to myself." Still in the dreamtime Tudee, enraged, picks up an iron bar to kill the symbolic "White Man." He is just about to strike but stops when Evey's daughter appears and points to an Indian woman emerging from a shaft of light. The woman beckons to Tudee "to follow" her. The voices of the spirits grow very loud. Suddenly we are back in real time. The five are still chanting "Rapper's Delight" but what we hear are the spirit whispers. Larry signals Farmer to fire into Tudee's head. A shot rings out. But it is Farmer who is lying injured on the ground; Perry has clipped him in the leg. Perry then releases the captives, telling his former cavalry compatriots that what they were doing was wrong. The film closes as the five now head once again for Washington, D.C. We learn that Freddy actually has taken the tomahawk: "It never belonged to them," he avers.

Follow Me Home is a ritual of reversal, as Teresa Córdova (1996, 16) recognizes: "The taking of the tomahawk is an act of retrieval, an act of recovery that symbolizes the first step in reversing the damages, the hidden pain, of colonial terrorism." While traditional Westerns continually reinscribe Manifest Destiny, *Follow Me Home* unravels it. Its seekers journey not toward the West but due East on a quest to restore honor to their ancestors who were victimized by that myth.

Follow Me Home's vision recenters the female principle. Evey's presence evokes and invokes the mythic Great Dark Mother as well as the original African mother (Birnbaum, 2001). Her memory is enshrined worldwide in the traditions of dark-skinned goddesses and Catholic Black Madonnas, who appear even in countries such as Italy, France, and Poland where the people are light-skinned. As with one of her manifestations, the Virgin of Guadalupe, the dark mothers are the deities of the common people of the earth (Birnbaum, 1993), goddesses whose presence persists despite suppression by patriarchal religions. Consistently, they signify justice, equality, and the rights to life and dignity for all people. Through her presentation of the original Dark Mother, Evey begins to heal Abel (and, concomitantly, viewers) of misogyny and ensuing alienations.

Follow Me Home is about healing, not searing, the soul. Peter Bratt (1997) cites the influence of Eduardo and Bonnie Durans' conception of the "soul wound" (1995, 45): "The core of Native American awareness . . . is the fabric of soul and it is from this essence that mythology, dreams, and culture emerge. Once the core from which soul emerges is wounded, then all of the emerging mythology and dreams of a people reflect the wound. The manifestations of such a wound are then embodied by the tremendous suffering that the people have undergone since the collective soul wound was inflicted half a millennium ago."

Marina Estrada-Meléndez (1997, 6) also speaks to this experience in explaining Chicanos' intense feeling of identification with the characters in *Follow Me Home*. She locates the "soul wound" specifically in Abel: "We are all like Abel, in too many ways. Displaced, out of place, in torn up cities, disconnected from any form of nature, smothered with pollution, diseases, drugs, tv, a death culture, a culture that is not our own, we find ourselves caught up in and completely lost at the same time by its insanity. In turn, we are eating ourselves alive, we are going insane." This "soul wound," however grievous, can be healed though not necessarily in conventional ways: "Since the soul wound occurred at the level of myth and dream, it follows that the therapy of transformation of the wound should also occur at the level of myth and dream" (Duran and Duran, 1995, 45). The Durans were executive producers of *Follow Me Home*, a film that consciously seeks to tap the mythic and dreamlike power of the medium to bring about healing.

As the film progresses, we see that Tudee has begun to take on a colonizing consciousness. He is becoming individualistic, greedy, deceptive, and egocentric, epitomized by his plan to sell out his collaborators by claiming sole credit and taking all the profits for their collective artwork. This alienation culminates in the moment in the dreamtime when he starts to go berserk and almost murders the mythic "White Man." Of course, had he done so, he would have fulfilled the oppressor's ceremony; becoming just like him. His soul wound would have been a fatal one.[9] The dreamtime Indian woman finds Tudee at that moment when he is most lost and about to lose his soul. She spins out a thread and asks him to follow her home, to health and wholeness.

Virtually every distributor in the United States turned down *Follow Me Home*. In a "Director's Statement," Bratt (1997) talks about his film's being dismissed as "too unmarketable," "too inflammatory," and "too alienating to mainstream audiences." The voice of one alienated viewer appeared in a review in the *New York Times*. Stephen Holden (1997) deemed *Follow Me Home* to be mired in "paranoid fantasies," epitomized by the "white racist stereotypes" that people the movie. Could

Bratt, I wonder, have presented the reality of racism in any way that would satisfy this reviewer? Aren't Larry and Farmer apt symbolic representations of such types as the two white soldiers, James Burmeister II and Malcolm Wright, who in December 1995 randomly selected and killed an African American woman and man, Jackie Burden and Michael James, in Fayetteville, North Carolina, to demonstrate their commitment to a racist organization? At the same time, Perry, the third white character, shows an alternative. He refuses to go along with the racists and takes definitive action to stop an injustice that he had originally, if passively, participated in.

"They have conceived the loony idea of painting a mural honoring their ancestors on the side of the White House," Holden fumes. "The notion of asking for permission to execute this artwork hasn't even crossed their minds." Alice Walker (1997, 171) sees this motif utterly differently: "The White House . . . has been a symbol of oppression to subjugated people of color since it was constructed during the colonial period; transforming it into a colorful expression of the presence of American people of color as we approach the next century (perhaps leaving one side of it white, as an example of fair representation) is a cheerful ambition in itself." And what of the dispossessed artists' disinclination to seek "permission"? This is a curious complaint in a culture that historically has claimed Manifest Destiny as a justification for its uninvited incursions into other people's homeplaces.

Social reality is constituted and reconstituted by acts of imagination. Parker Tyler, in *The Magic and Myth of the Movies,* calls our attention to cinema's "baroque energy and protean symbolism" (1947, xviii) and asks us to realize that popular films "are at least as important to the spiritual climate as daily weather to the physical climate" (xvii). Mythic narratives and ritual enactments, including those transmitted through the visionary art of film, do indeed "keep history alive," do continually recreate and regenerate certain realities, do, potentially, heal or sear souls. Artists, seeking ways to "counteract the destruction that seems to be getting so close to us" (as Linda Hogan puts it), deliberately tell stories and conjure images that recall alternative histories, invoke awareness and healing, and imagine a destiny that manifestly diverges from the apocalyptic trajectories plotted by the likes of *Forrest Gump* and *Natural Born Killers.*

8

The Gods We Worship
Sexual Murder as Religious Sacrifice

> As women we were meant to bleed
> but not this useless blood
> my blood each month a memorial
> to my unspoken sisters falling
> like red drops to the asphalt
> I am not satisfied to bleed
> as a quiet symbol for no one's redemption
> why is it our blood
> that keeps these cities fertile?
>
> Audre Lorde (1981, 67)

> In many rituals the sacrificial act assumes two opposing aspects, appearing at times as a sacred obligation to be neglected at grave peril, at other times as a sort of criminal activity.
>
> René Girard (1977, 1)

A man rapes and decapitates a teenage girl. He then flays her, wears her skin, and sings in falsetto. He proclaims that when he does this he becomes the living image of the fertility goddess. Later the skin and head are given a special place overlooking the city. The crowd approves.

Although this sounds like something right out of a Hollywood hit — say, *The Silence of the Lambs* (Jonathan Demme, 1986) meets *Gladiator* (Ridley Scott, 1999) — this is not fiction but the basic scenario of a religious ritual performed by a priest in the Aztec empire, a patriarchal, hierarchical, urban, and militarist civilization (Nash, 1978; Carrasco,

1999), which employed human sacrifice to effect political intimidation and inspire religious awe. My interest here is in human sacrifice in highly civilized cultures, where arguably many new forms of blood sacrifice are regularly performed, both legal and criminal: lynching, terrorism, the death penalty, war, and cancer deaths occasioned by pollution — all ceremonial killings propitiating gods of Ego, Progress, Power, Speed, and Domination.[1] My focus here is on those instances of modern blood sacrifice that make its gendered character most clear — serial sex murders.

I first introduced a discussion of serial sex murder of women as religious sacrifice in *The Age of Sex Crime* (1987). My principal argument is that such murder is a form of gynocide, the ritualized killing of women by men for purposes of hatred, envy, domination, possession, sexual gratification, energetic feeding, and symbolic statement. Gynocide, in its various historical forms, enacts the core patriarchal myth — the creation of the world through an original act of goddess murder (Daly, 1978). Many patriarchal creation myths (instituting a worldview as well as a world) tell of an original slaughter of a goddess/monster by a male god or hero. That act, then, must be ritually repeated in order to sustain the prevailing world/view. Mircea Eliade (1957, 100) explains: "*One becomes truly a man only by conforming to the teaching of the myths, that is, by imitating the gods. . . .* We have seen that certain blood sacrifices find their justification in a primordial divine act; *in illo tempore* the god had slain the marine monster and dismembered its body in order to create the cosmos. Man repeats this blood sacrifice — sometimes even with human victims" (emphasis in the original). In ritual, humans imitate the qualities that they ascribe to their gods so that they may become themselves godlike. Sylvain Levi identifies the foundational purpose of sacrifice as "the transformation of man into god" (cited in Smith, 2000, 6). By replicating this originary and divine act — in often spectacular and theatrically staged murders[2] — the sacrificer, sometimes a priest and sometimes a criminal, becomes godlike, having power over life and death. He becomes "immortal," at least in the word's current secular sense of enduring fame. Such a pattern is immediately discernible in one of the oldest myths known to modernity, that of Gilgamesh, the Sumerian culture hero who, motivated by his horror of personal death, sets out to slaughter Huwawa (the spirit or "demon" of a great cedar forest) and raze the forest in order to achieve "monumental fame" (Harrison, 1992, 14-18).

Both the quest for immortality and a foundational misogyny are inherent to blood sacrifice, whether it is males or females who are being killed, according to religious studies scholar Nancy Jay (1992). Such sacrifice, she argues, is a historically male practice meant to perform a variety of beneficial functions for men in general. In patriarchal cultures men are defined as a sex opposite to women, who are viewed as inferior, unclean, and dangerous. There must, then, be some way for men to rid themselves of the perceived dreadful consequences of having been born of women, including a continuing dependence on female reproductive and sustenance powers as well as the inevitability of death, as all who are born from women also die. According to Jay, blood "sacrifice can expiate, get rid of, the consequences of having been born of women (along with countless other dangers) and at the same time integrate the pure and eternal patrilineage." Sacrifice enables "a patrilineal group to transcend mortality in the same process in which it transcends birth" (40), to achieve its own notion of "male purity," and to connect generations of fathers and sons. In sum, blood sacrifice of males and/or females inspires male bonding, links men intergenerationally, ensuring and maintaining patrilineal descent, and separates men from the matristic cycle of birth and death, allowing them to achieve a sense of triumphant immortality.

Explicitly expanding upon Jay's work in his discussion of masculine psychology and sacrifice, William Beers (1992) suggests that the anxiety, envy, dread, and misogyny that Jay finds underlying traditional male sacrifice also motivate contemporary male violence against women. Using the insights of feminist psychoanalysis, he understands that masculine subjects must separate from the first omnipotent self/object they encounter, the mother. Because the path to her power through direct identification is blocked, and because the feminine represents a fundamental threat to the success of a male's individuation, masculine subjects seek to control and dominate the feminine, resulting in rape and other forms of abuse.

In sexist systems, masculinity is defined in total opposition to femininity, radically splitting what is originally a whole human psyche (Daly, 1973, 15). Simone de Beauvoir's (1953) key insight is that woman serves as man's "other," made to carry and represent those aspects of existence that are feared, despised, and disowned by men (e.g., nurturance, vanity, emotional range, intuitiveness, chaos, change, and death). "Woman" is "mysterious" to men because they can just barely glimpse in her image all that they have had to repress in themselves. Caught in this conundrum, sexist men proclaim women to be enigmatic even as they identify with them, are disgusted by women even as they want to be them, envy women even as they degrade them, fear women's power even as they dominate them, and beat them even as they idolize them.[3]

Yet the repressed always threatens to return. Men must ceaselessly maintain and "prove" manhood (Beneke, 1997) by ritually repudiating and defeating the feminine. This manifests itself not only in violence against women, but also in violence against other men (Gilligan, 1996), violence against the self (e.g., internalized homophobia, substance abuse), and violence against the feminine-identified elemental world (Mother Earth, Mother Nature). Clearly, some men can eschew misogyny and be comfortable with varying degrees of feminine identification. Others manifest misogyny by (psychically or physically) obliterating women, or a feminine (or feminized) substitute. This allows the sacrificing man, bizarrely enough, to then claim the feminine for himself. This is enacted literally in the Aztec ritual, but alluded to symbolically in the contemporary pop culture stereotype of the cross-dressing serial killer. In truth, actual cross dressers are far more likely to be murdered by homophobic and misogynist men than to be sexual murderers (MacKenzie, 1993).

Sacrificial priests act out the omnipotence they ascribe to their gods, and are themselves understood as "human gods," as the sacrificer, upon consecration, "passes from the world of men to the world of the gods" (Hubert and Maus, 1964, 20-22). This same aura also underlies serial killer mythos. "Jack the Ripper," the "father" of serial sex murder, tried to make his crimes as public as possible, horrifically mutilating the bodies and leaving four of them outside to be found. In the words of Tom Cullen (1965, 14), the Ripper "signposted" his murders, using them as a form of ritual communication. After his last murder, Colin Wilson (1969, 39-40) writes, "Jack the Ripper left 13 Miller Court and walked out of history." Leaving history behind, he entered legend, becoming immortal in the sense of attaining enduring fame.

Nowadays, legendary status is marked through the modern equivalent of the oral and mythic tradition, popular culture—film, fiction, comic books, pop music, trading cards, and so on. It is in popular images and stories about the serial killer, not in theoretical writings, that the core meanings of this figure are first articulated. These popular stories make it plain that the serial killer narrative graphically enacts the basic sacrificial paradigm identified by Nancy Jay: the male quest to attain numinous power through bloodletting, to confiscate female reproductive/creative powers, and to achieve immortality. Continually, we find a marked attention to an intergenerational lineage of killers/rippers/

stranglers, bonded and continuing each other's work; a matricidal imperative, desiring first to destroy and then incorporate the mother; the explicit recognition of the sacrificial character of the murders; the sacred and even godlike stature of the sex killer; and a blatant misogyny.

Manifest Misogyny

> It wasn't fuckin' wrong. Why is it wrong to get rid of some fuckin' cunts?
> Kenneth Bianchi, the "Hillside Strangler" (quoted in Schwarz, 1981, 370)

> Most men just hate women. Ted Bundy killed them. . . . When I was a sociopathic teenage hothead I used my words and actions to burst others into flames. This was a time when I could relate all too well to these books [about serial killers] and their detached feelings. Because Bundy, Gacy, Carr are in a way the ultimate men. Monuments of misogyny, homophobia, and self-hatred. These books are grotesque roadmaps to the Raging Bull boneyard. I'M A MAN, they scream.
> Jimmy McDonough (1984, 5)

> Then I cut her throat so she would not scream . . . at this time I wanted to cut her body so she would not look like a person and destroy her so she would not exist. I began to cut on her body. I remember cutting her breasts off. After this, all I remember is that I kept cutting on her body. . . . I did not rape the girl. I only wanted to destroy her.
> Sex killer James Lawson (quoted in Hazelwood and Douglass, 1980, 21)

Acts of sexual violence against women and feminine and feminized men and boys are frequently masked as crimes of monstrosity and deviance. But, however bizarre, these are crimes of misogyny, a hatred of women and the feminine that is all too normative in a sexist culture. Misogyny is overtly evidenced in the proclamations of killers, in responses by the police, in press coverage, and in the tendency in criminological profiles and fictional narratives to blame the killer's abusive and castrating mother figure for his criminality. It is also implicit in the widespread heroization of the killer, which usually takes one of two forms: he is celebrated as society's henchman, enforcing social norms; or he is adored as the "noble savage," the "natural born killer," the glamorous and supposedly libidinally free outlaw.

Jay links blood sacrifice to the misogynist stigmatization of women as "unclean" in patriarchal religious and moral systems. This belief surfaces regularly in cases involving the murder of prostitutes (Caputi,

1987). For example, in August 2001 *Newsweek* reported that a serial killer nicknamed "The Spider" had killed at least twenty-one prostitutes in Tehran. Many hard-line supporters of the Islamic regime publicly applauded these murders. "'Who is to be judged?' demanded the conservative newspaper *Jomhuri Islami*. 'Those who look to eradicate the sickness [as the killer is doing] or those who stand at the root of the corruption [the prostitute victims]?'" (Dickey and Baharai, 2001, 28). The standard combination of a belief in feminine evil, sex negativity and a sexist double standard regularly leads to an understanding of the serial killer as having "God on his side."

Sometimes, the serial killer is admired as a visionary, a genius, an exemplar of individualist freedom and verve. As I detail in chapter 5, "The New Founding Fathers," Ted Bundy epitomizes this type. The feature film *Ted Bundy* (Matthew Bright, 2002) continues the homage. Dave Kehr (2002) reviewing the film for the *New York Times,* finds that once again the killer is celebrated as someone free to "act out the impulses . . . that the rest of us are too cowardly and conventional to own up to. He's pure id, running loose in a society that is all repressive superego. And we're supposed to have a sneaky admiration for him." Kehr critically notes that this attitude would not be shared by the "women he killed nor by their families and friends." But it's the serial killer's, not the victim's, point of view that is centered here and elsewhere. Whether he is represented as a moral agent cleaning up female filth or, conversely, as an exemplar of sexual freedom and antiestablishment verve, the serial killer is celebrated by conservatives and liberals alike for his ongoing assertion of victory over the feminine.

Still, most scholarly commentators wouldn't lower their rigorous standards of academic objectivity (or obfuscation) to connect murder to misogyny. Some overtly dispute it. For example, Philip Jenkins (1994) dismisses the idea of the misogynist serial killer in part by pointing to the existence of female serial killers. Of course, only one female killer, Aileen Wuornos, has achieved iconic status, mostly because, as a highway prostitute with a long history of trauma and abuse, it was far more likely that she would be victimized by a serial killer (such as Gary L. Ridgway, the "Green River Killer") than to become one herself. Unlike the iconic male killers, Wuornos represents neither unrepressed id nor punishing superego. Her first victim was a convicted rapist. Wuornos claimed that he had beaten, anally raped, and was getting ready to kill her and that she killed in self-defense. She thus came to symbolize, for some, resistance to male sexual violence. Significantly, less sympathetic commentators had absolutely no trouble, in her case, recognizing another kind of sexual politics behind serial murder. Wuornos was immediately branded a "man hater" and typed as a "demon dyke."[4] Jenkins further chides feminists (among other interest groups) for seizing upon the subject of serial murder as a "symbolic weapon" to coerce others into accepting our cause (121)—a curious choice of words, displacing coercive aggression from serial killers to feminists.

Fascination with the serial killer as a cultural text to be interpreted produces not only conventional academic distance but also a confusing and alienating rhetoric in much academic writing on the subject. Mark Seltzer (1998, 33–34) exemplifies this approach: "[Serial killing] is inseparable from the problem of the body in machine culture: an intimacy with technology that will be set out in terms of the intersecting logics of seriality, prosthesis, and primary mediation. Yet such a 'situating' or 'contextualizing' of the serial killer . . . makes for some basic difficulties, not least because a sort of *hyperidentification with place, or context, or situation* seems typical in cases of serial violence. What seems typical in such cases, that is, is the subject's feeling of a radical determination from the outside in. In the most general terms, this amounts to an utter failure of distance or distinction between subject and scene. Which is to say that typical in these cases is the experience of a deep absorption in typicality itself: the serial killer . . . typifies typicality, the becoming abstract and general of the individuality of the individual" (emphasis in original).

Seltzer is not so obscure when he dismisses as stereotypic and wrong-headed the feminist association of misogyny with serial killers by reporting (relying on mostly secondary sources) that feminists regularly attribute to all men the desires of the serial killer. To be sure this is a common attribution, but it is not feminists who make it. Rather, it is male sex killers themselves (Ted Bundy and Richard Speck come to mind) as well as their male fans and scribes (e.g., Robert Bloch, Shane Stevens, Oliver Stone, Harlan Ellison, Lewis Shiner).

Seltzer claims the serial killer to be the product of a "wound culture," a machine world that confuses the being with the statistic, the thing with its representation, and the animate with the inanimate. Yet he neglects a large body of feminist criticism (Merchant, 1980; Mies, 1986; Sjöö and Mor, 1991; Caputi, 1987; Plumwood, 1993) interrogating how mechanization is itself linked to misogyny. Arguably, mechanization and its obsessions—control and order achieved by eliminating "dirt"; the worship of the light and the "clean"; the pursuit of artificial life and intelligence; the preference for the copy, soullessness and loss of sensuality—is a continuation of a misogyny that locates the feminine not only in women, but also in stigmatized men, and in what is seen as "nature" as opposed to "culture," that is, origins, darkness, death, emotions, change, and chaos.

Another scholar, Elana Gomel (1999, 27), focuses on the subjectivity of the serial killer, claiming that he "has become the postmodern subject par excellence," someone who generates narratives all out of proportion to his actual presence in the culture, "a self whose freedom lies neither in some impossible essence beyond the reach of cultural conditions, nor in the uniform 'resistance' to monolithic representation but rather in the inconsistencies, gaps and fissures within representation itself." Gomel's reading of serial killer narratives (both factual and fictional) leads her to propose a theory of an "irrevocably fragmented" postmodern subject, a self who remains a mystery (in this case, of evil), confounding rationality. Yet Gomel does not interrogate the masculine subjectivity of that paradigmatic self and the sexually political context out of which his (not really unprecedented or mysterious) evil emerges.

Clearly not all violence is male, not all victims are female, nor are all multiple murderers men. Yet to ignore the sexually political implications of the figure of the iconic male serial killer from Jack the Ripper on is at best ignorant. At worst it is to participate in misogyny through denial, distancing, and displacement. When scholarship on serial sex murder issues from a place of such remote surveillance, it is easy to forget that there are real victims, real torture, and real consequences.

Immortality/Paradise

But Males immortal live renewed by female deaths.
> William Blake [1797] (quoted in *Daly*, 1973, 160)

What I wanted to see was the death, and I wanted to see the triumph . . . the triumph of survival and the exultation over the death.
> Edmund Kemper, the "Coed Killer" (quoted in Seltzer, 1998, 272)

If the U.S.A. comes, I will tie a bomb to my body, I will smoke, and I will go to American camp. I will go to paradise and be famous.
> Thor Jan, Afghani refugee and opium addict (quoted in Laforet, 2001)

The desire for paradise or immortality propels terrorists of many different orientations—sexual, political, and religious—and is perhaps the most common theme in serial killer narratives. In innumerable Ripper and subsequent narratives, this theme is expressed fictionally via ritual human (female) sacrifice. One of the first is Robert Bloch's 1942 story, "Yours Truly, Jack the Ripper" (in Bloch, 1977, 1–20). The original Jack is alive and practicing psychiatry in Chicago. His continuing murders (attributed to others) are explicit blood sacrifices "to some dark gods" in exchange for eternal life. Bloch himself marveled at the endless reprintings, translations, anthologizations, and adaptations of this story: "For some reason, the notion of Jack the Ripper's survival in the present day touched a sensitive spot in the audience's psyche" (Ellison, 1967, 120). That spot remains responsive. For example, in Lewis Shiner's short story "Love in Vain," the killer, "Charlie," boasts: "You can't get rid of me that easy. . . . I been around too long. I was Springheel Jack and Richard Speck. I was Ted Bundy and that fella up to Seattle they never caught. . . . You can't never get rid of me because I'm inside you" (quoted in Gomel, 1999, 59).

A 2002 episode of the television series *Law and Order Special Victims Unit* again makes an explicit connection between immortality and serial sex murder. Two law enforcement representatives are interrogating a death-row serial killer about the meaning of his particular style. They ask: "Why was she cut so deeply?" The killer responds: "He has to take the thing and slice it open to see what's going on in there. The knife goes in like butter, so warm inside. But he has to be quick about it. It will be cold soon." They query: "Why does he have to be quick now?" His answer: "To be born again." One of his interrogators blurts out, "Are we talking religion now?" Indubitably, we are.

Shane Stevens's *By Reason of Insanity* (1979) revolves around a matricidal, misogynist, puerile, and sometimes transvestite serial killer. The detective pursuing him experiences a mystical identification, understanding him as someone who has "a supernatural power over natural forces," one of the "true magicians of our tribe." Another priest/magician/killer appears in *Seven* (David Fincher, 1995) — a deeply pious serial killer (and veritable performance artist) of ambiguous sexuality, who stages an elaborate series of murders dramatizing Catholicism's seven deadly sins. This artist/killer plots out elaborate murders that are dependent upon the victim's participation. For example, he forces a fat man to eat himself to death (gluttony) and a lawyer to cut away a pound of flesh from his body (greed). To provide a sign for the sin of pride, he cuts off the nose of a famous model and then glues one of her hands to a telephone and the other to a lethal dose of sleeping pills. She opts for suicide rather than life with disfigurement.

Two detectives are assigned to the case. Somerset (Morgan Freeman) is older, educated, pessimistic, world-weary, and single. Mills (Brad Pitt) is brashly optimistic, happily married, and impetuous. The detectives identify their erudite killer, John Doe (Kevin Spacey), through his library card; he has been reading Milton, Dante, Chaucer, and Thomas Aquinas. They go to the address on his card, but he escapes. The apartment is a shrine to religious sacrifice; a neon-red crucifix hangs over his single bed.

Seven ironically links the aims and desires of the serial killer to elite Western thought, particularly its theological reflections. According to the interpretation of the Genesis myth shared by Christianity, Judaism, and Islam, women are sexually impure and responsible for the introduction of sin into the world, a myth that fueled the massacre of hundreds of thousands of women in the early modern European Witch Craze (Caputi, 1987). Through its fixation upon a divine sacrificial victim in the person of Jesus, moreover, Christianity has instituted what the philosopher Mary Daly (1973, 76) identifies as the "scapegoat syndrome": "While the image of sacrificial victim may inspire saintliness in a few, in the many the effect seems to be to evoke intolerance. That is, rather than being enabled to imitate the sacrifice of Jesus, they feel guilt and transfer this to 'the Other,' thus making the latter 'imitate' Jesus in the role of scapegoat. . . . [T]hey . . . affirm themselves as 'good' by blaming others." The serial killer in *Seven* follows this logic with total precision.

Having completed five of the murders, Doe walks into the police station covered with blood and reports that there are two more bodies yet to be found. He proposes a deal. He will lead the police to these bodies and sign a full confession if Detectives Somerset and Mills accompany him to a site remote from the city. There is some unease—the killer might be setting them up—but Mills declares, "Let's go finish it."

During their drive beyond the city limits, the killer gets to expound on his sacrificial theology: "Only in a world this shitty could you say these [victims] were innocent people with a straight face. We see a deadly sin on every street corner, in every home and tolerate it because it's common, it's trivial. Not any more. I'm setting the example and what I've done is going to be puzzled over and studied and followed forever." They arrive at a place marked by high-tension electric towers. A dead dog lies in the road. Almost immediately, a van drives up. Somerset directs Mills to guard Doe and goes to query the driver. He is told that there is a package for Detective Mills. When Somerset opens the package, he finds the severed head of Mills's wife. Meanwhile, Doe is telling Mills that he visited his wife that morning and found himself irresistibly coveting Mill's happy, normal existence. That envy, he proclaims, caused him to kill her. Mills, reacting with no thought, becomes the embodiment of wrath and vengefully kills Doe.

Early on, Somerset understands that these are not ordinary crimes, that the killer has religious purposes, that he is "preaching." But soon it becomes clear that there is more here than a sermon. What this killer intends is to orchestrate a shamanic "personal quest" (in this case an evil one), the performance of a series of works or ordeals that will cause him to "die to the human condition and . . . resuscitate him to a new, a transhuman existence" (Eliade, 1958b, 87). Those who aspire to be shamans often exhibit strange behavior; they are solitary, seem insane, cut themselves with knives, and so on. Doe is a cipher; no one knows anything of his history. He lives a solitary existence in a dark, cavelike apartment. He regularly cuts off his fingerprints. During the final sequence, he tells the two detectives: "I did not choose, I was chosen," to perform what he calls his "special work." Doe comprehends what he is doing as a ritual that ensures that he will be remembered, transfigured, raised over the level of human existence—and, moreover, that his ritual will provide a model to be imitated.

At the site of the second murder, the killer writes in blood on the wall, "Help Me," which could be interpreted as a plea to help him stop himself. But that is not the case here. This killer intends his request literally, for the ritual cannot be completed without the collusion of those who pursue him, most specifically Detective Mills. Doe needs Mills not only to embody the sin of wrath but also to turn that fury on Doe in his embodiment of envy. Somerset sees this unfolding and warns Mills, "If you kill him, he will win." Mills thus condemns himself. At the same time, his action enables Doe to complete his ceremony and transform into his new "transhuman" immortality.

This scene in *Seven* is highly reminiscent of a penultimate scene in Leslie Marmon Silko's novel *Ceremony* (1977). The novel is based in Native American (Laguna) understandings of good and evil and an intricate ceremonial undoing of evil. The protagonist, Tayo, while bringing to completion a complex ritual of healing (for himself and the world), must resist an overwhelming impulse to murder an evildoer. He is able to restrain himself, but "it had been a close call. The witchery had almost ended the story according to its plan" (265). Had Tayo succumbed to the urge to kill, it would have brought destruction, not healing.

Although nominally fighting "the witchery," he would actually be ful-filling it. In *Seven,* there is no such resistance. The "witchery" wins; the ceremony of evil is completed.

Doe's ceremony hinges in every respect on the active participation of others. The victims must participate in their own murders. Of the detectives, Mills is the obvious participant, but Somerset is one as well. Rituals, including ritual sacrifices, are meant to be *observed,* meant to be witnessed. Somerset serves in the crucial role of witnessing the ceremony, authenticating it, solemnizing it, carrying the knowledge of it forever seared into his memory, and, finally, telling the tale.

One Internet reviewer, Bryant Frazer (1995), writes of the "palpable sense as the story winds down that something very real is at stake. . . . [T]he climax is likely to resonate in your head for hours, perhaps days after viewing. . . . *Seven* finds the dark heart of the soul and pokes at it til it bursts." Perhaps this sense of something very real at stake is due to the fact that the film not only represents or tells a story about a ceremony of soul-murder; it actually functions as such a ceremony, and one that is equally dependent upon participation—in this case that of the audience members also. "Help me," pleads John Doe. Have we?

The complex linking misogyny, sacrifice, magic/religion, and immortality can be found also in a PBS series from England, *Touched by Evil* (2000). The police are working with a tabloid reporter, Laney, who has been receiving letters from a serial killer, Emerson, and is secretly in league with him. The police close in on Emerson after he has kidnapped a young woman and taken her to an isolated cottage. As Emerson holds a knife to his bound victim's throat, a male detective freezes with fear and does not immediately shoot him. Emerson thus manages to slit the woman's throat.

Central to the serial killer myth is the notion of his genius and supernatural aura. Emerson is cast in this mold of the mystical, mesmerizing mastermind. When he speaks it is always with great authority and metaphysical flourish. When asked how many women he has killed, Emerson answers: "It doesn't matter how many have died. What matters is that I continue. What's the natural course of things? That the universe expands; so must we all. And like the universe there is a balance between us. We depend on one another to continue. A dance of the planets infinite and immortal. Do you understand? . . . Human logic doesn't apply to me. You can lock me up or you can even kill me. But you can never stop me. Energy can never be destroyed, only converted." Emerson's quest, then, is for immortality, and this quest is directly linked to his misogyny. He disdains a female detective, Taylor, pronouncing her a carrier of the "mark of death."

Laney initiates a sexual relationship with Taylor, but it soon becomes apparent that he has been in league with Emerson. Once again the detectives must petition Emerson for insight. He demands payment. Emerson has a fetish for women's hair and he collects it from his victims. He demands that Taylor sacrifice a lock of her hair in exchange for his cooperation. She complies. When the detectives then query him about the nature of Laney's "fixation," he deigns to answer: "Women in power. His drive and his weakness. He desires them and he despises that desire. How can a man reconcile his need for domination [by women] with his need to remain a man?" Taylor supplies the answer to this rhetorical question: "By killing the thing he desires." The detectives acknowledge to Emerson that Laney, through his reporting, has made Emerson a "household name," with a secure "place in the history books." Emerson coyly replies: "The power lives on. We simply serve it."

Laney soon kidnaps Taylor, recreating the scene of Emerson's last murder by taking Taylor to the cottage, tying her to the chair, and holding a knife at her throat. Taylor skillfully induces Laney to realize that Emerson is using him, and finally Laney drops the knife. But this time the male detective who had frozen the first time around shoots and kills the perpetrator. Taylor is devastated and screams: "He wasn't going to kill me." And Laney wasn't. The last image shows Emerson playing with the lock of Taylor's hair and looking consummately satisfied. The viewer realizes that Emerson has played with and deliberately sacrificed not only his female victims but also Laney to ensure that Emerson himself will "continue." PBS's *Mystery* series opts not to challenge but to promote the sacred serial killer mythos by giving all power, glory, and enduring mystery to Emerson; it too helps him to "continue."

The serial killer's sacredness and immortality take a different shape in the horrifying U.S. film *Frailty* (Bill Paxton, 2003). Here, the killer (who, by film's end, turns out to be the sheriff of a small Texas town) is a pure agent of the good, a devout Christian, explicitly chosen by "God," speaking through a manly angel (who kind of resembles Maximus in *Gladiator*). Beginning in childhood, and schooled by his father (the mother is long gone), this sacred serial killer methodically axe-murders numerous god-designated victims. Viewers might expect an ending revealing the killer as delusional; they might seek some opening for an ironic interpretation, some distance. But there isn't any. All of these victims, though seemingly innocent, are depraved killers. Peter Yoonsuck

Paik (2003) carefully analyzes the ways that *Frailty* provides a clear "vision of sanctified violence" that resonates not only with the religious terrorism of Islamic *jihads* but also with pronouncements of President George W. Bush "who self-righteously condemns the nations he considers hostile to his administration's interests as 'evil.'" *Frailty*'s narrative also fulfills the patriarchal sacrificial paradigm. At film's end, the sheriff/killer is shown with his pregnant wife. The implication is clear: He soon will have a son who will be able to continue his father's work.

Hungry for Blood

> Don't think that because you haven't heard from me for a while that I went to sleep. No, rather, I am still here, like a spirit roaming the night. Thirsty, hungry, seldom stopping to rest; anxious to please Sam.
>
> David Berkowitz, the "Son of Sam," letter to the *Daily News* (Klausner, 1981, 141)

> When her pupils darkened, Dr. Lecter took a single sip of her pain and found it exquisite.
>
> Thomas Harris (1988, 201)

> For men in the past—and most are living in the past rather than now—life has meant feeding on the bodies and minds of women, sapping energy at the expense of female deaths. . . . The priests of patriarchy have eaten the body and have drunk the blood of the Sacrificial Victim in their Mass, but they have not wished to know who has really been the Victim whose blood supported this parasitic life.
>
> Mary Daly (1973, 172)

An episode of the original *Star Trek* television series (1967–68) focused on a serial killer of women among the crew. It turns out that the killer is a supernatural entity, the same one who committed the original Ripper crimes in 1888. As the story has it, this entity terrorizes and kills not for sexual gratification, but for nourishment. It literally feeds on fear.

Once again, a popular narrative offers a key to a deeper understanding, reminding us that energetic exchange is at the core of sacrificial ritual. E. O. James (1926, 1) describes two modes that characterize such rites: "Sacrifice may be defined generally as a rite in the course of which something is forfeited or destroyed, its object being to establish relations between a source of spiritual strength and one in need of such strength, for the benefit of the latter. This relationship may be one of communion. . . . [O]r . . . it may be one whereby a human weakness is held to be withdrawn and neutralized. . . . An instance of the first type occurs whenever the victim is consumed in a sacred meal, of the second whenever it is treated as unclean and cast away." Both of these types of sacrifice characterize serial sex murder. The first is found when the victim is cannibalized. Physical cannibalism is relatively rare, but *psychical* cannibalism, whereby the sexual attacker feeds upon the energy of his prey, is common.

Nancy Venable Raine was raped in her home by a stranger wielding a knife. What she calls a depleting "energy exchange" (1998, 13) characterized the physical assault, particularly in the beginning, when she was surprised and utterly terrorized. Yet, she says, as the attack progressed: "[M]y terror seemed to implode and compress until it was like a hard dry seed. Once I was free of this devouring fear, a cold, even calculating awareness took its place, illuminating everything all at once and destroying all capacity for emotion." In this altered state of consciousness, she understood the rapist's universe as one literally "sustained by fear and pain. I had no emotional reaction to this universe and observed it with the detachment of a yogi. In this detachment, a state I reached the moment I knew I could not physically escape, I experienced his rage as if it were a separate entity, a shadow self to his physical being. I understood that this entity was hungry and that it was feasting on something from me—my terror, my physical and psychic pain. It got energy from me and in the initial moments of the attack, when my terror was uncontrollable, it had gained strength." Confronted with Raine's utter detachment, and therefore no longer able to feed off her emotion, the rapist lost his ability to terrorize her. She sensed, with surety, the very moment that *he* became afraid—too fearful, she realized, to kill her as he had originally threatened.

This kind of psychic cannibalization is a predominant feature of serial killer narratives. In *Psycho* (Alfred Hitchcock, 1960), the infantile and gynephobic son destroys the mother and then incorporates her, taking in/on her power and energy. Making himself over into her image, and using her voice, he murders young, desirable women. So complete is his consumption of the mother that other characters in the film, as well as most reviewers, accept as true his version of what she actually, in life, was like. Murdered by her own son, of course, she cannot speak for herself.

Both *Red Dragon* (1981) and *The Silence of the Lambs* (1988), novels by Thomas Harris and the films based on them, present serial murder as a ritual trajectory to "becoming" or "transformation" for the killer. Both use figures from the apocalyptic Book of Revelation: the Paschal Lamb and the Red Dragon. In *Red Dragon,* the more explicitly religious of the two novels, the killer understands himself as sacrificing his victims to the Dragon to enable that process of becoming.

The Silence of the Lambs concerns two serial killers, one whom we are supposed to like, Hannibal Lecter, and one whom we are supposed to despise, Jame Gumb. The "bad" serial killer is fixated on his dead mother. Though he is not a literal cannibal, he is close. Gumb, like the actual killer Ed Gein (and like an Aztec priest), skins his prey so that he can wear the skins and proclaim himself to be the embodiment of the feminine. The "good" killer, Hannibal Lecter—the genius, epicure, aesthete, and oddly feminine cannibal—plays teacher to Clarice Starling's student. But Lecter is simply a more polished and palatable version of Gumb, as well as an incestuous father-figure (see chapter 6 in this volume, "American Psychos"). Lecter, just like Gumb, seeks to dominate and incorporate the power of the feminine, a goal he achieves through his *psychic* cannibalization of Starling. He forces her to offer up her innermost self in trade for instruction. Taylor in *Touched by Evil* only had to sacrifice a lock of her hair to Emerson; Starling has to sacrifice her very soul to Lecter. Clarice, in truth, is not the heroine of this story but one of the titular silenced and sacrificial lambs. Lecter's total psychic consumption of Clarice is consummated in the novel *Hannibal* (Harris, 1999) when he marries her (a development that obviously was felt to be a bit too raw for the filmed version, which offered an altogether different ending).

The second type of sacrifice can be found when the victim is "treated as unclean and is cast away" (James, 1926, 1), for example, "throwaway" marginalized, poor, and/or prostituted women, a pattern established with the crimes of Jack the Ripper. For a popular scenario of this form of sacrificial murder (and its social invisibility and even acceptability) reflect, once again on the significance of the murdered and dumped prostitute "Skinny Marie" in the romantic comedy *Pretty Woman* (see chapter 2 in this volume, "*Sleeping with the Enemy* as *Pretty Woman Part II*?"). Consider also the words of the Green River Killer, Gary L. Ridgway, speaking of his forty-eight victims (whose average age was sixteen): "I'd much rather have white, but black was fine. It's just, just garbage. Just something [to have sex with and] kill her and dump her" (Kershaw, 2003).

We might reflect, as well, on the ongoing series of murders in Ciudad Juárez in Mexico, a border town where, as Gloria Anzaldúa (1987, 24) avers, "The Third World grates against the first and bleeds." The city is well known as a "playground" for the First World visitor who comes to sample any number of illicit pleasures (guns, drugs, sex). Simultaneously it is another kind of playground, a profit-making one, for the United States and other foreign-owned factories or *maquiladoras* that have set up shop there after the 1994 North American Free Trade Agreement (NAFTA) and now generate about $16 billion dollars annually in profit. Foreign companies are especially drawn to Ciudad Júarez and similar sites because they can pay the female workers, many who come from poor villages, an exceptionally low wage ($4-5 dollars per day), treat them as disrespectfully as they please, and pollute as much as they want (Pérez, 2003).

In the last ten years, anywhere from two hundred to four hundred girls and women (from age ten to forty-two) in Ciudad Júarez have been murdered, many raped and otherwise tortured and mutilated before being dumped in the outlying desert area (Portillo, 2001; Fragoso, 2003). Despite several arrests, the murders continue. Some feminist investigators boldly assert that many of the murders are the work of a gang (or gangs) of serial killers, composed of highly placed and wealthy Mexican men who kill for sport. Many people reiterate the widespread belief that the police, if not actually participating in the murders, are covering them up. Others contend that serial killers from the United States are taking advantage of the lax and inefficient Mexican justice system. And there is a persistent rumor that the killings are part of some kind of religious sacrifice.

All of these threads point to an underlying recognition of the political as well as the mythic/ritualistic nature of the crimes. The horrors visited upon these individual tortured female bodies enact the ongoing misogynist sacrifice of the feminine in the form of individual girls and women. At the same time, the murders are parallel enactments of concomitant sacrificial violences visited upon the dispossessed peoples of the world, and on the land and the elements. Like Ciudad Júarez, the victimized women become both "playground" and "waste dump" for their exploiters.

Ritual Drama

> To kill the victim was not enough; the execution became public theater, a participatory ritual of torture and death, a voyeuristic spectacle prolonged as long as possible (once for seven hours) for the benefit of the crowd. . . . The story of lynching, then, is more than the simple fact of a black man or woman hanged by the neck. It is the story of slow,

methodical, sadistic, often highly inventive forms of torture
and mutilation.

Leon F. Litwack (2000, 10-11, 14)

The murder [the shower scene in *Psycho*] is too erotic not to
enjoy, but too grisly to enjoy. . . . One does not so much watch
as participate in it, as one might in a religious ritual.

Raymond Durgnat (1978, 499, 505)

WOMEN'S TERROR IS NOT "JUST A MOVIE"
STOP FEMICIDE

Graffito by Chris Pocock, Berkeley, California, c. 1990

Earlier, I indicated that there are other modern practices that qualify as
human sacrifice. One of the most obvious is lynching—a public spectacle of the murder of black men and women, frequently accompanied by
castration and the taking of "trophies" from the victim's body. Huge
crowds of white people attended lynchings, including women and children. Families picnicked. Special excursion trains provided easy trans-
port. Employers sometimes let their workers have the afternoon off to
attend. Pictures were taken from which postcards were made. The terrorist effect of lynching was continued through these photographic representations, which are documented in the book *Without Sanctuary:
Lynching Photography in America* (J. Allen et al., 2000). Sexual murder,
obviously, is not practiced as a public spectacle. Nevertheless, its photographic representations are part of everyday entertainment culture, and
they function to continue its terrorist effects.

In spring 2002 I taught a class called "Sex, Violence, Hollywood."
One of the films we viewed was *Psycho*. A student, Sonia Quinapallo,
brought in an ad for home entertainment speakers that she found troubling (fig. 8.1). A luxurious room holds two chairs facing a giant screen
on which Janet Leigh, mouth open, screams in terror as she is knifed in
the shower. Can anyone imagine that if this film had as its centerpiece
the slashing death of a desirable, naked, screaming, and terrorized
young man it would be hailed as a classic of world cinema and be used to
signify the essence of home entertainment? In 1960 *Psycho* was somewhat shocking. Nowadays, it is everyday. Watching *Psycho* I often think
of a comment made to me by Chris Pocock, a radical feminist activist
who founded the informational Clearinghouse on Femicide in 1989. Pocock suggested that the filmed sexual murders of women, so relished by
audiences, and so normalized in the culture, were cinematic lynchings.

An extreme form of violent pornography is the snuff film or photograph, a document of someone actually being sexually tortured and murdered. A "virtual snuff" sensibility informs countless cultural images of

SPECIAL HOME ENTERTAINMENT SECTION

A WHISPER TO A SCREAM
The Right Speakers Will Deliver the Right Sound for You

8.1 "Special home entertainment section," *The Robb Report*, March 2002

women's bodies in what we might think of as everyday pornography—
in high art, fashion, tabloid journalism, popular movies, and so on. An
entire genre, the slasher film, is devoted to what Durgnat (1978, 505)
calls the "pornographic murder," each film trying to outdo its predeces-
sors in innovative ways to stage and prolong the gynocidal scene.

The *Scream* trilogy is frequently celebrated as a clever and funny
spoof of teen slasher movies. Each one opens with the drawn-out

terrorization and murder of a character. In the opening fifteen minutes of the first film, *Scream* (Wes Craven, 1996), Drew Barrymore plays the teenager who is psychologically tormented, stalked, knifed, and lynched. (Barrymore's boyfriend is also killed, but we see him already bound and gagged and then quickly dispatched.) In the last moments of her life, she is hung from a tree and disemboweled. Her parents return home to hear and witness her agony; her mother runs out the door to discover her daughter's strung-up body. Who exactly is laughing at this scene?

Calvin Hernton (1988) stresses that it is the body of the black person that obsessed the lynch mob—who castrated, mutilated, dismembered, and disemboweled that body. Symbolic dismemberments of female bodies and the taking of fetishized parts are also the characteristic actions of killers like Jack the Ripper and Ed Gein. A similar representational disrespect to the female body has long been the norm in fashion photography. We are so habituated to these glamorous and eroticized mutilations that their political meaning is obscured. We might recognize something unsavory if this were being done to white male bodies or children's bodies, or if a dominant ethnic group were doing it exclusively to a subordinated one, or if heterosexual men were doing it to gay men. But, for many, it just looks like sex when it is done to a woman's body.

And maybe it looks like something else too, though that meaning is apprehended mostly unconsciously. A ritual is a sign communicating beliefs, a spectacle demonstrating cultural hierarchies and norms. Victims of lynching, "more often than not, had challenged or unintentionally violated the prevailing norms of white supremacy" (Litwack, 2000, 25). In slasher films the women who suffer the most gruesome deaths are almost invariably the ones who have violated the norms of male supremacy by being sexually active.

Of course, being sexually active is also a code for any kind of assertion of sovereignty by a woman. Gynocide is meant to silence and punish women for an array of perceived transgressions against male domination, including seeking an education. Consider this instance recounted in a recent memoir by an Afghani woman, *My Forbidden Face* (Latifa, 2002). In 1996 her brother had visited Kabul University to help put it back in order following a siege by battling factions of the Islamic fundamentalist *mujahadeen* (most of whom opposed female education and all forms of female freedom). At the university he encountered a "completely naked woman. . . . She was . . . nailed to a pair of swinging doors at the university, they'd sliced her in half . . . into two pieces. There was half of her body on each door . . . and the

doors were opening and closing. . . . It was terrifying" (89). This gruesome display "said" in as graphic a way as possible that education was
forbidden to women.

Simulations of similar spectacles appear in any number of serial
killer fictions and films, from the schlocky film *Pieces* (J. G. Simon,
1983) to the artsy novel *American Psycho* (Ellis, 1991). It really is not so
difficult to read an analogous animosity against female freedom in such
cultural products. What is more difficult to understand is how that animosity can so often be enjoyed, ignored, denied, or rationalized.

The Gods We Worship

> Case 17: Jack the Ripper. . . . The murderer has never been
> found. It is probable that he first cut the throats of his victims,
> then ripped open the abdomen and groped among the intes-
> tines. In some instances he cut off the genitals and carried
> them away; in others he only tore them to pieces and left them
> behind. He does not seem to have had sexual intercourse with
> his victims, but very likely the murderous act and subsequent
> mutilation of the corpse were equivalents for the sexual act.
> Richard von Krafft-Ebing (1965, 58–59)

> The divinity of woman is still hidden, veiled. Could it be what
> "man" seeks even as he rapes it?
> Luce Irigaray (1993, 71)

In *Sex and Racism in America*, Calvin Hernton (1988, 117) does not flinch
from naming the energetic, pornographic, psychological, mythic, and
ritualistic dimensions of lynching: "The white man—the Southerner—
secretly worships and fears the sex image he has created in the Negro;
therefore, he must destroy that image. Castration represents not only
the destruction of a mythical monster, but also the partaking of that
monster. It is a disguised form of worship, a primitive pornographic
divination rite—and a kind of homosexualism in reverse. In taking the
black man's genitals, the hooded men in white are amputating that portion of themselves which they secretly consider vile, filthy, and most of
all, inadequate."

Hernton understands lynching as a "primitive pornographic divination rite" and discerns the hidden meanings and purposes of that ritual
in psychological projection, repressed worship, and overt sacrificial violence. All of these have ready analogues in sexual mutilations and
murders.

Just as white racism has created "sex monsters" of black women and men, so has sexism created femininity and even femaleness as an aberration (Tuana, 1993), with masculinity as the norm. "Women" are the so-called opposite sex: ideally emotional, nurturant, beautiful, decorative, intuitive, soft, warm, sexual, communicative. "Men" are phallic symbols: strong, silent, hard (or they are not really "men"). This conventional script of gender propriety causes many men to simultaneously love and hate women because women carry those aspects of men's selves that they themselves cannot manifest and still be "men."

Mutilation of the genitals is a key practice in both lynching and sexual murder. This only underscores the religious and sexually political meaning of these practices. The genitals are sacred sites and symbols in many world religions, ancient and current. Mircea Eliade (1969, 14) understands that sexuality's "primary and perhaps supreme valency is the cosmological function. . . . [E]xcept in the modern world, sexuality has everywhere and always been a hierophany, and the sexual act an integral action (therefore also a means of knowledge)." The mutilation of the vulva with the phallic knife, what Krafft-Ebing recognized as the Ripper's "equivalent of the [hetero]sexual act," like rape and other forms of phallocentric sexuality is not an "integral" action. Rather, it is a dissociative one, ritualizing an oppositional masculinity and consecrating a ripper way of knowledge. Perversely, that destruction is based in an underlying recognition of female divinity. As with rape, the act first seeks that divinity and then destroys it.

The Santa Cruz "Coed Killer," Edward Kemper, not only killed his mother but, as he put it, "humiliated her corpse," further amplifying: "I came out of her vagina. I came out of my mother and in a rage I went right back in" (Horvath, 1984). Feminist psychoanalytic theory (e.g., Nancy Chodorow, 1978) stresses the formation of masculine identity, the patriarchal family, in enmity to the feminine. To attain patriarchal masculinity, male infants need to separate from the mother and prevent any regression to the former state of unity by maintaining rigid ego boundaries and, throughout life, retaining a profound sense of discontinuous, nonrelational being. The vagina/womb is the female bodily zone that signifies to the patriarchal unconscious the threatening feminine, the confluence of life and death, the originating "slime" from which we all emerge and to which we all return. Control over and destruction of the female vagina/womb, like the destruction of the black man's penis, allows sacrificial agents to subliminally worship and literally destroy, separating themselves from what they have isolated as "nature" and achieving "civilization," masculinity, and immortality in the process.

Serial sex murder occurs in a patriarchal and profoundly sex negative culture where female sexuality is variously demonized, denied, and objectified. But, equally, serial sex murder reflects the ways in which male sexuality is objectified. The male organ, in its two phases of flaccid and erect, is denied and projected as the *phallus:* the hard-on that never dies, the weapon of invasion and destruction. As James Nelson (1994) realizes, this distortion has dire effects linked to both misogyny and violence, causing men to scapegoat women and to violently eschew those traits that both the vagina and the changeable penis symbolize—death/transformation, darkness, and softness.

This rigidity stretches all the way up to Heaven and its inhabitant. The patriarchal god, *"The Omnipotent"* as he is known in Catholicism, is made in the image and likeness of the phallus. Only in a phallic world can the penis be understood and used as a weapon and, concomitantly, can a weapon be understood and used as a penis. Only in that world can sex murder become a sacrificial rite and route to "immortality." A non-phallic and nonpatriarchal consciousness recognizes the genitals, both female and male, as congruent not opposite, and as the primary sacred sites on our bodies—evincing powers associated with divinity, including dynamism, desire, creativity, procreativity, and ecstasy. That same consciousness does not fear death and seek "immortality," but understands that "living and dying are twin beings, gifts of our mother, the Earth" (P. Allen, 1990, 52).

Curiously enough, something of that consciousness seeped into the mainstream Hollywood production *The Cell* (Tarsem Singh, 2001). Once again, the serial killer narrative is steeped in myth—but this time with a significant difference. Here goddess-identified death power metes out a sacrificial, though merciful, death to a pathetic, eminently unheroic killer.

The Cell's heroine, Catherine (Jennifer Lopez), is a dedicated though novice child therapist who, through elaborate technology, is able to enter into the minds of coma victims to help heal them. Catherine, although young and beautiful, seems lonely, with only a marijuana joint and a cat to help her make it through the night. She apparently pays a price for her powers.

And these powers are not those of the scientific establishment. Catherine, in keeping with both racialized and sexist expectations, is more intuitively brilliant than learned (Tapia, 2003). Her particular gift is her ability, enabled by an innovative technology, to actually enter the psyche of another. At film's opening, Catherine is employed by an exclusive psychiatric hospital, working to save a wealthy white boy rendered comatose by a rare form of schizophrenia. In his unconscious, she appears in regalia suggesting the presence of a sacred female figure, sometimes a pagan bird goddess, sometimes a traditional Catholic Madonna. A parallel plot concerns a tormented serial killer who kidnaps his victims and incarcerates them in a sealed chamber, where, after about a week, they are automatically drowned. This killer films his victim's extended torture so he can watch it later. A necrophile, he also bleaches their corpses, making them into doll-like objects that he can rape.

This is a typically outlandish myth narrative, so it turns out that the killer has the exact same rare form of schizophrenia as the child with whom Catherine is working. The killer manages to snatch another victim and enclose her in the chamber to await death. But after he goes back home, he has a seizure and becomes comatose just as the police close in on him. The detective working the case, like the killer, was sexually and physically abused as a child; he has devoted himself to tracking down abusers and advocating for victims. He brings the killer to Catherine, hoping she can enter into his unconscious to ascertain the whereabouts of the recently kidnapped victim.

When Catherine enters the killer's mind, she finds two personae: an omnipotent and misogynist adult self, stalking around in priestly drag, and a child self, fearful and traumatized. Catherine, terrorized by the adult, sympathetically bonds with the child and witnesses a formative moment when his father physically and verbally abuses him. The father disdains his son's "girlish" ways and forces him to look at his slovenly mother's vulva, pronouncing her sex organs a "place of evil." Her trip into the killer's psyche is harrowing, and Catherine is for a time possessed. The detective also has to enter into the killer's mind, not only to save Catherine, but to find the information that will lead him to the latest kidnapped victim. When they both emerge from the killer's psyche, he takes off to rescue the victim. But Catherine has an equally urgent task. Acting against orders, she "reverses the feed" of the machinery and for the first time ever brings a therapeutic subject into *her* unconscious mind, her world. There the child self begs her to kill him. Grieving, and in the guise of the *Mater Dolorosa*, the sorrowing Madonna, she does so, resulting in the death of the comatose murderer.

Patriarchal persecution and colonization has driven potent female deities underground. Behind the serene, sorrowing, and chaste mask of the Virgin Mary—or, more accurately, as Luisah Teish (1985, 103) advises, "beneath Mary's skirts"—can be found the archetypal life/sex/death goddess, known round the world by such names as Coatlicue, Kali, Oya, Yemonja, and Cybele, and bearing her twin gifts: life but also death. In the patriarchal religious sacrifice of sexual murder, this goddess is ritually slain. *The Cell*, then, "reverses the feed" of the all-too-familiar patriarchal myth and ritual. Its serial killer does not become heroic by denying death and attacking the despised feminine. Rather, the female divine sacrifices the one who has been so damaged that he can function only to destroy.

One such destroyer, Marc Lépine, in a notorious episode of overtly misogynist murder, shot fourteen female engineering students on December 6, 1989, in Montreal, screaming that he did so because they were all "fucking feminists." In the aftermath, Cardinal Paul-Émile Léger stated that the deaths of these women must be seen as an "offering made to God" (Côtè, 1991, 67). While I cannot know exactly what the cardinal meant by his words, I can wonder what manner of god would welcome such offerings. Although it is rarely admitted openly, the phallic god does indeed require the ritual sacrifice of women, sometimes called witches, sometimes prostitutes, sometimes feminists. The phallic god wears many masks, including Ego, Domination, Elitism, War, Speed, Capital, Power, Quantity, Size, and Progress. Understanding the religious/sacrificial nature of serial sex murder points inevitably to the realization that in order to change the reality of sexual violence, there must be a changing of the gods.[5]

Part 3

Myth and Technology

9

Seeing Elephants

The Myths of Phallotechnology

On January 24, Apple computer will introduce Macintosh and you'll see why 1984 won't be like "1984."

Television ad for Apple Computer

1984: Orwell Was Wrong

Ad for the Olivetti M20 personal computer, *Newsweek,* December 12, 1983

[Winston's] mind slid away into the labyrinthine world of doublethink. To know and not to know . . . to forget, whatever it was necessary to forget, then to draw it back into memory again at the moment when it was needed, and then promptly to forget it again, and above all, to apply the same process to the process itself—that was the ultimate subtlety.

George Orwell (1949, 36)

During election week of 1984, a particularly memorable commercial was shown on a nightly network news broadcast (*ABC World News Tonight,* November 5, 1984). It wasn't an overtly political commercial. It wasn't, for example, the Reagan campaign's red-baiting "Bear in the Woods" spot.[1] Rather, this one was about elephants. Elephants in the city. Elephants on Wall Street, to be exact.

The ad opens with an establishing shot of Wall Street. Centered directly in our view is Federal Hall, with its statue of George Washington standing midway up the entrance stairs. The scene is utterly deserted, desolate. There is a quick cut to an empty subway entrance; the wind is

blowing, and steam billows up from the underground system. An ominous drum resounds, soon accompanied by the ubiquitous male voiceover: "To help American business remember better / what American
business *has* to remember / help is on the way." During this exhortation,
trumpeting animal cries merge with the drum, and the camera turns to
introduce a herd of elephants now charging up Wall Street: "Introducing Elephant Premium Floppy Discs for business. They're designed to
protect your data when other discs won't. Elephant Premium Floppy
Discs. Because Elephant never forgets." The last shot places us back at
Federal Hall. There, a heavily tusked beast gives one last triumphant cry
in front of the statue of Washington, and the ad is over.

If elephants don't forget, neither did I, as images from the ad continued to replay in my mind. Indeed, the ad is all about *memory*. Fundamentally, it is about organic/animal memory being captive to, contained
by, and perhaps even replaced by artificial/computer "memory" — a process ineffably expressed by the image of elephants in a city. Moreover,
the ad is explicitly about *having* to remember; still, it wasn't until a few
days after the first viewing that I realized how deeply this ad is also
about *having* to forget.

On the morning after the elections, a friend told me a funny dream
she'd had the night before. Little baby elephants were running all
through her house, an image she immediately connected to the Republican presidential victory (Trisha Franzen, personal communication,
November 6, 1984). Only as I laughed did I connect her dream to my
commercial; only then did I remember what I had been forgetting all
along — that elephants are the well-known symbol of the Republican
party; and only then did I realize that the ad I had seen had been an un-
announced political message wrapped in the guise of a consumer product commercial. Recall the key words: *American, business, elephant, protect*. Link those to the presidential statue, Federal Hall, and the Wall
Street setting, and the message is not only blatant but, arguably, deliberately contrived.

Recalling the commercial's second image — the stairway down to the
subway system — we might also bear in mind this ad's entrance into our
own underground or subliminal system. For the communication
method here clearly involves what Wilson Bryan Key has termed "subliminal seduction" (1973; see also Key, 1980) — the implanting of hidden
messages into ads, billboards, newspaper and magazine copy and images, movies, and so on. Such messages are engineered so that they will
be perceptible only to the subconscious mind. Thus, they bypass the

critical faculty of the conscious, and the viewer is left unaware of even having received a message or suggestion.

Although Key is expressly critical of such methods, others endorse them, although usually not naming them as subliminal manipulations. Adman Tony Schwartz, for example (he designed the daisy countdown to nuclear explosion for the 1964 Johnson presidential campaign), explains what he terms the "resonance principle" (1973, 24–25): "The critical task is to design our package of stimuli so that it resonates with information already stored within an individual and thereby induces the desired learning or behavioral effect. Resonance takes place when the stimuli put into our communication evoke *meaning* in a listener or viewer. That which we put into the communication has no meaning in itself. The meaning of our communication is what a listener or viewer *gets out* of his experience with the communicator's stimuli. The listener's or viewer's brain is an indispensable component of the total communication system. His life experiences, as well as his expectations of the stimuli he is receiving, interact with the communicator's output in determining the meaning of the communication. . . . In communicating at electronic speed, we no longer direct information into an audience, but try to evoke stored information out of them, in a patterned way." The elephant commercial works by subconsciously evoking the viewer's stored memories linking elephants, Republicans, and big business. It probably was somewhat effective in inducing the "desired learning or behavioral effect"—that is, voting Republican, or, if you were already convinced, grafting your partisan enthusiasms to the product itself and causing you to favor Elephant Premium Floppy Discs.

Beyond these particulars, however, it is essential to realize that the ubiquity of subliminal messages creates an environment that in effect cracks the mind. In all subliminal ads there are deliberately constructed split-level meanings, and therefore the viewer's mind must divide in order to receive them. Thus, even if one disagrees with the hidden message, disregards it, and remains behaviorally resolute, such methods continually condition us to fragment our perception, to remember and forget at the same time, to keep a secret, effectively, by hiding it from ourselves. Again, in the elephant "package," viewers are called upon to remember that elephant equals Republican but simultaneously to forget/repress/hide that fact, for, as our expectations of the stimuli set us up to believe, this is *only* a commercial. George Orwell might recognize this structural mode of keeping secrets from oneself, of remembering and forgetting at the same time, as a form of doublethink. And computer company pronouncements notwithstanding, George Orwell might be right (fig. 9.1).

Moreover, Schwartz's description of the viewer's brain and the communication process itself, with his key words of *design, stimuli, information, component, system, output, stored*, and *patterned*, is reminiscent of that other, even deeper meaning of the elephant commercial—the replacement of organic memory by an artificial substitute. For Schwartz models the mind after the computer, not the other way around, as we might reasonably expect. However absurd such technological metaphors for the organic might seem, metaphors such as these—along with the more common *breaking down, turning on, screwing*, and even *accessing* or *interfacing*—are actively altering modern consciousness. For metaphor not only extends meaning through a sometimes ridiculous, if evocative, comparison, but, as Philip Wheelright argues, can actually lead to "the creation of new meaning by juxtaposition and synthesis" (1962, 72). Thus, metaphor can work to *create* a similarity, adjusting consciousness to perceive and feel a previously unknown and unfelt connection. David Edge comments, "To use a metaphor is to overlap two images . . . our sense of both is subtly altered, by a sort of elision" (1973, 33). Under the influence of such metaphors, humans and machines slur/blur ever into one another, the humans becoming more cold, the machines acquiring "soul."

Rather than merging with this vision, we can instead develop our own and even begin to "see elephants." Really *seeing* the elephants means seeing the ghosts that haunt mass communications, recognizing the apparitions beneath the bland and smiling surfaces. Seeing elephants means seeing through the doublethink and hearing beyond the doubletalk of mass communications. And, finally, seeing elephants means, as in the old story of the blind men and the elephants, no longer to be blind to the total picture through fragmentation. It means, taking a concept from Mary Daly, to *re-member* (1978, 23), no longer to accept the part as the whole, but to perceive and act upon essential connections.

Of course, once you start to look around, you find there are elephants everywhere. Here I will consider several of these, chosen particularly for the ways they involve remembering and forgetting, making connections, and the replacement of the organic with the artificial. These are, respectively: (1) the use of Charlie Chaplin's Little Tramp character to sell the IBM personal computer (2) the irresistible application of the nickname "Star Wars" to the Reagan administration's Strategic Defense Initiative (3) instances of what Marshall McLuhan designated as "mechanical

9.1 Olivetti M20 personal computer ad, 1983

bride" imagery, and (4) the use of the bitten, artificial apple as the trademark for Apple Computer.

Remembering and Forgetting

> Chiefly, we wanted something that people would remember.
> Using the Chaplin character was one way to create ads with
> stopping power.
>
> P. David McGovern, IBM ad director

> The Tramp campaign has been so successful that it has created
> a new image for IBM. The firm has always been seen as effi-
> cient and reliable, but it has also been regarded as somewhat
> cold and aloof. The Tramp, with his ever present red rose, has
> given IBM a human face.
>
> *Time*, July 11, 1983

> Soldiers! Don't give yourselves to these brutes. . . . Don't give
> yourselves to these unnatural men—machine men with ma-
> chine minds and machine hearts.
>
> Charlie Chaplin, *The Great Dictator* (1939)

Stuck with a multinational, cold, colossus-like, remote, and even totali-
tarian "Big Brother" public image, IBM took the plunge and set out to
manufacture some warmer and more sympathetic associations for itself
and its "personal" computer. Investing a quick $36 million, it mounted
one of the largest ad campaigns ever for a computer, producing ads calling the PC "a tool for modern times" and using Charlie Chaplin's inter-
nationally recognized and beloved character, the Little Tramp. These
ads proved to be both extraordinarily memorable and successful, winning not only business gains but also acclaim and awards from the advertising world.

The method of these spots, as with so many others, was to set up a
metaphor—to link a particular product with some positive symbol or
association already held by the viewers, to induce "resonance." Once
again, literal absurdity is by no means a disqualifier for such metaphors.
Consider cigarette advertising, whereby cigarettes are said to be "only
natural," to taste "like Springtime," or are consistently linked with fresh
air, the outdoors, and highly physical activities. Such ads use nature the
way the military uses camouflage. And although they may seem merely
ridiculous, metaphors such as these further the pollution and destruction of both environments—the body and the ecosystem—by bridging
our feelings about each with, of all things, a cigarette.

The absurdity of the smoking ads, however, is more than matched by the contradictions inherent in the IBM campaign. In these, the Little Tramp, "perhaps the most famous creation in any art medium of the twentieth century" (Pickard, 1971, 296), provides the positive associations, for Charlie the Tramp was a clown whose "appeal was virtually universal" (Giannetti, 1981, 83). His very image came immediately to signify humanity, survival, innocence, the beauty of the commonplace, and, above all, the soul or spirit. James Agee has written that "the Tramp is as centrally representative of humanity, as many-sided and as mysterious as Hamlet, and it seems unlikely that any dancer or actor can ever have excelled him in eloquence, variety, or poignancy of motion" (Agee, 1979, 542). Thus does IBM acquire a human face and graft a soul onto its new machine. The method is virtually indistinguishable from the way that Salem bonds itself to Springtime or Marlboro to the western landscape. All are highly *memorable* ads, ones with "stopping power."

But of course the IBM ads, like the elephant ad, are as much about forgetting as remembering, for, although they evoke those positive memories of Charlie, they simultaneously arrest and reverse the recollection that Chaplin himself was expressly opposed to big business, mechanization, and those technological goals and/or gods of timekeeping, speed, and efficiency. Those views, evident throughout much of his work, are nowhere more clearly expressed than in the 1936 *Modern Times,* Chaplin's last film to feature the Tramp, a character he had played for over twenty years. It was in *Modern Times,* as Parker Tyler has observed, that "the Machine was thoroughly identified [as the] enemy, the robber of art and poetry" (1972, 158). Now, however, in perfect accord with doublethink, the home computer is plugged as "a tool for modern times," and the image of the Tramp is made to perform as the thoroughly identified advocate, indeed *tool,* of the Machine—International Business Machines, to be precise.

In *Modern Times,* Chaplin as the Tramp is a worker in some colossal factory, his job to tighten the nuts on some unidentifiable product as it comes down an assembly line. The line becomes a synchronized mechanical dance, and each time Charlie takes a break, his shoulders and arms twitch in helpless repetition of the nut-tightening gesture. In one of the most celebrated scenes from the film, the Big Brother–like boss of the factory orders a speedup on the line, and Charlie snaps. Jumping onto the assembly line, he plunges headfirst into the machine and is swallowed though finally disgorged by the gigantic gears. Emerging from the machine, he frolics and spins out his own outrageous ballet in

9.2 IBM portable personal computer ad, 1983

response to the monotony of the line, spreading sheer chaos throughout the factory. The sequence closes with the Tramp's being taken off to a mental hospital.

Thus, in Chaplin's own account, the Machine might swallow him, temporarily, but it could not digest him and had to spit him out. Now, however, IBM figuratively swallows him whole, thoroughly assimilates and converts him, effectively erasing his original message by producing a doppelgänger who now befriends and promotes the Machine and its order—all accompanied by studied references to *Modern Times*. For example, one of the print ads in this series features the Chaplin figure dashing madly by on a bicycle; his hat flies off and his tie swings back to register his velocity (fig. 9.2). A computer is strapped to the back of his bike. The copy reads: "How to move with modern times and take your PC with you." A television spot portrays the Tramp straddling the intersection of two assembly lines in a bakery. He is placing decorated cakes from one line into boxes from the other. But the cakes don't match the boxes, the machinery starts going haywire, and chaos results. The scene then changes by means of a wipe taking the form of a hand sweeping around a clock face, and next we see the Tramp seated in front of a personal computer. His problems, we know, will soon be techno-magically solved. And, indeed, in the next shot he is back at the factory, but this time a baker has taken his place on the line. The Tramp is there only to put the decoration on a cake and present it to a purely decorative female. The moral of this thirty-second parable is clear. The Tramp, backed by the Machine, has *restored* Order; he is now the Owner, the Boss; he gets kissed by the Girl; the End.

These very specific and specifically reversed references to *Modern Times* indicate something of a willful effort to undercut the integrity of that film and indeed Chaplin himself. Although the question was raised early in the campaign whether the Tramp and this film represented "antitechnology sentiment," both IBM and the ad agency concluded, in the words of an IBM director, that the character actually "stands fear of technology on its head" ("Softening a Starchy Image, 1983). Of course, it is really the Chaplin character who is being stood on his head and shaken until the original content and message have been expunged, leaving only an empty if still appealing image to be infused with new meaning by IBM. Or, as O'Brien said to Winston in *1984*, "You will be hollow. We shall squeeze you empty, and then we shall fill you with ourselves" (Orwell, 1949, 260). The final punch or stopping power of these ads thus lies in their subtle suggestion that the dissident has been assimilated and converted. Just as Winston finally loves Big Brother, "Charlie" now loves the Machine.

Although the link between *Modern Times* and the IBM personal computer is a deceptive one, deliberately forged to induce a particular response, another metaphorical connection between a popular movie and a technology rings alarmingly true. I refer, of course, to *Star Wars*, which, obviously, isn't *only* a movie any more.

Seeing Stars

"What are the stars?" said O'Brien indifferently. "They are bits of fire a few kilometers away. We could reach them if we wanted to. Or we could blot them out."

George Orwell (1949, 269)

Star Wars (George Lucas, 1977) is one of the most phenomenally successful films in motion picture history. It has become a landmark of popular culture and has entered deeply into collective memory. When it was first released, most reviewers hailed its sheer entertainment value and pure escapism; it was, they stressed, a science fiction movie *without* a message, a fun, heroic, traditionally moral and optimistic fable in the best U.S. tradition. Vincent Canby (1977) spoke for many when he not only joined in the general applause but also further declared that the film "made absolutely no meaningful comment on contemporary concerns such as nuclear war, overpopulation, depersonalization and sex." Reversals abound here, however, for *Star Wars* is deeply about all of these and more.

One of the film's initially striking aspects is that it is science fiction (conventionally about the "future") set in the past; the action, we are told, takes place "a long time ago in a galaxy far, far away." Thus evoking mythic time, *Star Wars* serves as the perfect vehicle for implanting traditional patriarchal values in the present and future. The movie gives us powerful old men, both good and evil, and two young, blond, male heroes. All the human beings in the movie are white (although the embodiment of evil, Darth Vader, is encased in all-black garb and his voice is that of a black actor). There are machine slaves, robots with, as many critics delightedly pointed out, far more personality than their human counterparts. There are inferior and servile living species as well. Chewbacca the Wookie, one of the main characters, is an animalistic "primitive" who lives apart from any of his people and wordlessly plays the role of Tonto to Han Solo's space cowboy—a stereotyping as communicative of racism as the former formulaic duo. For female relief, we have virtually one woman in the entire movie, a princess in distress, the predictably spunky token in a movie whose sexual composition resembles that of a gang rape, a common media structure for subliminally communicating and constructing male dominance. The idealized future/past of *Star Wars* is an all-white, all-male world, and, like the Westerns and war movies it is modeled on, it reserves its principal commitments for violence, male bonding, and war. Indeed, *Star Wars* takes war figuratively and literally to the heavens and gives us not only a space combat but also a holy war, a just war, a war in which God or "the Force" is ultimately on "our" side.

As Dan Rubey (1978, 10) has noted, "If *Star Wars* is 'about' anything, it is about power—and the source of ultimate power in the films is the Force." Rubey identifies that power as a political one, inextricable from the patriarchal power passed from fathers to sons. The Force, of course, is also an explicitly religious power, and one taking form, as we might expect, along lines of oppositional dualism. Although the warrior-priest Obi Wan Kenobe explains the Force in quite attractive terms as an "energy field created by all living things that surrounds and penetrates us; it binds the galaxy together," the focus of the narrative is not on unifying in any sense, but on a dire split within the Force between a bad "dark" side and a good "light" side. Both warring camps, of course, use the Force for the same purpose: military conquest. The Force, like the patriarchal god, is basically about phallocentric power, in the sense of force against and domination over.

Star Wars is principally concerned that the "good" group should possess the Force and channel it into an energy aiding them in their righteous destruction of "evil." Translating from film symbol to social reality, the precise contemporary analogue of the Force is nuclear power, and *Star Wars*—Vincent Canby's pronouncements notwithstanding—is manifestly a film about *nuclear war.* Nowhere is this hidden message more evident than in the infectious nicknaming of the Strategic Defense Initiative (the proposed space-based missile defense system) as "Star Wars." That nickname was given to the SDI by its critics and then enthusiastically and irrevocably adopted by the mass media. Nearly all but those professionally connected to the Reagan administration regularly used it. Obviously there were *two* Star Wars, and although one is a movie, a commercial fantasy, and the other a "historic" technological, political, and military event, the two phenomena, as the naming reveals, are generically linked, culturally twinned. To illustrate this, we might begin by hearing some sample testimony from each side, for the rhetoric surrounding both Star Wars phenomena was astonishingly consistent.

Episode 4: A New Hope.[2] (Subtitle of *Star Wars*)

I have reached a decision which offers a new hope for our children in the twenty-first century. (Ronald Reagan, "Star Wars" speech, March 23, 1983)

It is a period of civil war. Rebel spaceships, striking from a hidden base, have won their first victory against the Evil Galactic Empire. (Introductory title from *Star Wars*)

So in your discussions of the nuclear freeze proposals, I urge you to beware the temptation blithely to declare yourself above it all and label both sides equally at fault, to ignore the facts of history and the aggressive impulses of an evil empire, to simply call the arms race a giant misunderstanding and thereby remove yourself from the struggle between right and wrong, good and evil. (Ronald Reagan, March 8, 1983)

The message of *Star Wars* is religious: God isn't dead, He's there if you want him to be. (Dale Pollock, 1983, 139)

Regrettably, our national debate over President Reagan's suggestion that the country develop a strategic defense against a Soviet nuclear attack is taking on a theological dimension. (Brzezinski, Jastrow, and Kampelman, 1985)

I thought: we all know what a terrible mess we have made of the world, we all know how wrong we were in Vietnam. We also know, as every movie in the last ten years points out, how terrible we are, how we have ruined the world and what schmucks we are and how rotten everything is. And I said, what we really need is something more positive. (George Lucas, quoted in Scanlon, 1977, 48)

Although President Reagan's proposal was dubbed Star Wars so its opponents could ridicule it, remarkably enough, a considerable proportion of the population took that designation in a most positive manner. (Edward Teller, 1984, 84)

It [*Star Wars*] was a subtle suggestion that opening the door and going out here, no matter what the risk, is sometimes worth the effort. (George Lucas, quoted in Pollock, 1983, 139)

My fellow Americans, tonight we are launching an effort which holds the promise of changing the course of human history. There will be risks, and results take time. But I believe we can do it. As we cross this threshold, I ask for your prayers and your support. Thank you, good night, and God bless you. (Ronald Reagan, 1983)

On March 23, 1983, Ronald Reagan, relying heavily on a rhetoric of *hope, defense, vision, peace, morality, promise, risk,* and the *future,* delivered what has subsequently registered in collective memory as his "Star Wars" speech. In it he called upon "the scientific community in our country . . . to give us the means of rendering . . . nuclear weapons impotent and obsolete" (Reagan, 1983). This presidential speech "on a new defense" succeeded in launching the most massive weapons research project ever, known officially as the "Strategic Defense Initiative." That project involved the development of a hypothetical "third generation" of nuclear weapons (in perfect harmony with the reigning doublethink, one scientist working on these arms passionately declared them to be "weapons of life"), as well as the construction of an equally hypothetical antimissile system in space, what Ronald Reagan's Secretary of Defense Caspar Weinberger dispassionately promoted as an "impenetrable shield."[3] We could think of it as a diaphragm in space (fig. 9.3). The Planned Parenthood ad took up a full page in the *New York Times* (October 23, 1984). Did the national debate over the "impenetrable shield" in space influence, however subtly, its format?

Within a few days of the presidential exhortation, Democratic opposition charged that Reagan was concocting a "'Star Wars' scenario" in

9.3 Planned Parenthood ad, 1984

order to incite fear of the Soviets. Considering not only the sci-fi aspects of the proposal itself, but also Reagan's characterization of the Soviet Union as an "evil empire," indeed the very "focus of evil in the modern world," that movie metaphor seemed completely appropriate. Still, the Democrats knew not what they had wrought. The "Star Wars" nickname proved both irresistible and irrevocable. And although Reagan and crew intermittently expressed pique about the name (after all, it does puts *war* into the title instead of *defense*), on the whole they had nothing to worry about. Even Edward Teller (a principal instigator of the SDI) affirmed that the linking of that project to one of the most mythic, popular, and all-American movies ever, one invariably described in terms of *vision, hope, optimism, positive messages, fun, morality,* and *universal themes,* a film that has become deeply embedded in our "shared media environment," could only serve to familiarize, popularize, and ultimately embed the project itself.[4]

Still, if the Democratic opponents of the SDI unwittingly stepped into the role of publicists for it, they were only giving utterance to an undeniable if largely subliminal connection; for there was far more than a superficial or fortuitous bond between *Star Wars* the symbolic fantasy and cinematic blockbuster and "Star Wars" the strategic vision and technomilitary extravaganza. Indeed, just as the movie *Star Wars* is fundamentally about nuclear war, its counterpart, "Star Wars," was fundamentally a fantasy, a political symbol produced for the purpose of manipulating emotions, budgets, perceptions, and behaviors. As one analyst observed, "The MX missile, whatever its military usefulness may be, is often seen as a weapon whose importance is largely symbolic, more a tool for manipulating perceptions than for fulfilling a real military need" (Goleman, 1985). Manifestly, the SDI, like the MX, performed primarily as a symbol, a motivating myth, for it is not the actual deployment or even the (much disputed) feasibility of the projected space shield that is the true significance of the "Star Wars" project. Rather, its actual meaning was to set new economic, military, and technological priorities, to legitimate the channeling of vast sums of money into weapons research, to step up the arms race, to cut off any movement toward disarmament, and to reenvision the Soviet Union as a diabolical enemy and global evil, with the United States as the true champion of morality and good.

The joint Star Wars phenomenon revealed not only the use of myth in politics but, equally, the mythic function of popular fictions and films. For gazing more deeply into *Star Wars,* we can see that film as itself a precursor of the SDI, the cultural herald of this giant step into both the space and nuclear ages, supremely entertaining propaganda and preparation for both war itself and its new theater—space.

The Joy of War

I loved the war. It was a big deal when I was growing up.
                                George Lucas (quoted in Pollock, 1983, 19)

Star Wars is the first war movie of a new age of electronic combat, a prediction of what war will feel like for combatants completely encased in technology.
                                Dan Rubey (1978, 10)

As many critics have noted, popular culture has rallied mightily to the cause of restoring/reshaping collective memory of the U.S. war on Vietnam, forgetting it as a hateful U.S. aggression and remembering it as a "call to glory." And although it appeared long before the 1985 *Rambo* and is not specifically about Vietnam, *Star Wars* should still be reckoned as one of the first and most powerful media forces in the restoration of that glorious image of war: war as a testing ground and initiation rite for young men; an arena of heroism; a struggle for the good; and just plain fun. Erasing the horror of Vietnam, Lucas painted us into a past that, as one critic noted, was actually "not so far away" (Rubey, 1978, 9). Rather, his principal imagery was taken from the popular storehouse of collective memories and images associated with a war Americans still felt good about, World War II: hence, the profusion of references to Nazi helmets and stormtroopers, dogfights and a romanticized air war, a nuclear explosion to end the action, and, astonishingly, a visual quotation from Leni Riefenstahl's 1935 *Triumph of the Will (Der Triumph des Willens)*, the key Nazi propaganda film and a precursor of both total Nazi domination of Germany and World War II. In the last scene, Lucas has his heroes parading in the footsteps of Adolf Hitler, Heinrich Himmler, and Viktor Lutze in a visual reenactment of their movement to the Nuremberg memorial monument. Those few critics who actually noted any of the many fascist themes in the film itself—its "Nazi mixture of heroism, self-sacrifice and mysticism," its sanctification of violence, its paeans to individual and triumphant will, its sexism and racism—nevertheless tended to attribute them to the former film student's good humor and boyish hijinks (e.g., Lubow, 1977, 20-21, who is most explicit in observing some of the fascist themes but then largely dismisses them). Post-1983, however, SDI should have opened our eyes and allowed us to see this filmic quotation not only as a structural acknowledgment of the film's underlying fascism but also as an internal prediction of the key propaganda role that *Star Wars* would soon come to play in the projected militarization of space.

Although visually reminiscent of much of World War II, *Star Wars* is really about much more modern warfares—both the contemporary and the futuristic. Writing in *Jump Cut*, Dan Rubey (1978) argues that the film's electronic warfare is the cinematic equivalent of the electronic battlefield that lay behind the air war in Vietnam. Drawing upon the writings of Robert Jay Lifton, he points to the state of mind induced by such technologies, particularly the "numbing" of sensibilities induced by the technological reduction of the enemy to mere blips on a radar screen as well as a concomitant sensorial merging between pilot and machine that allows the pilots to seem "to take on the machine's lack of moral sensibility as well" (10). Rubey quotes one flyer who participated in the bombing of Laos: "You become part of the machine as you really do it. . . . The key is to be able to bomb without really thinking about it, automatically . . . instinctively" (10). As Rubey notes, this statement is an apt description of Luke Skywalker's mystical consciousness during his final hazardous military mission—the attack on the Death Star space station. In this scene, he is part of a team of individual flyers who must travel up a long, narrow tunnel and try to shoot their missiles into a tiny hole, which will cause the gigantic, round Death Star to explode (this movie could also have been called "Sperm Wars"). After most of the flyers have died trying, Obi Wan Kenobe appears to Luke and exhorts him to turn off his computer and instead to rely upon the Force to guide his aim. Luke complies and, in Rubey's words, "releases the missile instinctively, in a fantasy of bionic fusion with his ship made possible by the Force" (10).

Leaving this admittedly fantastic film for a moment, we might also start to consider what actual forces in contemporary myth and metaphor work to cement this identification of man with machine or, more accurately, man with weapon. Susan Sontag has spoken of the "predilections of the fascist leaders . . . for sexual metaphor" (1980, 102), and such metaphors abound in the imageries of both *Star Wars* and "Star Wars." Recalling Reagan's oft-quoted vow to render nuclear weapons "impotent," we might wonder about this common conjunction of male sexuality and weaponry, as evident in slang, jokes, popular imagery, and erudite theory as it is in political oratory. Thinking about that fusion is particularly critical in this era, when manifestations of both the weaponry and male sexuality have paralleled each other in a continually accelerating lethality.

Sperm Wars: In the Image and Likeness of Man

Sex is the weapon of life, the shooting sperm sent like an army of guerillas to penetrate the egg's defenses—the only victory that really matters.

William Broyles, Jr. (1984, 62)

As you drove into town when it was lit up, you could see that missile standing straight up in the air, and it just gave you—I don't know—a warm, strong feeling about how strong a man he was.

"Shorty" Kiefer (quoted in Chamberlain, 1985, 63)

It makes me mad—it's a masculine thing—competing with each other to see who's got the biggest bomb.

Girl interviewed for the American Psychiatric Association survey of children's nuclear awareness (quoted in Lifton and Falk, 1991, 54)

A political cartoon by Lou Myers shows two military men dueling with extended penises, actually missiles, one marked "U.S.," the other "U.S.S.R." (Heller, 1983, 66). *Public Illumination* magazine, a small artists' publication, serves up a version of nuclear safety: a drawing of an exploding mushroom cloud with a diaphragm attempting to contain it (fig. 9.4). "Better Safe Than Sorry," the cartoonist advises (Mimi Smith, 1982, 14). What these cartoons mock, however, inspires a genuflection in a 1984 ad for a Northrop Tigershark fighter plane. This ad (appearing in the January 1984 *Atlantic*) features a black and white picture, not of the plane, but of its "control stick." That stick, in huge close-up, dominates the page. The copy reads: "Pilot and aircraft are one. He thinks; the plane responds. . . . Systems and human engineering . . . have coupled the pilot with the world's most advanced avionics through an anatomically designed control stick. All vital controls are strategically positioned on the stick and throttle. . . . The competitive edge is his." What Chaplin recoiled from in horror—the structural fusion between the mechanical and the organic—Northrop is promoting as a source of pleasure, epitomized in its flaunted "joystick." Moreover, this picture exposes the mythic force that is being used to facilitate that fusion, for this is manifestly a sexual fantasy. The key image is that "anatomically designed" stick, lovingly fashioned in the image and likeness of phallic

9.4 Illustration by Mimi Smith, *Public Illumination*, June 1982

man and thereby eliciting, or at least intending to elicit, unbending loyalty and support.

Reagan made supreme use of this mythic force in his postgame remarks at the Super Bowl in 1984. Speaking on split-screen television to Coach Flores of the Los Angeles Raiders, the president said, "I've already gotten a call from Moscow. They think Marcus Allen is a new secret weapon. They insist we dismantle it." Warming to his metaphors, the Great Communicator stated that the game "had given me an idea about that team of yours. If you would turn them over to us, we'd put them in silos and we wouldn't have to build the MX missile" (quoted in Bach, 1984). Idealized virility is thus gleefully fused to weaponry and to an unprecedented and earth-destroying lethality.

In her exquisitely titled *Missile Envy: The Arms Race and Nuclear War,* Helen Caldicott writes: "I recently watched a filmed launching of an MX missile. It rose slowly out of the ground, surrounded by smoke and flames and elongated into the air—it was indeed a very sexual sight, and when armed with the ten warheads it will explode with the most almighty orgasm. The names that the military uses are laden with psycho-sexual overtones: missile erector, thrust-to-weight ratio, soft lay down, deep penetration, hard line and soft line" (1984, 297). And "Star Wars," although confounded by the doublethink of *defense,* proudly carries on this tradition of missile envy. No longer content merely to competitively measure, the explicit vow is now to *unman* the enemy—a fate, however, that is intended only for the non-U.S. missiles. For however much "Star Wars" proponents want to emasculate their rivals, they desire only to bone up the home team. About 10 percent of the original budget was explicitly for nuclear weapons, what the *New York Times* coyly refers to as the "dark side" (Boffey, 1985). Such research included items such as advanced "penetration aids" to help the obviously still potent U.S. missiles reach their targets, as well as high-speed projectiles and the futuristic laser and particle beams. As laser expert and "Star Wars" advocate John D. G. Rather wrote in 1982, any country that was the sole possessor of space lasers would thus possess "the longest 'big stick' in history" (ibid.). This obsession with lengths, measurements, and comparisons of "sticks" points to one further supreme reversal: It is not *women* who have penis envy.[5]

There is one further connection I would like to make here. For this common bond between male sexuality, force, and destruction (as obvious in the words *fuck* and *screw* and the institution of rape as in the MX missile) clearly provides a touchstone for the identification of patriarchal ideologies, paradigms, and practices.[6] Hence, the patriarchal state's nuclear age began with a "fathered" bomb nicknamed "Little Boy" and dropped on a city chosen because it provided a "virgin" target. It has subsequently been marked by the development of ever more mature and destructive phallic devices. But at the same time, another form of that bond between sex and violence structures a parallel patriarchal age, an age I have elsewhere called the "age of sex crime" (Caputi, 1987). By this I mean the modern phenomenon of the random, serial, sexual murder (men killing predominantly women), which rose throughout the twentieth century.

Just as the nuclear age had a profoundly mythic initiating event—the Trinity explosion in the New Mexico desert in July 1945—the age of sex crime was blasted into being in London in 1888 with the essentially unprecedented crimes of Jack the Ripper.[7] That still-anonymous killer actually invented modern sex crime; we might think of him as its "father," providing a mythic paradigm for subsequent killers.

Jack the Ripper did not rape his victims; he first slit their throats and then mutilated their sex organs. Like their original model, the modern sex killers frequently do not actually rape their victims. Instead of using their penis as a weapon, they use a fetishized weapon as their penis: a knife, a gun, machine tools, a club, and so forth. This breed of sex killer, so well known today, was in 1888 an unprecedented anomaly, at first incomprehensible to his culture. Sex, weaponry, and mutilation were not yet interchangeable in the public consciousness. By 1891, however, Richard von Krafft-Ebing was able to articulate the soon-to-be-common consciousness: "He does not seem to have had sexual intercourse with his victims but very likely the murderous act and subsequent mutilation of the corpse were equivalents for the sexual act" (1965, 58–59). Within a few years, Sigmund Freud would lay down his theory of sexual symbolism, explicitly equating the penis with deadly force. He wrote that the male organ finds symbolic equivalents first in things that "resemble it in shape" and, second, in things that resemble it in function, "in objects which share with the thing they represent the characteristic of penetrating into the body and injuring—thus sharp weapons of every kind, *knives, daggers, spears, sabers,* but also fire-arms, *rifles, pistols,* and *revolvers*" (1953a, 154). Consider the consequences to female life now that the list has expanded to include nuclear weaponry. Consider as well the parallel consequences to *planetary* life now that cultural perceptions of male sexuality and weaponry have been metaphorically bridged by the likes of the MX missile. Listening carefully, we might realize that whenever the president or anyone else sexualizes/fetishizes his weaponry, he is actually pronouncing himself the political equivalent of Jack the Ripper.

Thus far, I have concentrated largely on the implicit aggression and destructiveness of "Star Wars." Yet what about this much vaunted *defense,* this "impenetrable shield," this diaphragm in space that will purportedly cover and protect us from the enemy emissions? Like Princess Leia in the otherwise all-male world of *Star Wars*, like Athena sprung from the head of Zeus, or like the Virgin Mary beside the men's association of the Christian trinity, the space shield seems to provide some traditional feminine symbolism—covering, protection, impregnability—to what is otherwise a flagrantly all-male venture. Yet although those other females—Space Princess, Warrior Goddess, Queen of Heaven—are indubitably token women, they also still manage to evoke some memories of archaic female power. The feminized space shield, however, moves beyond this level and into a more total realm of control, for it speaks without any memory and only to a future annihilation and replacement of female power and presence. The symbolic meaning of the feminized space shield resides precisely in what McLuhan was moving toward understanding when he identified the contemporary symbol cluster of the "mechanical bride."

Mechanical Brides . . . Or, Why a Space Shield Is Like a Beautiful Woman

> Why is a beautiful woman like a nuclear power plant? In order to remain beautiful she must take good care of herself. . . . She schedules her rest regularly. . . . When she is not feeling well she sees her doctor . . . she never lets herself get out of shape. . . . She is as trim now as she was ten years ago. . . . In other words, *she is a perfect example of preventative maintenance*.
>
> Ad for the Crouse group of companies, *Nuclear News Buyer's Guide*, mid–February 1976

It was McLuhan, in *The Mechanical Bride: Folklore of Industrial Man* (1951, 98, 101), who first pointed to "one of the most peculiar features of our world—the interfusion of sex and technology . . . a widely occurring cluster image of sex, technology, and death which constitutes the mystery of the mechanical bride." At the heart of this mystery, according to McLuhan, rests the pervasive sexualization (that is, feminization) of technology—engines, cars, "bodies by Fisher," even an atomic bomb nicknamed "Gilda" after Rita Hayworth—and the corresponding mechanization of the female body into a set of fragmented, fetishized, and replaceable parts—the legs, breasts, buttocks forming what is basically a plastic mechanism, a hot number, sex object, sex bomb, living doll, love machine.

Since 1951, the patterns that McLuhan pinpointed have only grown and prospered. In ads, fashion and pornography, on television, in popular novels, films, and songs, the mechanical bride is everywhere. To cite only a few of the more telling examples for his first category—the technological container of feminine symbolism—I would begin by pointing to those most explicit of mechanical come-ons, the car ads. One ad for a 1964 Pontiac told its viewers that "any car that is this responsive, obedient, and satisfying to drive simply has no right to be this good looking." More recently, an ad for Volvo urges: "Fall in love in 6.8 seconds flat," and one for Nissan informs us: "The headlights wink; the engine growls; the styling flirts." Recall as well National Airlines' sensational 1971 "Fly Me" campaign in which a woman and an airplane are posited as equals. A 1980s ad for Technics portable stereo shows its product surrounded by curling smoke and attended by a black cat; the copy reads: "Technology Made Seductive."

The second of McLuhan's categories—the fragmentation/mechanization of the images of women—continues full force. One of McLuhan's original illustrations is an ad for nylon stockings depicting frankly disembodied "legs on a pedestal" (1951, 100). Of course, this symbolic dismemberment has always been normative in pornography. Still, it is illuminating to realize how common the pornographic composition is in mainstream imagery. For example, a 1979 ad for "Tame" hair conditioner routinely chops up a female body in order to ask: "Is there a part of you that's overconditioned?" A 1981 ad for Almay eye shadow simply presents a V-shaped design of disembodied, although colorful, female eyes. A 1980 ad for Yves Saint Laurent stockings shows a pair of high-heeled legs, cut off at the waist and waving in the air.

Moreover, the woman need not be thus dismembered but can simply be presented as a mechanical doll, a perfect plastic copy (a mode superbly parodied by Ira Levin in his 1972 novel *The Stepford Wives*).[8] Consider, for example, a 1982 ad for Fuji audiocassettes (fig. 9.5). Against a grid of lines superimposed upon black space, a shiny, faceless mechanical woman is curled up in the fetal position. The copy reads: "Imagination has just become reality." And, indeed, it is partially through such contemporary creation myths, through the pervasion of such symbols and visualizations, that a new technological reality is summoned into being.

Another line from that same ad offers further testimony on the meaning of the mechanical bride: "Audiocassettes of such remarkable accuracy and clarity that differences between original and recording

9.5 Fuji audiocassettes ad, Fuji Photo Film U.S.A. Inc. © 1980

virtually vanish." Similarly, Memorex swears that its audio- and video-tapes will leave us forever wondering: "Is it live, or is it Memorex?" while Gould Electronics, a company that proclaims that it is "leading the way in nuclear power plant simulations," avers in a 1983 ad: "AT GOULD SIM-ULATION IS REALITY." Yet when life becomes so indistinguishable from its imitations, it is due not so much to the accuracy of the copy as to a willingness to forsake the original, as well as a fundamental alteration and atrophy of sense perceptions themselves (see Benjamin, 1969).

An identical message, and an identical use of mechanical bride symbolism, is eerily echoed in fashion photography. A late 1970s ad for Christian Dior sunglasses displays six "female" heads grouped in a clocklike circle. One, at the very bottom, seems conclusively real; four of the others are mannequins, clear fakes. Yet another at mid-left is questionable. Consider as well the fashion photography/pornography of such celebrated photographers as Helmut Newton and Guy Bourdin. Newton, for one, has made a specialty of using nudity, prosthetic props, and scenes of sexual slavery and ritual murder in his renowned fashion photography. Moreover, he regularly mixes wax mannequins in with his female models and shoots them as if they too were actual women. An introduction to one of his books meticulously explains that approach: "But above all, here is a man who loves women so passionately, so completely, that he has to carry this love to its ultimate conclusion. Look, he says, in a brace, a plaster cast, even in an artificial limb, she remains beautiful and desirable. And since models and mannequins are objects, to be manipulated at will, why not attempt the final manipulation, the mingling of real life and wax models? Do we really know the difference—not only here, but also in real life?" (Behr, 1978). Such abject objectification is but the extreme version of the normative objectification of women that structures phallic image production, most markedly in pornography and fashion. Moreover, as this passage indicates, the mechanical bride is as much an icon for the age of sex crime as it is for the age of mechanical reproduction. Indeed, such a final manipulator as serial sex killer Ted Bundy (who referred to his victims as *dolls, puppets, symbols,* and *images*) also refused to distinguish between life and its imitations. After his capture, Bundy frankly pointed to the mass objectification of women as both inducement to and clear justification for mass murder (see Michaud and Aynesworth, 1983, 130).

And the nuclear age itself ardently embraces the mechanical bride. In early 1984, the *New York Times* reported on a group of dedicated young scientists hard at work on "Star Wars" research at the Lawrence

Livermore Laboratory, young men striving to invent that "third generation" of nuclear weapons: "Behind fences topped with barbed wire and doors equipped with combination locks, dozens of young physicists and engineers at the Lawrence Livermore National Laboratory work late into the night, six and seven days a week, on classified projects aimed at creating the next generation of nuclear weapons. Their dream, they say, is to end the nuclear arms race" (Broad, 1984). That perfected doublethink is more than matched by many other such reversals throughout the article. For example, meet Mr. West, a physicist. Questioned about the morality of working on "weapons of death," he replies: "I don't think I fall into this category of working on weapons of death. . . . We're working on weapons of life, ones that will save people from weapons of death." That feat of inversion accomplished, we move on to learn that "here the average scientist is in his twenties and few, if any, wear wedding rings. No women are present except for secretaries. The kitchen has a microwave oven, a hot plate, a refrigerator, and a mountain of empty Coke bottles."

Here, surrounded by culinary evocations of the mechanical bride (but no actual women to disturb their security), these young priests swallow Coke, dream of their weapons, and tinker with world destruction. Their desires are for potency; they want to father that third generation of nuclear weapons. They happily follow the fathers before them: J. Robert Oppenheimer (named "Father of the Year" in 1945 by the American Baby Association for his "Little Boy"), Glenn Seaborg and the other four fathers of plutonium, Edward Teller ("Father of the Hydrogen Bomb"), and, of course, Dr. Victor Frankenstein. It can still give one pause to realize how prophetic, how hauntingly accurate Mary Shelley was when she conceived the exemplary monster of technological myth as a purely fathered (from dead flesh) and utterly unmothered creation.

McLuhan's "mysterious" mechanical bride is also a metaphor, one that links technology to creation via an artificial woman/wife/mother. As such, it cannot help but expose technological man's enmity not only toward living flesh-and-blood creation—nature, motherhood, the womb—but also for female *reality*.[9] It further signals the longed-for replacement of the elemental world by an indistinguishable artificial substitute, brought forth from that faked female, the controlled womb/ tomb of the mechanical bride. And assuredly this is "stale male mating," for the mechanical bride is absolutely empty of any genuine femaleness, as false a female as "Mother Church" or "Ma Bell" (Daly, 1978, 63). Rather, it is a technological Tootsie, veritably a transsexed image of themselves and their technology, for whom these young priests lust. It is "she" to whom they are truly wed, "she" with whom they couple to produce their inventions/sons/monsters. And, increasingly, the consummation of the union presages the destruction of the elemental earth and the final ensconcement in a totally artificial and dead environment— again, something like the parable of the Stepford husbands, who preferred to murder their wives and bury themselves in beautiful, acquiescent, man-made, and lifeless mechanical brides and, concomitantly, something like the ritual action of the sex killer who attacks and destroys the womb, the place of the original generation.[10] Finally, an inescapable meaning of the mechanical bride is that—as in the Lawrence Livermore Lab, the idealized world of *Star Wars*, the world of sex crime, and the Stepford world the phallotechnic fathers are wishing us into— in the deepest meaning of the word, no women are *present*.

The "Star Wars" fantasy is a variant on the mechanical bride motif in that it too is "technology made seductive"—not only by its implicit vision of potent, charging missiles but also by its subtle evocation of a companion feminine stereotype. The rhetoric surrounding the hypothetical space shield is strangely suggestive of a sort of Princess Leia-like space virgin, one who is untouchable, immaculate, impenetrable, impregnable, and, above all, moral.[11] "Star Wars" further evokes the mechanical bride in that it envisions a final technological container or envelope for the earth. This is the ultimate extension of the mall or bubble mentality—the consummate controlled environment, the planet as Astrodome, the world in a plastic bag, the earth itself contained by the artificial womb of the mechanical bride, the "Future Eve" finally ensconced in an artificial paradise.[12]

Eating Apples

> At Apple we only have one rule. Rules are made to be broken. . . . When you set out to change the rules, you wind up changing the world.
>
> Ad for Apple Computer, *Newsweek* (special edition), November/December 1984

> She's *changed*, Walter! She doesn't *talk* the same, doesn't *think* the same—and I'm not going to wait around for it to happen to me!
>
> Joanna (in Levin, 1972, 101)

> We do not merely destroy our enemies; we change them.
>
> O'Brien (in Orwell, 1949, 256)

To her who asks the nature of her crime they answer that it
was identical with that of the woman of whom it was written
that she saw that the tree of the garden was good to eat,
tempting to see, and that it was the tree requisite for gaining
understanding. . . . The women say with an oath, it was a trick
that he expelled you from the earthly paradise.

Monique Wittig (1985, 82, 110)

Let's go back once more to the time of the 1984 elections. To commemorate what it termed an "avalanche," *Newsweek* put out a special edition (November/December 1984) with only one sponsor — Apple Computer. Moreover, all the ads formed a continuum, telling the story of the new Macintosh personal computer. It is here that Apple announces that it intends to change the world. Of course, what we might immediately realize is that one of the ways it plans to accomplish this is through technological mythmaking, essentially (as evidenced by their logo — the artificial apple with the bite taken out) by altering the central creation myth of Judeo-Christian culture.

Clearly, that myth in its biblical version has functioned to make the world exactly what it is today. Elizabeth Cady Stanton (1968 [1896]), Karen Horney (1967), Kate Millett (1970), Mary Daly (1973), and many others have long pointed to the absurdities and misogyny of the Adam and Eve story: its negation and scapegoating of Eve; the ludicrous reversal of Eve's birth from Adam; the further reversal of blame and/or shame affixed to Eve's daring move toward knowledge, despite the deceptive injunctions of the gardener; and the myth's carte blanche legitimation of man's total domination over nature.

Yet within this myth linger stray memories of the earthly paradise, the snake/goddess, the Wilderness/Eden, the living food, the tree, and the daring originality of the woman.[13] And that original apple signified not only knowledge, but also a knowledge rooted in the earth. It signified a vital wisdom quite literally from the trees, something Mary Daly writes of in *Pure Lust* as an "Elemental" knowing or philosophy, "a form of philosophical be-ing/thinking that emerges together with metapatriarchal consciousness — consciousness that is in harmony with the Wild in nature and in the Self. . . . It is the force of reason rooted in instinct, intuition and passion . . . rooted in love for the earth and for things that are naturally on earth" (1984, 7-8). The original apple signifies as well the Elemental world *as* Paradise — the earthly paradise.

Apple Computer, however, neatly erases and reverses all of this. The symbol of knowledge disappears and is replaced by a plastic dummy—something like a Stepford wife. Now the apple represents artificial intelligence, and perhaps we will become what we eat as surely as we become what we behold. Moreover, what the Apple logo promotes and promises is an artificial paradise, indeed the artificial *as* paradise.

Laurie Anderson sings, "It's a sky blue sky; the satellites are out tonight" (1981). We now not only have satellite stars, mechanical brides, and plastic apples, but also nuclear power *plants* and *breeders, generations* of weapons, *smart* and *baby* bombs, electronic *bugs,* computer *memory,* mushroom *clouds,* space *pods,* missile *skin,* radar *eyes,* Ford *Mustangs,* black and acid *rains,* nuclear *winter*—all sorts of dummy replacements for the Elemental world. Moreover, all such "changes" are contingent upon the destruction, in memory and in fact, of the original sources, as well as our final inability to distinguish life from its replacements, imitations, and limitations.

This destructive opposition to a nature metaphorically bonded to women is marked throughout much of the patriarchal tradition (see Kolodny, 1975; Griffin, 1978; Merchant, 1980). Daly (1984) traces this theme throughout Western Christianity and demonstrates a distinctive Christian warfare against the "elemental spirits of the universe," citing Paul's demands that we not only "die to" such spirits but set our "mind on things that are above, not on things that are on the earth." Consider as well this letter from Peter (2 Peter 3:10): "But the day of the Lord will come like a thief, and then the heavens will pass away with a loud noise, and the elements will be dissolved with fire, and the earth and the works that are upon it will be burned up." Quoting this biblical Ripper, Daly comments that "as self-fulfilling prophecy and manifesto of necrophilic faith, this 'inspired' text is one among many that have paved the way for modern technological war against the elements, which takes such forms as nuclearism and chemical contamination" (1984, 10). Clearly the Apple update, that technological version of Genesis, is not so much a fundamental alteration of the original myth as a logical progression of the Christian credo, for it too implies and encourages the destruction of the "Elemental."

And indeed, that message is found everywhere today. In film, song, story, advertising, politics, language, and technique, from science fiction to fundamentalist religion, a complex of patriarchal symbolisms and practices propagate the diminishment, replacement, and destruction of the earth.[14] In the summer of 1984, for example, two very telling ads appeared in the business section of the *New York Times.* The first (25 June), for Saudia Airlines, used a split-screen composition. On the left hung an image of the earth, captioned: "And how we got round it." On the very next day, *Science* magazine took out an ad to promote its upcoming fifth anniversary issue, devoted to "20 DISCOVERIES THAT SHAPED THE 20TH CENTURY." To impress their significance upon potential readers, they visualized two gigantic male hands grasping, shaping, crushing, and dwarfing a puny, malleable, pathetic, and vulnerable Earth (fig. 9.6). Echoing the message, a 1984 ad for Perrier water shows a giant bottle triumphantly bursting out of the top of a now-dwarfed and violated planet. A 1984 ad for Cobra phone-answering machines depicts one floating over the surface of a planet that is no longer even composed of land and water but, instead, is covered by Cobra phone-answering machines. A 1984 ad for a *Newsweek* publication chops the globe in half, announcing that it is "ON TOP DOWN UNDER."

Such visualizations of the earth closely parallel many of the depictions of women as artificial and/or fragmented "mechanical brides," indicating here the presence of McLuhan's mysterious modern cluster of "sex, technology, and death." Further clues to that mystery can be found in two other nonadvertising images. The first illustrates an article in the *Nation* (February 25, 1984): a grinning Henry Kissinger raping a woman whose head is the planet Earth. The second image, from that crucial election month of November 1984, is the cover of *The Atlantic* (fig. 9.7). Referring to an article on nuclear winter, the illustration depicts a man (we see only his military arms labeled "U.S.") holding a glowing, irradiated earth in his hands. Moreover, the shrunken planet is now serving as the dot underneath a hovering question mark of black smoke; once again *he* has the whole world in his hands, once again the planet is diminutive in relation to the man. And just as a woman on her back with legs spread-eagled is the characteristic icon of female defeat in the age of sex crime, these images of the raped—the shrunken, violated, manipulated, and replicated—Earth are the characteristic icons in a pornography of the nuclear age.[15] And like that other age, the nuclear age presages the escalation of the paradigmatic rape of the "Mother" into a final act of sexual murder, for such images are meant not only to sell a particular product or illustrate a particular concept, but also to reflect, sell, and embed a worldview in which these products and conceptions attain a reality. Both Annette Kolodny and Carolyn Merchant have demonstrated the historical role of female metaphors for the earth and nature in influencing, constraining, legitimating, and even mandating certain behaviors. Such visualizations of a planet traditionally understood as

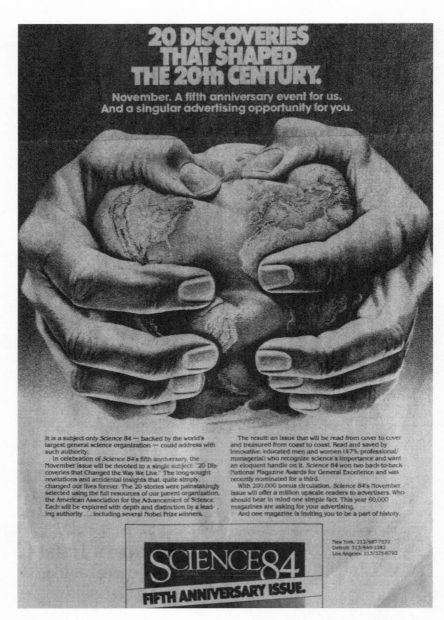

20 DISCOVERIES THAT SHAPED THE 20th CENTURY.

November. A fifth anniversary event for us.
And a singular advertising opportunity for you.

It is a subject only *Science 84* — backed by the world's largest general science organization — could address with such authority.

In celebration of *Science 84*'s fifth anniversary, the November issue will be devoted to a single subject: "20 Discoveries that Changed the Way We Live." The long-sought revelations and accidental insights that, quite simply, changed our lives forever. The 20 stories were painstakingly selected using the full resources of our parent organization, the American Association for the Advancement of Science. Each will be explored with depth and distinction by a leading authority . . . including several Nobel Prize winners.

The result: an issue that will be read from cover to cover and treasured from coast to coast. Read and saved by innovative, educated men and women (47% professional/managerial) who recognize science's importance and want an eloquent handle on it. *Science 84* won two back-to-back National Magazine Awards for General Excellence and was recently nominated for a third.

With 200,000 bonus circulation, *Science 84*'s November issue will offer a million upscale readers to advertisers. Who should bear in mind one simple fact. This year 60,000 magazines are asking for your advertising.

And one magazine is inviting you to be a part of history.

New York: 212/687-7632
Detroit: 313/646-1282
Los Angeles: 213/378-8792

SCIENCE 84

FIFTH ANNIVERSARY ISSUE.

9.6 *Science magazine* ad, 1984

9.7 *The Atlantic* cover, November 1984

"Mother Earth" not only legitimate male domination and violation of women but also enact and anticipate the domination/destruction of the earth and symbolically urge the actualization of that "ultimate" reality.

With this pattern in mind, let's return briefly to the movie *Star Wars*. Throughout most of that movie, the only colors we see are black and white, gold and silver; this is a mechanical universe. Moreover, we are usually out in space somewhere. Our longest time on a planet is spent on the bleak, desert world from which Luke happily escapes. But for one significant moment we do glimpse a resonant shimmer of blue and green. It happens when Darth Vader and his crew are trying to wrest information from Princess Leia. They show us her home planet of Alderaan on their space screen. "Tell us what you know, or we'll blow it up," they threaten. She pretends to comply, hoping to save her planet, but they blow it up anyway just so that they can demonstrate the destructive power of their "Death Star." Viewers of this most viewed of films then see a very graphic depiction of what a planet like the earth would look like being annihilated by a beam weapon. I suggest that, on some level, most viewers get the message that Alderaan equals Earth. It looks just like the earth, and frankly it is the only thing in the movie that does; moreover, it is linked with the only woman in the movie. Here we arrive precisely at the deep conjunction between *Star Wars*, the movie, and "Star Wars," the technomilitary extravaganza. The shared naming is completely logical, for each implicitly imagines the complete destruction of the earth.

And the ramifications of that "fantasy" go far beyond the movies. Consider the front page of the *Boston Globe* for Christmas Eve of 1984 (fig. 9.8). Two stories at the top of the page command our attention. The first, on the left, is about the Ethiopian famine. There is a photograph of a mother and her infant son grotesquely posed to look like the Christian Madonna and child. The headline reads: "Amid famine and war, hope and faith survive." If those key words sound familiar, our expectations are soon met, for when we turn to the immediate right there is a story about "Star Wars." Its headline reads: "Weinberger: No Give on 'Star Wars,'" and beneath that a quote from the man himself: "It's the one thing that offers any real hope to the world and we will not give that up."

Both stories are part of *one* continuing story.[16] One part is about the earth, the Mother, real food, Africa—the cradle of human life, the "primitive," the "past," the expendable. The other is about space, the Father, the Final Frontier, technology, the "future." No matter how many public tears are shed or publicity trips are taken by politicians, Africa

9.8 The *Boston Globe* front page, December 24, 1984

and its people are in the phallotechnical scheme of things completely, perhaps even necessarily, expendable. The white heavenly fathers pour $3 billion per year into Death Star research while those people starve; moreover, genocide in Africa is spurred not only by racism and neocolonialism, but also by the time-honored patriarchal war against the Elemental. For Caspar Weinberger, like Paul his brother before him, has set his mind "on things that are above, not on things that are on the earth."

Weinberger possessed hope; Reagan had a vision; computers are full of memory. But what of our own? If we see the world only through news, films, commercials, and the rhetorical reversals of bad actors and politicians, we see ourselves and the world objectified, mechanized, destroyed, and replaced. Must we then believe what we see? Do we become what we behold? Do we accept being mirrored in and by elephants trapped in the city, clowns replaced by puppets, shooting death stars, mechanical brides, artificial apples, and raped and shrunken earths? Siegfried Kracauer has written that "the deep feelings of uneasiness *Triumph of the Will* arouses in unbiased minds originates in the fact that before our eyes palpable life becomes an apparition" (1947, 303).

That very same intent and strategy inform every piece of propaganda discussed here. Moreover, under the influence of such systematic lying, we are expected to forget and forgo originality and/or reality, finally accepting the apparitions as the inevitable or preferred replacements for the palpable life.

In 1952 Rachel Carson drew a connection between the increasing artificialization of the environment and what she perceived to be an increasing destructiveness in "mankind."

> I myself am convinced that there has never been a greater need than there is today for the reporter and interpreter of the natural world. Mankind has . . . sought to insulate himself, in his cities of steel and concrete, from the realities of earth and water and the growing seed. Intoxicated with a sense of his own power, he seems to be going farther and farther into more experiments for the destruction of himself and his world.
>
> There is certainly no single remedy for this condition and I am offering no panacea. But it seems reasonable to believe—and I do believe—that the more clearly we can focus our attention on the wonders and reality of the universe about us the less taste we shall have for the destruction of our race. (Gartner, 1983, 124–25)

By "seeing elephants," then, I suggest that we are really doing two things. First, we can see through the unrealities, the deceptions. For example, we can realize that the rose-colored vision of "Star Wars" that Ronald Reagan so sincerely asked us to share with him is actually a lethal hallucination, that the apple in the computer is a man-made dummy, promoting knowledge that, if not wholly artificial, remains ontologically incomplete. Second, we can move on to focus our attention, to re-member and see the elephants, as well as the stars, apples, and the earth itself, not as possessed symbolic projections, but in their wonder, in their Elemental and continuing originality.

10

Sex, Radiation, and the Sacred

The feminine call for a new recognition [of the goddess] arises simultaneously with the [nuclear] violence that threatens to get out of hand. . . . [M]ythology unexpectedly comes to our aid. . . . The oldest deities of warfare and destruction were feminine, not masculine. . . . These archaic goddesses had dominion over both love and war [and] were not at all concerned with conquest and territorial expansion. Those were male obsessions. Rather, these goddesses monitored the life cycle throughout its phases: birth, growth, death, and rebirth. Evidently today our endangered life cycle again needs divine monitoring. In the depths of the unconscious psyche, the ancient Goddess is arising. She demands recognition and homage. If we refuse to acknowledge her, she may unleash forces of destruction. If we grant the Goddess her due, she may compassionately guide us toward transformation.

Edward Whitmont (1982, viii)

God is coming and is She pissed.

Bumper sticker, c. 1985

The most common and frequently intermingled sources of nuclear metaphor are the religious and the sexual, traditional repositories of the sacred. The concept of the sacred is a most complex one, bespeaking power, mystery, and ambiguity. The sacred is what Roger Caillois (1959, 22) understands as "the inexhaustible source that creates, sustains, and renews." The sacred is the cosmic potency to make things happen, the endlessly fruitful energy that creates life. At the same time, life is always in a process of growth, transformation, death, and rebirth. Thus, the sacred is a two-faced power—one that not only advances but also retreats, one that creates and sustains but also destroys and transforms.

In many tribal cultures, everything in the cosmos is understood as participating in the sacred; everything is imbued with consciousness and spirit and partakes in the greater power of being: "If the Great Spirit or Great Mystery holds everything in its thought, then everything is sacred" (Sanchez, 1993, 223). Though the sacred is omnipresent, it lodges most intensely in particular places, like the sun, trees, and animals. The most fundamental meaning of *sacred* in Native American philosophy is "entitled to reverence and respect: not to be profaned; inviolable" (224).

In the rationalist worldview systems, a great chasm exists between the sacred and the mundane. The elemental world, nature, and animals are desacralized, said to be lacking in soul, consciousness, and purpose— and, hence, can be exploited at will. Women, in patriarchal mythology, philosophy, and science, are deemed the "less noble sex" (Tuana, 1993), ontologically inferior to men. Female divinity is profaned, made into pornography, and god is conceptualized as most high, separate from creation, all-powerful, and all-male.

This reverence for what is "high" and what is most dominant is a central characteristic of phallic power systems. The *phallus*, of course, is the symbol of a penis in a state of permanent erection. The phallus—for both popular culture and high psychoanalytic theory—serves as the grandiose and universal signifier of male superiority, authority, law, and domination. Phallocratic systems are characterized by imperialism, fraternity, men's club models of power, and the sexual ownership and abuse of women and all that is identified as feminine (Keuls, 1985). Under this system, nuclear power frequently is imaged, both by those who applaud it and by those who criticize it, as phallic might.

At the same time, an alternative understanding of nuclear technology as rooted in *female* potency and divinity is suggested throughout popular culture. Sometimes that female power is domesticated and beneficial (as in 1950s "Miss A-Bomb" beauty pageants in Las Vegas), and sometimes it is unleashed, raging, and veritably castrating, as in the film *Eve of Destruction* (Duncan Gibbins, 1991). As I will detail, numerous commentators, male as well as female, understand nuclear power and nuclear materials, including reactors, bombs, and waste, as cosmically feminine. Moreover, they link these to a return of goddess energies that have long been suppressed and denied.

While these mythic contextualizations of nuclear technology are on the surface contradictory, they share the recognition that radiation and its technologies and effects are intimately connected to both sexuality and the sacred. In this chapter I examine both strains of the narrative and offer some thoughts on an integrated approach.

On Phallic Gods and Missiles

> I wish you were the town of Hiroshima and I *la bomb atomique*
> *pour tomer dessus* (the atomic bomb to fall on you).
> Master of ceremonies to a female performer in an Athens nightclub, 1945
> (Boyer, 1985, 246)

> NUKE THE BITCHES
> T-shirt worn by a counterdemonstrator at the antinuclear Women's Encampment
> for a Future of Peace and Justice (Putter, 1985)

> We have to prove that we are not eunuchs.
> Baloasaheb K. Thackeray, cheering the Indian nuclear tests
> (cnn.com, May 12, 1998)

Feminist criticism has focused on exposing what Diana Russell (1989) calls "nuclear phallacies" (fig. 10.1). Carol Cohn (1987) critiques the pervasively pornographic imagery and language of nuclear strategists. Feminist theologian Mary Condren (1989, 201) avers: "Nuclear destruction is intrinsic to the spirituality and theology generated by Western culture." Monica Sjöö and Barbara Mor (1991, 316) concur: "We suggest that the atomic or nuclear blast is man's final identification with the Sun God, the final annihilation of matter/mother—and that this is the ultimate goal of all patriarchal religion." The scientific quest that led to the development of nuclear technology was characterized by intense desire to split the atom, to break what the Cherokee thinker Marilou Awiakta (1986) understands as the "mother heart of the universe."

For about two centuries, *split*, an implicitly violent term, has served in "low slang" as a synonym for "copulate . . . as in . . . 'I'd like to split that one'" (Beale, 1989, 424). The environmental historian Caroline Merchant (1980) has traced the implicit sexual violence of the seventeenth-century scientific revolution as revealed through its characteristic metaphors of "mastering," "disrobing," and "penetrating" nature, understood as a female form. All such sexually violent imagery historically has

10.1 Photograph by Ruth Putter, 1985

marked nuclear metaphor. Atomic scientists are figured as investigating "the most intimate properties of matter," "penetrating hidden mysteries," tearing away veils to reveal inner secrets, and laying bare the structure of atoms. One scientist told of his "satisfaction in smashing a resistant atom" (Weart, 1989, 58).

Once that defiant atom was smashed and split, the resulting bomb at first was conceptualized as male. The original scientists working at Los Alamos took bets among themselves as to whether they would ultimately have a "boy" or a "girl"—that is, a success or a dud. A success it was: The bomb dropped on Hiroshima was called "Little Boy." In 1945 the War Department historian-journalist William L. Laurence won much acclaim for his eyewitness accounts of the first bomb blasts, which double as descriptions of a pornographic "come shot," glorying in the spectacle of male ejaculation: "The mushroom top was even more alive than the pillar, seething and boiling in a white fury of creamy foam, sizzling upward and then descending earthward, a thousand geysers rolled into one" (1946, 239).

A canny awareness of the sexual and sexually violent dimensions of nuclear imagery and practice unforgettably informs Stanley Kubrick's riotous 1963 film, *Dr. Strangelove: Or, How I Learned to Stop Worrying and Love the Bomb*. General Jack D. Ripper, paranoid and sexually impotent, insists that he avoids sexual intercourse with women only because it results in a "loss of essence." Ripper becomes obsessed with what he sees as a Soviet plot to pollute his "purity of essence" through fluoridation of water. He decides to wipe out the Soviet Union and orders airborne bombers to launch a nuclear attack, a move ultimately resulting in global apocalypse. General Ripper's namesake, Jack the Ripper, did not rape his victims, but slit their throats and tore apart their breasts and genitals, actions that soon were understood as sexually motivated. Similarly, General Ripper avoids sexual intercourse, but substitutes a sexualized weapon—in his case, a nuclear bomb. The mutilated female corpse is the planet Earth.

In 1948, when the United States was testing atomic weaponry on Bikini Atoll in the Pacific Ocean, the skimpy two-piece swimsuit was all the rage on the French Riviera. Popular jargon immediately joined the two phenomena. A long global history links the earth with the female body (Eliade, 1958a; Merchant, 1980). Such imagery is infused into cultural ideas about the Pacific Islands, which have long signified an erotic paradise to North Americans and Europeans, the original good place, the mother's body (Porter, 1991, 104–5). In travel writings, tourist advertisements, and popular film and fictions, the lush, volcanic islands are imaged as redolent with female sexuality, a "paradisiacal" sacred site on the body of earth akin to the sacred site of the vulva on the female body. To be sure, much of this sexual romanticism is overlaid with Orientalist (Said, 1987) longings for the "primitive" along with sexually avaricious desire. Yet these metaphors also grow out of the female character of the land itself. Indeed, the sexual potency and sovereignty of the land may have made it an especially attractive target for those who receive erotic gratification from destruction.

Recognition of such gratification from nuclear destruction can be found throughout popular culture in recurring images of the phallic identity of nuclear weapons, in any number of venues, both serious and jocular (see chapter 9 in this volume, "Seeing Elephants"). A most flagrant example is *The Incredible Mr. MX*, a pornographic film. An adult video catalogue hawked the film: "Take a long look at the real weapon of the '80s!!! . . . See his 16½ inch missile."

Similar sexual images surfaced in Indian culture after the successful 1998 tests of nuclear weapons, following twenty-four years of nuclear restraint. Bal Thackeray, leader of the militant Hindu Shiv Sena party and an open admirer of Hitler, boasted that the bomb explosions put permanently to bed the status of Indian men as "eunuchs." Historian Vinay Lal (1998, 7) traces this gendering of nuclear weapons to India's days under colonial rule, when "the British were apt to describe Indians as an 'effeminate' people, leading lives of indolence and womanly softness." Some Indian men have responded to this by embracing "a certain kind of hyper-masculinity," especially since they are aware that Pakistani Muslims are viewed as a "meat-eating, virile, robust and militaristic people."

Curiously enough, male sexuality that is read as feminine, gay, or having gay sex appeal is more frequently linked to nuclear reactors than to weaponry. *People* magazine ("Let the guy grin," 1986) quoted some "movie biggies" pronouncing on the incipient stardom of Tom Cruise (perceived by some as a gay icon): "He's like Three Mile Island inside, just ready to blow." *Time* movie critic Jay Cocks (1984, 59) had this to say about Michael Jackson: "Many observers find in the ascendancy of Michael Jackson the ultimate personification of the androgynous rock star. His high flying tenor makes him sound like the lead in some funked up boys' choir, even as the sexual dynamism irradiating from the arch of his dancing body challenges Government standards for a nuclear meltdown." Apparently, it is only a hypermasculine sexuality, one that is seen as targeting the feminine, which elicits the phallus/weapon metaphor.

Such sexual/nuclear metaphors are not really so astonishing. Sexual desire is almost universally experienced as a "sacred fire," akin to elemental forms of heat and, hence, electrical and nuclear energies. Still the phallic images—for the phallus (unlike the penis) is an artifact, not a thing of nature—owe more to sexist paradigms than to elemental correspondences. This correspondence between the phallus and the weapon of mass destruction speaks directly to the feminist insight that under male supremacy sex and violence are, as Catharine MacKinnon (1983, 650) argues, "mutually definitive," and "acts of dominance and submission, up to and including violence, are experienced as sexually arousing, as sex itself" (1987, 6). The gynocidal culture's image of woman as sex object and victim is paralleled by religious and scientific ideology that pictures the earth as feminine object/victim. In a symbol system in which the penis is identified with the cold, hard, unfeeling phallus and then consistently linked to weaponry, nuclear holocaust comes to be celebrated, however subtly, as ultimate orgasm, ultimate "snuff" scene, and men's acquisition of ultimate "godlike" power—*omnipotence*.

Ironically, however, the pursuit of omnipotence is based, as *Dr. Strangelove* suggests, not in sexual power and confidence, but in a profound feeling of *impotence*. Impotence itself is a natural enough response to the relentless demands for men to conform to the battery model of masculinity—"ever-ready," "die-hard" and able to "keep going and going." And impotence (spiritual and bodily), truth be told, is also the logical end product of the drastic alienation and desensualization of everyday life in the industrial and technologized world. At work, in our religions, our entertainments, and in our living places—there is little occasion for "sensual interactions with nature, with organic matter and living organisms" (Mies, 1998, 218). Instead, people interact mostly with machines—factory tools and devices, cars, computers, televisions, cell phones. Food is increasingly monotonous and flavorless. Theme parks offer canned versions of both nature and other cultures. The desirable woman is increasingly an artifact—body sculpted, hair dyed, lines on the face erased, breasts surgically enlarged but subsequently without much sensation, pubic bush shaved to look like a child's or waxed into the thinnest line of defense. Concomitantly, the programmatic desensualization demanded by conventional masculinity steers many men into obsessive relationships with both sex (Bearman, 1999) and violence (Hall, 1999). Marie Mies (1998, 218) argues that some men seek to "regain some bodily and emotional feeling by attacking women." Related outlets are pornography, violent media and video games, spectator sports like football, sadomasochistic sexuality (gay and straight), and, of course, war.

The exploitation of natural resources and forces that make nuclear weapons possible begins in this desensualization and concomitant enslavement of the erotic energies of human bodies. As theologian H. A. Williams understands it, the historical splitting of mind from body, and subsequent repression of the body and the force of Eros, has culminated in the nuclear threat. The split first takes effect when the body is condemned and made into a slave, understood alternately as an animal or machine, which is kept under the control of the mind. But this, Williams (1972, 33) warns, is a profoundly dangerous arrangement. For: "Being in hell, the place of undead, they [bodies] are always somehow planning and threatening their revenge, they may in the end catapult us into nuclear catastrophe. . . . The body deprived of Eros inevitably becomes the champion of thanatos."

This link between the diminishment of Eros and nuclear levels of human destructiveness informs the "classic" sex film *Café Flesh* (1982). The setting is a post-nuclear holocaust future. Most survivors have lost their capacity for bodily pleasure and, left only with voyeurism, enslave the few still functional "sex positives" to perform for them in Café Flesh. Further insight into the sex-nuclear conundrum can be gleaned by contemplating the meaning of *Mr. MX* as well as a "peace poster" from the 1980s by Japanese artist Takeshi Otaka. This depicts four increasingly distorted images of Marilyn Monroe's smiling face, forming an atomic mushroom cloud. Monroe and other desirable women are "sex bombs," while the most virile men are reckoned as kin to weapons of mass destruction. All such popular images direct us to a realization that nuclear weapons manifest our erotic energies—enslaved, repressed, reshaped and now aimed right back at us.

Nuclear Fundamentalism

[God] by His most powerful Hand, . . . holdeth backe the
Sythe of Tyme from destroying or imparying the Universe . . .
the same Hand shall at last destroy the Whole by Fire.
George Hakewill, 1630 (quoted in P. Miller, 1956, 220)

Atomic power, atomic power, was given by the mighty hand
of God.
"Atomic Power," song by the Buchanan Brothers (1946)

In the early 1980s, one of my students, a U.S. marine, brought me a poster that another marine had given him. The poster disturbed him, he said, because it made nuclear war seem desirable—religiously and sexually (fig. 10.2). The image is a spewing mushroom cloud. In the center is posed the ultimate nuclear question: "Is there a future?" At the bottom is our answer: a crucifix on a hill with the words, "Yes. I'm coming. Jesus Christ."

Here and in countless cultural references, nuclear technology is imbued with a sacred aura, frequently being cast as either a deity or a manifestation of the deity's will on earth. The historian of religion Ira Chernus (1986, 153) has argued that nuclear weapons carry symbolic meanings that are extremely similar to traditional religious categories describing attributes of divinity: "awesome and limitless power, omniscience, eternity, and omnipresence," as well as mystery and irrationality. Exploring the various symbolic ramifications of "the Bomb," Chernus concludes that this "technology culture has made a death machine its deity." Just as the images discussed earlier reveal a connection between patriarchal sexuality and nuclear weaponry and technologies, so also do the many manifestations of "nuclear fundamentalism," a term originated by Robert Lifton (Lifton and Falk 1991, 87), reveal an underlying bond between patriarchal religious tradition and Western men's invention and embrace of weapons that, they proudly claim, are capable of destroying the earth.

This association between patriarchal religion and nuclear technology goes back to Los Alamos: The chief scientist there, J. Robert Oppenheimer, code-named the first atomic explosion "Trinity," conjuring up in most people's minds the Christian god. Upon witnessing the first fireball, he broke into a recitation from the *Bhagavad Gita:* "The radiance of a thousand suns . . . like the splendor of the Mighty One. . . . I am become death, the shatterer of worlds." General Leslie Farrell, military chief for the project, had an equally revealing response: "We puny things were blasphemous to dare tamper with the forces heretofore reserved to the Almighty" (quoted in Jungk, 1958, 201). After ordering the first military use of the bomb, President Harry Truman informed the American public that this act represented the "harnessing of the basic power of the Universe." He further intoned: "We thank God that it has come to us instead of to our enemies: and we pray that He may guide us to use it in His ways and for His purposes" (quoted in Boyer, 1985, 6). Most melodramatic of all, once again, were the litanies of journalist William L. Laurence, describing his visions at the Trinity site: "It was as though the earth had opened and the skies had split. One felt as though he had been privileged to witness the Birth of the World—to be present at the moment of Creation when the Lord said: 'Let there be

10.2 Christian poster, c. 1979

Light'" (Laurence, 1945). Country, pop, and gospel musicians immediately incorporated many of these themes into their tunes, coming up with such winning numbers as "Jesus Hits Like an Atom Bomb."

Years later, it became clear that many Indian nuclearists approved of Oppenheimer's recitation. India's nuclear weapons program draws openly upon Hindu myth and symbolism: "The name of one Indian rocket, the Agni, means 'god of fire' in Sanskrit. Tirshul, another missile, stands for the trident of righteousness held by Vishnu. The nuclear bomb tests in May were code-named Shakti, which means cosmic [feminine] energy" (Marquand, 1998).

These metaphors, again, are not truly unexpected: The forces associated with nuclear technology recapitulate in many ways traditional tropes associated with divinity, most vividly in the common association of divinity with light, and with the near-universal understanding of "magicoreligious power as 'burning'" (Eliade, 1958b, 85). Divine power frequently has been conceptualized as unbearably *hot* and so filled with light as to be blinding. Humans are indeed unable to look upon the atomic fireball without going blind—rather like the standard punishment for those who foolishly gaze upon the nakedness of goddesses (Chevalier and Gheerbrant, 1994, 100).

The word *sacred* derives from the Latin *sacer*, which meant "untouchable" in the dual sense of both holy and unclean (B. Walker, 1983, 876). Roger Caillois (1959, 21) writes that the sacred "is always, more or less, 'what one cannot approach without dying,'" or, Paula Gunn Allen suggests, something not to be "touched or approached by any who are weaker than the power itself" (1986a, 28). The sacred must always be rigorously separated from what is profane. It is the essence of what is "taboo," something "empowered in a ritual sense" (ibid.). Caillois describes torments that would afflict the transgressor of the taboo: flesh withering, death with languor and convulsions, and other torments that sound very much like those afflicting someone in the throes of radiation sickness.

Throughout popular culture, radiation is linked to the sacred and the bomb to the divine. In the fabulous *Beneath the Planet of the Apes* (Ted Post, 1970), postholocaust mutants literally bow down before the bomb/ god that, by film's end, destroys them. That same metaphor appears in the U.S. cult comic book series *The Watchmen* (Moore, 1986), featuring a nuclear superhero, "Dr. Manhattan" (a scientist who disintegrated in a nuclear accident, only to reform as a "wholly original entity [with a] complete mastery of all matter"). This Dr. Manhattan, who clearly functions as a symbol of nuclear technology itself, is simultaneously understood as a divinity. In *The Watchmen*, a university professor discusses the global impact of this new superhero: "'*God* exists and he's American.' If that statement starts to chill you after a couple of moments' consideration, then don't be alarmed. A feeling of intense and crushing religious terror at the concept indicates only that you are still sane. . . . I do not believe we have made a man to end wars. I believe we have made a man to end worlds." *The Watchmen* is particularly interesting because it explicitly ties the cultural divinization of nuclear weaponry to the quintessentially patriarchal godlike power of unnatural death-dealing and that same god's penchant for arbitrarily destroying worlds.

The Jesuit Pierre Teillard de Chardin (1964, 151–53) recognized the importance of nuclearism to Catholic theology: "The fact remains that in laying hands on the very core of matter we have disclosed to human existence a supreme purpose: the purpose of pursuing, ever further, to the very end, the forces of Life. In exploding the atom we took our first bite at the fruit of great discovery, and this was enough for a taste to enter our mouths that can never be washed away: the taste for super-creativeness. . . . [T]he final effect of the light cast by the atomic fire into the spiritual depths of the earth is to illuminate within them the overriding question of the end of Evolution—that is to say, the problem of God."

Teilhard de Chardin is claiming that with the discovery of atomic fission, man drew nearer to being "super-creative"—essentially, nearer to being like God. Of course, what he perceives as "laying hands" on the very core of matter, feminists understand as a rape of nature, fulfilling a centuries-long (religious and sexual) tradition of science as forced penetration into female mysteries (Merchant 1980, 164–90; Weart 1989, 57–58). Man's "super-creativeness" is actually a "super-destructiveness." The pursuit of Life to which he refers is really a predatory hunt or a stalking. And the "end of Evolution" is the familiar earthly apocalypse to which Christianity historically has been committed. Reading between the lines, we might realize that the newfound nuclear grace is not really about furthering Life but, rather, about the extension of the power that patriarchal culture truly worships and understands as god-like: the power to *take* life in cosmic proportions, to birth death, to shatter worlds.

When trying to fathom why Western science invented the technology of atomic destruction, we first might recall Alice Walker's (1988, 148) insight that it is not "inventiveness" that characterizes "the Wasichu"

(Western patriarchal men), but rather "unnaturalness." She asks us to realize "that even tiny insects in the South American jungle know how to make plastic, for instance; they have simply chosen not to cover the Earth with it." When further contemplating phallotechnological culture's pronuclear choice, we might also recall Mary Daly's (1984, 10) argument that Christianity—with its commitment to necrophilia, systemic hatred of women, destructive opposition to nature, and consecrated warfare against the "elemental"—"paved the way for modern technological warfare against the elements, which takes such forms as nuclearism and chemical contamination."

Indeed, the history of Christianity is marked by a passion for earthly apocalypse. In his essay "The End of the World," Perry Miller (1956) traces Christian eschatological thought in Puritan America at the time of the scientific revolution, showing that after Kepler and Copernicus, theologians struggled mightily to demonstrate the continued "feasibility of destruction," arguing that an "explosion" rather than "arbitrary influence" now was required to destroy the earth, and proposing such forces as comets to do the job. Miller writes: "There is no more curious phenomenon in the history of our civilization than the fact that the triumph of modern physics over the imagination of mankind was achieved by a sustained effort to prove that such a triumph was not only compatible with the cherished hope [for the end of the world] but that actually it was confirmation, a veritable guarantee, of an approaching, colossally violent catastrophe" (222–23). Twentieth-century physicists made good on that guarantee: By inventing atomic power, they inarguably demonstrated the scientific "feasibility of destruction." By thus providing a practical means that they believe could incinerate the earth, the atomic scientists honored and perhaps unconsciously acted from patriarchal religion's unwavering desire for the apocalyptic fires. Atomic technology was invented not because Western patriarchy is the most "advanced" culture ever on earth. Nuclear and other apocalyptic technologies result more from cultural regression and the *loss* of an earlier, elemental wisdom and intelligence. Patriarchal men seek nuclear power not because they are so smart, but because that power fulfills the dominant paradigm of phallic sexuality, as well as the companion conception of male divinity.

Science fictions allow their authors to identify otherwise repressed or denied tendencies in the contemporary world by safely displacing them onto future ones. The intermeshing of the phallic sexual and sacred nuclear paradigms is vividly recognized in Russell Hoban's (1980) novel *Riddley Walker*. In this postholocaust world, humanity has lost much of its intelligence, evidenced by the vulgar orthography of current culture. On a quest for the nuclear power that destroyed the old world, the hero, Riddley Walker, journeys to Canterbury ("Cambry"), the site of the most powerful nuclear blast. Musing on the "Big Power"—alternately, the "Spirit of God"—that he seeks, Riddley undergoes an epiphany:

> Funny feeling come on me then I fealt like that Power wer a Big Old Father . . . I wantit it to come in to me hard and strong long and strong.
>   Let me be your boy, I thot.
>   Stanning on them old broakin stoans I fealt like it *wer* coming in to me and taking me strong. Fealt like it wer the han of Power clampt on the back of my neck, fealt the Big old Father spread me and take me . . .
>   And stil I fealt a nother way. . . . I knowit Cambry Senter ben flattent the werst of all the dead town senters it ben Zero Groun it ben where the wite shadderd stood up over every thing. Yet unnder neath that Zero Groun I lissent up a swarming it wer a humming like a millying of bees it wer like 10s of millyings. I begun to feal all juicy with it. Juicy for a woman. Longing for it hard and hevvy stanning ready. Not jus my cock but all of me it wer like all of me were cock and the worl a cunt and open to me. (158–59)

Two desires result from Riddley's two-pronged sacred/sexual experience of nuclear power as a Big Old Father: At first, he feels himself to be puny and willingly succumbs to that Father; second, he wants to take the Almighty phallic power and use it to destroy the earth (he does find that he is not yet man enough for that). This passage neatly expresses the pact that men have made with their God: If they bow/boy to the Big Old Father/God, the payoff will be their ultimate assumption of that divine paternal privilege to dominate, rape, and destroy all others.

This is the sexualized lure that, in part, drives the patriarchal culture's obsessive pursuit of nuclear weaponry: that weaponry's potential to externalize the (imagined) omnipotently destructive phallus as well as its ability to confer upon some men their own definition of divinity. Phallic notions of power, sexuality, and divinity collapse into one unholy trinity: god the rapist, god the ripper, god the shatterer of wombs and worlds. There are, however, other definitions of divinity, ancient ones and ones that are now emerging in response to nuclearism. I turn now to the wealth of metaphors that recognize a feminine force in nuclear power.

On Beautiful Women, Sex Bombs, and War Goddesses

What is sacred is simultaneously held in greatest esteem and greatest fear. It is the source of life and the power to take life away. From it man expects all rewards, success, and power; yet as a force greater than he, it might bring punishment, failure, and degradation. . . . Man is ambivalent toward the sacred; he respects that which is greater than himself, desiring to possess and control it; but, in addition, he fears it, wishing to avoid its negative powers.

> Richard Stivers (1982, 32)

Taboos against contact with "menstrous persons" [menstruating women] are worldwide, and occur throughout history. . . . In them, the woman is treated as a scientist treats a dangerous piece of radioactive material. . . . Radioactivity is the basic, archaic power of the universe. It is terribly destructive if incorrectly handled. Nevertheless, hydrogen fusion in the solar system created the planets, and the radiation from our star, which comes from the processes which are utilized in the hydrogen bomb, created life on our planet, and feeds us all day by day in the food chain beginning with photosynthesis. We would like to suggest that the analogy is worth following through, since an acknowledgment of paradoxical benefit and danger is also the characteristic of menstrual taboos.

> Penelope Shuttle and Peter Redgrove (1986, 57)

I am your best fear
I am your worst fantasy.

> Placard held by a Women's Liberation demonstrator, 1970

Though its initial imagery suggested that the atomic bomb was a "Little Boy," a sex change soon took place. The bomb dropped on Bikini Atoll in 1948 was named "Gilda," after a famous Rita Hayworth portrayal of a femme fatale, and a pinup image of Hayworth was painted onto the bomb itself (an act that enraged her). Film critic Michael Wood (1975, 51) muses: "The phallic agent of destruction underwent a sex change, and the delight and terror of our new power were channeled into an old and familiar story: our fear and love of women. We got rid of guilt too: If women are to blame, starting with Eve perhaps, or Mother Nature, then men can't be to blame."

Throughout the nuclear age a persistent imagery continues to link passive and subservient women with nuclear benevolence, and active and autonomous femmes fatales with destructive nuclear weaponry.

The historian Elaine May (1988, 110–11) notes that in the 1950s popular symbols made "connections between the fears of atomic power, sex, and women out of control." Concomitantly, political rhetoric and imagery associated the taming or containing of the atom with the domestication and control of women, with making women not only pliant but also productive and reproductive.

An exhibit in the Atomic Museum in Los Alamos is devoted to an early nuclear reactor named "Lady Godiva." A graphic depicts the lithesome lady on her horse, with luxuriant blond hair shielding her nakedness. There is an extensive goddess myth behind this familiar story. The name *Godiva* "is simply a combination of three different ways of saying 'Goddess'" (B. Walker, 1983, 347). The legend of Lady Godiva's naked ride evolved from the pre-Christian British goddess's annual May Eve procession. Sometimes there were two complementary Ladies, white and black, representing life and death, summer and winter: two inextricable aspects of one cosmic force. According to the story, Peeping Tom dared to spy on her nakedness and, for that act of disrespect, was struck blind.

Patriarchal myth sunders the harmonious dualism of the feminine principle represented by Godiva and other goddess figures, demonizing the "dark" side and attempting to corral the "light" side and put it to use. Such mythic structuring informs an unintentionally risible ad for nuclear power plants (Crouse, 1976). A drawing shows a superfeminine young white woman in a see-through negligee with a flower at her breast (fig. 10.3). Numerous viewers have told me that the ad reminds them of 1950s-era ads for sanitary napkins. Maybe it's the flower ("having your flowers" is a traditional euphemism for a menstrual period). Maybe it is the hyperbolic assertion of modesty and decorum. In any event, the ad unmistakably if subtly evokes the universal association of menstruation with cosmic forces of creation and destruction—here, forces that are firmly under the control of men. The "beautiful woman" is shy and submissive. She keeps her gaze down and to the side, and stands in a position of receptivity, with one leg out, emphasizing her hips and genitals. The copy reads:

> Why is a beautiful woman like a nuclear power plant? In order to remain beautiful she must take good care of herself . . . she schedules her rest regularly . . . when she is not feeling well she sees her doctor . . . she never lets herself get out of shape . . . she is as trim now as she was ten years ago . . . in other words, *she is a perfect example of preventative maintenance.*

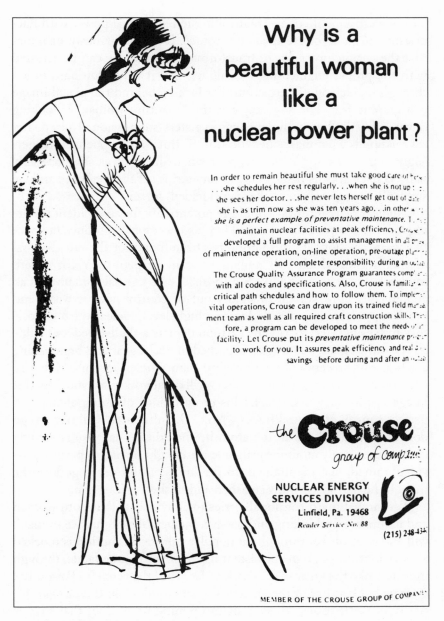

10.3 Crouse Group of Companies ad, 1976

This advertisement equates controlling female sexual power with harnessing the atom for use as a power source. It also, ludicrously, imagines that the cosmic processes of transformation somehow can be arrested with the proper engineering techniques. But it is not too hard to see through its illusion of perfection. For lurking behind the placid image is a graphic fear. For now, anyway, the "beautiful woman" is looking down—that is, her body language registers submission. Indeed, her submission is what makes her "beautiful." But what happens if she gets "ugly" and looks up? What happens when she ages, as she inevitably will? What happens if she gets hot and strips off that negligee and we suddenly have to face her naked (unshielded) force?

Nuclear reactors always hold the potentiality for an accident resulting in a catastrophic meltdown. They also necessarily produce radioactive waste. No long-term solution has been found for the safe disposal of that waste, which will remain toxic in perpetuity. With superb mythic logic, cartoonist Mike Smith (1988) uses a visual metaphor of an archetypally ugly woman to signify out-of-control nuclear waste and mock supporters of a plan to locate a high-level nuclear waste repository in Nevada (fig. 10.4). The cartoon depicts a skull-faced and wild-haired old woman, a Dominatrix garbed in S&M gear and brandishing a whip. She towers over a groveling man who proclaims: "Oh yes, Madam Nuke Dump, we pro-nukers will do anything for you." As this image vividly suggests, despite his protestations of omnipotence and perfect control of natural forces, "Mr. MX" ultimately will have to go down on bended knee to the atom he thought he had so masterfully split, to the unruly feminine principle he thought he had so perfectly divided, tamed, and maintained, to the life, sex, and death goddess he thought he had successfully smashed and trashed so long ago.

Patriarchal myth continually tries to convince us that both women and nature are unthinking and passive, ineluctably submissive to man's will and control. Yet throughout popular culture this notion is mocked as fallacious: through the persistent figure of the femme fatale, through monsters like the great white shark in *Jaws* and the vengeful Poison Ivy, a comic book avatar of the ancient Green Goddess, in the *Batman* series (Checkett, 2001). All such figures remind us, as does that snappy margarine commercial from the late 1960s: "It's not nice to fool Mother Nature."

The need to respect nature—and nature's profound ability to "fight back" if disrespected—is a foundational theme in oral traditions around the world. In 1991 the Cherokee thinker Marilou Awiakta gave a talk

10.4 Cartoon by Mike Smith, *Las Vegas Sun*, 1988

concerning her philosophical understanding of nuclear power as both feminine and sacred, of the need for respect, and of the earth's punitive response to human depredations. A Navajo lawyer in the audience, Leonard Tsosie, made this comment in response: "One time in listening to an elderly Navajo man talking about the atom, one of the things that I remember him saying is that Mother Earth is good, but Mother Earth also has to protect herself, and you can only go so far before you trigger Mother Earth's response. And one of the things that he was talking about—in Navajo we call it *'ant'iih*—meaning something that is bad. And if you keep digging and digging and digging, that elderly man said, eventually you will find Mother Earth's *'ant'iih*. And then that's when we all go. When we dig that up. We may have gotten to the *'ant'iih*, and, if that is the case, that may be the end."

Nuclearist thinking is filled with absurdities. The first is that the product of the collaboration of the very best international scientists, resulting in what is widely perceived as Western civilization's crowning technological achievement, is the Bomb: the ultimate mass murder and suicide machine. Another absurdity can be found in the belief, often held even by those who are antinuclear, that mankind somehow holds the very fate of the earth in its hands—and not the other way around. But the truth is that it is humans who are dependent on the earth for survival. The earth does not passively suffer human depredations. The earth fights back—with global warming, epidemics, natural disasters, and the radioactive toxicity of the very elements that humans, uninvited, wrest from her depths. Moreover, the earth has a fate, a purpose or destiny, which humans participate in but which they by no means control. The nuclear age and its transformations demand an end to such human-centric hubris and a new understanding of our relationship and place in the cosmos. Guidance for that neo/geocentric perspective can be found in abundance in Native American cosmologies.

Why a Thinking Woman Is Like a Nuclear Power Plant

Ts'its'tsi'nako, Thought-Woman
is sitting in her room
and whatever she thinks about
appears.

She thought of her sisters,
Nau'ts'ity'i and I'tcts'ity'i,
and together they created the Universe
this world
and the four worlds below.

Thought-Woman, the spider,
named things and
as she named them
they appeared.

She is sitting in her room
thinking of a story now.

I'm telling you the story,
she is thinking.

Leslie Marmon Silko (1977, 1)

Around the turn of the century . . . a few scientists began to observe the atom asserting its nature. . . . Perhaps the universe resembled a great thought more than a great machine.

Marilou Awiakta (1986, 185–86)

The universe is made of stories
not of atoms.

Muriel Rukeyser (1994, 231)

In much of Euro-American feminist thinking (including my own), the primary impulse has been to expose the phallic character of nuclear technology and weaponry and to oppose that force. Yet in the writings of some Native American thinkers—the novelists, essayists, and poets Paula Gunn Allen, Marilou Awiakta, Leslie Marmon Silko, and Carol Lee Sanchez—the predominant movement is to reclaim the atom from its immurement in phallocentric language, sexuality, and religion and to recall its repressed sacred gynocentric face.

Sanchez, a Laguna Pueblo (New Mexico) poet and artist, deplores the modern Western schism between the sacred and the profane and contrasts it with the tribal tradition that recognizes "all things in the known universe to be equally sacred" (1989, 346). She believes that modern peoples must not only acknowledge the sacredness of everyday life, but also "create new songs of acknowledgement as well as ceremonies that include metals, petrochemicals, and fossil fuels, electricity, modern solar power systems, and water power systems. . . .[I]t is very important to make sacred . . . the new ways and elements in our lives— from nuclear power . . . to plastics to computers . . . in order to restore harmony and balance to our out-of-control systems and, in particular, to our modern technologies" (352–53).

Of course, in one sense Western culture already holds "sacred" its technologies. "Songs" to nuclear power, reiterating the potent masculinity of the warhead, the promise of religious and sexual ecstasy in annihilation, and the captivity of female power, underlie many of the ads, popular tunes, and metaphors described in this chapter. Yet this brand of worship stems from a worldview that reveres splitting, domination, and hierarchy, not balance, as the basic principles of the universe. Sanchez insists that those who resist technological depredations must neither worship nor demonize technology but instead acknowledge its sacredness while thinking and acting in ways that restore harmony and balance. One way to achieve this is to understand atomic power through sacred gynocentric metaphor.

Like Sanchez, Marilou Awiakta points to modern culture's profound irreverence toward atomic power (manifested in the destructiveness of the bomb and the Three Mile Island disaster) and, correspondingly, toward women. Awiakta has long pondered the sacred significance of atomic power, which she understands as "the life force in process— nurturing, enabling, enduring, fierce. I call it the atom's mother heart" (1986, 186). As such, she feels herself to be neither pro- or antinuclear, but "pro-reverence" (Crowe, 1990, 45). Moreover, the atomic age has special, even ontological, significance for women: "The linear Western, masculine mode of thought has been too intent on conquering nature to learn from her a basic truth: *to separate the gender that bears life from the power to sustain it is as destructive as to tempt nature itself*.... But the atom's mother heart makes it impossible to ignore this truth any longer. She is the interpreter not only of new images and mental connections for humanity, but also, most particularly for women, who have profound responsibilities in solving the nuclear dilemma."

The "mother heart" is the first of several female metaphors through which Awiakta understands nuclear energy. Astonishingly, as a child growing up near the nuclear reservation in Oak Ridge, Tennessee, she too found a "woman" in a nuclear power plant. She recalls this scene from her childhood: "Scientists called the reactor 'The Lady' and, in moments of high emotion, referred to her as 'our beloved reactor.' 'What does she look like Daddy?' 'They tell me she has a seven foot shield of concrete around a graphite core, where the atom is split.' I asked the color of graphite. 'Black,' he said. And I imagined a great, black queen, standing behind her shield, holding the splitting atom in the shelter of her arms."[1]

The reference to the "black queen" suggests the Black Goddess or Madonna. Religious historian Ean Begg (1996, 27) notes that over four hundred of the world's images of the Madonna are black and that such figures represent the "elemental and uncontrollable source of life, possessing a spirit and wisdom of its own not subject to organization or laws of rationality." Instead of a possessed "beauty," Awiakta's vision is of an autonomous and infinitely powerful cosmic being, her experience a modern encounter with the ancient "Black Madonna."

The Laguna/Lakota philosopher Paula Gunn Allen similarly finds "elemental and uncontrollable" female power in nuclear power, not in the reactor but, boldly, in the bomb itself. In a published excerpt from her novel-in-progress *Raven's Road* (1986b, 56) two Native American lesbians, Raven and Allie, deliberately station themselves to watch the blast from an above-ground test. Allie, who has done this before and anticipates the response, asks Raven what she saw in the cloud. Scarcely believing herself, Raven remembers, "An old woman . . . I remember now. I saw an old woman's face." Through such daring figuration, Allen defies the masculinist hubris that sees only a fatherly face in cosmic force and figures the feminine only as passive and acquiescent.

The Keres people are a language group of Southwest Pueblo peoples, including Laguna and other New Mexico pueblos. In their theology, the original creator is Thought Woman, or Spider Grandmother, who continually thinks, dreams, and spins the world into being. Allen roots the exigencies of the nuclear age firmly in that spirituality: "I know that she's the lady that made the uranium and she's the lady that made radioactivity, and she's the lady that dreamed the dream of nuclear fission. She dreamed it. Men could not have found the idea if she didn't give it to them. What she dreams, and that's what Thought Woman does, what she says, what she dreams, becomes" (Caputi, 1990b, 62). Thought Woman is part of a *trinity* of sisters. Long ago, Naotsete, Sun Woman, quarreled with her sister Iyatiku, Corn Woman, and left. Allen continues: "Around Laguna they say she's come back. And they say it with respect to the bomb. And 'she' is Naotsete, who is Sun Woman. . . . I can't think of anything more vividly Sun Woman than the bomb."

Another Laguna thinker, Leslie Marmon Silko (1977), also addresses nuclear spirituality in her novel *Ceremony*. The narrative opens by recounting the creation narrative of Thought Woman (quoted above) and then tells the story (interspersed with further Laguna myth) of the psychic healing of a mixed-blood World War II veteran, Tayo. Ultimately, his restoration to health is tied to a healing for the planet, besieged by the "destroyers," forces of evil whose latest manifestation is nuclear weaponry. Silko does not find female energy in that weaponry; rather, the events leading to its discovery (including the creation of the white race) were set into motion by evil Indian "witches." Nevertheless, in *Ceremony* the advent of the nuclear age again signals the return of female divine force, embodied in Tayo's supernatural helper Ts'eh. Writing in *The Sacred Hoop*, Paula Gunn Allen (1986a, 118-19) identifies Ts'eh with primal female force: "There is not a symbol in the tale that is not in some way connected with womanness, that does not in some way relate back to Ts'eh and through her to the universal feminine principle of creation."

While Silko differs from Allen in her understanding of nuclear power, both intuit that the atomic age, begun in New Mexico on Native lands, is profoundly connected to the Native *trinity* of sister supernaturals, particularly the eldest, Thought Woman. All of these thinkers insist that we face nuclear technology as rooted in the feminine and in the sacred and, moreover, that we perceive that sacred as an active and mindful principle.

To do so requires that we shed the limits imposed by those deeply grooved sexist psychic patterns that, for example, project the feminine principle as some drudge who unthinkingly gives unconditional love, works for free, and patiently cleans up any mess left for her. An alternative sexist supposition regarding the "Mother" is that she is mindlessly fixed on her function of breeding. The psychiatrist Wolfgang Lederer, while recognizing the atom and bomb as female, roots his mythic analysis in a decidedly infantile point of view: He first portrays Mother Nature and women themselves as voracious breeders, worshipping at the "shrine of [their] . . . own sex" (1968, 246). It is these frenziedly fertile females who are threatening the planet with overpopulation and hence extinction, according to Lederer—not male leaders of world religions who prohibit birth control and abortion, not the mostly male scientists who plot chemical, biological, and nuclear devastations in their spotless laboratories, not the mostly male militarists who strategize their use, and not the mostly male-led corporations who mindlessly dump toxic wastes.

Lederer claims that the "natural" solution to the "human glut" produced by this mindless Mother Nature is her equally mindless death reflex: "And in the end the balance of this globe may yet again have to be redressed by the Great Mother herself in her most terrible form: as hunger, as pestilence, as the blind orgasm of the atom" (1968, 248). *Blind* here is a synonym for *thoughtlessness*. In patriarchal myths like this one, Thought Woman herself is rendered thoughtless. She becomes a mass sexual murderer, fixated only on her own "orgasm" at the expense of her victim (all of humanity!). But Lederer has it all precisely backwards: It is not the frenzied mindlessness of the feminine principle that threatens us, but human negation and ongoing disrespect of that principle. Furthermore, the monotheistic all-male godhead, the Big Old Father who has inspired nuclear domination, falls short in one key area: While he easily can be imagined as ending worlds, he cannot on his own accomplish a rebirth.

But what happens when we reintroduce the feminine principle into the nuclear stew? When we place nuclear technology in the context of a gynocentric sacred, the discussion can shift from "apocalypse now" to the possibility of continuance.[2] When we comprehend both nature and the feminine as the very quintessence of *Thought*, and as sacred, purposeful, and sovereign, we would have to put respect or reverence—not a quest for omnipotent/domineering power—at the core of our relationship to the atom and the elements.

Respect means using the earth's resources sparingly and with great caution. Frequently, resources should be left utterly alone. We should not dig up uranium without knowing how to rebury it sacredly/safely.

Right now, uranium returns to us as perpetually toxic waste, the un-shielded and outraged elements demanding justice. In nuclear waste we can recognize a modern manifestation of the Erinyes or Furies (B. Walker, 1983, 327), those three goddesses in Greek myth who enact ret-ribution after any act of disrespect against the Mother, most especially matricide, and any violations of the natural order.

I began this chapter with Edward Whitmont's reminder (1982, viii) that if we grant "the Goddess" her due and respect her, "she may com-passionately guide us toward transformation." Whitmont is mythically astute in putting the stress on transformation—the core metaphysical meaning of the nuclear age. This core meaning is signaled by the nature of radioactivity. For radioactivity itself is an energetic effect indicating that one element is transforming into another.

Any number of science fiction superheroes, beginning with Super-man and continuing through The Hulk, Poison Ivy, and the Teenage Mutant Ninja Turtles, transmute and subsequently acquire sacred/super powers after they have come into contact with radioactivity or chemical and nuclear waste. An ancient relative of this popular myth is the cycle of stories in which someone, usually by accident, beholds the naked goddess. As with Peeping Tom, they might be struck blind. Sometimes, though, they are transformed into the other sex or into a creature— something that might kill them or that might make them stronger.[3]

The myth is still true. Humans cannot look upon the naked goddess (including, in her nuclear manifestations, the exploding Bomb and toxic waste) and "live"; that is, they cannot remain psycho-physically unchanged. The still-unfolding mythic fallout of the nuclear event is the radical reordering of perceptions and identities, the smashing not only of atoms, but also inevitably of the paradigms that brought us to this moment.

Patriarchal civilization is finished/dead. But, like the ghouls in George Romero's 1968 film *Night of the Living Dead*, it doesn't fully re-alize it yet.[4] This system no longer guarantees a future; indeed, it prom-ises only futurelessness. It is biting the breast that feeds it, eating its own Mother (Sjöö and Mor, 1991, 412). Its final cause, epitomized in the invention of the bomb, is an utterly apocalyptic one; its wasteful and rapist practices are ravaging the earth and the elements. This real-ization, whether conscious or not, motivates, on the one hand, a des-perate and futile attempt to find salvation by reverting to patriarchal political and religious fundamentals. On the other, it has caused the eruption of manifold, ongoing liberation movements—civil rights, women's liberation, gay, lesbian, and transgender liberation, animal rights, green consciousness—seeking to transform those fundamentals.

Having gazed uninvited upon the sacred, humans have been issued an ironic invitation, one that cannot really be refused, an invitation to change our way of life, or end our existence. Perhaps civilization will take all of us out with it. But perhaps it will turn out that the world that patriarchy shatters is its very own. In her poem "The Fifties," the Hopi poet Wendy Rose (1989, 60–61) recalls her childhood during the Cold War years, when she and other schoolchildren practiced "how to die / in a foetal position" under their desks at school. All grown up, she now muses:

> Once again
> We scan our western expanse of sky
> Not for bombers and Russians
> But for a thing more final
> Than antique atom bombs.
> Like earthquakes
> Crawling up the Richter scale
> The ghosts of our future
> Are unpredictable
> And out of control.
>
> This is a weather report:
> Who knows what will end
> In the fury of the storm?

11

Unthinkable Fathering

Connecting Incest and Nuclearism

> Like the arms race during the Cold War, the incestuous father
> is also out of control. He fails to honor his most basic respon-
> sibility as a parent—to protect the child. . . . His fathering is
> unthinkable.
>
> Amy Estelle (1991)

Newsweek's cover for October 7, 1991, focuses on the post–Cold War
nuclear world order. It features a mushroom cloud. Inscribed over that
cloud are the words "The Future of the Bomb." Underneath are three
questions: "Will Bush's Plan Work? Can We Trust the Soviets? What Is
Saddam Hiding?" This is fairly ordinary weekly news magazine matter.
Yet the whole meaning of this communiqué changes when we factor in
the blurb at the top of the page. Above the *Newsweek* logo, referring to
another story, is the headline: "Surviving Incest. Can Memories Be
Trusted?" Elsewhere, I have argued that media messages, broadcast and
print, are constructed via a process of flow (Caputi, 1991). By this I
mean that in order to apprehend the full meaning of any media text, we
have to see it, literally, in its context. We have to take into account the
influence of whatever precedes and follows it, whatever surrounds it.
Essentially, this, or any, magazine cover is a complex package of interconnecting items that often must be read together in order to comprehend a total message. The covert message here is that there are profound bonds between incest and the Bomb.

Normative discourse denies such a connection, rendering it unspeakable, even unthinkable. Yet the repressed will return, and the truth will out—if not in official channels, then in unofficial ones. The *Newsweek* cover is by no means unique. My extensive examination of cultural productions with nuclear themes—popular films, novels, visual art, songs, and so on—reveals the regular recurrence of the theme of incestuous fatherhood. Feminist theorists have long argued that there are profound interconnections between personal forms of patriarchal violence (such as rape and sexual murder) and institutional, frequently technological and militaristic, violence (see Daly, 1978; Griffin, 1978; Caputi 1987; Davis, 1989; Russell, 1989). In this chapter I extend this approach by using popular culture, incest survivors' accounts, scientific metaphor, and feminist theoretical writings to analyze the connections between the practices of incest and nuclearism.[1]

The Nuclear Father: Warhead of the Family

An uncanny image appears on the cover of *The Outsiders* (Thomas, McFarlane, Hernandez, 1985), a D.C. comic book. A band of tiny costumed heroes, ready for battle, approaches an enormous mushroom cloud, upon which is inscribed a face that is broadly reminiscent of a 1950s sitcom dad. A pipe juts from his mouth and his expression is a lordly and sadistic know-it-all smirk. Here is a prime portrait of the cultural figure whom I call the "nuclear father"—the quintessential patriarch, the man who nominally provides for and protects his dependents but who actually threatens and violates them. This "nuclear father" figure can be found ruling over a family, a laboratory, a corporation, a military force, a church, or a nation.

In his astute study *Fathering the Unthinkable* (1983), Brian Easlea, a physicist and historian, points to a predominance of metaphors of male birth and fatherhood in the language of the Manhattan Project, the U.S. government's mission to develop the atom bomb. He and Carol Cohn (1987) perceive these metaphors as indicators of the masculinist bias steering the development of nuclear weapons. For example, in 1945, as Los Alamos scientists struggled to produce the bomb before the war ended, they took bets on whether they would produce a dud or a success—in their lingo, a "girl" or a "boy." The bomb dropped on Hiroshima was nicknamed "Little Boy," and the National Baby Association reacted to this birth/explosion by naming J. Robert Oppenheimer "Father of the Year." Oppenheimer remains the paradigmatic father figure in a select nuclear club that includes Edward Teller, "father of the U.S. H-bomb"; Glenn Seaborg, one of the "five fathers of plutonium"; Andrei Sakharov, "father of the Soviet H-bomb"; and Admiral Hyman B. Rickover, "father of America's nuclear navy."

Oppenheimer, Teller, and other such scientific nuclear fathers were widely heroized after World War II. "[M]ass murderers have always commanded the attention of the public," their colleague Leo Szilard observed, "and atomic scientists are no exception to this rule" (cited in Boyer, 1985, 61). This linkage of fatherhood and mass murder is eerily reflected in the contemporary nuclear family, where murderous mayhem is an increasingly common event.

Another kind of nuclear father was exemplified by forty-one-year-old Ernie Lasiter of Roswell, New Mexico, who in January 1992 strangled his wife and four of his children and then shot himself. A couple of days earlier, his seventeen-year-old daughter had been removed from the home by the police, who were investigating her complaint of incestuous assault by Lasiter. In the aftermath of the atrocity, a number of friends confirmed, as is typical in such cases, that Lasiter was a "good guy" and fine family man. A secretary in the highway department where he worked added, "He was very conscientious and a hard worker. He was almost like a machine" (Jadrnak, 1992). The machine that a family (war)head like Ernie Lasiter most resembles is the unendingly lethal nuclear weapon. Not only does the apocalyptically raging nuclear father have an immediate mass kill from his "blast," but the effects of his lethality linger forever in the bodies and psyches of his survivors. Eerily, the mass murder/suicide pattern of the nuclear father presages the probable fate of any nation that initiates nuclear war.

Nuclear-family men such as Lasiter seem omnipresent these days. Other family mass murderers include John List, Jeffrey MacDonald, Ramon Salcido, George Franklin, and Gene Simmons. This lethally abusive nuclear father is also represented by fictional "pop" figures such as Leland Palmer in *Twin Peaks* (1989–90), Jerry Blake in *The Stepfather* (1988), "De-Fens" in *Falling Down* (1993), and Freddy Krueger in the *Nightmare on Elm Street* film series.

Moreover, in all sorts of stories with explicit themes of nuclear weaponry and power — from comic books to popular films to elite literature — abusive fathers appear as prime metaphors for the bomb. Examples include the novels *The Nuclear Age* by Tim O'Brien (1985), *Falling Angels* by Barbara Gowdy (1990), *The Mosquito Coast* by Paul Theroux (1982), *The Prince of Tides* by Pat Conroy (1986), *A Thousand Acres* by Jane Smiley

(1991), the films *Star Wars* (1977), *Forbidden Planet* (1956), and *Desert Bloom* (1986), and even, humorously, the television show *The Simpsons*.

Of course, in his original mythic manifestations, primarily in television sitcoms, the fictionalized head of the nuclear family is the benevolent patriarch who always "knows best." During the 1950s, the heyday of the atomic culture, fatherhood became a much valorized role, and Father's Day became for the first time a holiday of national significance (May, 1988, 146). In *The Feminine Mystique* (1963) Betty Friedan connected the cult of the (white, middle-class) nuclear family with a national psyche scarred by "the loneliness of the war and the unspeakableness of the bomb." These conditions, she argued, made women particularly vulnerable to "the feminine mystique," the belief that the highest value for women was fulfillment in a femininity characterized by "sexual passivity, male domination, and nurturing maternal love" (37). At the same time, women and men also were vulnerable to a "masculine mystique," the illusion that man's rightful position was head of the family, where he was all-powerful, protective, a provider, benevolent, omniscient, essentially godlike—attributes simultaneously ascribed to America's newest weapon.

In truth, the bomb, while purportedly protecting, actually threatens. So too does the nuclear father. Just as those seeking refuge in a fallout shelter from an atomic bomb attack might instead find themselves roasted alive, those seeking security in the nuclear family might instead find themselves under attack in the form of battery, rape, incest, and mass murder. Affirming the connection of the political to the personal, and in subliminal recognition of the often apocalyptic experience of American family life, the phrase "nuclear family" established itself firmly in the national vernacular by 1947.

The film *Atomic Cafe* (Rafferty, Loader, Rafferty, 1982) is a witty compilation of clips from 1950s government and military disinformation films. These clips demonstrate the efficacy of that inflated Great White Father image in such nuclearist propaganda. Over and over, they present heavily iconic white family images: dads coming home from work; moms in the kitchen, cooking and serving; and Dick-and-Jane-type kids in the living room, watching TV. Simultaneously, we see white governmental father figures blithely assuring us of the safety of radiation and indeed of nuclear war itself. This genuflection to paternal authority was equally apparent in mainstream popular culture. Television boasted popular shows with such masterfully subtle titles as *Father Knows Best* and *Make Room for Daddy*. So dominant was the image of the white, middle-class, patriarchally ordered family that one critic claimed that "Dad's authority around the house appeared to be the whole point of the spectacle" (M. Miller, 1986, 196). Of course, that televised paternal authority also served to legitimate and ordain "Dad's" authority around the globe.

Benevolent nuclear father imagery was resurrected with great vigor during the Reagan-Bush era, when the federal government spent $4 billion per year on the Strategic Defense Initiative or "Star Wars"—Reagan's proposed space-based nuclear "defense" system. In order to persuade Americans to place their trust in him and his utterly specious project, Reagan smoothly donned the mask of the father protector, promising that his plan would offer a "new hope for our children in the twenty-first century" (1983).

Reagan's "good father" image continued in a 1985 television commercial produced by High Frontier, a pro-Star Wars lobbying group. The spot opens with a childlike drawing of a simple house. Stick figures represent a family, and there is a gloomy-faced sun. A syrupy little girl voice chirps, "I asked my daddy what this Star Wars stuff is all about. He said that right now we can't protect ourselves from nuclear weapons, and that's why the president wants to build a Peace Shield." At this point, larger red missiles appear to threaten the house, but they harmlessly disintegrate when met by a blue arc in the sky. Like magic, the grumpy sun begins to smile and the arc is transformed into a shimmering rainbow. This scenario was about as believable as Reagan's hair color. Yet credibility was not really the point. The essential message of this little package was that we, the much vaunted "American people," are children, in need of the loving protection of the all-powerful father/president. See, he can even make the sun smile.

Reagan again assumed the mask of the benevolent nuclear father in his 1984 address to the peoples of Micronesia, acknowledging the cessation of their "trust" relationship with the United States. In 1947 the United Nations had made the United States the administrator of Micronesia (which encompasses more than two thousand islands) as a "strategic trust." This action authorized the United States to use the area for military purposes. In exchange, the United States would "protect" the islands from invaders. Ironically, over the next eleven years, the real invader was the protector—the United States itself. The U.S. government tested sixty-nine atomic and hydrogen bombs on the islands, rendering some of them permanently uninhabitable. Diana Davenport, a native of Rongelap Atoll, remembers witnessing the blast of the hydrogen bomb

Bravo, dropped on neighboring Bikini Atoll in 1954: "Electricity crackled through my father's body, and during the flash my mother saw all her bones, her arms and legs, and hips, glowing through her skin. Windows shattered, animals bled through their eyes. Bikini Atoll became debris. . . . Six hours after the 'Bravo' blast, something rioted down on us, on our water and food. Like starflakes, or shavings of the moon. We danced in it, we played with it. It didn't go away. . . . We were caught in the fallout that scientists named 'Bikini Snow'" (1989, 61).

Within twenty-four hours, everyone on Rongelap showed signs of radiation sickness. The legacy of this contamination continues in the form of all sorts of health calamities: "Blindness. Thyroid tumors. Miscarriages. Jelly-fish babies. Mental retardation. Sterility. Lung cancer. Kidney cancer. Liver cancer. Sarcoma. Lymphoma. Leukemia. . . . Retardation. Infants born who leaked through one's fingers like breathing bags of jelly. Others with long, twisted pincers like crabs" (Davenport, 1989, 62). More than 50 percent of the deaths on Rongelap each year occur among children under five.

Childbirth has become, in Davenport's word, a "metaphor" for the monstrosity of the future in a post-nuclear world. With no sense of irony, nuclear father Reagan employed a metaphor of healthy children growing up and leaving home in his formal 1984 goodbye to the Marshall Islands: "Greetings. For many years a very special relationship has existed between the United States and the people of the trust territory. . . . Under the trusteeship, we've come to know and respect you as members of our American family. And now, as happens to all families, members grow up and leave home. I want you to know that we wish you all the best. . . . We look forward to continuing our close relationship to you in your new status. But you'll always be family to us" (*Half-Life* [film], Dennis O'Rourke, 1986). Here Reagan revealed himself as the ultimate unthinking and unthinkable father. His own role and the "American family" to which he referred represented, on a global scale, the "toxic parenting" and "dysfunctional family" of scores of best-selling recovery books. The "family" he described is one afflicted by a severely disordered and abusive father—one who more or less destroys the next generation, physically and/or psychically, and then denies his own horrendous behavior and tries to coerce everyone else into the denial as well.

Incest is the atrocity most paradigmatic of fatherly abuse. In her essay "The Color of Holocaust," the novelist Patricia A. Murphy uses nuclear metaphors to describe both her incest experience and the interior self of her father/perpetrator: "The nuclear winter resonates through our culture reaching into our global imagery as expressed through television. It extends into the secret heart of the family and finally into that private space inside our own skins. The color of this winter is ash, which seems to be the color of all holocausts public and private. My father and I were once children of the sky. That great blue bowl which hangs over the limitless prairie where we both experienced our childhoods a generation apart. He is the color of ash now like a stain on that sky. He smudges life itself. . . . My father has surrendered to the nuclear winter within. (1985, n.p.). Murphy reminds us that there would not be an external bomb unless a bomb also existed in the hearts of men, and that the nuclear winter is a psychic state of blight as well as a physical one. Her father, she tells us, is an artificial season, a destroyed atmosphere, a stifler of breath, life, and color, a sorry substitute for that older, original, nurturing father she simultaneously invokes: Father Sky. Barbara Gowdy's *Falling Angels* (1990) also sets up a metaphoric link between nuclear devastation and incest. This novel tells the story of a 1960s nuclear family consisting of a tyrannical and crazed father, a nearly catatonic alcoholic mother, and three daughters. One Christmas, the father bestows minimal and despised presents on his daughters, telling them that in the summer they will take a trip to Disneyland. However, in the spring, heeding media messages of an imminent Soviet attack, the father begins frenzied work on a basement A-bomb shelter. When summer arrives, his daughters find that instead of going to one newly constructed, controlled environment, Disneyland, they are to spend two weeks together in another such environment—their father's brand-new bomb shelter.

The experience in the bomb shelter is, of course, hell on earth: the water supply is insufficient and everyone drinks whiskey incessantly; the oldest daughter gets her first period, to her unbearable shame; the tyrannical father grows increasingly cranky, angry, and unpredictable; the air is foul; the toilet backs up, and the stench is unbearable. The metaphor is unmistakable: Nuclear family life, while advertised, like Disneyland, as "the happiest place on earth," actually is a lot more like life in a bomb shelter, waiting in cramped quarters amid insane behavior for the bomb to drop. In Gowdy's novel, of course, some years later the bomb does drop: The father makes incestuous advances toward the oldest daughter, and the mother kills herself by jumping off the roof of the house. The daughters, with varying degrees of damage, manage to survive.

The incest-nuclear connection also appears in the 1986 film *Desert Bloom*, a movie that could easily be subtitled *Or, How I Learned to Stop Worrying and Love My Stepfather*. Set in Las Vegas in the early 1950s as the city awaits a bomb test, the film focuses on a family composed of a mother, Lilly, her three daughters, and a stepfather, Jack. Jack is a World War II veteran, wounded in both body and spirit, who desperately seeks esteem and power through possession of "secret" information obtained via his short-wave radio. Significantly, the family keeps a number of secrets of its own. Jack is an alcoholic and a bully, lording it over his stepdaughters and his wife, who placatingly calls him "Daddy." Jack's relationship with Rose, the "blooming" pubescent oldest daughter, is charged with sexual tension: We see him verbally and physically abuse her. Moreover, Rose tells us that "Momma had a way of not seeing things." In these and other ways, the film strongly implies Jack's sexual abuse of Rose.

Eventually Rose, seeking safety, runs away. Ironically, she ends up camping out at the eminently dangerous nuclear test site, where she is found by the authorities and returned to Jack, who has followed her trail. As they drive back to the house, he tells her that he just wants to "protect" her. "From whom?" Rose asks pointedly. The film's parallel between the incestuous/abusive father and nuclear weapons is extremely persuasive. Each purportedly protects the family, and yet each, in reality, invades it and threatens to destroy its members.

"Trust Me"

> A world once divided into two armed camps now recognizes one sole and preeminent power, the United States of America. And they regard this with no dread. For the world trusts us to be on the side of decency. They trust us to do what's right. . . . As long as I am president we will continue to lead in support of freedom everywhere, not out of arrogance and not out of altruism, but for the safety and security of our children.
> George Bush, State of the Union Address, 1992

> The incest survivor can be said to be incapable of experiencing trust. She has in fact learned that words don't mean what they say, that things are not always what they seem, and that what appears safe is generally not to be believed.
> E. Sue Blume (1990, 243)

"Trust" is one of the key words linking incest and the bomb on *Newsweek*'s "Future of the Bomb" cover. Witness the similarity between the incest headline, "Can Memories Be Trusted?" and the bomb headline, "Can We Trust the Soviets?" Frankly, both of these questions desperately displace the really important concern about trust. That is: Can we trust our fathers, grandfathers, uncles, brothers, priests, old family friends, neighbors, doctors, and teachers around issues of safety for children? At the same time, based on past deceptions by nuclear authorities, it is absurd to place much trust in the U.S. government, military, and associated nuclear facilities around issues of nuclear safety.

When I was about twelve, the older boys in my neighborhood used to sexually harass girls by playing a game called "Trust Me." A boy would put his hand on the top button of a girl's blouse, unbutton it, and ask, "Trust me?" The girl was supposed to say "yes," even as he proceeded to uncover her breasts or shove his hand down her pants, all the while reiterating, "Trust me?"

During the 1950s U.S. military and government officials played "Trust Me" not only with the Pacific peoples of the United Nations "trust territory" but also with countless U.S. citizens, including lower-echelon military personnel, who, as part of their duties, were exposed to radiation from bomb tests; the residents of northern Arizona, Nevada, and Utah, who regularly were hit with fallout from above-ground bomb tests; uranium miners (a great number of whom were Lakota, Kaibab Paiute, Navajo, and Pueblo Native Americans); and the residents of areas where nuclear production facilities such as Hanford and Oak Ridge were located.

Throughout the era of above-ground testing (1951–63), the Atomic Energy Commission and the U. S. government engaged in a "sustained and wide-ranging effort" (Boyer, 1985, 318) to fool the public about the dangers associated with nuclear development and bomb testing. In the aftermath of the attacks on Japan, the U.S. government actually denied the lethal and disabling effects of the radiation from the Hiroshima and Nagasaki bombs, dismissing statements about them as "Japanese propaganda." By 1950, the Federal Civil Defense Agency was claiming that nuclear war survival was simply a matter of "keeping one's head" and making sure to "duck and cover." In 1953, President Eisenhower advised the Atomic Energy Commission to keep the public "confused" about any hazards associated with radiation. Despite warnings from scientists such as Linus Pauling, the official line was that "low" levels of radiation were perfectly safe, that people could trust the government to protect them, and that bomb tests were in our best interest. By and large, U.S. citizens believed the government, embraced the bomb through a million popular songs and artifacts, and accepted the notion of the "peaceful atom." Many of these people later developed cancer, sterility, and other serious and frequently lethal health problems in return for their trust (Gallagher, 1993).

Now, after decades of enforced secrecy, information is being released about this massive betrayal of trust by the nuclear industry, the Atomic Energy Commission, and their supporters throughout the government. Tom Bailie is a resident of the desperately contaminated area in Washington State around the Hanford Nuclear Reservation. He characterizes his experience as a virtual rape since the day he was born: "As 'downwinders,' born and raised downwind of the Hanford Nuclear Reservation in Washington, we learned several years ago that the government decided—with cold deliberation—to use us as guinea pigs by releasing radioactivity into our food, water, milk and air without our consent. Now, we've learned that we can expect continuing cancer cases from our exposure in their 'experiment.' Is this what it feels like to be raped? The exposure began the same day our lives began" (Bailie, 1990).

Bailie observes that even after the government admitted that radioactivity had been released, residents were continually reassured that there would be no "observable" health consequences. Health effects were indeed not observed—*not* because harm was absent, but because the consequences of radioactive contamination were perceived as normal: "Unknowingly, we had been seeing the effects for a long time. For us, the unusual was the usual!" (Bailie, 1990). Bailie recalls nuclear cleanup crews, "men dressed in space suits," wandering around his town throughout his childhood, nice guys who gave him candy. He remembers the "neck massages" he and other children received from the school nurse, who was actually looking for thyroid problems. He remembers farm animal mutations, a high rate of human and animal miscarriage, and a high local cancer rate. To Bailie, all of this was "normal," including his own underdeveloped lungs and numerous birth defects. Eventually he "underwent multiple surgeries, endured paralysis, endured thyroid medication, a stint in an iron lung, loss of hair, sores all over my body, fevers, dizziness, poor hearing, asthma, teeth rotting out and, at age eighteen, a diagnosis of sterility."

Bailie's perception of the normalcy of abuse corresponds almost perfectly with testimony from people who literally were raped from birth. One incest survivor, Kyos Featherdancing, was raped by her father from the time she was a baby. Until she was nine years old, she thought that "every father did that with their daughter" (in Bass and Davis, 1988, 395). Just as Bailie "thought all kids lived with death and deformity,"

Featherdancing assumed that all kids lived with incest. She too mistook the abnormal for the normal and suffered long-term damage from the normalized abuse. In her case, this included drug addiction, alcoholism, and self-hatred.

Lifton points to the shame of many Hiroshima survivors, their "sense of impaired body substance." He observes: "Radiation effects . . . are such that the experience has had no cutoff point. Survivors have the possibility of experiencing delayed but deadly radiation effects for the rest of their lives. That possibility extends to their children, to their children's children, indefinitely into the future" (Lifton and Falk, 1991, 45–46). Like many survivors of Hiroshima, the survivors of incest often are frightened to have children, for the effects of incest, like the effects of radiation, are insidious, long term, and transmitted through generations. They, too, often lie harbored in the victim until they later erupt into disease or disorder. Some of the long-term effects of incest include fear, anxiety, anger, and hostility; eating disorders; allergies and asthma; shame; low self-esteem; guilt; depression; inability to trust or to establish relationships; phobias; multiple personality disorder; sexual dysfunction; a tendency toward revictimization through participating in such activities as prostitution, drug addiction, alcoholism, self-mutilation, and suicide (Wyatt and Powell, 1988).

Official Secrecy

Except possibly for the word *silence* and maybe the word *safety,* the word *secret* recurs more than any other in feminist discussions of incest. Florence Rush (1980), a psychiatric social worker, calls the sexual abuse of children patriarchy's "best-kept secret." The sociologist Diana Russell (1986, 16) speaks of incest as "the secret trauma," marked by "a vicious cycle of betrayal, secrecy, unaccountability, repetition, and damaged lives." Similarly, as any analyst of nuclear culture knows, an unprecedented and profoundly enforced official secrecy is the most prominent feature of the history of nuclear development (Lifton and Falk, 1991, 26).

Secrecy is fundamental to the abuse of power—sexual and otherwise. Protected by the cult of secrecy, fathers molest their daughters; priests violate their flocks; governments test nuclear weapons on human populations, including their own; and weapons laboratories and defense contractors plan, manufacture, and mismanage weapons without public knowledge, scrutiny, or criticism. Secrecy in the nuclear world, moreover, creates a select club of those "in the know," bestows a sense of privilege, and fosters in-group loyalty. It encourages the arms race, allows safety problems to remain uninvestigated and unresolved at any number of nuclear weapons facilities in both the United States and the former Soviet Union, and has enabled disastrous accidents to be completely covered up.

So, too, the truth about child sexual abuse is covered up regularly, by individual perpetrators and the enabling culture. At the outset, children are told by abusers that their sexual activity is a secret that must never be told, frequently under threat of abandonment or death (for themselves or loved ones). If the children disregard that prohibition and tell the truth, they all too often are not believed. The invalidation of children's words, the characterization of their reports as fantasy, and massive community denial and resistance to believing in the abusive practices of paternal authorities (individual or institutional) have long histories in psychoanalytic theory and everyday practice (Summitt, 1988).

This scenario of silence, secrecy, denial, avoidance, erasure, initial embrace of the trusted father-figure abuser, and victim blaming unerringly mirrors the typical responses of nuclear communities to complaints against the institutional abusers in their midst. Since Tom Bailie's family blew the whistle on the devastation caused by Hanford, "Our patriotism has been impugned, our credibility questioned. . . . We have been slandered as the 'glow in the dark family' by friends and strangers alike. . . . Moscow was condemned for its three days of silence after the Chernobyl nuclear accident. What about Washington's forty years of silence?" (Bailie, 1990).

Marylia Kelley is a resident of Livermore, California—home of the Lawrence Livermore Laboratory. She is also a founder of Tri-Valley CARE—Citizens Against a Radioactive Environment. When she moved to Livermore in 1976, she knew there was some "super-secret government facility" where almost everyone worked, but neither she nor anyone she spoke to seemed to have a clear idea about what went on there. There was some awareness of ongoing nuclear weapons work, but most people dismissed it as constituting only a small proportion, maybe 10 percent, of the lab's actual endeavors. (In truth, weapons work accounted for about 90 percent of the lab's activities.) As antinuclear activists increasingly converged upon Livermore in the 1980s, local residents like Kelley became interested in finding out the truth. Yet local activism faced resistance, since so many community members were economically dependent on the nuclear facility. After several years of deliberate noncooperation, some of the churches agreed in 1989 to sponsor a series of talks entitled "Pathways to Peace," to be held in neighboring Pleasanton. Lectures were given over a six-week period, but, Kelley reports, not once did anyone mention Lawrence Livermore Lab. As she told me in a 1993 conversation, "I felt like the community was keeping a dirty secret, and it was breaking a taboo to speak the name Livermore in a public way."

In other words, making genocidal bombs isn't taboo, but speaking out against them is. So too, as many observers note, incest is not really taboo in our culture, but speaking out against it is. The "dirty secret" scenario Kelley describes parallels the protection by family members of a trusted and/or economically powerful child abuser and the concomitant silencing of victims. Kelley concludes that one of the most important features of CARE's activism is to overcome this obeisance to secrecy and get people to "name things by their true names, to find their voice." Indeed, in order to thwart both child sexual abuse and nuclearism, we must, in the phrase commonly used by survivors, "break silence." We must begin to spill those long-held and closely guarded secrets and, concomitantly, believe the unbelievable, be it that a fine church-going family man is sexually abusing his daughter or that high rates of thyroid and brain cancer (such as those in Los Alamos) are due to radioactive contamination.

Keeping Secrets From Oneself

> "What was your family life like, Savannah?" I asked, pretending I was conducting an interview.
> "Hiroshima," she whispered.
> "And what has life been like since you left the warm, abiding bosom of your nurturing, close-knit family?"
> "Nagasaki," she said, a bitter smile on her face.
> Pat Conroy (1986, 8)

Victims of incest often seek temporary refuge in numbing, denial, and repression, keeping their worst secret even from themselves because confronting incest in their own lives is truly "thinking about the unthinkable." Pat Conroy's best-selling novel *The Prince of Tides* elaborates a complex narrative, encompassing nuclear devastations, the secrets of family life, and child rape. The book's narrator, Tom Wingo, tells us that he and his twin sister, Savannah, "entered the scene in the middle of a world war at the fearful dawning of the atomic age" (1986, 9). Their childhood was simultaneously haunted by a terror of their father's recurrent brutality, directed against them and their mother.

While the world anticipated nuclear war, their "childhood was spent waiting for him to attack."

Tom further reveals that his is "a family of well-kept secrets and they all nearly end up killing us" (97). His father, Henry Wingo, relentlessly batters his family. His mother, Lila Wingo, adamantly forbids her three children to reveal their father's brutality. She also conceals the fact that she has been stalked by a rapist and murderer. Yet the repressed returns, this time with apocalyptic virulence. The stalker and two other men escape from prison and come to the family's home while Henry is absent. They rape and try to kill Lila, Tom, and Savannah and are thwarted only because Luke, the oldest son, manages to disrupt the assaults and lead a lethal attack against the invaders. Lila orders everyone to render the event permanently unspeakable and unthinkable, meaning that everyone must wipe it from memory. Tom can't stop himself from remembering; still, he brackets that knowledge and refuses to deal with its implications or speak of it. Savannah completely expunges this and other horrific memories from her consciousness. She goes on to become an extraordinarily gifted poet, yet she regularly attempts suicide. Some years later, Lila conspires to sell off the Wingo family's South Carolina island home to the U.S. government so that it can build a nuclear weapons facility there. Utterly opposed to nuclear weapons, Luke becomes a one-man guerrilla army, battling the construction of the plant. Within a few months, he is shot and killed.

Savannah Wingo's name is not arbitrary. One of the primary U.S. nuclear weapons facilities is the Savannah River Plant, located in South Carolina. For years, Savannah River was the major source of tritium for U.S. nuclear weapons, but it was closed for the first time in 1988 because of its unsafe practices: a "long and shocking record of serious incidents of radioactive contamination and unsafe disposal of waste," hazards that the Department of Energy "has long attempted to keep . . . from public view" (Glenn, 1988, 266). The Savannah River, like the Columbia, is one of the most toxic bodies of water in the world.

Numbing, repression of memory, and denial characterize the Wingo family, patterns that serve as microcosmic mirrors for larger nuclearist abuse. Robert Jay Lifton and Eric Markusen (1990, 13) demonstrate in detail that denial, numbing, dissociation or splitting, and even "doubling" ("the formation of a functional second self") are not only classic responses of victims of genocidal practices but also characterize victimizer consciousness. In special circles, these ways of numbing are actually celebrated and encouraged. For example, General Curtis

LeMay, who oversaw the Hiroshima bombing and the creation of the Strategic Air Command (SAC), was popularly portrayed, with no onus attached, as "more machine than man." Spencer Weart notes that in his capacity as head of SAC, "LeMay took care to select only officers like himself, men who kept their feelings under strict control" (1989, 149). Bombing, as one writer explained in the *Saturday Evening Post,* "had to be done 'mechanically, with swift, sure precision, undisturbed by emotion, either of fear . . . or pity'" (ibid.). LeMay himself recalled that when he flew bombers over Germany, "his imagination had caught a picture of a little girl down below, horribly burned and crying for her mother. 'You have to turn away from the picture,' he said, 'if you intend to keep on doing the work your Nation expects of you'" (ibid.).

I wager that unapologetic incestuous abusers might sound very much like LeMay—riveted on their own conquest or pleasure and steeling themselves to turn away from the "little girl down below," crying, injured, and annihilated. Just as the survivor splits into a "day child" and a "night child" (Atler, 1991, 90), so does the abuser create a second self, enabling him to perform atrocities and to keep the secret of his depredations even from himself. With such abusers, psychic numbing means never having to say you're sorry.

Another method of inculcating nuclear numbing is to render weapons work an always unfinished jigsaw puzzle. General Leslie Groves, who was the military chief of the Manhattan Project, initiated a policy of "compartmentalization of knowledge." This policy ensured that "each man should know everything he needed to know about doing his job and nothing else" (Lifton and Falk, 1992, 26). The internalization of this mentality among nuclear workers guarantees that none of them needs to face what he or she is doing. Nearly everyone claims to perform some specialized, unrelated task. Even those technicians who acknowledge that they are making weapons often mute their awareness with truly stunning doublethink. As one weapons designer at Lawrence Livermore told an interviewer, "We're working on weapons of life, ones that will save people from weapons of death" (cited in Broad, 1985, 47). Similarly, many who commit incest deny that they are grievously injuring children. In their minds, they are pleasuring the children, helping them to attain adulthood, loving them, giving them only what they want, responding to their initiation of sex play, and so on.

In January 1991 *Time* magazine opted to name George Bush "*Men* of the Year" and actually depicted a two-faced presidential image on its cover. Such doubling nominally referred to Bush's disparate record on international and domestic affairs. Yet this image simultaneously portrayed the "doubling" propensity of nuclear fathers and prepared the nation for Bush's role as commander-in-chief of the Persian Gulf War and mass slaughter by the U.S. military. A similar construction appeared in a 1991 advertisement for the Army National Guard. It depicted a young man whose face was split precisely down the middle. On the right, it was a relatively normal face. On the left, the face was heavily painted camouflage-style; the wide-open eye stared threateningly. This ad was stark testimony to the military's normative inculcation of a secret "killer self" within the soldier. It also portrayed the fissioned configurations not only of official femininity, but also of official masculinity in the nuclear-fathered world.

Taboo Violation: Just Do It

Our mission: to boldly go where no man has gone before.
Star Trek

In scores of nuclear movies such as the 1958 *Teenage Caveman* and the 1968 *Planet of the Apes,* a recurrent motif is the "forbidden zone," an area closely guarded by taboo that no one may enter. Usually, this area is contaminated by radiation from some long-ago nuclear war. In pro-technology films like *Teenage Caveman,* the hero is the one who disregards the taboo and boldly strides into the proscribed area.

The 1956 film *Forbidden Planet* puts a different twist on this theme. A scientist, Morbius, lives alone on the paradisiacal planet Altair with his full-grown daughter, Altaira. Domestic chores are performed by a marvelously efficient robot named Robby. A spaceship from Earth arrives to find out what happened to the original landing party that came to the planet twenty years ago. Morbius attempts to make them go away. He tells them that, in essence, the entire planet is taboo to them, for there is a deadly force on the planet that killed everyone in the landing party except himself and his daughter. Nevertheless, the captain of the ship refuses to leave.

As a sexual attraction develops between the captain and the daughter, the deadly planetary force again makes an appearance, threatening the men and their ship. Ultimately, we learn that the lethal force is generated by the jealous Morbius's own mind. The planet Altair formerly was inhabited by members of a technologically superior civilization, the Krell. Although they wiped themselves out years ago "in a single night," the Krell left behind the agent of their own destruction, a vast nuclear-powered machine. Morbius, lusting for the Krell's technological knowledge, has been able to tap into the machine's power, allowing him to produce externally all that he can imagine, such as the marvelous Robby. But Morbius is operating under a mantle of denial. He is transgressing profoundly against self-, family-, and planetary-preservative taboos in his unbounded quest for both sexual and technological knowledge. The Krell machine manifests in material reality not only his conscious wishes but also his most awful unconscious thoughts and desires, unleashing "monsters from the id." The lethal planetary force, then, is actually an externalization of Morbius's unconscious. When his incestuous paradise with his "forbidden partner," his daughter, is threatened, his unconscious strikes out to eliminate the threat. In the film's climactic moment, Morbius faces his own evil self, and the experience does indeed destroy him. Romance, however, "saves" Altaira. She and the captain escape into space, bringing Robby with them, while Morbius and the planet that shares Altaira's name are blown to bits.

The word *forbidden* in the film's title speaks not only to the archetypal "forbidden knowledge" that structures both ancient myths and mad-scientist movies, but also to the forbidden incestuous relationship that the father imposes on his daughter. *Forbidden Planet* is basically a conservative movie: It sets up pairs of false dichotomies and then in a tidy resolution replaces the "bad" heterosexual domination (incest with her father) with "good" heterosexual domination (marriage to the captain). Similarly, the "bad" nuclear technology (represented by the Krell machine) is replaced with "good" nuclear technology—in the form of Robby the Robot.

Yet, however conventional, *Forbidden Planet* once again holds up for scrutiny the connection between the incestuous father and nuclearism. If we look past the film's false oppositions, we can discern an unmistakable parallel between Morbius's unbounded quest for knowledge and his incestuous depredations. As Catharine MacKinnon sums it up: "Sexual metaphors for knowing are no coincidence. . . . Feminists are beginning to understand that to know has meant to fuck" (1983, 636). Manifestly, in the patriarchal tradition, knowledge is power (domination), just as space exists to be invaded. It was this reigning pornographic paradigm of knowledge that fired the drive to gain nuclear knowledge or, as the most common scientific metaphors put it, "to penetrate the hidden mysteries," to investigate "the most intimate properties of matter," and even to "smash resistant atoms" (Weart, 1989, 58).

While social lip-service is widely given to the incest taboo, Diana Russell (1986, 16) suggests that a minimum of one of every six women in the United States has been incestuously abused. The violation of life-preservative taboo so characteristic of incestuous practice equally underwrites much technological adventuring. "[W]hen you see something that is technically sweet," J. Robert Oppenheimer avowed, "you go ahead and do it, and you argue about what to do about it only after you have had your technical success" (cited in Lifton, 1979, 425). Under the reigning ideologies of knowledge, power, and progress, there is no ethic of respect for others, no limit on phallic desires, no prudent calculation of future consequences. Whether advancing upon the "final frontier" of outer space, probing the "most intimate properties of matter," taking possession of desirable and colonizable "virgin land," or staking a claim on the body of a child, patriarchal men routinely disregard any notion of taboo or limitation and continually give themselves permission to "boldly go where no man has gone before."

Family Values

The word *survivor* began to be used by incest victims sometime in the late 1970s or early 1980s. *Survivor* sheds some of the pain of the word *victim* and focuses on the time when the immediate danger is over and healing can begin. It also affirms a link between incest/child sexual abuse and what are, at least for the Western world, the two defining horrors of the twentieth century: the Nazi death camps and the U.S. use of atomic weaponry against Japan. While such an association may seem extreme, one medical expert, Dr. Judith Herman, who has been working on issues of incest and battery since 1976, affirms a profound connection. She describes the link "between public and private worlds" and the commonalties "between rape survivors and combat veterans, between battered women and political prisoners, between the survivors of vast concentration camps created by tyrants who rule nations and the survivors of small, hidden concentration camps created by tyrants who rule their homes" (Herman 1992, 2–3). Just as neo-Nazis attempt to deny the reality of the Holocaust, so a confluence of forces consistently try to deny the reality and harm of incest. Most recently, there has been a growing movement to discredit memories recovered by victims after years of forgetfulness (Tavris, 1993). Survivors of incest must then bear witness to atrocity, renouncing numbing, and nurturing awareness. The word *survivor* as applied to incest also demands that we fathom the magnitude of the inescapable day-to-day devastation caused by this atrocity. We must understand its ongoing psychic and cultural consequences, its metaphorical enactment on the global scale, and its connection to other apocalyptic depredations.

A poem by Roseann Lloyd, "Not Even a Shadow on the Sidewalk" (1991, 84–87), makes the connection between incest and the bomb more powerfully than anything else I have encountered. The poem opens as Lloyd recalls her reaction to a *PBS Frontline* investigation of incest. In this televised news story, a woman returns to the room where she was repeatedly raped by her father, points to a wall, and describes how she would project herself into it during the assaults. Lloyd remembers that she was "jealous" when she heard this account:

> Because I didn't go anywhere in particular
> when my dad climbed on my bed
> It's not that I can't remember where I went
> I didn't go anywhere
> I was just gone   like the people in Japan
> blown away by the atom-bomb
> Annihilated
> There wasn't even a shadow left
> on the sidewalk
> to say   someone's missing
> My symptoms developed   like the side-effects
> of nuclear war—numb hands   missing hands
> disconnected synapses
> wheezing chest
> damaged vision: staring at the white light
> weak limbs
> reamed out like the inside of a sewer pipe
> aphasia   memory loss   splitting
> headaches.

Lloyd and others tell us that incest is an apocalyptic, annihilating experience for the individual sufferer. Moreover, it signifies a greater apocalyptic event. For a society that fucks and fucks over its children is not only acting out an extreme form of male supremacy; it is also fucking its own future, eating up the next generation, and indulging in the grossest excesses of consumerism, individual gratification, and final-frontierism.[2] Ellen Bass (1988, 43), a poet and counselor who has worked with incest survivors for decades, points to the apocalyptic significance of nuclear development (from war to toxic waste) and comments: "It is not odd that men whose desire for profit has superseded their own instinct for survival should so abuse their young. To stunt a child's trust in people, in love, in her world, to instill a fear that may take a lifetime to overcome, may never be overcome, to force one's body into the body of a child, of a baby, to desecrate children so is consistent for people who desecrate all life and the possibility of future life."

A stunning display of this desecrating dynamic occurred early in June 1992 at an oil recycling plant in California, during a speech by George Bush, the once self-proclaimed "environmental president." Some weeks earlier, the Bush administration had issued, in essence, a death sentence for many of the region's spotted owls by opening up a good portion of their northwestern old-growth-forest home for logging. Bush referred to this during his speech, not by explicitly mentioning the owl, but by gesturing toward the sky and declaring that he cared as much as anyone else about those "little furry-feathery" things, but that if those furry-feathery things got in the way of jobs and the mighty "family" (here a code word for corporate interests), they just had to go.

Mythically, the owl is a particularly powerful presence, long regarded in many traditions, including the European and the Aztec, as the embodiment of wisdom and a favorite familiar of witches. In some Native American lore, particularly in the Northwest, the owl represents the powers of death. In his oration at the oil recycling plant, George Bush dared not speak the spotted owl's name, but the Owl was calling his name. For, in truth, the witless leadership that Bush and his ilk have offered over the past century has resulted in widespread desecration and destruction of forests. The result is harm for trees, creatures, and working-class humans whose jobs have been chainsawed out of existence through unregulated corporate greed and mismanagement. Bush's foolish pronouncements sounded a death knell, not only for his failed administration, but also, perhaps sooner than we think, for the consummately wasteful "American way of life."

Despite all the 1992 Republican presidential campaign jabbering about honoring "family values," Bush's administration transgressed against the original and most essential "family value"—the equal sacredness of all life, a respect for future generations, and the commitment to what Carol Lee Sanchez calls humanity's "*familial* relationship with all creatures, elements, plants, and minerals, as well as humans" (1993, 213; emphasis added). The original theory of relativity is that *everything is a relative . . .* and one *never* fucks one's relatives.

12

On the Lap of Necessity

Myth and Technology through the Energetics
Philosophy of Teresa Brennan

> It is thus to the Mother that man owes the World of Forms or
> Universe. Without Her as material cause, Being cannot dis-
> play itself. It is but a corpse. . . . [P]rimacy is given to the
> Mother, and it is said, "What care I for the Father if I but be
> on the lap of the Mother?"
> Arthur Avalon (1978, 419–20)

> We sit in the lap of our Mother. . . . We shall soon pass, but
> the place where we now rest will last forever.
> Lakota saying (Gottlieb, 1996, 47)

Maternal origins and the feminine principle have been marginalized,
distorted, suppressed, trivialized, and denied, as Teresa Brennan (1993),
Mary Daly (1978, 1984, 1998), Alice Walker (1983), Luce Irigaray (1985,
1993), Paula Gunn Allen (1986a), Gloria Anzaldúa (1987), Monica Sjöö
and Barbara Mor (1991), Vandana Shiva (1988), Donna Wilshire (1989),
and Nancy Tuana (1993) have revealed, with varying emphases, perspectives, and degrees of explicitness. This reconstruction/destruction
of the Mother, in the realms of the sacred, scientific, social, philosophical, psychological, technological, and cultural has contributed to such
deleterious characteristics of modern societies as hierarchical and oppositional consciousness (light and dark, masculine and feminine, self and
other, spirit and matter, culture and nature, high and low, mind and

body, life and death, heaven and earth); a corresponding denigration of all that is associated with the feminine (the second part in these oppositions); exploitation of the elements and nature; and a pervasive cultural necrophilia. That necrophilia is evidenced in an identification of both knowledge and pleasure (from science to sexual murder) with invasion, torture, bondage, dismemberment, and destruction (Merchant, 1980; Caputi, 1987; Harding, 1999), the preference for the imitation over the original, and the proliferation of consumer objects that necessitate the degradation of the elemental world.

In *History after Lacan* (1993) and *Exhausting Modernity* (2000), Teresa Brennan identifies what she terms a "foundational fantasy" that drives this massively destructive and ultimately suicidal worldview. As she defines this fantasy: The "ego comes into being and maintains itself partly through the fantasy that it either contains or in other ways controls the mother; this fantasy involves the reversal of the original state of affairs, together with the imitation of the original" (1993, 167). Drawing upon the psychoanalytic insights of Melanie Klein, Brennan highlights Klein's notion of the "splitting" found in infantile aggression against the mother. Splitting provides a strategy whereby the infant can disown in the self what it fears or dislikes, separating it from the "good." The "bad" is then projected onto the other, and specifically onto the "bad breast" of the mother as the infant divides the mother (the breast) into "good" and "bad" (Klein, 1975). Furthermore, the infant desires to "abject" the mother, to "poison or dismember her, to spoil and poison the breast (and the mother) with its own excrement" (Brennan, 1993, 93). The bad breast, then, is the one contaminated by the excrement that he has dumped in it. Brennan extends this notion of splitting, arguing that through the foundational fantasy we come to know the world through such schisms as those between the mental and the physical, the social and the natural.

Because, as Brennan argues, the mother's body is correlated with "living nature," the enactments and effects of this fantasy in the technological era have become ever more environmentally disastrous. Brennan argues for the development of "a vocabulary which constrains manifestations of a destructive psychical fantasy, as well as one that symbolizes the relation to maternal origin" (1993, 174). My purpose here is to explore one aspect of that emerging vocabulary: that which concerns the symbolization of relation to the original/the mother/living nature. This vocabulary, consisting of both words and images, takes shape, potentially, in a variety of forms: reinstatements of life-preservative taboos;[1]

the revival and reconceptualization of potentially helpful concepts (for example, "Mother Earth," "Mother Nature," the "feminine principle");[2] criticism and reconceptualization of notions such as the hierarchical *high* and *low* (Christian, 1997), *light* and *dark* (Anzaldúa, 1987); the invention of wholly new words and phrases (Daly, 1978; Irigaray, 1985); as well as deliberate discursions into realms the foundation fantasizes as obscene (for example, the artwork by Chris Ofili discussed below).

Brennan's call for a new vocabulary, her theorization of energetics, and her emphasis on maternal origin all invite an application of feminist mythmaking and mythic analysis. For it is myth—*living* symbols and stories—I shall argue, that is most capable of speaking about the original, and it is myth that is the form of language and imagery most charged with the energy to transform consciousness.

Myth and the Original

Come out of their language. Try to go back through the names they've given you. I'll wait for you, I'm waiting for myself. Come back.
Luce Irigaray (1985, 206)

Myths are the deepest, innermost cultural stories of our human journeys toward spiritual and psychological growth. An essential part of myth is that it allows for our return to the creation, to a mythic time. It allows us to hear the world new again.
Linda Hogan (1995, 51)

Time comes into it.
Say it.   Say it.
The universe is made of stories,
Not of atoms.
Muriel Rukeyser (1994, 230-31)

Lucia Chiavola Birnbaum, in a talk at Florida Atlantic University in April 2000, described the characteristic form taken by processions in honor of the Black Madonna in Sicily: participants take three steps forward and then two steps back. One way to interpret the meaning of this ritual movement is that it teaches that progression must be based in the past—a zone understood not only as a historical past but as a mythic source of origins. Similarly, Linda Hogan (1995) explains that in order to create the new—in consciousness and culture—we must first go back to the time/space of the original. Myth is one vehicle to accomplish this intricate passage.

While primarily informed by psychoanalytic theory and Marxism, Brennan shares with other key feminist thinkers a reliance on such a mythic frame. In her emphasis on the *original* (about which I have much more to say), Brennan participates in a stream of feminist theory that articulates a mythic space to "go back to," one that preexists master-slave/patriarchal/colonial definition and occupation—a space/time that is variously imaginative, ideal, historical, emergent, and/or psychical.

Myths can be understood as coded transmissions communicating "certain basic, universal meanings" that exist in an ongoing process of manifestation, interpretation, and reinterpretation (O'Flaherty, 1988, 31). Even to tell a myth is to interpret it. Hence meanings expand, shift, and are revealed over time. Donna Wilshire finds primal myth to be a particularly vital source for feminist interpretation. The retelling of myths can itself be transformative, she asserts, opening "doors long-closed on the riches of the so-called 'female' perspective. . . . [P]rimal Myth exposes a way of thinking and being in the world that dissolves dualism, neutralizes coercive hierarchies, and puts some old taboos (especially about women's blood and bodies with their dark interiors) into new and positive frameworks" (1989, 96–97). Feminist reinterpretations of myths of origin demand, as we shall see, radical reconsiderations of the maternal and related concepts including darkness, descent, dependence, dirt, and death.

Of course, so much of primal myth seems to be mired in gynephobic, misogynist, and frankly infantile points of view. Over and over, we find a masculine inability to face the mother, horror at femaleness, and fantasies of heroic slaughter of the feminine (Neumann, 1963; Lederer, 1968). These myths, Mary Daly argues (1978), point to a paradigmatic act of "goddess murder" serving to legitimate consanguineous attacks against female bodies and psyches throughout global history. Yet, Daly continues, patriarchal myth also contains stolen energies. Feminist interpreters can see through the "foreground" deceptions of patriarchal myth, reverse their characteristic reversals, and thereby tap into the *Background* (1978, 3, 26)—which we might recognize as one face of the *original*—a realm of wild, inimitable, and inviolable reality.

Interpreting myth, then, not only challenges established meanings but connects interpreters to a transformative ideational energy. Challenging traditional rationalist notions, Paula Gunn Allen argues that myths are stories that are sacred not only because they are meaningful but because they are able to influence reality, imbued with the "power to transform something (or someone) from one state or condition to another" (1986a, 103). Here we again find a key link between feminist theories of myth and Brennan's philosophical work. For Brennan bases her thought in a recognition of *energetics:* "All beings, all entities in and of the natural world, all forces, whether naturally or artificially forged, are connected energetically" (2000, 41). Myths and mythic images must be comprehended as energetic phenomena; they are *living* symbols, forces with which we interact, powers capable of opening up "levels of reality otherwise closed to us and . . . unlock[ing] dimensions and elements of our souls which correspond to these hidden dimensions and elements of reality" (Daly, 1984, 25). Daly further asserts that the act of "Re-membering and decoding" certain primal myths and images can itself "conjure vortices of force" (1998, 187). Hence, I turn to a mythic vocabulary for the two reasons I have just outlined: the capacity of myth to speak of and to the original; and the unique transformational powers of mythic dialogue and interpretation. The energetic elements of this mythic vocabulary can be found, read, and communicated with in both ancient and contemporary forms, from the worlds of religion as well as art and popular culture.

The Foundational Fantasy

Brennan argues that an egocentric paradigm of consciousness (masculine) subjectivity as we know it, is crucial to this culture of objectification, fragmentation, and domination. What she calls, after Lacan, the "ego's era" derives from a foundational fantasy in which the masculine-identified and infantile subject imagines himself as the "locus of active agency and the environment as passive" (1993, 11). This begins with the mother, as the subject makes her into an object that the subject in fantasy commands. At the same time, the subject denies its history "in so far as that history reveals its dependence on a maternal origin" (101). This includes dependence not only on the actual mother but also upon living nature. Brennan further explains: "I am positing that the desire for instant gratification, the preference for visual and 'object'-oriented thinking this entails, the desire to be waited upon, the envious desire to imitate the original, the desire to control the mother, and to devour, poison and dismember her, and to obtain knowledge by this process, constitute a foundational psychical fantasy" (ibid.).

A postmodern current (for example, Baudrillard, 1981; Haraway, 1991, 150–51) explicitly rejects any notion of an "original." Yet Brennan asserts her belief in an *"original,"* a "living nature" (1993, 14) that is correlated with the mother's body. This *original* preexists the foundational fantasy and is first known in the earliest experiences of the mother's body. Psychoanalysis and deconstruction have characterized any notion of a foundation as laden with narcissism, inscribing the white male modern subject as the source of all meaning. Yet such a critique actually promotes that same narcissism by implying that if the white male modern subject is not the source of meaning, then there is *no* meaning and *no* origin. Brennan's articulation of the "foundational fantasy," instead, explains how it is that we have come to think of the elite masculine subject as the source of meaning and agency. Moreover, it points us toward necessary knowledge of the original that the fantasy would deny and distort.

The foundational fantasy rivals and reverses the original in any number of ways—for example, via the common notion of the man as the provider on whom the woman depends, masking masculine envy, appropriation, control of, and imitation of the mother's powers. Both of these arguably motivate and structure not only interpersonal relations (consider Ronald Reagan's pet name for his endlessly adoring and acquiescent wife, Nancy—"Mommie Poo Pants"), but also much economic, religious and technological activity (Daly, 1978, 57–64; Easlea, 1983). Later, I consider Brennan's analysis of the relationship of the foundational fantasy to technological development. For now, however, it might be instructive to contemplate these themes as they coalesce in a 1996 advertisement for British Airways (fig. 12.1).

This ad uses a collage that is overtly fantastic. An idealized white, young, properly coifed and tastefully, if suggestively, sweater-clad mother is shown in sepia tones. The seated mother holds in her lap an infant, upon whom she gazes adoringly. The diapered infant's head and upper torso are replaced with a full-color insert of an old, bald white man, wearing a white shirt and red tie. He smiles in his sleep. A headline touts the "New Club World cradle seat" and adds this disclaimer: "Lullaby not included."

In the overt text of this ad, the mother is controlled by being rendered a phantasm, an unrealistic sentimentalization, the narcissistic projection of a perpetually infantile elder. On a less visible level, the mother, with her capacity to carry, is imitated, rivaled, and replicated by the airplane, a device that Marshall McLuhan (1951) would recognize as a "mechanical bride."

Here as elsewhere, denial and control of the mother is effected through promoting the image of an idealized angel-mom, nurturant, passive, devoted, young, beautiful, and ever so happy to clean up "baby's" messes. Yet the fantasy itself inevitably contains the splitting that is

The new Club World cradle seat. Lullaby not included.

Introducing the unique new business class cradle seat. It doesn't simply recline but tilts as a whole raising your knees and relieving your body of stress and pressure. Pity you may not be awake to enjoy all the other changes on new Club World.

BRITISH AIRWAYS
The world's favourite airline

Introduced throughout this year. ©1996 British Airways

12.1 British Airways ad © 1996

endemic to masculine subjectivity and egocentric consciousness. Just as the "whore" lurks behind every "virgin," so too the mad, bad, and devouring monster-mother (Hitchcock's *Psycho* is a key text here) is the perverse underside of this idealized maternal fantasy.[3]

It doesn't take long to discover the "dark side" of this ad. The ad is for a "cradle" seat; its headline mentions a deliberately excluded "lullaby." "Rock-a-bye Baby" might come to mind. In that hardly restful ditty, the bough notoriously breaks and the cradle fatefully falls. And indeed, much to the masculine subject's dismay, mothers can abort; airplanes, cars, computers, stock markets, and egos can crash.

The entire ad, again, is manifestly chimerical, signposting the presence of the destructive psychical fantasy. In Brennan's view, that fantasy produces a "complex physical alternative world which papers over the original" (1993, 195). Yet, she cautions, this virtual reality should "not blind us to the existence of the original" (196). In this virtual world, the ordinary one we inhabit, Brennan cautions, we "cannot know the original with certainty." Still, we can begin to discern it through "tracing the inverted path of the imitation." This is possible because "an unconscious knowledge of the original informs the direction and content of its competitive contender" (195–96)

Hence, if we wend our way back, regressing through the mythic image, we can recover knowledge of the *original*. Returning to the airline ad, for example, we can look behind the foreground opposition of the angel-mom/monster-mom and find its symbolic etymology in a complex mythic conception of the maternal divine. In any number of world figures—Kali from the Hindu tradition (Dalmiya, 2000), Isis from the Egyptian (Baring and Cashford, 1991, 264), Demeter from the European, Tlazolteotl, Coatlicue, and Tlaelcuani from the Aztec (Anzaldúa, 1987, 46), Oya from the Yoruban (Gleason, 1987), even the vernacular "Mother Nature" (Caputi, 1993, 46–47)—the unsplit, original Mother is equally and always creator, preserver, destroyer, and transformer (Baring and Cashford, 1991; Sjöö and Mor, 1991). And she knows exactly what she is doing.

The Unsplit Mother

> Kali is thus the paradox: She is the Primal Mother who brings forth all life even while she signifies Death. Everything that there is, everything "natural," is the vale of Death even though it is nothing other than Kali/*Prakṛti*, the source of life.
>
> Vrinda Dalmiya (2000, 136)

In *The Sacred Hoop* (1986a, 13–14; emphasis added), Paula Gunn Allen describes the primal or original force, known variously as Old Spider Woman, Thought Woman, Serpent Woman, Earth Woman, and Corn Woman: "There is a spirit that pervades everything, that is capable of powerful song and radiant movement, and that moves in and out of the mind. The colors of this spirit are multitudinous, a glowing, pulsing rainbow. . . . Her variety and multiplicity testify to her complexity: she is the true creatrix for she is thought itself, from which all else is born. *She is the necessary precondition for material creation,* and she, like all of her creation, is fundamentally female—potential and primary. . . . To assign to this great being the position of 'fertility goddess' is exceedingly demeaning: it trivializes the tribes and it trivializes the power of woman. Woman bears, that is true. She also destroys."

As Allen's language suggests, this quintessential power can also be known by the name of *Necessity*. Proverbially, necessity is the mother of invention, that is, of everything that comes into material being. In the Greek tradition, Necessity is the mother of the Fates or *Moirae,* the three ancient goddesses who are older than all the gods and to whose dictates even Zeus must yield. Euripides (cited in Ann and Imel, 1993, 148) calls Necessity "the most powerful of the deities." Plato in the last chapter of his *Republic* tells the "Myth of Er," in which individual souls participate in a lottery presided over by the Fates. According to a number falling to it by chance, each soul chooses a life or destiny, proceeds under the hand of each of the three Fates, and then passes under the lap or throne of Necessity before emerging into material existence.

Although she does not refer to them explicitly, Brennan's work is informed by the knowledge encoded in these ancient myths: that the *original,* the primal creative source, is correlated with the biological mother. Yet what do we mean by "the mother"? In her feminist interpretation of Kali, Vrinda Dalmiya distinguishes between biological and metaphysical motherhood, with Kali epitomizing the latter. "Kali/*Prakṛti* is the Ultimate monistic stuff from which everything emerges but which nevertheless is distinct from and transcends these emergents" (2000, 134). Biological motherhood, Dalmiya explains, requires impregnation by a male and is constructed, however erroneously, as being passive. But "emanation from *Prakṛti* is not dependent on a male being the source of everything. *Prakṛti* is prior to even the male . . . [and] is definitely the active principle in generation" (135). A culture inimical to female genius, divinity, and creativity distorts the concept of motherhood, narrowing it to a solely biological, passive, and mindless activity.[4] This is pure reversal. *Thought*, as Allen reminds us, is the first principle of cosmic or metaphysical motherhood.[5]

Brennan also addresses this distortion. She points to the splitting at the core of the foundational fantasy as producing the notion that "direction or agency is . . . mental and mindful, while activity, paradoxically, is . . . something that lacks intelligence" (2000, 28). Outrageously, the *activity* of women as mothers is (mis)understood as passive, as something that is directed from elsewhere—by the sperm, by the fetus, by the doctor, by god. Concomitantly, as Brennan recognizes, this dismissal of maternal agency "can be extended readily to living nature overall" (ibid.). Contemplating the oft-repeated association of women with nature, Brennan argues that this "can be explained not by what women and nature have in common, but by the similar denial imposed upon both of them. In the case of women, it is one's will that is denied. In the case of living nature, its own inherent direction is disregarded" (ibid.). In short, the envy of the masculine subject for the creativity and power of the original drives it to deny the intelligence of nature, and to impose a notion of motherhood as thoughtless activity.

Deepening our notion of motherhood to include the intelligent, mindful, and metaphysical, we can reconsider the innumerable religious icons (including the subliminally sacred imagery of the British Airways ad) that display a (sometimes remote and sometimes tender) mother/goddess with a (frequently nursing) child on her lap—for example, the Yoruban First Ancestor and child; the Egyptian Isis and Horus, Catholicism's Mary and Jesus, and Haitian Vodou's Ezili Dantò and daughter Anaïs (Neumann, 1963, plates 37–47; Austen, 1990, 22; Houlberg, 1995, 273; Graham, 1997, 51–62). Although we might be tempted to focus on the child or even the mother in these images, that would be a mistake. These *really* are not family portraits. Rather, they are living symbols communicating complex concepts regarding the nature of the cosmos.

Erich Neumann explains that the Great Mother "as a whole is a symbol of creative life and the parts of her body are not physical organs but numinous symbolic centers of whole spheres of life" (1963, 128). The key element in these icons is not the foreground figures; rather it is the lap.[6] The lap, seemingly the most passive of all places, is in truth the most active. The mother/lap represents the *original*, the intelligent matrix or cosmic womb. In ancient Sumerian the word for *womb, vulva, loins*, and *lap* is the same (Wolkstein and Kramer, 1983, 146). The name of the Egyptian goddess *Isis* possibly derives from a word meaning *seat*, *lap, throne* (Lurker, 1980, 71). Isis characteristically appears with the throne on her head and is "goddess of the throne upon whose sovereign lap the king sat as her infant child in the image of all humanity" (Baring and Cashford, 1991, 225). She is always behind him, making possible not only his rule but also his life—his very coming into the "World of Forms" or material existence. As a praise-song to this goddess avowed, everything is "because of Isis" (Monaghan, 1999, 145).[7]

Understanding the metaphysical mother as the ultimate cause, as Necessity herself, we recognize that while the original bears, nurtures, and sustains life, that same original also ultimately takes back all of life into her lap. There, she decomposes and recomposes these elements, resulting in ceaseless action, movement, and transmutation. Returning to the lap icons, we find that sometimes a son is dead. Consider the resonant mystery of Michelangelo's *Pieta*. Even the bizarre collage of the British Airways ad, linking the infant and the old man, suggests the mother's lap as the beginning and end of life. Here, the mother represents the eternal, the infinite, mindful primal potency and potential; the son represents the transitory and finite.[8] The process signified by the mother's lap is the ceaseless intelligent movement of life, growth, and change. This quintessential process—one that *encompasses* organic death—*is* the life force.

Death and the Ego

Kali is she who swallows the universe. She consumes your smallness, your pain, your guilt, and finally your ego, if you will allow her to. Kali is the Black Mother, the dark mother of the night. It is she who kills the ego dead.

Ma Jaya Sati Bhagavati (1998, 18)

Although Brennan does not specifically link the modern notion of the self-contained individual to the ego, arguably the two are synonymous. The splitting involved in the foundational fantasy includes a rupture between subject and object, resulting in the ego that imagines himself as separate and contained. This self-concept is intrinsic to oppressive and splitting practices such as objectification, prostitution, racism, abandonment of the homeless and elderly, and genocide (P. Williams, 1991, 62). Concomitantly, the ego imagines himself able to poison the mother/nature without simultaneously destroying himself. This conception of the self-contained bounded individual, while found in ancient thought, has "hardened" through time (Brennan, 2000, 47). In the West, such individuality is now accepted as the standard version of subjectivity.

Yet the conception of the maternal/original evoked here radically challenges that model. One theorist of myth and consciousness, Gloria Anzaldúa, finds that when she attends to the "darkness that was 'present' before the world and all things were created," the darkness "equated with matter, the maternal, the germinal, the potential," she is "led back to the mystery of the Origin" (1987, 49). Descending into the "Coatlicue state," Anzaldúa finds that she is able to move beyond the "conscious I" that looms as a boulder in her path of becoming (50).

Particularly in her manifestation as the cruel hag, Kali also "dashes to pieces the finite world of individual egos" (C. M. Brown, 1987, 121–22). As the ego is annihilated, a different conception of the self is freed to emerge. In other words, when understanding of the *original* transforms and deepens, so necessarily does understanding of the self. Drawing upon environmental philosopher Val Plumwood (1993), Dalmiya identifies the ego or "master identity" as a self-construction formed in response to fear of death, opposition to nature, and a failure to acknowledge that life and death are intertwined (2000, 140). The mythic mother-child bond with Kali, she argues, bespeaks a radically different self-construction, a "'relational identity' that may well curb the excesses of the domineering self" (142) and aid in "ethico-political struggles for justice" (25).

Hence, the "terrible mother" generated by the foundational fantasy is so horrific to masculine subjectivity as we know it because she signifies not only natural death, but also the "death" of the ego and the alternative world built in its image. Curiously enough, this theological understanding is coded into that mysterious lullaby "Rock-a-bye Baby." Its implicit mother does not impel the actual death of her child. Rather, she ends the infantile stage. As baby comes "down," the illusory ego and its "cradle" are dashed to bits. The mature being is now able to emerge. And, we might recall, in worldwide myth, *descent* is a principal way of knowledge. Referencing the Myth of Er, and the passing of the soul under the lap of Necessity, James Hillman identifies a need for individuals to mature, to "grow down" into this world (1996, 41–62).

The figure of the inexorable and ego-shattering mother/hag, embodied in such mythic figures as Coatlicue and Kali, is crucial to a re-symbolization of the maternal—and thereby of the self—that would counteract the foundational fantasy. Having established this, we can now turn our attention to the material effects of the fantasy itself. As Brennan outlines this, unable to face the shattering of self-important subjectivity and the illusion of omnipotence, the ego constructs an "alternative psychophysical world," one that "guarantees a self which sees things from its own standpoint" (1993, 185). This fantastic, self-centered consciousness attempts to keep at bay all fears of falling and demonizes the very process of maturation that would render that fear bearable if not moot. The construction of this world, and its characteristics, dynamics, and implications, are theorized in Brennan's clarifying article "Social Pressure" (1997).

Psychical Matters

> The capacity for growth, exuberant expression, and transcendence, symbolized esthetically as well as sexually by the flowering plants—this is the primal gift of life; and in man it flourishes best when living creatures and equally living symbols are constantly present.
>
> Lewis Mumford (1970, 383)

According to Brennan, it is an error to believe that the social is "immaterial, . . . lacking matter and/or energy" (1997, 257). Rather the social is "physical, a force that interacts with and affects the biological body" (258) and the material world. Brennan theorizes the energetic forces and patterns, both fluid and bound, which exist between humans, between humans and objects, and between humans and nature, arguing that "affects and desires can be communicated from the one to the other, and . . . both the one and the other can be born into affects that pre-exist them" (2000, 41).

Brennan's use of the term *social pressure* shares in its traditional meanings but expands these to comprehend the energetic, physical pressures exerted by bound energies or fixities (1997, 257, 275). These fixities first take the form of pathways in the psyche that result from repression. Energy is bound in pathways that are created as a result of experience as well as habitual fantasies, thoughts, and behaviors, including the foundational fantasy. While some are necessary in order to learn, bound pathways also leave the subject less access to freely mobile energy and presumably less ability to change and adapt. This can cause one to age poorly, to become numb, entropic, uniform, inert, and deathlike. At the same time, this binding of energy leaves us in a "world with different energetic coordinates" (263). The recurrent binding of energies and subsequent exploitative relationships changes the external world, creating the alternative physical world.

This dreary world is manufactured as the foundational psychical fantasy makes itself *materially* true, Brennan explains, through an exploitative transaction. The binding of energy into fixed pathways causes rigidity, a kind of psychophysical waste. Carrying this rigidity can make the subject ill, entropic, and so on. The master identity then finds a solution in exploitation. Exploitation always demands an "energetic transfer that depletes one agency while enriching the other. . . . One is empowered, subjectified, by the energy of the other. At the interpersonal level of image, and imaginary fixing, one 'makes it to subject' by directing aggression and a negative image outwards, freeing oneself to move" (1993, 185). In other words, the subject dumps his negative affect onto and into the other (the subject is masculine, Brennan writes, though both females and males can assume that position). At the same time he is enriched by mining the resources of loving attention (living energy) of the other. This exploitative relationship is clearly a political one. The "other" is variously compelled — economically, socially, or psychologically — to act as a repository, carrying the subject's shame, pain, impotence, and feelings of inferiority. Any hierarchically gendered relationship — the colonial relationship, the battering relationship, the incest relationship, the relationship of prostitute to john, of servant to mistress or master, the normative heterosexual relationship — is paradigmatic here.[9]

If we turn to literature, we can find an almost exact description of this process in D. H. Lawrence's *Women in Love,* originally published in 1920. A lovemaking scene between Gerald and Gudrun is noteworthy for its portrayal of what Brennan terms the transmission of affect or "dumping," the energetic transfer whereby the masculine partner is both relieved of his waste and revivified, while the feminine is depleted: "Into her he poured all his pent-up darkness and corrosive death, and he was whole again. . . . This was the ever-recurrent miracle of his life, at the knowledge of which he was lost in an ecstasy of relief and wonder. And she, subject, received him as a vessel filled with his bitter potion of death. . . . As he drew nearer to her, he plunged deeper into her enveloping soft warmth, a wonderful creative heat that penetrated his veins and gave him life again. He felt himself dissolving and sinking to rest in the bath of her living strength. It seemed as if her heart in her breast were a second unconquerable sun, into the glow and creative strength of which he plunged further and further" (Lawrence, 1996, 384). After this

transference, Gerald sleeps the "sleep of complete exhaustion and restoration. But Gudrun lay wide awake, destroyed into perfect consciousness." Later she feels "old, old" (385).[10]

Fathers of the Catholic Church quite openly acknowledged the operation of an exploitative energetic relationship in the institution of
prostitution. Mary Daly (1973, 60–61) points out that Augustine and
Thomas Aquinas scapegoated the prostitute as unclean but useful.
Augustine excoriated prostitutes as the most sordid, immodest, and
shameful of all women, yet warned that their removal from human affairs would result in a pollution of "all things with lust" (cited ibid., 60).
The celibate Thomas Aquinas, who entered the monastery at age six,
drew upon Augustine to compare the social function of prostitution to
that of sewers in a palace (61). Contemporary popular imagery remains
infused with the stereotype of the prostitute as contaminated scapegoat.
But, simultaneously, it is suggested that she is able to contain and even
recycle that "pollution," for she is not only a human dump but also a
therapist, mother figure, nurse, and midwife assisting at death. She is
said to possess a "heart of gold," but the alchemical transformation she
performs is all to the psychophysical benefit of the "john" who, in countless Hollywood films, deposits his refuse into her and emerges from the
encounter cleansed, healed, energized, and otherwise transformed—as
in *Pretty Woman* (Garry Marshall, 1991), *L.A. Confidential* (Curtis Hanson, 1995), *He Got Game* (Spike Lee, 1998), and *Leaving Las Vegas* (Mike
Figgis, 1995).

And it is not only interpersonal relationships that must be considered in a theory of energetics. Brennan proposes that paralleling the fixity or bound energy of the psychophysical pathways, and the dumping
of the subject's rigidity into the other, is the unbalanced and destructive
energetic patterns brought into being by the mass production of consumer goods. Consumer objects, dominating our habitats and made in
the image and likeness of the ego and its desires (for instant gratification, narcissism, perpetual youth, speed, power, etc.), are characterized
by bound energies. In these commodities, living energies are fixed,
slowing down their motion and reentry into the life cycle. Similarly, I
would add, in many mass-mediated images the living energy of myth
and symbol is fixed into stereotype and objectification, promoting
super-self-absorption for those positively portrayed and what Patricia J.
Williams (1991, 73) calls "spirit murder—disregard for others whose
lives qualitatively depend on our regard"—for those victimized by images of deviance, stupidity, sinfulness, hate, and fear.

The proliferation of bound energies—pavement, buildings, objects, images, machines—is attended inexorably by the diminishment of the ever-fluid natural world of living, reproducing, and decomposing plants, soil, creatures, elements, ideas. The replacement of this mobile force by bound energies then constitutes social pressure. Brennan explains: "Socially constructed fixities [are] . . . felt as a pressure, and not just in the sense that they are pollutants. Their very existence means there is less that is living in the atmosphere. This new dead weight must be felt as a pressure for the reason that any presence which cannot escape, which is confined by its inability to re-enter the flow, is felt as a pressure" (1997, 274–75).

While Brennan allies social pressure with "death" and the "death drive" (1997), that which obliterates distinctiveness and yields inertia and uniformity, I would prefer to call this *deathlessness,* which is, of course, equally *lifelessness.*[11] The oppositional split between life (good) and death (bad) might itself be a product of the foundational fantasy. In this fantasy, death, identified with the demise of the ego, is demonized, while struggles against "evil" (a mask for that which causes death) are heroized, resulting in tragedy and the causation of genuinely evil consequences (Becker, 1975, 146–70).

Yet organic death, the inevitable outcome of life, cannot reasonably be understood as evil. Death releases energies back into the flow of life, into the regenerative lap of Necessity. These energies then reconstitute in new forms. A fear of flowing (as well as falling/dying) is everywhere manifested in the monocultures, objects and objectifications, commodities, and other such monuments to the ego that Brennan so astutely identifies.

Technological (In)Toxication

Before the advent of a Western technology capable of fulfilling the desires embodied in the foundational fantasy, it is contained. The advent of that technology is prompted by the fantasy and represents an acting out of it on an increasingly global scale, an enactment that reinforces the psychical power of the fantasy.

Teresa Brennan (1993, 11)

The exploitation of resources, annihilation of living beings, and generation of toxic waste that characterize technological development provide touchstones to identify the operation of the foundational fantasy. So too is another technological tendency—that which seeks to immortalize the ego through its personification in the artificial intelligence machine. Fear of ego death, resulting in the attempt to deny death and to control matter, the body, and the maternal, is nowhere more apparent than in contemporary technological "posthuman" or "postbiological" discourse. Technicians such as Hans Moravec and Ray Kurzweil fantasize a "postbiological future" where computers and other machines surpass humans in intelligence and render us, in a word, unnecessary. Moravec (1988) plans the obsolescence of the mother and welcomes the fading away of humans, who are to be replaced by "mind children," future machines invented by (male) artificial intelligence engineers. Kurzweil, in his 1999 book *The Age of Spiritual Machines,* eagerly anticipates a cyborgian future in which human beings merge with machines, downloading their consciousness into computers and becoming, literally, software. The fantasy that turns him on involves abandoning the body, spurning living nature, and encasing the ego in an idealized fixity, the computer, and a completely virtual reality. In so doing, the self can become like god. This new species will eventually consider the "fate of the universe" (Kurzweil, 1999, 280).

In these frantic fantasies, the ego not only makes a new species but, blatantly rivaling the biological and metaphysical mother, overcomes the powers of the Fates, Necessity, and death. Kurzweil's model for the "god" he wants to become is the familiar immutable heavenly father. That god lives in bodiless heaven, neither on the Earth nor immanent in matter. This notion of omnipotent divinity is made in the image and likeness of the ego and leads inexorably to loneliness, alienation, objectification of the body, and destruction of the environment.

Noting that humans are becoming increasingly inert while our machines are becoming more lively, Donna Haraway (1991), in her influential "A Manifesto for Cyborgs," raises not an alarm but a flagpole. Creatively attempting to shake up received categories and concepts, she claims the cyborg, a fusion of animal, machine, and human, as a revolutionary feminist identity. While noting its origins in the military-industrial complex, Haraway nonetheless claims the cyborg to be "the illegitimate offspring of militarism and patriarchal capitalism" (1991, 151), and hence potentially disloyal to these "inessential" fathers. It seems that there are no maternal origins for the cyborg. Haraway chides other feminists who "insist on the organic, opposing it to the technological," and celebrates the cyborg for its abandonment of the spurious organic: "The cyborg would not recognize the Garden of Eden; it is not made of mud and cannot dream of returning to dust" (ibid.). The machines with which we are urged to identify also are removed from the earth and matter: "Our best machines are made of sunshine; they are all light and clean because they are nothing but signals, electromagnetic waves, a section of a spectrum. . . . People are nowhere near so fluid, being both material and opaque" (153).

As her metaphors suggest, Haraway's cyborg might well be a product of the destructive fantasy. The imagination of the cyborg persists in the foundational denial of the maternal source, here disregarded as the dust, matter, the dark, the low, the earth. Although cast as fluid, Haraway's cyborg is fixed, outside of Necessity—the cycle of life, death, regeneration. It neither begins nor ends. Some years earlier Lewis Mumford lamented that an egomaniacal technological culture, dominated by the "myth of the machine," has long idealized "a world of light and space, disinfected of the human presence" and fit only for machines (1970, 33). Moravec, Kurzweil, and even Haraway are disturbingly close to this ideal of disinfection and, hence, a cosmic sterility.

What might we make of Haraway's ascription of a desirable disassociation from "dust" to the cyborg? The neocolonial/militaristic/patriarchal culture, with its seemingly limitless capacity to generate toxins (material and psychic) and dump these onto others, is characteristically obsessed with promoting itself as the "light" and the "clean." High-tech and often futuristic spaces—in ads and other such iconic images for nuclear power plants, cloning, and biotechnologies—are conventionally presented as sterile places with "clean" functional lines and a total absence of color. There is no acknowledgment of the carnage and waste that is necessarily behind this façade.

In *Tar Baby*, Toni Morrison scathingly points to a colonizing culture's characteristic movement: "to defecate over a whole people and come there to live and defecate some more. . . . That was the sole lesson of their world: how to make waste, how to make machines that made more waste, how to make wasteful products, how to talk waste, how to study waste, how to design waste, how to cure people who were sickened by waste so that they could be well enough to endure it, how to mobilize waste, legalize waste and how to despise the culture that lived in cloth houses and shit on the ground far away from where they ate" (1981, 175).[12] With the inversion and denial typical of the foundational fantasy, the colonizers imagine themselves as clean, advanced, white, pure, and progressive and those they subjugate, exploit, foist their psychophysical waste upon, and *depend upon* for sustenance as foul, dirty, smelly, dark, and backward. A key component of the foundational fantasy is a desire to poison, to piss and shit on the source—technologically, verbally, literally, and virtually. This superficial fixation on cleanness and lightness masks the colonial and technological obsession with its own waste and a concomitant denial and projection, resulting in the production of unprecedented toxins—nuclear waste, PCB's, dioxin, and so on. Behind the façade of every shiny consumer "good" is a "slimy bad by-product" (Sofia, 1984, 46), bound and poisonous fixities, a strip mine, a clear-cut forest, a wasted species, a pile of nuclear droppings (Caputi, 1993, 223–24).

Consuming the Source/Feeding the Ego

This ego-driven world, Brennan writes, characteristically refuses to acknowledge indebtedness to and dependence on the mother and, correspondingly, "on the extraordinary creativity of the 'God as Nature'" (1993, 194). This parallel factor makes the "feminist concern with symbolizing divinity in maternal terms an imperative" (ibid.). A world in denial of responsibility to the Mother is a world in which Being does not readily display itself. This world, founded upon reversal and imitation, is a world of "body snatchers" and the "living dead," as shown to us in mythically intuitive horror films.[13] These virtual corpses take even such everyday and familiar forms as TVs, VCRs, sport utility vehicles, and computers, as well as dehumanizing images, objectifications, and stereotypes.

Again, turning to the world of popular culture, we find an extraordinarily vivid enactment of the foundational fantasy, which "accords certain attributes to the subject, and dispossesses the other of them as and by the process that makes the other into an object, a surround . . . an absent background against which it is present" (Brennan, 2000, 36). It is one of a series of television commercials for Radio Shack (November 2000). These all feature a pretend married couple, ex-football star Howie Long and actress Teri Hatcher. In one, Hatcher, dressed all in white, invites Long, garbed all in black, into a stark, all-white space. She seats him in a thronelike black chair and swivels it around so that he can focus his attention on the large black television screen and speakers. She powers a remote control, switching on the TV, hands him a drink and popcorn, and then remains, standing behind him. Long watches an outer-space machine fight scene from a *Star Wars*-ish movie. Zap, zap, zap go the laser beams. There is nothing alive anywhere in sight. He visibly glazes over, thoroughly engrossed in the fantasy. But, he smirks at her, something is missing: "a cup holder." Without even turning to look at her, he reaches back and deposits his cup into her outstretched hand. In this thirty-second hallucination, the *original* (represented by the woman) seems to be utterly controlled. The instantaneously gratified ego (represented by the man) reposes in a completely denatured environment, happily and perhaps permanently lost in the infantile fantasy. Of course, the real matrix, the original, is still behind him, supporting him, feeding him, making him possible. But he can't face her or his dependence. Instead, he treats her as a serviceable object and depository. And, in the fantasy, she doesn't even object to her abjection. It's "Mommie Poo Pants" all over again. While this scenario masquerades as a utopia of total consumer fulfillment, it actually is a vision of profound dissociation, sensory deprivation, and disaster.

In a balanced world, one guided by respect for death, an appreciation of the necessary energetic connections between living beings and forces, and respect for the need to check egocentric greed and self-indulgence, consumer items and images would not be fetishized and production would be kept at a sustainable level.[14] Yet in this bizarre, artificial world, these fixities not only are endlessly reproduced, but themselves masquerade as the Source. For example, a 1999 ad for computer software available through the Internet company Amazon.com displays a giant computer screen with these words writ large: "Feed Me." "Feeding" the computer is an elaborate means of feeding the foundational fantasy, nourishing the ever-rapacious ego. This, of course, is the exact inverse of the *original* pattern whereby humans should nourish the Source, give energy back to the Mother.

The poet, novelist, and essayist Linda Hogan writes that humans estranged from the land are lonely and alienated because we "have been split from what we could nurture, what could fill us" (1995, 82). Still, she continues, many of us do "desire to see the world intact, to step outside our emptiness and remember the strong currents that pass between humans and the rest of nature, currents that are the felt voice of land, heard in the cells of the body" (84). Hogan is not being metaphorical here. It is through participating in these *currents*, which Brennan understands as those very *real* energetic transactions between living beings and forces, that we not only attain nourishment, energy, and ecstasy but ourselves feed the life force. This worldview and practice requires adult accountability and the abandonment of infantile fantasies. It recognizes that humans are not simple dependents on the original but participants in a complex interdependence. It is our responsibility to nurture the earth and the elemental, to feed the Green as it feeds us. Numerous ancient and still-vibrant world traditions guide humans to nourish the gods, to "give back" to the earth.[15] Our job as humans, according to Hogan, is to offer prayer, which we can understand as *energetic* communication with the life force (1995, 81). It is also through our simple life processes, including sexual exuberance, excretion, respiration, and final expiration that we feed the primal source—for example, by replenishing the soil as our waste and bodies decompose.

Holy/Shit

At the outset of this chapter, I indicated that I would return to the consideration of a maternal concept that challenged the foundational fantasy. A radical symbolization of the original/Mother and a meditation on the cycling of energies, wastes and affects, cohere in one controversial recent artwork. In November 1999 Mayor Rudy Giuliani of New York City threatened to close down the Brooklyn Museum because of its presentation of the "Sensation" exhibit. All of the items in the show, works from young British artists, concerned the body—waste, sex, shit, death, and decay. The most inflammatory to Giuliani was a painting by Chris Ofili, *The Holy Virgin Mary*. It figures a standing Madonna with a flower-like form, dressed in a flowing blue robe. She is black, with pronounced African features. One eye gazes into those of her viewers; the other is cosmically remote. Surrounding the Madonna are cutouts of buttocks from pornographic magazines. Moreover, the painting rests on two mounds of elephant dung, on which, with colored pins, the name *Holy Virgin Mary* is spelled out. Her right breast is exposed; it too is composed of a blob of dung with a spiral shape painted on it. A golden aura radiates around her form, enhanced by the addition of glitter and resin to the paint. Here, the invisible energetic patterns are made visible; an alchemical transmutation (from shit to gold) is invoked.

Ofili is of African ancestry. He indicates that his work is anticolonialist, that he deliberately plays with racist expectations of black art, and that the elephant dung is a reference to its use in some African art as well as a way of connecting his paintings to the earth. Enormous tension shadowed the exhibit. Protestors prayed outside daily. In late December 1999, an elderly man threw white paint onto the Madonna's face and shoulders. His wife told the *New York Times* that her husband is a devout Roman Catholic who is opposed to abortion. He considered the painting blasphemous and attacked it to "try to clean it" (McFadden, 1999).

Brennan observes: "The splitting that secures subjective identity is replayed at all the levels on which the fantasy is acted out" (1993, 194). As we have seen, the mother, including the sacred mother, is viciously divided into two. In the Catholic tradition, the Virgin Mary is identified with purity, asexuality, and life, while Eve is identified with sin, sex, dirt, and death. The Virgin Mary dogmatically is declared to be a product of "Immaculate Conception"—that is, she was conceived without *original* sin. In this perverse fantasy, the Great Mother herself is rendered spotless, clean, utterly severed from the soil and mud, and, we might note with some astonishment, from the *original*. She is *purified*, as Mary Daly observes, of autonomous be-ing (1984, 104).

Despite her dogmatic whitewashing, the Virgin Mary still ineluctably suggests the presence of the ancient Great Mother Goddesses. Even in the Catholic tradition, the continuing presence of the dark Earth/Mother survives, often in the figure of a Black Madonna: for example, the Virgins of Montserrat, Notre-Dame-aux-Neiges, and Czestochowa (Begg, 1996; Birnbaum, 1993).

Swearing fealty only to their fantasy of a virginal, immaculate Madonna, Spanish Catholic conquistadors in Mexico deplored and defaced the "obscene" goddesses they encountered, such as Tlazolteotl. In her aspect as confessor she also was know as Tlaelcuani, the "Filth Eater" (Cisneros, 1996, 49). The goddess bore this name because, like Kali, she is able to absorb the sins, ego, corruption, disease, and waste of human beings. Tlaelcuani is equally a metaphysical mother; her core icon is a naked woman squatting and giving birth (Cisneros, 1996, 49). Like Kali and other mythic mothers, Talzolteotl/Tlaelcuani takes filth (pollutions of all types, psychical as well as material) back into herself and cosmically recycles it, transforming and energizing the cosmos, and rebirthing matter. The Dark Mother, be she Kali, Tlaelcuani, the Ephesian Diana, or the "dirty" Virgin of Ofili's painting, is the original unpurified, unrefined Thought/Sex/Source/Shit goddess.[16] She unifies the realms: sex and mind, matter and energy, heaven and earth, food and waste, life and death.[17] The exploitative "dumping" strategy of the ego that Brennan theorizes, whereby the masculine subject, aided by social inequality, dumps his negative affect into a feminine object who recycles it, keeping him invigorated, is a perverse imitation if not a thwarting of the transmutational powers and processes of the Original/Mother.

Returning to Morrison's *Tar Baby*, we find an extraordinarily revealing confrontation between the white colonizer, Valerian, his wife, Margaret, and their servants, Sydney and Ondine, a black island husband and wife. Valerian is rude and condescending to Ondine. Sydney, speaking up for his wife, asserts that Ondine should have the same respect as Margaret. Ondine interrupts the conversation to tell all sorts of truths. She effectively defends against Valerian's and Margaret's attempted "spirit murder" by naming the profound inversion that governs the exploitative relationship and claiming the honor she deserves: "More . . . I should have more respect [than Margaret]. I am the one who cleans up her shit!" (Morrison, 1981, 178).

Brennan suggests that when the subject refuses its appointed role "to impose a negative image on the other . . . resist[s] and reverse[s] moments of objectifying aggression . . . these decisions may reverberate throughout the cosmos, like Lorenzo's butterfly" (1993, 188). So, too, the aggressed-against "object," like Ondine, can talk back, refusing to carry the waste and sustain the fantasy, becoming a subject and insisting that all understand the world from her standpoint. Such resistance, the kind of reverse "dumping" Ondine engages in here, also releases psychical energies that previously have been bound. These everyday resistances powerfully "perturb the established pathways which otherwise guide and limit understanding" (Brennan, 1997, 283).

In the same way, realizing the significance of a symbol whose meaning has been forgotten or discredited, or discerning a Background presence that has been frozen into a stereotype, releases bound energy back into the cosmic flow.[18] Feminist poets and philosophers (for example, Mary Daly, 1973 and 1978; Luce Irigaray, 1985 and 1993; Gloria Anzaldúa, 1987, 66–75; bell hooks, 1989 and 1992; Muriel Rukeyser, 1994, 217) have long insisted that naming, truth-telling, talking back, breaking silence, oppositional gazing, the decoding of myths and symbols, and transformative mythmaking can cause the world to "split open" (Rukeyser, 1994, 217). Brennan's elegant theory affirms these central propositions of feminist thought and provides a framework of energetics to understand how, precisely, this happens.

If we attend to Ondine's words in *Tar Baby*, we recognize the voice of Necessity. So, too, we can absorb her glowing, pulsing presence when gazing upon the beauty and mystery of Ofili's *Holy Virgin Mary*. This Madonna overturns and renders moot what Brennan identifies as the *splitting* at the core of the foundational fantasy. The realms of dark and light are connected; sex, the earth, and even dung are not separated from the Holy. Yet I also suspect an accompanying admonition. At this advanced stage of the ego's era, perversely, all esteem, power, and gain is given to those who, overtly or collaboratively, deny dependence upon nature, produce toxic waste, ravage the land, bind energy into fixities, engage in exploitative dumping, cannibalize the earth, and (suicidally) deny death. Is this why the bared breast of the Virgin is made of dung? Has the "infant" finally succeeded in poisoning the breast with his own excrement? Or is there a more *original* interpretation?

Let's get down. Let's be real. Ultimately, humans are not capable of poisoning the source, the "Ultimate monistic stuff from which everything emerges" (Dalmiya, 2000, 134). We can, however, poison ourselves. Fatally. As Ofili's Virgin suggests, perhaps even She grows weary of the ego's assault, immaturity, and disrespect. Change direction, She warns. Grow down, clean up, or you might soon be eating shit.

Part 4

Female Potency

13

Goddesses and Monsters

The male-dominated *Azteca-Mexica* culture drove the powerful female deities underground by giving them monstrous
attributes . . . thus splitting the female Self and the female
deities. They divided her who had been complete, who possessed both upper (light) and underworld (dark) aspects . . .
into chaste virgins and . . . *putas*, into Beauties and the Beasts.
Gloria Anzaldúa (1987, 27–28)

Years ago, along with much of the nation, I went to see *Jaws* (Steven
Spielberg, 1975) and was overcome with recognition. I had been reading
widely in ancient myth, stories of snapping *vaginas dentata* disabled by
manly culture heroes—when they weren't otherwise engaged slaying
similarly fanged (female) dragons and sea serpents. *Jaws'* great white
shark/monster of the depths had much in common with the ancient
goddess, recognizable by her dangerous mouth/vagina, her serpentine
affect, her underworld dwelling, and her appetite.

The likelihood of actually being bitten let alone killed by a shark is
tiny. Nonetheless, *Jaws* struck a resonant chord; it had mythic power,
the subterranean potency to communicate deeper beliefs and ideas than
were obvious in the characters and plot line. One of its mythic themes is
the ongoing warfare against a feared and demonized female divine. The
predictable parade of sequels suggests not only a continuance of that
war, but, ironically, the immortality of the goddess—by which I mean,
in part, a force of female and feminine energy, potency, and resistance.

It's not really so surprising to find myth at the movies, especially
in richly symbolic movies like horror films. Mythic consciousness is

especially enabled by the cinematic experience (Tyler, 1947). Viewers sit in the dark in a space that is both collective and set apart from other activities. Dramas, fantasies, and dreamlike stories and images are enacted, often by charismatic, larger-than-life "stars," immortals, archetypal personas existing in a realm of light, apart from ordinary reality. While most popular culture myth narratives prescribe values and roles that support the status quo, astute critics have consistently noted an undercurrent of dissent, as in the "gangster film" that mocks the American ideal of success (Warshow, 1979). Feminist critics, in particular, have uncovered subversive potential and/or archetypal presence in the disruptive rampages of aliens and monsters (e.g., Rushing, 1989; Keesey, 1997).

A core, if currently taboo, figure of worldwide myth that is of particular significance for feminist interpretation is the female divine, the goddess, a figure who signifies not only female potency but also the feminine principle: the vital, active, creative, diverse, and interconnecting force in nature as it is also in women and men (Shiva, 1988, 38–42). Negated in many contemporary male-dominated religions and psychologies, this figure remains with us in the world of popular culture, albeit frequently in the form of a caricature, a fetish, or a monster.

Drawing upon Julia Kristeva's understanding of feminine abjection, Barbara Creed (1996, 51) demonstrates that much monstrosity in the horror film is rooted in patriarchal denial, dread, and derogation of the "generative, parthenogenetic mother—that archaic figure who gives birth to all living things," she who "exists in the mythology of all human cultures as the mother-goddess who alone created the heavens and earth." In patriarchal myth, that figure is turned into a monster, a particularly sexual monster as the "generative mother [is] seen only as the abyss, the monstrous vagina" (54). Indeed, the vulva becomes the very model of monstrosity and informs the form of monsters in numerous science fiction (Sobchak, 1990) and horror films: *Jaws*, *Aliens* (James Cameron, 1986), *Species* (Roger Donaldson, 1995), *Independence Day* (Roland Emmerich, 1996), and more. This background might help us to understand why some unruly viewers tend to identify not with the putative heroes and slayers (usually male, sometimes female), but with the monsters.

In her powerful anthem/poem "Monster," Robin Morgan (1972, 81–86) recalls a moment when her not-yet-two-year-old son, catching sight of her naked for the umpteenth time, "suddenly / thought of the furry creature who yawns through / his favorite television program; / connected that image with my genitals; laughed, / and said, 'Monster.'"

Morgan registers the impact and then claims this identity as one signifying her resistance to a social system that devalues the female: "May I
realize that I / am a / monster. I am / a / monster. / I am a monster. /
And I am proud."

Bertha Harris (1977), the lesbian novelist and poet, also avows her
monster identification, but differently. The monster, in her argument, is
the emblem, not of "the mother," but of that really scary figure in the
world made by what she calls "phallic materialism" (1977, 6): the lesbian.
The lesbian/monster is all that is "unassimilable, awesome, dangerous,
outrageous, different"—in short, all that is unfuckable, all that remains
chaotic beyond the ordering, taming, controlling power of what she
calls the "cock" (ibid.). The lesbian/monster, the fusion of maiden, beast,
and nature, according to Harris, represents the greatest threat to patriarchal men's social control.

Film critic Robin Wood (1986) and essayist and poet Gloria Anzaldúa (2000) also seek depths of monster identification. Each argues
that many women and men find in the monster those aspects of the self
that society and civilization, in the service of social inequalities, have
required both women and men to lose, to repress, stigmatize, and disown. Both point to the repression of female sexuality, bisexuality, cross-
gender identification, racial difference, and all that is identified with the
feminine and our animal natures as traits of the "other," monstrous by
establishment standards. Despite social pressure, many women and men
still long to unearth these buried aspects of the self and traverse these
sacred/monstrous routes to knowledge.

The Goddess Becomes Monster

David Leeming and Jake Page set out to restore the sacred context of
the female divine. They conceptualize that task as writing the "biography of an archetype, a potential being who exists in all of us" (men as
well as women), one who takes various forms, including those found in
contemporary popular culture (1994, 7). Their "biography" begins with
a prehistory of the feminine principle understood as the "source of life
and death and regeneration" (ibid.).

Originally, the female divine is honored; then, Leeming and Page
contend, as the patriarchal era takes hold, femaleness, animality, sexuality, nature, death, and darkness are increasingly seen as something abject, chaotic, "dirty," to be feared and controlled if not eradicated. For
example, dutiful motherhood and (exploitable) fertility are honored

while free sexuality is labeled "whoredom." Death becomes the very essence of evil, not respected as an inevitable part of life. Concomitantly, the paradoxical nature of female divinity is no longer respected; "goddess" is split into two aspects. Sovereign, complex, and wild deities are simplified, chastened, straightened, married off, raped, degraded, abused, and demoted in stature. At the same time, in the religious and popular imaginations, the unpacified, insubordinate, and uncontrollable goddess appears as "whore," femme fatale, dragon, beast, devil, and monster.

In popular movies the goddess origins of the monstrous figure are usually disguised, but occasionally specific goddesses from world traditions are caricatured and slandered. For example, in *Bird of Paradise* (King Vidor, 1932), Pele, the volcano goddess, still revered in Hawaii, is turned into a savage male deity demanding the sacrifice of female virgins.

Another type of goddess presence—the earth/death goddess—is announced by the horror film's preoccupation with the world below. Conventional hierarchical dualisms separate up from down, male from female, light from dark, life from death—and then demonize the second part of these pairs. But an older mythic pattern suggests that it is only by descending into the darkness of the underworld and encountering the death goddess that one attains true wisdom, which, of necessity, requires facing all aspects of the cycle of existence. In patriarchal myth that descent is rendered as horrific, and the hero does not face but tries to annihilate the goddess.

This scenario is enacted with some camp overtones in *Vamp* (Richard Wenk, 1986). The film opens as a cadre of white fraternity boys (along with one caricatured Japanese exchange student) embark on a journey from a suburban campus into a seedy part of a city. Their quest is to find a prostitute to dance at a party. In a bar, they encounter the black vampire queen (Grace Jones), who appears in spiraling breastplate and with her face powdered white as she performs her dance. This beautiful, seductive, and ferocious Vamp is a predatory vampire who takes both female and male victims (in other words, she is bisexual). Not too surprisingly, at film's end the young hero ritually kills this goddess/whore. Key signs (like the powdered face) reveal the Vamp as Oshun/Erzuli (Hurston, 1983, 145), the orisha (goddess or spirit) of Africa and the African diaspora, she who is both Mother and Sacred Harlot (Teish, 1985, 79, 121). Jones's Vamp is seductive but also death-dealing; although she is beautiful, her final visage is that of a corpse.

From a gynocentric perspective all of these paradoxes evince divinity. Natalie King-Pedroso (2000, 64) reminds us: "[Oshun's] beauty and charity are legendary, but one should not be deceived by her charms." For, Oshun is often "insensitive, capricious, and voluble, and she can even become nasty and treacherous; in these darker apparitions, we also see her as an old carrion-eating witch and as the orisha of death" (Benitez-Rojo, 1988, 14). It is this inexorably paradoxical nature of Nature—whose twin and inseparable gifts are life and death—that Oshun represents. This cosmic complexity historically has engendered dread in more puerile minds and cultures, represented here by the self-serving "fraternity." *Vamp* unwinds like countless tales of patriarchal initiation where a hero becomes "the man" by slaying the dragon/monster. But from a gynocentric perspective this is a failed initiation. Were the fraternity boys able to face the dark goddess and accept her wisdom, they would have been able to complete their transition to adulthood. But by denying and trying to kill what they fear, they, and the culture they represent, remain in a state of arrested development.

These themes of infantile dread also appear in *Indiana Jones and the Temple of Doom* (Steven Spielberg, 1984). Kali Ma, the great Hindu mother goddess, is cast as a force of cosmic evil, demanding human sacrifice and child slavery, and making strong men like Indiana weak. Incidentally, Kali Ma just happens to be uniting her people in resistance to British colonialism and the three major patriarchal religions. At one point the conventionally creepy leader of the Kali "cult" avows that first the Muslim religion will fall, then the Hebrew God and then the Christian. Soon, he avers, "Kali Ma will rule all the world." Clearly, he will have to be killed by our hero.

Ironically, the cosmic force that the dancing Kali Ma manifests—change, death, and regeneration—has always ruled the world, despite the best efforts of patriarchal gods and heroes. Vrinda Dalmiya (2000, 136) explains: "The dance of Kali . . . suggests . . . constant movement or change. Etymologically, Kali is a feminine form of *kala*, which means time. But time and change are just euphemisms for decay and death. Kali is thus the paradox: She is the Primal Mother who brings forth all life even while she signifies Death. Everything that there is, everything 'natural,' is the vale of Death even though it is nothing other than Kali/*Prakṛti*, the source of life." In Indiana Jones's world, this complex theology is reversed and ridiculed. Female potency, motherhood, and natural death are so feared that they must be denied and reconfigured into a fantasy about a monstrous goddess demanding child slavery, the emasculation of heroes, and human sacrifice.

Killing the Soul

> The movie *Alien* affected me greatly. . . . My sympathies were
> not with the people at all; they were with the alien. I think
> that's how the soul is: It's treated like an alien because we don't
> know it. It's like a serpent; it's slimy and bad. That's what they
> did with women's sexuality and with women.
>
> Gloria Anzaldúa (2000, 40)

The serpent is generally taken to be a symbol of evil, particularly through its association with the Tempter in Genesis. Yet some linguists suggest that the serpent *is* Eve and that together they represent the primordial goddess who gives birth to all humanity (Bennett, 1926, 607). The serpent, moreover, has a global, ancient, and honored lineage as the "principle of life itself" and "the holiness of nature" (Chevalier and Gheerbrant, 1994, 845). The serpent is also the archetypal image of the human soul, the emblem of healing, the emblem of the bisexuality of divinity (that is, containing both female and male; see Hurston, 1983, 142), and the guardian of the sacred.

In her lively and informative illustrated history of the femme fatale, *Vamps*, Pam Keesey (1997) locates the origin myth of modern vamps and vampires in goddess/serpent imagery: fangs, caves, the underworld, darkness, the night, blood, sex—all formerly sacred attributes of female divinity. The goddess appears again as vampire queen in *From Dusk to Dawn* (Richard Rodriguez, 1996). This Mexican monster/goddess, named "Santanico Pandemonio," is played by Salma Hayek in a feathered headdress and accompanied by a giant albino serpent. She is a pop culture avatar of Snake Woman (Olaguibel, 2000), the primal Aztec-Mexica deity. At a climactic moment Hayek's character transforms from a desirable woman into a hideous, serpent-headed, bloodsucking monster. The male heroes, who have been ogling her, then righteously annihilate her. Haven't we seen this all before?

In *Gyn/Ecology*, Mary Daly (1978, 100) posits the epic event of "goddess murder"—for example, the slaughter of the sea serpent/goddess Tiamat by Marduk in the Babylonian epic—as the paradigmatic moment of worldwide patriarchal myth. This mythic model then legitimates continuing violence—such as witch-burnings and sex murders—against the "goddess," whom Daly (11) understands ontologically as the affirmative being and becoming of the female self. In countless monster films as well as any Disney movie in which a witch is climactically destroyed, the myth of mandatory goddess murder is replayed.

One such Disney film is *The Little Mermaid* (John Musker and Ron Clements, 1989), whose "sea witch" Ursula is murdered in a scene that symbolically suggests rape-murder. We meet Ursula as she lurks in her cave/womb, surrounded by a voluptuary of vulva symbols. The mermaid heroine, Ariel, has come to Ursula seeking to change her destiny, to become human. Ursula too is a type of mermaid, but with her bottom half taking shape in octopus tentacles (with a central black hole) rather than a fish tail. Ursula, like innumerable world goddess figures, is accompanied by two serpentine figures (here, two eels). Like mermaids everywhere, she is associated with a mirror.

Ursula, as well, is an unmistakable avatar of a complicated figure (Amadiume, 2003), the water goddess, known popularly in Africa as "Mammy Water." Still revered in West Africa (Jell-Bahlsen, 1997), the "Water Monarch" also appears in the Americas, where she is known by many names, including *Erzulie* (a figure we will return to later and of which *Ursula* is an obvious variation). Two serpent forms (in this case pythons) traditionally accompany Mammy Water. She often takes the form of a mermaid, is associated with mirrors, is able to alter a supplicant's destiny, and is worshiped frequently by women who refuse to lead conventional lives. Mammy Water, like Ursula, lives at the bottom of deep waters and holds power over life, death, and destiny.

As the film's narrative has it, Ursula (who perhaps is Ariel's denied mother) has been exiled from the kingdom. Through all sorts of nefarious machinations, she finally manages to seize King Triton's crown and scepter, reclaiming her place and sovereignty. Rising out of the sea, she then begins to grow, attaining gigantic proportions and becoming ever more fearsome, as she recites: "I am the ruler of all the oceans. The waves obey my every whim. The sea and all its spoils bow to my power."

Curiously enough, Ursula's speech and her manifestation vividly recall the Egyptian Isis, as recounted in a second-century novel, *The Golden Ass*. The narrator, Apuleius, has made an oration when the moon is full to this most "puissant goddess," who, in response, appears to him as if "from the midst of the sea." First she manifests as a "divine and venerable face" and then as the "whole figure of her body, bright and mounting out of the sea." The goddess speaks: "I am Nature, the universal Mother, mistress of all the elements, primordial child of time, sovereign of all things spiritual, queen of the dead, queen also of the immortals, the single manifestation of all gods and goddesses that are. My nod governs the shining heights of Heaven, the wholesome sea-breezes, the lamentable silences of the world below" (Baring and Cashford, 1991, 270). These words of Isis eerily resonate in Ursula's assertion. Were they uttered by Triton, they might be taken as "just the facts." Here, in a patriarchal context, and coming from the lips of a "sea witch," they are heresy, punishable by death, which the film promptly metes out to her. Ariel's prince handily steers the prow of his ship so that it pierces her belly/womb, penetrating, splitting her much as Marduk killed Tiamat in the Babylonian myth.

Another contemporary film that has its female villain speak words uncannily reminiscent of an ancient goddess is *Star Trek First Contact* (Jonathan Frakes, 1996). The essayist and novelist C. S. Lewis (1959, 13) gives voice to a specifically masculinist horror that pops up in this film: "In the hive and in the ant-hill we see fully realized the two things that some of us most dread for our own species—the dominance of the female and the dominance of the collectivity." In the *Star Trek* saga this fear takes shape in the Borg, a perennial antagonist of Star Fleet. The Borg are part machine and part flesh; they eschew individuality and live as a collective. Their ruler is an eerie and intensely sexual queen (there is no king). We first encounter her as a head and shoulders about to be attached to a voluptuous female body (presumably she could also connect to a male body). From her torso trails a glowing connector that flagrantly resembles a serpent. This Borg queen (Alice Krige) has kidnapped the android Data (Brent Spiner), a machine/man without emotions. The sci-fi dominatrix ties him down, installs an "emotion chip," and grafts human skin onto his arm. In close up, we see her ruby red lips blow breath across this newly sensate zone. Data shivers with both fear and desire. "Who are you?" he beseeches. The queen replies: "I am the beginning and the end; I am the one and the many." The Borg queen's speech distinctly recalls the words of the goddess Sophia, speaking as Wisdom in "Thunder, Perfect [Whole] Mind," found in a memorable Gnostic text. Here Sophia/Wisdom names herself in her integrity, despite those who would split her into warring oppositions: "I am the first and the last / I am the honored one and the scorned one / I am the whore and the holy one / I am the wife and the virgin" (Baring and Cashford, 1991, 630).

Following patriarchal paradigms, popular stereotypes reflect the splitting of the goddess's "perfection" or *wholeness*, into warring oppositions. One side, the "light," is made good; the other, the "dark," stands for the bad. Dark-skinned actors are conventionally used to represent the bad (as in *Star Wars*, where the "dark side" of the Force, personified by Darth Vader, is given voice by James Earl Jones). *Star Trek First Contact* challenges this convention. The "evil" Borg queen is preternaturally white. Her opposite number, the "good" woman (naive, chaste, sidelined, and subservient to the men) is played by an African American actress, Alfre Woodard. Despite this innovation, the feminine principle remains vividly divided against itself. For the Borg queen is yet another phobic fantasy of the "eternal feminine," the monstrous *Ewig Weibliche*, who drags men, reason, and civilization down with her into a horrific underworld of sex, instinct, rot, and death. At film's climax, the Borg Queen attempts, literally, to pull Data and Captain Picard *down* into the mists and mystery of sex and communalism, but these stalwart defenders of masculine ascendancy over the feminine triumph. The bald, hard, and erect Picard (Patrick Stewart), veritably a walking phallus, deftly destroys this queen by snapping her snakelike spine in two.

The Witch

Some feminists reclaim witchcraft as a religion based in respect for femaleness, sexuality, the elements, and nature (Starhawk, 1989). This view recognizes the traditional witch not as the servant of the devil—the justification for the massive and lethal persecution by state and church that took place over several centuries in early modern Europe (Caputi, 1987)—but as the priestess for a goddess-centered, earth-based, and nature-respecting religion. Reflecting the feminist and environmental movements, a vivid popular culture has generated how-to books, television shows, and movies featuring young women as powerful witches. Two television series originating in the 1990s, *Charmed* (Spelling Productions) and *Buffy the Vampire Slayer* (Joss Whedon, Executive Creative Producer), feature young witches whose potency increases when they act in conjunction with one another, either as sisters *(Charmed)* or as lesbian lovers *(Buffy)*. This is a qualitative leap beyond the closeted witch of the late 1960s series *Bewitched* (Screen Gems), who tried to mute her powers in order to appease her husband and live a happy suburban married life. The witches of *Buffy* and *Charmed* regularly wage spiritual warfare, defeating cosmic versions of serial killers and other misogynist or power-mad demons.

These television productions are far friendlier to the witchy wisdom tradition than a popular film on the same theme. In *The Craft* (Andrew Fleming, 1996), four outcast high-school girls at first bond with each other to conjure magic and avenge the racist and sexist insults heaped on them. An extraordinary image shows the four grouped in front of a mural of the Virgin of Guadalupe, whom Ana Castillo (1996) calls the "Goddess of the Americas." The four are most powerful when they are bonded. Their rituals are respectful of nature, the elements, and the four directions. The most talented witch, Sara (Robin Tunney), has inherited her gifts from her dead mother, acknowledging the continuance of gynocentric knowledge and traditions.

This could have been a helpful initiation story, giving useful warnings about the dangers of overstepping boundaries and misusing power. However, the narrative devolves into a faceoff (no surprises here) between the "good girl," Sara, and the "bad girl," Nancy (Fairuza Balk). Sara is a virgin, white, pretty, and middle class. Nancy is "white trash," grandiose and insatiable in her quest for money, magic, and power, dark in mood and visage, sexually abused, enraged, infected with a sexually transmitted disease, and transparently lesbian. She acts out violently against the men who have abused her. But socially stigmatized bad girls can only come to a disastrous end in this drearily familiar formula. By film's end Nancy is raving and in a straitjacket, drugged and incarcerated in a mental institution.

Thomas Szasz (1970), criticizing the "manufacture of madness," argued that modern psychiatry's stigmatization of women as especially prone to insanity is analogous to the social-control function of the witch persecutions. Another critic of psychiatry, Phyllis Chesler, pointedly observes that much of what is defined as women's "madness is essentially an intense experience of female biological, sexual, and cultural castration, and a doomed search for potency" (1997, 71). Her description of the forms that women's madness takes in misogynist cultures is a blueprint for Nancy's bad-witch behavior in *The Craft:* "The search often involves 'delusions' or displays of physical aggression, grandeur, sexuality, and emotionality—all traits which would probably be more acceptable in female-dominated cultures. Such traits in women are feared and punished in patriarchal mental institutions." *The Craft's* "happy ending"—with Nancy, the most rebellious and "dark" witch, tortured and confined in a mental institution—is a neo-witch burning.

The Sex Goddess

> She was so extraordinarily beautiful that I nearly laughed out loud. She [was] famine, fire, destruction and plague . . . the only true begetter.
>
> Richard Burton on his first sight of Elizabeth Taylor (quoted in J. E. Rodgers, 1999)

Today, Lanier Graham (1997, 246) notes with some chagrin, the word *goddess* "is used more often in association with movie stars than in any other context." And that context is often narrowly sexual and objectified. A paradigmatic sex goddess from the ancient world is Inanna of Sumer (ca. 3500–500 B.C.E.). Inanna, as a sex goddess should, inspires and emanates the "desire that generates the energy of the universe" (Wolkstein and Kramer, 1983, 169). The sex goddess is banned from the world's patriarchal religions, but "pagan" Hollywood still offers a site for her manifestations (Paglia, 1994, 164). Still, unlike male stars, she is susceptible to being fetishized and sacrificed—turned into pornography, humiliated, constrained, abused, and discarded if she lives long enough to age visibly.

Marilyn Monroe openly lamented her treatment as an objectified "sex symbol" and begged interviewers not to make her into a "joke." The much-mocked Carmen Miranda, in her signature fruit and vegetable headgear, served as "a virtual fertility goddess," cynically exploited to signify the availability of Latin American resources for U.S. expropriation (Shohat and Stam, 1994, 158). The expatriate Resistance fighter Josephine Baker, the sex goddess known as the "Black Venus," is made into an exotic wild thing and literally caged in *Zou Zou* (Marc Allégret, 1934). Dorothy Dandridge, whom the *New York Times* headlined as "Hollywood's First Black Goddess and Casualty" (Weinraub, 1999), was dead at forty-two, after being consistently subjected to sexual and racial harassment. The anglicized Latina Rita Hayworth learned to her horror that her image was painted on an atomic bomb, which was nicknamed "Gilda" after her most popular film. Monroe, Dandridge, and Hayworth all suffered childhood sexual abuse. The qualities so deeply associated with "sex goddesses" in our misogynist culture are really the effects of sexual damage (Steinem, 1991): vulnerability, sadness, inability to resist another's definition of her, and a pronounced aura of sexual availability.

The deeper meaning of Monroe's status as "sex goddess" informs an astonishing image illustrating an essay on books about aliens and UFOs (*New York Times Book Review*, August 9, 1998). Thomas Fuchs's drawing uses a familiar image of Marilyn Monroe from *The Seven Year Itch* (Billy Wilder, 1955). Monroe stands in her white dress over the subway grating, clutching and holding down her swirling skirt so that it just covers her vulva (fig. 13.1). There is one hugely dissonant note, though: Monroe's face has been filled in as a bug-eyed, bald alien.

Before hazarding an interpretation of this strange image, let's check out the scene from the film. Monroe (the sex symbol whose character

13.1 Illustration by Thomas Fuchs, *New York Times Book Review,* August 9, 1998

remains unnamed) and her date, a married man who is trying to work up his courage to have a fling with her, have just seen a monster movie, *The Creature from the Black Lagoon.* The marquee, with a giant image of the monster, looms over them. Monroe expresses empathy with the Creature, whom she recognizes as being in need of love. Immediately after communicating this sentiment to her bemused date, who is played as distinctly foppish and unerotic by Tom Ewell, Monroe takes her position above the subway grating, welcoming the air as her skirt blows up around her hips. Although Hollywood censors allowed only a quick shot of the skirt billowing above her knees, the intent of this scene is to focus all viewers' attention on Monroe's sex organ. We go from the image of the "Creature" to a vivid suggestion of her vulva. Now let's return to the drawing that references this scene. We can see that the artist has brought to the surface what is implicit in that cinematic moment: the identity of the "monster" with the vulva of the (sex) goddess.

Of course, one could object, it is Monroe's face that is made monstrous here. But the familiar iconic and fabricated face of Marilyn Monroe—with all the emphasis on fake blond hair and large, made-up, moist, and parted lips—has always represented the vulva, albeit a desperately made-up and commodified one (much less threatening that way). Joyce Carol Oates (2000, 347) makes this clear in *Blonde,* her fictionalization of Monroe's life. One of Marilyn's lovers thinks to himself as he watches her performance in *Niagara:* "She's got her legs spread and you swear you can see her blond cunt through the sheet. You're just mesmerized, staring. And her face, that's a special kind of cunt. The wet red mouth, the tongue." This connection between the monster-face and the vulva is not new. Sigmund Freud (1955b) famously linked the maternal vulva to the face of the Gorgon Medusa, the snake-haired goddess/monster of Greek myth.

In Monroe's familiar iconography, then, the sex goddess's *sex,* both overtly and covertly, is emblematized as the face of the monster for a culture that can face neither active female desire nor divinity. Luce Irigaray (1993, 71) poignantly asks: "The divinity of women is still hidden, veiled. Could it be what 'man' seeks even as he rapes it?" The same culture that fears female divinity embraces Marilyn Monroe as its consummate "sex goddess," with a star persona based in damage, availability, vulnerability, and eroticism that is "all responsiveness and no desire" (L. Miller, 2000, 6). Monroe is never allowed to be sexually sovereign or demanding; rarely is she acknowledged as smart or even very grown up. No wonder it rings so true when her character in *The Seven Year Itch* identifies with the hunted and maligned Creature. Both the Creature and Marilyn herself represent the besieged (animal, feminine, sexual) *soul* that suffers in a world made by a phallic consciousness that splits male and female, human and animal, spirit and matter, sex and mind.

The Fatal Woman

Give me the demonic any day—Anna May Wong as a villain slithering around in a slinky gown is at least gratifying to watch, neither servile nor passive.

Jessica Hagedorn (1994, 74–75)

The word *fatal* is etymologically linked to fate and the Fates, three ancient goddesses who regulate birth, life, death, change, and regeneration—the cycle of existence. The femme fatale is a popular incarnation of the Fates. The historical distortion and degradation of female divinity, Leeming and Page (1994) contend, is the backdrop for the popular manifestations of women as snaky femmes fatales, dragon ladies, monsters, and witches. Pam Keesey (1997) also links "vamps" to the Fates and to sex/death goddesses.

Patriarchal "good girls" are associated with niceness and all-around impotence, toothlessness. The "bad girl" or femme fatale is the always dangerous abyss, the black hole, and the *vagina dentata*—the one that still has some bite. Jessica Hagedorn speaks for many women when she expresses her preference for the serpentiform "bad girl" over her defanged counterpart. The femme fatale, witch, or vamp represents an outlawed form of female divinity, potency, genius, sexual agency, independence, vengeance, and death power. Hagedorn is not alone in finding a liberatory feminist message in the femme fatale; Lynda Hart (1994) reminds us of the (usually unspoken) lesbian presence informing representations of aggressive and lawless women.

Despite her overwhelming characterization as a "white woman" (with one obvious exception in the Asian Dragon Lady), the political background of the femme fatale is a colonialist one (Lalvani, 1995). Indeed, the characteristics attributed to her as a "deviant" white woman are the ones attributed to "normal" women of color: treachery, excessive sexuality, and so on. While white femmes fatales are sometimes victorious, the femme fatale of color is usually vanquished: Grace Jones in *Vamp*, Tia Carrere in *True Lies* (James Cameron, 1994), and the rest (see chapter 3).

One of the most famous of all white femmes fatales was Catherine Trammel (Sharon Stone) in *Basic Instinct* (Paul Verhoeven, 1992).

Trammel is a female genius, but this is no *Good Will Hunting* happy kind of male genius story. In patriarchal myth all female geniuses are of the criminal/lesbian variety (see also *Wild Things*, John McNaughton, 1998). In *Basic Instinct* Trammel's threat is established in the very first scene, where a mysterious blonde writhes "on top" in heterosexual intercourse. Large statues of jungle beasts with bared fangs watch over the happenings. The woman (whom we later find out to be Trammel) binds the man's hands with a scarf and stabs him to death. The film's key scene occurs when the bisexual Trammel is interrogated by an assembly of male cops and attorneys. With consummate cool Catherine crosses and uncrosses her legs, flashing her unclad vulva and utterly intimidating her inquisitors. In this fabulously "Gorgonesque" moment, the femme fatale virtually turns her inquisitors to stone.

Mythically, the exposure of the genitals is the quintessential apotropaic act, one that averts evil, promises defiance, and asserts power. In his essay on the "Medusa's Head," Freud (1955b, 173) differentiates between the male and female genitals in terms of their power to avert danger. According to him, the apotropaic effect of the vulva is due to the beholder's horror at its exposed impotence, whereas the display of the penis boldly manifests phallic potency: "To display the penis (or any of its surrogates) is to say: 'I am not afraid of you. I defy you. I have a penis.'" Savvy readers might allow themselves a snicker before returning to that remarkable scene where Catherine's brazen gesture can only be interpreted as saying: "I am not afraid of you. I defy you. I have a vulva" (although this character would probably use a more wicked word for her sex organ). This scene also suggests, contra Freud, that it is the sovereign and even lesbian vulva, not necessarily the maternal one, that has this most potent and Gorgonic affect and effect.

In her discussion of abjection and its relation to gender, Julia Kristeva (1986, 70) comments: "[I]t is always to be noticed that the attempt to establish a male, phallic power is vigorously threatened by the no less virulent power of the other sex, which is oppressed. That other sex, the feminine, becomes synonymous with a radical evil that is to be suppressed." The association of evil with Eve and her descendants continues, as *Basic Instinct* once again links an instinct for evil to the feminine sex. Regardless, resistant viewers still appreciate the "power of the other sex" as that sex announces and pronounces its presence, refusing to be reduced to or contained by caricature (pornography) or named as a "lack" (as in psychoanalytic theory). Rather, "the abyss" looks and talks back, potent and full of presence.

Cinderella Stories

The folklore scholar Harold Bayley (1996, 1:190) avers that ancient fairy tales and myths issued "from the soil," that is, from the dark mother tongue of women's oral tradition, from enduring, if now marginalized, wisdoms. Marina Warner (1996) suggests that female storytellers used the world of conventional fantasy to create multiple meanings and negotiate their uncertain place in an unfriendly world that splits the female self into, on the one hand, sinful carnality (Eve) and, on the other, impossible purity (the Virgin Mary). Clarissa Pinkola Estés (1992) points to fairy and folk tales as guides to female initiation, growth, knowledge, and strength.

The fairytale princess is a quintessential figure in popular culture, frequently signifying female passivity. Regarding Sleeping Beauty Andrea Dworkin asks (1974, 42): "He fell in love with her while she was asleep, or was it because she was asleep?" Still, investigation of this tale and others yields a gynocentric substory. Cinderella especially is a core story of female potency and hope for the restoration of the refused and abused soul to glory. Writing in 1912, Bayley (1996, 2:194–95) reveals that in its origins and essence the Cinderella narrative is about the soul's journey, an ancient, global myth that combines elements from goddess culture, the pagan world, the Wisdom literature of Judaism, Gnosticism, mystical Christianity, alchemy, the Grail legends, and fairytales (see also Baring and Cashford, 1991, 655). Bayley links Cinderella to the Black Shulamite of the Song of Songs, the exiled Shekinah in the Judaic tradition, Diana, goddess of light, and the Black Virgin, among others. He finds in the story the soul's suffering because of the splitting of earth, nature, and physical body from spirit: "Cinderella, the bright and shining one, who sits among the cinders and keeps the fire alight, is a personification of the Holy Spirit dwelling unhonoured amid the smoldering ashes of the Soul's latent, never totally extinct, Divinity, and, by patient tending, fanning them into flame" (Bayley, 1996, 2:194–95). Gradually, the soul awakens to the full radiance of its divinity. Cinderella's glorious and diverse gowns symbolize the various gateways of initiation, the differing aspects of acquired elemental Wisdom.

Alice Walker's *The Color Purple* (1982) and the film made from the novel (Steven Spielberg, 1985) convey a radical reinterpretation and reclamation of the Cinderella myth. Celie (Whoopi Goldberg), whose name recalls the celestial radiance of Cinderella, overcomes incestuous rape, the theft of her children, battery, destruction of her self-worth, and separation from all she loved. Aided by a "fairy godmother" (and lover) in the form of Shug, a philosophical blues singer, Celie claims her self through her experiences of lesbian Eros, a revisioning of her religious understandings, creative endeavor, and economic self-sufficiency. Vividly, she transforms from a state of degradation to one of exaltation, symbolized not so much by glorious gowns as by the comfortable, individually beautiful, and well-designed pants that she makes. Celie emerges from the "cinders" of profound feelings of unworthiness, lovelessness, injustice, abuse, and despair to blaze, with the beauty of the soul's radiance, for the world to see. Viewers and readers, as if in a ritual, participate in her process. As Walker herself sees the character: "When Celie comes in from the cold of repression, self-hatred, and denial, and only when Celie comes in from the cold—do I come in. And many of you as well" (1985, 96).

The promotional copy for the Jamaican film *Dancehall Queen* (Don Letts and Rick Elgood, 1997) tells viewers that they are about to see a "Cinderella story." Marcia (Audrey Reid) is a plainly dressed street vendor and a poor, single mother. When the film opens, Marcia and her friends are talking, celebrating the fact that a group of squatters, forewarned, have successfully resisted an anonymous landlord's attempts to remove them from their homes. Suddenly, a menacing interloper, "Priest" (Paul Campbell), appears and tries to evict Marcia from her vending site. Marcia and her friends hold him off, but he comes back later and kills one of them, Sonny. Priest then continuously sexually harasses Marcia and threatens her brother. Contributing to the support of Marcia's family is Larry (Carl Davis), a local man whom she perceives as a "businessman" although he is, in actuality, the corrupt landlord and implicitly a pimp. In return, Larry expects Marcia to allow him to sexually use her teenage daughter. At first Marcia goes along with this, seeing loss of educational opportunities, hunger, and homelessness as the only alternative. After one session with Larry, the daughter refuses to see him again. Besieged and the target of her daughter's fury, and realizing that no one is going to "save" her, Marcia decides to make some changes. A moment of revelation occurs: She sees the glamorous reigning Dancehall Queen, Olivine, out of her transformative clothing, looking just like an ordinary woman. Marcia realizes that she too can work some glamour. Like the mythic Cinderella, she dons a disguise and goes to the "ball," finding a route to transformation and potency in the dancehall culture of Kingston.

In Jamaica, vibrant song and music, flashy costuming, and "dirty" dancing characterize the dancehall. Although moral majorities and cultural elites scorn it as irredeemably vulgar, the Jamaican scholar Carolyn Cooper applauds the dancehall as a place where nonconformist class and gender politics take shape. She calls dancehall culture "an innocently transgressive celebration of freedom from sin and law" (1995, 11). This type of transgression has particular relevance for female potency: "Liberated from the repressive respectability of a conservative gender ideology of female property and propriety . . . women lay proper claim to the control of their own bodies" (ibid.). Women wear wildly colored wigs, flashy jewelry, glittery, revealing and body-hugging costumes. Marcia, who normally dresses in gender-neutral slacks, shirts, and caps, begins to outfit herself for a change. At first she is secretive, dancing at home alone, but soon she engages the help of a local fairy-godmother-like seamstress. An attractive photographer at the dancehall comes on to her, but Marcia puts him off. When he offers to manage her, she vehemently retorts: "I manage myself." During her ride home in a taxi, Marcia hurriedly strips off her finery, becoming once again a poor "street vendor" as she enters her house.

But Larry has become smitten with the costumed and unrecognizable Marcia, calling her his "sexy bitch." In hopes of sexual conquest, he assists her financially with her increasingly expensive outfits. He also foolishly reveals that Priest is working for him. Marcia realizes that he is the corrupt landlord whom the squatters were resisting and also the one who ordered the hit on Sonny in retaliation for his warnings to the squatters. Marcia is appalled but realizes that she can use this information to her advantage.

The film climaxes on the night of a contest for the title of Dancehall Queen between Olivine and Marcia, who is dubbed "The Mystery Lady." Hoping to take her down in advance, Olivine pays an informant to find out who Marcia is. Just before the contest is to begin, she reveals Marcia's true identity, scorning her as a mere "street vendor." Now everyone knows, and Marcia is so humiliated that she feels unable to continue. But, encouraged by her daughter and her "fairy godmother," Marcia realizes that she can claim her identity and still merge it with her erotic persona. Her commonness is not a liability but a source of strength, for if she wins it will be a victory for "all of we." Of course, Marcia triumphs, and this Jamaican Cinderella is crowned Queen of the Dancehall. As the dance contest takes place inside, Larry and Priest square off outside, and Larry kills him. When Larry comes in to claim his "sexy bitch," Marcia reveals herself to him and laughs in his face. Larry, now a suspect in a murder case, is no longer a threat.

When we first meet her, Marcia is poor, buffeted by circumstances and manipulated by powerful and violent men. Moreover, as she reveals to a friend, it has been a very long time since she has "gotten any." By film's end, Marcia, winner of a large cash prize, vindicated in her identity, and glowing with energy, now takes the initiative and invites the eager photographer home with her.

Marcia, much like Celie, undergoes a glorious transformation. Her dance is a song of herself. Indeed, the purpose of her sexually jubilant dance—to tap into her deepest sources of strength—is best understood by comparing it with the spiritless and pornographic movements of the women working for Larry in his strip club, women who must offer themselves up as visual "meat" for gawking male patrons. Marcia's dance channels a very different type of untrammeled and unbought power that Audre Lorde (1984, 53) understands as the *erotic:* "a resource within each of us that lies in a deeply female and spiritual plane, firmly rooted in the power of our unexpressed or unrecognized feeling." As Lorde sees it, the erotic also is linked to "sources of power within the culture of the oppressed that can provide energy for change" (ibid.).

The erotic is what the ancient myth of the "sex goddess" is all about. It is the force of desire that engenders life. It is the wellspring of hope, the glorious energy enabling connection and communion, an ineffable source that we recognize manifesting in color, dance, glitter, glow, and music. It is the radiance that Cinderella/Marcia has had to bury underneath the metaphorical coat of ashes. Marcia is not a conventional glamour queen—she is thirty years old, a mother, physically strong, dark-skinned, and not especially beautiful. But she is the "Mystery Lady," with all that that title implies. *Mystery* not only refers to the enigma of her identity, but speaks to the deeper theme: the hidden erotic potential in all beings, the innate resiliency, creative power, and strength of purpose that can triumph over domination. When Marcia wins, one of the latest in the ancestral line of Cinderellas, all oppressed people win.

Goddesses and Mammies

A stock figure of racist and sexist imagery is the "mammy," the devoted servant and cook, and the loving nurturer of white children. Musing on the persistence of the racist stereotype of Aunt Jemima in an essay titled "Giving the Party," Alice Walker (1997, 139) finds that the "black woman is herself a symbol of nurturing." She proposes a radical reconceptualization of the ubiquitous stereotype of the mammy or "Aunt

Jemima." For the big black woman with the steaming pot of food represents the Origin, abundance, the source of all being: "Her big tits right next to the big black pot; a potent symbol, the big black pot, in itself. For isn't the black pot of a black woman's womb the vessel from which white men secretly fear they came, just as the big black hole in the cosmos is the black pot into which they fear they will disappear?" (141). Behind the distorting and racist image, Walker recognizes Aunt Jemima as the ultimate ancestor, the ancient dark universal Goddess, the food source, the endlessly fruitful life force, and the feminine principle. In a patriarchal world, the directive has been to enslave this quintessentially sovereign figure: She who nurtures and loves all.

In this light let us reconsider the figure of the stereotypic mammy, Delilah (Louise Beavers) in *Imitation of Life* (John Stahl, 1934), a film based on a best-selling novel by Fannie Hurst, who for a time employed Zora Neale Hurston as a companion/secretary. Perhaps Hurston's knowledge of and respect for African folk wisdom influenced, in a roundabout way, Hurst's characterizations of black women. *Imitation of Life* involves a white woman, Miss Bea (Claudette Colbert), who becomes a millionaire by mass-producing a pancake mix based on a "secret recipe" given to her by her African American servant, Delilah. Delilah is a large, self-sacrificing stereotypic mammy, seemingly too simple-minded to grasp the complexities of business. When Miss Bea offers Delilah the chance for a home and car of her own and a 20 percent share of the business, Delilah refuses, saying that she wants to stay on working for Miss Bea. When Miss Bea points out that all their success is due to Delilah's recipe, Delilah acknowledges this but reminds her: "I gives it to you, honey; I made you a present of it." One cannot approach this scene without first recognizing the flagrant racism of its rendition of a happy slave who is utterly content with her "place" (Caputi and Vann, 1987). Yet, if we look into the deepest *Background* layers of this character, we can perceive some resonance of the dark goddess, the source of all nurturance, the epicenter of the life force—and her rebuke to the domineering and soulless slaveholders (and neo-slaveholders) who seek to possess and exploit the life force. Consider Delilah's words in conjunction with a core understanding of Cherokee philosophy, as expressed by Marilou Awiakta (1993, 252): "The life force cannot be owned as property, used and consumed—or merchandised. Period." The life source feeds us all with infinite generosity. Delilah, the only character in the film who holds sacred knowledge, encoded as the "secret recipe," speaks as and for the life force—its ethic of munificence and its refusal of commerce. The supreme folly of patriarchal/capitalist culture is to act as if the life source can be enslaved, endlessly ripped off, packaged, and sold, without dire consequences ultimately unfolding. The life force can always choose to quit or, far more accurately, can ask disrespectful humanity to leave her house. For as Walker so truly tells it, it is She (Mammy/Aunt Jemima) who actually is "giving the party." We exist at Her invitation.

Toni Morrison (1984, 343) finds the "presence of the ancestor" to be one of several "distinctive elements" in African American narrative. That ancestor is located behind the façade of the traditional mammy in Cheryl Dunye's scintillating film *The Watermelon Woman* (1997). Dunye plays herself in a mock documentary about an aspiring black lesbian filmmaker's quest to uncover the identity of a compelling actress who played mammies in 1930s films (like *Imitation of Life*) but appeared in the credits only as "The Watermelon Woman." Getting no help from either the library or a black gay male specialist on African American film, Dunye goes to the primal source—the oral tradition in the person of her mother. Through Mom's stories from the old days, Dunye learns that the "Watermelon Woman" was Fae Richards, an actress and singer. Delving further, she finds out that Fae was a lesbian. One of Fae's friends (played by the poet Cheryl Clarke) exhorts Dunye: "She paved the way for kids like you. Make our history before we are all dead and gone."

Because the history of black lesbian creativity has been so systematically erased, Dunye cannot find actual antecedents. Rather, she must script and film her own myth/history, populating her cinematic world with black lesbian artists such as Clarke and the musician Toshi Reagon. Such mythmaking generates its own kind of power. In the fictional story Dunye tells, Fae Richards comes to represent the real artists who have been and are being silenced, kept out, and/or confined to mammy roles and permanent anonymity. When Richards is claimed and named, she becomes the mythic ancestor who can provide hope, inspiration, history, and possibility for black lesbian creativity (Sullivan, 2000). She becomes someone who, like the mother in Alice Walker's germinal essay "In Search of Our Mothers' Gardens," leaves a "legacy of respect . . . for all that illuminates and cherishes life. She has handed down respect for the possibilities—and the will to grasp them" (Walker, 1983, 241–42). *The Watermelon Woman*, like Walker's essay, is itself a ritual honoring "goddess"—that is, the vital, active, erotic principle that nurtures creativity, connection, and resistance. Dunye delves into the suggestive space behind the mammy stereotype and unearths a mythic black lesbian ancestor. In her ritual of respect, the ancestor is restored, her gift to the community is acknowledged, and a sacred place for her is created in communal memory.

"Another Way of Knowing Things"

While gynocentric and goddess-oriented myths and stories have been largely disguised, suppressed, caricatured, or demonized in mainstream popular culture, filmmakers like Dunye seek the *Background* story and move it forward. Many others—critics, writers, artists, performers— also follow this winding route, diving into the memory pool and bringing up elements of a resistant, affirming, and transformative oral and wisdom tradition to ensoul their works (P. Allen, 1986a; Brooks De Vita, 2000, Singer, 2001).

Kasi Lemmons, writer and director of *Eve's Bayou* (1998), discusses her conscious incorporation of such elements in her film: "Folklore is the legacy of power handed down from woman to woman" (Muhammad, 1998, 75). The folklore in *Eve's Bayou* concerns female wisdom/ witchcraft, healing, fate, family secrets involving adultery and incest, and those legacies of power. The Louisiana town and the protagonist, a ten-year-old girl, are named for a powerful ancestor, Eve, an African slave who used "powerful medicine" (both physical and metaphysical) to save her master's life. He then freed her and gave her a tract of land. She, "perhaps in gratitude," bore him sixteen children. In the film's opening moments, a series of black and white images reveal the slave cabins and the fields, where the ancestral Eve stands on the path with the bayou in view. Eve's female descendants, another Eve (Jurnee Smollett) and her aunt Mozelle (Debbi Morgan), have inherited her potency. Both are associated with creatures that traditionally have signified witchcraft *and* female divinity—snakes and spiders. Both have second sight—activated by taking the hands of another. And both have a fateful influence.

These supernatural elements in *Eve's Bayou* are intrinsic to an African American cosmology. Toni Morrison has spoken of the ways in which she blends an "acceptance of the supernatural and a profound rootedness in the real world at the same time with neither taking precedence over the other. It is indicative of the cosmology, the way in which Black people looked at the world. We are very practical people, very down-to-earth, even shrewd people. But within that practicality we also accepted what I suppose could be called superstition and magic, which is another way of knowing things. But to blend those two worlds together at the same time was enhancing not limiting. And some of those things were 'discredited knowledge' that Black people had, discredited only because Black people were discredited and what they knew was discredited. And also because the push toward upward social mobility would mean to get as far away from that kind of knowledge as possible" (1984, 342). "Discredited knowledge" characterizes three mythic female characters in *Eve's Bayou*. All participate in what Karla Holloway (1992, 2) recognizes as "the recovered metaphor . . . of the goddess/ancestor," which appears over and over in the literary (and filmic) works of contemporary African American and West African mythmakers.

First is Eve herself. The name *Eve* signifies not only the primordial goddess/monster, the serpentine mother of all the living (Bennett, 1926, 607), but also the West African Mammy Water, known in Togo as Evhe Mammy Water (Jell-Bahlsen, 1997, 109). Second, there is Mozelle (whose name recalls the goddess Erzulie), who has a flourishing practice as a psychic healer, working mostly with female clients. Although popular and efficacious, she is socially unrecognized. Mozelle is young, loving and beautiful but, like her brother, has been habitually unfaithful and has occasioned lethal violence due to her love affairs. Her husbands have all died—through murder or accident. She is childless. The third is Elzora (Diahann Carroll), another witch/conjure woman. Elzora (whose name also invokes Erzulie as well as "Eze Mimri" in Africa) chalks her face white and runs a fortune-telling stand at an outdoor market. She is poor and lives apart from the town, in an old home in the midst of the swamp. Mammy Water and Erzulie, along with their (usually childless) priestesses, habitually appear with white mask or lightened aspect, an attribute indicating numinous qualities, transitions from life to death and vice versa, and depth of spirit involvement and communication (Jell-Bahlsen, 1997, 110). Like all elemental deities, they are of ambivalent character, light and dark, beautiful and ugly, reflecting the very nature of Nature. There are two distinct faces of Erzulie. Sometimes she is "gentle and ministering, above all in women's matters and those of love" and other times she appears as "an older woman and terrible to look at" (Hurston, 1983, 147), known to be "insensitive, capricious . . . nasty and treacherous," more like a "carrion-eating witch and . . . *orisha* of death" (Benitez-Rojo, 1988, 14). Together, Elzora and Mozelle manifest this divine presence.

Mozelle's brother (Eve's father) is Louis (Samuel L. Jackson), a conventional, accredited healer—a medical doctor. Louis openly mocks

Mozelle's unsanctioned medical practices, reminding the family that she is "not unfamiliar with the inside of a mental institution." His words remind us of the punishment all too frequently meted out to medicine women in misogynist and racist systems. The world that refuses to honor Mozelle also permits Louis to become only the "best colored doctor" in the area (as a friend innocently comments to his mother). And perhaps because of these racist blows to his narcissism, he describes himself as a man with an insatiable "need to be a hero." He finds that he is able to realize that yearning only by being desired by scores of women. Eve witnesses his sexual betrayal of her mother with his lover Maddy Meroux (Lisa Nicole Carson). She also watches jealously as Louis pays special attention to her sister, the thirteen-year-old Cisely (Meagan Good), selecting her for dances at family parties while ignoring Eve. Cisely's behavior alters in response to her father's attentions. She begins to dress in alluring nightgowns and wait up for Louis so that she can greet him with a drink when he returns home late at night after his romantic assignations. She meets her father secretly while he is at work and cuts and restyles her hair, making herself look not only older but more like her mother. Soon Cisely inexplicably suffers a breakdown and, under pressure from Eve, tells her that Louis has kissed her sexually. She then moves away from the family home to stay with relatives. Enraged, Eve takes action. She first asks Mozelle how Voodoo might kill someone. Mozelle, shocked, demands that Eve give her her hands. They touch for a second only. Nothing seems to be revealed, and Mozelle says to Eve: "OK, keep your secrets." The next day Eve goes to the outdoor market, where she happens upon Lenny (Roger Guenveur Smith), Maddy Meroux's husband. She hints broadly to him that when he is out working in the evening, his wife is having a good time with Louis. Eve takes leave of him and immediately encounters the fortuneteller Elzora. She goes back to Elzora's swamp home with her and requests a spell to kill her father. Elzora at first demurs, telling Eve that people have a "way of dying at their own speed." But when Eve persists, Elzora takes her money and tells her to return in a few nights for her hex. When Eve comes back, expecting to be given a Voodoo doll or some other object to set things in motion, she still thinks that she can change her mind. But Elzora, all forbidding and nasty death Hag now, laughs at her and tells her that the spell has already begun. And indeed it has.

Panic-stricken and now regretting her action, Eve goes in search of her father and finds him in a bar with Maddy. At this point, Lenny shows up, tells Maddy to leave, and orders Louis never to speak to her again. Louis deliberately disobeys, and Lenny shoots him dead. Viewers are left to debate whether any magic was operative at all. Many might conclude that Louis's murder was ordained not by a spell, but by Eve's betrayal when she first told Lenny about the affair. And, moreover, wasn't it Louis's cockiness and bad judgment that really got him killed?

Although these are reasonable suppositions, the film requires a more complex understanding of the way things happen—neither wholly rationally (one is in complete control) nor wholly magically (one is the hapless victim of another's ill will). The spell that Elzora and Eve cast takes lethal shape only when Louis foolishly lends his energy to it, when he becomes a participant in it. Had Louis refrained from speaking to his lover as her husband had demanded, he could have remained unscathed. Instead, he completes the spell through his own actions and ends up dead.

Afterward, doubt is cast on Cisely's accusation of incest. Although she said nothing when she took Eve's hands, Mozelle had clearly gleaned some insight into Eve's suspicion and had confronted Louis. Louis had replied to her in a letter, which Eve finds and reads. As he explains it, Louis was astonished when Cisely initiated the sexual kiss. He ruefully acknowledges that he had perhaps welcomed his daughter's comfort after a terrible fight with his wife, but he truly never anticipated or desired the kiss. Indeed, when Cisely kissed him, Louis shouted at her and slapped her away violently. He regrets the terrible effect this blow has had on her, but says that he nonetheless allowed Cisely to depart from the home to live with relatives without breaking his silence, in order to spare her further humiliation. Upon reading the letter, Eve is outraged and demands that Cisely tell her the truth. Sobbing, Cisely confesses that she really doesn't know the truth. Eve, mirroring Mozelle, demands that Cisely give her her hands. As she does, Eve "sees" the events as they really happened, including Cisely kissing her father. While one might think that this only confirms Louis's account, Eve does not respond with anger. Instead, she embraces her sobbing sister, comforts her, and tells her that everything will be all right.

How can we understand this? What does Eve realize? Lemmons (Muhammad, 1998, 75) frankly tells us that this part of her story is not about incest, but about "something infinitely more common . . . inappropriate behavior between adults and children." This occurs when the adult is irresponsible, not creating or respecting boundaries between adult and child. Louis, although he does not commit overt incest with his daughter, is guilty of a type of emotional incest. He has long neglected his wife while sexualizing his relationships with patients and neighbors. Simultaneously, he has been behaving seductively with his daughter, relishing her hero worship, treating her in subtle ways as a substitute for his wife. When Cisely sits on his lap and kisses him, she has only played out the part her father had scripted for her. When Louis slaps her for this, he transfers to her all responsibility and shame, furthering his error and his mistreatment of his daughter.

D. Soyini Madison (2000, 325–26) remarks upon the film's complex explorations of phallic narcissism, racism, and sexual responsibilities as these play out against a background of mythic consciousness and culture. Reimagined here are African American and gynocentric traditions of knowledge and power: "Blackness is located in second sight and in the conjuring powers of Mozelle, Eve and Elzora. They represent a long history of New Orleans black conjure women; they are the sphinx, the chorus, the black widow spider, and fate. They are also the burning of witches avenged!" *Eve's Bayou* restores the honor not only of the fate goddess and the witch, but also that of the mythical Eve, the black female ancestor who is the potent "mother of all living," the original monster/goddess. That ancestor's continuing presence, manifesting in the young Eve, is recognized as the original and enduring source of life and death, magic, power, and fate.

Eve's Bayou defies a reductive reading that would find one character lying all the time and one telling the complete truth, or one that would see only the world of material reality and not the one of magic and medicine. Toni Morrison, we might recall, speaks of an African American sensibility and knowledge that characteristically blends two worlds—the magical and the real. That same blending pervades *Eve's Bayou*, drenched, as it is, with the overwhelming presence of the bayou. Deep waters are the home of the female divinities whose presences permeate the film. And the waters are not only the home of the goddess; they also are her magic mirror, serving as a portal between the worlds of the numinous and the mundane. The ancestral Eve's bayou—deep, shimmering, and mysterious—reflects the happenings as the narrative unfolds, consistently reminding viewers of the reality of the spirit world. The final image of the film has Cisely and Eve holding hands and looking out at the water as they stand between twin trees on a strip of land jutting out into the bayou. The water is thus before and behind them. The camera draws back, showing the ordinary world on top, and its reflection mirrored below. Viewers are invited to contemplate the dual nature of existence—magical *and* real.

Another film by an African American director and writer—Julie Dash's *Daughters of the Dust* (1992)—also speaks to the transmission of power from the ancestors and the manifestation of gods and goddesses in everyday life. The story concerns a Gullah family at the turn of the century. Some of the members are about to leave the islands and settle in the North. They gather for a final ritual of solidarity and community with the grandmother. Looking at Dash's (1992) notations in the margins of the script, we learn that the ostensibly mundane characters all signify different Yoruban deities in this consciously mythic drama. The lesbian prostitute Yellow Mary manifests Yemayá, the African "Mother of the Sea, the Great Water, the Womb of Creation . . . the Mother of Dreams, the Mother of Secrets" (Teish, 1985, 118). Nana Peazant, the eighty-eight-year-old grandmother, is Obatala, the "supreme deity of the Yoruba pantheon, the androgynous creator. S/he is envisioned as an ancient wo/man . . . most benevolent, most wise, and infinitely powerful" (117). Trula (Yellow Mary's companion) is Oshun. Eli, Nana's grandson, is Ogun, the "architect, the builder of civilization" (126); his unborn child is Elegba, "the divine trickster-linguist" (113).

References to other mythic characters and stories, old and new, are threaded through *Daughters of the Dust*. The viewer is immediately prepared for an experience of film as myth/ceremony when it opens with a sacred recitation. The voice that we hear belongs to Yellow Mary/Yemayá, making new once again the words of the goddess in the Gnostic poem "Thunder, Perfect Mind": "I am the first and the last. I am the honored one and the scorned one." With these words, Sophia/Yemayá pronounces herself as whole, as balanced in her duality. The goddess and the monster, once again, are one.

14

The Second Coming
of Diana

Today the fact that Diana once had for the pagans a reality she
does not have for us means merely that the myth lives in another form. It is an ideal archetype, a part of human experience that has its home in the imagination. And yet . . . that
which was true once may become true again. What was symbolized by the Diana myth . . . is a permanent legacy of the
race. So the essence of myth also has the status of permanent
possibility.

Parker Tyler (1947, xx)

What sort of religious forces are beginning in this era of death
for the great male gods? Surely new gods will be born. . . . [A]s
our range of the possible expands so must our pantheon.

Naomi R. Goldenberg (1979, 9)

A new world asserted itself and made a goddess. . . . I'll tell my
grandchildren I was there . . . but . . . it will seem so obvious to
them: of course Diana changed the world.

Brian Appleyard (quoted in MacArthur, 1997, 166)

A *New York Times* editorial (September 7, 1997) spoke for many when it
confessed: "The source of Diana's remarkable hold on the public remains something of a mystery." The choice of the word *mystery*, however, itself provides a clue. *Mystery* signifies not just inexplicability but
also a religious truth or ritual. It is the realm of the mythic or sacred that
arguably provides the power source for Diana Spencer's remarkable

interaction with a global public and with history. This will be clear once we draw out the parallels between the myth surrounding Princess Diana and the ancient myth and representations of the World Goddess Diana.

First, however, let us survey some instances of this sacred response. Upon word of Princess Diana's death, a group of Aboriginal people at Millingimbini performed a ritual dance to recognize her passing (Grace, 1997, 2). One year later, the Spanish-language television network Univisión featured a story on indigenous Peruvians incorporating Diana's image into a religious ceremony and tendering offerings to that image.[1] Rationalist-identified cultures are often loath to notice their own mythic behaviors, preferring, in both sexist and racist fashion, to ascribe these only to the "primitive" and/or the "feminine." Yet the spontaneous displays of public mourning that overtook London (and much of the world) in the week after Diana's death—the seemingly limitless "flower revolution" and stream of offerings from around the world (MacArthur, 1997)—must be recognized as modern mythoreligious behaviors. Half of the world's people watched her televised funeral. I saw shop windows—from fabulous Hollywood, California, to the rich and famous reserve of Palm Beach, Florida—displaying window "altars" to the Princess. Visiting Luxor, Egypt, in October 2000, I found the "Princess Diana Factory of Alabaster," the name emblazoned just above a full-length image of the goddess Isis with outspread wings (fig. 14.1). Diana fetishes, talismans, and sacred icons, so-called memorabilia, now constitute a $200 million annual industry. Visual artists merge Diana's image with that of the Virgin Mary, Leonardo's Mona Lisa, Delacroix's Liberty, Cinderella, and Che Guevara, as well as their own features (Turner, 1998, 184). Shrines, official and unofficial, private, public, and fictional (Rathbone, 1998) flourish.

Commentary on this phenomenon is decidedly mixed. Dr. Christiane Northrup, author of *Women's Bodies, Women's Wisdom,* writes in her monthly newsletter: "In a world saturated by the male point of view, Diana's life represented feminine wisdom, beauty, vulnerability and nurturing. She was as close as our planet is likely to come to having a Goddess figure" (1997, 1). Mark Steyn, writing in the *National Review,* abhors the "sanctification" of Diana as a "repellent" example of "American Oprahfied psychobabble" (1997, 38). ("Oprahfied" presumably means both primitive and feminine.) Unity Minister Nancy Clark likens Diana to ancient mother goddesses who gave birth to sons offering hope to the world (1997, 11), while an Internet essayist denounces Diana as a New Age avatar of the Goddess Diana, and fears that her death

14.1 Photograph by Helene Vann, 2000

might signal the emergence of the Antichrist (Despatch, 1997). Similarly soured on the female sacred, the Archbishop of York calls for an end to the "cult of Diana," admonishing: "We should be careful that she is not worshipped. That worship should be directed to the God who created her" (C. Morgan, 1998, 1). Indeed.

Patriarchal hegemony generally insists upon the primacy of a solely male principle, the worship of god only. Males then are divinely legitimated in ruling the world and women (Daly, 1973). However, a global feminist movement asserts an end to male-supremacist orders and envisions qualitative shifts in possibilities for both women and men. This necessarily is accompanied by transformations in religious symbolism. The old gods are dead and dying, and multiple new ones are emerging. I reserve further inquiry into the personae of that emerging pantheon for a future study. My focus here is on one of its personalities: a new goddess, though based on a very old one, discernible in the legend forming around Princess Diana.

Recognition of the religious signification of Diana predated her death. In a 1992 essay entitled "Diana Regina," an ancient appellation of the Roman Goddess Diana (Gimbutas, 1989, 318), Camille Paglia zeroes in on Diana as possibly "the most powerful image in world popular culture today, a case study in the modern cult of celebrity and the way it stimulates atavistic religious emotions" (1994, 164). Reading Andrew Morton's *Diana: Her True Story* (1992; reprinted 1997), she points to the ways in which his text is structured by conventional types drawn from the worlds of myth and fairytale: Cinderella, the betrayed wife, the princess in the tower, the *Mater Dolorosa,* the pagan goddess Artemis/Diana, the Hollywood queen, the beautiful boy.

Morton's standard-bearing biography of Diana, like much of the oral, written, and image culture surrounding the Princess, thus gathers force through the elaboration of a story steeped in familiar images from the worlds of myth, religion, and fairytale. To some, this story—like the popular affection for the Princess—suggests only naiveté, conventionality, feminine frivolity, and media manipulation. However, it is myth, archetype, and icon that enable the expression of otherwise remote or ineffable concepts and emotions. Moreover, folk and fairy stories can be understood as constituting a tradition of female wisdom (Estés, 1992). The ancient fairytales issued "from the soil," according to the folklorist Harold Bayley (1996, 1:190), and they represent enduring, though marginalized, wisdoms. However much some forms of popular culture serve as a means of social control, *popular* at its root means *people's,* and some aspects of popular culture function, albeit in coded form, as a repository for knowledges discredited by racism, upward mobility, male supremacy, misogyny, elitism, colonialism, and heterosexual order. (Toni Morrison speaks of "discredited knowledge" [1984, 342].) We can note the resurgence of this tradition in the popular exaltation of other women, including Oprah Winfrey and Selena from the United States, Argentina's Evita Peron, India's "Bandit Queen" Phoolan Devi, Mexico's Frida Kahlo, and Egypt's Oum Kolthoum. The popular rendering of Diana, the "People's Princess," into sacred myth is another prime example of a form of popular culture pronouncing the sovereignty of the Queen, upholding the value and values of the Mother, and reclaiming respect for female sacrality.

Both Paglia and Alice Walker (1998, 56) point to the fateful coincidence of the Princess's name with that of the ancient Goddess Diana. As I am arguing, there is an uncanny resonance between the ancient archetype and the modern myth unfolding around Diana Spencer. According to Carl Jung (1968, 5), archetypes are the contents of the collective unconscious, "universal images that have existed since the remotest times," expressions of psychic realities. One such archetype, that of the Great Mother, takes many characteristic forms, both creative and destructive, and continuously emerges in the image life of cultures. Key aspects of the Great Mother or Goddess archetype abound in the evolving legend around Princess Diana.

It is the archaic myth and its embeddedness in the collective psyche that is responsible, I suggest, for the form and potency of the modern myth. The parallel is evident, as I will show between Princess Diana and (1) Goddess Diana as the people's Goddess, beloved especially by the unprivileged, women, and gender-variant men; (2) Goddess Diana as the Lunar Goddess of Light and Dark; (3) Goddess Diana as the Lady of Beasts, Divine Bitch; (4) Cinderella/Goddess Diana, enacting the journey of the soul from self-loss to wholeness; (5) Goddess Diana as the bestower of sovereignty; (6) Goddess Diana as wanderer, sufferer, and homecomer; (7) Goddess Diana as Soteira (divine female redeemer); and (8) Goddess Diana as World Goddess.

Queen of People's Hearts/Goddess of the Folk

The compassionate goddess whose prevailing presence can breathe solace in times of grief and pain, and inspire hope to the weary and heavy hearted. Such is the holy Mary in Christian worship, with her almost exact counterpart among the Iroquois, Aztecs, and Mayas of America and elsewhere.

Edwin D. Starbuck (1926, 828)

Queen of the Coloured Hearts, Queen of the Devastated, Queen of the Unloved Ones, Queen of the Unknown, Love from the Unknown.

Written tribute to Princess Diana, left at Kensington Palace (Mica Nava, 1997, 20)

If Diana's image, persona, and "fairytale" story make up a cultural "text" to be read, it is helpful to approach that text as a sort of palimpsest, one whose power is based in infinite background layers of older tales that infuse the surface narrative with memory, color, nuance, soul, and metamorphic power.[2] Values associated with Princess Diana include compassion, love, and recognition of the primacy of the common people, particularly those who are rejected by mainstream patriarchal society. These same values are associated with ancient as well as contemporary goddesses, who are now actively worshipped. Exemplary here is Oshun, the Yoruban orisha and crowned sovereignty divinity known throughout the African diaspora. Under the name "Mamma Oxum" in Brazilian Umbanda, she is recognized as sheltering those "who have suffered in body and soul the pain visited upon those disenfranchised by a patriarchal system: specifically a man said to be gay and a woman said to be lesbian, some women beaten and ill-supported by the fathers of their children, another woman dogged by men on account of her beauty" (Hale, 2003, 219).

Princess Diana's namesake, the ancient Goddess Diana, was understood throughout Europe as goddess of the folk, "the protectoress of the plebeians, and in particular the guardian of slaves, outlaws, and thieves" (Sjöö and Mor, 1991, 84). Her lineage is ancient. The name *Diana* recalls a string of pre-Roman goddesses from Sumer on—*Anna, Anatha, Anat, Nana, Dinah.* As *Dé Ana, Dana, Danu, Ana,* or *Anu,* she was the central Celtic deity, the mother of the gods. The mythic fairy ancestors of the Irish people were the *Tuatha Dé Danann,* whose name translates as "People of the Goddess D[i]ana."[3] By Middle Irish times she had become Brigit, the Triple Goddess. In the ancient world, August 15 was widely recognized as the day sacred to both Dana/Diana and Danu/Brigit. As we will see, August 15 was later appropriated by the Catholic Church as the feast day of the Virgin Mary.

Diana was the Roman name for the Triple Moon Goddess—Lunar Virgin, Mother of Creatures, and Destroyer/Huntress (B. Walker, 1983, 233–34; Begg, 1996, 50–56). As the moon, she wanders, disappears, and transforms regularly, often under the names of Selene in the heavens, Diana/Artemis on earth, and Persephone in the underworld. Roman imperialism meant that towns all over Europe habitually called the local Mother goddess "Diana." Her characteristic sacred site was a grove of oak trees. Legend has it that her famous shrine at Ephesus (one of the Seven Wonders of the ancient world) was built by Amazons in 900 B.C. There she was worshipped originally in the form of a black meteoric stone. When given human form, like Isis and Cybele, Diana is frequently imaged as black. The later Ephesian Diana is a woman with a black face, hands, and feet. On her dress are images of creatures, including bulls, goats, deer, and a bee. Saint Paul attempted to persuade the people of Ephesus to turn away from Diana, "whom all Asia and the world worship" (Acts 19:26–27). To combat Diana's sovereignty, the church distorted her cult while assimilating her least threatening aspects to the Virgin Mary. In the fourth century, Ephesus was appropriated by the church and rededicated to Mary. In 1950, the Catholic Church declared August 15 (Diana and Danu/Brigit's day) to be the feast of the Assumption of Mary into heaven. Although the church has continuously diverted reverence for the Goddess to the Madonna, the memory of her origins persists in the tenacious "cult of the Black Virgin" (Birnbaum, 1993; Begg, 1996). The principal symbols associated with Princess Diana, the *rose* and the *heart*, are complex ones evoking Eros, compassion, sexuality, love, and beauty. Both the heart and the rose are symbols of the vulva, and, concomitantly, both archetypally are linked to female divinities, including the Virgin Mary, who is also known as the "Mystic Rose."

Randy Conner (1993, 84) observes Goddess Diana's appeal to "women and gender-variant men, some of whom appear to have been homoerotically inclined. This may have been due in part to their exclusion from positions in the state priesthood . . . [and] an apparent desire on the part of some women and gender-variant men for a more intimate relationship with the deity than was promoted in patriarchal religions." Centuries later, Christianity's antagonism to Goddess Diana, and a concomitant hostility to women and gender-variant men, took shape in the European witch burnings. Beginning in the early tenth century, a string of documents instructed church authorities to root out various beliefs and practices. This, for example, dates from 906: "One mustn't be silent about certain wicked women who become followers of Satan . . . and insist they ride at night with Diana, goddess of the pagans" (Ginzburg, 1991, 89–90). Throughout the Middle Ages reports of nighttime visits with Goddess Diana centered on "beneficent female figures who bestow prosperity, wealth, knowledge" (100) and are venerated, above all, by women. These stories were distorted by Inquisitors in their manufacture of a prejudicial stereotype of the witches' Sabbath. Diana was labeled the "Queen of the witches" and "Goddess of the heathen."

This brief narrative of Goddess Diana sets the stage for an examination of the resonance between that narrative and the one that has accreted around Diana Spencer. Though Diana as Princess of Wales was meant to serve as an icon of whiteness, privilege, and race and class superiority, she countered this expectation and evolved into what Mica

Nava (1997) calls "Princess of Others." In the famous 1995 BBC *Panorama* interview, her first after her separation from Charles, Diana spoke of finding her "role" as she became "more and more involved with people who were rejected by society—with . . . drug addicts, alcoholism, battered this, battered that," realizing an "affinity there" far more than with the royal establishment (BBC, 1995). She avowed her primary loyalty to "all those people who have loved and supported me throughout the last fifteen years." She also claimed that there was a whispering campaign against her: Charles's friends (who mocked Diana by calling her the "mad cow") were "indicating that I was unstable, sick, and should be put in a home of some sort." Diana understood this as an attempt to "dismantle" her through isolation. This "whispering campaign" continues after her death, most rancorously in Sally Bedell Smith's (1999) best-selling biography, *Diana in Search of Herself*. Smith, who has no psychological credentials, smugly diagnoses Diana as a "borderline personality" who should have committed herself to psychiatric treatment, silent and daily "toil in an East London hospice or shelter," or both. To Smith's chagrin, Diana instead had the nerve to run around, "spread her magic," and make her mark as the most celebrated woman in the world (for further commentary see Caputi, 2001).

In the 1995 interview, Diana acknowledged that the establishment opposed her being queen of the country. No matter—she would much rather be "queen of people's hearts, in people's hearts" (BBC, 1995). Princess Diana's understanding of her own celebrity/myth as rooted in her connection to the common people, and especially the marginalized or besieged, was utterly validated by public behavior after her death. Skeptics and antagonists from afar insist that the whole mourning phenomenon was somehow produced by the media and did not truly reflect a spontaneous response. Still, journalist Andrew Marr (1998) affirms that the devotion to Diana "wasn't 'got up' by the press. It was real, and unchoreographed." And her public *was* composed of "ordinary people: families, generations, ethnically diverse" (Silverstone, 1998, 83). Even the style of mourning—emotional display, candles, flowers, incense, and outpouring of words—departed from British tradition. A *New York Times* editorial called this a "Latin" style of grief (September 7, 1997). More accurately, it is one steeped in "neo-heathen" traditions—feminine, folk, gay, and otherwise non-elite.

Princess Diana, famously, interacted socially and physically with "others." She visited the sick and the poor, deeply affecting public consciousness when she touched those afflicted with leprosy, AIDS, and other feared diseases. A leader of an AIDS advocacy group in Australia assesses her impact: "The Princess of Wales was one of the first international figures to have the courage and compassion to reach out to people with AIDS. With one simple gesture, she not only changed the life of one sick man but of people with AIDS around the globe" (Benzie, 1997, 128). It was due particularly to her involvement with AIDS that her compassionate *touch* became legendary. This was only amplified when she took up a crusade to abolish landmines and traveled into Angola and Bosnia, holding, visiting, and comforting those who had been maimed. Many commentators have expressed doubt regarding Diana's sincerity. Was she just another upper-class white woman doing charity work? Was she merely lighting upon public actions that would be sure to enrage Prince Charles? Her brother, Charles, said in his eulogy that she took up charity work as a means of resolving "deep feelings of unworthiness." Mica Nava believes that "[h]er life experiences and personal suffering led her to identify with the marginalised and needy, and they in turn identified with her" (1997, 21). Those who participated in this flow of identification included people with AIDS, the young urban homeless, the injured, the socially marginalized, the poor, the imprisoned, the depressed, and the unloved. Just as the Goddess Diana was known as the special patron of the enslaved, downtrodden, sick, and poor, so too was her celebrated twentieth-century namesake.

At the same time, Princess Diana, like the Goddess Diana, was especially beloved by women and gender-variant men. Feminist Liz Kelly (1997/98, 68) reminds us that her public was "overwhelmingly female." Gay scholar Tim Benzie (1997) claims Diana as a "gay icon" and interprets her public process of self-realization as one with great resonance for gay men: In her initial imagery, Diana is plain, shy, and horribly "ordinary." But as she grows into her true self, she becomes fabulous, glamorous, and stylish. Paglia recognizes Diana's "androgynous charisma" (1994, 169), an essential attribute of divinity throughout much of the nonpatriarchal world (Teish, 1985, 54–55). The gay actor Sir Ian McKellen reads Diana's *Panorama* interview, as she recounts her successful journey out of self-loathing and hostile family relations and into self-discovery and transformation, as a veritable "coming out" (Benzie, 1997, 130). Clearly, as with the ancient Goddess Diana, both women and gender-variant men could have a more "intimate relationship with the deity than was promoted in patriarchal religions" (Conner, 1993, 84).

Nava continues: "[Princess Diana's] psychic formation, her powerful identification with outsiders extended . . . also to her lovers" (1997, 21).

Diana had mockingly referred to Charles as the "great white hope" (Morton, 1994, 9), and she struck a most subversive chord by erotically linking herself to Dodi Al-Fayed, a Muslim in a time when Islamic peoples are increasingly positioned as the enemy of the West, a man of color from Egypt, a former British colonial possession. His father, millionaire Mohammed Al-Fayed, had been rejected in his quest for British citizenship. Whether Dodi's motivation was love, fame, or trophy acquisition, and whether Diana sought love, riches, a trophy, or political shock value, their union constituted a spectacular blow against traditional racial and religious bigotry and snobbery and a challenge to the division of the world into opposing religious and racial camps.

Indeed, their deaths spawned a series of assertions that they had been assassinated. Moammar Gadhafi immediately charged that they had been deliberately killed, soon seconded by Dodi's father. Well-known Cairo writer Anis Mansour gave the general view: "The British intelligence service killed them. They could not have let the mother of the future king marry a Muslim Arab" (quoted in N. Morris, 1997, 54). The word continues to spread in graffiti at the death scene, popular books, artworks, and Internet discussions. Post–September 11 the theory was given a new and flamboyant spin. The December 18, 2001, cover of the American tabloid *The Globe* declared: "Bin Laden Killed Diana!" According to this article, a French government antiterrorist department had released a report revealing that Osama Bin Laden had arranged the crash. *The Globe* explains this with the help of a former FBI agent: "Diana was Bin Laden's worst nightmare. . . . She inspired female Muslims around the world to fight for change—and that may have cost her her life" (Herz, Robinson, and Gibson, 2001, 28).

All of these theories revolve around the idea that a politically active and powerful woman such as Diana will be perceived as dangerous by the male powers that be—on all sides of the warring patriarchal factions. Diana herself had made this point in the *Panorama* interview, pointing out that she and other "strong women in history" are characteristically viewed as a "threat" (BBC, 1995). Indeed, just a month or so before her death, a member of the British Parliament labeled her a "loose cannon" (Nava, 1997, 21). A 1998 poll by *The Times* found that "more than a third of British people do not accept that she died as the result of an accident and a quarter think there was a conspiracy to have her murdered" (Morgan and Smith, 1998, 4). Whatever one thinks of the credibility of these beliefs, rumors and gossip form part of a contemporary oral tradition pointing to a recognition that patriarchal powers respond with violence to feminist challenges. Such conspiracy theorizing is also based in recognition of the racist/sexist/colonialist foundation of the British monarchy and its ceremonial function as representative of empire, white supremacy, "purity" of "blood," and patriarchal family values (B. Campbell, 1998). All of this Diana profoundly challenged.

Goddess of Light and Dark

[F]or nonwhite Britons, she was like a beacon in the darkness.
Trevor Phillips (quoted in Elliott, 1997, 106)

She's special because she bring light to the world.
Mourner, a middle-aged Afro-Caribbean woman (BBC, 1997)

Now the stars spell out your name.
"Candle in the Wind 1997," sung by Elton John (John and Taupin, 1997)

Fire, the stars, the moon and the sun, the bedazzling luminosity of elemental forces—all are associated archetypally with divinity and figure prominently in sacred narratives, including the one centered on Goddess Diana and the one now evolving around Princess Diana. The fatal crash took place in a Parisian tunnel on August 31, 1997. Directly above the tunnel is a life-sized replica of the flaming beacon of the Statue of Liberty. That site is now an unofficial shrine. Mourners have brought thousands of bouquets, cards, and prayers to Princess Diana, held vigils, and written messages all over the flame. Weirdly enough, the Statue of Liberty is a modern version of Goddess Diana, a deity of Light. One of her titles was Diana Lucifera, and in this persona she was represented as a woman bearing a beacon (Neumann, 1963, plate 161).

Another instance of the recurrent association of "light" with Princess Diana appears in Naomi Segal's (1998, 132–33) survey of popular commentary on the Princess: "'An instant radiance' is said to have emanated . . . 'when she walked into the room.' Put another way, 'she glittered, and the glittering sucked you in.' She had a 'stellar luminescence,' was 'shining' and 'golden,' 'illuminated our lives.' . . . Commentators from all political sides have compared her to a light source: a 'beacon' (Margaret Thatcher), a 'comet' (Simon Jenkins), a 'shining light' or a 'bright star' (Lords Archer and Hurd), a 'crescent moon' (Simon Hoggart), a 'paper lamp' and the 'sunshine' (Maya Angelou, Donatella Versace and the *Bury Free Press*)."

Of course, the world knows Diana best through her photographs, and commentators often speak of her "photogenic" quality, through which the subject herself actually appeared to give off light (Grace, 1997, 8). Yet this concept of light cannot be extricated from sexually racist photographic conventions. "[T]he aesthetic technology of the photographic media," Richard Dyer (1997, 122) argues, "not only assumes and privileges whiteness but also constructs it." An extreme instance of this is "the use of light in constructing an image of the ideal white woman within heterosexuality." "Pretty" white women, like Princess Diana, are conventionally shown in ways that bathe them in light, make them seem permeated with light: "In short they glow." Indubitably, some of the associations of the Princess and "light" can be traced to this prejudicial motif. Still, the convention itself is an appropriation and distortion of an enduring and complex correspondence between the sacred and a twinned luminosity/darkness, whiteness/blackness.

The name *Diana* means "shining one" or "dual-Ana" (Begg, 1996, 56). Her duality is not oppositional but paradoxically unified. She has inextricably twinned faces, one bright and one dark. Lightness is not linked with "whiteness" as the antithesis of a dirty, obscene, and inferior "blackness." Darkness is not the opposite, but the very necessary womb, root, or source of light. Light is the manifest face of darkness. Under the influence of oppositional hierarchy, Diana's balanced duality is repressed. In European patriarchal culture, she and the dark are demonized. Diana becomes Goddess of Witches and Queen of the Night for this puerile culture that persecutes what it fears. Still, as Begg (1996, 27) reminds us, something of her original signification lives on in the beliefs and traditions around the Catholic image of the Black Virgin, "a symbol older and more formidable than King or Pope, of that elemental and uncontrollable source of life, possessing a spirit and wisdom of its own not subject to organization or the laws of rationality." The Goddess Diana's "light in the darkness" signifies creation, birth from the necessarily dark womb/earth. Black originally "had a good signification. Isis was frequently represented as black, and Diana, the Goddess of Light, was represented indifferently as white and black" (Bayley, 1996, 1:213). Blackness has nothing to do with evil and indecency, as modern symbology, steeped in racism, decrees. Rather, it is "a symbol of 'the Divine Dark' of Inscrutability, of Silence, and of Eternity" (214). It is instructive also to recall what is said of the Hindu goddess Kali, the representation of *Prakṛti* (creative and dynamic nature): "I've heard the hue of Her skin is black—A Black that lights the world" (Ramprasad, cited in Dalmiya, 2000, 130).

In the wake of her death, several depictions of Diana as a darkened figure have appeared. Egyptian artist Fathi Hassan has painted a portrait of Diana as an African princess; she still has blond hair, but the familiar face is now brown (Turner, 1998, 184). A leaflet for a London conference, "Death of a Princess: Postmodern Spirituality and the Gospel," reproduced in *After Diana* (Merck, 1998) depicts Diana as a black Queen of Hearts. The silhouette of Diana gracing the façade of the lakeside "temple" at her gravesite is black (fig. 14.2). Beside it is a plaque bearing her words: "Whoever is in distress can call on me. I will come running, wherever they are."

Such configurations, both verbal and visual, recall the traditional iconography, characteristics, and powers of the Black Diana and the Black Madonna. The "Dark Mother," Alice Walker (1998, 66) reminds

14.2 Photograph by Jane Caputi, 1999

us, "is none other than the human symbol for the dark earth." The City of Paris plans an official memorial to Diana in the form of a nature garden for children. As a radio report put it, this will recognize the Princess's close association with the earth and with nature. Here, public memory of the contemporary Princess corresponds far more with archetypal promptings than with the actual life of Diana Spencer.

The Great Bitch

In a *cosmogynic* worldview, that "of an ordered universe arranged in harmony with gynocratic principles" (P. Allen, 1991 xiii–xiv), nature is not the soulless creation of a transcendent god. Rather, divinity is immanent in nature, both wild and human. Expressing this intuition, the Goddess archetypally is envisioned not only as Dark Mother but as Lady of the Beasts, one who appears not just in the company of creatures, but sometimes as an animal herself—snake, fish, frog, bird, mammal (Neumann, 1963; Gimbutas, 1989). An image from the Ionian period (500–600 B.C.) portrays Hecate-Artemis (Diana) in purely animal form: as a whelping Bitch (Neumann, 1963, plate 51). "Bitch became a naughty word in Christian Europe because it was one of the most sacred titles of the Goddess, Artemis-Diana," Barbara Walker (1983, 109) informs us. In Christian terms, "son of a Bitch" was insulting because it meant a "spiritual son" of the Goddess Diana.

Commenting upon Princess Diana's persona in the *Panorama* interview, Simon Schama (1996, 143) uses wildly mythic language, evoking the dual (black/white) face of the Di-Ana and her character as Lady of Beasts and Huntress/Destroyer (cast here as the sexist stereotype, the *castrator*): "Here's the thing about Diana the Huntress. . . . Treat her badly and she'll treat you to a quiverful of arrows, for all that she looks so demure, so white, so chaste. . . . The makeover has been from desperate molting swan into bird of prey . . . an exterminating angel. . . . Katharine Hepburn as the wronged Eleanor of Aquitane . . . comes to mind. What did the estranged Queen want? . . . The king's 'vitals on a plate of lettuce.'" Such hyperbole reflects the threat that Diana posed in manifesting those most denied, feared, and potent aspects of archetypal female sacred power.

The emerging oral tradition around Diana also highlights the quintessential "Bitch" connection. The gossip from a former housekeeper at Althorp, the Spencer estate, is that the island on which Diana is buried was used for years as a pet cemetery and is known to the household staff as "Dog Island" (*Newsday*, 1998)![4] All such stories, however apparently trivial, bolster the emerging mythic narrative linking Princess Diana with her divine namesake.

Virgin/Whore

Both the blackness and the animality of Goddess Diana signify soul, mystery, and depth, not degradation. At the same time, the *virginity* of the Goddess does not signify chastity: "The Virgin Goddess is Life itself, and Life, like the cycles of the moon, appears out of itself without union with anything external to itself" (Baring and Cashford, 1991, 192). Under Christianity, the fructifying, potent, and autonomous sexuality of the Goddess is severed from her compassionate, nurturing powers. Two distortions result: the Virgin and the Whore. Black Virgins who still manage to represent some of the original wholeness are frequently perceived to be "masculine" (Begg, 1996, 134).

Not surprisingly, Princess Diana's "whorish" character and "witchy" pursuits have been attacked by religious advocates of chastened female sexuality and diminished powers. In August 1998, two evangelical Christian Sunday school teachers told a group of British children that Diana was in hell! In interviews, the two churchmen decried her growing cult as a form of idolatry, denounced her mortal sins, including sexual relationships with men outside marriage, and condemned her "New Age" beliefs, including the diabolical practice of "visiting a medium" (Landesman, 1998, 7). Such censure recalls the ire directed at Goddess Diana and women in general by Inquisitors and witch-burners.

The former Archbishop of Canterbury, Lord Coggan, became explicitly misogynist in attacking the worship of Princess Diana as a "false goddess" and bemoaning the neglect of patriarchal religion: "Our nation has become godless. Man is made with a hollow which only God can fill. Then along came this false goddess and filled the gap for a time. But like all false gods, she could not last. The British people identified with someone who had pretty loose morals and certainly loose sexual morals" (Morgan and Smith, 1998, 1). In other words, all women who are sexually self-determining are "whores," and all female gods are false. These naysayers reflect the historical male hysteria over autonomous and refulgent female sexuality and the sex/love goddesses who represent this cosmic force. Nonetheless, the tradition remains adamant, if symbolically coded. The heart and the rose are such recurrent symbols of Goddess, and appear so prominently in Diana's cult, because they so fully suggest the divine *yoni* (vulva). Diana is buried, moreover, on an island surrounded by a pond (called the "Round Oval") whose elliptical shape recalls the *mandorla*, the vulva-shaped outline that typically encloses the figures not only of ancient goddesses but also of the saints, Christ, and the Madonna in Catholic imagery (Chevalier and Gheerbrant, 1994, 16). Even in the patriarchal context, the evocative presence of the sex/love goddess is needed to confer divine legitimacy.

The Queen

The historical derogation of Goddess Diana—her powers of dark and light, her animality, her Virgin gender (lustful, sovereign, primordially female, but containing also the male)—is recapitulated in the accusations against Princess Diana. But the attack neither begins nor ends here. Disrespect for goddess traditions, those that uphold female sovereignty and potency, are inscribed heavily into racist stereotypes of women of color (both lesbian and straight, mothers or not) who are damnably associated not only with that disreputable darkness but also with greater animality, sexuality, masculinity, and bitchiness (hooks, 1992, 61–77; Collins, 1998, 123–46).

Sappho called Goddess Diana "the Queen." That title designates a goddess who rules in her own right, not through connection to any divine king or husband (Gimbutas, 1989, 318). It also signifies one who has completed an initiation. The word is used both negatively and positively in gay slang. It can be linked with prostitution, but alternately *queen* "attributes a grandeur akin to that experienced by a female ruler to a gay man" (Conner, Sparks, and Sparks, 1997, 277). *Queen* also figures prominently in a discourse of empowerment chosen by many women of African descent, including singers Queen Latifah and India Arie, who sings: "I ain't built like a supermodel / But I learned to love myself unconditionally / Because I am a queen" (quoted in DeCurtis, 2002, 1). Luisah Teish (2002) educates audiences about the history of African goddesses and queens and then asks them to "learn how the goddesses and queens live on in the psyches of women today, and how these ancient feminine powers operate in our personal lives and our communities." She urges others to "honor the queen within, naming and claiming this powerful icon of power, transformation, and healing."

Oppressive regimes of consciousness deliberately disparage and discredit sites—spatial, bodily, mythic, and verbal—of sacred gynocentric significance. Not too surprisingly, the word *queen* is often appropriated for racist discourse, besmirching not only black female sovereignty, but womanliness itself. "[W]e black women," Patricia J. Williams declares, "bear the burden of being seen as pretenders to the thrones of both femininity and masculinity, endlessly mocked by the ambiguously gendered crown-of-thorns imagery of 'queen'—Madame Queen, snap queen, welfare queen, quota queen, Queenie Queen, Queen Queen Queen. We black women are figured as stand-ins for men, sort of like reverse drag queens: women pretending to be women but more male than men—bare-breasted, sweat-glistened, plow-pulling sole supporters of their families" (1996, 97).

These sexist/racist uses of *queen* convey a mockery of the past, present, and future of black female rule, leadership, motherhood, influence, autonomy, power, and authority while simultaneously betraying a rank fear of those realities and their ramifications for the white, masculinist power structure. In these ritualistic insults, we might also recognize some of the most virulent attacks upon female divinity. Via these epithets, Goddess qualities of Blackness, sovereignty, fruitfulness, androgyny, self-completeness, and sufficiency are reconfigured into sexist/racist projections: regressive matriarchy, prostitution, savagery, greed, lasciviousness, unfemininity. Obviously, the search for contemporary narratives of female divinity cannot be confined to honored and technologically illuminated lives such as Princess Diana's, but, as in Walker's *The Color Purple* (1982), must be recognized as most at home in the colonized, impoverished, exiled, caged, enslaved, raped, denigrated, and denied beings of the world—the gynocentric, the butch, the queer, the dark, the aged, the elemental, the common.

The worldwide myth of Cinderella, who transforms from a persecuted girl, consigned to the ashes, into a radiant Queen, is a prime example of the survival of the gynocentric oral tradition. The Cinderella story promises the coming restoration of the oppressed to a place of honor, the recognition of the divinity in the commonplace, the second coming of the Queendom. Princess Diana has frequently been linked to Cinderella. A deeper understanding of that complex story identifies its ancient connection to the legend of the wandering and transforming Goddess Diana and further illuminates the power of the archetypal forces accreting around Princess Diana and the meaning of her legend.

As amplified in chapter 13, the Cinderella myth is not about heterosexual romance; it is about the soul. The soul is suffering because of the splitting of earth, nature, and physical body from spirit. Its light smolders but is never extinguished. Gradually, the soul awakens to the

full radiance of its divinity. Cinderella's glorious and diverse gowns—
rather like Princess Diana's relic-like dresses, displayed at her museum
at Althorp—symbolize the various gateways of initiation from princess
to Queen, the different aspects of acquired elemental Wisdom. At Althorp, the last item of dress is not a gown at all but the jeans, shirt, and
protective garb Diana donned during her campaign against landmines,
signifying her increasing politicization. In her well-known narrative,
Diana emerges from the "cinders" of profound feelings of unworthiness,
lovelessness, injustice, abuse, and despair to blaze for all the world to see
with the beauty of the soul's radiance. Such stories then light the way
for others' becoming.

Female Sovereignty

In *Planet Diana* Zoë Sofoulis (1997, 16–17) identifies a discourse around
Diana's death that continuously references "the world" and "Diana as a
world symbol." Via the mass media, Diana has become "part of the *ha-
bitus* of many people. . . . The loss of Diana was experienced as a loss
not just of a person but a part of the world." The title of the anthology
is from a press statement issued by the McGillicuddy Serious Party of
New Zealand, which suggested that we "not go through the bother of
naming all these different parks, flowers, airports, etc. after Diana, but
to simply rename the world 'Diana.'" A classical tradition, of course,
personifies institutions, cities, and lands as goddesses—Europe and Eu-
ropa, Athens and Athena, Ireland and Eire. In the Tarot deck (originating in fourteenth-century Europe), the last trump of the Major Arcana
is the "World." Its central image is a naked woman, signifying the
"World Mother of a thousand names," one of which is "Diana" (B.
Walker, 1984, 13).

The archaic habit of imaging the city, nation, or world as a goddess,
along with the custom of crowning her queen, are emblematic of an
underlying principle of female *sovereignty*—a sacred concept embracing
autonomy, self-rule, integrity, and radiance or resplendence (Benard
and Moon, 2000, 20). The sovereignty goddess traditionally is the
source of power behind a worldly queen or king. Goddess Diana is "bestower of sovereignty" (Monaghan, 1990 98). No ruler is considered legitimate unless the Goddess, the ultimate guardian of the land, confers
sovereignty upon him. Echoes of this tradition can be discerned in public feelings about Princess Diana. Though she only married into the ruling family, Princess Diana soon superseded Prince Charles and Queen

Elizabeth in the people's affection. It was she who came to be seen as symbolizing the nation. In the *Panorama* interview, Diana implied that Charles might never reign. Many commentators in the weeks after her death suggested that the public would prefer that William—the direct line from Diana—succeed to the throne, and not Charles.

By naming Diana divine, women and men symbolically reclaim and recognize female sovereignty, subjectivity, and selfhood. The sovereignty of the individual and collective female body is mythically rooted in the sovereignty of the World Goddess. This means not only that she governs creation, but that her body is sacred and inviolate and that to enjoy her bounty requires permission and respect for her limits. Disrespecting these leads to pollution, malaise, and ultimately disaster, personal and global. Her sovereignty bespeaks the sanctity of matter and of all life.

Mary Daly has identified the mythic paradigm underlying patriarchal order as a primordial act of goddess murder/dismemberment, the original *gynocide* (1978, 109-12) by a male god. Such violence is, simultaneously, the "murder-dismemberment of the Self-affirming be-ing of women" (111). Gynocide and *rapism*, "invasion, violation, degradation, objectification, and destruction of women and nature" (Daly with Caputi 1987, 91), are implicit in the slang employed by the paparazzi who specialized in taking pictures of Diana. Two of them, Mark Saunders and Glenn Harvey (1996), published *Dicing with Di*. They unapologetically describe life among the paparazzi who chased Diana despite her demand to be left alone. *Dicing with Di* means "taking pictures of Diana." Other terms include *bang, blitz, hose, rip, smudge,* and *whack*—all describing rapid and invasive photography. They deny Diana any right to privacy and believe she was silly to have expected any.

The lingo employed by the Diana-chasing paparazzi is neither incomprehensible nor shocking: The camera is well understood through the conventions of fashion and the horror/thriller genre to function as weapon as well as voyeur, objectifier, rapist, and/or murderer (Sontag, 1977). Violence itself has increasingly been comprehended as a form of sexual expression, most vividly enacted in the well-publicized exploits of "sex-killers" from Jack the Ripper on (Caputi, 1987). Salman Rushdie proffers a markedly feminist analysis of Diana's death. Western culture eroticizes the star, the consumer object, the car, and even (referencing the novel and film *The Crash*) the car crash. "Think of it this way, and the pornography of Diana Spencer's death becomes apparent. She died in a sublimated sexual assault" (1997, 68).

Mary Daly factors in both the pornographic and the sacred in interpreting the symbolic significance of Diana's demise: "In grieving for Diana, women are also grieving for themselves, because so many things that happened to Princess Diana have happened to every woman. They are grieving over the loss of a Gynocentric society. . . . [O]ver the loss of Goddess. Princess Diana triggered all those unconscious memories. Diana was stripped of her titles, betrayed, mistreated, abused, chased by the paparazzi, and killed. Everything that happened to her happened to Goddess" (1998, 14). The "sexual assault" death of Diana thus recapitulates a primal rape-murder of Goddess.

Yet this violence did not end Diana's story. Stories of healings and apparitions have already circulated. The museum at Althorp (housed in the former stables) and her egg-shaped lake island burial site, which can be viewed only at a distance, have all the makings of a shrine. Just across from the island, a Doric temple, upon which is inscribed her name, displays Diana's black silhouette. Thirty-six oak trees (the sacred tree of the Goddess Diana), one for each year of her life, flank the long drive. Pilgrims visit, bringing flowers, written and sketched prayers, and remembrances to a Diana whom we might recognize as an emerging deity, both ancient and new. Althorp is accessible to the public only during the months of July and August, opening on the day of her birth and closing the day before her death. August may one day again be heralded as the sacred festival month of the Goddess Diana.

Despite the violence of her demise, Princess Diana's narrative does not necessarily lead to horrific world-ending visions. Rather, perhaps because of the oft-remarked-upon — and even predicted (Paglia, 1994, 171) — "sacrificial" nature of her death, the dominant postdeath image of Diana is one associated with a "Soteira," or "Savioress," a title of Persephone in her role as "annual bride of Pluto, or Hades, who took her underground" (B. Walker, 1983, 953). A banner unfurled outside Kensington Palace after Diana's death read boldly "Savior of the World." Threaded through the grief is a reclamation of Diana as a sign not only of female becoming, but also of a concomitant world *be-coming*. Here and there, we glimpse sketches of utopian, not apocalyptic, visions, of redemptive, not destructive, stories.

Be-Coming Diana

Feminist invocation of various ancient Goddess traditions is often dismissed as naive, simplistic, static, essentialist. Yet a fuller understanding of these traditions reveals them to be not only complex and dynamic, but antecedents of contemporary ideas regarding the moving, becoming, and sovereign female subject, both human and divine. The lunar Goddess Diana was one of several "Mystery" goddesses, a Soteira because "the story of the wanderings, sufferings, and finally homecoming of the universal goddess offered the possibility that one's own wandering and suffering might . . . end in a . . . homecoming" (L. Martin, 1987, 59).

Ideas of a moving and transformative Goddess provide background to the most vital of contemporary feminist theologies. In 1973, Mary Daly moved *Beyond God the Father*, inventing new words, such as *Being*, to express her understanding of God as neither man nor noun: "Ultimate/Intimate Reality, the constantly Unfolding Verb of Verbs which is intransitive, having no object that limits its dynamism"; *be-ing* is "participation in Be-ing" (Daly with Caputi, 1987, 64). Feminist thinkers continue to explore the significance of the dynamism and gender of divinity. "To become means fulfilling the wholeness of what we are capable of being," Luce Irigaray writes. "But as long as woman lacks a divine made in her image she cannot establish her subjectivity or achieve a goal of her own. She lacks an ideal that would be her goal or path in becoming" (1993, 61, 63–64). Irigaray too stresses the necessity of a moving and changing deity with whom women can be in relationship: "In order to become, we need . . . not a One postulated to be immutable but rather a cohesion and a horizon that assures us the passage between past and future" (67).

Kath McPhillips, guided by Morny Joy's perception that the "other" we need in this process may well be disavowed parts of the female self, argues that Diana's mass-mediated narrative enacts precisely this dynamic of female becoming. Its key elements—an unhappy childhood, a loveless marriage, bulimia, loneliness, and insecurity—elicited unprecedented popular identification. As Diana faced and healed these wounds, she performed what McPhillips calls a "great redemptive action." By "the heroic act of connecting up the damaged parts of her self, she held out to all of us the possibility of becoming divine through achieving selfhood." McPhillips summarizes: "It seems to me that Diana represents this potential of expressing our collective desires for God/other where God . . . 'enters the process of becoming a woman.' In this scheme of things, Diana partakes of divinity" (1997, 91).

The idea of a female divinity realized and participated in through the process of becoming a whole female subject is undeniably powerful. Yet despite what these thinkers may intend, the modern mind tends to read *becoming* as signifying a psychological process of self-development, isolated from larger cosmic movements and transpersonal implications. In *Pure Lust* (1984), Daly calls forth a flock of *be-* words in which the prefix *be-* "signifies ontological depth" (Daly with Caputi, 1987, 63). In this vein, then, we might speak of the *be-coming* of Diana. As Diana so publicly faced troubled aspects of self and worked at achieving integrity, becoming ever more completely Diana Spencer, she was, mysteriously to be sure, simultaneously *be-coming* another Diana, a mythic one. *Be-coming* means the emergence not only of the individual self, but also that of a self manifesting Goddess, those female essences of Be-ing that have been raped, reviled, rejected, and fragmented now openly expressed, embraced, revalued, restored.

As Diana be-comes, so does the culture, for she is herself a sign of "changes happening already" (Marr, 1998, 1). To Irigaray, the female God that "we have yet to make actual, as a region of life, strength, imagination, creation . . . exists for us both within and beyond, as our possibility of a present and a future" (1993, 72). Diana's be-coming is a sign of a concomitant be-coming of women and women-identified men—and indeed of world be-coming. It signifies the possibility of present and future transformations in human ways of relating to the society, the natural world, and the cosmos.

The Once and Future Diana

> That community answering to Diana in that way was a sign. . . .
> I believe that the future is feminine.
> Gaetano Pesce, architect (quoted in Mead, 1998, 40)

When I first began speaking of the mythic import of Diana, my Catholic father astutely asked if I regarded Diana as a "sign." The theological meaning of *sign* was explained by Pope Paul VI in a characteristically sexist 1977 declaration on the impossibility of a female priesthood: "The priest is a sign . . . that must be perceptible and which the faithful must be able to recognize with ease. The whole sacramental economy is in fact based upon natural signs, on symbols imprinted upon the human psychology. . . . There would not be this 'natural resemblance' which must exist between Christ and His minister if the role of Christ were not taken by a man" (quoted in Goldenberg, 1979, 5–6). As a manifestation of Goddess, the be-coming Princess Diana is a sign, easily recognized, highly perceptible, of the natural correspondence between femaleness and the divine, and concomitantly, the insufficiency of solely masculine and patriarchal signs of the sacred. The resemblance of the modern Diana to the ancient Diana and the ongoing "divinization" of the Princess herald a return, a second coming if you will, of female sacred powers, concomitant with a revisioning of human possibility.

In *The Once and Future Goddess,* Elinor Gadon argues that the world is now in a time of "epochal changes like those at the time of the coming of the Buddha and the birth of Jesus when human realities are being reshaped by a vision of far-reaching consequences" (1989, 376). At the core of that vision is some recognition of universal female Powers: sometimes understood as appearing in the principles of quantum physics (Baring and Cashford 1991, xiii–xiv), nuclear power and chaos theory (Caputi, 1993), environmental science (Lovelock, 1979; Gadon 1989, 341–68); sometimes understood as Goddess; and sometimes understood as associated values and behaviors: the dissolution of hierarchical opposition; balance; Eros; respect; female sovereignty; communitarianism; compassion; healing; the equality of all creatures; equitable distribution of goods; tolerance for diversity (P. Allen 1986, 2–3); the honoring of "gay, queer archetypal energy" (Conner, 1993, 304); and female be-coming in a world that has too long denied and persecuted this movement.

Unity minister Nancy Clark makes explicit the parallel I have been drawing when she declares that Diana in life was a woman "with whom we could identify, and in death she is the goddess for whom we long" (1997, 11). But this is no quest simply for infantile bliss, static worship. Clark, like many others, likens Diana to the descending/disappearing Goddess Persephone: "as we reclaim the spirit of Diana, the spirit of our Persephone, aliveness and fruitfulness will return" (ibid.). Those who reverence Diana are called upon to take responsibility for calling into being a world that corresponds to the values she represented.

These values include the banishing of invidious racial distinctions. One rumor is that Diana was pregnant at the time of her death, conjuring a mental picture of a child of Diana and Dodi, a mixed-race sister or brother to the future king of England. Mica Nava (1997, 24) imagines that child along with Diana as queen of a "modern rainbow nation . . . a post colonial one where the descendants of the colonisers can no longer be distinguished from the descendants of the colonised, where cultural and racial differences are transformed by their interaction and merger with each other: where sexual desire and intermarriage produce a new generation of racially indeterminate Britons."

Another vision speaks to a revaluation of social ideals. For at least one week, the world became something of a queendom. Beliefs, behaviors, and ideals that snools spurn as feminine, maudlin, trivial, frivolous, and "Oprahfied" ruled the world stage.[5] The World Sikh Council called Diana "the queen of universal love" (Black, 1997) and that archetypal pronouncement rang many responsive chords. Remarking on a banner in the mourning crowd reading "Diana of Love," Sofoulis reads Diana herself as a sign of Eros, a "force that bound people together, a force of sociality. Diana in her aspects as mother, humanitarian and lover becomes a sign of sexual, maternal and communitarian love. The participatory global rituals of mourning for 'Diana of Love' might well entail delusional components, but are nevertheless effective in building—or at least prefiguring—a world where the joys and sufferings of [ordinary] beings . . . are not confined to the 'trivial' realms of tabloids and women's magazines, but outrank . . . the dominant values of greed, territoriality and war" (1997, 18).

In her powerful essay on the dangers to human survival posed by environmental and political crises in the current era, the historian Gerda Lerner explores the value of feminism as a transformative worldview. She draws attention to the dangers to human survival generated by the patriarchal model of hierarchical and imperialistic leadership as well as its severance of feeling and action, and affirms that "the qualities of leadership needed by persons of both sexes in the coming period of transition will be closer to those developed by women over the centuries, due to their historical marginality to power: sensitivity to others and the ability to persuade, patience, peacefulness, and a nonconfrontational style of authority, the ability to be nurturant and to care for conservation, protection of the earth and its resources and of people in need of help" (1997, 111). The worldwide embrace of Diana is profoundly connected to her ability to manifest this emerging vision of a transformative human subjectivity and a related political practice.

The mass grief for Diana flows from what many believe to be archetypal if unconscious memories. Still, that torrent of emotions is as much about the future as about the past, about redemption as much as loss. It is about possibility: hopes for a be-coming world very different from the one to which we are habituated, a world made in the image of a sovereign Goddess. Historian Luther Martin reminds us that the story of the suffering, wandering, and ultimately homecoming universal Goddess serves as a "paradigm of salvation" (1987, 59). Kath McPhillips predicts that Diana's journey will prove to be a "curiously redemptive one for the whole world in ways that may take us a long time to fully appreciate" (1997, 19). There is no great "mystery": By claiming Diana as world symbol, divine sign, People's Queen, Savior/Goddess, many women and men signify a commitment to transform/save not only the self, but also the world.

15

Facing Change
African Mythic Origins in Octavia Butler's Parable *Novels*

the house on fire
poison waters
earthquake
and the air a nightmare

momma
help me
turn the face of history
to your face.

June Jordan (1989, 76)

Parables, traditionally, are mysterious, often riddling stories whose full meaning can be grasped only by those who are in the know. When teaching Octavia Butler's *Parable of the Sower* (1994) and *Parable of the Talents* (1998), I ask students to consider the many ways in which Butler's nightmarish vision of a future United States (2024-2090) is grounded in past and present realities: the legacy of African enslavement, including the systemic raping of women and men; the abduction and forcible adoption of Native American children, and their reeducation in Euro-American churches, institutions, and homes; the ongoing flight from southern "third world" countries to northern "first world" ones because of poverty and political repression; the homophobic, misogynist, and frequently white-supremacist religious right; antilesbian and antigay violence; the vast and growing chasm between rich and poor; the burgeoning of gated communities; racist, corrupt police; the use of electric stun belts and restraint chairs on U.S. prisoners; worldwide sex trafficking and enslavement of women and children; anti-immigrant sentiment and legislation; and the current flourishing of new and alternative communities and spiritualities.[1]

It is on that last feature that I concentrate here. James Walborn has responded to Butler's works by claiming *Parable of the Sower* to be an extended prayer to the Goddess of Fire.[2] A new religious movement, which Luisah Teish (1985) calls the global WomanSpirit Movement, recognizes female divinity and redefines it as encompassing not only nurturance and forgiveness but also turbulent, destructive, and transformative power. Of course, this is also a very old religious movement. Although the big three global religions, Judaism, Islam, and Christianity, recognize only male divinity, worldwide oral traditions have always spoken of and with female Powers. Fate or Destiny—a concept that predates male divinity—is almost everywhere understood as female, as are Chaos, Chance, Luck, the Void, Justice, and Necessity. Indeed, as Dr. Bankole notes in *Parable of the Talents* (Butler, 1998, 50), this feminine power is again being recognized under new names: chaos theory, evolution, and quantum physics.

The Parable of the Talents (Butler, 1998, 7) begins with the scornful voice of Larkin: "THEY'LL MAKE A GOD of her." She is referring to her mother, Lauren Oya Olamina, who has founded a religion, Earthseed, against a backdrop of fascist Christian fundamentalism, environmental devastation, and the complete breakdown of civil society. In the Earthseed belief, God is Change, inexorable but malleable. Earthseed itself has no recognizable mythic personages, no promised afterlife, no comforting, caring parental deity. It does, however, offer guidelines for a way of life. For the relationship between humans and divinity is a mutual and dialogic one: God shapes us, and we can shape God.

Despite the absence of mythic personages in the Earthseed religion, we can discern some homage to African ancestry in the underlying presence of the Yoruban goddess Oya. Larkin reminds us that her mother's second name is "Oya" and muses: "I wonder whatever possessed my Baptist minister grandfather to give her such a name. What did he see in her? 'Oya' is the name of a Nigerian Orisha—goddess—of the Yoruba people. In fact, the original Oya was the goddess of the Niger River, a dynamic, dangerous entity. She was also goddess of the wind, fire, and death, more bringers of great change" (Butler, 1998, 50).

According to Judith Gleason (1987, 7), Yoruba sages say that when a person is born, she or he "'chooses a head,' thereby becoming endowed with a portion of cosmic essence, which is the soul's matrix." The essences, or orishas, "are numinous archetypal forces. They are wounds that heal us, sanctifying madnesses." (Butler [1996] might say "positive obsessions.") "The Orisha with whom we have prenatally chosen to be consubstantial," Gleason continues, "is called the 'owner of the head'" (1987, 7).

It is Oya, it seems, who owns Olamina's head. Oya, Gleason (1987, 11) reminds us, traveled to the Americas along "with other African gods, in the heads of worshipers chained in the holds of slave ships." Oya at her most awesome is a weather goddess, and the weather is notoriously beyond scientific predictability and control. "The diviners who recite the praises to Oya are concerned not only with getting people who ought to be worshipping her to do so, but with keeping Oya herself in line" (2). Just as "she" shapes us, we shape her. In this complex theology, Fate does not absolve humans of responsibility; rather, it necessitates it.

As elemental goddess, Oya appears as the consuming fire and attendant winds that burn a great deal of California in *Parable of the Sower*. Oya manifests in *Parable of the Talents* as the destructive but liberating storm that triggers a landslide that allows Olamina and the Earthseed community to escape from a concentration camp organized by "Jarrett's Crusaders," a Christian/fascist militia. The landslide disrupts the electrical current during the night, shutting off the power to electronic slave collars that have enabled the incarceration. The men of Jarrett's Crusaders, ironically enough, helped shape their own fate by cutting down all the trees on the hillside and making the conditions ripe for a landslide.

Oya is always associated with pointed speech and fiery truth-telling, as one of her praise-songs makes clear: "Mother, Oya / She's the one who employs truth against wickedness / She stands at the frontier between life and death" (Gleason, 1987, 3). Oya is said to tear lies to pieces. Olamina, too, is a truth-teller. For example, she tells the truth about sexual sadism as an underlying motivation for both slavery and male-supremacist religion. Moreover, she transgresses the Christian patriarchal tradition forbidding women leadership positions in religion— from Saint Paul to the Promise Keepers—by preaching and founding a religion.

The Goddess Oya is a warrior, fierce and sometimes bearded. Like many of the oldest deities in Africa and the Americas, she incorporates masculinity. We spot "Oya" manifesting herself when Olamina passes as male, fights physically, and experiences attraction for and from women as well as men. Oya is matron/patron of gender-variant and homoerotically inclined males (Conner, 1993, 242–43). Marc, Olamina's gay brother, who reacts to the trauma of being raped and enslaved by allying himself with the Christian leadership, is one such male who could not face himself and accept Oya's guidance.

Larkin acidly writes of Earthseed's God of Change: "This is a terrifying God, implacable, faceless, yet malleable and wildly dynamic. I suppose it will soon be wearing my mother's face" (Butler, 1998, 49). Olamina undoubtedly would reject any attempt to deify her, but Change/Oya will find its way and have its say.

In Taoism, too, Change is the universal principle: When something goes beyond its extremes, it inevitably changes into its opposite (Huang, 1998, 26). The *Parable* books suggest that patriarchy itself—a society based in male supremacy—has gone beyond its extremes. Patriarchy's core icon is the omnipotent and immutable male divinity. The message is clear: When god is male, the male is god (Daly, 1973). The presiding genius/deity of the *Parable* books is black, masculine, female, ever-changing, untrammeled, and untrammelable. One of the open secrets of Butler's *Parables* is the power of the living Oya archetype to upend the established order, to revolutionize consciousness and culture.

Oya travels all over, in books as well as heads.

16

The Naked Goddess
Pornography, Female Potency, and the Sacred

> Thinking of sex as an it and women as sex objects is one of the
> grooves most deeply carved in the Western mind. This groove
> in the national mind of America will not accept the concept of
> sex as part of the sacred generative power of the universe—and
> of woman as bearer of this life force. The life force cannot be
> owned as property, used and consumed—or merchandised.
> Period. For all of its sweetness, the Corn-Mother's line is im-
> placably drawn.
>
> Marilou Awiakta (1993, 252)

> In order to perpetuate itself, every oppression must corrupt or
> distort those various sources of power within the culture of the
> oppressed that can provide energy for change.
>
> Audre Lorde (1984, 53)

Catharine MacKinnon and Andrea Dworkin (Dworkin, 1989, 253–75)
originally shifted the debate around pornography from questions of
morality and chastity to questions of power relations by defining pornography as the "sexually explicit subordination of women," as well as
those used in the place of women (racialized men, transsexuals, etc.).[1]
Pornography, in a radical feminist view, is not about the appreciation of
women and the "joy of sex" but about the "denigration of women and a
fear and hatred of the female body" (Kaplan, 1991, 322). It is ultimately
not about arousal but about desensitization. Adding a dimension from
sexual thealogy, we can further understand pornography as that most

deeply carved mental "groove" (in Awiakta's formulation) that makes us think of and practice sex as an "it" instead of as an ontological event—a coming and becoming.[2]

By connecting sex to nonbeing, mindlessness, and misogyny, pornography seeks to discredit an alternative sexual cosmology. That cosmology recognizes the body as sacred, and the genitals as a site where the sacred lodges with a special intensity. It perceives sexual desire not as "sin," but as a manifestation of the cosmic energy that drives the universe. And it knows the feminine principle, lodged particularly in women but in which both women and men participate, as mysterious, potent, the cosmic source of life, something that must be inviolable, reverenced, and respected. These ideas come together in the imagination of the sex/love/death goddess, a symbolic form that reveals realities otherwise ineffable, taking shape in a deity like Inanna of Sumer. Diane Wolkstein (Wolkstein and Kramer, 1983, 169), a folklorist working with texts from the third millennium B.C., describes this figure in these terms: "Inanna is the Goddess of Love. Formed from all of life, the Goddess of Love gives forth desire that generates the energy of the universe." Divine power is not, as the phallic imaginary would have it, the absolute power to dominate all others while remaining curiously detached and insensate; divine potency is energetic, communicative and connective, desiring, sexual, intelligent, ecstatic.

Conventional (moralistic *and* pornographic) notions of sex are steeped in a mind/body hierarchical split that deems the body inferior to mind and spirit. "Sex" is limited to the inferior physical, associated particularly with women ("the sex") and with the stigmatized low as opposed to the valorized high, with the dark as opposed to the light, with the emotional as opposed to the rational, even with the demonic as opposed to the sacred. Yet this reverses the wisdom traditions of most of human history. The religious historian Mircea Eliade (1969, 14) explains: "Everywhere and always it [sexuality] is a polyvalent function whose primary and perhaps supreme valency is the cosmological function. . . . [E]xcept in the modern world, sexuality has everywhere and always been a hierophany, and the sexual act an integral action (therefore also a means to knowledge)." Sexuality, then, is the indelible mark of the sacred on our bodies, an endlessly evocative epigram written on the flesh, to both delight and puzzle us so that we might feel and know god/dess.

In *Goddess: Myths of the Female Divine*, David Leeming and Jake Page (1994) trace an ancient history of goddess worship followed by systematic degradations during the patriarchal era. Nevertheless, they note the continuing presence of goddess imagery, albeit displaced and distorted, in such popular figures as the femme fatale and, I would add, the drag queen and the porn "star." In order for the male to become "God" and for patriarchal religion to triumph, it was imperative that Goddess and feminine sacrality be disrespected, explicitly profaned, and distorted. Thus pornography (in both its overt and everyday manifestations) appropriates, stigmatizes, or refigures in oppressive forms such characteristic features of goddess-centered spiritualities as: sexual exuberance and orgiastic, including same-sex, activity; an honorific association between sexuality and "nature"—animality, dirt, the elements, the night sky; nakedness to indicate potency (B. Walker, 1983, 706; Marinatos, 2000); the honoring of male femininity and ceremonial transvestitism (Conner, 1993); the sensual, sexual, and/or naked dance to invoke power (Omolade, 1983, 350); same-sex whipping as part of an initiatory ritual (Reis, 1991, 206–12); the spread legs of a woman or goddess as a sign of *yoni* worship (Marglin, 1987, 330); and the proscription against gazing unbidden or unceremoniously on the nakedness of goddesses, specifically the vulva or *yoni*, an act traditionally punished by blinding (Chevalier and Gheerbrant, 1994, 200).

The Sanskrit word *yoni* has various meanings, including "womb, vulva, vagina, place of birth, source, origin, spring; abode, home, lair, nest; family, race, stock, caste" (Marglin, 1987, 330). Many cultures venerate icons representing overt depictions of *yonis* as well as symbolic ones (downward pointing triangles, caves, concentric ovals, spiral patterns, sea shells, fruits), recognizing in these the original animating, generative, and transformative matrix (533), god herself—not the playmate of the month.

The *yoni* plays a prominent role in Zora Neale Hurston's (1983, 137) account of her initiation into Voodoo: "'What is the truth?' Dr. Holly asked me, and knowing that I could not answer him he answered himself through a Voodoo ceremony in which the Mambo, that is the priestess, richly dressed, is asked this question ritualistically. She replies by throwing back her veil and revealing her sex organs. The ceremony means that this is the infinite, the ultimate truth." Under a pornographic paradigm this complex rite gets turned into the "beaver shot" in *Hustler*, the "monster shot" in a porn film, a ceremony not of revelation but of degradation, not of mystery but of exposure. Pornography, as Melissa Raphael has argued, is intended to profane the sacred, to deliberately desecrate "womanhood in order to establish the male as the ultimately privileged god-like subject within a spiritual hierarchy" (1996, 110). In this hierarchy, the *yoni* becomes the very epitome of what is "down there," the lowest of the low, and a whole genre of "taboo" materials is generated to make that point continually. Ironically enough, the god being celebrated in the sacred texts and worshipped as occupying the very tip-top of that hierarchy is himself a thinly veiled phallus.

Revering the Phallus/Profaning the Cunt

> peg my vulva
> my star-sketched horn of the dipper
> moor my slender boat of heaven
> my new moon crescent cunt beauty.
> Sacred song of Inanna, 2300 B.C. (Meador, 2000, 11)

> But if woman is seen as revolting, how much more so that which makes her a woman—her genital. The revolting, of course, was once the sacred.
> Wolfgang Lederer (1968, 42)

The *phallus* is the symbolic double of the penis—well, sort of, anyway. It is a simulation, often symbolic, of a penis in a state of permanent erection, and, for both popular culture and psychoanalytic theory, serves as the lofty and universal signifier of male superiority, authority, and law, "all greatness and goodness, 'the power and the glory,' the intellect and all superior capacities and attributes" (Sillman, 1966, 165). As such inflated language reveals, the phallus is the not-so-hidden model for the patriarchal god, the euphemistically called "most high." The (supposedly nonpornographic) title for this male god in the Catholic religion is "The Omnipotent."

I am all in favor of encountering divinity in the genitals, male and female, but the phallus is another matter. The always hard and detached phallus is adamantly not a true representative of the penis, which is definitely attached, sometimes hard but more often soft, changeable and responsive, fertile. The modern phallus, Susan Bordo argues (1999, 89), in contrast to ancient male fertility symbols, is the emblem of the rejection of sexuality and the body by patriarchal religion. In keeping with modern forms of racist and rationalist systems, the phallus was detached from the "lower" biological body and associated with the superiority of (the usually white) "male intellect, rationality, mind" (90). Detachment/ splitting is the core function of the phallus; for psychoanalysis it is the instrument of separation, the thing that forces the disjuncture of mother and child. Mythically, it is the instrument separating humanity from (Mother) nature, resulting in a profound alienation.

Only elite men can really have the phallus. Men of "lower" races and classes hold phallic power in relation to women and subordinate men, and, when expedient, can be embraced as fellow phallus-holders by elite men. But when necessary in order to justify their subordination, "low" class or racially stigmatized men can be deemed by the elite to be either pure brute and instinctual "penis," as with black men (Fanon, 1967, 120), or as "sexless" and phallus-less, as with so-called Orientals (Fung, 1991).

The idolization of the phallus has dire effects linked to both misogyny and violence, causing many men to scapegoat women as revolting, profane, and the "most low" and to allot to despised men that same fate, deeming them "bitches," "pussies," and "cunts." The phallus also disrespects and shames the actual penis, and ordains the demonization of softness, darkness, and death (Nelson, 1994), for these are the properties not only of the vulva but also of the penis. The phallic imaginary stigmatizes all who can be linked to these factors, not only women, but also "unmanly" men, ethnic others, animals, nature. The phallic imaginary encourages the worship of the controlled artifact, feeds anxieties about castration (after all, the phallus is detachable) as well as fears of death, and demands the derogation if not sacrifice of wild nature—internal and external.

While the phallus is deified, its female symbolic equivalent—which is largely unnamed but which we might think of as "the cunt"—is everywhere stigmatized. This includes all that is symbolically associated with "the cunt," including darkness, smell or "essence," instinct, irrationality, chaos, the depths, and the common.

The ancient word *cunt*, though now obscene, was not always so mortified. Until the fourteenth century, *cunt* was Standard English for the vulva and only became obscene in the seventeenth century because of its "powerful sexuality" (Partridge, 1961). Sex-negative pornographic/religious thinking obviates female being and becoming by reversing the original power of the word and then branding women "cunt," the vulva viciously detached from the whole body/mind/soul, without powers of speech or cognition. The pornographic construction of woman as "cunt" further suggests that women are perpetually vulnerable and available and thus strips them physically and metaphysically, ritually divesting them of full humanity.

The phallus, Bordo (1999, 89) writes, "stands for a [male] superiority that is not just biological, but partakes of an authority beyond." Correspondingly, in the phallic/pornographic imaginary, the "cunt" signifies a female inferiority that is both metaphysical and biological. This paradigm leads to a common sexually racist characterization, a "pious pornography (Hernton, 1988, 136) that idealizes a good, "cuntless," woman—the Virgin Mother, the immaculate, white Southern lady, the Barbie doll, the futuristic "fembot" (Daly with Caputi, 1987, 198).

Concomitantly, the pornographic fantasy of woman as pure "cunt" has been literally enacted, most commonly on the bodies of racially targeted women, prostituted women, and women in war zones. The so-called Hottentot Venus, the southern African Sarah Baartmann, was displayed naked, as a freak, to jeering crowds in Europe from 1810 to 1815. When she died in 1815 at the age of twenty-five, her genitals and buttocks were cut from her body and exhibited (Gilman, 1985, 215–16; hooks, 1992, 63). Eyewitness accounts from the Sand Creek Massacre report that the invading European Americans mutilated the sex organs of Native American women and men and displayed trophies made of women's "private parts" (D. Brown, 1981, 88). The founding father of serial sex murder, Jack the Ripper (Caputi, 1987), did not rape the prostituted women he victimized; rather, he slit their throats, mutilated their genitals, and even carried off the womb of Annie Chapman. Such actions must also be understood as rites, ceremonies of degradation and annihilation targeting the feminine principle, based not only in hatred but, even more fundamentally, in fear and ontological impotence.

Mary Gossy (1994, 23) issues this challenge: "Let those of you who are not lesbians just try to imagine a response to a cunt that is not determined by castration anxiety." Some famous nonlesbians evince this anxiety throughout the annals of Western thought. Aristotle philosophized that woman "is as it were an impotent male, for it is through a certain incapacity that the female is female" (cited in Agonito, 1977, 4). Saint Augustine preached that woman, in her sexual difference from man, and apart from her husband, was not exactly made in the image of "God" (Power, 1996, 165). The existentialist philosopher Jean-Paul Sartre (1957, 86) looks down on woman, locating the "obscenity" of her sex in the fact that she is in the form of a "hole." Freud describes women's sexuality as the "dark continent" (cited in Doane, 1991, 210), an image that hinges upon the interrelated racism and sexism in the colonialist idea of Africa, linking the feminine with the very "heart of darkness."

Colonization, of course, has everything to do with the pornographic paradigm. In *The Sacred Hoop: Recovering the Feminine in American Indian Traditions,* Paula Gunn Allen argues that worldwide there were and are "gynocracies" — "woman-centered tribal societies in which matrilocality, matrifocality, matrilinearity, maternal control of household goods and resources and female deities of the magnitude of the Christian God were and are present and active features of traditional tribal life" (1986a, 3–4). She further argues that genocide directed against American Indian tribes must be understood as a type of *gynocide,* hate-based assaults against the feminine, because genocide "is and was mostly about patriarchal fear of gynocracy" (2).

The novelist John Updike (cited in Keller, 1985, 105), speaking generally of and for (presumably heterosexual) men, once remarked: "We want to fuck what we fear." As a popular obscenity, *fuck* means not only a sexual penetration but also an act of (sexualized) conquest, violation, injury, destruction. Colonizing forces fearing gynocentrism try to "fuck" it, not only through murder and theft of land and resources, but also by profaning its sacred — appropriating holy sites, seizing and exhibiting sacred things, forbidding native languages, demonizing native divinities, and, finally, making the sacred into property and selling it.

So profound is the influence of the pornographic worldview that it is almost impossible to step out of it. Yet it is from this outsider position that new visions of divinity, pleasure, sex, and power can be imagined. For rebellious women and men (straight or gay) to get to this place, part of the passage must include taking back gynocentric holy sites (on the body and outside the body), languages, and divinities. While the idea of "goddess" might seem irrelevant to those not particularly interested in religion, it has everything to do with cultural understanding of women's (and nonmisogynistic men's) capacity to be — precisely what pornography is intent on destroying. The philosopher Luce Irigaray (1993, 61, 63–64) writes: "To become means fulfilling the wholeness of what we are capable of being. . . . But as long as woman lacks a divine made in her image she cannot establish her subjectivity or achieve a goal of her own. She lacks an ideal that would be her goal or path in becoming." All men too, arguably, need a feminine ideal "for the good of their souls," in order to relate to that aspect of their being and to avoid being "overwhelmed" by it (Begg, 1996, 135).

In much academic writing, including feminist and queer writing, unqualified support for pornography is much in evidence. What is taboo, curiously enough, is support for female divinity. This itself is a result of the reigning pornographic worldview. Carol Christ (1997, 78) has pointed to the reluctance of scholars to take seriously the notion of female divinity "because they have been taught to view the body and sexuality, especially the female body and female sexuality, as being 'lower' than the rationality that is associated with divinity and 'man's' 'higher' nature." In other words, they have been schooled by the pornographic worldview to view the feminine as a dumb, demonic, and dirty "cunt," while consciously or unconsciously reverencing and romancing the ultra-clean and veritably sterile high phallus.

The Dirty/Earth Body

The pornographic desacralization of what formerly was sacred is evident in the use of the word *dirty* to refer to sexual thoughts, words, and deeds. *Dirty* means not only the soil/earth itself but also something that is befouled, contaminated, profane, and profaned. The earth and sexuality, in this framework, are the very antithesis of the sacred. This seemingly reverses a long human history in which "the mere existence of the soil was seen as significant in the religious sphere"; and the Earth (as both soil and planet) is understood "as a religious 'form' . . . repository of a wealth of sacred forces" and "the *foundation* of every expression of existence" (Eliade, 1958a, 242), the very flesh of a goddess, the cosmic womb that begets us and to which we ultimately return. In truth, the Earth is still understood in this way and that is precisely why Earth is under such attack by those in the grip of the phallic imaginary.

Common metaphors negatively link sexuality to both animals and Earth—both of which are said to be "lower" than humans. Louise Erdrich (2001, 134) tells us that in the Ojibwe language the word for *vagina* derives from the word for *earth*. This does not mean that the Ojibwe consider sex to be "dirty" in the sense of sinful. Rather, it recognizes and honors the profound connection between the sexual body and the generative earth, both physical and metaphysical. When *dirty* is used to disgrace and desacralize sexuality, nature, and darkness—and all those who are seen to embody these—*cleansing* emerges as the most apt metaphor for genocide, gynocide, and geocide.

Henry Kissinger, Richard Nixon's Secretary of State, and still a powerful political figure, once noted that "power is the ultimate aphrodisiac." A political cartoon by David Levine in *The Nation* (February 25, 1984) visualizes Kissinger's power by showing him "fucking" the earth (a woman's naked body with the earth as her head). In advertising imagery both the landscape and the female body are regularly shown as conquered, rendered into property that can be taken, owned, and mapped. A 1999 ad for car stereo speakers shows a naked, curvy, and inert, perhaps dead, young white woman lying on the ground. Inscribed over every inch of her body are roadmaps. The headline reads: "Feel the raw, naked power of the road." Such imagery signifies an overall pornographic assault on the "naked goddess," the cosmic feminine principle, what Vandana Shiva (1988, 40) defines as the active and creative principle in which both women and men participate. Here that principle is stripped of all reverence; the dancing is stilled. What madness is this?

The Bitch/Goddess

A 1977 poster for the New York Erotic Film Festival surfaces an underlying trope characterizing both pornography and patriarchal religion. It displays the bare outline of a naked woman's body. Her genital area, though, is highly detailed—the face of the devil, replete with protruding tongue and animal-like horns. Significantly, the characteristic attributes of the devil—the horns, protruding tongue, and serpentine nature—are originally associated with female divinity: the Greek Medusa, the Hindu Kali, the Aztec Coatlicue, the Yoruban First Ancestor, and others (Anzaldúa, 1987; Baring and Cashford, 1991; Sjöö and Mor, 1991; Graham, 1997), as well as with nature gods such as the Greek Pan. The pornographic/theological association of "God" with sexual prohibition is paralleled by the linkage of the "Devil" with sex.

The hairy, instinctual, and very animated sex organs are understood as the least godly parts of our bodies. Yet gynocentric sexualities/spiritualities would hold otherwise. The sex organs (and animals themselves) are understood as imbued with both intelligence and divine powers. Barbara Walker (1983, 109) reveals that *Bitch* was "one of the most sacred titles of the Goddess Artemis-Diana," who often appeared as a dog herself, or in the company of hounds. Indeed, around the world, the Lady of the Beasts assumed the full or partial form of an animal (e.g., with or carrying horns) or appeared with characteristic animals, such as birds, fish, pigs, snakes (Neumann, 1963, 268). This ancient, powerful Bitch is the sacred archetype behind the contemporary profanity, reflecting fear of the "bitch goddess" (as well as the sexually sovereign, creative, autonomous woman).

In patriarchal religions, the Bitch is demonized. In the secular world, she is turned into pornography, the dominatrix, a controlled fetish despite appearances of power. We find her, for example, on the cover of the fetish magazine *Bizarre* (c. 1953; reproduced in Keesey, 1997, 21): a dark-haired seductress, her eyes lined with kohl, clad in a corset-like teddy, long black gloves, and perilously high stiletto heels, and wielding a snakelike whip. A stuffed tiger sits at her feet. The message is a mixed one, of course. Female power is invoked, but immediately contained, for, as her outfit and shoes indicate, she is tightly bound and ultimately immobile. Her tiger is only a toy, and so, the image proclaims, is she.

Reclaiming the Dirty Mouth

> The fertile Earth is symbolized by the sex organs, which dis-
> play the power of generation as well as an indecent boldness.
> > Hildegard of Bingen, 1098–1179? (1987, 114)

> [Phallic power is] really womb power that men stole. A man
> standing with his legs apart is impersonating a woman. Men
> all have womb envy. We don't have penis envy. My psychic
> penis is way larger than any man's. My attitude is, I have a va-
> gina and therefore I have the bigger penis. . . . I was the filthi-
> est act ever. I would do anything. People say to me, "You're not
> very feminine." Well, they can suck my dick.
> > Roseanne (quoted in Lahr, 1995, 44)

In patriarchal myth, enacted in sacred texts as well as pornography, the female sex is no longer divine, but is aligned with evil, monstrosity, and obscenity, said to be the devil's gateway, the mouth of hell. The "Great Goddess" becomes the "Great Whore." Female sexual mysteries are identified with immorality and pagan savagery and eventually become the very stuff of pornography. There, these mysteries, private and usually female-only, are made massively public and purveyed specifically to men. The attendant moralities of pornographic cultures mandate female modesty and expressly forbid to "good" women the realm of sexual talk and imagery as well as sovereign, self-determining sexual expression. In these mutually reinforcing ways, women are robbed of our voices and of our "mysteries," vehicles for both individual growth and the creation of gynophilic space and community.

In her profoundly impudent *SCUM Manifesto*, originally written in 1967, Valerie Solanas challenges women to "trust only their own animal, gutter instincts" (1995, 177). Conversely, ladylike propriety enjoins girls and women to keep our minds and language "out of the gutter." Yet in a quest to transform pornographic consciousness, that metaphorical site may well deserve our most intense devotion.

The word *impudence* is derived from the Latin *pudendum*, "the vulva," which in turn is derived from *pudere*, "to feel shame." Raped, occupied, sold, colonized, turned into pornography, unable to claim our own space, mortified—generations of women referred to our genitals as "down there" (Steinem, 1998, vii), or as nothing at all. In a revelatory moment in Colette's *Gigi* (1952), the teenaged Gigi refers to her "you know what." Madame Alvarez vehemently cuts her off: "Silence! Aren't you ashamed to call it your you-know-what?" Gigi replies that she wouldn't "mind calling it by any other name, only . . . " Madame doesn't let Gigi finish her sentence. "There is no other name," she tells her (cited in Callander, 1996, 53). Colette here is explicitly making a connection between the imposition of female modesty and its attendant social institutions— marriage, pornography, and prostitution. The literary critic Margaret Callander analyzes this scene. Because Gigi's "'you-know-what'" is about to be "sold intact to a male owner, it must remain outside language," for naming it would "subvert the proprieties of that world" (1996, 53). To aid in counteracting centuries of sexual sales, silencings, alienations, and shamings, it might be beneficial to gravitate to the loud, the *impudent*, the guttural, the base, the vulgar, the earthy, the shameless, reclaiming this territory for women and redefining it in the process.

Eve Ensler describes the liberating effect of what she calls "vagina-talking" in an interview regarding her play, *The Vagina Monologues*. The play, a popular phenomenon, consists of a series of vignettes shaped by Ensler from stories and perceptions she collected from women whom she had asked to think about (and, implicitly, *with*) their vaginas. Ensler told the *New York Times* that she has been pondering what she calls "the vagina brain," a separate brain whose "understanding of the world comes through the body. The reason we're in so much trouble on earth is that the vagina intelligence has been damaged by rape, battery, sexual abuse and terror" (Boxer, 1998).

In her "Introduction" to *The Vagina Monologues*, Ensler elaborates: "I say 'vagina' because when I started saying it I discovered how fragmented I was, how disconnected my body was from my mind. My vagina was something over there, away in the distance. I rarely lived inside it, even visited. I was busy working, writing; being a mother, a friend. I did not see my vagina as my primary resource, a place of sustenance, humor, and creativity. It was fraught there, full of fear. I'd been raped as a little girl, and although I'd grown up, and done all the adult things one does with one's vagina, I had never really reentered that part of my body after I'd been violated. I had essentially lived most of my life without my motor, my center, my second heart" (1998, xxi). In order to reclaim her integrity, and as part of a process of stopping the shame and the violation, Ensler found herself saying *vagina,* over and over, no matter how "dirty" it sounded.

Going Down

> Much, of course, can be learned by all of us from all of us who speak, read, write, including those of us who look high. But as we look high, we might also look low, lest we devalue women in the world.
>
> Barbara Christian (1997, 56)

Once we dislodge the phallus from its position as the source of all signification, we can cease gazing only on what is above and turn our attention to what is below. In so doing, we steep ourselves in traditions scorned and dismissed by elites: an underground wisdom tradition still found in the background of words, in myth, and in contemporary oral, popular, artistic and literary outpourings.

Feminine modesty forbids the use of obscenity by women. Yet the gynocentric oral tradition instructs us in alternative female significations and strategies. In the summer of 2002, Nigerian women, outraged at the exploitation of international oil companies, threatened to march naked in order to shame the neocolonial abusers. This tactic is not an unprecedented or isolated one.

Shirley Ardener, a British anthropologist living in Cameroon, found that Bakweri women, in defense of their sexual honor, would demonstrate in ways that might otherwise be considered obscene. For example, when a man insults a woman's vulva—perhaps "by saying that it smells"—that woman calls out all the other women of the village. "Converging upon the offender, dressed in vines, they demand immediate recantation and a recompense of a pig, plus something extra for the woman who has been directly insulted. The women then surround him and sing songs which are often obscene by allusion, and accompany them by vulgar gestures" (1987, 115). Even more extravagantly vulgar gestures are employed by another Cameroonian people, the Balong. If a man insults his wife's lower parts, "it is like insulting all women." The women gather and "they will take all their clothes off. They will shame him and sing songs. . . . [T]he term used for this phenomenon *(ndon)* is probably derived from a root meaning 'beautiful'" (117).

Ardener is concerned with tracing a historical phenomenon whereby women employ deliberately vulgar "'ritual games' and gestures . . . in an idiom which reverberates across time and space, to defend their corporate identity" (114-15). Her essay begins with examples of African women collectively signifying sexual dignity and ends with the visual art of Judy Chicago, Suzanne Santoro, Niki de Saint-Phalle, and others who deliberately use honorific vulva images in their work in order to, in Chicago's words, "state the truth and beauty of . . . [female] identity" (1982, 143-44) against the insults of the pornographic world. Ardener concludes that this traditional use of deliberate vulgarity constitutes a form of oppositional discourse invented by groups who are "muted" and negated by dominant others. Significantly, Chicago's art was soon condemned by the postmodern and/or misogynist academic elite as "essentialist" and disparaged by art historians and critics as not "high art" but as the lowest of the low, veritably "cunt art" (Amelia Jones, 1996). In the U.S. Congress, ironically enough, her work was denounced as "pornographic."

Ardener also refers to a Greek myth featuring an old woman figure, Baubo, the Goddess of Obscenity, who is associated with lewd jokes and the exposure of the vulva. Baubo's name is said to derive from a word meaning a body cavity, belly, womb, vulva. Images show her sometimes as a full-bodied old woman lifting her skirt, sometimes only as a vulva, and sometimes as the lower half of a female body with a face in place of the vulva. Baubo stars in the climax of one version of the story of the goddess Demeter, who, distraught at the rape and loss of her daughter Persephone, wandered the earth and caused all earthly fertility to cease. Finally, Demeter encountered the dancing Baubo, who lifted her skirt, revealing her vulva and making the goddess laugh. This gesture and Demeter's delight resulted in the return of the Green—earthy fertility (Lubell, 1994).

The sacred potency of the vulva is recognized by the Baule people of the Ivory Coast. In their art, naked female figures with spread legs are highly unusual. When these do occur, their "aggressive nudity may express an implied threat. The female body as the source of life is one of the most potent *amuin* (energetic or spirit force) the Baule have, and clandestine or brazen looking at a woman's sexual organs can be fatal to men" (Vogel, 1997, 60). The most powerful *amuin* is recognized as belonging to the women's deities, notably *Adyanun*. One Baule commentator relates: "The women dance Adyanun as a last recourse in times of impending calamity—epidemics, war, drought, a president's death—because it is more potent than all the other *amuin*. . . . The women's *amuin* is danced 'naked because its locus of power is every woman's sexual organs'" (59).

A Japanese myth draws upon similar themes. Amaterasu, the sun goddess, is outraged by sexual violence against her younger sister and withdraws her face from the land. To prevent world demise, an old hag goddess, Uzume, invents music and dance and then performs a sacred striptease that is both comic and deeply serious, ending with the exposure of her genitals, making the divine spirits laugh. Hearing the laughter, Amaterasu comes back, and the sun shines once again (Monaghan, 1994, 10-11). In the stories of Baubo and Uzume, the revelation of the cunt, the fleshy epiphany of the divine source of life, is both comic and serious, vulgar yet infinitely efficacious.

In her popular work *Women Who Run with the Wolves*, Clarissa Pinkola Estés (1992, 336, 340) tells Baubo's story, urging her readers to reclaim the "Dirty Goddess," the female divine who is both sexual and sacred: "There is a powerful saying: *Dice entre las piernas*, 'She speaks from between her legs.' . . . '[S]peaking from the vulva' . . . is, symbolically, speaking from the *primae materia*, the most basic, most honest level of truth—the vital *os*. What else is there to say but that Baubo speaks from the mother lode, the deep mind, literally the depths?" Estés' words directly inspire the novelist and essayist Sandra Cisneros (1996) in her exquisitely brazen essay, "Guadalupe, the Sex Goddess." Trained by Mexican Catholicism to be alienated and estranged from her female body, coming into adulthood she at first rejects Guadalupe as a lofty, unrealistic, asexual "goody-goody meant to doom me to a life of unhappiness" (1996, 48). Overcoming those prohibitions leads to literary creativity and spiritual becoming. Thus awakened, she critically reinterprets the *Virgen* and her pre-Columbian antecedents—a pantheon of sex, life, and death goddesses who were deemed obscene by the church—Tonantzin, Coatlicue, Tlazolteotl (see also Anzaldúa, 1987, 27-28). She affirms that Guadalupe is herself a continuation of "the sex goddess, a goddess who makes me feel good about my sexual power, my sexual energy, who reminds me I must, as Clarissa Pinkola Estés so aptly put it, '[speak] from my vulva' . . . and write from my *panocha*" (Cisneros, 1996, 49).

A few years earlier, and with a most impressive impudicity, Chicana lesbian Victoria de los Santos Mycue reinterpreted the iconic image of *La Virgen de Guadalupe* as her own vulva. In 1993, de los Santos Mycue published and later performed "A Little Prayer" as an erotic reading, understanding *La Virgen* in this way: "I could understand and love you better once I understood you in relation to my love for other women, once I understood you in relation to myself. . . . Your gently tilting face, your beautiful visage, is my clitoris. Our sensors of head and pleasure are one. Your flowing garment and folded arms are the wings of my vagina, the labia. Your belly, framed by your hands held in prayer, is your womb, like the precious entrance to me. . . . Once I began to see you as my vagina, I began to see you as the symbol for all women, as a deity advocating our empowerment on earth, and not as a repressive silencing force. . . . I begin to understand you as advocating 'Pussy Power' and thus advocating for both my sex and sexuality" (quoted in Trujillo, 1998, 225). De los Santos Mycue reverses the reversals of the pornographic imaginary, decolonizing sacred imagery and intimate space by understanding the vulva as speaking/advocating. She shamelessly locates the godhead in female sex and lesbian sexuality.

While de los Santos Mycue responds with ecstasy to her vision of the vulva in *La Virgen,* Cisneros is repelled by the image of the vulva proffered to her by a porn movie: "The film star's *panocha*—a tidy, elliptical opening, pink and shiny like a rabbit's ear. To make matters worse, it was shaved and looked especially childlike and unsexual. . . . [M]y own sex has no resemblance to this woman's. My sex, dark as an orchid, rubbery and blue purple as *pulpo,* an octopus, does not look nice and tidy, but otherworldly" (1998, 51). Cisneros recognizes that both pornography and patriarchal religion celebrate the "cuntless" woman. She reclaims not only Guadalupe's sex but also her own in all its "otherworldliness"—that is, its kinship with cosmic sacrality. The adult sexuality of her *panocha,* from which she writes/speaks, invokes once again the ancient wisdom tradition that recognizes cosmic forces of energy, thought, and creation in the genitals, both female and male.

The Feminine Principle

> A common recollection of former slaves was the sight of a woman, often the reporter's mother, being beaten for defying her master's sexual advances. . . . Minnie Folkes remembered watching her mother being flogged by her overseer when she refused "to be wife to dis man." Decades after her emancipation, Minnie repeated with pride her mother's teaching: "Don't let nobody bother yo principle; 'cause dat wuz all yo' had."
>
> Dorothy Roberts (1997, 45)

> The name of the Female Principle is "Thought."
>
> Paula Gunn Allen (1993, xx)

While both patriarchal morality and pornography hinge upon an understanding of the genitals as inferior, animalistic, mindless, instinctual, low, dirty, and disgusting, this is only credible under the reign of the bizarrely artificial, sterile and morbidly dispassionate high/white phallus. The genitals, in truth, are the mark of divinity on the body, manifesting forces of desire, ecstasy, exuberance, cyclic movement, creativity, and procreativity as well as those of thought, speech, and truth. Both the penis and the vulva—which are not opposites but correspondents—are manifestations of the primal source of being, something in which both men and women participate and something that has been understood in many parts of the world as the feminine principle (Shiva, 1988).

To refer to the female sex organs, Minnie Folkes's mother used the extremely evocative word *principle. Webster's* (1986) defines *principle* as "a general or fundamental truth . . . on which others are based and from which others are derived . . . basic or primary source of material or energy: ultimate basis or cause." The mother's use of *principle* understands the vulva to be precisely that: an incarnation of the truth; a physical manifestation of the cosmic source, basis, and cause of life; the source and heart of matter and energy, reflecting infinitely in the shapes and creative forces of the universe.

Paula Gunn Allen explains that it is profoundly limiting to understand "sex as sex" in the (pornographic) ways that we are used to. Rather, "sexual connection with woman means connection with the womb, which is the container of power that women carry within their bodies" (1986a, 24). This power, Allen cautions, "is not really biological at base. It is the power of ritual magic, the power of Thought, of Mind, that gives rise to biological organisms as it gives rise to social organizations, material culture, and transformations of all kinds" (28). Southwestern Native peoples recognize the basic power of the universe as "Thought Woman." This is a way of expressing that the "true creatrix . . . is thought itself, from which all else is born" and that the universe, "like all of her creation, is fundamentally female—potential and primary" (14). Moreover, this cosmic power of Thought/Conception is manifested in the powers of the womb/vulva as well as the brain. This vision is not unique to the Southwest. Edwin Starbuck (1926), writing in the *Encyclopedia of Religion and Ethics* on the "Female Principle," notes that the name of *Minerva*, goddess of wisdom and contemplation, is from the Latin, Greek, and Sanskrit words for "mind," and that among the Tzentals of Mexico the greatest goddess is *Alaghom Naom,* literally "she who brings forth mind." Starbuck further tells us that this pervasive quality of goddesses "causes them to burrow in the depths of things" (828). Indeed.

James B. Nelson (1994), Carol Christ (1997), Beverly Clack (2001), and Melissa Raphael (1996) have all argued that radical shifts occur when we conceptualize the divine based in values drawn from the female body and a nonphallic understanding of the male body. I would add that this process is furthered when we once again recognize sex not as antithetical to divinity, but as an essential part of cosmic thinking/desiring, not domineering, powers of being. From such perspectives, divinity can be understood not so much as male transcendent, changeless, solitary, and commanding, but as fluid, bisexual, immanent, connective, energetic, and thoughtful. The powers of mind are akin, not opposed, to the powers of sex. I take heart from the response of a six-year-old girl interviewed by Eve Ensler, included in the *Vagina Monologues*. When Ensler asked her, "What's special about your vagina?" she replied: "Somewhere deep inside I know it has a really really smart brain" (1998, 88–89).

17

The Cyborg or the Goddess?

I would like to define biology as the history of the earth and all its life—past, present, and future. To understand biology is to understand that all life is linked to the earth from which it came; it is to understand that the stream of life, flowing out of the dim past into the uncertain future, is in reality a unified force, though composed of an infinite number and variety of separate lives. The essence of life is lived in freedom. Any concept of biology is not only sterile and profitless, it is distorted and untrue, if it puts its primary focus on unnatural conditions rather than on those vast forces not of man's making that shape and channel the nature and direction of life.

Rachel Carson (1998a, 193)

Though both are bound in the spiral dance, I would rather be a cyborg than a goddess.

Donna Haraway (1991, 181)

Seeking to understand the lives of women who work for minimum wage at the most unappreciated and demeaned (though necessary) jobs, the social critic Barbara Ehrenreich worked in several of them for a while. She describes her experience in *Nickel and Dimed* (2002). While employed as a housecleaner with the "Maids" company in Maine, Ehrenreich was shown a video promoting a vacuum cleaner that could be strapped right onto the maid's back. The inventor, a man, puts it on and "then says proudly into the camera: 'See, I *am* the vacuum cleaner'" (74). This horrific statement comes easily for him, since he doesn't have to vacuum for a living. The fusion of the maid with the machine might not make it easier for the working woman to vacuum, but it indubitably makes it easier for employers to depersonalize her, making her very being synonymous with her service.[1]

However grotesque, this implied woman/machine fusion seems almost quaint when compared with an image promoting a more high-end technology. A 1993 ad is emblazoned with the headline: "Eclipse FAX: If It Were Any Faster, You'd Have to Send and Receive Your Faxes Internally" (fig. 17.1). The vision this ad presents is the decapitated head of a deathly pale white woman. Her snaky hair fans out around her head, invoking memories of Medusa, who symbolically represents, among other things, the vulva. Two electrodes are attached to her forehead. Jammed into her eyes, ears, and mouth are large and cruel metal pipes with wires going in multiple directions. Every visible opening is penetrated. The image seems to make no sense—until one realizes that it is a kind of scrim for a type of pornographic image. On the world wide web, for free, one can easily find examples of what is called "geni-torture," photos of women with legs spread, and vagina and anus penetrated by thick electrodes, labia wrenched apart by clamps, and wires attached in order to electro-shock and torture. This scenario, in both versions, is not only about the sexual torment of women, but about the torture of the life force itself. The last line of the ad sneers: "[T]o fax any faster, you'd have to break a few laws. Of physics." *Physics* is from the Greek *phusis,* "nature." This eerie image valorizes (as it visualizes) a kind of cosmic rape of nature/goddess.

An especially uncanny machine/woman synthesis appears in an ad that promotes high-tech tomorrows: a 1985 promotion from the Canned Food Information Council (fig. 17.2). A video version premiered during the high-profile Super Bowl; in the print variants, a shiny European-featured fembot (Daly with Caputi, 1987, 198) with sculpted porno-fantasy body—semireclining with legs opened, and "naked" except for fetish ornamentation and stiletto heels—announces: "In the year 3000, food will come in . . . cans." The overt meaning concerns the durability of the canning process, but what is simultaneously being transmitted is a *prophecy.* For this strangely cold sex symbol also betokens the future. Like most prophecy, the message is ambiguous. Peering into her empty eyes, imagining the touch of her "skin," we might well wonder exactly what sort of future she presages.

This fantasy of the artificial female sex object, a fusion of woman and machine, is a recurring and complicated one with an extensive

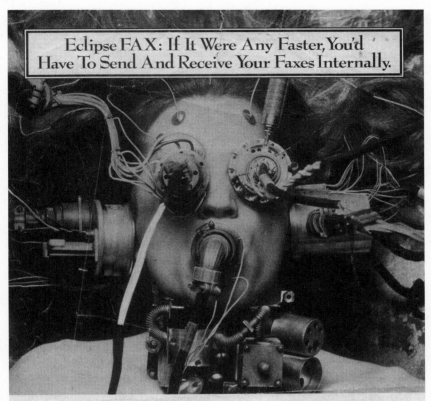

17.1 Eclipse FAX software ad, Phoenix Technologies Ltd. © 1993

history (Caputi, 1987, 176–88). Marshall McLuhan (1951, 101), in *The Mechanical Bride: The Folklore of Industrial Man*, put forth his view that this symbol, what he called "the mechanical bride," indicated a troubling cultural confusion of sex, technology, and death. Its pervasiveness, he warned, indicated our culture's tendency to invest necrophilic sexual desires into technology (like nuclear bombs). The mechanical

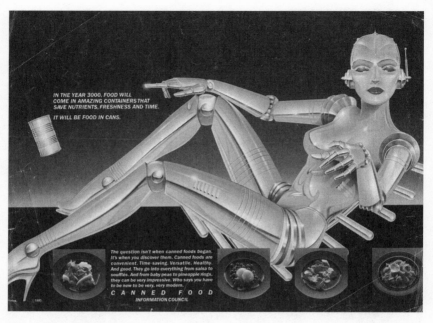

17.2 Canned Food Information Council ad © 1985

bride further betokened, he conjectured, the pervasion of a numbed cultural sensibility, a kind of soullessness, leaving many unable to experience pleasure, or perhaps any sensation at all, without extreme speed or
sadism.

A very different view was put forth in a much-reprinted and much-
quoted article, "A Manifesto for Cyborgs," first published by Donna
Haraway in 1985. Haraway, writing from what she calls a deliberately
"ironic" and "blasphemous" position, eschews beliefs in original wholeness and connection to nature and swears that we are already cyborgs,
fusions of machine, animal, and human. The cyborg, even though it
originated in the military industrial complex, can be claimed, Haraway
argues, as a liberatory symbol, signifying the feminist seizure of technological tools to change the world and to collapse oppressive gender and
species boundaries. Haraway celebrates what she understands as contemporary "boundary breakdowns" between animals, humans, and machine and finds that "the cyborg appears in myth precisely where the
boundary between human and animal is transgressed . . . signals disturbingly and pleasurably tight coupling" (1991, 152).

Haraway also understands the cyborg mythically as a "trickster" figure (4), one whose actual meaning is contrary to appearances. Although
the cyborg might most obviously be read, with McLuhan, as a sign of
desensitization, alienation from nature, and even apocalypse, Haraway
argues that the cyborg actually hints at the "ways that things many feminists have feared most can and must be refigured and put back to work
for life and not death . . . for earthly survival!" (ibid.). Her "Manifesto"
concludes with the challenge cited at the opening of this chapter, expressing a personal preference for identification with a cyborg rather
than a goddess.

Haraway's recognition of the cyborg as mythically important is undeniably apt, and she is right to ask that we develop a feminist cosmology (and myths and rituals), acknowledging our interactions with technology and our artifacts.[2] But this manifesto does not provide it.
Earlier, I quoted Rachel Carson's warning about the folly of focusing on
"unnatural conditions," rather than on those "vast forces not of man's
making that shape and channel the nature and direction of life." Haraway might be as dismissive of Carson's distinction as she is of similar
ones made by "American radical feminists" who, as she characterizes them, "insist on the organic, opposing it to the technological" (174).
But the contemplation of these "vast forces"—all that humans *cannot*
make—is a great antidote to human arrogance. It encourages not only
wonder but also *humility* (from *humus*, "earth"), both individually and as
a species, in our practices and in our fantasies. From that fundamentally
bio-logical stance of humility, we might ask: Are all boundaries subject
to human transgression and reconstruction, or are some rightfully beyond our intervention? Have animals expressed any interest in this fusion, frequently enacted as a *literal* and lethal fusion (Chelland, 2000b),
with humans and/or machines? Why should humans get to say what
happens to animals? Has the cyborg appeared at this moment because it
is a harbinger of a liberated and revolutionary future, a new and shiny
alternative to an obsolete past of tired old goddess/nature myth? Or is
the cyborg, strangely enough, that same old goddess, although with a
newly dreadful face?

In all of the cyborgian images that I have cited so far, the boundaries
of the female figure, the universal signifier of nature, are violated. In the
first, she is identified completely with the tool she uses. In the second,
she is penetrated through every possible aperture by some type of hard-
ware. In the third, a more subtle violation is implied, since the "can" is a

"container technology" (Sofoulis, 2000), gendered feminine and suggestive of the womb/vulva. The reclining pornographic cyborg here seems to be promising that she, like the can, is made to be opened.

An essential component of goddess myth worldwide—*sovereignty*—provides some instruction about this disrespectful notion of perpetual openness and violability. The concept will also help to initiate our contemplation of this conundrum of the cyborg and the goddess.

Female Sexual Sovereignty

> To woman, by nature, belongs the right of sexual determination. When the instinct is aroused in her, then and then only should commerce follow.
> Victoria Woodhull (quoted in Dworkin, 1987, 136)

> The painful, patient, and silent toil of mothers to gain a fee simple title to the bodies of their daughters, the despairing fight, as of an entrapped tigress, to keep hallowed their own persons, would furnish material for epics.
> Anna Julia Cooper, 1893 (quoted in Roberts, 1991, 3)

> Once women are free to bestow their favours and affections where they will, the whole structure of patriarchal society starts to crumble.
> Ean Begg (1996, 137)

The title of the 1997 film *The Fifth Element* (Luc Besson) refers to a female "supreme being" who takes mortal form as a woman in order to save the earth and the cosmos from some apocalyptic evil. The manly-man hero, played by Bruce Willis, is attracted to her and tries to kiss her while she is sleeping. Instantaneously she disarms him and, pointing his own weapon at his head, utters a warning in her own language. He later gets the translation: "Never without my permission." In other words, the "supreme being" is a sovereignty goddess.

The word *sovereignty* has numerous significations. In its most ancient meanings *sovereignty* signifies self-rule, autonomy, excellence, radiance, and self-realization; it was associated specifically with goddess figures (Benard and Moon, 2000, 11–12). More modern definitions include "supreme power esp. over a body politic: dominion, sway" (*Webster's*, 1986). Politically, the term is integral to discussions of nationhood, colonialism, law, and governance; it speaks of a nation's inherent right to self-rule, to be inviolable by any other sovereignty, to be "free and independent . . . entirely self-governed, self-directed."[3] In regard to personal matters—the body—*sovereignty* means pretty much the same things.

Control of women's sexual and reproductive capacities is the core patriarchal practice. It takes various forms: the sexual double standard; female-subordinate marriage; rape, incest, sexual harassment, and spousal abuse; birth control and abortion, sometimes forbidden, sometimes mandated; pornography, prostitution and trafficking. Slurs aimed at women are often based in an open contempt for personal, political, and sexual female sovereignty: the epithet *bitch* castigating any assertive or potent woman; the diminutive *princess* marking a woman as a product of her father's or husband's class; the scornful *matriarch* and *welfare queen* stigmatizing and disempowering poor African American mothers.[4] This tradition of contempt reverses numerous mythic legacies in which respected goddess figures are seen as the very "source of sovereignty" (Benard and Moon, 2000, 3–4).

Both concepts of sovereignty, the sexual and the political, commingle in a sacred story from pre-Christian Ireland (Green, 1996, 84–85). Four thirsty brothers are wandering about in the woods. They come upon a well, which happens to be guarded by a hideous hag. The hag offers them a drink in exchange for a kiss. Three of the brothers are repulsed (whether by her visage, her age, or her sexual assertiveness we don't know); they flee. Niall, however, senses something else and agrees readily. She then grants him what the oral tradition recognizes as the "ultimate favor" that is bestowed by women, sexual intercourse, and he accepts.[5] In the midst of their sexual exchange, the Hag turns into a beautiful and fertile young woman. When Niall asks her name, she replies, "I am Sovereignty." Due to and contingent upon her continuing favor, Niall becomes king and acquires the right to rule. Here and elsewhere the sovereignty goddess is regarded as the source of the king's power (Benard and Moon, 2000, 74). Moreover, political sovereignty is intimately and ultimately linked to the goddess's—and the land and women's—favor and choice, to her determination of sexual partner and her bodily integrity.

Around the world, the name of the land and/or nation is linked to that of a goddess or mythical heroine. James Lovelock (1979) reinvents this tradition in the "Gaia hypothesis," invoking the Greek earth goddess and recognizing planet Earth as a living, self-creating, and sovereign being.

Native American cultures impress upon us a strong sense of female sovereignty. The Iroquois Constitution recognizes sovereignty as the special property of women and gender balance in governance as the norm: "The lineal descent of the people of the Five Fires [the Iroquois Nations] shall run in the female line. Women shall be considered the progenitors of the Nation. They shall own the land and the soil. Men and women shall follow the status of their mothers. . . . If a disobedient chief persists in his disobedience . . . the [War] Chiefs shall then take away the title of the erring chief by order of the women in whom the title is vested. . . . The women will then select another of their sons as a candidate and the chiefs shall elect him" (cited in P. Allen, 1986a, 212). Attesting to the centrality of women to a nation's sense of self, the Cheyenne oral tradition avows, "We will not be conquered until the hearts of our women are on the ground" (ibid.). In global oral and iconographic traditions, *heart* is often synonymous with *vulva* (24).

A particularly patriarchal definition of *sovereign* is "a husband in relation to his wife" (*Oxford English Dictionary*, 1971). Although this distasteful meaning is now considered obsolete linguistically, it is practiced and promulgated in households around the world. Ayesha Imam documents the ways in which the "Muslim religious right (like Christian and Hindu religious-right groups) has been reconstructing patriarchal control over women and their sexuality" (2001, 26). She notes that "all practices that relate to managing fertility are removed from women's control and handed over to men and the state. These range from decisions over whether or when to have intercourse, to decisions over knowledge of and access to different types of contraception, to the permissibility or impermissibility of pregnancy termination. . . . Wives may never refuse to have sexual intercourse with their husband; it is their husbands who have the right to decide" (25). In the United States, Southern Baptists officially declared in 1998 that a wife must "submit herself graciously" (Niebuhr, 1998) to her husband's leadership, implicitly in the bedroom as well as the family room.[6] The international feminists who met in Beijing in 1995 at the Fourth World Conference on Women expounded the revolutionary ramifications of female sexual sovereignty. In their declaration on the human rights and fundamental freedoms of all women, the very *first* provision focused specifically on its necessity: "Women have the right to decide freely all matters related to their sexuality and child-bearing; forced sterilizations and abortions are condemned" (Faison, 1995).

Female sexual sovereignty is a core concern for the political theorist and antipornography activist Andrea Dworkin. In *Intercourse* Dworkin (1987) boldly argues that heterosexual coitus, defined and delimited by male power, operates as a sexually political practice, a ritual that is meant to subvert and destroy sovereignty. In her view, intercourse positions women as space to be invaded, bonds eroticism to dominance and submission, requires female objectification, works to destroy female freedom, and induces women to collaborate in our own oppression.

Another feminist theorist, bell hooks (1994, 109) recognizes the rape of women by men as "a ritual that daily perpetuates and maintains sexist oppression and exploitation." At the same time, normal heterosexual relations reflect and reenact the structures and concerns of that "rape culture." Hooks considers her own relationships, where she often "felt compelled to engage in sexual intercourse" when she didn't want to (111). She questions the conventional construction of heterosexual erotic desire and suggests an alternative "where his pleasure and his hard-on is decentered and mutual pleasure is centered instead," and where "coitus" is not viewed "as the ultimate expression of desire" (112). The assertion of female sexual sovereignty is not only a lesson in personal autonomy but a powerful political strategy: "By refusing to function within the heterosexist framework that condones male erotic domination of women, females would be actively disempowering patriarchy" (113).

The "rape culture" extends even beyond the violation of individual female sovereignty and into a sexualized attack on all that is perceived or can be projected as feminine—a subordinated man, a stigmatized ethnic group and culture, a colonized land and people. The abuse and domination of individual female and feminized bodies is a practice that also is continuous with scientific/technological domination of animals, elements, matter/energy, and of the body of Earth. Rena Swentzell (1993, 167), a Native American scholar from Santa Clara Pueblo in New Mexico, scoffs at the normal but fundamentally rapist belief in "power as an integral part of sexuality." She demands that we recognize the historical implications of that belief: "That is what the inquisition was all about. That is what the whole conquest of the Southwest was about—power and control by males."

These ideas, explicitly theorized by anticolonial thinkers and feminists, are also open secrets within mainstream culture. Advertising imagery for all sorts of products shows white men as "cowboys" and white women, as well as women and men of color, as "Indians." A *Time* magazine cover (September 4, 1995) depicts a gray "polluted and plundered" wasteland. The headline reads: "The Rape of Siberia." Nuclear warheads, chainsaws, handguns, SUVs, and space rockets: All are regularly and often risibly flaunted as invasive and destructive phalli. Everyone gets the joke, but lots of us are not laughing.

Elemental Sovereignty

The definition and use of the female body is the paradigm for
the definition and use of all things; if the autonomy of the female body is defined as sacred, then so will be the autonomy of
all things.

Monica Sjöö and Barbara Mor (1991, 384)

You can't go to Mother Clay without the cornmeal and ask her
permission to touch her. Talk to Mother Clay.

Corn Blossom (Margaret Tafoya), Pueblo potter (quoted in D. Martin, 2001)

The early language of the scientific worldview, exemplified by the writings of Francis Bacon, is explicitly a language of "sexual domination"
(Keller, 1985, 34); scientists are applauded for harassing and hounding
nature, and ultimately penetrating to her "inner chambers." Scientific
work is metaphorically understood as taming, subduing, and enslaving
a female nature, the "bride." These activities, in Bacon's words, promise
"the restoration and reinvesting of man to . . . *sovereignty* and power"
(quoted in Keller, 1985, 35; emphasis added).

In both religious and scientific worldviews, all that is categorized as
natural—the land and animals, as well as those echoes of the "vast
forces" of nature within our own psyches and bodies—is figured as the
enemy, that which must be beaten into submission, civilized, married/
enslaved, and put to work for the "man." The future envisioned by reproductive, genetic, and bio-technology is one of total control of a totaled
nature, one where dirty and wild (that is, fecund and sovereign) nature
has been finally "cleansed" through various projects. Sovereign nature is
then replaced by a tamed substitute or simulation. These projects include control of reproduction for sociopolitical purposes through artificial wombs, cloning, genetic manipulations; the colonization, patenting,
and piracy of the "genetic codes" of living beings, from microbes to humans (Shiva, 1997); the supposed "creation" of species through genetic
engineering. All of this, of course, takes places against a background of
the destruction of original species, plant and animal, and wild spaces.

Exemplifying this worldview is the ontologically oxymoronic "sterile seed." Actual patented "sterile seeds" now exist, although ferocious
criticism has held them back for the time being. Environmentalists have
dubbed this technology "The Terminator," after the cyborg played by
Arnold Schwarzenegger. *Sterility* and *termination* are apt associations
indeed. Boosters of this product have promoted the sterile seed—with
no apparent fear or even a sense of irony—as guaranteeing that "the
next generation will be the last" (Feder, 1999).

A parallel soullessness and disrespect for sovereignty inform human treatment of the animal world. In 1964 Rachel Carson wrote a preface to *Animal Machines,* by the activist Ruth Harrison, who was one of the first to point to the horrendous abuses of factory farming. Carson names the technological society as one that "worships the gods of speed and quantity, and of the quick and easy profit" (1998, 194). In service to such mechanistic gods, power and profit-seeking humans treat animals as "inanimate objects," forcing them to lead a horrific existence without "ever feeling the earth beneath their feet, without knowing sunlight, or experiencing the simple pleasures of grazing for natural food" (194–95). In these and other situations, humans not only treat animals as machines, but also use real machines to effect their total domination over and incorporation of the animals. A typical techno-fantasy of this worldview is a genetically engineered hen, featherless, headless, and void of a digestive track, able to crank out eggs until its ovaries collapse (Daly, 1998, 123). Despite Haraway's blandishments, this is what the cyborgian fusion of animal, human, and machine really looks like.

Haraway argues that modern scientific breakthroughs in fields such as animal language have overcome ignorance and breached a longstanding separation between humans and animals. But this same knowledge has been richly understood and theorized for millennia by many indigenous cultures. Oral traditions around the world affirm a shared original language of humans and animals and a kinship between the two that carries with it, for humans, a set of sacred obligations. This respectful relationship is something that is missing from the cyborgian master plan.

The U.S. nature writer Barry Lopez writes of Eskimo cultures who "sometimes see themselves as still not quite separate from the animal world" and "who regard us as a kind of people whose separation may have become too complete" (1986, 39). Ironically enough, as Fran Chelland (2000a) argues, it is Haraway's refusal to recognize "original wholeness" that leads her to propose "the transgression and violation of the physical boundaries of others as the answer to the profound alienation we now feel from the rest of the 'natural' world." Cyborg consciousness emerges out of a disastrous perception of human separation from animals. It allows cyber-humans to "harvest" animals disrespectfully and gluttonously, not only for necessary food, but for excessively grand and graceless consumption as well as for torturous and grossly gratuitous experiments (Collard with Contrucci, 1988). It allows them to splice one species' genes into another's, leading to the absurd claim that scientists "create" new species. It allows the engineering of such horrors as "roborats," rats implanted with electrodes so that scientists can maneuver them via remote control (Lemonick, 2002, 61). Those contemplating cyborg identification might ask if the animals have invited any such mergers with humans and our machines. They might ask how the cyborgian fusion of humans with animals that Haraway alludes to is any different from these profitable and no doubt sadistically pleasurable transgressions against animal sovereignty.

Soullessness along with sterility is the teleology of the cyborg worldview. When humans wage such thoughtless and insensitive campaigns against animals, they are acting out (and acting out of) what has already happened to their own psyches, the destruction of soul—empathy and awareness of connectedness and interdependence among all beings. The word *animal* is derived from the Latin *anima,* "soul." Humans have habitually associated animals with soul—the spark of consciousness that is the metaphysical equivalent of bodily breath. Alice Walker suggests that free and wild animal life is "the spiritual equivalent of oxygen," allowing "'Magic,' intuition, sheer astonishment at the forms the Universe devises in which to express life . . . to breathe in us" (1988, 191–92). Like the sun, the moon, and the tides, animals evince regularity in harmony with cosmic rhythms. They inspire human imaginations. In his novel *London Fields,* Martin Amis realizes a core truth. He asks: "How will we teach the children to speak when all the animals are gone? Because animals are what they want to talk about first. Yes, and buses and food and Mama and Dada. But animals are what they break their silence for" (1989, 97).

In the cyborg worldview, Fran Chelland (2000a) notices, "animals are viewed only as a means to an end/telos, the nature of which remains solely at the discretion or whim of human will, inventiveness, or imagination." But when humans humbly recognize that animals have their own telos, and their own souls, we enter into an "encounter" that allows us to "experience the full presence of another, of the not-self," of *nonhuman* consciousness/purpose. This "encounter," Chelland suggests, is a necessary basis for imagination, relation, empathy, and knowledge. As encounter is denied and replaced with use, dissection and torture become paradigms for the pursuit of both "knowledge" and "pleasure."

Ironically enough, a resistant strain of science fiction mythos continually warns human beings of the dangers to the body/soul associated with cyborg identification, cyborg techniques of mechanical reproduction, and artificial intelligence. Significantly, these all take place against a backdrop of the destruction of the animal and elemental world. *Blade Runner* (Ridley Scott, 1982), *The Terminator* (James Cameron, 1984), and *The Matrix* (Andy and Larry Wachowski, 1999) all deliver the same basic message. Just as elite humans, aided by their machines, have enslaved and destroyed other humans, animals, and the green world, so too will humans inevitably be enslaved by machines and made over into their image, left to forage futilely for any remnants of soul remaining in a gray, paved, and polluted world.

Let us recall once again Carson's insistence that any notion of biology is "sterile" as well as "distorted and untrue if it puts its primary focus on unnatural conditions rather than on those vast forces not of man's making that shape and channel the nature and direction of life" (1998, 193). We need not reject all things technological in favor of the "organic," but we need to keep our relations in the right proportion, maintain a respectful and balanced interconnection with the animal and elemental world, and not put our *primary* focus on human-made things. We become cyborgs (and lose our souls) by interacting *primarily* with the products and reflections of our own consciousness (Mies, 1998; Chelland, 2000b). Ironically, we then are at a loss to explain why our society is so characterized by narcissism, arrogance, insensitivity, desensualization, alienation, and escalating violence.

Gail A. Norton, the interior secretary in the George W. Bush administration, reflected such a cyborg consciousness when she described the Arctic Wildlife Refuge as "flat white nothingness" (Firestone, 2003), fit only for oil drilling. Barry Lopez—after having an "encounter," in Chelland's sense, with a seal on sea ice in the high Arctic—has another perspective altogether. Speaking directly against drilling, he warns: "To contemplate what people are doing out here and ignore the universe of the seal, to consider human quest and plight and not know the land, I thought, to not listen to it, seemed fatal. Not perhaps for tomorrow, or next year, but fatal if you looked down the long road of our determined evolution" (1986, 13). By disrespecting the sovereignty of nonhuman beings and ignoring the soul and voice of the land, many believe humans are acting in our self-interest, but in the long run we are doing the very opposite. In truth, the cyborg, "mechanical bride," or fembot suggests not the future but, rather, *futurelessness*. The cyborg presages not "earthly survival" (Haraway, 1991, 4), but earthly sterility.

The Sterility Goddess: Or, What Goes Around, Comes Around

> She is the true creatrix for she is thought itself, from which all
> else is born. She is the necessary precondition for material

creation, and she, like all of her creation, is fundamentally female—potential and primary. She is also the spirit that informs right balance, right harmony, and these in turn order all relationships in conformity with her law. To assign to this great being the position of "fertility goddess" is exceedingly demeaning; it trivializes the tribes and it trivializes the power of woman. Woman bears, that is true. She also destroys. That is true.

Paula Gunn Allen (1986a, 14)

As Paula Gunn Allen reminds us, goddess theology is a way for human beings to know and understand cosmic processes of thought, creation, and destruction. Imaging goddess as a simple, mindless "fertility" figure is part of a larger project to deny and contain elemental powers. And this is not only trivializing; it is profoundly foolish. Goddess/cosmos/nature also has a very thoughtful Destroyer aspect, signifying the most awesome, feared, and envied of those "vast powers not of man's making"—death itself.[7]

Embedded throughout the oral tradition is the knowledge that the Earth reacts to the violation of its sovereignty with the withdrawal of fertility. This is the gist of the still-told story of Demeter and Persephone. In the earliest understandings of this divine pair, they are dual aspects of one chthonic being (from Greek *chthōn*, "earth"), with Demeter symbolizing "the kindly earth yielding food for man" and Persephone "the gloomy depths of Hades," the underworld (Geffcken, 1926, 673). Together, they represent the necessary cycles of life and death, the cyclic advances and retreats of the life force. Later versions personify Demeter as the mother, and Persephone as the daughter, who is raped by a personified god, Hades, and taken into the underworld against her will. When Persephone is seized, Demeter turns instantly into the Destroyer, an ancient, forbidding Hag, who causes a cessation of all fruitfulness, Eros, and joy. The world is on the verge of apocalypse. Only when Demeter relents, supposedly striking a deal with Hades, does fertility return. This later version revises the dual aspect of the Earth goddess, making her into two separate persons and denying Persephone's original position as queen of the underworld by putting her down there against her will. Nonetheless, the story accurately conveys the Earth's inevitable response to the violation of sovereignty: the withdrawal of fertility, not in the familiar cyclical way that promises its predictable return, but in a way that promises a sterility of cosmic proportions.

With this background in mind, let's turn once more to the shiny cyborg from the year 3000, the one making an appearance in the Canned Food ad. At first glance it might seem that Earth/Nature/Goddess has finally been married/enslaved, and then replaced by an cosmic Stepford Wife. Yet however "clean," shiny, seductive, and superficially sexually available this image might initially appear, she is no such thing.

To understand the meaning of this tricky cyborg, we might examine again the Celtic story of the sovereignty goddess and apprehend a key feature of the Hag's character. Like Demeter/Persephone she has a dual or two-faced nature. Miranda Green writes that the sovereignty goddess's "concern with life, fertility and death was symbolized by her ability to shape-shift, particularly between the image of the young, beautiful girl and the ancient, hideous hag." The Hag form she assumes is "associated with the death aspect of the goddess" (1996, 84). Frequently the hero in such tales, as in the story of Gawain, is presented with a choice: Which will he have her be, the beautiful young woman or the ugly Hag? The only mythically correct answer—the only sacred and respectful one—is for him to reply, "I recognize your Sovereignty" and leave the decision up to her.[8]

The superficially seductive cyborg in the ad for the Canned Food Information Council is Sovereignty herself. But here she is wearing her Destroyer face. Reflecting the exigencies of the technologically enhanced attack on her integrity, the grimness of that face goes far beyond the necessity of individual death. Now she is veritably a sterility goddess, signifying the sterile seed, a de-souled and *anima*/animal-less world, a cessation of generation, deathlessness as well as lifelessness.

This cyborg's expressionless face is profoundly more terrifying than that of the Hag in the Celtic myth. Mired in false opposition, phallotechnic myth promotes "progress" via its vision of a good, pure, clean, white world with bad, wild, dirty nature finally eliminated. While this porno-cyborg seems to promise such a "utopia," a second look might make us realize that her fleshless, cuntless, wombless body holds no potential for energy, ecstasy, or fruitfulness. Recognizing her as one face of the Destroyer aspect of goddess impels us to ponder the possibility of an apocalyptic future far more distressing than mere individual death—one marked not by human triumph over nature but by the retreat of the Green, the end of imagination, and the spread of material privation and pollution—all inevitable consequences of the continuing rape of energy/matter and exploitation of the elements.

The cyborg, as Haraway intuited, is indeed bound to the goddess. But all those interested in continuance might think twice before blithely proclaiming cyborg identification. The cyborg, as the Destroyer face of the shape-shifting sovereignty goddess, issues an admonition that we ignore at our greatest peril. Only if we choose to recognize ritually, fully, and with all due respect her cosmic integrity might she grant us "the ultimate favor," shifting back to lust, life, and ongoing possibility/fertility.

Notes

Bibliography

Index

Notes

Introduction

1. Because these essays were all written over a long period and for diverse occasions and publications readers will encounter some repetition, for which I apologize.

2. Others who have who interpreted popular culture through a mythic and folkloric lens are Tyler (1947), McLuhan (1951), Fiedler (1982), Lorde (1994), Paglia (1994), Cooper (1995), Keesey (1997), Haynes and Shearer (1998), Kittelson (1998), Rushing (1989), Creed (1993), Rushing and Frentz (1995), Osherow (2000), Schechter (2001), and Frentz and Rushing (2002).

3. The movie *The Long Kiss Goodnight* (Renny Harlin, 1996) is particularly suggestive. The script, written by Shane Black, has it that the CIA plotted the 1993 World Trade Center bombing and blamed it on Arab terrorists so that it could get funding for its programs, a rumor that eerily anticipated a much more prevalent one that circulated in the wake of September 11.

4. "Yip" Harburg, lyricist for "Somewhere over the Rainbow" from *The Wizard of Oz* (Victor Fleming, 1939), was a Russian Jew who immigrated to the United States. He was blacklisted during the McCarthy era.

5. Thanks to Colleen Coughlin for helping me to remember this with her wonderful paper on Amazons in popular film (manuscript, Bowling Green State University, 1995).

6. For some male perspectives see Briffault (1927), Whitmont (1982), Conner (1993), and Begg (1996).

7. This feminine/masculine complementarity also figures in many other world traditions, including Native American theology (Allen, 1991, 107–8) and Haitian Voodoo (Hurston, 1983, 143).

8. For further commentary see Sjöö and Mor (1991) and Raphael (1996, 40).

9. The documentary *Half Life* (Dennis O'Rourke, 1986) is about the nuclear poisoning of the Pacific islands Rongelap and Utirik by American nuclear testing in the 1950s. One elder comments: "I used to think the Americans were smart, but now I think they are crazy." She laughs and adds, "Well, yes, they're smart, smart at doing stupid things."

Chapter 1. *Jaws* as Patriarchal Myth

1. Neumann (1963, 187) writes, "In the westerly symbol group of the Terrible Mother—night, abyss, sea, watery depths, snake, dragon, whale—all the symbols color one another and merge with one another."

2. Graves recounts the numerous rapes of the goddesses and suggests that these rapes represent the usurpation of shrines as well as the seizure of control of agriculture, fishing, and other arts.

3. For a translation of the Babylonian epic, see Long (1963, 88–93).

4. I have explicated this point further in "The Glamour of Grammar" (1977).

5. Bertha Harris places *Jaws* in a literary tradition that includes *Beauty and the Beast* and *Dracula,* in which the monster represents the fusion of maiden, beast and nature, a lesbian image whose being represents the greatest challenge to men's sexual control, for "the monster [is] the quintessence of all that is female; and female enraged" (1977, 7).

Chapter 2. *Sleeping with the Enemy* as *Pretty Woman Part II*?

1. Shved states: "Girls now have few opportunities yet great freedom. They see *Pretty Woman* or a thousand movies and ads with the same point, that somebody who is rich can save them" (Specter, 1998).

2. Feminist analyses of trafficking and prostitution include Barry (1995), Jeffreys (1997), Hodgson (1997), and Hynes and Raymond (2002).

3. Similar tactics of psychological abuse were experienced by Charlotte Fedders and described in her book *Shattered Dreams* (Fedders and Elliot, 1987).

4. Madonna reportedly left Sean Penn because of his physical abuse, alluded to in her 1989 video "Oh Father." In verbal capsules accompanying a Steven Meisel (1991, 196) photo spread in *Vanity Fair,* Madonna alluded to the abuse but still defended her former husband: "Sean was very protective of me. He was like my father in a way. He patrolled what I wore. He'd say, 'You're not wearing that dress. You can see everything in that.' But at least he was paying attention to me. At least he had the balls. And I liked his public demonstrations of protecting me."

5. The opening scene is a posh party given by Edward's lawyer, Philip. After a magician pulls a coin from behind a glamorous woman's ear, Philip jokes: "A penny for the ear but how much for the rest of her?"

6. Barbara Omolade (1990, 284) revises the notion of *griot* (historically an African male courtier who praised royal lineage) to mean "a symbolic conveyor of African oral and spiritual traditions."

Chapter 3. Femme Noire

1. It is useful here to take into consideration Robin Wood's insightful analysis of the tragic figure of Jake LaMotta in *Raging Bull* (Martin Scorsese, 1982). Using Freud's understanding of paranoia based in homosexual repression, Wood (1986, 252–54) argues that LaMotta manifests the familiar forms of paranoia linked to denial of homosexuality, including extreme violence against other men, a "Don Juan" complex, megalomania, and extreme jealousy.

2. According to findings from the National Violence Against Women (NVAW) Survey, "approximately 4.8 million partner rapes and physical assaults are perpetrated against U.S. women annually." Also, "nearly 25 percent of surveyed women and 7.6 percent of surveyed men said they were raped and/or physically assaulted by a current or former spouse, cohabiting partner, or date at some time in their lifetime. . . . Almost 5 percent of surveyed women and 0.6 percent of surveyed men reported being stalked by a current or former spouse, cohabiting partner, or a date at some time in their lifetime." Moreover, "violence perpetrated against women by intimates is often accompanied by emotionally abusive and controlling behavior. The survey found that women whose partners were jealous, controlling, or verbally abusive were significantly more likely to report being raped, physically assaulted, and/or stalked by their partners" (Tjaden and Thoennes, 2000, iii–iv).

Chapter 4. The Pornography of Everyday Life

1. I want to thank my sister Mary Caputi, my brother Daniel Caputi, and the friends and students who have brought some of these ads to my attention: Valentina Bruno, Ana Rodriquez, J. D. Checkett, Heather Stewart, Natalia Gago, Augusta Walden, Fran Chelland, Angelina Dicello, Mia Hale, and Erica Woerner. I especially thank Ann Scales for our many fruitful conversations on this topic. See also Scales (2000).

2. Some of these are faked, as in the notorious 1976 film *Snuff.* But numerous sex killers document their tortures and murders with audiotape, film, and video (Caputi, 1987).

3. Many feminist thinkers connect sexual abuse to the silencing of women. Charlotte Pierce-Baker (1998) titled her book *Surviving the Silence: Black*

Women's Stories of Rape. Nancy Venable Raine (1998) called her memoir *After Silence: Rape and My Journey Back.*

4. An educational video, based on this article, is available (Siren Studios, 2004). Contact jcaputi@fau.edu.

Chapter 5. The New Founding Fathers

1. One of the worst offenders was NBC's *Ted Bundy: The Deliberate Stranger* (see P. Brown, 1989). I have provided commentary on the Rolling Stones' salute to the Boston Strangler, "The Midnight Rambler," and other songs elsewhere (see Caputi, 1987). Jimmy McDonough (1984, 3–5) is an example of the horror fanzine. *Hustler* is discussed in *The Age of Sex Crime* (Caputi, 1987, 53–62). Peter Sotos, the publisher of the sadist magazine *Pure,* was interviewed by Adam Parfrey (1987, 125–27).

2. This is Tom Cullen's phrase regarding Jack the Ripper (1965, 4).

3. Jan Brunvand (1981) analyzes urban legends, including "The Hook." For reports about the "Son of Sam" structured by that narrative, see Lawrence Klausner's book about Berkowitz (1981, 222–27).

4. Bundy's biographer Ann Rule says that after NBC broadcast its made-for-TV movie *Ted Bundy: The Deliberate Stranger,* she received "letters and phone calls from women who . . . had 'fallen in love' with Ted Bundy" (see P. Brown, 1989).

5. I define *gorenography* as nonsexually explicit material that nevertheless sexualizes objectification, subordination, domination, and/or violent behavior (e.g., battering, torture, mutilation, dismemberment, and murder) so as to arouse the viewer and endorse and/or recommend the behavior as described, represented, or documented. It is murder, torture, and mutilation presented in a context that makes murder, torture, and mutilation sexual (Caputi, 1992).

6. The poem and illustration were given to me by the boy's grandmother. He may have copied the first part of the poem from another source, but the part where Freddy comes and slaughters everyone is the boy's invention.

Chapter 7. Small Ceremonies

1. For information on genocide in American history, see Thornton (1987). *Gynocide* or *femicide* is the sexually political murder of women, individually or *en masse,* for reasons of misogyny, sense of ownership, objectification, or enforcement of male supremacy (see Caputi [1987]; Radford and Russell [1992]).

2. Communications scholar James Carey (1975, 6) characterizes "a ritual view of communication" as one that "is not directed toward the extension of messages in space but the maintenance of society in time; not the act of imparting information but the representation of shared beliefs . . . the construction and maintenance of an ordered meaningful cultural world which can serve

as a control and container for human action." In this view, the archetypal communicative act is "the sacred ceremony which draws persons together in fellowship and commonality."

3. Paula Gunn Allen (1986a, 36) argues that the genocide was largely motivated by a "gynocide," for native cultures were largely "gynocentric," based in principles that included the centrality of women to political, religious, and social life, communitarianism, tolerance for diversity, and balanced relation to the environment. All that had to be disappeared and discredited for the conquering, phallocentric and consumer culture to become established.

4. For example, a Utah teenager murdered his stepmother and half-sister after becoming "obsessed" with *Natural Born Killers*. Before the killings, he shaved his head and started to wear tinted granny glasses like those worn by Mickey (Associated Press, 1994). The most notorious case involved two young lovers who killed one man and permanently disabled a woman. They told police that they had been inspired by *Natural Born Killers* (Gibeaut, 1997).

5. Early on, Mickey describes himself as "Mr. Rabbit," a creature that symbolically suggests apocalypse, a consumer who devours even the seed, thwarting regeneration. Lucy Young (1997, 51), a member of the Lassik tribe of California told of her grandfather's prophetic dream foretelling the arrival of Europeans: "My grandpa say: 'White Rabbit'—he mean white people—'gonta devour our grass, our seed, our living. We won't have nothing more, this world.'"

6. For commentary on *The Birth of a Nation*, see Bogle (1974) and Rogin (1987).

7. After writing the essay on which this chapter is based, I came upon James Hillman's similar critique linking *Natural Born Killers* and *Forrest Gump* (1996, 247–48). Hillman also refers readers to Elaine Pagels, *The Origin of Satan* (1995) for her relevant analysis of the development of scapegoating and projection of all evil onto the "other" in early Christian thought.

8. See Cara MariAnna (1993), "The Seven Mythic Cycles of *Thelma and Louise*," for a superb mythic analysis. Other films that it might be fruitful to analyze in this way include *Daughters of the Dust* (Julie Dash, 1991); *Sugarcane Alley* (Euzhan Palcy, 1983); *The Watermelon Woman* (Cheryl Dunye, 1997); and *A Nightmare on Elm Street* (Wes Craven, 1984).

9. See also the analysis of *Seven* and its comparison to a crucial scene in Leslie Silko's 1977 novel *Ceremony* in chapter 8 in this volume, "The Gods We Worship."

Chapter 8. The Gods We Worship

1. On the death penalty see Brian Smith (2000); on war, where combatants make the "ultimate sacrifice," see Ehrenreich (1997). Areas fatally contaminated with toxic waste are known as "National Sacrifice Areas." Cancer deaths,

arguably, are sacrifices to the gods of Progress and Capital. A provocative coincidence of stories in the *New York Times* on April 8, 1999, inadvertently suggests the sacrificial nature of cancer deaths. On the front page, a headline announced: "Entirely Preserved Inca Mummies Found." We learn that three mummies of murdered children, aged eight to fifteen, have been found in Peru, offerings to the "sacred mountains." Readers might temporarily be assured that these were the barbaric practices of a tribal people. On an inside page we encounter a story about the fears of the local community surrounding Brookhaven National Laboratory on Long Island. The lab has a history of toxic contamination, radioactive and chemical, and has been designated a Superfund site. Local parents blame the laboratory for causing an extremely rare form of cancer—rhabdomyosarcoma—that afflicts eighteen children in the area. One of the parents, Randy Snell, states: "They've always said, 'Trust us,' and then they poisoned us. . . . They say the risks are minimal. For what? What is to be achieved? I have to sacrifice my child for progress. I never agreed to that."

2. For example, a marked theatricality attended the killings of Jack the Ripper, the Boston Strangler, and the Hillside Stranglers.

3. This became clear to me once when listening to an expert on wife abuse on a Christian radio show (I was unable to get his name). Much of what he said was consistent with feminist analysis—that this was an exercise in control and power for the man, that he battered her not because he felt strong but because he felt weak, needing her presence and approval in order to maintain his sense of self. His interviewer, seemingly impatient with the secular and political discussion, pressed the guest to name the precise "sin," according to Christian belief, that the batterer was committing. The answer was "idolatry": By giving the woman this much power over his sense of being, the man was putting her in the place of "God."

4. An early article about these murders, before any arrests were made, referred to a killing spree by "man-haters" (Associated Press, 1991). After Wuornos was arrested she was characterized as a "demon dyke" (Brownworth, 1992), whose homosexuality, a former FBI agent speculated in *Glamour* magazine, possibly contributed to an "intrinsic hatred of males . . . as well as an identification with male violence" (cited in O'Sullivan, 1992, 7).

Aileen Wuornos was executed in Florida on October 8, 2002. She contended for years that she killed only those men who had raped her or tried to rape her. In 2001 Wuornos retracted this claim and said that her motive had been robbery. Still, in Nick Broomfield and Joan Churchill's 2004 documentary, *Aileen: Life and Death of a Serial Killer,* Wuornos believing she is off camera, affirms that her original testimony was true.

In an interview a couple of months before she was executed (Cundiff, 2002), Wuornos said that she needed extra money to get an apartment. Living in motels and RV parks was no longer viable, because, once the management realized that she and her lover were lesbians, they regularly threw her out. Although

Wuornos sometimes claimed, as in this last interview, to have had an idyllic childhood, there is ample evidence that she was sexually abused on numerous occasions, had a child at the age of thirteen, was homeless throughout her teens, and developed an early addiction to alcohol and drugs.

Aileen Wuornos changed her story so often that it is difficult to have any certainty about her motivation. Even though she probably did not kill any but the first victim in self-defense, the life of a street prostitute is one marked by exceptionally high rates of victimization (Silbert and Pines, 1982), sexual and otherwise. Wuornos refers to this when she gives her recollection of Richard Mallory, her first victim, who had a previous conviction for rape. He was, she said, a "woman-hater," evidenced through his "nasty" talk about his wife: "When I looked at him, I looked at all the guys ever (expletive) with me, man . . . I thought, well I've always wanted to kill somebody for everything they ever done to me in my life, so here goes." She adds: "They were all killed to rob, and they were killed in pure hatred for all past experiences I ever had with guys, in life or anything" (Cundiff, 2002, 6).

Because of her history of abuse, because of her status as a lesbian, a sexual minority in a country in which minorities are much more likely to receive the death penalty, and because many women identify with her rage, if not her actualization of it, against sexually abusive men, Wuornos has become iconic. She is the only female serial killer to have attained this status, with a made-for-TV movie, two documentaries, an opera, a sympathetic play based on her saga (Gates, 2002, B4), and the much publicized feature film *Monster* (Patty Jenkins, 2003). As I will explore in a future work, Wuornos fulfills not only the role of the sacrificed, but also that of the sacrificial victim.

5. Representative works on the feminist challenge to patriarchal religion include Daly (1978); Goldenberg (1979); Sjöö and Mor (1991); Caputi (1993); Raphael (1996); Clack (2000).

Chapter 9. Seeing Elephants

1. This political spot was fairly obvious in its play upon anti-Soviet sentiments. A Native American was shown in the woods. The voiceover spoke of the danger of the "bear" (i.e., Russia) and warned that although some denied that "the bear" even existed, it was best to be prepared.

2. Although it was the first in the series, *Star Wars* is actually episode four of a projected nine-part series.

3. "Third-generation" nuclear technology is different from "first-generation" (the atom bomb) and "second-generation" (the hydrogen bomb) in that it is based on devices such as X-ray lasers, directed microwave weapons, and others still undisclosed. These weapons will have a small nuclear bomb at their core; the explosive energy, it is posited, can be channeled into tight beams of radiation that can then be directed at targets (see Broad, 1984).

4. Somewhat later, President Reagan himself came around to acknowledging the positive propaganda value of the "Star Wars" nickname. Doublespeaking to the National Space Club, he reminded his listeners: "The Strategic Defense Initiative has been labeled 'Star Wars,' but it isn't about war, it's about peace. It isn't about retaliation, it's about prevention. It isn't about fear, it's about hope . . . and in that struggle, if you will pardon my stealing a film line, the force is with us" (*Albuquerque Tribune*, March 30 1985).

5. For a new definition of *penis envy*, see Mary Daly in cahoots with Jane Caputi, *Websters' First New Intergalactic Wickedary of the English Language* (1987, 215–16).

6. Feminist theorists who have made this point include Kate Millett, *Sexual Politics* (1970, 44); Andrea Dworkin, especially *Pornography: Men Possessing Women* (1981, 129–98); and Catharine A. MacKinnon, "Feminism, Marxism, Method, and the State: Toward Feminist Jurisprudence" (1983).

7. This point is made by Colin Wilson in his introduction to *The Complete Jack the Ripper* (Rumbelow, 1975, vii). The assertion that the Ripper's crimes were unprecedented and at first incomprehensible can be substantiated by a review of newspaper reporting at that time (see Caputi, 1987, 4–6, 10–12). Although assuredly there were prior isolated instances in which men murdered and mutilated women, the crimes of the Ripper—the single, territorial serial killer who victimized a socially stigmatized class of women in a ritual manner—transformed cultural consciousness, entered into cultural mythology, and provided an initiating myth for future emulation. For additional commentary on the mythic role of Jack the Ripper, see Walkowitz, 1982, 543–74.

8. See also the 1974 film directed by Bryan Forbes. This is a parable of an upper-middle-class suburban "Men's Association" whose members, with the help of high technology and skills learned at Disneyland, bond to kill their wives and replace them with beautiful, eminently screwable, and very clean robot wives. A new version of this film, starring Nicole Kidman and Bette Midler, is to be released in 2004.

9. For an analysis of technological attempts to both control and replace biological motherhood, see Corea (1985).

10. Jack the Ripper not only mutilated female genitals and wombs, but he also took the womb from the body of one of his victims, Annie Chapman.

11. For example, Paul C. Warnke stated that "Star Wars" is "all things to all people. . . . To Defense Secretary Weinberger, it is a technological stepping-stone from missile defense to the President's larger conception of *immaculate* defense. . . . To . . . the President, it is *untouchable*" (quoted in Gelb, 1985; emphasis added).

12. In *The Future Eve* (1887), by Philippe Villiers de l'Isle Adam, a rejected lover asks the inventor Thomas Edison to construct a perfect mechanical replica of his lost love. Edison complies (see Bergler, 1953, 271–72).

13. See Alice Walker's poem "Without Commercials," in *Horses Make a Landscape Look More Beautiful* (1984, 55–58), for the phrase "Wilderness/Eden."

14. See Arthur C. Clarke's classic science fiction novel *Childhood's End* (1953), and Hal Lindsey with C. C. Carlson, *The Late Great Planet Earth* (1970).

15. The original "spread eagle"—the figure of an eagle with wings and legs spread—is the emblem on the Great Seal of the United States. *Webster's Unabridged Dictionary* (1986) reports that as a verb, *spread eagle* means "defeat completely."

16. A basic principle of media analysis is that media content is organized according to *flow;* that is, stories and commercials on television and in other media are arranged for comprehensive comment and counterpoint in order to achieve a unified experience. Raymond Williams discusses flow in television content in *Television: Technology and Cultural Form* (1974, 78–118).

Chapter 10. Sex, Radiation, and the Sacred

1. Compare the experience of Henry Adams, who, "nostalgic for the twelfth-century Virgin of Chartres, unexpectedly found her at the St. Louis World's Fair in 1904. There, faced with a huge electric dynamo, he removed his hat and pronounced the dynamo the twentieth-century equivalent of the twelfth-century 'cult of the Virgin'" (McLuhan, 1951, 96).

2. Here I am extending Paula Gunn Allen's concluding argument in *The Sacred Hoop* (1986a) to nuclearism.

3. An example of this type of myth is the Greek story of Actaeon, who, after stumbling upon Artemis at her bath, was transformed by her into a stag and later killed by his own men and his own dogs.

4. Gerda Lerner, in a talk at the Harvard Divinity School, Cambridge, Massachusettes, November 2, 2002, during a conference on "Religion and the Feminist Movement," told her audience: "Patriarchy is dead. It just doesn't know it yet." She pointed out that the original bargain patriarchy offered women was that men would go to war and that women would be dominated but protected, ensuring that there would be future generations. Patriarchy is no longer keeping this bargain. It is civilians—women, children, and the elderly—who are the targets in contemporary warfare.

Chapter 11. Unthinkable Fathering

1. *Nuclearism* is a word first used by Lifton (1979, 39) to mean "the passionate embrace of nuclear weapons as a solution to death anxiety and a way of restoring a lost sense of immortality." I use it to mean a worldview combining disrespect for the atom with the exploitation, eroticization, and worship of nuclear

technology as a means to extend elite men's domination over the elements and the earth.

2. I use the word *fuck* deliberately. In common parlance, *fuck* can mean either "to have sex" (paradigmatically, a penis penetrating a vagina) or "to destroy utterly." No other word conveys the eroticized domination and destruction so characteristic of patriarchal sex and violence.

Chapter 12. On the Lap of Necessity

1. In *Gossips, Gorgons, and Crones* (Caputi, 1993, 160–93) I discuss the Gorgon face as a symbolic marker of taboo with special relevance for taboos on nuclear development.

2. Nancy Tuana traces a centuries-old tradition within Western intellectual thought—scientific, philosophical, and theological—that views woman as inferior to man. For example, in Greek patriarchal myth, "the primal creative force, the female principle is ultimately demoted to very minor participation" (Tuana, 1993, 121). Vandana Shiva speaks of nature as the embodiment of the female principle in Indian cosmology. She further notes that "the feminine principle is not exclusively embodied in women, but is the principle of activity and creativity in nature, women and men. . . . One cannot really distinguish the masculine from the feminine, person from nature. . . . Though distinct, they remain inseparable in dialectical unity, as two aspects of one being" (1988, 52).

3. In *Psycho* (1960) a perpetually infantile son murders his mother and then imitates her. He dresses as the mother, murders in her name, and acts out his version of her personality. The masquerade is lost on most male critics, however, who accept Norman's representation of "the mother" as an authentic version of his permanently silenced mother.

4. For feminist critiques and reconceptualizations of motherhood see Dorothy Dinnerstein (1976), Sara Ruddick (1989), Emily Martin (1991), and Danah Zohar (1985; 1990).

5. As Allen further clarifies, the womb itself is a manifestation of a cosmic power that "is not really biological at base; it is the power of ritual magic, the power of Thought, of Mind, that gives rise to biological organisms as it gives rise to social organizations, material culture, and transformations of all kinds" (1986a, 28).

6. My thinking on the interpretation of these icons has been influenced by fruitful conversations with Fran Chelland, Boca Raton, Florida, September 2000.

7. The full text reads: "Because of Isis, there is a heaven. / Because of Isis, there is an earth. / Because of Isis, winds blow on the desert. / Because of Isis, the river floods in spring. / Because of Isis, plants bear fruit. / Because of Isis, we live and grow strong. / Because of Isis, we have breath to give thanks" (Monaghan, 1999, 145).

8. I reserve for a future time contemplation of any different symbolic meanings that might emerge when it is a daughter on the mother's lap.

9. Questions inevitably occur. How does the feminized, passive, and receptive subject survive this dumping process? Why doesn't she just wither away under the onslaught of psychic toxins? Indeed, why do feminine subjects often seem more possessed of life energy than the masculine? One answer might be that the feminine is inherently more energetic than the masculine. Another might be that it takes an enormous amount of psychic energy to sustain the fantasy. Hence masculine subjects, those with the most to gain from the fantasy, expend an enormous amount of energy in repressing their awareness that it is, alas, just a fantasy. Feminized "objects," on the other hand, know, albeit sometimes unconsciously, the truth. Because the feminine subject is not expending as much energy in repressing awareness, she has more accessible energy and resiliency.

10. Hegemonic heterosexuality makes this complementary relationship attractive to some women as well as to men. The bargain is this: While the man is thus cleansed and revivified, the women, his servant-goddess, receives his private worship and emotional dependence. In Lawrence's *Women in Love*, the artist Gudrun, a "new woman," coldly refuses this old role. Moreover, Lawrence wants to punish his character Gerald for refusing the purity of man-to-man love with the author's surrogate, Birkin. Hence, Gerald is killed off, literally frozen, at the novel's end.

11. Conversation with Fran Chelland, Boca Raton, Florida, December 1999.

12. I thank Helene Vann for alerting me to this passage in *Tar Baby*.

13. *Invasion of the Body Snatchers* (Don Siegel, 1956) is about seedpods from outer space that emigrate to Earth. While humans sleep, the pods replicate their bodies and consume their souls. The pod then takes over, an entity without soul, emotion, or imagination. In the extraordinary trilogy by director George Romero—*Night of the Living Dead* (1968), *Dawn of the Dead* (1979), and *Day of the Dead* (1985)—the recently dead reanimate and, soulless and without emotion, concentrate on eating the flesh of the living.

14. For an understanding of principles of balance and respect and their relation to modern wasting of the environment and consumer production, see Carol Lee Sanchez (1989, 1993).

15. Linda Alcoff speaks of her grandmother, a peasant and sharecropper whose hands had never worn jewelry. "But her hands could sift and test the dirt of a particular area and sense whether or not it was a good place for her family. She always kept a bucket to collect every bit of vegetable scrap that was generated and would take these and toss them around the yard. This was not primarily a practical gesture; it was not a piling up of compost. Rather, it was a practice communicating buckets of knowledge about a way of life. As she tossed a scrap under a tree, she would tell her granddaughter: 'We take so much from the

earth. We have to give something back.'" Conversation with Linda Alcoff, Boca Raton, Florida, September 2000.

16. For a discussion of the Aztec Shit Goddess, see Randy Conner (1993, 322–23). See also the discussion by David Carrasco on the ancient vision of the "cosmos as compost heap" (1999, 178) with the constant transformation of waste into humus, death into life.

17. Thanks to Ceti Boundy for the phrase "unifying the realms," conversation, Boca Raton, Florida, October 1999.

18. See Sandra Cisneros's (1996) reading of the meaning of the Virgin of Guadalupe and Alice Walker on Aunt Jemima (1997, 137–43). See also chapters 13 and 16.

Chapter 14. The Second Coming of Diana

1. Conversation with Bettina Molina, Boca Raton, Florida, September 1, 1998. I thank also Helene Vann, Peggy Spurlock, Lauri Sagle, Karman Kregloe, Mary Daly, Kate Cook, J. D. Checkett, and Rita Butler for alerting me to significant information. I thank Kate Cook for her great hospitality and Fran Chelland, the late Teresa Brennan, and the readers at the *NWSA Journal* for their editorial assistance.

2. Conversation with Karima Ridgley, Deerfield Beach, Florida, October 10, 1998.

3. Telephone conversation with Cara MariAnna in Albuquerque, New Mexico, September 15, 1997.

4. *Gossip* (Daly with Caputi 1987, 132–33; Caputi 1993) is a form of gynocentric speech, a key feature of the sacred aspects of story.

5. *Snool* was first used by Mary Daly in *Pure Lust* (1984, 20–21). Snools are characterized by "sadism and masochism combined" and are "the stereotypic saints and heroes of the sadostate."

Chapter 15. Facing Change

1. For amplification see Roberts (1997); Crossette (1998); Niebuhr (1999); Sterngold (1999); Brinkley (2000); Olson (2000).

2. James Walborn made this observation in a class I taught at Florida Atlantic University, "Women, Myth, Power and Popular Culture," summer 1999.

Chapter 16. The Naked Goddess

1. Ron Long (2002) claims that gay pornography derives a spiritual dimension from its ideal vision of beauty, perfection, and happiness. He evocatively argues that for gay men the experience of watching porn can be at least

as spiritually compelling as going to church. My discussion here centers completely on paradigmatic pornography: that is, the heterosexist variety. Gay and lesbian pornographies frequently differ from heterosexist pornography in that they affirm the beauty, dignity, and exuberance of sexualities that mainstream religions and moralities condemn. Yet questions remain. Do the gay and lesbian pornographies under consideration participate in the same habit of thought as regular pornography? Do they have objectifying, voyeuristic, and other-subordinating structures? Are viewers getting off (deliberately or inadvertently) on someone else's prostitution and oppression? Are sexually racist, classist, and misogynist notions indelibly marking the images? If we are in church, what god are we worshipping? Long's article has no consideration of the ways in which racism enters into gay porn's ideals of beauty and ideal happiness. An important article by Richard Fung (1991) criticizes the racist standards and "visual apartheid" of gay pornography, which celebrates only "*white* male beauty" and "Aryan, blond, shaved good looks." Fung also contends that the sexuality of men of color in gay porn is appropriated, not affirmed, and that scenarios of dominance and submission reflect the power imbalances of racist relation. For example, the Asian man is shown "getting fucked" in a way that suggests punishment or domination, or is scripted as "house boy" to an older, wealthier, and more powerful white man.

2. *Thealogy* refers etymologically to a female, instead of a male, divine.

Chapter 17. The Cyborg or the Goddess?

1. Thanks to Holly Larson for bringing this to my attention.

2. I deal with this more thoroughly in "Sex, Radiation, and the Sacred," chapter 10 in this volume. Most helpful is the thought of Carol Lee Sanchez, who believes that modern peoples must not only acknowledge the sacredness of everyday life, animals, and the elemental world, but also "create new songs of acknowledgement as well as ceremonies that include metals, petrochemicals, and fossil fuels, electricity, modern solar power systems, and water power systems. . . . [I]t is very important to make sacred . . . the new ways and elements in our lives—from nuclear power . . . to plastics to computers . . . in order to restore harmony and balance to our out-of-control systems and, in particular, to our modern technologies" (1989, 352–53). Making technologies sacred often means leaving them alone, not developing them, and being committed to using them only in a balanced way that recognizes all of their implications and consequences. Cyborg theory does not seem to have any sense of such respectful limitation.

3. This 1828 description of sovereignty by U.S. Attorney General William Wirt is cited in Morris (1992, 65). Obviously, exceptions to the rule of national sovereignty can exist: for example, if a government is engaged in the ethnic cleansing and rape of its own people.

4. "American culture reveres no Black madonna," the legal theorist Dorothy Roberts points out. "It upholds no popular image of a Black mother tenderly nurturing her child" (1997, 15, 19). Black motherhood, instead, is pathologized and scapegoated as responsible for the ills of the country. Particularly, poor black mothers are stigmatized as overfertile, sexually lax, degenerate, and inferior, and are mocked, in ways that demean female sovereignty itself, as "matriarchs" and "welfare queens." All sorts of programs, both private and public, attempt to control black women's reproductive and family life. The reality is that black women, having been enslaved and subjected to repeated rapes and forced childbearing, have post-slavery been disproportionately victimized by rape, forced childbearing, forced sterilizations, birth-control experimentation, and health-care neglect.

5. One of the definitions of *favor* in *Webster's* (1986) is explicitly sexual and explicitly based in female sovereignty: "sexual privileges or sexual intercourse usu. as granted by a woman—usu. used in pl. or in the phrase '*the ultimate favor.*'"

6. The October 5, 1997, installment of NBC's *Meet the Press* featured Bill McCartney, the former football coach and founder of the evangelical Christian men's group, Promise Keepers. The host asked McCartney if men were meant to be "head of the household." McCartney replied: "When there needs to be a decision made where it can't be reconciled, then tenderly and gently the man needs to take authority. And it isn't any different than any other structure that has been ordained by God, that we all operate within."

7. Indeed, it is patriarchal men's envy of that power that causes them to identify themselves solely with unnatural death power—with violence, mass and serial murder, and the technological means of megadeath (Caputi, 1993).

8. I thank Marta Weigle, a fine storyteller and keeper of the myths, for first telling this story to me, Albuquerque, New Mexico, 1983.

Bibliography

Abrahamsen, David. 1983. Confessions of "Son of Sam." *Penthouse,* November, 60.

Adam, Nathan M. 1981. To catch a killer: The search for Ted Bundy. *Reader's Digest,* March, 210–39.

Adams, Carol. 1990. *The sexual politics of meat: A feminist–vegetarian critical theory.* New York: Continuum.

Agee, James. 1979. Comedy's greatest era. In *Film theory and criticism,* ed. Gerald Mast and Marshall Cohen: 535–58. New York: Oxford University Press.

Agonito, Rosemary. 1977. *History of ideas on woman: A source book.* New York: Berkeley Publishing Group.

Allen, James, Hilton Als, John Lewis, and Leon F. Litwak. 2000. *Without sanctuary: Lynching photography in America.* Santa Fe: Twin Palms.

Allen, Paula Gunn. 1986a. *The sacred hoop: Recovering the feminine in American Indian traditions.* Boston: Beacon Press.

———. 1986b. *Raven's Road.* In *The new Native American novel: Works in progress,* ed. Mary Bartlett: 51–63. Albuquerque: University of New Mexico Press.

———. 1990. The woman I love is a planet the planet I love is a tree. In *Reweaving the world: The emergence of ecofeminism,* ed. Irene Diamond and Gloria Feman Orenstein: 52–57. San Francisco: Sierra Club Books.

———. 1991. *Grandmothers of the light: A medicine woman's sourcebook.* Boston: Beacon Press.

———. 1993. Foreword. In *Gossips, gorgons and crones: The fates of the earth,* Jane Caputi: xi–xx. Santa Fe: Bear & Company.

Alloula, Malek. 1986. *The colonial harem.* Translated by Myrna Godzich and Wlad Godzich. Minneapolis: University of Minnesota Press.

Amadiume, Ifi. 2003. Bodies and choices: African matriarchs and Mammy Water. In *Feminist futures: Re-imagining women, culture and development*, ed. Kum-Kum Bhavnani, John Foran, and Priya Kurian: 89–106. New York: Zed Books.

Amis, Martin. 1989. *London fields*. New York: Harmony Books.

Anderson, Laurie. 1981. Let x = x. *Big Science* (recording). Warner Bros.

Ann, Martha, and Dorothy Myers Imel. 1993. *Goddesses in world mythology*. Santa Barbara, Calif.: ABC-CLIO, Inc.

Anzaldúa, Gloria. 1987. *Borderlands/ la frontera*. San Francisco: Spinsters/Aunt Lute Press.

———. 1990. Haciendo caras: Una entrada. In *Making face, making soul haciendo caras: Creative and critical perspectives by feminists of color*, ed. Gloria Anzaldúa: xv–xviii. San Francisco: Aunt Lute Press.

———. 2000. *Interviews/entrevistas*. Edited by AnaLouise Keating. New York: Routledge.

Ardener, Shirley. 1987. A note on gender iconography: The vagina. In *The cultural construction of sexuality*, ed. Pat Caplan: 113–42. New York: Tavistock.

Associated Press. 1991. Man-haters suspected in slayings. *Albuquerque Tribune*, January 12.

———. 1994. Police seize suspect obsessed by movie. *New York Times*, November 4.

Atler, Marilyn Van Derbur. 1991. The darkest secret. *People Weekly*, June 10, 88–94.

Austen, Hallie Iglehart. 1990. *The heart of the goddess: Art, myth and meditations on the world's sacred feminine*. Berkeley, Calif.: Wingbow Press.

Avalon, Arthur. 1978. *Shakti and Shakta*. New York: Dover.

Awiakta, Marilou. 1986. Baring the atom's mother heart. In *Homewords: A book of Tennessee writers*, ed. Douglass Paschall and Alice Swanson: 183–88. Knoxville: Tennessee Arts Commission and the University of Tennessee Press.

———. 1993. *Selu: Seeking the Corn Mother's wisdom*. Golden, Colo.: Fulcrum.

Bach, Bob. 1984. Letter to the editor. *New York Times*, February 2.

Bachofen, Johann Jakob. 1967. *Myth, religion, and mother right: Selected writings of J. J. Bachofen*. Translated by Ralph Manheim. Princeton, N.J.: Princeton University Press.

Bailie, Tom. 1990. Growing up as a nuclear guinea pig. *New York Times*, July 22.

Baker, Mark. 1982. *Nam: The Vietnam war in the words of the men and women who fought there*. New York: William Morrow.

Baker, Nancy V., Peter R Gregware, and Margery A. Cassidy. 1999. Family killing fields: Honor rationales in the murder of women. *Violence against Women* 5, no. 2: 164–84.

Bambara, Toni Cade. 1993. Reading the signs, empowering the eye: *Daughters of the Dust* and the black independent cinema movement. In *Black American cinema*, ed. Manthia Diawara: 118–44. New York: Routledge.

Baring, Anne, and Jules Cashford. 1991. *The myth of the goddess: Evolution of an image.* New York: Penguin Books.

Barry, Kathleen. 1995. *The prostitution of sexuality.* New York: New York University Press.

Bass, Ellen. 1988. Introduction: In the truth itself, there is healing. In *I never told anyone: Writings by women survivors of child sexual abuse,* ed. Ellen Bass and Louise Thornton: 23–60. New York: Harper and Row.

Bass, Ellen, and Laura Davis. 1988. *The courage to heal: A guide for women survivors of child sexual abuse.* New York: Harper and Row.

Bataille, George. 1962. *Death and sensuality: A study of eroticism and the taboo.* New York: Walker and Company.

Bauman, Zygmont. 1989. *Modernity and the holocaust.* Ithaca, N.Y.: Cornell University Press.

Bayley, Harold. 1996 [1912]. *The lost language of symbolism.* 2 vols. New York: Barnes and Noble.

BBC. 1995. Diana the BBC Interview. http://scoop.evansville.net/diana.html.
————. 1997. *Diana 1961–1997, a celebration.* Video. Fox/CBS.

Beale, Paul, ed. 1989. *Partridge's concise dictionary of slang and unconventional English.* New York: Macmillan.

Bearman, Steve. 1999. Why men are so obsessed with sex. In *Male lust: Pleasure, power, and transformation,* ed. Kerwin Kay, Jill Nagle, and Baruch Gould: 215–22. New York: Harrington Park Press.

Beck, Peggy V., and A. L. Walters. 1977. *The sacred: Ways of knowledge sources of life.* Tsalie (Navajo Nation), Ariz.: Navajo Community College Press.

Becker, Ernest. 1975. *Escape from evil.* New York: The Free Press.

Beers, William. 1992. *Women and sacrifice: Male narcissism and the psychology of religion.* Detroit: Wayne State University Press.

Begg, Ean. 1996. *The cult of the black virgin.* New York: Penguin Books.

Behr, Edward. 1978. Introduction. In *Sleepless nights,* Helmut Newton. New York: Congreve.

Bello, Walden. 1992. From American lake to a people's Pacific. In *Let the good times roll: Prostitution and the U.S. military in Asia,* ed. Saundra Pollock Sturdevant and Brenda Stoltzfus: 14–21. New York: New Press.

Benard, Elisabeth, and Beverly Moon. 2000. Introduction. In *Goddesses who rule,* ed. Elisabeth Benard and Beverly Moon: 3–13. New York: Oxford University Press.

Benchley, Peter. 1974. *Jaws.* Garden City, N.Y.: Doubleday.

Beneke, Timothy. 1997. *Proving manhood: Reflections on men and sexism.* Berkeley: University of California Press.

Benitiz-Rojo, Antonio. 1988. *The repeating island: The Caribbean and the postmodern perspective.* Translated by James Maraniss. Durham, N.C.: Duke University Press.

Benjamin, Walter. 1969. The work of art in the age of mechanical reproduction. In *Illuminations,* ed. Hannah Arendt: 217–51. New York: Schocken.

Bennett, W. H. 1926. Eve. In *Encyclopedia of religion and ethics,* ed. James Hastings, 5: 607–608. New York: Scribner's.

Benzie, Tim. 1997. Diana as gay icon. In *Planet Diana,* ed. Re: Public: 127–32. Kingswood, Australia: Research Centre in Intercommunal Studies.

Berg, Charles Ramírez. 1989. Immigrants, aliens, and extraterrestrials: Science fiction's alien "other" as (among other things) new Hispanic imagery. *CineAction* (fall): 3–17.

Berger, John. 1972. *Ways of seeing.* London: BBC and Penguin Books.

Bergler, Edmund. 1953. *Fashion and the unconscious.* New York: Robert Brunner.

Bhagavati, Ma Jaya Sati. 1998. Kali who swallows the universe. *Parabola* 23, no. 3: 18–21.

Bierman, Judy. 1991. Pieces of the night sky: My body's legacy. In *She who was lost is remembered: Healing from incest through creativity,* ed. Louise M. Wisechild: 189–94. Seattle: Seal Press.

Binder, David. 2002. In Europe, sex slavery is thriving despite raids. *New York Times,* October 20.

Birnbaum, Lucia Chiavola. 1993. *Black Madonnas: Feminism, religion, and politics in Italy.* Boston: Northeastern University Press.

———. 2001. *Dark mother: African origins and godmothers.* San Jose, Calif.: Authors Choice Press.

Black, Ian. 1997. Memorials planned across globe. *The Guardian,* September 6.

Black Elk, Wallace, and William S. Lyon. 1991. *Black Elk: The sacred ways of a Lakota.* San Francisco: HarperSanFrancisco.

Blake, Richard A. 1996. Redeemed in blood: The sacramental universe of Martin Scorsese. *Journal of Popular Film and Television* 24, no. 1: 2–9.

Bloch, Raymond. 1986. Portents and prodigies. In *The encyclopedia of religion,* ed. Mircea Eliade, 11: 454–57. New York: Macmillan.

Bloch, Robert. 1977. Yours truly, Jack the Ripper. In *The best of Robert Bloch,* ed. Lester del Rey: 1–20. New York: Ballantine.

Blok, Josine H. 1995. *The early Amazons: Modern and ancient perspectives on a persistent myth.* New York: E. J. Brill.

Blume, E. Sue. 1990. *Secret survivors: Uncovering incest and its aftereffects in women.* New York: Ballantine.

Boffey, Philip M. 1985. Dark side of "Star Wars": System could also attack. *New York Times,* March 7.

Bogle, Donald. 1974. *Toms, coons, mulattoes, mammies, and bucks.* New York: Bantam.

———. 1988. *Blacks in American films and television: An illustrated encyclopedia.* New York: Simon and Schuster.

Bordo, Susan. 1993. *Unbearable weight: Feminism, Western culture, and the body.* Berkeley: University of California Press.

———. 1999. *The male body: A new look at men in public and in private.* New York: Farrar, Straus, Giroux.

Boxer, Sarah. 1998. From cringing to comfort: A word has its day. *New York Times,* February 14.

Boyer, Paul. 1985. *By the bomb's early light: American thought and culture at the dawn of the atomic age.* New York: Pantheon.

Bratt, Peter. 1993. *Follow me home.* Screenplay.

————. 1997. Publicity materials for *Follow Me Home.*

Brennan, Teresa. 1993. *History after Lacan.* New York: Routledge.

————. 1997. Social pressure. *American Imago* 54, no. 3: 257–88.

————. 2000. *Exhausting modernity: Grounds for a new economy.* New York: Routledge.

————. 2004. *The transmission of affect.* Ithaca, N.Y.: Cornell University Press.

Briffault, Robert. 1927. *The mothers: A study of the origins of sentiments and institutions.* New York: Macmillan.

Brinkley, Joel. 2000. Vast trade in forced labor portrayed in C.I.A. report. *New York Times,* May 18.

Broad, William J. 1984. The young physicists: Atoms and patriotism amid the Coke bottles. *New York Times,* January 31.

————. 1985. *Star warriors.* New York: Simon and Schuster.

Brooks De Vita, Alexis. 2000. *Mythatypes: Signatures and signs of African/diaspora and black goddesses.* Westport, Conn.: Greenwood Press.

Brown, C. MacKenzie. 1987. Kali, the mad mother. In *The book of the goddess past and present,* ed. Carl Olson: 110–23. New York: Crossroad.

Brown, Dee. 1981. *Bury my heart at wounded knee: An Indian history of the American West.* New York: Washington Square Press.

Brown, Elsa Barkley. 1997. "What has happened here": The politics of difference in women's history and feminist politics. In *The second wave: A reader in feminist theory,* ed. Linda Nicholson: 272–87. New York: Routledge.

Brown, Lyvia Morgan. 1975. Sexism in western art. In *Woman: A feminist perspective,* ed. Jo Freeman: 307–15. New York: Mayfield.

Brown, Peter H. 1989. Calendar: Murder most glamorized. *Los Angeles Times,* April 2.

Brownmiller, Susan. 1975. *Against our will: Men, women and rape.* New York: Simon and Schuster.

Brownworth, Victoria. 1991. Florida lesbian charged in serial killings. *San Francisco Bay Times,* September.

————. 1992. Crime and punishment. *QW,* October 24, 24–27.

Broyles, William, Jr. 1984. Why men love war. *Esquire,* November, 55–65.

Brunvand, Jan. 1981. *The vanishing hitchhiker: American urban legends and their meaning.* New York: Norton.

Brzezinski, Zbigniew, Robert Jastrow, and Max M. Kampelman. 1985. Defense in space is not "Star Wars." *New York Times Magazine,* 27 January.

Burt, Martha R. 1980. Cultural myths and support for rape. *Journal of Personality and Social Psychology* 38: 217–30.

Butler, Octavia E. 1987. *Dawn*. New York: Warner Books.

————. 1994. *Parable of the sower*. New York: Seven Stories Press.

————. 1996. Positive obsession. In *Bloodchild and other stories:* 123–36. New York: Seven Stories Press.

————. 1998. *Parable of the talents*. New York: Seven Stories Press.

Caillois, Roger. 1959. *Man and the sacred*. Translated by Meyer Barash. Glencoe, Ill.: Free Press.

Caldicott, Helen. 1984. *Missile envy: The arms race and nuclear war*. New York: Morrow.

Callander, Margaret. 1996. Colette and the hidden woman: Sexuality, silence, subversion. In *French erotic fiction: Women's desiring writing, 1880–1990,* ed. Alex Hughes and Kate Ince: 49–68. Washington, D.C.: Berg.

Cameron, Debbi. 1988. That's entertainment? Jack the Ripper and the celebration of sexual violence. *Trouble and Strife* 13: 17–19.

Cameron, Deborah, and Fraser, Elizabeth. 1987. *The lust to kill: A feminist investigation of sexual murder*. New York: New York University Press.

Campbell, Beatrix. 1998. *Diana Princess of Wales*. London: Women's Press.

Campbell, Joseph. 1968. *The hero with a thousand faces*. Princeton, N.J.: Princeton University Press.

Canby, Vincent. 1977. Not since "Flash Gordon conquers the universe." *New York Times,* June 5.

Caputi, Jane. 1977. The glamour of grammar. *Chrysalis* 4 (winter): 35–43.

————. 1987. *The age of sex crime*. Bowling Green, Ohio: Bowling Green State University Popular Press.

————. 1988. Films of the nuclear age. *Journal of Popular Film and Television* 16, no. 3: 100–107.

————. 1990a. Advertising femicide: Lethal violence against women in pornography and gorenography. In *Femicide: The politics of woman killing,* ed. Jill Radford and Diana E. H. Russell: 203–21. Boston: Twayne.

————. 1990b. Interview with Paula Gunn Allen. *Trivia: A Journal of Ideas* 16/17: 50–67.

————. 1991. Charting the flow: The construction of meaning through juxtaposition in media texts. *Journal of Communication Inquiry* 15, no. 2: 32–47.

————. 1993. *Gossips, gorgons, and crones: The fates of the Earth*. Santa Fe: Bear & Company.

————. 1999. The pornography of everyday life. In *Mediated women: Representations in popular culture,* ed. Marian Meyers: 57–80. Cresskill, N.J.: Hampton Press.

————. 2001. Review of *Diana in search of herself: Portrait of a troubled princess,* by Sally Bedell Smith. *Women's Review of Books,* January, 17–18.

————. 2003. "Take back what doesn't belong to me": Sexual violence and the "transmission of affect." *Women's Studies International Forum* 25, no. 6: 1–14.

————. 2005. Sexuality, religion and nature. In *Encyclopedia of religion and nature,* ed. Bron Taylor. New York: Continuum.

Caputi, Jane, and Helene Vann. 1987. Questions of race and place: Comparative racism in *Imitation of Life* and *Places in the Heart. Cineaste* 14, no. 4: 16–21.

Carey, James. 1975. A cultural approach to communication. *Communication* 2: 1–22.

Carrasco, David. 1999. *City of sacrifice: The Aztec empire and the role of violence in civilization.* Boston: Beacon Press.

Carse, James P. 1986. Shapeshifting. In *The encyclopedia of religion,* ed. Mircea Eliade, 13: 225–29. New York: Macmillan.

Carson, Rachel. 1998a [1960]. To understand biology. In *Lost woods: The discovered writing of Rachel Carson,* ed. Linda Lear: 193–94. Boston: Beacon Press.

————. 1998b [1964]. Preface to *Animal Machines.* In *Lost woods: The discovered writing of Rachel Carson,* ed. Linda Lear: 194–96. Boston: Beacon Press.

Castillo, Ana. 1996. *Goddess of the Americas la Diosa de las Americas: Writings on the Virgin of Guadalupe.* New York: Riverhead Books.

CBS News. 2003. Porn in the U.S.A. www.cbsnews.com/stories/2003/11/21/60minutes/main585049.shtml, November 21.

Chamberlain, David. 1985. Missile Center—USA. *Harper's,* March, 61–67.

Checkett, J. D. 2001. The green goddess returns: Batman's Poison Ivy as a symbol of emerging ecofeminist consciousness. M.A. thesis, Florida Atlantic University.

Chelland, Fran. 2000a. "Are the animals happy?": An inquiry into the diminishment of presence and the death of the imagination. Student paper for graduate course, Myth, Magic, and Popular Culture, at Florida Atlantic University. In author's possession.

————. 2000b. The souls of animals: Or, why cyborgs don't matter. Student paper for graduate course, Myth, Magic, and Popular Culture, at Florida Atlantic University. In author's possession.

Chernus, Ira. 1986. *Dr. Strangegod: On the symbolic meanings of nuclear weapons.* Columbia: University of South Carolina Press.

Cheshes, Jay. 2002. Hard-core philanthropist. *Mother Jones,* November/December, 68–73.

Chesler, Phyllis. 1997. *Women and madness.* New York: Four Walls Eight Windows.

Chevalier, Jean, and Alain Gheerbrant. 1994. *The Penguin dictionary of symbols.* Translated by John Buchanan-Brown. New York: Penguin Books.

Chicago, Judy. 1982. *Through the flower.* New York: Anchor/Doubleday.

Chodorow, Nancy. 1978. *The reproduction of mothering.* Berkeley: University of California Press.

Christ, Carol P. 1997. *Rebirth of the goddess.* Reading, Mass.: Addison-Wesley.

Christian, Barbara. 1997. The highs and lows of black feminist criticism (1990). In *Feminisms: An anthology of literary theory and criticism,* ed. Robyn R.

Warhol and Diane Price Herndl: 51-56. New Brunswick, N.J.: Rutgers University Press.

Chumo, Peter. 1995. "You've got to put the past behind you before you can move on": Forrest Gump and national reconciliation. *Journal of Popular Film and Television* 23, no. 1: 2-7.

Cirlot, J. E. 1962. *A dictionary of symbols*. Translated by Jack Sage. New York: Philosophical Library.

Cisneros, Sandra. 1996. Guadalupe the sex goddess. In *Goddess of the Americas la Diosa de las Americas: Writings on the Virgin of Guadalupe*, ed. Ana Castillo: 52-55. New York: Riverhead Books.

Clack, Beverly. 2001. Human sexuality and the concept of the god/ess. In *The good news of the body: Sexual theology and feminism*, ed. Lisa Isherwood: 115-35. New York: New York University Press.

Clark, Nancy Hiscoe. 1997. Princess Diana as the great mother. *The Quest* 85, no. 12: 10-11.

Clarke, Arthur. 1953. *Childhood's end*. New York: Ballantine.

Clover, Carol J. 1987. Her body, himself: Gender in the slasher film. *Representations* 20 (fall): 187-228.

Coakley, Tom. 1988. After slaying, fears disrupt Halloween in Greenfield. *Boston Globe*, October 27.

Cocks, Jay. 1984. Why he's a thriller. *Time*, March 19, 54-60.

Cohn, Carol. 1987. Sex and death in the rational world of defense intellectuals. *Signs: Journal of Women in Culture and Society* 12, no. 4: 687-718.

Colette. 1952. *Gigi. Julie de Carnelhan. Chance acquaintances*. New York: Farrar, Straus and Young.

Collard, Andrée, with Joyce Contrucci. 1988. *Rape of the wild: Man's violence against animals and the earth*. Bloomington: Indiana University Press.

Collins, Patricia Hill. 1998. *Black feminist thought: Knowledge, consciousness, and the politics of empowerment*. New York: Routledge.

Condren, Mary. 1989. *The serpent and the goddess: Women, religion and power in Celtic Ireland*. San Francisco: Harper and Row.

Conner, Randy P. 1993. *Blossom of bone: Reclaiming the connections between homoeroticism and the sacred*. San Francisco: HarperSanFrancisco.

Conner, Randy P., David Hatfield Sparks, and Mariya Sparks. 1997. *Cassell's encyclopedia of queer myth, symbol, and spirit: Gay, lesbian, bisexual, and transgender lore*. London: Cassell.

Conroy, Pat. 1986. *The prince of tides*. New York: Bantam.

Cooper, Carolyn. 1995. *Noises in the blood: Orality, gender, and the "vulgar" body of Jamaican popular culture*. Durham, N.C.: Duke University Press.

Córdova, Teresa. 1996. Trying to keep us silenced — again: A review of *Follow Me Home*. *Voces Unidas (Southwest Organizing Project, Albuquerque, New Mexico)*, November, 16.

Corea, Gena. 1985. *The mother machine: Reproductive technologies from artificial insemination to artificial wombs*. New York: Harper and Row.

Corliss, Richard. 1988. Did you ever see a dream stalking. *Time,* September 5, 66–67.

Cortez, Jayne. 1984. Tell me. In *Coagulations: New and selected poems:* 106–109. New York: Thunder's Mouth Press.

Côtè, Andrée. 1991. The art of making it work for you. In *The Montreal massacre,* ed. Louise Mallette and Marie Chalouh: 67–70. Charlottetown, Prince Edward Island: Gynergy Books.

Cousteau, Jacques-Yves, and Phillippe Cousteau. 1970. *The shark: Splendid savage of the sea.* Translated by Francis Price. Garden City, N.Y.: Doubleday.

Crawley, A. E. 1926. Human sacrifice. In *Encyclopedia of religion and ethics,* ed. James Hasting, 6: 840–45. New York: Scribner's.

Creed, Barbara. 1993. *The monstrous feminine: Film, feminism, psychoanalysis.* New York: Routledge.

————. 1996. Horror and the monstrous-feminine: An imaginary abjection. In *The dread of difference: Gender and the horror film,* ed. Barry Keith Grant: 35–65. Austin: University of Texas Press.

Crenshaw, Kimberlé Williams. 1993. Beyond racism and misogyny: Black feminism and 2 Live Crew. In *Words that wound: Critical race theory, assaultive speech, and the first amendment,* ed. Mari J. Matsuda: 111–132. Boulder, Colo.: Westview Press.

Cromer, Mark. 2001. Porn's compassionate conservatism. *The Nation,* February 26, 25–28.

Crossette, Barbara. 1998. Most consuming more, and the rich much more. *New York Times,* September 13.

Crowe, Thomas Rain. 1990. Marilou Awiakta: Reweaving the future. *Appalachian Journal* 18, no. 1: 40–54.

Cullen, Tom. 1965. *When London walked in terror.* Boston: Houghton Mifflin.

Cundiff, Rick. 2002. "I'll kill again and again and again." *Oclala Star Banner,* June 30.

Dalmiya, Vrinda. 2000. Loving paradoxes: A feminist reclamation of the goddess Kali. *Hypatia* 15, no. 1: 125–50.

Daly, Mary. 1973. *Beyond God the Father: Toward a philosophy of women's liberation.* Boston: Beacon Press.

————. 1978. *Gyn/ecology: The metaethics of radical feminism.* Boston: Beacon Press.

————. 1984. *Pure lust: Elemental feminist philosophy.* Boston: Beacon Press.

————. 1997. A manifestation of goddess. *On the Issues* (spring): 14–15.

————. 1998. *Quintessence . . . realizing the archaic future: A radical elemental feminist manifesto.* Boston: Beacon Press.

Daly, Mary, with Jane Caputi. 1987. *Websters' first new intergalactic wickedary of the English language.* Boston: Beacon Press.

Dash, Julie. 1992. *Daughters of the dust: The making of an African American woman's film.* New York: New Press.

Dauphin, Gary. 1997. Homeward bound. *Vibe,* March, 119–20.

Davenport, Diana. 1989. Snow (Marshall islands). *Ikon* 10: 60–64.

Davis, Angela. 1989. *Women, culture, and politics.* New York: Random House.

Davis, Elizabeth Gould. 1971. *The first sex.* New York: Putnam.

Daws, Gaven. 1968. *Shoal of time: A history of the Hawaiian Islands.* Honolulu: University of Hawaii Press.

de Beauvoir, Simone. 1953. *The second sex.* New York.

DeCurtis, Anthony. 2002. A soul singer with a vision of beauty. *New York Times,* September 22.

Delaney, Carol. 1988. Mortal flow: Menstruation in Turkish village society. In *Blood magic: The anthropology of menstruation,* ed. Thomas Buckley and Alma Gottlieb: 75–93. Berkeley: University of California Press.

Denby, David. 1996. Buried alive. *New Yorker,* July 15, 47–58.

Despatch. 1997. The emergent goddess — Diana myth-religion of Antichrist. http://www.despatch.cth.com.au/Despatch/vol93_diana_myth.html.

Dickey, Christopher, and Maziar Bahari. 2001. And along came a spider. *Newsweek,* August 20, 28.

Dijkstra, Bram. 1996. *Evil sisters: The threat of female sexuality and the cult of manhood.* New York: Knopf.

DiMassa, Diane. 1992. *Hothead Paisan: Homicidal lesbian terrorist* 5. New Haven: Giant Ass Publishing.

Diner, Helen [Eckstein-Diener, Bertha]. 1965. *Mothers and Amazons: The first feminine history of culture.* Edited and translated by John Philip Lundin. New York: Julian Press.

Dinnerstein, Dorothy. 1976. *The mermaid and the minotaur.* New York: Harper and Row.

Doane, Mary Ann. 1991. *Femmes fatales: Film, feminism, psychoanalysis.* New York: Routledge.

Doria, Charles. 1974. The dolphin rider. In *Mind in the water: A book to celebrate the consciousness of whales and dolphins,* ed. Joan McIntyre: 33–34. New York: Scribner's.

Dowd, Maureen. 2003. Look good, act cool. *New York Times,* May 11, web edition.

Doyle, Laura. 2000. *The surrendered wife: A practical guide to finding intimacy, passion, and peace with a man.* New York: Simon and Schuster.

Dozois, Gardner, and Susan Casper, eds. 1988. *Ripper.* New York: Tom Doherty.

duCille, Ann. 1997. The unbearable darkness of being: "Fresh" thoughts on race, sex, and the Simpsons. In *Birth of a nation'hood: Gaze, script, and spectacle in the O. J. Simpson case,* ed. Toni Morrison and Claudia Brodsky Lacour: 293–338. New York: Pantheon.

Duran, Eduardo, and Bonnie Duran. 1995. *Native American postcolonial psychology.* Albany: State University of New York Press.

Durgnat, Raymond. 1978. Inside Norman Bates (1967). In *Great film directors: A critical anthology,* ed. Leo Braudy and Morris Dickstein: 496–506. New York: Oxford.

Dworkin, Andrea. 1973. *Woman hating.* New York: E. P. Dutton.

――――――. 1981. *Pornography: Men possessing women.* New York: Perigee.

――――――. 1987. *Intercourse.* New York: Free Press.

――――――. 1989. *Letters from a war zone.* New York.: E. P. Dutton.

――――――. 1991. *Mercy.* New York: Four Walls Eight Windows.

――――――. 2000. *Scapegoat: The Jews, Israel, and women's liberation.* New York: Free Press.

Dworkin, Andrea, and Catharine A. MacKinnon. 1988. *Pornography and civil rights: A new day for women's equality.* Minneapolis: Organizing Against Pornography.

Dyer, Richard. 1997. *White.* New York: Routledge.

Dyke, Marty O. 1983. Yeah, I'm blaming you. In *I never told anyone: Writings by women survivors of child sexual abuse,* ed. Ellen Bass and Louise Thornton: 113. New York: Harper.

Easlea, Brian. 1983. *Fathering the unthinkable: Masculinity, scientists, and the nuclear arms race.* London: Pluto Press.

Edge, D. O. 1973. Technological metaphor. In *Meaning and control,* ed. D. O. Edge and J. N. Wolfe: 31–59. London: Tavistock.

Ehrenreich, Barbara. 1997. *Blood rites: Origins and history of the passions of war.* New York: Metropolitan Books.

――――――. 2002. *Nickel and dimed: On (not) getting by in America.* New York: Henry Holt.

Eliade, Mircea. 1957. *The sacred and the profane: The nature of religion.* Translated by Willard R. Trask. New York: Harper and Row.

――――――. 1958a. *Patterns in comparative religion.* Translated by Rosemary Sheed. New York: World.

――――――. 1958b. *Rites and symbols of initiation: The mysteries of birth and rebirth.* New York: Harper and Row.

―――――― 1964. *Myth and reality.* New York: Harper and Row.

――――――. 1969 [1961]. *Images and symbols: Studies in religious symbolism.* Translated by Philip Mairet. New York: Sheed and Ward.

――――――. 1975. *Myths, rites, symbols: A Mircea Eliade reader,* ed. Wendell C. Beane and William G. Doty. 2 vols. New York: Harper and Row.

Eller, Cynthia. 2000. *The myth of matriarchal prehistory: Why an invented past won't give women a future.* Boston: Beacon Press.

Elliott, Michael. 1997. Heroine of a new Britain. *Newsweek* (commemorative edition), September, 106–7.

Ellis, Bret Easton. 1991. *American psycho.* New York: Vintage.

Ellison, Harlan. 1967. Afterword to "The prowler in the city at the edge of the world." In *Dangerous visions,* ed. Harlan Ellison: 154. Garden City, N.Y.: Doubleday.

Ellison, Harlan, and Gahan Wilson. 1989. In pursuit of pure horror. *Harper's,* October, 45–53.

Ellroy, James. 1986. *Killer on the road.* New York: Avon.

Enloe, Cynthia. 1990. *Bananas, beaches and bases: Making feminist sense of international politics.* Berkeley: University of California Press.

Ensler, Eve. 1998. *The vagina monologues.* New York: Villard.

Erdrich, Louise. 2001. *The last report on the miracles at Little No Horse.* New York: Harper Collins.

Estelle, Amy. 1991. Incest and the bomb. Student paper for graduate course, Nuclear Technology and American Culture, at University of New Mexico. In author's possession.

Estés, Clarissa Pinkola. 1992. *Women who run with the wolves: Myths and stories of the wild woman archetype.* New York: Ballantine Books.

Estrada-Meléndez, Martina. 1997. Reconnecting people of color to spirit and ancestors through film. *La Voz de Berkeley* 6, no. 4: 6.

Eugene, Toinette M. 1994. When love is unfashionable: Ethical implications of black spirituality and sexuality. In *Sexuality and the sacred: Sources for theological reflection,* ed. James B. Nelson and Sandra P. Longfellow: 105-14. Louisville, Ky.: Westminster/John Knox Press.

Faison, Seth. 1995. Women's meeting agrees on right to say no to sex. *New York Times,* September 11.

Fanon, Frantz. 1967. *Black skin white masks.* New York: Grove Press.

Featherdancing, Kyos. 1988. In *The courage to heal: A guide for women survivors of child sexual abuse,* ed. Ellen Bass and Laura Davis: 396-99. New York: Harper and Row.

Fedders, Charlotte, and Laura Elliot. 1987. *Shattered dreams.* New York: Harper and Row.

Feder, Barnaby J. 1999. Plant sterility research inflames debate on biotechnology's role in farming. *The New York Times,* April 19.

Fenn, Richard K. 1995. Soul-loss in antiquity. In *On losing the soul: Essays in the social psychology of religion,* ed. Richard K. Fenn and Donald Capps: 23-38. Albany: State University of New York Press.

Fiedler, Leslie. 1982. *What was literature? Class culture and mass society.* New York: Touchstone.

Firestone, David. 2003. Republicans resigning themselves to defeat on drilling plan for Alaska wildlife refuge. *New York Times,* March 23.

Fo, M. 1988. Interview: Robert Englund. *Thrasher,* February, 72-77.

Fragoso, Julia Monárrez. 2003. Serial sexual femicide in Ciudad Juárez, 1993-2001. *Aztlan: A Journal of Chicano Studies* 28, no. 2: 153-78.

Frazer, Bryant. 1995. Review of *Seven.* www.deepforus.com/flicker.

Frentz, Thomas S., and Janice Hocker Rushing. 2002. "Mother isn't quite herself today": Myth and spectacle in *The Matrix. Critical Studies in Mass Communication* 19, no. 1: 64-86.

Freud, Sigmund. 1953a. Dreams (1940 [1922]). In *Standard edition of complete psychological works of Sigmund Freud,* vol. 15: 154. London: Hogarth Press.

―――. 1953b. Medusa's head (1940 [1922]). In *Standard edition of complete psychological works of Sigmund Freud,* vol. 18: 273–74. London: Hogarth Press.

Friedan, Betty. 1963. *The feminine mystique.* New York: Dell.

Fung, Richard. 1991. Looking for my penis: The eroticized Asian in gay video porn. In *How do I look: Queer film and video,* ed. Bad Object Choices: 145–68. Seattle: Bay Press.

Gadon, Elinor. 1989. *The once and future goddess: A symbol for our time.* New York: Harper and Row.

Gallagher, Carole. 1993. *American ground zero: The secret nuclear war.* Cambridge, Mass.: M.I.T. Press.

Gartner, Carol B. 1983. *Rachel Carson.* New York: Frederick Ungar.

Gates, Anita. 2002. A killer, yes, but she's a good old girl. *New York Times,* June 5.

Geffcken, J. 1926. Eumenides, erinyes. In *Encyclopedia of religion and ethics,* ed. James Hastings, 5: 573–75. New York: Scribner's.

Gelb, Leslie H. 1985. Vision of space defense posing new challenges. *New York Times,* March 3.

Gerbner, George. 1978. The dynamics of cultural resistance. In *Hearth and home: Images of women in the media,* ed. Gaye Tuchman, Arlene K. Daniels, and James Benet: 46–50. New York: Oxford.

Giannetti, Louis. 1981. *Masters of the American cinema.* Englewood Cliffs, N.J.: Prentice-Hall.

Gibeault, John. 1997. Deadly inspiration. *ABA Journal* 83: 62–67.

Gilligan, James. 1996. *Violence: Reflections on a national epidemic.* New York: Vintage Books.

Gilman, Sander L. 1985. Black bodies, white bodies: Toward an iconography of female sexuality in late nineteenth-century art, medicine, and literature. *Critical Inquiry* 12: 204–42.

Gimbutas, Marija. 1989. *The language of the goddess.* San Francisco: Harper and Row.

Ginzburg. Carl. 1991. *Ecstasies: Deciphering the witches' sabbath.* New York: Pantheon Books.

Giobbe, Evelina. 1990. *A facilitator's guide to prostitution: A matter of violence against women.* Minneapolis: WHISPER (Women Hurt in Systems of Prostitution Engaged in Revolt).

Girard, Rene. 1977. *Violence and the sacre*d. Translated by Patrick Gregory. Baltimore: Johns Hopkins University Press.

Gire, Dan. 1988. Bye, bye, Freddy! Elm Street creator Wes Craven quits series. *Cinefantastique* 18, no. 5: 8–10.

Gleason, Judith. 1987. *Oya: In praise of the goddess.* Boston: Shambhala.

Glenn, John. 1988. Joint hearings on nuclear reactor safety at the DOE's Savannah River plant, opening statement to the House of Representatives Environmental, Energy, and Natural Resources Subcommittee of the

Committee on Government Operations and the Senate Committee on Government Affairs. Washington, D.C.: GPO.

Goldenberg, Naomi. R. 1979. *The changing of the gods*. Boston: Beacon Press.

Goleman, Daniel. 1985. Political forces come under new scrutiny of psychology. *New York Times*, April 2.

Gomel, Elana. 1999. Written in blood: Serial killing and narratives of identity. *Post Identity* 2, no. 1: 24–70.

Gossy, Mary. 1994. Gals and dolls: Playing with some lesbian pornography. *Art Papers* 18: 21–24.

Gottlieb, Roger S., ed. 1996. *This sacred earth: Religion, nature, environment*. New York: Routledge.

Gowdy, Barbara. 1990. *Falling angels*. New York: Soho Press.

Grace, Helen. 1997. Introduction: The lamenting crowd. In *Planet Diana*, ed. Re: Public: 1–12. Kingswood, Australia: Research Centre in Intercommunal Studies.

Graham, Lanier. 1997. *Goddesses*. New York: Abbeville Press.

Graves, Robert. 1960 [1955]. *The Greek myths*. 2 vols. Baltimore: Penguin Books.

———. 1966. *The white goddess*. New York: Farrar, Straus, Giroux.

Green, Miranda. 1996. *Celtic goddesses: Warriors, virgins and mothers*. New York: George Braziller.

Griffin, Susan. 1971. Rape: The all-American crime. *Ramparts*, September 10, 26–35. Reprinted in *Made from this Earth: An anthology of writings* (1983), 39–58. New York: Harper and Row.

———. 1978. *Woman and nature: The roaring inside her*. New York: Harper and Row.

———. 1989. Split culture. In *Healing the wounds: The promise of ecofeminism*, ed. Judith Plant: 7–17. Philadelphia: New Society Publishers.

Grossberg, Lawrence. 1986. On postmodernism and articulation: An interview with Stuart Hall. *Journal of Communication Inquiry* 10, no. 2: 45–60.

Guns N' Roses. 1988. Used to love her. *G N' R Lies*. Geffen Records.

Gutfield, G. 1999. The sex drive: Men who are hooked on cyberpornography. *Men's Health*, October, 116–21.

Hagedorn, Jessica. 1994. Asian women in film: No joy, no luck. *Ms.*, January/February, 74–79.

Hale, Lindsay. 2003. Mama Oxun: Reflections of gender and sexuality in Brazilian Umbanda. In *Òsun across the waters: A Yoruba goddess in Africa and the Americas*, ed. Joseph M. Murphy and Mei-Mei Sanford: 213–29. Bloomington: University of Indiana Press.

Hall, Chris. 1999. God is a bullet. In *Male lust: Pleasure, power, and transformation*, ed. Kerwin Kay, Jill Nagle and Baruch Gould: 159–66. New York: Harrington Park Press.

Hall, Stuart. 1992. Cultural studies and its theoretical legacies. In *Cultural studies*, ed. L. Grossberg et al.: 277–94. New York: Routledge.

Hamamoto, Darrell Y. 1994. *Monitored peril: Asian Americans and the politics of representation*. Minneapolis: University of Minnesota Press.

Hanh, Thich Nhat. 1988. *The heart of understanding*. Berkeley, Calif.: Parallax Press.

Hannsberry, Karen B. 1998. *Femme noir: Bad girls of film*. Jefferson, N.C.: McFarland.

Haraway, Donna J. 1991. *Simians, cyborgs, and women: The reinvention of nature*. New York: Routledge.

Harding, Sandra. 1999. Is science multicultural? Lecture. Florida Atlantic University, Boca Raton, Florida.

Harmon, Amy. 2001. The search for intelligent life. *New York Times*, September 23.

Harris, Bertha. 1977. What we mean to say: Notes toward defining the nature of lesbian literature. *Heresies: A Feminist Publication on Art and Politics*, September, 5-8.

Harris, Thomas. 1981. *Red dragon*. New York: Bantam.

———. 1988. *The silence of the lambs*. New York: St. Martin's.

———. 1999. *Hannibal*. New York: Delacorte.

Harrison, Robert Pogue. 1992. *Forests: The shadow of civilization*. Chicago: University of Chicago Press.

Harron, Mary. 2000. The risky territory of "American psycho." *New York Times*, April 9.

Hart, Lynda. 1994. *Fatal women: Lesbian sexuality and the mark of aggression*. Princeton, N.J.: Princeton University Press.

Hartsock, Nancy C. M. 1983. The feminist standpoint: Developing the ground for a specifically feminist historical materialism. In *Discovering reality: Feminist perspectives on epistemology, metaphysics, methodology, and philosophy of science*, ed. Sandra Harding and Merrill B. Hintikka: 283-310. Boston: D. Reidel.

Haskell, Molly. 1975. The claptrap of pearly whites in the briny deep. *Village Voice*, 23 June.

Hawkins, Harriet. 1993. Maidens and monsters in modern popular culture: *The Silence of the Lambs* and *Beauty and the Beast*. *Textual Practice* 7, no. 2: 258-66.

Hayles, N. Katherine. 1999. *How we became posthuman: Virtual bodies in cybernetics, literature, and informatics*. New York: Routledge.

Haynes, Jane, and Ann Shearer, eds. 1998. *When a princess dies: Reflections from Jungian analysts*. London: Harvest Books.

Hazelwood, Robert R. , and John E. Douglass. 1980. The lust murderer. *FBI Law Enforcement Bulletin* 49, no. 4: 18-22.

Heller, Steven. 1983. *War heads: Cartoonists draw the line*. New York: Penguin Books.

Herbert, Bob. 1994. In America: Throwing a curve. *New York Times*, October 26.

Herman, Judith Lewis. 1992. *Trauma and recovery: The aftermath of violence from domestic abuse to political terror.* New York: Basic Books.

Hernton, Calvin C. 1988 [1965]. *Sex and racism in America.* New York: Anchor Books.

Herz, Steve, J. D. Robinson, and Rod Gibson. 2001. Bin Laden had Diana murdered! *Globe,* December 18.

Hildegard. 1987. *Book of divine works with letters and songs.* Edited by Matthew Fox. Santa Fe: Bear & Co.

Hillman, James. 1996. *The soul's code: In search of character and calling.* New York: Random House.

Hoban, Russell. 1980. *Riddley Walker.* New York: Pocket Books.

Hoch, Paul. 1979. *White hero black beast: Racism, sexism and the mask of masculinity.* London: Pluto Press.

Hodgson, James F. 1997. *Games pimps play: Pimps, players and wives-in-law: A qualitative analysis of street prostitution.* Toronto: Canadian Scholars' Press.

Hogan, Linda. 1995. *Dwellings: A spiritual history of the living world.* New York: Touchstone.

Holden, Stephen. 1997. Uneasy riders with plenty to fear. *New York Times,* February 28.

Holloway, Karla. 1992. *Moorings and metaphors: Figures of culture and gender in black women's liberation.* New Brunswick, N.J.: Rutgers University Press.

Holmlund, Christine. 1994. A decade of deadly dolls: Hollywood and the woman killer. In *Moving targets: Women, murder and representation,* ed. Helen Birch: 127–51. Berkeley: University of California Press.

hooks, bell. 1989. *Talking back: Thinking feminist, thinking black.* Boston: South End Press.

————. 1992. *Black looks: Race and representation.* Boston: South End Press.

————. 1994. *Outlaw culture: Resisting representations.* New York: Routledge.

Hoppenstand, Gary. 1992. Yellow devil doctors and opium dens: A survey of the yellow peril stereotypes in mass media entertainment. In *Popular culture: An introductory text,* ed. Jack Nachbar and Kevin Lause: 277–91. Bowling Green, Ohio: Bowling Green State University Popular Press.

Horney, Karen. 1967. The distrust between the sexes. In *Feminine psychology,* ed. Harold Kelman: 107–18. New York: Norton.

Horvath, Imre. 1984. *Murder: No apparent motive.* HBO.

Houlberg, Marilyn. 1995. Magique marasa: The ritual cosmos of twins and other sacred children. In *Sacred arts of Haitian Vodou,* ed. Donald J. Cosentino: 267–83. Los Angeles: UCLA Fowler Museum of Cultural History.

Huang, Alfred. 1998. *The complete I Ching.* Rochester, Vt.: Inner Traditions.

Hubert, Henri, and Marcel Mauss. 1964. *Sacrifice: Its nature and function.* Translated by W. D. Halls. Chicago: University of Chicago Press.

Hunt, Lynn. 1993. Introduction: Obscenity and the origins of modernity, 1500–1800. In *The invention of pornography: Obscenity and the origins of modernity, 1500–1800,* ed. Lynn Hunt: 9–45. New York: Zone Books.

Hurst, Fannie. 1943 [1932]. *Imitation of life*. Cleveland: World.

Hurston, Zora Neale. 1983 [1938]. *Tell my horse*. Berkeley, Calif.: Turtle Island.

Hutchings, Patrick. 2002. 11 September and the "s[ublime]" word. *Sophia* 41, no. 1: 71–72.

Hynes, H. Patricia, and Janice G. Raymond. 2002. Put in harm's way: The neglected health consequences of sex trafficking in the United States. In *Policing the national body: Race, gender, and criminalization,* ed. Jael Silliman and Anannya Bhattacharjee: 197–230. Boston: South End Press.

Imam, Ayesha M. 2001. The Muslim religious right ("fundamentalists") and sexuality. In *Good sex: Feminist perspectives from the world's religions,* ed. Patricia Beattie Jung, Mary E. Hunt, and Radhika Balakrishnan: 15–30. New Brunswick, N.J.: Rutgers University Press.

Interview. 1995. BBC interview with Princess Diana. http://scoop.evansville.net/diana.html.

Irigaray, Luce. 1985. *This sex which is not one*. Translated by Catherine Porter. Ithaca, NY: Cornell University Press.

———1993. Divine women. In *Sexes and genealogies*. Translated by Gillian C. Gill: 57–72. New York: Columbia University Press.

Jadrnak, Jackie. 1992. Social workers' actions proper in Roswell case. *Albuquerque Journal,* January 24.

James, Caryn. 1991. Now starring, killers for the chiller 90s. *New York Times,* March 10.

James, E. O. 1926. Sacrifice. In *Encyclopedia of religion and ethics,* ed. James Hastings, 11: 1–8. New York: Scribner's.

Jane's Addiction. 1988. "Ted, Just Admit It." *Nothing's shocking*. Warner Bros.

Jay, Nancy. 1992. *Throughout your generations forever: Sacrifice, religion, and paternity*. Chicago: University of Chicago Press.

Jayawardena, Kumari, and Malathi de Alwis, eds. 1996. *Embodied violence: Communalising women's sexuality in South Asia*. New Delhi: Kali for Women.

Jeffords, Susan. 1987. "The battle of the big mamas": Feminism and the alienation of women. *Journal of American Culture* 10, no. 3: 73–84.

Jeffreys, Sheila. 1997. *The idea of prostitution*. North Melbourne, Australia: Spinifex.

Jell-Bahlsen, Sabine. 1997. Eze mmiri di egwu, the water monarch is awesome: Reconsidering the Mammy Water myths. In *Queens, queen mothers, priestesses, and power: Case studies in African gender,* ed. Flora Edouwaye S. Kaplan: 103–34. New York: New York Academy of Sciences.

Jenkins, Philip. 1994. *Using murder: The social construction of serial homicide*. New York: Aldine De Gruyter.

Jensen, Robert. 1998. Using pornography. In *Pornography: The production and consumption of inequality,* ed. Gail Dines, Robert Jensen, and Ann Russo: 101–46. New York: Routledge.

Jensen, Robert, and Gail Dines. 1998. The content of mass-marketed pornography. In *Pornography: The production and consumption of inequality,* ed. Gail Dines, Robert Jensen, and Ann Russo: 65-100. New York: Routledge.

Jermyn, Deborah. 1996. Rereading the bitches from hell: A feminist appropriation of the female psychopath. *Screen* 47, no. 3: 251-67.

John, Elton, and Bernie Taupin. 1997. Candle in the wind.

Johns, C. H. W. 1926. Purification (Babylonian). In *Encyclopedia of religion and ethics*, ed. James Hastings, 10: 466-68. New York: Scribner's.

Johnston, D. 1992. Survey shows number of rapes far higher than official figures. *New York Times*, April 24.

Jones, Amelia. 1996. The "sexual politics" of the *Dinner Party:* A critical context. In *Sexual politics: Judy Chicago's Dinner Party in feminist art history*, ed. Amelia Jones: 81-118. Berkeley: University of California Press.

Jones, Ann. 1994. *Next time, she'll be dead: Battering and how to stop it.* Boston: Beacon Press.

Jordan, June. 1981. Against the wall (1978). In *Civil wars:* 147-49. Boston: Beacon Press.

———. 1989. Getting down to get over. In *Naming our destiny: New and selected poems:* 67-76. New York: Thunder's Mouth Press.

Jung, C. G. 1968. *The archetypes and the collective unconscious.* Translated by R. F. C. Hull. Bollingen series 20. Princeton, N.J.: Princeton University Press.

Jung, C. J., and Carl Kerenyi. 1963. *Essays on a science of mythology.* Translated by R. F. C. Hull. Bollingen series 22. Princeton, N.J.: Princeton University Press.

Jungk, Robert. 1958. *Brighter than a thousand suns: A personal history of the atomic scientists.* Translated by James Cleugh. New York: Harcourt, Brace.

Junod, Tom. 2001. The devil in Greg Dark. *Esquire*, February, 129-35.

Kagan, Norman. 1995. *The cinema of Oliver Stone.* New York: Continuum.

Kaplan, Louise J. 1991. *Female perversions: The temptations of Emma Bovary.* New York: Doubleday.

Keesey, Pam. 1997. *Vamps: An illustrated history of the femme fatale.* San Francisco: Cleis Press.

Kehr, Dave. 2002. The life and violent times of a 1970s serial killer. *New York Times*, September 13.

Keller, Evelyn Fox. 1985. *Reflections on gender and science.* New Haven, Conn.: Yale University Press.

Kelly, Liz. 1988. *Surviving sexual violence.* Cambridge: Polity Press.

———. 1997/98. Including others. *Trouble & Strife* 36: 67-68.

Kerenyi, Carl. 1949. The primordial child in primordial times. In *Essays on a science of mythology*, ed. C. J. Jung and Carl Kerenyi: 46-51. Translated by R. F. C. Hull. Princeton, N.J.: Princeton University Press.

Kershaw, Sarah. 2003. In deal for life, man admits killing 48 women. *New York Times*, November 6.

Keuls, Eva C. 1985. *The reign of the phallus: Sexual politics in ancient Athens.* Berkeley: University of California Press.

Key, Wilson Bryan. 1973. *Subliminal seduction.* Englewood Cliffs, N.J.: Prentice-Hall.

————. 1980. *The clam-plate orgy.* Englewood Cliffs, N.J.: Prentice-Hall.

King, Stephen. 1979. *The dead zone.* New York: Viking.

King-Pedroso, Natalie. 2000. "I-tie-all my people-together": New World appropriations of the Yoruba Deity Oshun in Toni Morrison's *Tar Baby* and Derek Walcott's *Omeros. Journal of Caribbean Studie*s 15: 61–93.

Kipnis, Laura. 1996. *Bound and gagged: Pornography and the politics of fantasy in America.* New York: Grove Press.

Kiselyak, Charles. 1996. *Chaos rising: The storm around* Natural Born Killers (film included with the director's cut version of *Natural Born Killers* released on VHS).

Kittelson, Mary Lynn, ed. 1998. *The soul of popular culture.* Peru, Ill.: Carus Publishing.

Klapp, Orinn E. 1962. *Heroes, villains, and fools: The changing American character.* Englewood Cliffs, N.J.: Prentice-Hall.

Klausner, Lawrence D. 1981. *Son of Sam.* New York: McGraw-Hill.

Klein, Melanie. 1975. *Envy and gratitude and other works 1946–1963: The writings of Melanie Klein.* London: Hogarth Press.

Knight, Chris. 1988. Menstrual synchrony and the Australian rainbow snake. In *Blood magic: The anthropology of menstruation,* ed. Thomas Buckley and Alma Gottlieb: 232–55. Berkeley: University of California Press.

Kolodny, Annette. 1975. *The lay of the land: Metaphor as experience and history in American letters.* Chapel Hill: University of North Carolina Press.

Kracauer, Siegfried. 1947. *From Caligari to Hitler: A psychological history of the German film.* Princeton, N.J.: Princeton University Press.

Krafft-Ebing, Richard von. 1965. *Psychopathia sexualis.* Translated by Franklin S. Klaf. New York: Stein and Day.

Kristeva, Julia. 1986. *The Kristeva reader.* Edited by Toril Moi. New York: Columbia University Press.

Kupers, Terry A. 1993. *Revisioning men's lives: Gender, intimacy, and powe*r. New York: Guilford Press.

————. 2001. Rape and the prison code. In *Prison masculinities,* ed. Don Sabo, Terry A. Kupers, and Willie London: 111–17. Philadelphia: Temple University Press.

Kurzweil, Ray. 1999. *The age of spiritual machines: When computers exceed human intelligence.* New York: Viking.

Lacy, Suzanne. 1982/83. In mourning and in rage (with analysis aforethought). *Ikon* (fall/winter): 60–67.

Laforet, Vincent. 2001. Army of addicts, at Kabul's door. *New York Times,* October 7.

Lahr, John. 1995. Dealing with Roseanne. *New Yorker,* July 17, 42–61.

Lal, Vinay. 1998. Now are we men, not eunuchs? *Humanscape (Bombay)* 5, no. 7: 6–9.

Lalvani, Suren. 1995. Consuming the exotic other. *Critical Studies in Mass Communication* 12: 263–86.

Lamar, Jacob V. 1989. I deserve punishment. *Time,* February 6, 34.

Landesman, Cosmo. 1998. Giving the godless absolute hell. *The Times* (London), August 23.

Larned, Deborah. 1974. The greening of the womb. *New Times,* December 27, 35–39.

Larsen, Richard W. 1980. *Bundy: The deliberate stranger.* Englewood Cliffs, N.J.: Prentice-Hall.

Latifa. 2001. *My forbidden face: Growing up under the Taliban: A young woman's story.* Translated by Linda Coverdale. New York: Hyperion.

Laurence, William L. 1945. Eyewitness account of bomb test. *New York Times,* September 26.

———. 1946. *Dawn over zero: The story of the atomic bomb.* New York: Knopf.

Lawrence, D. H. 1996 [1920]. *Women in love.* New York: Bantam Classic.

LeBoyer, Frederick. 1976. *Birth without violence.* New York: Knopf.

Lederer, Wolfgang. 1968. *The fear of women.* New York: Harcourt Brace Jovanovich.

Lee, Helen Elaine. 1994. *The serpent's gift.* New York: Scribner's.

Lee, Susan, and Sondra Till Robinson. 1980. *Dear John.* New York: New American Library.

Leeming, David, and Jake Page. 1994. *Goddess: Myths of the female divine.* New York: Oxford University Press.

Lemonick, Michael D. 2002. Send in the roborats. *Time,* May 13, 61.

Leo, John. 1991. Toxic feminism on the big screen. *U.S. News and World Report,* June 10, 20.

Leonard, John. 1979. Review of *Confessions of a lady-killer. Village Voice,* December 24, 46.

León-Portilla, Miguel. 1963. *Aztec thought and culture.* Translated by Jack Emory Davis. Norman: University of Oklahoma Press.

Lerner, Gerda, ed. 1972. *Black women in white America: A documentary history.* New York: Vintage Books.

———. 1986. *The creation of patriarchy.* New York: Oxford University Press.

———. 1997. *Why history matters: Life and thought.* New York: Oxford University Press.

Let the guy grin. 1986. Let the guy grin. *People,* December 22–29, 24.

Levin, Ira. 1972. *The Stepford wives.* New York: Random House.

Levine, Sylvia, and Joseph Koenig. 1980. *Why men rape.* Toronto: Macmillan.

Lewis, C. S. 1959. *Surprised by joy.* London: Fontana Press.

Lewis, R. W. B. 1965. *The American Adam: Innocence, tragedy, and tradition in the nineteenth century.* Chicago: University of Chicago Press.

Lifton, Robert Jay. 1979. *The broken connection: On death and the continuity of life.* New York: Simon and Schuster.

Lifton, Robert Jay, and Richard Falk. 1991 [1982]. *Indefensible weapons: The political and psychological case against nuclearism.* New York: Basic Books.

Lifton, Robert Jay, and Eric Markusen. 1990. *The genocidal mentality: Nazi holocaust and the nuclear threat.* New York: Basic Books.

Lil' Kim. 1996. Queen bitch. *Hard core.* Atlantic Records.

Lindsey, Hal, with C. C. Carlson. 1970. *The late great planet Earth.* Toronto: Bantam.

Lindsey, Robert. 1984. Officials cite rise in killers who roam U.S. for victims. *New York Times,* January 21.

Litwack, Leon F. 2000. Hellhounds. In *Without sanctuary: Lynching photography in America,* ed. James Allen et al.: 8–37. Santa Fe: Twin Palms Publishers.

Lloyd, Roseanne. 1991. Not even a shadow on the sidewalk. In *She who was lost is remembered: Healing from incest through creativity,* ed. Louise M. Wisechild: 84–87. Seattle: Seal Press.

Long, Charles. 1963. *Alpha: The myths of creation.* New York: Braziller.

Long, Ron. 2002. A place for porn in a gay spiritual economy. *Theology and Sexuality* 16: 21–31.

Lopez, Barry. 1986. *Arctic dreams.* New York: Vintage.

Lorde, Audre. 1981. Need: A choral of black women's voices. In *Fight back: Feminist resistance to male violence,* ed. Frédérique Delacoste and Felice Newman: 63–67. Minneapolis: Cleis Press.

———. 1984. *Sister outsider.* Trumansburg, N.Y.: Crossing Press.

Lovelock, J. E. 1979. *Gaia.* London: Oxford University Press.

Lowndes, Marie Belloc. 1940 [1913]. *The lodger.* New York: Longmans, Green.

Lubell, Winifred Milius. 1994. *The metamorphosis of Baubo: Myths of women's sexual energy.* Nashville, Tenn.: Vanderbilt University Press.

Lubow, Arthur. 1977. A space "Iliad": The *Star Wars* war: 1. *Film Comment,* July–August, 20–21.

Lurker, Manfred. 1980. *The gods and symbols of ancient Egypt: An illustrated dictionary.* Translated by Barbara Cummings. New York: Thames and Hudson.

MacAllister, Pam. 1978. Wolf whistles and warnings. *Heresies: A Feminist Publication on Art and Politics* 6 (summer): 37–39.

MacArthur, Brian, ed. 1997. *Requiem: Diana, Princess of Wales 1961–1997.* London: Pavilion Books.

MacKenzie, Gordene. 1993. *Transgender nation.* Bowling Green, Ohio: Bowling Green State University Press.

MacKinnon, Catharine A. 1983. Feminism, Marxism, method, and the state: Toward feminist jurisprudence. *Signs: Journal of Women in Culture and Society* 8, no. 4: 635–58.

———. 1987. *Feminism unmodified: Discourses on life and law.* Cambridge: Harvard University Press.

————. 1989. *Toward a feminist theory of the state*. Cambridge: Harvard University Press.

MacPherson, Myra. 1989. The roots of evil. *Vanity Fair*, May, 140.

Madden, Mary. 1990. "Pretty woman": Disney turns out Cinderella. Minneapolis: WHISPER (Women Hurt in Systems of Prostitution Engaged in Revolt).

Madison, D. Soyini. 1995. *Pretty Woman* through the triple lens of black feminist spectatorship. In *From mouse to mermaid: The politics of film, gender, and culture*, ed. Elizabeth Bell, Lynda Haas, and Laura Sells: 224–35. Bloomington: Indiana University Press.

————. 2000. Oedipus Rex at *Eve's Bayou* or the little black girl who left Sigmund Freud in the swamp. *Cultural Studies* 14, no. 2: 311–40.

Magill, Marcia. 1975. Jaws. *Films in Review* 26 (August/September): 436.

Maguire, Gregory. 1995. *Wicked: The life and times of the wicked witch of the west*. New York: Regan Books.

Marcus, Michelle I. 1996. Sex and the politics of female adornment in pre-achaemenid Iran (1000–800 B.C.E.). In *Sexuality in ancient art: Near East, Egypt, Greece, and Italy*, ed. Natalie Boymel Kampen: 41–54. Cambridge: Cambridge University Press.

Marglin, Frédérique Appfel. 1987. Yoni. In *The encyclopedia of religion*, ed. Mircea Eliade, 15: 530–35. New York: MacMillan.

MariAnna, Cara. 1993. The seven mythic cycles of *Thelma and Louise*. *Trivia: A Journal of Ideas* 21: 82–99.

————. 1996. Initiatory themes in popular film: The mythic roots of a national destiny. M.A. thesis, University of New Mexico.

Marinatos, Nanno. 2000. *The goddess and the warrior: The naked goddess and mistress of animals in early Greek religion*. New York: Routledge.

Marquand, Robert. 1998. Hinduism and the atomic bomb. *Christian Science Monitor*, June 4, web edition.

Marr, Andrew. 1998. The way we are now. *The Guardian*, August 22.

Martin, Bernice. 1995. Whose soul is it anyway? Domestic tyranny and the suffocated soul. In *On losing the soul: Essays in the social psychology of religion*, ed. Richard K. Fenn and Donald Capps: 69–96. Albany: State University of New York Press.

Martin, Douglas. 2001. Margaret Tafoya, 96, Pueblo potter whose work found a global audience. *New York Times*, March 5.

Martin, Emily. 1991. The egg and the sperm: How science has constructed a romance based on stereotypical male-female roles. *Signs: Journal of Women in Culture and Society* 16, no. 3: 485–501.

Martin, Luther. 1987. *Hellenistic religions*. New York: Oxford University Press.

Martinez, Michael. 2000. Xena online resources. www.xenite.org/xor/home.shtml.

Mast, Gerald. 1977. *Film, cinema, movie: A theory of experience*. New York: Harper and Row.

May, Elaine Tyler. 1988. *Homeward bound: America in the cold war*. New York: Basic Books.

McAllister, Pam, ed. 1982. *Reweaving the web of life: Feminism and nonviolence*. Philadelphia: New Society Publishers.

McCaskill, Barbara, and Layli Phillips. 1996. We are all "good woman!": A womanist critique of the current feminist conflict. In *"Bad girls"/"good girls": Women, sex, and power in the nineties*, ed. Nan Bauer Maglin and Donna Perry: 106–24. New Brunswick, N.J.: Rutgers University Press.

McCaughey, Martha. 1997. *Real knockouts: The physical feminism of women's self-defense*. New York: New York University Press.

McCaughey, Martha, and Neal King, eds. 2001. *Reel knockouts: Violent women in the movies*. Austin: University of Texas Press.

McDonough, Jimmy. 1984. I can teach you how to read the book of life. *Bill Landis' Sleazoid Express* 3, no. 4: 3–5.

McDowell, Edwin. 1991. All the rage in fiction: Serial murder, multiple murder, hideous murder. *New York Times*, April 15.

McFadden, Robert. 1999. Angry man attacks painting in a disputed Brooklyn show. *New York Times*, December 17.

McLuhan, Marshall. 1951. *The mechanical bride: Folklore of industrial man*. Boston: Beacon Press.

———. 1964. *Understanding media: The extensions of man*. New York: New American Library.

McNamara, Mark. 1991. Kiss and kill: Out of Florida's recent wave of horrific crimes comes a dark version of *Thelma and Louise* in a rare case of a female serial killer. *Vanity Fair*, September, 91–106.

McPhillips, Kath. 1997. Postmodern canonisation. In *Planet Diana*, ed. Re: Public: 19–26. Kingswood, Australia: Research Centre in Intercommunal Studies.

Mead, Rebecca. 1998. Postcard from Paris. *New Yorker*, May 11, 40.

Meador, Betty De Shong. 2000. *Inanna lady of largest heart: Poems of the Sumerian high priestess Enheduanna*. Austin: University of Texas Press.

Meisel, Steven. 1991. The misfit. *Vanity Fair*, April, 196.

Merchant, Carolyn. 1980. *The death of nature: Women, ecology and the scientific revolution*. San Francisco: Harper and Row.

Merck, Mandy. 1998. *After Diana: Irreverent elegies*. New York: Verso.

Merkin, Daphne. 1990. Prince charming comes back. *New York Times Magazine*, June 14, 18–19.

Michaud, Stephen G., and Hugh Aynesworth. 1983. *The only living witness*. New York: Simon and Schuster.

Michener, James. 1946. *Tales of the South Pacific*. New York: Pocket Books.

Mies, Maria. 1998 [1986]. *Patriarchy and accumulation on a world scale: Women in the international division of labour*. New York: Zed Books.

Miles, Margaret. 1989. *Carnal knowing: Female nakedness and religious meaning in the Christian West*. New York: Vintage Books.

Miller, Laura. 2000. Norma Jeane (review of Joyce Carol Oates's *Blonde*). *New York Times Book Review*, April 2.

Miller, Mark Crispin. 1986. Deride and conquer. In *Watching television*, ed. Todd Gitlin: 183–228. New York: Pantheon.

Miller, Perry. 1956. *Errand into the wilderness*. Cambridge: Harvard University Press.

Millett, Kate. 1970. *Sexual Politics*. New York: Ballantine.

Modleski, Tania. 1982. *Loving with a vengeance: Mass produced fantasies for women*. New York: Methuen.

Monaghan, Patricia. 1990. *The book of goddesses and heroines*. St. Paul, Minn.: Llewellyn.

———. 1994. *O mother sun! A new view of the cosmic feminine*. Freedom, Calif.: Crossing Press.

———. 1999. *The goddess companion: Daily meditations on the feminine spirit*. St. Paul, Minn.: Llewellyn.

Moon, Beverly. 2000. Inanna: The star who became queen. In *Goddesses who rule*, ed. Elisabeth Benard and Beverly Moon: 69–81. New York: Oxford University Press.

Moore, Alan. 1986. *The watchmen*. New York: D. C. Comics.

Moravec, Hans. 1988. *Mind children: The future of robot and human intelligence*. Cambridge: Harvard University Press.

Morgan, Christopher. 1998. Archbishop urges end to "cult of Diana." *The Times* (London), July 1.

Morgan, Christopher, and David Smith. 1998. Coggan brands Diana "a false goddess with loose morals." *The Times* (London), August 23.

Morgan, Robin. 1972. *Monster*. New York: Vintage Books.

Morgan, Ted. 1974. Sharks. *New York Times Magazine*, April 21, 10–11, 85–96.

Morland, Nigel. 1966. *An outline of sexual criminology*. New York: Hart.

Morris, Glenn T. 1992. International law and politics: Toward a right to self-determination for indigenous peoples. In *The state of Native America: Genocide, colonization, and resistance*, ed. M. Annette Jaimes: 55–86. Boston: South End Press.

Morris, Nomi. 1997. A jet-setting Don Juan. *Macleans*, September 15, 54–55.

Morrison, Toni. 1981. *Tar baby*. New York: New American Library.

———. 1984. Rootedness: The ancestor as foundation. In *Black women writers (1950–1980)*, ed. Mari Evans: 339–45. New York: Anchor.

———. 1992. *Playing in the dark: Whiteness and the literary imagination*. Cambridge: Harvard University Press.

Morrow, Lance. 1991. A moment for the dead. *Time*, April 1, 82.

Morton, Andrew. 1994. *Diana: Her new life*. New York: Simon and Schuster.

———. 1997 [1992]. *Diana: Her true story*. New York: Simon and Schuster.

Muhammad, Erika. 1998. Kasi Lemmons: The woman behind *Eve's Bayou*. *Ms.*, March/April, 74–75.

Mumford, Lewis. 1970. *The myth of the machine: The pentagon of power.* New York: Harcourt Brace Jovanovich.

Murphy, Patricia A. 1985. The color of holocaust. Unpublished manuscript. In author's possession.

———. 1988. *We walk the back of the tiger.* Tallahassee, Fla.: Naiad Press.

Nash, June. 1978. The Aztecs and the ideology of male dominance. *Signs: Journal of Women in Culture and Society* 1, no. 21: 349–62.

Naslund, Sena Jeter. 1999. *Ahab's wife, or: The star gazer.* New York: William Morrow.

National Bulletin on Police Misconduct. 1994. Officers leave naked boy with Jeffrey Dahmer—boy later murdered. *National Bulletin on Police Misconduct* 11, no. 8: 2.

Nava, Mica. 1997. Diana, princess of others: The politics and romance of 'race'. In *Planet Diana,* ed. Re: Public: 19–26. Kingswood, Australia: Research Centre in Intercommunal Studies.

Nelson, James B. 1994. Embracing masculinity. In *Sexuality and the sacred: Sources for theological reflection,* ed. James B. Nelson and Sandra P. Longfellow: 195–215. Louisville, Ky.: Westminster John Knox Press.

Nelson, Jill. 1993. *Volunteer slavery: My authentic Negro experience.* Chicago: Noble Press.

Neumann, Erich. 1963. *The great mother: An analysis of the archetype.* Translated by Ralph Mannheim. Bollingen series 47, 2d ed. Princeton, N.J.: Princeton University Press.

New Millennia Films. 1997. About the production [*Follow Me Home*]. Unpaged.

Newton, Michael. 1990. *Hunting humans: An encyclopedia of modern serial killers.* Port Townsend, Wash.: Loompanics Unlimited.

Niebuhr, Gustav. 1998. Southern Baptists declare wife should "submit" to her husband. *New York Times,* June 10.

———. 1999. Alternative religions as a growth industry. *New York Times,* December 25.

Nitzsche, Jane Chance. 1975. *The genius figure in antiquity and the middle ages.* New York: Columbia University Press.

Nordheimer, Jon. 1978. All-American boy on trial. *New York Times Magazine,* December 10, 46, 110–30.

Northrup, Christiane. 1997. Dear reader. *Health Wisdom for Women,* October, 1.

Nussbaum, Martha C. 1999. "Secret sewers of vice": Disgust, bodies, and the law. In *Passions of law,* ed. Susan Bandes: 19–62. New York: New York University Press.

Oates, Joyce Carol. 2000. *Blonde.* New York: Ecco Press.

O'Brien, Tim. 1985. *The nuclear age.* New York: Dell, Laurel Trade.

O'Flaherty, Wendy Doniger. 1988. *Other people's myths: The cave of echoes.* Chicago: University of Chicago Press.

Olaguibel, Jennie. 2000. The legacy of snake woman. Student paper for graduate course, Women, Myth, and Reality, at Florida Atlantic University. In author's possession.

Olson, Elizabeth. 2000. Geneva panel says U.S. prisoner restraints amount to torture. *New York Times,* May 18.

Omolade, Barbara. 1983. Hearts of darkness. In *Powers of desire: The politics of sexuality,* ed. Ann Snitow, Christine Stansell, and Sharon Thompson: 350–67. New York: Monthly Review Press.

————. 1990. The silence and the song: Toward a black woman's history through a language of her own. In *Wild women in the whirlwind: Afra-American Culture and the contemporary literary renaissance,* ed. Joanne M. Braxton and Andrée Nicola McLaughlin: 282–98. New Brunswick, N.J.: Rutgers University Press.

Opie, Iona, and Peter Opie. 1959. *The lore and language of schoolchildren.* Oxford: Clarendon Press.

Orwell, George. 1949. *1984.* New York: Harcourt, Brace and World.

Osherow, Michelle. 2000. The dawn of a new Lilith: Revisionary mythmaking in women's science fiction. *National Women's Studies Association Journal* 12, no. 1: 68–83.

O'Sullivan, Gerry. 1992. Down the memory hole. *Lies of Our Time,* April, 8–9.

Oxford English Dictionary. 1971. Oxford: Oxford University Press.

Pagels, Elaine. 1988. *Adam, Eve, and the serpent.* New York: Vintage.

————. 1995. *The origin of Satan.* New York: Random House.

Paglia, Camille. 1994. *Vamps and tramps: New essays.* New York: Vintage Books.

Paik, Peter Yoonsuk. 2003. Smart bombs, serial killing, and the rapture: The vanishing bodies of imperial apocalypticism. *Postmodern Culture* 14, no. 1: www.iath.virginia.edu/pmc/contents/all.html.

Pareles, Jon. 1997. Nusrat Fateh Ali Khan, Pakistani Sufi singer, 48. *New York Times,* August 17.

Parfrey, Adam, ed. 1987. *Apocalypse culture.* New York: Amok Press.

Pechter, William S. 1975. Movies: Man bites shark and other curiosities. *Commonweal* 60, November, 68–72.

People. 1998. *Newsday,* July 7.

Pérez, Emma. 2003. So far from God, so close to the United States: A call for action by U.S. authorities. *Aztlan: A Journal of Chicano Studies* 28, no. 2: 147–52.

Peterson-Lewis, Sonja. 1990. Paradoxes of violence in spousal relationships: The role of characteristics of initial attraction in subsequent battering. Paper presented at the annual Popular Culture Association Conference, St. Louis, April.

Pickard, R. A. E. 1971. *Dictionary of 1,000 best films.* New York: Association Press.

Pierce-Baker, Charlotte. 1998. *Surviving the silence: Black women's stories of rape.* New York: W. W. Norton.

Plagens, Peter. 1991. Violence in our culture. *Newsweek,* April 1, 46–52.

Plato. 1992. *Republic.* Translated by C. D. C. Reeve. Revised by G. M. A. Grube. Indianapolis: Hackett.

Playboy Forum. 1989. Ted Bundy's original amateur hour. *Playboy,* June, 49–50.

Plumwood, Val. 1993. *Feminism and the mastery of nature.* New York: Routledge.

Pollock, Dale. 1983. *Skywalking: The life and films of George Lucas.* New York: Harmony.

Porter, Dennis. 1991. *Haunted journeys: Desire and transgression in European travel writing.* Princeton, N.J.: Princeton University Press.

Portillo, Lourdes. 2001. *Señorita extraviada.* Women Make Movies.

Power, Kim. 1996. *Veiled desire: Augustine on women.* New York: Continuum.

Price, Nancy. 1987. *Sleeping with the enemy.* New York: Simon and Schuster.

Pukui, Mary. 1973. *Nana I ke kuma (Look to the source).* Honolulu: Hvi Hanai.

Putter, Ruth. 1985. Nuke the bitches. *Heresies: A Feminist Publication on Art and Politics* 5, no. 4, back cover.

Pyne, Stephen J. 1991. Review of *Trees of life,* by Kenton Miller and Laura Tangley. *New York Times Book Review,* April 21, 19.

Radford, Jill, and Diana E. H. Russell, eds. 1992. *Femicide: The politics of woman killing.* New York: Twayne.

Radin, Paul. 1957 [1937]. *Primitive religion.* New York: Dover.

Raine, Nancy Venable. 1998. *After silence: Rape and my journey back.* New York: Three Rivers Press.

Randall, Alice. 2001. *The wind done gone.* Boston: Houghton Mifflin.

Raphael, Melissa. 1996. *Thealogy and embodiment: The post-patriarchal reconstruction of female sacrality.* Sheffield, England: Sheffield Academic Press.

Rathbone, Julian. 1998. *Trajectories.* London: Golancz.

Re: Public, ed. 1997. *Planet Diana.* Kingswood, Australia: Research Centre in Intercommunal Studies.

Reagan, Ronald. 1983. Speech on a new defense. *New York Times,* March 24.

Reis, Patricia. 1991. *Through the goddess: A woman's way of healing.* New York: Continuum.

Roberts, Dorothy. 1997. *Killing the black body: Race, reproduction, and the meaning of liberty.* New York: Pantheon.

Rodgers, Jeann. 1975. Rush to surgery. *New York Times Magazine,* September 21, 34–42.

Rodgers, Joan Ellison. 1999. The science of flirting. *Sun-Sentinel* (Fort Lauderdale), April 10.

Rogin, Michael. 1987. *Ronald Reagan, the movie and other episodes in political demonology.* Berkeley: University of California Press.

Roof, Judith. 1999. We want Viagra. *Post Identity* 2, no. 1: 5–23.

Rose, Wendy. 1989. The fifties. In *Women on war: Essential voices for the nuclear age from a brilliant international assembly,* ed. Daniela Gioseffi: 60–61. New York: Simon and Schuster, Touchstone Books.

Rubey, Dan. 1978. "Star wars": Not so far away. *Jump Cut* 18: 9–14.

Ruddick, Sara. 1989. *Maternal thinking: Toward a politics of peace.* Boston: Beacon Press.

Rukeyser, Muriel. 1994. *A Muriel Rukeyser reader.* Edited by Jan Heller Levi. New York: Norton.

Rule, Ann. 1980. *The stranger beside me.* New York: New American Library.

Rumbelow, Donald. 1975. *The complete Jack the Ripper.* Boston: New York Graphic Society.

Rush, Florence. 1980. *The best-kept secret: Sexual abuse of children.* New York: McGraw-Hill.

Rushdie, Salman. 1997. Crash. *New Yorker,* September 15, 68–69.

Rushing, Janice Hocker. 1989. "Evolution of the new frontier in *Alien* and *Aliens:* Patriarchal co-optation of the feminine archetype." *Quarterly Journal of Speech* 71: 1–24.

Rushing, Janice Hocker, and Thomas S. Frentz. 1995. *Projecting the shadow: The cyborg hero in American film.* Chicago: University of Chicago Press.

Russell, Diana E. H. 1975. *The politics of rape: The victim's perspective.* New York: Stein and Day.

––––––––. 1986. *The secret trauma: Incest in the lives of girls and women.* New York: Basic Books.

––––––––, ed. 1989. *Exposing nuclear phallacies.* New York: Pergamon.

––––––––. 1998. *Dangerous relationships: Pornography, misogyny, and rape.* Thousand Oaks, Calif.: Sage.

Saadawi, Nawal El. 1980. *The hidden face of Eve: Women in the Arab world.* Translated by Sherif Hetata. New York: Zed Books.

––––––––. 1983. *Woman at point zero.* New York: Zed Books.

Sack, Kevin. 2001. Epidemic takes toll on black women. *New York Times,* July 3.

Sade, Marquis de. 1987. *The 120 days of Sodom and other writings.* Translated by Austryn Wainhouse and Richard Seaver. New York: Grove Press.

Safire, William. 2003. Shock and awe. *New York Times Magazine,* March 30, 10.

Said, Edward. 1987. *Orientalism.* New York: Penguin.

Sanchez, Carol Lee. 1989. New world tribal communities: An alternative approach for recreating egalitarian societies. In *Weaving the visions: New patterns in feminist spirituality,* ed. Judith Plaskow and Carol P. Christ: 344–56. San Francisco: Harper and Row.

––––––––. 1993. Animal, vegetable, and mineral: The sacred connection. In *Ecofeminism and the sacred,* ed. Carol J. Adams: 207–28. New York: Continuum.

Sartre, Jean-Paul. 1957. *Existentialism and human emotions.* New York: The Philosophical Library.

Saunders, Mark, and Glenn Harvey. 1996. *Dicing with Di: The amazing adventures of Britain's royal chasers.* London: Blake Publishing.

Scales, Ann. 2000. Avoiding constitutional depression: Bad attitudes and the fate of Butler. In *Feminism and pornography*, ed. Drucilla Cornell: 318–45. New York: Oxford University Press.

Schama, Simon. 1996. Makeovers: Royal flesh. *New Yorker*, February 26/March 4, 142.

Schechner, Mark. 1979. Male chauvinist romp. *New York Times Book Review*, November 18, 15.

Schechter, Harold. 2001. *The bosom serpent: Folklore and popular art*. New York: Peter Lang.

Scherr, Appolinaire. 2001. Making a career with one eye on a gender gap. *New York Times*, November 4.

Schiff, Stephen. 1994. The last wild man. *New Yorker*, August 8, 40–55.

Schneemann, Carolee. 2002. *Imaging her erotics: Essays, interviews, projects*. Cambridge: MIT Press.

Schwartz, Tony. 1973. *The responsive chord*. New York: Anchor.

Schwarz, Ted. 1981. *The Hillside Strangler: A murderer's mind*. Garden City, N.Y.: Doubleday.

Segal, Naomi. 1998. The common touch. In *After Diana*, ed. Mandy Merck: 131–45. New York: Verso.

Seltzer, Mark. 1998. *Serial killers: Death and life in America's wound culture*. New York: Routledge.

Shalit, Wendy. 1999. *A return to modesty: Discovering the lost virtue*. New York: The Free Press.

Shiva, Vandana. 1988. *Staying alive: Women, ecology and survival in India*. London: Zed Books.

———. 1997. *Biopiracy: The plunder of nature and knowledge*. Boston: South End Press.

Shohat, Ella, and Robert Stam. 1994. *Unthinking Eurocentrism: Multiculturalism and the media*. New York: Routledge.

Shulins, Nancy. 1991. A new breed of heroine. *Albuquerque Journal*, July 13.

Shuttle, Penelope, and Peter Redgrove. 1986. *The wise wound: Myths, realities, and meanings of menstruation*. New York: Bantam.

Silbert, Mimi, and Ayala Pines. 1982. Victimization of street prostitutes. *Victimology: An International Journal* 7: 122–23.

Silko, Leslie Marmon. 1977. *Ceremony*. New York: Viking/Penguin.

———. 1981a. Language and literature from a Pueblo Indian perspective. In *English literature: Opening up the canon*, ed. Leslie A. Fiedler and Houston A. Baker, Jr.: 54–71. Baltimore: Johns Hopkins University Press.

———. 1981b. *Storyteller*. New York: Arcade.

Sillman, Leonard R. 1966. Femininity and paranoidism. *Journal of Nervous and Mental Disease* 143: 163–70.

Silverstone, Roger. 1998. Space. *Screen* 19, no. 1: 81–84.

Simpson, Kevin. 1989. Scenic gorge belies what jumpers see as final solution. *Denver Post*, August 13.

Simurda, Steven. 1988. Seventy-five horror films found in slay suspect's home. *Boston Globe,* December 9.

Singer, Beverly R. 1996. Film and video made by Native Americans. Dissertation, University of New Mexico.

———. 2001. *Wiping the war paint off the lens: Native American film and video.* Minneapolis: University of Minnesota Press.

Sjöö, Monica, and Barbara Mor. 1991. *The great cosmic mother: Rediscovering the religion of the earth.* San Francisco: HarperSanFrancisco.

Slater, Philip E. 1968. *The glory of Hera.* Boston: Beacon Press.

Slotkin, Richard. 1973. *Regeneration through violence: The mythology of the American frontier 1600–1860.* Middletown, Conn.: Wesleyan University Press.

Smiley, Jane. 1991. *A thousand acres.* New York: Fawcett Columbine.

Smith, Andy. 2003. Not an Indian tradition: The sexual colonization of native peoples. *Hypatia* 18, no. 2: 70–85.

Smith, Brian K. 2000. Capital punishment and human sacrifice. *Journal of the American Academy of Religion* 68, no. 1: 3–26.

Smith, David C. 1998. Belief in Diana "murder" grows. *The Times* (London), August 23.

Smith, Mike. 1988. Madam nuke dump (cartoon). *Nevada Nuclear Waste Newsletter* 4, no. 2: 1.

Smith, Mimi. 1982. Better safe than sorry. *Public Illumination,* June, 14.

Smith, Sally Bedell. 1999. *Diana in search of herself.* New York: Random House.

Sobchak, Vivian. 1990. The virginity of astronauts: Sex and the science fiction film. In *Alien zone: Cultural theory and contemporary science fiction cinema,* ed. Annette Kuhn: 103–15. New York: Verso.

Sofia, Zoë. 1984. Exterminating fetuses: Abortion, disarmament, and the sexosemiotics of extraterrestrialism. *Diacritics* 14, no. 2: 47–59.

Softening a starchy image. 1983. *Time,* July 11, 54.

Sofoulis, Zoë. 1997. Icon, referent, trajectory, world. In *Planet Diana,* ed. Re: Public: 13–18. Kingswood, Australia: Research Centre in Intercommunal Studies.

———. 2000. Container technologies. *Hypatia* 15, no. 2: 181–201.

Solanas, Valerie. 1995 [1967]. *The SCUM manifesto.* In *I shot Andy Warhol,* ed. Mary Harron and Daniel Minahan. New York: Grove Press.

Sonkin, Daniel Jay, Del Martin, and Lenore E. Auerbach Walker. 1985. *The male batterer: A treatment approach.* New York: Springer.

Sontag, Susan. 1977. *On photography.* New York: Delta.

———. 1980. Fascinating fascism. In *Under the sign of Saturn:* 73–108. New York: Farrar, Straus, and Giroux.

Sophocles. 1954. Oedipus the king. In *Greek tragedies,* ed. David Grene and Richmond Lattimore, vol. 1. Chicago: University of Chicago Press.

Specter, Michael. 1998. Traffickers' new cargo: Naive Slavic women. *New York Times,* January 11.

Stade, George. 1979. *Confessions of a lady-killer*. New York: Alpha/Omega.

Stanton, Elizabeth Cady. 1968 [1896]. Letter to the editor, *The Critic*. In *Up from the pedestal: Selected writings in the history of American feminism*, ed. Aileen S. Kraditor. Chicago: Quadrangle Books.

Starbuck, Edwin D. 1926. The female principle. In *The encyclopedia of religion and ethics*, ed. James Hastings, 5: 827–33. New York: Scribner's.

Starhawk. 1989. *The spiral dance: A rebirth of the ancient religion of the great goddess*. San Francisco: HarperSanFrancisco.

Steinem, Gloria. 1991. Women in the dark: Of sex goddesses, abuse, and dreams. *Ms.*, January/February, 35–37.

Stember, Charles Herbert. 1976. *Sexual racism*. New York: Harper Colophon.

Sterngold, James. 1999. Police corruption case draws quiet response. *New York Times*, February 15.

Steyn, Mark. 1997. The transfiguration of Diana. *National Review*, September, 38.

Stivers, Richard. 1982. *Evil in modern myth and ritual*. Athens: University of Georgia Press.

Stone, Edward. 1975. Ahab gets the girl, or Herman Melville goes to the movies. *Literature/Film Quarterly* 3, no. 2: 172–81.

Sullivan, Laura L. 2000. Chasing Fae: The watermelon woman and black lesbian possibility. *Callaloo* 23, no. 1: 448–60.

Sullum, Jacob. 1997. Victims of everything. *New York Times*, May 23.

Summitt, Ronald. 1988. Hidden victims, hidden pain: Societal avoidance of child sexual abuse. In *Lasting effects of child sexual abuse*, ed. Gail Elizabeth Wyatt and Gloria Johnson Powell: 39–60. Newbury Park, Calif.: Sage.

Sutton, Ward. 2003. Donald Rumsfeld, between press briefings (cartoon). *Village Voice*, March 24. www.villagevoice.com/issues/0313/sutton.php.

Swentzell, Rena. 1993. Commentaries on *When Jesus came the corn mothers went away: Marriage, sex, and power in New Mexico, 1500–1846*, by Ramón Gutierrez, compiled by Native American studies at the University of New Mexico. *American Indian Culture and Research Journal* 17, no. 3: 141–77.

Swofford, Anthony. 2003. *Jarhead: A marine's chronicle of the Gulf War and other battles*. New York: Scribner.

Szasz, Thomas. 1970. *The manufacture of madness: A comparative study of the Inquisition and the mental health movement*. New York: Harper and Row.

Tajima, Renee. 1989. Lotus blossoms don't bleed: Images of Asian women. In *Making waves: An anthology of writings by and about Asian American women*, ed. Asian Women United of California: 308–17. Boston: Beacon Press.

Takaki, Ronald. 1989. *Strangers from a different shore: A history of Asian Americans*. New York: Penguin Books.

Talk of the Town. 1977. *New Yorker*, August 15, 21.

———. 1989. *New Yorker*, February 27, 23.

Tapia, Ruby. 2003. Maternalizing sex, taming horror: J. Lo's butt in the cell of dominant visualties. Paper presented at National Women's Studies Association Conference, New Orleans, June 21.

Tavris, Carol. 1993. Beware the incest-survivor machine. *New York Times Book Review,* January 3, 16–17.

Teilhard de Chardin, Pierre. 1964. *The future of man.* Translated by N. Denny. New York: Harper and Row.

Teish, Luisah. 1985. *Jambalaya: The natural woman's book.* San Francisco: HarperSanFrancisco.

———. 2002. Discover the history of African goddesses and queens, and realize the goddess within. www.ciis.edu/lifelong/fall02/fall02.

Teller, Edward. 1984. Bringing stars down to earth. *Popular Mechanics,* July, 84–87.

The random killers. 1984. *Newsweek,* November 26, 100–106D.

Theroux, Paul. 1982. *The mosquito coast.* New York: Avon.

Theweleit, Klaus. 1987. *Male fantasies.* Vol. 1, *Women, floods, bodies, history.* Minneapolis: University of Minnesota.

Thomas, Roy, Todd McFarlane, and Mike Hernandez. 1985. *The outsiders* 1, no. 2/2. New York: D.C. Comics.

Thornton, Russell. 1987. *American Indian holocaust and survival: A population history since 1942.* Norman: University of Oklahoma Press.

Tjaden, Patricia, and Nancy Thoennes. 2000. *Extent, nature, and consequences of intimate partner violence.* Washington, D.C.: U.S. Department of Justice.

Tolkien, J. R. R. 1954a. *The fellowship of the ring.* New York: Ballantine.

———. 1954b. *The two towers.* New York: Ballantine.

Trinh, T. Minh-ha. 1989. *Woman, native, other: Writing postcoloniality and feminism.* Bloomington: Indiana University Press.

Tripp, Edward. 1970. *The Meridian handbook of classical mythology.* New York: New American Library.

Trujillo, Carla. 1998. La Virgen de Guadalupe and her reconstruction in Chicana lesbian desire. In *Living Chicana theory,* ed. Carla Trujillo: 214–31. Berkeley: Third Woman Press.

Tuana, Nancy. 1993. *The less noble sex: Scientific, religious, and philosophical conceptions of woman's nature.* Bloomington: Indiana University Press.

Turner, Jonathan. 1998. Portraits of a lady. *ARTNews,* November, 184.

Tyler, Parker. 1947. *Magic and myth of the movies.* New York: Simon and Schuster.

———. 1972. *Chaplin: Last of the clowns.* New York: Horizon Press.

Vietnam Veterans Against the War. 1972. *The winter soldier investigation: An inquiry into American war crimes.* Boston: Beacon Press.

Vogel, Susan M. 1997. *Baule: African art western eyes.* New Haven, Conn.: Yale University Press.

Walker, Alice. 1980. Coming apart. In *Take back the night: Women on pornography,* ed. Laura Lederer: 95–104. New York: Bantam.

————. 1982. *The color purple.* New York: Washington Square Press.

————. 1983. In search of our mothers' gardens. In *In search of our mothers' gardens: Womanist prose:* 231–43. San Diego: Harcourt Brace Jovanovich.

————. 1984. *Horses make a landscape look more beautiful.* New York: Harcourt Brace Jovanovich.

————. 1985. Finding Celie's voice. *Ms.,* December, 71–72, 95–96.

————. 1988. *Living by the word: Selected writings 1973–1987.* San Diego: Harcourt Brace Jovanovich.

————. 1989. *The temple of my familiar.* San Diego: Harcourt Brace Jovanovich.

————. 1997. *Anything we love can be saved: A writer's activism.* New York: Random House.

————. 1998. *By the light of my father's smile.* New York: Random House.

Walker, Barbara G. 1983. *The women's encyclopedia of myths and secrets.* Edison, N.J.: Castle.

————. 1984. *The secrets of the Tarot: Origins, history, and symbolism.* San Francisco: HarperSanFrancisco.

Walker, Hollis. 2001. Like una Virgen: Chicana artists update Our Lady. *Ms.,* September, 85–87.

Walkowitz, Judith. 1982. Jack the Ripper and the myth of male violence. *Feminist Studies* 8: 543–74.

Wallace, Michele. 1990. *Invisibility blues: From pop to theory.* New York: Verso.

Warner, Marina. 1996. *From the beast to the blonde: On fairy tales and their tellers.* New York: Farrar.

Warren, Karen J. 1997. Introduction. In *Ecofeminism: Women, culture, nature,* ed. Karen J. Warren: xi–xvi. Bloomington: Indiana University Press.

Warshow, Robert. 1979 [1964]. *The immediate experience.* New York: Atheneum.

Watts, Alan W. 1968. *Myth and ritual in Christianity.* Boston: Beacon Press.

Weart, Spencer. 1989. *Nuclear fear: A history of images.* Cambridge: Harvard University Press.

Webster's third new international dictionary of the English language unabridged. 1986. Edited by Philip Babcock Gove. Springfield, Mass.: Merriam-Webster.

Wedekind, Frank. [1904]. *The first Lulu.* Translated by Eric Bently. New York: Applause Theatre Books.

Weinraub, Bernard. 1999. Hollywood's first black goddess and casualty. *New York Times,* August 15.

Wheelwright, Philip. 1962. *Metaphor and reality.* Bloomington: Indiana University Press.

Whitmont, Edward C. 1982. *Return of the goddess.* New York: Crossroad.

Wiener, Norbert. 1954. *The human use of human beings: Cybernetics and society.* New York: Doubleday.

Williams, H. A. 1972. *True resurrection.* New York: Holt, Rinehart and Winston.

Williams, Lena. 1989. For more U.S. youths, it's always Halloween. *New York Times,* October 30.

Williams, Patricia J. 1991. *The alchemy of race and rights: Diary of a law professor.* Cambridge: Harvard University Press.

————. 1995. *The rooster's egg: On the persistence of prejudice.* Cambridge: Harvard University Press.

————. 1996. My best white friend. *New Yorker,* February 26/March 4, 94–97.

————.1997. American Kabuki. In *Birth of a nation'hood: Gaze, script, and spectacle in the O.J. Simpson case,* ed. Toni Morrison and Claudia Brodsky Lacour: 273–92. New York: Pantheon.

Williams, Raymond. 1974. *Television: Technology and cultural form.* London: Fontana/Collins.

Wilshire, Donna. 1989. The uses of myth, image, and the female body in revisioning knowledge. In *Gender/body/knowledge: Feminist reconstructions of being and knowing,* ed. Alison M. Jaggar and Susan R. Bordo: 92–114. New Brunswick, N.J.: Rutgers University Press.

Wilson, Colin. 1969. *A casebook of murder.* London: Leslie Frewin.

Wines, Michael. 2003. Fourteen arrested in the sale of organs for transplant. *New York Times,* December 8.

Winn, Steven, and David Merrill. 1980. *Ted Bundy: The killer next door.* New York: Bantam.

Wittig, Monique. 1985 [1971]. *Les guérillères.* Translated by David Le Vay. Boston: Beacon Press.

Wolf, Naomi. 2003. The porn myth. *New York Magazine,* October 20. www.newyorkmetro.com/nymetro/news/trends/n_9437/index.html.

Wolkstein, Diane, and Samuel Noah Kramer. 1983. *Inanna: Queen of heaven and earth.* New York: Harper and Row.

Wood, Michael. 1975. *America in the movies.* New York: Basic Books.

Wood, Robin. 1986. *Hollywood from Vietnam to Reagan.* New York: Columbia University Press.

Woolf, Virginia. 1957. *A room of one's own.* New York: Harcourt, Brace and World.

Wyatt, Gail Elizabeth, and Gloria Johnson Powell, eds. 1988. *Lasting effects of child sexual abuse.* Newbury Park, Calif.: Sage.

Young, Lola. 1996. *Fear of the dark: "Race," gender and sexuality in the cinema.* New York: Routledge.

Young, Lucy. 1997. Out of the past: Lucy Young's story. In *No rooms of their own: Women writers of early California, 1849–1869,* ed. Ida Rae Egli: 47–58. Berkeley, Calif.: Heyday Books.

Zahavi, Helen. 1991. *The weekend.* New York: Donald I. Fine.

Zernike, Kate. 2002. Experts debate the sniper's links to popular culture. *New York Times,* October 11.

Zohar, Danah. 1985. Quantum physics and motherhood. In *About time,* ed. Christopher Rawlence: 169–78. London: Jonathan Cape.

———. 1990. *The quantum self: Human nature and consciousness defined by the new physics.* New York: Quill/William Morrow.

Index

A RAY AND PAT BROWNE BOOK

Series Editors
Ray B. Browne and Pat Browne
